DEDICATION

To my parents, who started my life toward outcomes that I could not imagine at the time.
–RLD

To my mother, Leone Evert, and my father, Oswald Marcic, who created in me the desire to manage chaos and learn to create structure.
–DM

BRIEF CONTENTS

Building Management Skills: An Action-First Approach

Richard L. Daft
Vanderbilt University

Dorothy Marcic
Columbia University

Australia • Brazil • Japan • Korea • Mexico • Singapore • Spain • United Kingdom • United States

Building Management Skills,
First Edition
Richard L. Daft and Dorothy Marcic, with the assistance of Patricia G. Lane

Vice President of Editorial, Business: Jack W. Calhoun

Publisher: Erin Joyner

Executive Editor: Scott Person

Developmental Editor: Jennifer King

Editorial Assistant: Tamara Grega

Marketing Manager: Jonathan Monahan

Marketing Coordinator: Courtney Doyle Chambers

Senior Content Project Manager: Emily Nesheim

Media Editor: Rob Ellington

Manufacturing Planner: Ron Montgomery

Senior Marketing Communications Manager: Libby Shipp

Production Service: MPS Limited

Sr. Art Director: Stacy Jenkins Shirley

Cover and Internal Designer: Joe Devine, Red Hangar Design

Cover Image: iStock Photo

Rights Acquisitions Specialist: Amber Hosea

Cengage Learning is a leading provider of customized learning solutions with office locations around the globe, including Singapore, the United Kingdom, Australia, Mexico, Brazil, and Japan. Locate your local office at: **www.cengage.com/global**

For product information: **www.cengage.com/international**

Visit your local office: **www.cengage.com/global**

Visit our corporate website: **www.cengage.com**

© 2014 South-Western, Cengage Learning

ALL RIGHTS RESERVED. No part of this work covered by the copyright herein may be reproduced, transmitted, stored, or used in any form or by any means graphic, electronic, or mechanical, including but not limited to photocopying, recording, scanning, digitizing, taping, web distribution, information networks, or information storage and retrieval systems, except as permitted under Section 107 or 108 of the 1976 United States Copyright Act, without the prior written permission of the publisher.

For product information and technology assistance, contact us at
Cengage Learning Customer & Sales Support, 1-800-354-9706
For permission to use material from this text or product,
submit all requests online at **www.cengage.com/permissions**
Further permissions questions can be emailed to
permissionrequest@cengage.com

Exam*View*® is a registered trademark of eInstruction Corp. Windows is a registered trademark of the Microsoft Corporation used herein under license. Macintosh and Power Macintosh are registered trademarks of Apple Computer, Inc. used herein under license.
© 2014 Cengage Learning. All Rights Reserved.

Cengage Learning WebTutor™ is a trademark of Cengage Learning.

Library of Congress Control Number: 2012937324

ISBN-13: 978-1-285-18822-5
ISBN-10: 1-285-18822-5

Cengage Learning International Offices

Asia
www.cengageasia.com
tel: (65) 6410 1200

Australia/New Zealand
www.cengage.com.au
tel: (61) 3 9685 4111

Brazil
www.cengage.com.br
tel: (011) 3665 9900

India
www.cengage.co.in
tel: (91) 11 30484837/38

Latin America
www.cengage.com.mx
tel: +52 (55) 1500 6000

UK/Europe/Middle East/Africa
www.cengage.co.uk
tel: (44) 207 067 2500

Represented in Canada by Nelson Education, Ltd.
www.nelson.com
tel: (416) 752 9100 / (800) 668 0671

Printed in Canada
1 2 3 4 5 6 7 16 15 14 13 12

CONTENTS

40260.COM/ALAMY

PART 2 Managing Relationships 259

© CLOVER/A.COLLECTIONRF/ AMANA IMAGES INC./ALAMY

Chapter 7 Motivating for Performance 260

Chapter 8 Getting Things Done through Networks, Relationships, and Soft Power 296

Chapter 9 Developing People with Coaching, Delegation, and Deliberate Practice 332

FANCY ALAMY

ABOUT THE AUTHORS

Richard L. Daft, Ph.D., is the Brownlee O. Currey, Jr., Professor of Management in the Owen Graduate School of Management at Vanderbilt University. Professor Daft specializes in the study of organization theory and leadership. A Fellow of the Academy of Management, Dr. Daft has served on the editorial boards of *Academy of Management Journal, Administrative Science Quarterly, and Journal of Management Education*. He was the associate editor-in-chief of *Organization Science* and served for three years as associate editor of *Administrative Science Quarterly*.

Professor Daft has authored or co-authored 13 books, including *The Executive and the Elephant: A Leader's Guide to Building Inner Excellence* (Jossey-Bass, 2010), *Organization Theory and Design* (South-Western, 2013), *The Leadership Experience* (South-Western, 2011), and *What to Study: Generating and Developing Research Questions* (Sage, 1982). He published *Fusion Leadership: Unlocking the Subtle Forces That Change People and Organizations* (Berrett-Koehler, 2000) with Robert Lengel. He has also authored dozens of scholarly articles, papers, and chapters. His work has been published in *Administrative Science Quarterly, Academy of Management Journal, Academy of Management Review, Strategic Management Journal, Journal of Management, Accounting Organizations and Society, Management Science, MIS Quarterly, California Management Review*, and *Organizational Behavior Teaching Review*. Professor Daft is also an active teacher and consultant. He has taught management, leadership, organizational change, organizational theory, and organizational behavior.

Professor Daft has served as associate dean, produced for-profit theatrical productions, and helped manage a start-up enterprise. He has been involved in management development and consulting for many companies and government organizations, including the American Bankers Association, Bridgestone, Bell Canada, the Transportation Research Board, Nortel, TVA, Pratt & Whitney, State Farm Insurance, Tenneco, the U.S. Air Force, the U.S. Army, J.C. Bradford & Co., Central Parking System, Entergy, Bristol-Myers Squibb, First American National Bank, and the Vanderbilt University Medical Center.

Dorothy Marcic, Ed.D., MPH, is a professor at Columbia University and former faculty member at Vanderbilt University. Dr. Marcic is also a former Fulbright Scholar at the University of Economics in Prague and the Czech Management Center, where she taught courses and did research in leadership, organizational behavior, and cross-cultural management. She has taught courses at the Monterrey Institute of International Studies and has taught courses or given presentations at the Helsinki School of Economics, Slovenia Management Center, College of Trade in Bulgaria, City University of Slovakia, Landegg Institute in Switzerland, the Swedish Management Association, Technion University in Israel, and the London School of Economics. Other international work includes projects at the Autonomous University in Guadalajara, Mexico, and a training program for the World Health Organization in Guatemala. She has served on the boards of the Organizational Teaching Society, the Health Administration Section of the American Public Health Association, and the *Journal of Applied Business Research.*

Dr. Marcic has authored 12 books, including *Organizational Behavior: Experiences and Cases* (South-Western Publishing, 6th edition, 2001), *Management International* (West Publishing, 1984), *Women and Men in Organizations* (George Washington University, 1984), and *Managing with the Wisdom of Love: Uncovering Virtue in People and Organizations* (Jossey-Bass, 1997), which was rated one of the top ten business books of 1997 by *Management General.* Her most recent book is *Love Lift Me Higher* (George Ronald). In addition, she has had dozens of articles printed in publications such as *Journal of Management Development, International Quarterly of Community Health Education, Psychological Reports,* and *Executive Development.* She has recently been exploring how to use the arts in the teaching of leadership and has a book, *RESPECT: Women and Popular Music* (Texere, 2002), which serves as the basis for the musical theater production *Respect: A Musical Journey of Women.* Her newest artistic endeavor is *SISTAS: The Musical,* which has played for over a year Off-Broadway and was nominated as the Best New Musical. She has appeared on television networks C-Span, CMT, and BRAVO.

Professor Marcic has conducted hundreds of seminars on various business topics and consulted for executives at AT&T Bell Labs, the governor and cabinet of North Dakota, the U.S. Air Force, Slovak Management Association, Eurotel, Czech Ministry of Finance, the Cattaraugus Center, USAA Insurance, State Farm Insurance, and the Salt River–Pima Indian Tribe in Arizona.

PREFACE

A Zen master poured tea into a cup until it overflowed, spilling tea onto the saucer and tray. The master asked a student, "What is the lesson here?" The student shook his head, not knowing. The master gave him the lesson: *"You can't pour new tea into the cup until you empty out what is already there."*

The master's teacup lesson is a metaphor for educating students. Students arrive in our classrooms full of concepts, beliefs, habits, distractions, life experiences, worries, skepticism, mental criticalness, and defensiveness—all blocks to learning and change. A mind already full doesn't have much room for the new knowledge, skills, and techniques of management. One solution is to allow students to empty out their own ideas and thinking before introducing them to a new concept. The effectiveness of this simple technique for teaching adults has been established in social science research and is the premise for this book.[1] Indeed, emptying oneself first is often a precursor to any significant personal change.[2]

Our vision for this book is to provide management instructors with a new set of tools and techniques from which to teach students the difficult and challenging application of managerial theories and concepts. The application of good management principles is a lot harder than it looks, as are most endeavors that require new skills. We discovered in our classrooms that student engagement and learning increase when students first empty out their ideas with an introductory problem or challenge. Each chapter of this book gives instructors a menu of teaching resources for student challenges, feedback, applications, and learning. Moreover, students will learn a great deal about themselves as potential managers.

There are many ways to teach management skills. The prevalent model is to (1) introduce students to conceptual models and principles, followed by (2) student attempts to apply concepts to an exercise, case, or video, and concluding with (3) an exam that provides feedback on test performance. A questionnaire to provide feedback about a student's style is often included as a pre-assessment or during the learning process.

This traditional approach has been successful for decades, but it does not reflect the most up-to-date developments or technology for student learning. Much research on pedagogy and learning has generated new insights. This book is organized around a new learning philosophy, new technology, and a coherent learning package for students to acquire management skills. This integrated textbook package may appear novel to some users because it is based on the latest research findings about how people learn. The approach and materials have also been tested in our own classrooms. The basis of the new approach is action, as in "first do, then learn." Adding to this basic principle of learning are the following ideas: less is more, tight integration, and the power of new techniques such as the manager challenge and the student's personal learning log. Instructors may adopt all or part of this new approach, or use this text's rich array of teaching materials within their own approach for teaching management skills.

[1] John D. Bransford, Ann L. Brown, and Rodney R. Cocking, eds., *How People Learn: Brain, Mind, Experience, and School* (Washington DC: National Academy Press, 2000).

[2] Carl Rogers, *On Becoming a Person: A Therapist's View of Psychotherapy* (Boston: Mariner Books, 1995).

WHAT IS ACTION-FIRST?

Action-first means for the learner to take action early and often. This text is loaded with opportunities for students to learn via the principle of "first do, then learn." The importance of real world action-first and "doing" is visible in the rise of teaching innovations such as service learning projects and student-based consulting projects. A significant development in teaching new skills in the field of higher education is problem-based learning (PBL).[3] Problem-based learning started in medical schools and has since been adopted in schools of engineering, architecture, social work, law, and nursing.[4] The essence is simple—start with a problem upon which a student takes action rather than with a theory. In recent years, medical and nursing schools have found that putting students into a clinical setting very early is more effective than waiting until after heavy in-class work, memorization, and testing.

Traditional academic learning is based on the principle "first learn, then do." Through lectures and reading assignments, students digest and memorize conceptual material that they hope to apply to a case problem, a final exam, or on the job. Problem-based learning reverses this sequence into "first do, then learn." Students start with a realistic problem scenario upon which they take action *before* learning a concept or skill. Action on the problem reveals to students their *learning gap*—how little they know—which opens the students' minds to knowledge and synthesis, completing a learning cycle. Conceptual material is used in support of solving the problem and synthesizing lessons for future applications. Concepts are not expected to be an end in themselves.

A PBL application can be as simple as having students analyze and problem-solve a brief written case using their own thoughts and opinions, followed by the instructor explaining a theory or model that shows how to resolve the problem. In other applications of action-first learning, instructors might assign students individual deliberate practice exercises or team exercises either inside or outside the classroom. Completing these exercises will often lead to better retention and skill building than a traditional lecture.

PBL or action-first learning works as follows:

1. Learners are given an exciting and realistic problem at the start of the class session about which to brainstorm and discuss practical solutions.[5]
2. Learners' prior knowledge is surfaced and used, to which new knowledge is then added. Learners are more in charge of their own learning, including self-direction for handling problems in their own lives.
3. Trying to respond correctly to a video challenge or case "problem" immediately answers the question implicit in the student's mind: "Why do I need to know this material?"[6]
4. PBL engages students in *active* rather than passive learning, trying things to learn what works, improving their skills through mental repetition and physical practice. Learning with action is consistent with the action nature of managerial work.

[3] Barbara J. Duch, Susan E. Groh, and Deborah E. Allen, eds., *The Power of Problem-Based Learning* (Sterling, VA: Stylus Publishing, 2001).

[4] Gerald F. Smith, "Problem-Based Learning: Can It Improve Managerial Thinking?" *Journal of Management Education* 29, no. 2 (April 2005): 357–378.

[5] Roland K. Yeo, "Leading Through Problems: Recognizing the Potential of Getting Their Hands Dirty," *Industrial and Commercial Training* 42, no. 3 (2010): 128–134.

[6] Gerald F. Smith, *op. cit.*

The teaching materials within this text provide instructors with an opportunity to empty each student's cup before trying to fill it. Each chapter begins with an engaging manager video challenge that lets students empty their cups of personal beliefs and opinions about the right way to handle a manager incident. By taking action on the problem, a student learns what he or she does *not* know. Then the lesson is given by the instructor, or can be provided by the follow-up video, by discussion with other students, or by the text. *First do, then learn,* a simple reversal in the typical learning sequence, is a powerful tool enabling students to experience personal transformation in their management skills in a short time.

Research into adult learning supports the high payoff from starting with a problem to solve rather than with lectures and readings. For example, recent research in psychology revealed that trying and failing a test before being exposed to readings and lectures increased student learning.[7] There are real benefits to taking action without preparation and getting it wrong. The mind suddenly opens to new knowledge. Moreover, evidence from the science of learning suggests the importance of helping people become involved in the control of their own learning. Effective instruction builds on what learners bring to the setting, including previous experiences, cultural practices, and knowledge of academic content. Problem-based learning helps students make connections between previous knowledge and current assignments. Solving a problem also activates a student's independent thinking that will apply concepts to new problems beyond the classroom. Learning experiences premised on action create a stimulating and effective learning environment.[8]

LESS IS MORE

This skills text is highly focused. There are 16 chapters rather than the traditional 10, and the mass of research material has been distilled and refined into shorter chapters that capture the essence and critical points for each topic. Each chapter is accompanied by a robust menu of exercises and activities to engage students. The opening video challenge relates directly to chapter competencies and is followed by a menu of brief questionnaires from which students discover their personal styles and characteristics. Likewise, the cases and exercises are original and written to focus on issues directly relevant to each chapter's content.

Academic authors often feel the need to be comprehensive by mentioning every relevant research concept and citation in a subject matter area. Concept may be piled on concept to include "everything" in a single textbook chapter, which can make a chapter seem pointless as well as endless for students. The same is true of questionnaires and other text features. Is it necessary to use 40 questions when 10 will make the point for the student? Why use a complete article from a business magazine as a case for analysis when a shorter, more pointed incident or dilemma would make for a better class discussion? Students have shorter attention spans than ever and want to get to the point quickly. The goal of this book is to provide greater focus and more options.

[7] Henry L. Roediger III and Bridgid Finn, "The Pluses of Getting It Wrong," *Scientific American Mind* (March–April 2010): 39–41.

[8] Bransford, et al., *How People Learn.*

TIGHT INTEGRATION

The seven elements of the learning cycle used in this book for building management skills are summarized in Exhibit 6 on page 14 (in the Introduction). These seven pieces comprise a tightly integrated learning system. Each chapter begins with an opening *Manager Challenge* that can be presented as a video. After students watch the video challenge, they respond with *Initial Thoughts* to solve the problem. This action step also provides a benchmark for the student's later realization of how much has been learned. The next piece is made up of *Discover Yourself* questionnaire assessments that are specifically tailored to the content of each chapter. The feedback and interpretation of each questionnaire's score is located in the relevant section of the chapter so students will link their scores to chapter content. Next comes the *Discover Knowledge* section—the chapter text, providing research-based concepts, theories, and lively examples. This is followed by *Action Learning*—individual deliberate practice exercises and team exercises through which students can apply and test their new knowledge and skills.[9] The next section, *Test Your Mettle*, enables students to apply their acquired competencies to new problems, role plays, and cases. Students again learn based on their own actions rather than from text memorization. The last piece in each chapter is the *Personal Skills Log* that encourages students to record what they have learned. This step crystallizes the learning experience and brings it to a close.

SUGGESTIONS FOR STUDENTS

Whether you are a student or a practicing manager in business, education, engineering, nursing, or some other field, the management concepts and skills in this book are relevant to your development. Here are some suggestions for getting the most from the material in this book.

- **Manager Challenge and Initial Thoughts.** Make it a point to write down a specific answer in response to the opening Manager Challenge. Also write down your response to exercises and case incidents assigned by your instructor. Clarifying your responses by writing them down will improve your learning and make subsequent discussion and feedback more valuable.
- **Discover Yourself.** Complete each questionnaire in the Discover Yourself section carefully and thoughtfully. Be as honest as you can. Your scores on these questionnaires will improve your self-awareness and identify areas you may want to change or improve. The interpretation for your answers appears within the chapter text in the section pertaining to that specific concept and skill.
- **Deliberate Practice.** The Deliberate Practice exercises are something you can use to build management skills and self-insights. New behavior requires stretching yourself, followed by repetitions that allow the new behavior to become part of your management skills repertoire. Deliberate practice is an essential element of skill development in all professions and sports.[10]

[9] Geoff Colvin, *Talent Is Overrated: What Really Separates World-Class Performers from Everybody Else* (New York: Penguin, 2010).

[10] K. Anders Ericsson, Ralf T. Krampe, and Clemens Tesch-Römer, "The Role of Deliberate Practice in the Acquisition of Expert Performance," *Psychological Review* 11, no. 3 (July 1993): 363–406.

- **Personal Skills Log.** We cannot overstate the value of the Personal Skills Log near the end of each chapter. Taking a few moments to write down your new learning and insights from each activity in the chapter will pay large dividends in your development. Taking the time to focus your mind on your specific learning takeaways from chapter material and exercises will increase your retention and enable you to use that insight in the future.
- **Don't Hold Back.** This book is designed for a course in which students are engaged in the practice of management skills. Don't hold back from fear of embarrassment or failure. The exercises provide you an opportunity to take action, receive feedback, and improve your skills in a safe environment. The more freely you can experience these activities, the more learning outcomes you can receive from the course.

SUGGESTIONS FOR INSTRUCTORS

Each chapter provides a menu of small items that can be packaged to suit your teaching style. You can choose various elements from the menu for each chapter to reflect your interest or to provide variety in the classroom. The array of items also provides various ways to use the problem-based, action-first approach that has worked so well in our classrooms. Our personal shift from starting classes with concepts to starting with a problem happened gradually. For example, we originally used videos primarily to illustrate theoretical concepts to students. One day we decided to write down the video scenario as a two-paragraph case incident on which students could take action before watching the video. They became fully engaged as they offered up their ideas and solutions. Then we showed the video, and student interest was higher than ever because they could compare their own thinking and solutions to what actually happened. That was the initial step in our journey toward the teaching power of "first do, then learn" that eventually became this book.

Here are some suggestions based on how we use the features in each chapter:

- **Manager Challenge Video Incident.** The video incident is a fun way to open a class session and challenge students with a problem. You can also ask students to complete the Initial Thoughts questions that follow the written version of the manager challenge at the beginning of each chapter. The cases, role plays, and other exercises within each chapter provide other options with which to challenge students.
- **Discover Yourself Questionnaires.** Students receive value from completing questionnaires on their own and comparing their scores to benchmark data. You can get even more impact by periodically inviting students to compare key scores in class and discuss what scores mean among themselves, and then briefly recording scores on the whiteboard so students can see where they stand. This might take only ten minutes of class time.
- **Discover Knowledge Text Material.** The text chapters contain quite a bit of new content compared to other texts, including topics that capture student interest, such as networking, difficult conversations, robust dialogue, manager strengths and weaknesses, soft power, accountability, right people on the bus, counterdependence,

personal change, courage, and self-management. We personally have moved away from heavy reliance on lectures, but students still want to know our take on chapter ideas and models, especially when we can share our own experience about how to use them in practice. While comprehensive lectures about text material typically are not needed, students do want to hear what you think is important.

- **Deliberate Practice Exercises.** These action learning exercises can be especially important for helping individuals stretch beyond their comfort zone and practice some repetitions to form a new skill. Moreover, some deliberate practice exercises involve serious reflection, which will balance out students' action experiences.[11]
- **In-Class Team Exercises.** These exercises are always fun, but they do use a lot of class time. We have tried to design exercises that will take less than an hour so there will be time for discussion and another class activity.
- **Field Team Exercises.** Most of these outside-of-class exercises involve a lot of time, and you might assign only one or two of them in a semester or quarter. You can choose a field exercise based on the chapter content and type of group activity you think more important.
- **Case Incidents.** The case incidents are all new and written to reflect the material in the chapter. These cases are short and to the point and are based on real and challenging manager problems to be solved.
- **Role-Play Simulations.** We have found that instructors differ widely regarding their preference for role plays. We sometimes use a role play by asking two or three students to role play in front of the class, which heightens the excitement for everyone. Other times we divide students into small groups so everyone can have the role-play experience. If role plays are part of your teaching portfolio, you will have lots of options to choose from.
- **Personal Skills Log.** This log asks students to crystallize and write down their learning "takeaway" for each activity completed. This technique provided unexpectedly high value for our students. Student insights disappear into the ether if not written down. Crystallizing what they learned in order to write it down increases retention. At the end of the course, we typically ask students to write a short paper analyzing the patterns and themes within each vertical column (e.g., takeaway, strength, weakness, application) across all the logs. This activity captures and summarizes each student's major learning from throughout the term.

The *Instructor's Manual* provides more details about how you might use each item in the learning model. It also provides detailed ideas on how to use the specific videos, cases, deliberate practice exercises, role-play simulations, and group exercises in each chapter. We have provided as much support material as possible to help you use the text effectively.

The book and support materials will support diverse teaching styles. We invite you to try starting a class with the video challenge. Let students rely on their own ideas and experiences until they are empty of ideas. See how that works for you and them. Then you could present key concepts and how they may apply to the situation.

[11] Christian Berggren and Jonas Soderlund, "Management Education for Practicing Managers: Combining Academic Rigor with Personal Change and Organizational Action," *Journal of Management Education* 35, no. 3 (2011): 377–405.

FINAL NOTE

Many instructors in the field of management and organization behavior have expressed a yearning for a next-generation skills text, with shorter chapters and a better menu of exercises. This book is designed to meet that need. We have worked extensively to develop materials based on our own classroom experiences after we underwent a change in teaching paradigm toward an action-first approach. Many parts of the book were developed and tested in our classes. Cengage has developed the requisite technology to support each instructor in using the many techniques and activities in the text and *Instructor's Manual* to guide students' skills learning.

There is a great truth in the Chinese proverb, "*When I hear, I forget. When I see, I remember. When I do, I understand.*" Well-focused problem-based educational instruction can noticeably improve a person's management skills. In this approach, students have frequent opportunities to "do" rather than sit passively. Programs that have used a focused action-first approach have demonstrated educational and practical significance for participants. In one study, participants experienced a 48 percent increase in communication skills, 37 percent increase in personal effectiveness, and 33 percent increase in self-esteem.[12] Various other studies have also shown the superiority of problem- and experience-based learning of management skills compared to traditional lecture-discussion approaches.[13] We request your feedback on your experience with this text as we work to continuously improve it.

Dick Daft
Dorothy Marcic

SUPPLEMENTARY MATERIALS

Instructor's CD-ROM. Key instructor ancillaries (*Instructor's Manual*, Test Bank, ExamView, and PowerPoint® slides) are provided on CD-ROM, giving instructors the ultimate tool for customizing lectures and presentations.

Instructor's Manual. Designed to provide support for instructors new to the course, as well as innovative materials for experienced professors, the *Instructor's Manual* includes chapter outlines, annotated learning objectives, lecture notes, and sample lecture outlines. Additionally, the *Instructor's Manual* includes answers and teaching notes to end-of-chapter materials, including the exercises and cases. This resource is available on the Instructor's Resource CD-ROM or on the companion Web site.

Test Bank. Scrutinized for accuracy, the Test Bank includes hundreds of multiple-choice, true/false, short-answer, and essay questions. Each question is tagged based on learning outcomes, national guidelines, and Bloom's Taxonomy. This resource is available on the Instructor's Resource CD-ROM or on the companion Web site.

[12] Rowena Crosbie, "Learning the Skills of Leadership," *Industrial and Commercial Training*, 37, no. 1 (2005): 45–51.

[13] Richard E. Boyatzis, Scott S. Cowan, and David A. Kolb, *Innovation in Professional Education: Steps on a Journey from Teaching to Learning* (San Francisco: Jossey-Bass, 1995); G. R. Norman and H. G. Schmidt, "The Psychological Bases of Problem-Based Learning: A Review of the Evidence," *Academic Medicine*, 66 (1992): 557–565.

ExamView. Available on the Instructor's Resource CD-ROM, ExamView contains all of the questions in the printed Test Bank. This program is easy-to-use test creation software. Instructors can add or edit questions, instructions, and answers, and select questions (randomly or numerically) by previewing them on screen.

PowerPoint Lecture Presentation. Available on the Instructor's Resource CD-ROM and the companion Web site, the PowerPoint Lecture Presentation enables instructors to customize their own multimedia classroom presentation. Each slide deck includes key points as well as exhibits from the text. Material is organized by chapter and can be modified or expanded for individual classroom use.

Video DVD. Put management in action with this set of video clips created exclusively for use with this text. Students gain an insider's perspective on issues that managers face and the skills they need to be effective leaders.

Instructor's Companion Web Site. Instructors can access important teaching resources on this companion Web site. For your convenience, you can download electronic versions of the instructor supplements at the password-protected section of the site, including the *Instructor's Manual*, Test Bank, and PowerPoint presentations. Additionally, many more self-assessments, role-play exercises, and other activities are included on this Web site.

Instructors can access these additional course materials and companion resources by visiting www.cengagebrain.com. At the CengageBrain.com home page, search for the ISBN of your title (from the back cover of your book) by using the search box at the top of the page. This will take you to the product page where free companion resources can be found.

Student's Companion Web Site. Students will find useful study aids, such as learning objectives, on this Web site, as well as additional self-assessments, role-play exercises, and other activities that the instructor may choose to assign.

Students can access these additional course materials at www.cengagebrain.com. At the CengageBrain.com home page, search for the ISBN of your title (from the back cover of your book) using the search box at the top of the page. This will take you to the product page where free companion resources can be found.

MANAGEMENT CourseMate. Engaging, trackable, and affordable, the new MANAGEMENT CourseMate Web site offers a dynamic way to bring course concepts to life with interactive learning, study, and exam-preparation tools that support this printed edition of the text. Watch student comprehension soar with all-new flash cards and engaging games, audio summaries, self-assessments, streaming videos, and more in this textbook-specific Web site. A complete e-book provides you with the choice of an entire online learning experience. MANAGEMENT CourseMate goes beyond the book to deliver what you need!

CengageNOW. This robust, online course management system gives you more control in less time and delivers better student outcomes—NOW. CengageNOW for *Building Management Skills, First Edition* includes teaching and learning resources organized around lecturing, creating assignments, grading, quizzing, and tracking student progress and performance. Flexible assignments, automatic grading, and a gradebook option provide more control while saving you valuable time. A Personalized Study diagnostic tool empowers students to master concepts, prepare for exams, and become more involved in class.

ACKNOWLEDGMENTS

Textbook writing is a team enterprise. This book has integrated ideas and support from many people whom we want to acknowledge. First, we want to recognize Pat Lane, without whom we could not have completed this book. Pat seemed to do everything, including skillful drafting of chapter materials, finding sources, incorporating last minute changes, and handling the copyedited manuscript, art, and page proofs. We also give a special thanks to DeeGee Lester, who used her creative writing talent to draft the exceptional cases for the chapters. Thank you also to Jeanne Lawson who helped us with drafts of key materials when we were in a crunch.

R.L.D. Here at Vanderbilt I want to extend special appreciation to my assistant, Barbara Haselton. Barbara provided excellent support and assistance on a variety of projects, which gave me time to write. I also want to acknowledge an intellectual debt to my colleagues, Bruce Barry, Rich Oliver, David Owens, Tae-Youn Park, Ranga Ramanujam, Bart Victor, and Tim Vogus. Thanks also to Melinda Allen in the Leadership Development Program for her partnership and to Deans Jim Bradford and Ray Friedman who have supported my writing projects and maintained a positive scholarly atmosphere in the school.

D.M. There have been numerous people who have given time and support on this project, including my assistant, Allison Greer. On this project, I must thank Don Downie, director and film-maker extraordinaire, who brought to life the scripts for CAFFEINE AND CRULLERS and made them better with his filming and editing skills. Many thanks also to Ryan Lash, who took such good photos of the video shoot that the production staff decided to use them in the text, rather than only in marketing materials.

Friends and colleagues who gave invaluable support include Janice Maffei, Adrienne Corn, Peter Neamann, Victoria Marsick, Patricia McGraw Romano, Bill Franzblau, Hinton Battle, Kaylie Jones, Matt Klamm, Franky Grebacher, Georgia Sauer, Jane Faily, Lynn Lobban, Gail Phanuf, Bob and Debby Rosenfeld, Nick Ritchie, Karen Streets-Anderson, Andi Seals, Mark and Maxine Rossman, Adrienne Ewing-Roush, Hillary Chapman, Mehr Mansuri, and Shidan Majidi. How can one do such a project without family love and support? My sister, Janet Mittelsteadt, is a true friend; my cousin Shannon Stordock, who is almost my doppelgänger—and her sweet mother Jennylle, Aunt Maxine Shroeder, cousin Marilyn Nowak (a bright light), Michael Shoemaker (the genealogist who has helped me find my own roots), and Katherine Runde (who is so precious); and my Aunt Babe, who is forever a link to the past. There is no way to imagine my life without my three beautiful daughters—Roxanne, Solange, and Elizabeth—who have taught me more than all my degrees combined.

We both want to express our deep appreciation to the team of dedicated professionals at South-Western who were committed to the vision of producing the best management skills text ever. We are grateful to Scott Person, executive editor, whose interest, creative ideas, and assistance kept this book's spirit alive. Erin Guendelsberger and Jennifer King, developmental editors, provided encouragement, superb project coordination, and excellent ideas that helped the team meet a demanding and sometimes arduous schedule. Jon Monahan, Market Development Manager, provided valuable ideas throughout the project. Emily Nesheim and Cliff Kallemeyn, content project managers, expertly managed the production phase and ensured that everyone working on the production process adhered to high standards of quality. Tippy McIntosh and Stacy Shirley, art directors, contributed their graphic arts skills to create a visually dynamic design. Thanks also to media editor Rob Ellington, print buyer Ron Montgomery, and rights specialist Amber Hosea.

Another group of people who made a major contribution to this textbook are the management experts who provided advice, reviews, answers to questions, and suggestions for changes, insertions, and clarifications. We want to thank each of these colleagues for their valuable feedback and suggestions on this first edition:

Joe S. Anderson
Franke College of Business, Northern Arizona University

Kathryn Archard
University of Massachusetts Boston

Don Ashbaugh
Fort Hays State University

John H. Barr
Keuka College

Gregory O. Bruce
La Salle University

Jonathan Bundy
University of Georgia

Denise Daniels
Seattle Pacific University

Christine R. Day
Eastern Michigan University

Joseph V. DePalma
Fairleigh Dickinson University

Ivan Filby
Greenville College

David Glew
University of North Carolina Wilmington

Kimberly Goudy
Central Ohio Technical College

George Griffin, Ed.D.
Spring Arbor University

Melissa L. Gruys
Wright State University

Pamela Buckle Henning
Adelphi University

Joanne Hix
Dallas Baptist University

Diane Holtzman
Richard Stockton College of New Jersey

Jonathan Jelen
Parsons The New School for Design

Jim Jolly
Idaho State University

Antoinette S. Knechtges
Eastern Michigan University

Jerry Luckett
Dakota Wesleyan University

Erin Makarius
Canisius College

Karen S. Markel
Oakland University

Cheryl Meheden
University of Lethbridge

Morgan R. Milner, Ph.D.
Eastern Michigan University

David M. Nemi
Niagara County Community College

Joseph Seltzer
La Salle University

Elaine M. Tweedy
The University of Scranton

Maria Vitale
Chaffey College

Paula Weber
St. Cloud State University

INTRODUCTION

A New Approach to Management Skills

Lisa Drakeman was happy teaching religion courses at Princeton when her husband asked her to help out at Medarex, a new biotechnology company he founded to develop antibody-based medicines for cancer and infectious diseases. Drakeman began performing various tasks part-time, and soon found herself appointed as CEO of a spinoff company, Genmab AS of Denmark.

Drakeman had to quickly learn about management. One key to her survival was to ask "dumb" questions, such as "What is a clean room?" and not worry about appearing stupid. She also observed and borrowed management techniques from established pharmaceutical companies, such as how to flexibly reassemble employees for new projects. One of her toughest challenges was learning not to do everything herself the way she did as a teacher. In the beginning, Drakeman attended every meeting, interviewed every job candidate, and read every draft of clinical trial designs. She soon realized that she couldn't master every detail, and that trying to do so was clogging the company's growth. Although it was hard to step back, Drakeman made the transition to performing as a manager. Instead of trying to keep track of every stage of product development, she established procedures and delegated the details of new products and clinical trials to others. Rather than interviewing job candidates herself, she set up human resources systems to enable others to interview, hire, and train employees. By changing from individual performer to manager, Drakeman helped Genmab grow from 25 employees to around 200 within a few years.[1]

Lisa Drakeman learned the skills to become a successful manager. She learned how to hire the right people, delegate authority, and ask questions to learn about the pharmaceuticals business. The transition from individual performer to manager or executive is a challenge for most people. The purpose of this introduction is to explain the nature of management and explore the dynamics associated with successful and not-so-successful managers. By the end of this introduction you will recognize some of the skills managers use to keep organizations on track and begin to understand how managers can achieve astonishing results through people. The chapters of this textbook will focus on specific management insights and skills to help you develop competence as a manager.

MANAGERS PERFORM THE EXECUTIVE FUNCTION

Management as we know it today probably arrived fairly recently on the calendar of social evolution. An early manager in a tribal society might have been a respected elder who helped resolve disputes among members. Early industry was made up mostly of individual craftspeople doing their own work in a feudal or tribal society. Early warfare may have looked like William Wallace's efforts in thirteenth-century Scotland to overthrow English rule, as depicted in the movie *Braveheart*. Warfare was mostly a large horde of medieval clansman, each fighting an individual battle with an enemy combatant. The leader served as a warrior in the battle rather than directing strategy from the rear.

The executive function includes direction, organization, and coordination for an entire system.[2] The need for a management function, sometimes called the organization's *executive function*, was born when organizations grew into large armies, large industrial firms, and large governments. The executive function is responsible for the organization itself. Some people learned to master the executive function, which became a specialized role. As Lisa Drakeman discovered, managers are responsible for the organization as a whole. Rather than focus on the accomplishment of a single task, a manager's responsibility is to organize and make the most of all the people and tasks in combination. The executive function is intangible and multidimensional, yet vital to an organization's success. For example, in a manufacturing company, employees perform activities such as operations, marketing, finance, and human resources (HR). The executive function is to provide the overall vision and strategic direction, set goals, and implement plans of action to achieve the company's desired outcomes from all these work units. The executive function is forward-looking, provides a strategic beacon for other departments, builds teams, engages employees, shapes the culture, mediates conflicts, and coordinates the various activities of an organization.

To understand the executive function, consider the coach of a sports team. Pat Summitt, head coach emeritus of the University of Tennessee Lady Vols basketball team, is recognized for winning more games than any other NCAA basketball coach in history, but she didn't do it by scoring three-point shots, stealing balls, snagging rebounds, or making expert defensive moves on the court. Summitt couldn't go in and make a free throw for a player, steal the ball, or guard against a competing team member. Instead, her role was to shape the team culture, motivate people, provide overall coordination and direction, and guide the players to perform well. When she was head coach of the Lady Vols, Pat Summitt fulfilled the executive function that brings disparate parts together to achieve goals. That is the manager's role in any organization.

There is a huge difference between performing the executive function and performing a regular task. Consider Alina, who loves making cupcakes. People tell Alina her cupcakes are delicious, so she decides to bake and sell cupcakes for a living. As sales increase, she hires people and assigns them to duties in the kitchen and the front counter. As the business grows and adds new bakery products, Alina becomes stressed out. She is now overwhelmed with operational problems, people issues, and customer concerns. Alina started the business because she loves making cupcakes, and now she is overloaded with management responsibilities that she does not enjoy at all. There is little time to create recipes and do the baking—tasks she enjoys. Alina, unlike Lisa Drakeman and Pat Summitt, cannot embrace the executive function so long as her mind thinks of baking cupcakes as her primary job and feels resistance to all the management issues.

Just as a basketball coach's job is not to make three-pointers or play defense, as a manager, Alina's job is not to make cupcakes. Rather, the role of the executive function *is to design and manage the organization to make cupcakes.*[3] As much as Alina loves to make and sell cupcakes, her focus of responsibility as CEO has to be bigger, and without a mental shift, her new business is likely to fail. The ideal manager performing the executive function loves designing and managing an organization in the same way Alina loves designing recipes and making cupcakes. The manager has to have a sense of how basic tasks fit together to achieve the organization's purpose. The manager is concerned with hiring and training people so the business has the right people to provide efficient operations and market cupcakes to customers. To make the transition in mental focus, Alina must learn to think of the "organization" as the real product of her efforts, as an entity separate from herself, as a human system that she designs to make cupcakes, hamburgers, software, or whatever.

For any organization to succeed, the organization as a whole and each of its major divisions or departments must have someone paying attention to the executive function. Exhibit 1 illustrates the role of the executive function. Even though today's more participative organizations strive to harness the intellectual capital of all employees, *the executive function itself cannot be abandoned or delegated away*. Managers who become entangled mostly in non-management tasks and decisions are not performing the executive function. If managers do not perform a vital executive function distinct from other work activities, they are not doing their job.

Exhibit 1 Managers Provide an Executive Function for Each Part of the Organization

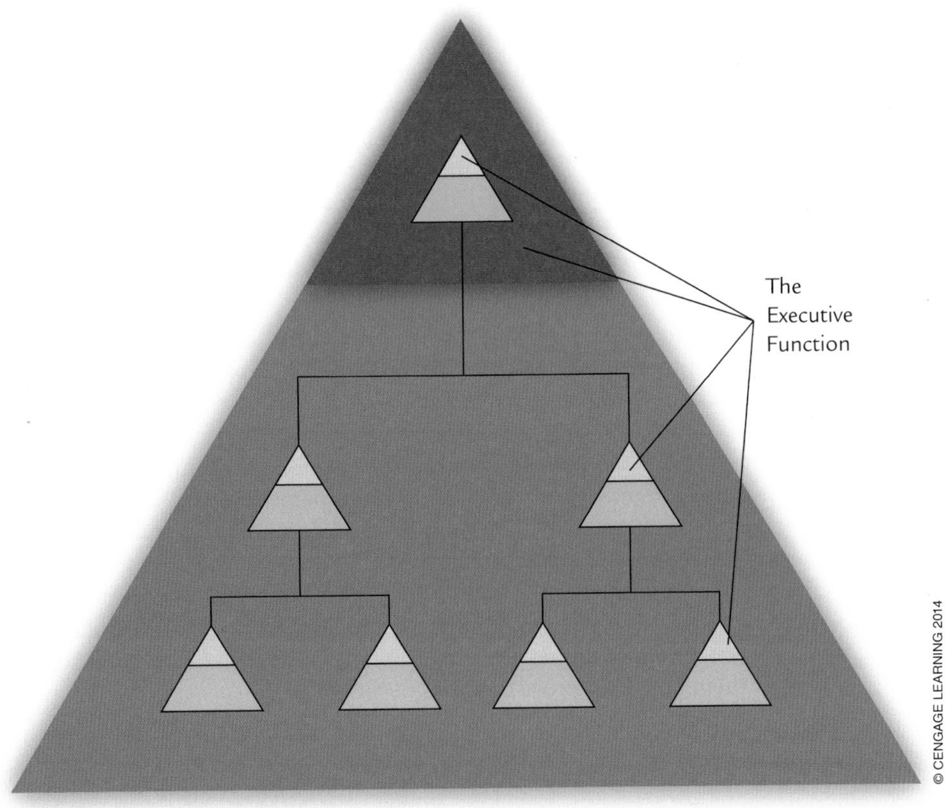

© CENGAGE LEARNING 2014

SKILLED MANAGERS ARE ESSENTIAL

Good managers make an enormous contribution to society by engaging people and resources to produce valued outcomes. Managers are custodians of society's most powerful institutions, and thus must act responsibly and hold themselves to a higher standard of skill and performance. Managers venture into uncharted territory and must appreciate the larger importance of their organization, profession, community, and society.[4] Consider the following examples:

- **Knowledge Is Power Program (KIPP) Schools** The KIPP Schools were started in 1994 when two teachers, Mike Fienberg and Dave Levin, launched a new school program in inner-city Houston, Texas. There are now 82 KIPP schools in the United States serving 20,000 students. KIPP schools serve the most disadvantaged students and produce seemingly miraculous transformations. Managers have created an organization in which low-income students regularly outperform their public school counterparts in math and reading tests. Fewer than one in five low-income students attend college nationally, yet KIPP's college matriculation is above 80 percent for students who complete the eighth grade. Nearly 95 percent of KIPP students who complete the eighth grade go on to college-prep high schools. Waiting lists are commonplace because parents want their children exposed to the marvel of effective management at KIPP schools.[5]
- **New York City Police System** Another revolution brought about by highly competent managers has transformed community policing. In the 1990s, then-New York Police Commissioner William Bratton devised a proactive system of police work designed to reduce crime. Bratton delegated to his precinct commanders the responsibility for everything that went wrong in their geographical area. He also installed a computer system called Compstat that tracked crime trends to help precinct personnel spot problems and brainstorm sophisticated solutions. Active police work made New York City one of the safest cities in North America. Crime plummeted. Over an 11-year period, murders in New York declined an astonishing 76.2 percent, and robberies dropped 74.2 percent. Municipal police managers around the country adopted these management techniques, contributing to the steadily declining crime rate in the United States.[6]
- **Best Companies** The companies on *Fortune* magazine's annual list of 100 best companies to work for are also the best managed companies. One study of these companies revealed that investing each year in the best companies to work for would have produced a return nearly twice the market average.[7] One company that quickly zoomed to the upper ranks of *Fortune*'s list of best companies to work for is Zappos.com. Fed up with working in a poor corporate culture, Tony Hsieh started a new company to sell shoes and decided that Zappos.com would be devoted to making employees and customers happy. The managers at Zappos made a happy culture their number one priority. Employees were engaged in defining core values and encouraged to come up with ideas for building "their" culture. Building on the success of its efforts, Zappos now offers seminars to managers from other companies to show them how to improve their business cultures.[8]

As another example of the role of good management, when CEO Alan R. Mulally joined Ford Motor Company as an outsider, his management competence resolved many problems, including the infighting among Ford divisions. Mulally pulled together diverse global managers into a single team, had the foresight to borrow $24 billion to avoid the bankruptcy that plagued rivals General Motors and Chrysler, reduced factories and jobs to better align production with demand for autos, and championed a line of smaller, lighter, and environmentally friendly passenger cars.[9]

At the other extreme, bad managers can create catastrophes for their organizations and for the larger society. Consider the finance manager who was promoted to financial controller of the company after proving himself as a top contributor in his department. Unfortunately, this manager held tightly to the reins of decision making, not trusting others to make good judgments. He insisted that all information go through him and that everyone check with him before taking action. Consequently, field operators couldn't get the information they needed, decision making slowed to a crawl, performance slipped precipitously, and business was lost.[10]

On a societal level, bad management caused the Wall Street meltdown that contributed to a worldwide financial crisis. Managers at home loan originators aggressively pushed subprime and no-documentation loans to borrowers who could not afford them. Managers at investment companies such as Bear Stearns, Lehman Brothers, and Merrill Lynch got into serious trouble by buying subprime assets and repackaging them into bond-like securities sold to investors as rated very safe. Managers at investment rating companies contributed to the calamity by praising the investments, the companies, and their leaders. Executives paid themselves huge salaries and bonuses even as losses mounted into the billions. The whole episode reflects a failure of responsible management. As Harvard's Bill George said: "The . . . crisis was not caused by subprime mortgages, credit default swaps, or failed economic policies. The root cause is failed leadership."[11]

WHAT DOES IT TAKE TO BE A SKILLED MANAGER?

One management theorist may describe the essence of management as people—leading and developing people. Another may focus on the need for control, and yet another on the importance of strategy. Another theorist may focus on the "action" aspect of management and study the amount of hard work. Yet another may focus on decision-making. As Henry Mintzberg describes in his book, *Managing*, all of these views are correct. An effective manager does all of these things blended together.[12] Many studies of managerial work have successfully identified specific activities and roles that a successful manager performs. What are the required competencies that are common to all managers? Exhibit 2 shows a summary of some key manager competencies.

One striking aspect of the activities shown in Exhibit 2 is the variety. A manager is called upon to do many different things. One early researcher struggling to make sense of managerial work commented that executive behavior is "so varied and so hard to grasp" that "it is more practical art than applied science."[13] Every manager has to face a broad diversity of demands and master many varied skills.

Managing Yourself

These are personal competencies that include self-awareness, reflective thinking, and knowing one's own strengths and weaknesses. Time management and self-organization bring the manager's thought processes to life in the form of a calendar or schedule that

Exhibit 2 Some Key Competencies for Managers

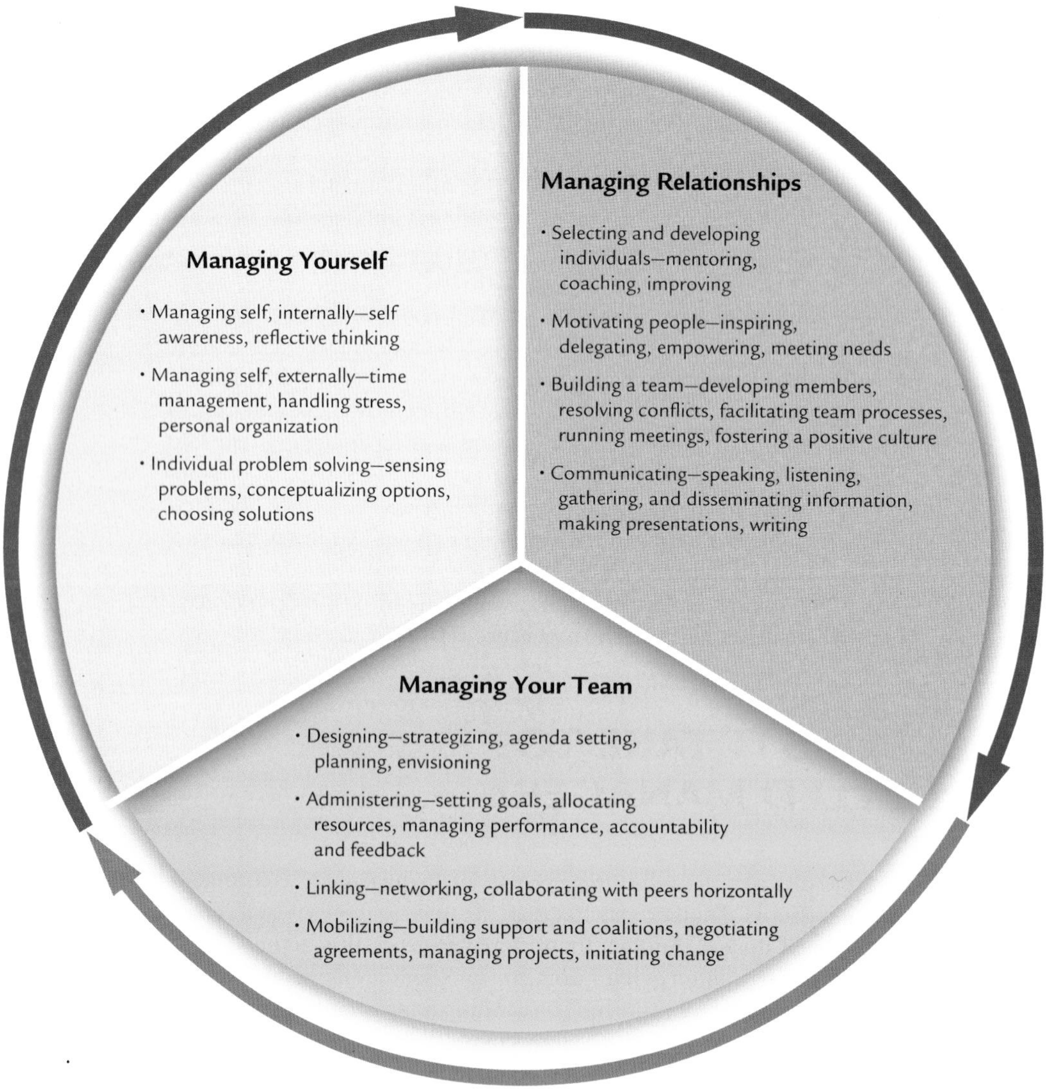

Source: Based on Henry Mintzberg, *Managing* (San Francisco: Berrett-Koehler Publishers, 2009), Chapter 3.

signals intention to other people. Thoughtful problem solving and decision making also fall into the realm of managing yourself. Indeed, some managers have been known to systematically tabulate and count their own time allocation as a way to maintain their time-management goals.

Managing Relationships

These are the interpersonal competencies, which include social skills to deal effectively with other people, such as selecting the right people for the job and developing and coaching them to higher performance. Motivating people is similar, including the need to energize, inspire, and delegate. A manager identifies what needs to be done but can leave the decisions and specific activities to someone else. Building a team may be the biggest challenge in this category, because people have to give up some individuality for the success of a group. The manager's job is to help people play as a team rather than be a collection of individuals. Communicating takes the most time, perhaps 40 percent of a manager's day. Managers find themselves frequently getting information as well as informing and advising other people about relevant events and activities.

Managing Your Team

These management competencies often pertain to design and administration. A manager acts as the architect of organizational purpose by formulating strategies and plans for others to implement. Administering is often seen as the routine work of setting goals, allocating resources, analyzing paperwork and documents, and holding people accountable for desired outcomes. The manager is responsible for instituting specific directions and controls. One of the least understood competencies is linking to numerous people and groups in other parts of and outside the organization. Networking is a pervasive aspect of management. Compared to non-managers, managers have large networks. They develop these networks on a peer level and with senior people. Finally, managers champion the needs of their unit upward and outward in the organization, lobby for its causes, and advocate on its behalf. Managers use their networking skills to build support, negotiate deals, and manage ongoing change projects.

The trick for mastering the many competencies in Exhibit 2 is to maintain balance, to not focus on one competency to the exclusion of others. The ideal for a manager is to be well-rounded. A manager may have specific strengths, such as for strategizing, administering, or building a team. However, it is the ability to play multiple roles that produces the best performance.[14] Too much thinking and self-reflection can weigh a manager down. Too much communicating without a thoughtful purpose becomes empty and aimless rhetoric. A manager who spends too much time administering may bog the unit down with rules and bureaucracy and thereby overlook the need to motivate people and build a team. The manager's job is best seen holistically, with the need to develop some competency in each area of managing oneself, managing relationships, and managing a team.

WHY IS GOOD MANAGEMENT SO DIFFICULT?

Management is harder than it looks. Life as a manager looks appealing, and most people think of the step into a managerial role as a positive move both personally and professionally. When you're toiling away in a low-level position, it's easy to think that managers have it made. They get to make the decisions and issue the orders rather than being at the mercy of someone else telling them what to do. Yet being a good manager is exceedingly demanding, sometimes frustrating, and downright difficult.

New managers are often surprised at how difficult management is. FedEx found that 10 percent of new managers asked to leave their managerial position in less than a year, prompting the company to start a course called "Is Management for Me?" to give people a better understanding of what management entails. Between 30 and 40 percent of those who take the course decide *not* to pursue a management career.[15] And many people who are already managers are ready to jump off the management track.

"I hated all the meetings," said Bill White, who left his post as an award-winning manager of a real estate office to return to selling. "And I found the more you did for people who work for you, the more they expected. I was a counselor, motivator, financial advisor, psychologist." Likewise, MacKenzie Walker of Portland, Oregon, left his management job last year. "I was told 50 hours a week was not enough and that I had to work my people harder. The few dollars more were not worth the pain."[16]

Why is a manager's job so tough? One reason is the array of manager competencies needed to succeed, as just discussed and shown in Exhibit 2. Managers have to be good at many different things. A manager good with people might drop the ball on strategy or efficient management of time. An effective administrator may assert too much control and alienate rather than motivate direct reports. Dirk Meyer, former CEO of Advanced Micro Devices (AMD), provides an illustration. After he was appointed CEO in 2008, Meyer provided superb management of AMD's existing operations but seemed unable to set a vision and strategy for taking the company in new directions, skills that were needed to help AMD thrive in a rapidly changing industry. Meyer resigned in early 2011 after the board said it would begin searching for a more visionary top leader.[17] No individual can be good at everything, but effective managers thrive on many different skills rather than developing one or just a few competencies. Two other reasons managers sometimes struggle are the fragmentation and unrelenting pace of the job, and the lack of preparation for the dramatic change compared to non-management work.

Fragmented Multitasking on Speed Dial

Manager activities are characterized by variety, fragmentation, and brevity.[18] The average time spent on any one activity is less than nine minutes. Managers shift gears quickly. Significant crises are interspersed with trivial events in no predictable sequence. For example, a human resources manager may be studying press clippings about her department when a colleague stops by to tell her about a possible sexual harassment problem. After they discuss how to handle the issue, the manager starts preparing an important briefing for the board of directors when she is interrupted by a phone call asking about the company's upcoming employee picnic. Every manager's job has essential similarities. Consider the diverse events in a typical few hours for Marine Captain Sean Miller in Fallujah, Iraq as he manages reconstruction efforts.[19]

- Begins the day meeting with tribal sheiks and local officials to decide which projects to pursue
- Drives to check the status of a job that a contractor has left unfinished
- Walks to a nearby school to discuss awards for students who recite passages from the Koran
- Is interrupted by a handful of people who have come with questions or demands
- Finally returns to the discussion of student awards
- Agrees to a tour of the school, where a contractor requests a $50,000 generator that Miller believes can be obtained for $8,000
- Checks the recently cleaned grounds at another school and finds that trash once again litters the area
- Notices a man running a pipe from his roof and intervenes to warn him against running his sewage to the school
- Calms his Marines, who grow skittish as teenage students rush from the school building

- Takes photos of a still-damaged cemetery door that contractors have been paid to repair
- Stops by a café to hear young men's complaints that they are asked to pay bribes to get a job

In addition to the variety, managers also work at an unrelenting pace. Effective managers work quickly and expend great energy. A typical manager observed by Mintzberg processed 36 physical pieces of mail each day (before e-mail), attended eight meetings, and took a tour through a building or plant. As soon as the daily calendar was set, disturbances erupted and new meetings were required. There is no escape from relentless demands. During time away from the office, executives catch up on paperwork, phone calls, and e-mail. For example, Brett Yormark of the New Jersey Nets typically responds to about 60 e-mail messages before he even shaves and dresses for the day.[20]

Not Prepared for the Promotion

Many people promoted into a management position have little idea what the job actually entails and receive little training. Organizations often promote their star performers into management, both to reward the individuals and to bring new talent into management. But the shift from worker to manager is not easy. Diane Baker, an expert nurse who was promoted to supervisor, quickly found herself overwhelmed by the challenge of supervising former peers, keeping up with paperwork, and understanding financial and operational issues.[21] Harvard professor Linda Hill followed a group of 19 managers during their first year of management. She found that becoming a manager involved a profound transformation in the way people think of themselves and their work. Exhibit 3 outlines the transformation experienced by many new managers.

Recall the earlier discussion of the role of manager as fulfilling the executive function by building systems and coordinating activities rather than doing specific tasks. The individual contributor's mind is conditioned to think in terms of doing specialized tasks as expertly as possible. The manager, on the other hand, has to be a generalist and learn to coordinate a broad range of activities to achieve a unified purpose. In addition, the individual performer gets things done mostly through his or her own efforts, developing the habit of relying on self rather than others. The manager, though, gets things done by influencing other people.

Exhibit 3 Why New Managers Face a Rude Awakening

Expectations Based on Non-Management Job	Reality of the Manager's Job
Specialist doing specific tasks	Be friendly, be liked
Get things done through own efforts	Generalist coordinating diverse tasks
An individual actor	Gets things done by influencing others, using diplomacy
Work independently	A network builder
Use formal control	Depends on others
Managing one-on-one	Energizes others, uses persuasion
Keep operation in working order	Pulls together a team
Hold others accountable	Initiates changes for better performance

Source: Based on Linda A. Hill, *Becoming a Manager: Mastery of a New Identity*, 2nd ed. (Boston, MA: Harvard Business School Press, 2003).

New managers typically go through the transition via "trial by fire," learning on the job as they go, making frequent mistakes. The following sections describe some common mistakes new managers make.

Mistake #1: Trying to Do Too Much

Many new managers try to do all the work themselves rather than delegate and persuade others to do the work. Alan Mulally, CEO of Ford, had to learn this lesson. In his first job as an engineering supervisor, he forced other engineers to redo their work many times until one engineer quit. When Mulally asked why, the engineer told Mulally he might make a good supervisor someday, but right now, he said, "this is just too much for me to be supervised this tightly."[22] Mulally quickly learned that his job as supervisor was to focus on the engineering mission and let people be in control of their own work.

Mistake #2: Failing to Appreciate Interdependence

A successful individual contributor can focus on his or her own work and stay independent of others. A manager, by contrast, proactively builds a broad network while at the same time depending on direct reports to accomplish work for which the manager is responsible. New managers often expect to take advantage of the hierarchy for exerting authority, and then find themselves being ignored until they learn how to motivate and energize their direct reports. As Linda Hill commented in her study, "Being a manager means not merely assuming a position of authority but also becoming more dependent on others."[23]Another false expectation is that new managers will deal with direct reports one on one. Yet to succeed, managers have to think and work as a team rather than focusing on individual relationships. A big shift in thinking is from "I" to "we."

Managers may appear to have control over their time and be able to get rid of the undesirable aspects of their jobs to concentrate on big, important issues. In reality, most managers find themselves much more constrained than they were as non-managerial employees.[24] Rather than having more independence, they actually have less. They still have a boss to deal with, but they also have to manage relationships with subordinates, managers in other departments, and people outside the organization, all of whom make relentless and often conflicting demands on their time and energy. Byron Reimus, a former corporate communications manager, says he gave up his management job because he got tired of being "pulled in 15 different directions."[25]

Mistake #3: Expecting to Have Power

The new manager soon learns that just because she has a door with her name on it doesn't mean people are going to follow her suggestions. After a promotion, managers often encounter resentment from former colleagues, particularly if they try too hard to assert their new authority. People get promoted because they are well liked, and then have to hold previous friends accountable for performance, a potentially unpleasant task.

New managers are under constant scrutiny as employees analyze their every statement and action for signs of the new boss's motives and abilities.[26] Good managers listen to employees, build trust, and find ways to help people contribute and perform effectively, both as individuals and as a team. Steve Bennett, former CEO of Intuit, says he spent about 50 percent of his time coaching employees.[27]

Mistake #4: Maintaining the Status Quo

Although it is important to keep things running smoothly, managers also have to initiate change for better performance rather than accept the status quo. Being a good manager means coming up with new ideas and proposing and implementing changes that can help the team and the organization do even better in the future. This means learning to influence people all across the company and even outside the organization. A manager might have terrific ideas, but the ideas are worthless unless he can get them implemented.

The Challenge of Juggling Multiple Demands

For new managers, the multiple demands can seem overwhelming. And moving up the hierarchy doesn't make things any easier. Ray Sarnacki, who had a long career at General Electric and Lockheed Martin and now teaches management at St. Joseph's University, thought being a manager meant he'd have more influence at work and more control over both his work and home life, but he found the opposite to be true. The higher he moved up in the organization, Sarnacki says, "the less control I seemed to have over anything, including my own life."[28] For many managers, traveling incessantly, attending endless meetings, and dealing with mountains of paperwork seem to leave little time for anything else—but they still have to be a coach, motivator, and counselor for their employees; manage relationships with superiors and colleagues; and mediate between upper management and the workforce. Winona French, a manager at a large U. S. media company, refers to the experience as "like you are in final exams 365 days a year."[29]

A PROBLEM-BASED METHOD FOR LEARNING MANAGEMENT SKILLS

As a manager, your job will be fast moving, complex, and people oriented. Will you be ready for it? Management education has been criticized for being too theoretical and disconnected from management practice. Students are often trained in objective and factual knowledge, including quantitative analysis and calculation typical of "hard" subjects such as finance and accounting. Courses in "soft skills" are often taught in a similar fashion with lectures and objective tests. The term *soft skills* refers to an individual's people skills, including communication, collaboration, teamwork, self-reflection, ethical judgment, leadership, initiative, influence, people development and coaching, problem solving, and personal effectiveness.

The Primacy of Soft Skills

Some evidence suggests that soft or people skills will account for at least 80 percent of your job success, compared to about 15 percent accounted for by technical skills and functional expertise. Managers who want to advance in their careers pay attention to developing soft skills.[30] A recent survey comparing the importance of managerial skills today with those from the late 1980s found a decided increase in the role of soft skills, particularly skills for building relationships with others and skills for managing one's own time effectively.[31]

Even at a company such as Google that depends on technical expertise, soft skills are essential. Google analyzed performance reviews and feedback surveys to find out what makes a good manager of technical people and found that technical expertise ranked dead last among a list of eight desired manager qualities, as shown in Exhibit 4. The exhibit lists eight effective behaviors of good managers. Notice that almost all of them relate to soft skills such as communication, coaching, and teamwork. People want managers who listen to them, build positive relationships, help them learn by asking questions rather than dictating answers, and show an interest in their lives and careers.[32]

Exhibit 4 Google's Rules: Eight Good Behaviors for Managers

To know how to build better managers, Google executives studied performance reviews, feedback surveys, and award nominations to see what qualities made a good manager. Here are the "Eight Good Behaviors" they found, in order of importance:

1. Be a good coach.
2. Empower your team and don't micromanage.
3. Express interest in team members' success and personal well-being.
4. Don't be a sissy: Be productive and results-oriented.
5. Be a good communicator and listen to your team.
6. Help your employees with career development.
7. Have a clear vision and strategy for the team.
8. Have key technical skills so you can help advise the team.

Source: Reprinted with permission from Google, Inc.

The intangible soft skills such as those on the Google list in Exhibit 4 cannot be mastered through factual memorization. Personal mastery of soft skills involves deeper learning, including cognitive understanding plus actual practice inside and outside the classroom. This text offers a new approach for mastering the skills you will need to be a good manager.

Problem-Based Learning

A significant innovation in teaching management skills, called problem-based learning (PBL), started in medical schools and has since been adopted in schools of engineering, architecture, social work, law, and nursing.[33] The essence is simple—rather than starting with a "theory," you have the opportunity to start with a problem upon which to take action.

Traditional learning is based on the principle, "first learn, then do." Through lectures and reading assignments, students digest and memorize conceptual material that they hope to apply on the job after their coursework is finished. PBL reverses this sequence into "first do, then learn." Action comes first. With action-first learning, you will start with realistic problem scenarios and take action to solve them. Conceptual material can come later in support of solving the problem and synthesizing lessons for future applications. One reason action-first learning based on PBL is so effective is that it actualizes your existing knowledge, and then adds new knowledge to it. PBL engages you in *active* rather than passive learning. That is, you try things to learn what works, improving your skills through repetition and practice. This action-first learning is consistent with the action-oriented nature of the work you will experience when you become a practicing manager.

FRAMEWORK FOR THE BOOK

The content of this book may appear to be similar to a typical course in management, leadership, or organizational behavior. This book differs from other textbooks by providing a coherent skill-learning system for each topic, and each topic provides opportunities to learn the relevant skills via an action-first approach.

Plan of the Book

The book is divided into three major sections, each with a different focus to which management skills apply. The major sections along with chapter titles are illustrated in Exhibit 5. Note that these sections address the three areas of key competencies for managers outlined at the beginning of this introduction in Exhibit 2.

Part I, Managing Yourself, contains the chapters on personal skills. Personal skills pertain to what goes on inside you, such as your strengths and weaknesses, self-awareness, self-organization, creativity and problem solving, the ability to communicate, and your ethical foundation. Of course these skills involve other people, but the primary focus of these topics is on you.

Exhibit 5 The Essential Skills of Management

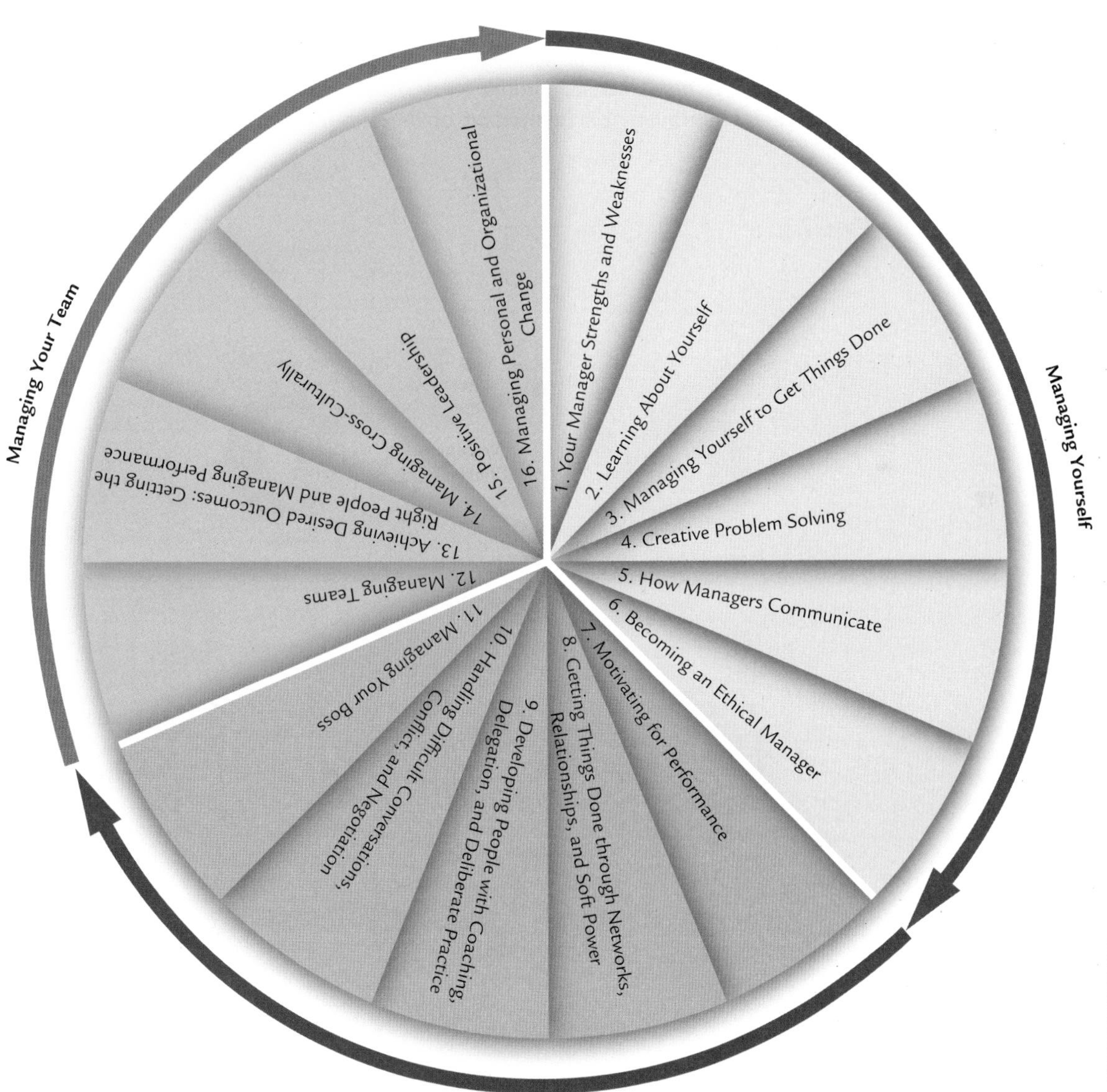

© CENGAGE LEARNING 2014

Part II, Managing Relationships, focuses on interpersonal skills, which represent the skills that define how you interact with and relate to other people. The interpersonal domain is the arena of the soft skills that can make or break a manager. These skills include motivating direct reports, building networks and managing relationships, providing coaching and feedback, influencing others, handling difficult conversations and conflict, and managing upward. These chapters cover interpersonal skills in all directions and deal with most possible contingencies.

Part III, Managing Your Team, includes chapters for managing a team or an organization. These skills focus more on how to get work accomplished. The topics include building a team, getting things done through performance management, getting things done through delegation and engagement, managing people from diverse cultural backgrounds, positive leadership, and managing change. These topics encompass much of the executive function of an organization.

Building Block Plan of Each Chapter

Each chapter is organized according to the management skills learning sequence illustrated in Exhibit 6. Each element of the learning sequence in Exhibit 6 is a

Exhibit 6 The Skills Learning Model

Source: This learning model is based on John D. Bransford, Ann L. Brown, and Rodney R. Cocking, Eds., *How People Learn: Brain, Mind, Experience, and School* (Washington, D.C.: National Academy Press, 2000).

building block for learning management skills. The seven building blocks create an integrated learning system that begins with a problem and ends with clearly defined skill-based and knowledge-based takeaways, as explained in Exhibit 7.

Building block 1 is a learning challenge based on a real-world problem faced by a manager (Manager Challenge). The innovation here is that the management problems and incidents are provided as short videos for classroom viewing. After watching the Manager Challenge video, you are asked to craft a solution to the problem, either through written analysis, discussion, or role-play, which is building block 2 of the model (Initial Thoughts). This also provides a benchmark of current skill so you can later see how much you have learned.

Building block 3 consists of using survey instruments to assess your current style and competency concerning the subject matter presented in that chapter (Discover Yourself). You are provided the interpretation of your scores in the relevant content section of the text.

Building block 4 (Discover Knowledge), provides research-based knowledge and ideas that may be useful in solving the type of learning challenge confronted in building blocks 1, 2, and 3. These learning resources include text material, instructor's lecture, video streams, Web links, and perhaps outside readings depending on instructor preference. These resources expose you to multiple perspectives on how the current problem and future problems might be solved.

Building block 5 gives you a chance to put new knowledge into practice (Action Learning). By participating in individual deliberate practice exercises and team exercises, you can apply and test your new knowledge and skills.[34] Action learning means learning by doing, individually or in teams, both inside and outside the classroom.

Exhibit 7 The Integrated Building Blocks for Learning Management Skills

Building Block	Elements	Purpose
1. Manager Challenge	Video incidents Written incidents	Students challenged with a critical incident
2. Initial Thoughts	Role-play it Write it down Group discussion	Students try out own ideas Benchmark starting knowledge Become aware of own learning gap
3. Discover Yourself	Survey instruments	Benchmark students' current style
4. Discover Knowledge	Read text Class lecture Videos, other resources	Resources from which to learn conscious knowledge
5. Action Learning	Deliberate Practice Exercises In-Class Team Exercise Field Team Exercise	Apply concepts Practice Gather feedback Gain competence
6. Test Your Mettle	Role Play Simulations Video Application Case Incidents	Broader, stretch-yourself applications for students and groups
7. Personal Skills Log	Write down new insights and skills gained from chapter	Students record new mastery compared to initial manager challenge

Source: This learning model is based on John D. Bransford, Ann L. Brown, and Rodney R. Cocking, Eds., *How People Learn: Brain, Mind, Experience, and School* (Washington D.C.: National Academy Press, 2000).

Building block 6 stretches you further by asking you to apply your new skills to new problems, role plays, and cases (Test Your Mettle). This step of the learning sequence challenges you in a way that will deepen and expand your learning. Again, you will be learning based on your own actions rather than from text memorization.

Building block 7 encourages you to sum up and write down the takeaways you have learned from the parts of the chapter you completed (Personal Skills Log). An insight quickly disappears if it isn't written down. By writing down your learning takeaways immediately after class, you crystallize what you have learned compared to your initial response to the opening Manager Challenge video. Your instructor may ask you to aggregate and analyze these takeaways at the end of the course so both you and your instructor can see and appreciate your progress.

NEED TO KNOW

- Managers perform the executive function for a team, department, or organization rather than performing specific job tasks; that is, they provide direction, organization, and coordination for the entire system.
- Skilled managers are essential to organizations and the larger society. Key competencies for managers fall into three broad categories: managing yourself, managing relationships, and managing teams or organizations.
- A manager's job is extremely varied and fragmented. Managers have to be good at many different things and often have to shift gears quickly.
- Many people who are promoted to manager positions are not prepared for the transition from being an individual performer to being a manager who must get things done through other people.
- Four common mistakes new managers make are doing too much rather than delegating, failing to appreciate the interdependent nature of management, expecting to have power and control, and maintaining the status quo rather than promoting new ideas for change.
- Soft skills, including communication, collaboration, teamwork, self-reflection, ethical judgment, leadership, initiative, influence, people development and coaching, problem solving, and personal effectiveness, will account for as much as 80 percent of your success as a manager.
- Problem-based learning is an innovative approach to developing management skills that starts with a problem upon which to take action rather than with a theory. Problem-based learning starts with what you bring to the learning situation, gives you opportunities to learn actively rather than passively, enables you to make connections between your own experience and new knowledge, and helps you apply what you learn to future problems and situations.

ADDENDUM: YOU AND THE MANAGER'S JOB

YOUR MANAGER APTITUDE

Instructions: Think back to a time when you were a team leader. If you have not been a leader, imagine how you would have led a specific team you were part of that completed a major project or task. Rate how accurately each statement describes you based on whether the statement is clearly true or accurate, clearly false or inaccurate, or in the middle as somewhat true and somewhat false.

Part A	True	Somewhat	False
1. I am patient and helpful when giving complicated explanations.	○	○	○
2. I provide frequent, ongoing feedback to let members know how they are doing.	○	○	○
3. I give encouragement and support when a person has a difficult task.	○	○	○
4. I have regular one-on-one meetings to discuss and develop members' competencies.	○	○	○

Total Score Part A ________. (Sum questions 1–4, giving 3 points for each True, 2 points for each Somewhat, and 1 point for each False.)

Part B	True	Somewhat	False
5. I foster cooperative relationships among team members.	○	○	○
6. I give others a great deal of freedom to decide how they work.	○	○	○
7. I show confidence in others by letting them make important decisions on their own.	○	○	○
8. I give stretch assignments that allow people to handle big problems.	○	○	○

Total Score Part B ________. (Sum questions 5–8, giving 3 points for each True, 2 points for each Somewhat, and 1 point for each False.)

Part C	True	Somewhat	False
9. I convey a warm, interpersonal style.	○	○	○
10. I know about my team members' families and lives outside work.	○	○	○
11. I work hard to maintain good interpersonal relationships with all team members.	○	○	○
12. I show good understanding of new team members' needs.	○	○	○

Total Score Part C ________. (Sum questions 9–12, giving 3 points for each True, 2 points for each Somewhat, and 1 point for each False.)

Part D

	True	Somewhat	False
13. I spend much time making sure that people on the team adhere to the goals and standards we agreed upon.	○	○	○
14. I hold people accountable for achieving our goals.	○	○	○
15. I use my influence to remove roadblocks to team performance.	○	○	○
16. I stay focused on team goals and how to help members achieve those goals.	○	○	○

Total Score Part D ________. (Sum questions 13–16, giving 3 points for each True, 2 points for each Somewhat, and 1 point for each False.)

Part E

17. I actively listen to members' concerns about proposals or plans without getting defensive.	○	○	○
18. I encourage open dialogue and listen to issues and concerns.	○	○	○
19. I over-communicate relevant information members may want or need about decisions and plans.	○	○	○
20. I consult with people to get their reactions and suggestions before making a major decision.	○	○	○

Total Score Part E ________. (Sum questions 17–20, giving 3 points for each True, 2 points for each Somewhat, and 1 point for each False.)

Part F

21. I frequently inquire about members' career progress and next steps.	○	○	○
22. I consciously help people get assignments that will advance their careers.	○	○	○
23. I delegate many assignments to help people grow.	○	○	○
24. I observe and discuss members' progress on their strengths and weaknesses.	○	○	○

Total Score Part F ________. (Sum questions 21–24, giving 3 points for each True, 2 points for each Somewhat, and 1 point for each False.)

Part G

25. I engage team members in setting a vision and the strategy to get there.	○	○	○
26. I make the team's mission attractive and attainable.	○	○	○
27. I help the team stay focused on clear goals and actionable plans.	○	○	○
28. I maintain a broad view and communicate where we are headed.	○	○	○

Total Score Part G ________. (Sum questions 25–28, giving 3 points for each True, 2 points for each Somewhat, and 1 point for each False.)

Part H

	True	Somewhat	False
29. I actively solicit feedback and criticism from my team's customers about the job we are doing.	○	○	○
30. I answer requests for technical information.	○	○	○
31. I understand technical quality and help define ways to improve.	○	○	○
32. I periodically check on the progress and quality of my team's work.	○	○	○

Total Score Part H ________. (Sum questions 29–32, giving 3 points for each True, 2 points for each Somewhat, and 1 point for each False.)

Check the interpretation of your scores on page 20.

INTERVIEW A MANAGER

Locate a manager who is willing to be interviewed about being a manager. This person should be a full-time manager, such as a business owner, a manager in a non-profit, or a manager in a larger firm, such as a department head or vice-president. Be sure to explain that you are a student completing an assignment for a class in management. Be sensitive to confidentiality issues.

Your goal is to get an idea about what it is like to manage, which means to get things accomplished through the work of others rather than doing it yourself. Below are some questions that may help you obtain relevant information.

1. What is a typical day like for you at work? How do you spend your time all day?

2. How would you describe your management style?

3. What are the most important elements of your job as a manager?

4. What are some typical problems with which you must deal?

5. What was the biggest change you had to make when you first became a manager? What new skills did you need to learn?

6. In your experience, what are the most difficult aspects of being a manager?

7. What are the most satisfying aspects of being a manager?

8. Do you like making decisions as a manager? Do you prefer to make decisions by yourself or as a group with people you supervise? Please explain.

9. If you had to hire someone to replace you, what skills and strengths would you consider most important?

10. How do you motivate employees?

11. What ethical issues do you encounter?

12. What does it mean to be an effective manager?

DISCOVER YOURSELF

Interpret Your Score: Google's Rules for Team Managers

Your eight scores reflect Google's rules for effective team managers as illustrated in Exhibit 4. Higher scores reflect a manager competency closer to the Google ideal. The eight rules are in descending order of importance.

Part A: "Be a good coach" measures the extent to which you provide constructive feedback and instruction to team members along with encouragement and support. Comparative data: Thirty person Mean score = 10.1; Top Quartile = 11–12; Bottom Quartile = 7–10.

Part B: "Empower your team and don't micromanage" reflects the extent to which you delegate appropriate freedom to motivate employees, along with providing stretch assignments. Comparative data: Thirty person Mean score = 10.1; Top Quartile = 11–12; Bottom Quartile = 8–9.

Part C: "Express interest in team members' success and personal well-being" measures the extent to which you know and care about your team members as people, welcome new people, and express a warm interpersonal style. Comparative data: Thirty person Mean score = 10.2; Top Quartile = 11–12; Bottom Quartile = 8–9.

Part D: "Don't be a sissy: Be productive and results oriented" is the extent to which you set appropriate standards, use your influence to clear the way, and keep your team focused on performance. Comparative data: Thirty person Mean score = 10.2; Top Quartile = 11–12; Bottom Quartile = 5–10.

Part E: "Be a good communicator and listen to your team" means you communicate to listen and share information, encourage open dialogue, and over-communicate to keep people informed. Comparative data: Thirty person Mean score = 10.2; Top Quartile = 11–12; Bottom Quartile = 8–9.

Part F: "Help your employees with career development" means that you are concerned with career progress beyond members' current jobs and find ways to develop them for future roles. Comparative data: Thirty person Mean score = 8.4; Top Quartile = 9–12; Bottom Quartile = 4–7.

Part G: "Have a clear vision and strategy for the team" measures the extent to which you involve the team in setting a vision and keep the team's focus on goals and strategy to achieve the vision. Comparative data: Thirty person Mean score = 10.3; Top Quartile = 12–12; Bottom Quartile = 5–9.

Part H: "Have key technical skills so you can help advise the team" measures your involvement and concern for the technical aspects of the team's work. Technical knowledge is important but is considered less important to effective management than the other factors above. Comparative data: Thirty person Mean score = 10.5; Top Quartile = 11–12; Bottom Quartile = 8–10.

© CENGAGE LEARNING 2014

Your instructor may ask you to write a brief report on what you learned from your manager interview or to work with others to combine results from multiple interviews in a single group paper.

STEP INTO A MANAGER'S SHOES

Astrix Games, Inc. In-Basket Exercise[35]

You—William Masterson—have been with Astrix Games for one year as sales manager in the Santa Monica office. Ricardo Salas, the general manager of the Austin branch, has been taken into custody in a foreign country with political instability. He went

Partial Organization Chart for Astrix Games Inc.

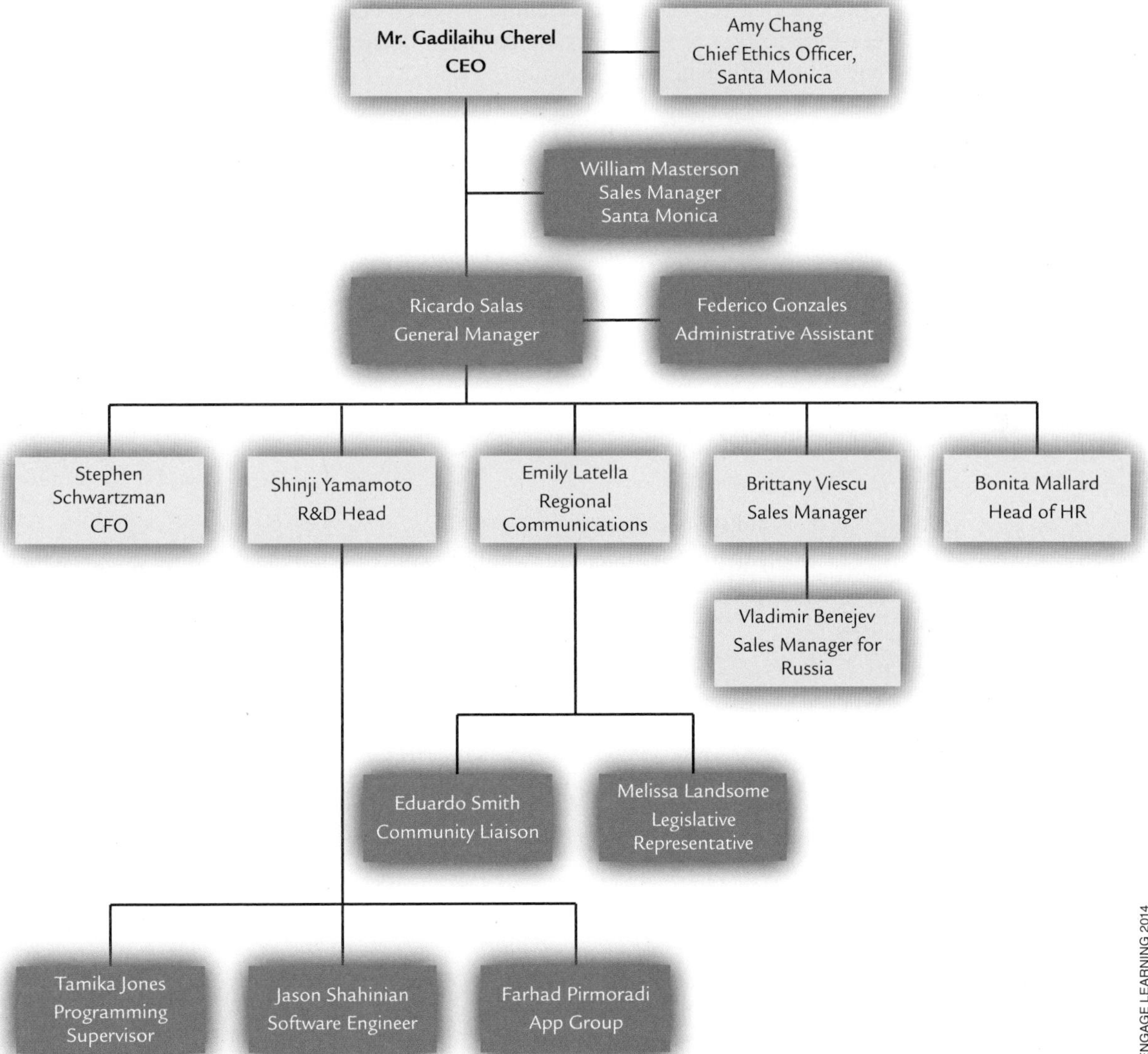

© CENGAGE LEARNING 2014

there to try and negotiate with the government to build a new factory for component parts. That country is making demands in order to release Salas, and no one knows when he'll be back. He left Tuesday and was arrested (on false charges) on Thursday. The U.S. State Department and Interpol are involved, trying to resolve the situation. In the meantime, you've been called to Austin to take over Salas's job for a few weeks. You worked with Salas some years ago when you were both in IT with IBM in Russia, but you haven't seen him much in the interim. Astrix Games' Austin office handles design, licensing, sales, and off-shore manufacturing of the education- and business-oriented games for the larger conglomerate of Astrix Games, Inc. You really believe in Astrix and feel this is a great opportunity to show headquarters that you can be more than sales manager.

Astrix Austin has seen sales decline during the past year. They haven't had a certifiable hit in three years. Despite the introduction of eight new games and 24 apps during this time, none has been as big as ROBOT IQ. You've seen reports about one of the new games that everyone expects to be a runaway success. GUITAR DANCE has been in development for two years and is sort of a cross between Air Guitar and Just Dance, with a YouTube component. It has been endorsed by music and dance teachers. Introduction of the new game has been delayed by some programming glitches and contractual issues with YouTube.

It is 8 A.M. on Monday, March 15th. You find a pile of e-mails with urgent matters, and your job now is to go through the correspondence and do the following for each e-mail message:

1. Decide whether you will:
   a. Call
   b. E-mail
   c. Meet personally
   d. Delegate (and to whom)
   e. No response needed
2. Decide whether you will do so:
   a. Immediately
   b. Within two to three days
3. Briefly write down how you would handle each problem and what your major concerns are.

E-mail message
From: Federico Gonzales, Administrative Assistant to Ricardo Salas
To: William Masterson
Subject: Your schedule
Date: March 15

Please note that I have forwarded the most important e-mails sent to Mr. Salas since he left the country. I am, of course, happy to follow-up with any of the issues that arise, either in the e-mails or otherwise.

One other item: Would you like me to cancel the event tomorrow afternoon? It is a celebration honoring the three years since ROBOT IQ (Austin's most successful game to date) hit the market. Everyone from the Austin site is scheduled to be in attendance.

Please let me know any other way I may be of assistance.

E-mail message
From: Melissa Landsome, Legislative Representative, Washington, D.C.
To: Ricardo Salas
Subject: Tax break for Astrix
Date: March 9

A bill is being voted in the House of Representatives on Wednesday, March 17, regarding tax breaks for companies employing U.S. software engineers and game designers. I worked out the figures and it could mean a savings to Astrix of $3.56 million per year, plus we'd be moving several hundred jobs onshore.

It would really help if you could send two of your most articulate software engineers or programmers to Washington to speak with individual members of Congress on Tuesday, March 16. In fact, I think the best choice is to send that amazing Sanjay Anand. He always knocks 'em dead. Without this, I fear the chances of this bill passing are slim.

E-mail message
From: Vladimir Benejev, Sales Manager for Russia, St. Petersburg
To: Ricardo Salas
Subject: Russian confiscation
Date: March 12

Urgent: Our new game, Acid Wipeout, which was selling 10,000 units per week, has been stalled by the Russian government. Over 200,000 units have been confiscated by the local authorities and will not be released until we agree to share all our user data with the government.

I am writing to you because of your years of work with IBM in Russia, your command of the language, and all the contacts you developed during your time here. Several people I talked to said that you, and possibly someone in Santa Monica named William Masterson, who also has some Russian experience, might be able to help. I don't know Masterson, but I know you.

I have tried to convince the government officials—petty bureaucrats, really—that our user data is not like that of Google or Yahoo, that we only know names, frequency of plays, who they play with, and scores. But they demand we give them this information.

Our CEO, Mr. Cherel, has stressed to me how important Russia is to our overall strategy, and I don't want our sales to stall. There are two competitors with similar games ready to launch in Russia. Even if we resume, it might be too late, and we could lose our standing in the market here.

If we want this to go away quickly, I recommend we pay three of the people $150 each. They are lowly paid bureaucrats and that will satisfy them. I can do this immediately when someone in authority gives approval, and then we can move forward. Otherwise this could drag on for months.

Phone message
From: Brittany Viescu, Sales Manager
Date: March 9
Transcribed message:

I hope you get this before you leave the country. I'm just getting so fed up with Shinji Yamamoto. You and I have talked so many times about GUITAR DANCE. This is our one chance to dig out of the financial hole we've . . . we've fallen in. And Shinji . . . he . . . you know that saying: Perfection is the enemy of good or whatever. That's Shinji. All we need is "good enough," right? Can you get him and Brad Horowitz to move? I've got stores all over the world that are waiting, and waiting. We've been advertising for six weeks and I've got 25,000 orders with irate vendors.

Sorry to go on and on, but you've got to do something about these guys.

E-mail message
From: Farhad Pirmoradi, App Group
To: Ricardo Salas
Subject: Michael Townshend, Head of Business Applications
Date: March 11

Michael Townshend has been pushing our group to collaborate on developing an app that would track and analyze engagement in social media, along with brand interaction. He claims it would help business clients to cut through complicated data with lightning speed and help the clients make better business decisions. I tried to get him to explain what that means, but I still don't get it.

I don't necessarily believe he knows what he is talking about. This is the guy, after all, that lost the company $2.1 million last year when they insisted on (and wasted three of our people's time for six months) developing a business app that would let employees buy drinks and food from vending machines by waving their phones in front of the vending machine and having PayPal send money to the vending company. He didn't think through how much it was going to cost the vending companies to change their machines so they'd be compatible with the app.

The other issue here, if I understand a little of what he is trying to do, is one of privacy. Tracking our clients' (and their clients') engagement in social media sounds like there would be data gathered on many people. While I know this is helpful in business, we'd want to be mindful of how the news media will react to this.

E-mail message
From: Dr. Marion P. Wanchowski, University of Chicago
To: Ricardo Salas
Subject: Media exposure
Date: March 8

Do you remember me from the Video Learning Conference last year? You might recall that I've been doing research for several years on learning and have started recently to look at the effects of video games on the development of adolescent brains. Just yesterday I was asked to fill in for the keynote speaker at a symposium called Digital Impacts on Learning on March 22.

Because I remember your passion for letting the world know that video games aren't just, as I think you put it, "dumb fun," I naturally thought of you after I got the call.

Would you mind forwarding to me any research you've done in this area, or even insights that your people have gained about teenagers and how video games affect their brains and learning? I would, of course, reference you. The symposium is always filled with reporters, so I expect much of what I as keynoter say will be printed in various media and on numerous blogs. There's been talk in the blogs that Astrix has some innovative new game on the way, and it would be wonderful if I could mention it in my talk.

I know this is a last-minute request and I'll understand if you decline. But if you can send me something by March 18, I'd be able to consider it as part of my presentation.

Thanks in advance for your helpfulness.

E-mail message
From: Jason Shahinian, Software Engineer
To: Ricardo Salas
Subject: Lack of discipline
Date: March 12

I'm sorry to bother you, but my boss, Judith Mendez, is not easy to talk to. She sulks when anyone tries to give her feedback and just tells us to do our work. But that's the problem. No one seems to be doing any work. I think she wants to be everyone's friend and is afraid to lay down the law on work habits. People are taking two-hour lunches, napping at their desks, updating Facebook and posting images with Instagram. I doubt if Judith even knows what a productivity report looks like.

Again, so sorry to bother you, but I really care about Astrix.

E-mail message
From: Eduardo Smith, Community Liaison
To: Ricardo J. Salas
Subject: Austin Domestic Violence Housing Options Center
Date: March 12

You can see from the forwarded message below, that we have an opportunity to serve Austin's non-profit sector, which is part of our mission statement and something headquarters has been championing more lately.

The Austin Domestic Violence Housing Options Center, which provides long-term housing assistance to victims of domestic violence, is in a programming crisis. Since we have some of the best programmers in the city, I thought it would be part of our mission and help our standing in the community if we offer to help them. Sanjay Anand and Hong Cho have just finished an intense game app and they have several days before their next assignment starts, so I took the liberty of offering their services to the Center.

Begin forwarded message
From: Amelia Callispell, CEO of ADVHC
To: Eduardo Smith, Astrix
Subject: Programming needs
Date: March 12

It was great to see you last night at the Rotary meeting, and I really appreciated you listening to me go on and on about our funds being cut and our programmer quitting, with management freezing all positions for now. As I told you, we are left at a time when our accounting software needs updating. Without it, I fear we cannot pay employees nor keep track of our donations. Your offer to lend us two programmers for three days will fix the problem, and I thank you in advance. Please e-mail me back with their names and other details, so I can get this set up ASAP.

Again, many thanks.

E-mail message
From: Amy Chang, Chief Ethics Officer, Santa Monica
To: Ricardo Salas
Subject: CONFIDENTIAL: violations investigation
Date: March 12

We are closing in on the two employees stealing our code and selling it to one of our main competitors. As of this afternoon, we've identified that they both work in the Austin location. Because of the security of our own firewall, we are so far unable to identify the exact people, so I need you to do some low-key digging around to figure out who they are. We do know that they seem to send portions of our code every two weeks, on either Thursday or Friday, and that would mean the next "drop" would be either March 18 or 19.

We can't afford to let this go on. Each time they sell code, we estimate that it costs us about $1.2 million dollars in development costs that someone else steals and uses in their products. We don't want to go to the police yet. We've decided it might spook the thieves, and they would steal more quickly and then disappear.

Please help us find out the names of these two people who work at your branch, so that we can take the proper measures to protect Astrix.

E-mail message
From: Tamika Jones, Programming Supervisor
To: Ricardo Salas
Subject: My job
Date: March 9

Mr. Salas, I want you to know how much I appreciate all you've done for me. When you were programming chief, you hired me straight out of school and gave me a chance to work for a great company. My job was everything I dreamed of. Then I got promoted last year and now I am miserable. None of my friends at work treat me the same. They don't invite me out anymore, and I know they talk behind my back. Also, I find I don't really like the planning and all the meetings. And if I have to do another performance review, I might scream. I don't think I can last much longer. My cousin told me about a job as a programmer in a new company. In fact, she sent them my resume without telling me, and they called me two days ago and I am scheduled for an interview April 5. I really don't know what to do. But like I said, I do appreciate all you've done for me.

E-mail message
From: Shinji Yamamoto, R&D Head
To: Ricardo Salas
Subject: Our games
Date: March 11

This is something I've been worrying about for months. We used to have a reputation (maybe we still do) as being the smartest game developer. Our marketing has emphasized the intelligence of the games and helped parents see their kids can learn from them. But lately I'm seeing that we are sinking to the lowest common denominator and pandering to the "WOW! Bang Bang Bang" crowd.

I know this is important to you, because we have talked about it many times. If you'd like to talk more about where I see us heading, I'd be most happy to. We've got a big game convention coming up in the fall, and I'd like for us to have some smart games in the works that we can talk about there.

And if there's any way to speed up the development of GUITAR DANCE, I'd love to hear about it. You know one of the biggest stumbling blocks is the licensing deal with YouTube, and I honestly think Brad Horowitz doesn't get the sense of urgency that most of us feel. Sanjay Anand is making great progress on the software problems, but, I'll tell you, it's really complicated. Still, he does get how important it is, but if I push him too much, it will backfire.

I think that game will put us back in the game, as it were, and help our reputation in the learning field. Otherwise, we're just turning out one special effects game after another.

E-mail message
From: Emily Latella, Regional Communications
To: Ricardo Salas
To: Amy Chang, Chief Ethics Officer
Subject: Working conditions in Chengdu, China
Date: March 11

I got another call from the investigative reporter who has been writing a piece on Astrix's major supplier of manufactured goods in Chengdu, China. The article, which is scheduled to print on Sunday, March 21, will be a PR nightmare for Astrix. To make matters worse, the reporter has a quotation by one of your employees (I don't know who it is—the reporter lists it as an "unnamed source") who claims that you (Ricardo Salas) supposedly told hardware engineers that "Astrix was not concerned about worker safety, only that our products would be produced and sold at the lowest possible cost with the highest possible profits." I feel certain you did not make any such comment, but you need to talk to the reporter to deny the quote. Please call me first and let's talk it through before you talk to her.

We've got to call the reporter before the article is filed, which I understand is Thursday, March 18. Or we will have lots more problems to worry about.

E-mail message
From: Bonita Mallard, Head of HR
To: Ricardo Salas
Subject: Potential loss of programmer
Date: March 12

I've just accidentally learned, from one of my colleagues at SHERM, that Sanjay Anand has been offered a position with Gangbuster Media at twice his pay. His wife wants to move to Boston, but he doesn't, as I understand, but the lure of the salary is tempting. He's supposed to let them know by Tuesday, March 30. We all know that Sanjay is one of the top programmers in Texas, and maybe even the whole country, which is why he's being poached.

I've looked over our budgets and figured out how we can squeeze out more money for him, but I fear it's not enough. Maybe you can take some out of your budget? No one, and I mean NO one, wants to lose Sanjay. Without his expertise, the introduction of GUITAR DANCE will be delayed at least another six months, and I don't need to tell you what that will do to our bottom line.

E-mail message
From: Stephen Schwartzman, CFO
To: Ricardo Salas
Subject: Cutting Middleware costs
Date: March 12

You mentioned at our last management meeting the importance of looking into all areas for cost-cutting. I've spent a whole week looking at the numbers and doing some research.

We currently spend 10.3 percent of our costs on Middleware, including game engines, foundation graphics, and audio technologies. Most of this comes from three main vendors, who have just informed us their prices are rising anywhere from 10 to 15 percent, starting next month.

This has serious implications for us. I have found four other vendors that can provide these services, and I recommend you have some engineers look into them for quality and standards.

In addition, I've been talking to two professors at USC, which has, as you know, the top video design school in the country. We are trying to put together a program where their students would work with us, helping us with some of what we would otherwise outsource to Middleware. This could save us millions over the coming years.

I'm trying to set up a meeting in coming weeks with you, one software engineer (How about Sanjay?), a game designer, and the two professors. Can you let me know which people you'd like to include and I'll facilitate setting up the meeting. We'd all meet in our conference room and Skype in the profs.

E-mail message
From: Bonita Mallard, Head of HR
To: Ricardo Salas
Subject: Inappropriate language
Date: March 9

Several (well, actually about six) female employees have come to me about the crude language that Rowland Wallinger uses in meetings. They feel it is degrading and makes them uncomfortable. Further, they've seen some questionable magazines lying around, in plain sight, in his office.

Rowland is a good sales manager. Actually, he's a GREAT sales manager. He is kind of crude and crusty, I know, but it is hard to replace him and the results he gets. So, I'd like to work on keeping him.

He hasn't responded to talks I've had with him. Perhaps if a MAN sits him down, it would help? Otherwise I am afraid two of the women involved may file a lawsuit.

Let's talk.

E-mail message
From: Gadilaihu Cherel, CEO
To: William Masterson
Subject: Scouting trip
Date: March 15

I trust you have arrived safely and are getting settled in. None of us know how long it's going to take the State Department to secure the release of Salas, who isn't even allowed visitors right now. The two engineers he was traveling with are under house arrest in their hotel. Hopefully that won't get worse.

It is near the top of our agenda to get another factory up this year, to meet anticipated demand for GUITAR DANCE, in a place where we can manufacture at low cost. So, we have to find a new country. Our strategy team had put second choice as Vietnam, and we need to send some location scouts in the next couple weeks to start looking. We've always found it helpful to send two software or design engineers along on the trip, as it positively impacts the host country and makes it easier for us to negotiate.

Because we are down two engineers in Santa Monica, I'd like you to find two of your staff you can send on this next trip. This is very important for Astrix, as this new factory will make the difference next year in whether we are profitable or not. I am counting on you to find good people.

And don't worry at all about their safety. I've been assured by our risk-management people that Vietnam is generally one of the more stable countries in the region.

REFERENCES

1 Jeanne Whalen, "Chance Turns a Teacher into a CEO; Religion Lecturer Leaves Academic Path and Learns to Run a Biotech Start-Up" (Theory & Practice column), *The Wall Street Journal*, October 17, 2005.

2 Elkhonon Goldberg, *The Executive Brain: Frontal Lobes and the Civilized Mind* (New York: Oxford University Press, 2001).

3 Michael D. Gerber, *The E-Myth Revisited: Why Most Small Businesses Don't Work and What to Do About It* (New York: HarperCollins, 2001).

4 C. K. Prahalad, "The Responsible Manager," *Harvard Business Review* (January–February 2010): 36.

5 "Kudos for KIPP," *The Wall Street Journal*, March 26, 2007; and KIPP Web site, http://www.kipp.org/ (accessed March 15, 2011).

6 Heather MacDonald, "A Crime Theory Demolished," *The Wall Street Journal*, January 5, 2010; and William Bratton and Peter Knobler, *The Turnaround: How America's Top Cop Reversed the Crime Epidemic* (New York: Random House, 1998).

7 Noshua Watson, "Happy Companies Make Happy Investments," *Fortune* (May 27, 2002): 162.

8 Adam Bryant, "On a Scale of 1 to 10, How Weird Are You?" *The New York Times*, January 10, 2010.

9 Bill Vlasic, "Ford's Bet: It's a Small World After All," *The New York Times*, January 10, 2010.

10 Reported in Stephen L. Cohen, "New Leaders: Coach Them for Success," *Leadership Excellence* (October 2008): 10.

11 Bill George, quoted in David Gergen, "How Business Can Stand Tall Again," *Fortune* (May 11, 2009): 25.

12 Henry Mintzberg, *Managing* (San Francisco: Berrett-Kohler, 2009), pp. 43–44.

13 S. Carlson, *Executive Behaviour: A Study of the Work Load and the Working Methods of Managing Directors* (Stockholm: Strombergs, 1951; reprinted by Uppsala University, with comments by H. Mintzberg and R. Stewart, Uppsala: Uppsala University, 1991).

14 S. L. Hart and R. E. Quinn, "Roles Executives Play: CEOs, Behavioral Complexity, and Firm Performance," *Human Relations*, 46 (1993): 543–574.

15 Victoria Griffith, "FedEx Search for Bosses Who Can Deliver the Goods: Business Education Test for Would-Be Managers," *Financial Times* (April 27, 1998).

16 Timothy D. Schellhardt, "Off the Ladder: Want to Be a Manager? Many People Say No, Calling Job Miserable—They Cite Stress of Handling Bosses and Subordinates, Ending Up in the Middle: The Dilbert Factor at Work," *The Wall Street Journal*, April 4, 1997.

17 Don Clark and Joanna S. Lublin, "AMD CEO's Board Fallout: Directors Grew Concerned with Meyer's Strategy Nearly a Year Before His Ouster," *The Wall Street Journal*, January 12, 2011.

18 Henry Mintzberg, *Managing* (San Francisco: Berrett-Kohler, 2009); and Henry Mintzberg, "Managerial Work: Analysis from Observation," *Management Science* 18 (1971): B97–B110.

19 Based on Damien Cave, "A Tall Order for a Marine: Feeding the Hand That Bit You," *The New York Times*, December 30, 2007.

20 Matthew Boyle and Jia Lynn Yang, "All in a Day's Work," *Fortune* (March 20, 2006): 97–104.

21 Erin White, "Learning to Be the Boss: Trial and Error Is the Norm as New Managers Figure Out How to Relate to Former Peers," *The Wall Street Journal*, November 21, 2005.

22 Adam Bryant, "Planes, Cars, and Cathedrals," *The New York Times*, September 6, 2009.

23 Linda A. Hill, *Becoming a Manager: How New Managers Master the Challenges of Leadership*, 2nd ed. (Boston: Harvard Business School Press, 2003), p. 262.

24 This discussion is based on Linda A. Hill, "Becoming the Boss," *Harvard Business Review* (January 2007): 49–56; Schellhardt, "Off the Ladder: Want to Be a Manager? Many People Say No"; and Jared Sandberg, "Down Over Moving Up: Some New Bosses Find They Hate Their Jobs," *The Wall Street Journal*, July 27, 2005.

25 Schellhardt, "Off the Ladder."

26 Hill, "Becoming the Boss."

27 Carol Hymowitz, "Business Is Personal, So Managers Need to Harness Emotions" (In the Lead column), *The Wall Street Journal*, November 13, 2006.

28 Quoted in Sandberg, "Down Over Moving Up."

29 Hill, "Becoming the Boss."

30 Robert Bolton, *People Skills* (New York: Touchstone Books, 1986); Rowena Crosbie, "Learning the Soft Skills of Leadership," *Industrial and Commercial Training*, 37, no. 1 (2005): 45–51; and Boris Groysberg, L. Kevin Kelly, and Bryan MacDonald, "The New Path to the C-Suite," *Harvard Business Review* (March 2011): 60–68.

31 William A. Gentry, Lauren S. Harris, Becca A. Baker, and Jean Brittain Leslie, "Managerial Skills: What Has Changed Since the Late 1980s?" *Leadership and Organization Development Journal* 29, no. 2 (2008): 167–181.

32 Adam Bryant, "The Quest to Build a Better Boss," *The New York Times*, March 13, 2011.

33 Gerald F. Smith, "Problem-Based Learning: Can It Improve Managerial Thinking?" *Journal of Management Education*, 29, no. 2 (April 2005): 357–378.

34 Geoff Colvin, *Talent Is Overrated: What Really Separates World-Class Performers from Everybody Else* (New York: Penguin, 2010).

Addendum: You and The Manager's Job

35 Based on Taylor Clark, "The Most Dangerous Gamer," *The Atlantic* (May 2012): 40–51; Joseph Seltzer, Susan Schorr, and Jim Smither, "SSS Software," in Dorothy Marcic, Joseph Seltzer, and Peter Vaill, *Organizational Behavior: Experiences and Cases* (Mason, OH: Southwestern Publishing, 2001), pp. 265–276; A. B. Shani and James B. Lau, *Behavior in Organizations* (Chicago: Irwin, 1996), pp. M17–45, 46; Dafna Eylon and Susan Herman, "Exploring Empowerment: One Method for the Classroom," *Journal of Management Education* 23, no. 1(February 1999): 80–94; "New CDAA President Talks up Australia as 'Best' Location for Making Games," *Wireless News* (March 8, 2007): 1; "Actian and Unruly Media Bring Big Data to Social Video," *Business Wire Web site*, April 26, 2012, http://www.businesswire.com/news/home/20120426006110/en/Actian-Unruly-Media-Bring-Big-Data-Social; and Michael Arrington, "Middle Ground," *Computer Graphics World* (December 2006): 34–35.

PART 1

Managing Yourself

40260.COM/ALAMY

CHAPTER 1

Your Manager Strengths and Weaknesses

Chapter Outline

RYAN LASH

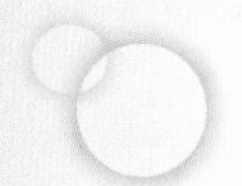

MANAGER CHALLENGE

VIDEO INCIDENT: BAKERY RIVALRY

Jane Sutton is the general manager of a chain of restaurants and bakery/coffee shops called Caffeine and Crullers, based in Madison, Wisconsin, and reporting to corporate headquarters in Milwaukee, Wisconsin. For the past eight months, Jane has been trying to keep her team motivated, while at the same time meeting the "numbers" she gets from corporate. Too often she feels caught in the middle of competing needs. She's just hired a new sales manager, Jason Wong, who came with an impressive sales record from two respected companies. Jason replaced the well-liked Jim Honeyman, who left because of some murky problem at the corporate office. Jason's first staff meeting was rocky. HR director Heather Carreau came in late. People were talking fast and over one another. Though Jane tried to include Jason in the discussions, CFO Carlos Hernandez kept interrupting when Jason talked and often re-interpreted what Jason was saying. Heather would often back up what Carlos was saying, but then seemed to lack focus the rest of the time. Director of operations Carrie Fishman was getting frustrated with Carlos because she felt the meeting was getting off track. But she avoided open confrontation, instead just giving compliments to Jason when he said something reasonable and cutting off Carlos when he was too abrupt. Jason could see Carrie was upset, and that she was watching out for him, and he often smiled with a silent "thanks." Because of all this disruption, Jane found it difficult to finish the agenda, and now there are two key items that still need to be addressed by the end of the business day.

Initial Thoughts

1. If you were Jane, how would you have handled the meeting?

2. What do you see as each person's strengths and weaknesses based on the above information?

Your instructor may ask you to be part of a role play based on the Bakery Rivalry incident.

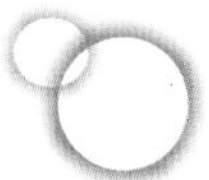

DISCOVER YOURSELF

For those students using CourseMate or CengageNOW, you can access the Daft/Marcic Assessment Library to take the questionnaires online and view dynamically updated comparative data.

Questionnaire 1[1]

Instructions: Think in general about your life and behavior and then indicate your response to each of the statements below based on whether the statement is clearly true or accurate, clearly false or inaccurate, or in the middle as somewhat true and somewhat false.

Part A

	True	Somewhat	False
1. I am able to do things as well or better than most people.	○	○	○
2. My body language projects confidence.	○	○	○
3. I easily ask those in authority for what I want.	○	○	○
4. Given time, I can figure out any task.	○	○	○
5. I am pretty sure of myself.	○	○	○

Total Score Part A ________. (Sum questions 1–5: 3 points for each True, 2 points for each Somewhat, and 1 point for each False.)

Part B

	True	Somewhat	False
6. I take my time before making up my mind.	○	○	○
7. I make sure I have all the facts before I take action.	○	○	○
8. I usually handle confrontations calmly.	○	○	○
9. When feeling frustrated or angry, I keep my cool.	○	○	○
10. I never interrupt when someone is speaking.	○	○	○

Total Score Part B ________. (Sum questions 6–10: 3 points for each True, 2 points for each Somewhat, and 1 point for each False.)

Part C

	True	Somewhat	False
11. When I have a job to do or a task to finish, I work diligently until it is completed.	○	○	○
12. I often find myself thinking about other things when I should be paying attention.	○	○	○
13. I typically stay focused for a couple of hours on any task.	○	○	○
14. When someone brings up an unrelated topic in a meeting, I bring the discussion back to the task.	○	○	○
15. New e-mail messages don't distract me from the task on which I am working.	○	○	○

Total Score Part C ________. (Sum questions 11–15: 3 points for each True, 2 points for each Somewhat, and 1 point for each False.)

Part D

	True	Somewhat	False
16. I treat opposite viewpoints as equal to my own.	○	○	○
17. I look at the big picture rather than push my own viewpoint.	○	○	○
18. I typically step back and remove my feelings from a situation in order to make an unbiased decision.	○	○	○
19. I often review a situation and see where I could have done things differently.	○	○	○
20. I welcome criticism without getting upset or hurt.	○	○	○

Total Score Part D ________. (Sum questions 16–20: 3 points for each True, 2 points for each Somewhat, and 1 point for each False.)

Part E

	True	Somewhat	False
21. I often show appreciation to other people.	○	○	○
22. I frequently reach out to engage people, even strangers.	○	○	○
23. My relationships are what help me succeed.	○	○	○
24. I am genuinely interested in and concerned about others.	○	○	○
25. I frequently smile and laugh with other people.	○	○	○

Total Score Part E ________. (Sum questions 21–25: 3 points for each True, 2 points for each Somewhat, and 1 point for each False.)

Part F

	True	Somewhat	False
26. Once I've been given a job or task, I typically start it immediately.	○	○	○
27. Procrastination is not a problem for me.	○	○	○
28. I am typically the one to take the initiative to start a new project.	○	○	○
29. If I see something broken, I fix it.	○	○	○
30. I involve myself in changes to improve whatever group or organization I am in.	○	○	○

Total Score Part F ________. (Sum questions 26–30: 3 points for each True, 2 points for each Somewhat, and 1 point for each False.)

Part G

	True	Somewhat	False
31. It is easy for me to stick to my aims and accomplish my goals.	○	○	○
32. I have formulated goals and priorities for the next two months.	○	○	○
33. I frequently create a vision or mission that gives purpose to other people.	○	○	○

	True	Somewhat	False
34. I set aside enough time to define goals and plan a project.	○	○	○
35. I have a clear idea of what I want to accomplish during the next week.	○	○	○

Total Score Part G ________. (Sum questions 31–35: 3 points for each True, 2 points for each Somewhat, and 1 point for each False.)

Part H

	True	Somewhat	False
36. People say that I am an organized person.	○	○	○
37. I regularly create my own systems for organizing my work.	○	○	○
38. I am typically the one to break out and assign tasks when working in a group.	○	○	○
39. I keep my work space in good order.	○	○	○
40. I take the time to stay organized.	○	○	○

Total Score Part H ________. (Sum questions 35–40: 3 points for each True, 2 points for each Somewhat, and 1 point for each False.)

Part I

	True	Somewhat	False
41. At the end of the day, I've usually finished what I set out to do.	○	○	○
42. I stay caught up on all my projects.	○	○	○
43. I stay in control of my time throughout each day.	○	○	○
44. I seldom waste any time.	○	○	○
45. There is little room for improvement in how I use my time.	○	○	○

Total Score Part I ________. (Sum questions 41–45: 3 points for each True, 2 points for each Somewhat, and 1 point for each False.)

Part J

	True	Somewhat	False
46. I consider myself to be highly flexible and adaptive.	○	○	○
47. I instantly adjust to new people on my team.	○	○	○
48. I change my mind easily.	○	○	○
49. I do not tense up or resist changes in my daily schedule.	○	○	○
50. After I have started implementing a plan, I don't mind changing it.	○	○	○

Total Score Part J ________. (Sum questions 46–50: 3 points for each True, 2 points for each Somewhat, and 1 point for each False.) Go to page 50 to interpret your scores.

Questionnaire 2[2]

Instructions: When confronting someone with whom you have a very serious difference of opinion that will be difficult to discuss, indicate your response to each of the statements below as True, Somewhat, or False.

Part A

	True	Somewhat	False
1. If I make a mistake or disappoint someone, the feeling stays with me for a while.	○	○	○
2. I tend to deflect compliments rather than just say, "Thank you."	○	○	○
3. Sometimes I avoid saying what I'm really thinking.	○	○	○
4. There are some things I would change about myself if I could.	○	○	○
5. I am nervous about meeting important people.	○	○	○

Total Score Part A ________. (Sum questions 1–5: 3 points for each True, 2 points for each Somewhat, and 1 point for each False.)

Part B

	True	Somewhat	False
6. I am quick to encourage people who are feeling down.	○	○	○
7. I sometimes say what an authority figure wants to hear rather than what I am really thinking.	○	○	○
8. It is hard for me to hold people accountable for inappropriate behavior.	○	○	○
9. I have a hard time saying no to people.	○	○	○
10. I find it difficult to say something that might hurt another person, even if it needs to be said.	○	○	○

Total Score Part B ________. (Sum questions 6–10: 3 points for each True, 2 points for each Somewhat, and 1 point for each False.)

Part C

	True	Somewhat	False
11. I often interrupt when people are speaking.	○	○	○
12. Being strong-willed enables me to get my way.	○	○	○
13. I can be pushy and hardheaded because usually I'm right.	○	○	○
14. I know the best thing to do in most situations.	○	○	○
15. I push people pretty hard to meet our goals.	○	○	○

Total Score Part C ________. (Sum questions 11–15: 3 points for each True, 2 points for each Somewhat, and 1 point for each False.)

Part D

	True	Somewhat	False
16. People have a responsibility to do their job without personal encouragement from me.	○	○	○
17. I am not considered an affectionate person.	○	○	○
18. Showing nurturing behavior is awkward for me.	○	○	○
19. I rarely do nice things for other people.	○	○	○
20. I do not wear my emotions on my sleeve.	○	○	○

Total Score Part D ________. (Sum questions 16–20: 3 points for each True, 2 points for each Somewhat, and 1 point for each False.)

Part E

	True	Somewhat	False
21. Staying on task is hard for me once I lose interest.	○	○	○
22. My impulsive nature has been a source of conflict in my relationships.	○	○	○
23. I am much better at starting things than I am at finishing them.	○	○	○
24. I have experienced impulse buys and lack of planning while shopping.	○	○	○
25. I usually don't think through an idea before acting.	○	○	○

Total Score Part E ________. (Sum questions 21–25: 3 points for each True, 2 points for each Somewhat, and 1 point for each False.)

Part F

	True	Somewhat	False
26. I notice when things are not right or as good as they could be.	○	○	○
27. People don't seem genuinely excited or happy to see me.	○	○	○
28. I can find fault with most ideas.	○	○	○
29. I tend to notice the quirks and shortcomings that other people have.	○	○	○
30. My mind often has critical thoughts about other people.	○	○	○

Total Score Part F ________. (Sum questions 26–30: 3 points for each True, 2 points for each Somewhat, and 1 point for each False.) Go to page 55 to interpret your scores.

Questionnaire 3[3]

Instructions: When dealing with people, especially those with whom you have a serious difference of opinion, check your response to each of the statements below as True, Somewhat, or False.

Part A

	True	Somewhat	False
1. I know when I am about to become angry or upset.	○	○	○
2. I can always tell when I am in a good or bad mood.	○	○	○
3. I know what causes my emotions to change.	○	○	○
4. I pay a lot of attention to how I feel.	○	○	○
5. I know when I start to become defensive.	○	○	○

Total Score Part A ________. (Sum questions 1–5: 3 points for each True, 2 points for each Somewhat, and 1 point for each False.)

Part B

	True	Somewhat	False
6. When I start to get angry, I step away and continue the discussion later.	○	○	○
7. I try to understand my feeling by analyzing them.	○	○	○
8. I easily motivate myself to move through uninteresting work.	○	○	○
9. I stay calm even when I am the target of anger from others.	○	○	○
10. I try to think good thoughts no matter how bad I feel.	○	○	○

Total Score Part B ________. (Sum questions 6–10: 3 points for each True, 2 points for each Somewhat, and 1 point for each False.)

Part C

	True	Somewhat	False
11. I nearly always pay attention to the impact of my words or behavior on others.	○	○	○
12. I can tell my friends' moods from their behavior.	○	○	○
13. I pay attention to the emotional expressions on the faces of others.	○	○	○
14. I often sense the impact of my words or behavior on others.	○	○	○
15. I can tell how someone is feeling by the tone of his or her voice.	○	○	○

Total Score Part C ________. (Sum questions 11–15: 3 points for each True, 2 points for each Somewhat, and 1 point for each False.)

Part D

	True	Somewhat	False
16. I frequently initiate the successful resolution of a conflict.	○	○	○
17. I make it a point to build a consensus with other people.	○	○	○
18. I frequently compliment others.	○	○	○

	True	Somewhat	False
19. I take the initiative to arrange small events that others will enjoy.	◯	◯	◯
20. I am open with others about my feelings.	◯	◯	◯

Total Score Part D ________. (Sum questions 16–20: 3 points for each True, 2 points for each Somewhat, and 1 point for each False.) Go to page 58 to interpret your scores.

GO ONLINE to find additional questionnaires at www.cengagebrain.com, search for Daft/Marcic Building Management Skills 1e, click on Free Online Resources, click on Additional Self-Assessments.

- Am I Ambitious?
- Am I a Jerk?

DISCOVER YOURSELF

SHUTTERSTOCK #53973379

Chapter 1: Your Manager Strengths and Weaknesses

DISCOVER KNOWLEDGE

Tami Heim, vice president of Thomas Nelson Publishers in Nashville, Tennessee, believes managers can do their best work when they know and apply their strengths. Heim completed a questionnaire called the StrengthsFinder,[4] which identifies 34 key strengths, and asked her entire management team at Thomas Nelson to do the same. Each member of the team discovered a different set of strengths, and each manager knew everyone else's strengths. When new projects came up, people were asked to participate, or volunteer, based on the tasks for which they had a natural ability, which made projects fun and kept people motivated. Heim's managers were also free to stretch themselves by taking unusual assignments to develop new strengths.

Heim was profiled in the book *The One Thing You Need to Know* by Marcus Buckingham. She began her career with a part-time job during high school, working in a retail store because retail was her passion. Even doing rotten jobs early on did not diminish Heim's love of the immediate feedback of retail and the drama of putting on a show every day for customers. This love led her to study retail management in college, after which she progressed rapidly to regional vice president of Federated Department Stores. Then Borders offered Heim a job as territorial vice president for the western United States. Her next stop was Thomas Nelson Publishers, where her strengths-based approach has created a powerful and effective senior management team.[5]

Just as the executives on Tami Heim's senior management team boosted their potential by understanding where their natural capabilities lie, you will develop into an effective manager much more quickly if you discover your own unique set of strengths and capabilities and learn how to make the most of them in an organizational setting. Each individual has some abilities that seem to come naturally. One person might be particularly good at analyzing complex situations and making good decisions under time pressure. Another might have a hard time getting a grasp on big problems but could be a whiz at organizing and managing details. Some people find it easy and comfortable to communicate with direct reports, peers, and superiors to build networks of relationships. Others struggle with verbal communication and networking but are experts at analyzing data and planning projects. Everyone has strengths, whether or not they pertain to management, but many of us fail to recognize and apply them. Benjamin Franklin referred to these wasted strengths as "sundials in the shade."[6] Only when we know our own strengths can we use these abilities effectively in our work and personal relationships.

Recall from the introductory chapter our discussion of key manager competencies in the areas of managing oneself, managing relationships, and managing a team. These competencies rely on various skills such as communicating, managing your time, solving problems, setting goals, managing conflicts, and so forth. The personal strengths that support these skills lie deep within you. Your challenge as a future manager is to find those strengths and use them.

DISCOVER YOUR STRENGTHS

Warren Buffett finds investing so much fun that he would do it for free. Buffett tried other work early in his career but found it so unsatisfying that he knew he wouldn't want to do it for any amount of money. The legendary self-made billionaire and chairman of Berkshire Hathaway was the third richest person in the world in 2010.[7] Yet it isn't the money that drives him, but the love of the work. "I do not want to live like a king," Buffett says. "I just love to invest."[8] Each year, Buffett hosts in his hometown of Omaha, Nebraska, about 160 business students from many universities worldwide. He answers whatever questions the students ask, one of which is typically about how to know what career to pursue. How did the great man know that investing was the right career for him? Buffett answers in two parts. First, he says his "natural wiring" was made for capital allocation—that is, he just had a knack for knowing how to allocate financial resources into companies or other entities as a way to generate wealth. Buffett says that if he had been born in a country such as Sudan or Cambodia, without abundant private capital and a system of capital allocation, he would never have gotten to use his natural talents.

Nor would he have succeeded in a different era when there was no capitalism. Buffett is very clear in recommending that people need to do what fits their natural mental makeup. How did he know that his wiring fit investing? The key was his *love* for it. His career advice is to find work or a career that you really enjoy and it will fit the natural strengths of your mental wiring.[9]

Talent, Knowledge, and Skills

Using a natural talent comes easily, but talent alone is not enough. A true **strength** arises from natural talent that is supported and reinforced with both learned knowledge and skills.[10]

Natural Talent is a Starting Point

Certain abilities come naturally to each of us, just as investing came naturally to Warren Buffett, who bought his first stock at the age of 11 and invested in a business owned by his father while he was still in high school. This innate aptitude or ability is what we refer to as talent. As used here, **talents** can be thought of as your naturally recurring patterns of thought, feeling, or behavior. These patterns happen naturally and don't have to be forced. Thus, if you are naturally outgoing and easily make friends, that is a talent. Similarly, an instinctive ability to organize things is a talent, as is a relentlessly inquisitive nature, an innate sense of responsibility, or a knack for recognizing when someone is in a bad mood. Once we recognize our innate talents, we can turn them into strengths by consciously developing and enhancing them. Until they are honed and strengthened and put to use, talents are merely aspects of our potential.

Add Knowledge to Put Talent to Use

Knowledge consists of facts, information, and experiences that are linked together to become meaningful. Facts and information can be gained from books, classrooms, Web sites, lectures, or workshops. However, these become knowledge only when we absorb them, link them with experience, and apply them.[11] Warren Buffett studied business administration and economics in college and combined what he learned with his experiences and observations.

Solidify Your Strengths with Skills

The term **skills** refers to accumulated knowledge that has been formalized into behavior steps needed to adequately perform an activity. You might recall from a high school English class the steps for writing a short theme paper: Start with an introductory paragraph with a one- or two-sentence theme statement that tells the reader what the paper is going to be about; develop the theme in the main body of the paper, two or three paragraphs that support the argument you make in your introduction; then write a concluding paragraph that restates the theme you presented in your introduction and summarizes your arguments and ideas. Learning a skill such as this writing sequence can't make you a great writer if you have no natural writing ability, but applying the steps can help you write an adequate theme paper. And if you do have a natural writing ability, combining that talent with knowledge and skills can help you attain excellence. The same is true for many other activities, whether it be selling magazines door-to-door, resolving a conflict among employees, or developing a marketing plan for a new Web site. Although not all activities can be broken down into specific steps, it's important to recognize that strengths express themselves through tangible skills. Skills are the final outcome from developing your strengths.

LEADING WORDS

"Although men are accused of not knowing their own weakness, yet perhaps few know their own strength. It is in men as in soils, where sometimes there is a vein of gold which the owner knows not of."
—Jonathan Swift,
author of *Gulliver's Travels*

"I have no special talent. I am only passionately curious."
—Albert Einstein,
theoretical physicist

"You cannot run away from weakness; you must some time fight it out or perish; and if that be so, why not now, and where you stand?"
—Robert Louis Stevenson,
Scottish novelist, author of *Treasure Island*

"Talent is cheaper than table salt. What separates the talented individual from the successful one is a lot of hard work."
—Stephen King,
novelist

Why Discover Your Strengths?

The reason that learning about strengths is so important is that many people are in a form of denial, especially about themselves. It is hard to see ourselves clearly and objectively. Consider that when individuals rate dimensions of their own personality, the ratings typically do not correlate very strongly with other people's ratings of them.[12] You might consider yourself highly conscientious but find that others rate you as only moderately so. Your boss may think she is agreeable and approachable, but you and your colleagues might consider her bad-tempered and inaccessible. Most people, managers included, tend to have an inflated or distorted view of themselves. Interestingly, though, most people can enumerate their weaknesses much more readily than their strengths.

You may have to think carefully and intentionally to identify your strengths, or use one of the instruments or exercises in the Discover Yourself or Action Learning sections of this chapter. A good first step is to use questionnaire-type instruments to gain self-insight, such as what Tami Heim did with her senior management team. There are many survey instruments and exercises throughout this book that will help you discover your strengths. They all have value.

The Role of Positive Psychology

Much of the recent explosion of interest in college classrooms and in the popular press concerning the importance of "strengths" began with the advent of positive psychology, founded by Martin Seligman in 1998. Positive psychology represented a significant shift from psychology's historic focus on negative aspects, weaknesses, and the dark side of the human psyche. As a place to start, Seligman joined with Chris Peterson of the University of Michigan to map out a list of human strengths and virtues. They surveyed every list they could find (major religions, Boy Scout Oath, etc.) and made large tables to see which strengths were common across lists.[13] They boiled it all down to six higher-level virtues that embodied 24 personal strengths, which are listed in Exhibit 1.1. You can measure your own strengths based on this list by completing the Brief Strengths test at the Authentic Happiness Web site (http://www.authentichappiness.sas.upenn.edu/), as instructed at the bottom of the exhibit.

DISCOVER KNOWLEDGE

Exhibit 1.1 Twenty-Four Personal Character Strengths

Strengths of Wisdom and Knowledge:

1. Creativity
2. Curiosity
3. Love of learning
4. Open-mindedness
5. Perspective

Strengths of Courage

6. Authenticity
7. Bravery
8. Persistence
9. Zest

Strengths of Humanity

10. Kindness
11. Love
12. Social intelligence

Strengths of Justice

13. Fairness
14. Leadership
15. Teamwork

Strengths of Temperance

16. Forgiveness/mercy
17. Modesty/humility
18. Prudence
19. Self-regulation

Strengths of Transcendence

20. Appreciation of beauty and excellence
21. Gratitude
22. Hope
23. Humor
24. Religiousness/spirituality

Identify Your Character Strengths: To measure your own character strengths as listed in this exhibit, complete the Brief Strengths test at **http://www.authentichappiness.sas.upenn.edu/Default.aspx.** (You will have to register, but there is no fee.)

Source: This list is from Christopher Peterson, *A Primer in Positive Psychology* (New York: Oxford University Press, 2006), pp. 142–146; and University of Pennsylvania, Authentic Happiness Web site, http://www.authentichappiness.sas.upenn.edu/Default.aspx

What, exactly, does one of these strengths feel like, if you happen to have it? The criteria for a person's signature strength, such as creativity or persistence, would typically include:

1. A sense of ownership of the strength ("This is the real me.")
2. A feeling of excitement while displaying or using the strength
3. A rapid learning curve when using the strength
4. A yearning to use the strength
5. Invigoration rather than exhaustion when using the strength
6. A feeling of motivation to use the strength[14]

Data have been gathered about these signature strengths from people around the world. The rankings of strengths from nation to nation are very similar from Azerbaijan to Zimbabwe. Which strengths do you think would rank highest and lowest across all the countries? Kindness and fairness rate highest and self-regulation rates lowest. Kindness and fairness are nearly universal strengths. And self-regulation—the ability to control oneself—ranks lowest all over the world. Techniques for self-regulation will be discussed in Chapter 3.

DISCOVER KNOWLEDGE

Focus on Strengths

One neat thing about understanding your strengths is the philosophy—*concentrate on your strengths, not your weaknesses*. You excel in life by maximizing your strengths, not by fixing your weaknesses. When you live and work from your strengths, you are more motivated, competent, and satisfied. Strengths are important because you can refocus your life around them rather than devoting your energy to judging, regretting, and trying to fix your weaknesses. You can put yourself in the place of greatest potential to use your strengths.

When you are engaging your strengths, tasks, activities, and relationships proceed smoothly without much effort. A task seems almost like second-nature. On the other hand, when you're performing tasks that don't match your strengths, they take much more effort, thought, and intention. Many "effortful tasks" are still doable, but they are much more difficult to accomplish, don't give you the same sense of capability, and don't enable you to be your best.[15]

When people use their strengths, they feel good because they are performing activities they enjoy, that come without excessive effort, and that provide feelings of *self-efficacy*, which means that people feel they are being effective and making a positive contribution. Indeed, when you understand your strengths, you can give your best to your job, volunteer activities, and personal relationships. You can be a happier, more successful person—and a better manager—when you put yourself in jobs and situations that play to your strengths.

TEN STRENGTHS RELATED TO MANAGER PERFORMANCE

Lani Hay is the founder and CEO of Lanmark Technologies, a company that provides technological and administrative support to a dozen or so U.S. government agencies, including the Nuclear Regulatory Commission and the Department of Defense. Hay wanted to be a pilot and fly with the Blue Angels (the U.S. Navy's flight demonstration squadron) but was medically disqualified before she graduated from the Naval Academy. Disappointed, yes, but Hay was by no means dispirited. She just started looking for the next opportunity. She started Lanmark Technologies with a goal of making it a $15 million company within five years, and she "knocked on doors and forced people to take meetings" with her. She isn't troubled by the "old boy's club" mentality she often encounters in Washington, and she'll try any approach to build the connections she needs to reach her goals.[16]

Lani Hay is applying several key management strengths as CEO of Lanmark Technologies. It takes self-confidence, determination, focus, and initiative to start a company, negotiate the tricky world of government contracting, make cold calls to various agencies, and convince high-ranking people to meet with her. Hay is a master networker. Whenever she meets someone new, she asks for a business card and jots down on the back the date, the event, and how the person might be relevant to her or the company.

No one can be good at everything, but each of us, like Lani Hay, has some areas of strength. Recognizing your strongest areas can help you understand where you can make your best contribution. In this section, we briefly discuss ten key executive attributes, some of which may be strengths for you.[17]

1. Self-confidence. Self-confidence is the foundation for many important manager behaviors. **Self-confidence** refers to assurance in one's own ideas, judgments, and capabilities. Being self-confident doesn't mean being arrogant and prideful, but rather knowing and trusting in yourself. A manager with self-confidence inspires respect and admiration and is able to meet challenges and solve problems in order to achieve goals. Self-confident managers enjoy the freedom to make mistakes without feeling the world has come to an end or feeling down on themselves. Without the confidence to move forward, even if an occasional decision is wrong, a manager can be paralyzed into inaction. A manager who lacks self-confidence is more likely to avoid difficult decisions and confrontations and may tend to over-control subordinates, which is called micromanaging. A lack of self-confidence also leads to less trust in others, less sharing of information, and less time spent developing capable people. Self-confident managers, by contrast, believe in themselves and can more easily delegate responsibility, take risks, give credit to others, confront problems, and assert themselves for the good of their team.

2. Emotion Control. Emotion control refers to being able to keep one's emotions in check so that they don't interfere with relationships and goal attainment. Some people seem naturally able to balance their emotions so that worry, desire, frustration, anxiety, fear, or anger do not get in the way, thus enabling them to think more clearly and be more effective. These people can remain calm under pressure, hopeful when confronted with disappointments, and optimistic in the face of trials and tribulations. Managers who are low on emotion control may be easily hurt by criticism, may be overly emotional in difficult situations, and may experience negative thinking prior to an important presentation.

Self-restraint is one outward manifestation of emotion control. A manager's job is typically fast paced and pressure packed. It is easy to react too quickly or to overreact. **Self-restraint** is the ability to think before you speak or act. Self-restraint means you can resist the impulse to say or do something that may harm rather than help. It means you can take a moment to evaluate the situation and how your response may affect things. A lack of self-restraint means that a manager may fire off an angry e-mail before having time to cool down or impulsively buy the latest expensive gadget before she understands how it can benefit her. Self-restraint means being able to resist that emotional urge, giving you time to evaluate the circumstances you're in and decide the wisest course of action. Self-restraint also involves the ability to delay immediate gratification in the pursuit of important long-term goals.

3. Focus. Bill Gates and Warren Buffett were attending the same dinner party. Bill Gates's dad posed a question to the table: What factor was most important in getting to where they were in life? Warren Buffett answered that it was his "focus." Bill Gates gave the same answer.[18] The executive strength of focus means that you can keep your attention centered on a topic, situation, or task, screening out distractions and completing the job rather than becoming sidetracked by less important activities. A manager's job is highly fragmented, with interruptions every few minutes. People with high focus are able to give their attention to the immediate problem and then go back to the long-term task without losing speed. People high in focus such as Gates or Buffett are able to ignore distractions such as e-mail, text messages, and phone calls in order to complete a project. These people typically find it easy to say "no" to requests that interfere with accomplishing their priorities. People low in focus tend to look for distractions rather than stick with a project to completion. People low in focus are likely to start cleaning out the refrigerator rather than finishing a research paper for class, or will answer routine e-mails rather than completing an important project at work. People high in focus are typically good at meeting deadlines because, even if they find a job tedious, they are able to push through boredom and fatigue to see it through.

4. Objectivity. Are you able to look at yourself objectively? If so, this is likely one of your strengths because it means you're also able to observe other people and situations impartially. Psychologist Jonathan Haidt wrote that a "like-o-meter" is constantly running in the brains of human beings.[19] Each of us has a tendency to view things based on our personal likes and dislikes, even though we're not aware of it. For example, a physician low on objectivity will find that the mere liking or disliking of a patient may influence treatment.[20] If a doctor likes a patient, she may be inclined to skip a test that would cause discomfort. If she dislikes a patient, she may blame the patient's behavior for his illness, and assign less treatment. Likewise, managers who make decisions based only on like/dislike are low on objectivity for decision-making.

People high in objectivity have the ability to mentally stand back and take a bird's-eye view of self and others to understand the rational basis for how to solve a problem. Rather than act on personal likes and dislikes, they can typically come up with multiple solutions, evaluate the pros and cons, and make sensible decisions based on what they think will work best. This strength allows managers to see a bigger picture that includes other people's perspectives. Managers with objectivity are also able to take an unbiased view of their own performance, looking at how well they're doing and analyzing why something went wrong to learn from it. A person high in objectivity often has a pretty good understanding of his or her own abilities.

5. **Relationship Building.** New managers quickly discover that management means getting things done through other people. A lot of time has to be spent in the "care and feeding" of people, including direct reports and colleagues. Exhibit 1.2 shows the results of an exercise in which people reported what they do to show they care about others and what it feels like to be cared about. People who fail in new management jobs often do so because they are blind to the importance of the items in Exhibit 1.2. These struggling managers have poor working relationships or they misjudge management philosophy or cultural values. A manager low on relationship building may be insensitive to the needs of other people, be too critical and negative toward others, or stay isolated while working on tasks of personal importance. An important point to learn as a manager is that you can't do everything yourself. Your job is to reach out to others and influence them in a way to create the environment and conditions for accomplishing goals. After a year or so in a managerial role, successful managers learn that more than half their time is spent networking and building successful relationships. Managers high on relationship building typically like and care about people and are likable; are empathetic toward other people's needs; and treat people with respect, compassion, and kindness. For example, Bob Iger, CEO of Disney, wins praise for his skills at building relationships. He is a good listener with a calm, diplomatic, and collaborative approach to leadership that has built a collegial culture at Disney and mended relationships with executives in partner companies.[21]

6. **Initiative.** Initiative means having a strong capacity to begin an activity without procrastinating. If

7 STEPS TO... Fixing a Damaged Relationship

1. **Determine the cause and strive for objectivity.** Don't automatically blame the other person; accept that you might be at fault. If you don't know what went wrong, ask.
2. **Watch your step.** When a relationship is under strain, the smallest misunderstanding can ruin any chance for reconciliation. This isn't the time for jokes and sarcasm.
3. **Apologize like you mean it.** If you are at fault, apologize sincerely and specifically for your behavior and the impact it had on the other person.
4. **Make the first move.** If you truly don't think you are at fault, you can still be the bigger person and express regret for the breakdown in the relationship. Replace "I'm sorry for . . ." with "I regret that . . .".
5. **Don't give up too soon.** Repairing a severely damaged relationship takes time, patience, and consistency.
6. **Take personal responsibility.** For at least a week, take responsibility for improving every interaction you have with the other person. Particularly if the falling out is due to a personality clash, don't expect it to be solved collaboratively.
7. **Know when to move on.** Sometimes, a relationship is beyond repair. Some people will never see eye to eye. If the other person clearly doesn't want to make peace, it may be time to move on.

Sources: Based on "Career Masterclass: Fix Broken Relationships," *Management Today* (October 1, 2010): 15; and "Your Route to the Top: Admitting a Mistake," *Management Today* (February 1, 2009): 14.

Exhibit 1.2 The Practical Aspects and Outcomes of Caring About Others

What do you do when you care for someone?*	What does it feel like to be cared about?*
1. reach out	1. valuable
2. embrace, hug	2. alive
3. be there with them	3. responsive
4. compassion	4. positive outlook
5. acceptance	5. exhilarated
6. share dreams	6. respect
7. acknowledge accomplishments	7. free
8. trust	8. important
9. encourage	9. good
10. be a cheerleader	10. safe
11. tell you care	11. more open to express yourself
12. relate feelings	12. elevates self-esteem
13. respect them	13. boosts morale
14. be positive	14. proud
15. give them a smile	15. loved
16. give them time	16. worthy
17. give them recognition	17. blessed
18. protect	18. you make a difference
19. reassure	19. fulfilled
20. celebrate with	20. happy

*These are the actual, unedited words called out by participants and written on a white board during a seminar at which people were asked these two questions.

Source: Marilyn R. Zuckerman and Lewis J. Hatala. Reprinted with permission from *Incredibly American: Releasing the Heart of Quality* © 1992 American Society for Quality. No further distribution allowed without permission.

you have initiative, it is easy for you to get started on things, even when it's something you're not looking forward to doing. People high in task initiative tend to hit the ground running as soon as they get to work, rather than chatting with colleagues or lingering over an extra cup of coffee before getting down to the business of the day. Managers high in initiative will flow into necessary work rather than experience an internal struggle based on a desire to avoid a task that needs doing. Initiative is revealed in the ability to reach out and include people, the willingness to confront someone when needed, the readiness to start a new project, and the ability to take personal responsibility to act on one's own.

7. **Goal-Directed Mindset.** The strength of being goal directed refers to the ability to look forward and define a goal or vision for the future, then formulate plans and action steps needed to accomplish it. People high in this strength can see the desired future outcome, establish the steps needed to reach it, and stay on target without letting themselves be distracted by competing interests. They are typically task-focused, reliably complete the tasks they commit to, and can focus on the long term rather than being pulled away by short-term opportunities. For managers, an important role is setting clear goals and establishing plans for how to accomplish them. People low on this ability have trouble focusing beyond immediate outcomes. They have a hard time conceptualizing the desired result and how to achieve it. They easily lose sight of long-range goals and get off track when they are excited by some new opportunity.

8. **Ability to Organize.** Organizing is the capacity to arrange people, resources, and activities into a system. People with a high capacity for organizing can clearly identify the activities and arrange the resources needed to accomplish plans and goals. They can identify the most important work elements and how they should be structured. In a group getting organized, the person high on organizing skill will immediately see

and suggest which people should perform each specific task, the resources needed, and when the task should be completed. Organizers are efficient and disciplined in how they approach tasks, and they are clear about which tasks to focus on and which to ignore. They are good about creating a personal filing system, keeping a daily to-do list, sticking to time limits for meetings and phone calls, and establishing deadlines for themselves and others. They quickly assess situations and reorganize for efficiency. A manager low in organizing skill might not be sure where to start, be reluctant to organize people to accomplish the task, or be hapless about how to structure activities and manage resources.

9. Time Management. People high in this strength are almost always on time for appointments, meetings, or events; dependably meet deadlines; and usually approach things in a methodical way. They are able to estimate the amount of time it will take to accomplish a project and can juggle tasks to complete the most important jobs first and still have time to finish other necessary activities. If you have this strength, you are probably high on self-regulation, mentioned earlier. You are able to allocate and use your time efficiently. If you're low on time management abilities, you probably have trouble being on time for appointments, often miss deadlines, and don't accomplish as much during a day as you expect because you underestimate the time requirements of certain activities. One woman started an errand business for busy mothers but quickly learned she wasn't cut out for the job. No matter how many times she had driven a particular route, she consistently underestimated the time it would take. She routinely failed to complete all the errands she agreed to accomplish because of her weakness in time management.

10. Agility. If you quickly adapt to changing conditions, you possess the strength of agility. You don't panic when a book you need for a class presentation fails to arrive; you calmly find another approach. You don't get annoyed or flustered if someone drops by unexpectedly while you're trying to cook dinner or get the kids to bed. **Agility** means that you are able to revise and adjust your plans and change course when faced with obstacles, setbacks, new data, or mistakes. Agility is related to one's ability to adapt to change and to incorporate new information. People high in agility take unexpected events in stride and adapt easily to change, whereas those low in agility aren't comfortable with the unexpected, have a harder time adapting to changing situations, and are less willing to incorporate new information that might alter their plans. Managers high in agility are able to cope with uncertainty and high pressure without becoming stressed out. For example, a manager high in agility would not be fazed by an accelerated deadline for completion of an important project, whereas someone low in agility would likely experience a high level of anxiety.

DISCOVER YOURSELF

Interpret Your Score: Manager Strengths (Questionnaire 1)

Your answers to these 50 questions provide information on the ten strengths described in the chapter. A higher score on each of the Parts A–J means that you likely possess more of that strength; a lower score probably means less of that strength. Comparative data for the ten manager strengths are: **Self-confidence** (Part A) Thirty person Mean score = 13.5, Top Quartile = 14–15; Bottom Quartile = 11–13. **Emotion Control** (Part B) Mean = 11.7, Top Quartile = 13–14; Bottom Quartile = 8–10. **Focus** (Part C) Mean = 11.2; Top Quartile = 12–15; Bottom Quartile = 7–11. **Objectivity** (Part D) Mean = 12.4; Top Quartile = 14–15; Bottom Quartile = 8–11. **Relationship Building** (Part E) Mean = 13.7, Top Quartile = 15–15; Bottom Quartile = 10–13. **Initiative** (Part F) Mean = 11.9, Top Quartile = 14–15; Bottom Quartile = 7–10. **Goal-Directed Mindset** (Part G) Mean = 11.7; Top Quartile = 14–15; Bottom Quartile = 7–10. **Ability to Organize** (Part H) Mean = 13.1; Top Quartile = 15–15; Bottom Quartile = 8–12. **Time Management** (Part I) Mean = 11.2, Top Quartile = 13–15; Bottom Quartile = 6–10. **Agility** (Part J) Mean = 11.9, Top Quartile = 13–14; Bottom Quartile = 9–11. No manager is expected to score high on all strengths. The important thing is for you to identify and take advantage of the strengths that you have. How do your strengths compare to those of other students? How well do your strengths align with your desire to be a manager? CNOW and CourseMate users can access dynamically updated comparative data through www.cengagebrain.com.

© CENGAGE LEARNING 2014

WHAT ABOUT PERSONAL WEAK POINTS OR LIMITATIONS?

Entrepreneur Michael Arrington started TechCrunch, the company that publishes the influential blog of the same name, as a hobby in 2005. Within five years, it had become the go-to source for breaking news about technology companies and Internet startups and was bringing in annual revenues of around $10 million. Arrington started the blog because he enjoys the research and writing, and he admits he isn't very good at the people management part of his job. "It's hard to be a coach and a player at the same time," Arrington says. "Plus, I'm moody." Recognizing his weak point in being a manager of other people, Arrington hired Heather Harde as CEO of the company, which enabled TechCrunch to grow and allowed Arrington to focus on what he was best at doing.[22]

As important as it is to discover the areas in which you have managerial strengths, it is also essential to recognize your weak points. Achieving excellence means not only playing to your strengths but also upgrading or compensating for areas in which you don't do well. Many people are held back because they fail to recognize the constraints that limit their ability to be their best at work and in their personal lives.[23]

Internal Constraints Limit You

A key weakness can derail a career in management. The **theory of constraints** says that every system or process has one or a few weaknesses that prevent it from achieving maximum performance. The weakness or flaw acts as a serious limitation on the system's performance. Assume, for example, that you own a small cafe. When coffee sales pick up during lunch, it takes about five minutes to make a fresh pot of coffee. However, if there is no coffee on hand, the process takes 30 minutes because someone has to drive to the store to buy coffee. Thus, the lack of coffee is a key "constraint" that has to be corrected in order for coffee making to be efficient. Keeping a supply of coffee beans on hand would resolve this constraint. Another constraint that would slow the coffee-making process would be washing the coffee pots. Again, this constraint could be eliminated by devising a way to always have clean coffee pots ready to go. These examples show that the weakest link in a system limits performance, and correcting the weakest link will have a big payback.[24]

Everyone Has Internal, Personal Constraints

Personal constraints typically fall into three basic groups:[25]

- There are minor constraints that don't affect your work or management ability. For example, an introverted college professor is fairly typical so introversion is not a key constraint on performance. Moreover, a minor constraint is easy to fix, such as when psychologist Timothy Wilson decided to become more extroverted. In baby steps, he made more of an effort to chat with people he did not know at social get-togethers, and he became more extroverted as a result.[26]
- There are constraints that managers can hire someone else to do for them. A manager who is disorganized may have an assistant who is highly organized, for example. A manager who is weak at planning can make sure a strong planner is a member of the team. Hiring an assistant or direct report who offsets your specific constraints will ensure that the team has all of the competencies needed to succeed.
- There are major constraints that can prevent a manager from performing as needed. Such a constraint can derail your personal life and professional success. Attributes such as dishonesty, low self-control, or lack of self-confidence can seriously prevent a manager from executing effectively. A manager may have only one or two constraints of this severity, and resolving them will significantly improve manager performance.

You Cannot Correct What You Don't See or Understand

When people don't acknowledge a serious weak point, they can't do anything to ameliorate it. A person who has a significant weakness in any of the executive strengths discussed above will find that it can hinder his performance and success unless he finds a way to minimize or deal with it. A manager who has a strong weakness in the area of focus, for example, might do fine as long as she isn't under pressure, yet fail to meet an urgent deadline because she is easily distracted from the project. Similarly, someone who is significantly weak in the area of agility would have a difficult time if his department or organization suddenly became immersed in a major transformation. Recognizing and admitting your weaknesses, and understanding when and why they create problems for you, is a significant step toward finding ways to mitigate them.

What's Your Problem?

Q: I have been happily working as a pricing analyst for four years. I was doing so well that I was promoted six months ago to manage a five-person team. It's hard to admit, but I hate it. Administrative work is bad, bad. Plus there are constant problems. People have conflicts they want me to solve. One person resents my authority. My boss wants me to manage more with my head and less with my heart. I am ready to quit management, but I don't want to lose my job with this company.

A: Don't quit. It takes most people at least one year to adjust to handling people full-time. What did your boss see in you when he asked you to be a manager? First, make a careful assessment of your strengths. It sounds like your natural gifts are heart and people skills. Build on those by networking, reaching out, and connecting with people on a personal level. Second, reframe this as an opportunity to learn and grow. Your style may be rather soft like a marshmallow. Ask your company to provide some personal coaching on assertiveness and handling conflicts and ask for some training on the administrative stuff. Recognizing your strengths and weaknesses and getting help are admirable. With guidance and repetition you will master the hard parts, and your fulfillment will arise from your relationships with your team.

© CENGAGE LEARNING 2014

DISCOVER KNOWLEDGE

A Manager Who Learns to Minimize or Resolve a Significant Constraint Will Be a Winner

A significant constraint can get in the way of your work effectiveness and relationships on a regular basis. It is important to know and build on your strengths, and equally important to understand that a significant constraint will undercut those strengths. No one can be strong in every area, and most of us have one or two areas of significant weakness that we need to address to achieve our best. In addition, there are some weaknesses or flaws that can be deadly to a management career. One area in which it is essential that managers overcome personal constraints is people and relationship skills. Inadequate skill or strength in building positive relationships is a frequent cause of manager failure.

The Problem of Poor People Skills

Research into management failure suggests that lack of human skills is a major constraint on being an effective manager.

Why Managers Derail

A few clues to the importance of human skills were brought to light by the Center for Creative Leadership in Greensboro, North Carolina.[27] The study compared 21 derailed executives with 20 executives who successfully arrived at the top of a company. The derailed managers were successful people who were expected to go far, but they reached a plateau, were fired, or were forced to retire early. They were all bright, worked hard, and excelled in a technical area such as accounting or engineering. The striking difference between the two groups was the ability to use human skills. Only 25 percent of the derailed group were described as being good with people, whereas 75 percent of those who arrived at the top had good people skills. Several of the top reasons for failure reflected the central role of people skills in successful management. Unsuccessful managers were insensitive to others, abrasive, cold, arrogant, untrustworthy, overly ambitious and selfish, unable to delegate or build teams, and unable to acquire appropriate staff to work for them. The inability to surround oneself with good people and help them learn and contribute can doom any manager. The best managers are those who are genuinely interested in other people and find ways to bring out the best in them.[28]

A Survey of Failures

A survey of more than 1,000 managers from approximately 100 organizations undergoing change used focus groups to ask participating managers the following question: *Based on your experience, why do managers fail to get the desired results in rapidly changing organizations?*[29] Exhibit 1.3 shows the ten most frequent causes of managerial failure as reflected in this survey. The top two causes of failure, mentioned by 81 percent and 78 percent of participants respectively, are ineffective communication skills and poor work relationships. Managers fail when they cannot communicate effectively to share critical information with

Exhibit 1.3 Primary Causes of Manager Failure in Fast-Changing Companies

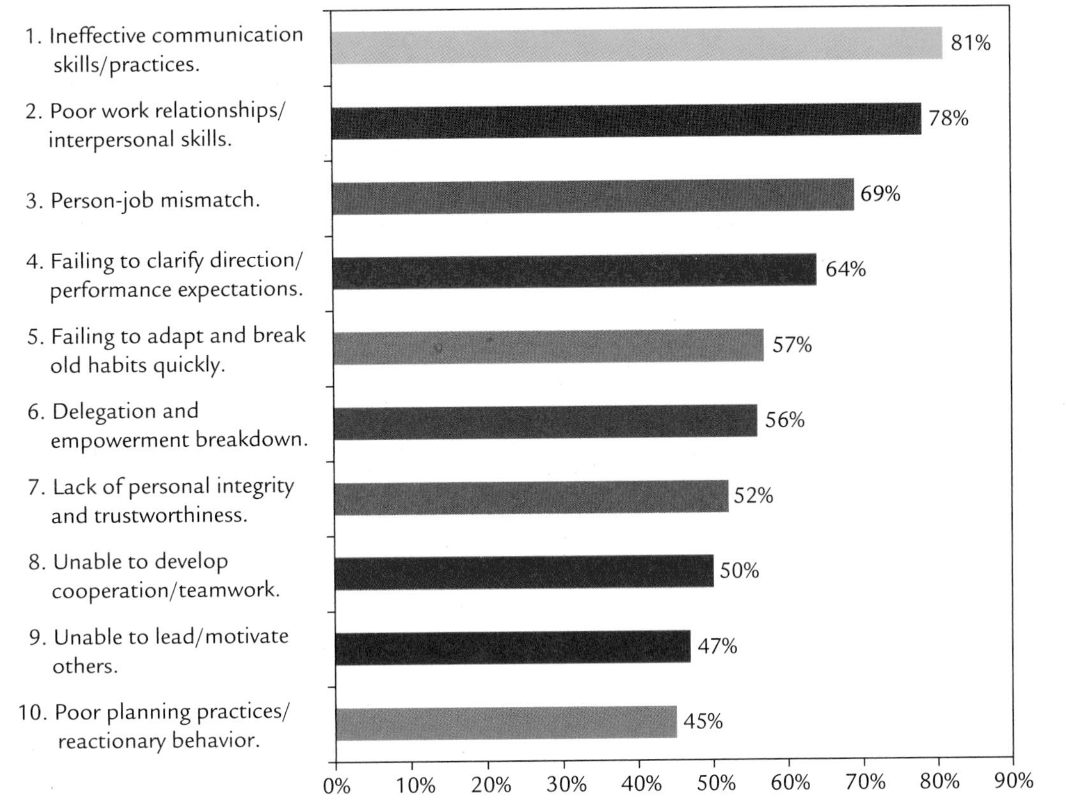

Source: Reprinted from Clinton O. Longnecker, Mitchell J. Neubert, and Lawrence S. Fink, "Causes and Consequences of Managerial Failure in Rapidly Changing Organizations," *Business Horizons*, 50 (2007): 145–155 with permission from Elsevier.

employees or work teams. Moreover, they may fail to listen to the concerns of people around them, with potentially devastating results. One manager said, "Change brings increased levels of busyness and busyness can breed communication problems of all sorts, which can only spell trouble for any leader."[30]

More than ever, effective working relationships, interpersonal skills, and building networks are critical for managers to achieve results. The inability to gain the commitment and cooperation necessary to plan and implement change initiatives is the second-leading cause of failure. The inability to create and nurture effective working relationships creates barriers and impediments to getting things done. Other causes of failure in Exhibit 1.3 also play a role. Person-job mismatch means that the manager did not have sufficient training and was in over his or her head. The inability to clarify expectations, to break old habits, to delegate, to act with integrity, to develop teamwork, to motivate, or to plan also lead to manager failure. The importance of developing skills for dealing with people successfully cannot be over-emphasized. Managers who have weak human skills are headed for career derailment. In addition, there are some personal weaknesses in the area of people skills that are so damaging that, if not corrected, they will totally wreck a manager's career.

SIX KILLER CONSTRAINTS

Ruth Namie and her husband Gary founded the Workplace Bullying Institute because they know first-hand how damaging it can be to work for a boss who is a bully. Ruth suffered years of verbal abuse in her job as a clinical psychologist before she finally quit. One of their recent clients also has a bully for a boss: He loads her down with excessive work, constantly belittles her in front of others, and neglects to inform her about important meetings so she will miss them and then be faulted for it. It is likely this manager does the same

Exhibit 1.4 The Six Killer Constraints

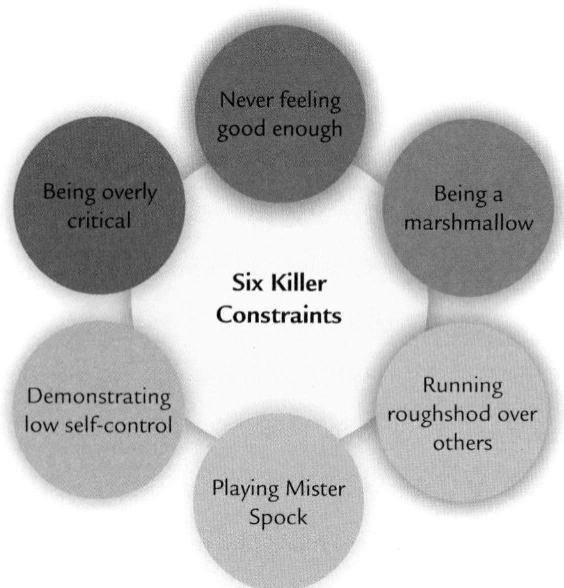

© CENGAGE LEARNING 2014

with other employees, and the company will lose good people because of it.[31]

Everyone has weaknesses, and some of them don't matter all that much. However, when a manager is a bully, as Ruth Namie's manager was, employees and the company alike suffer. There are six weak spots, shown in Exhibit 1.4, that matter tremendously for both your personal life and your career as a manager.[32] These *killer constraints* or *fatal flaws* are more than a poorly developed skill or a weakness in a key area; they are patterns of thought or behavior that if left unchecked can cause pain, frustration, and real damage for yourself and others. As you review the constraints that follow, you will notice that they pertain to how managers relate to other people rather than how they handle technical matters.

1. Never Feeling Good Enough. In recent years, we've heard too many stories about executives with out-sized egos, but not having *enough* self-confidence can be just as damaging. This pattern is so subtle that people may not see it in themselves. They sabotage their own careers and happiness because they don't feel quite good enough. You might have noticed someone from a working-class background who was decidedly uncomfortable interacting with colleagues who attended prestigious universities. This person's lack of confidence reflects an underlying fear or insecurity. Without self-esteem, a manager may second-guess himself and be afraid to speak out or to take initiative for fear of failure or disapproval. A manager who doesn't take needed action for fear of failure will not lead a team to excellent performance.

In a work setting, this limitation becomes dangerous when people achieve a level of status and responsibility beyond where they think they belong (even though they may have eagerly sought the advancement). They may unconsciously do things to prove that they don't deserve the promotion, such as procrastinating, acting uncertain, failing to exercise initiative, or simply doing a bad job. When he was a middle manager at a publishing company, Scott Flanders (currently the CEO of Playboy Enterprises and former CEO of Columbia House) learned in therapy that although he craved success, he felt unworthy of it. These feelings of unworthiness were causing him to wage intense rivalries with peers to prove himself rather than treating them as teammates. He later became friends with many people whom he had earlier "encouraged to hate me." Flanders says he probably wouldn't be a CEO today if he hadn't overcome the stumbling block of never feeling good enough.[33]

Are you guilty of never feeling good enough? See if you recognize yourself in any of these statements:

- "When peers give me good feedback, I believe it is not true. My inner critic says, 'they don't know the real me.' I am afraid people will find out that I really have no idea what I'm doing."
- "I was amazed at the number of times I criticize myself in one day. Many times, I blame myself and feel guilty for procrastination and falling short of my plan."
- "Everything I do I am comparing, judging, wishing, regretting. I hold myself to perfection and strive to meet that goal."[34]

Negative self-judgments such as these will limit your potential and impair your performance as a manager by blocking your underlying creativity and initiative. Negative self-judgment is like a bad headache, which, if removed, will yield a big increase in management creativity and capacity.

2. Being a Marshmallow. Can a person ever be *too* nice? The surprising answer is yes. Sometimes, a person's nurturing and care-giving goes far beyond what is good for them or for those around them. If you find yourself always covering for the mistakes of others, taking over for irresponsible people, or being physically and emotionally drained from your inability to say "no," you might be a marshmallow. Over-nurturing people can sometimes hurt those they're trying to help. For example, let's say you overhear a colleague, Adam, complaining about having to work late every night to finish a project. You genuinely want to help so you go to the boss and ask if there's any way to lighten Adam's workload. Now, the boss is wondering why Adam is falling behind in his work, Adam is embarassed and angry that the boss found out that he's behind, and both of them resent your meddling.[35] Marshmallows don't make good managers. They can't offer the constructive criticism needed to help employees develop and improve. In addition, they frequently end up coddling poor performers at the expense of more responsible workers and the overall success of the company.

3. Running Roughshod Over Others. The flip side of being a marshmallow is just as bad. Some people are dominant in the extreme. These are the bullies of the school yard, lunch room, or corporate hallway. One author tells a story of a partner in a prestigious law firm who walked through the corridors literally swinging a baseball bat, which he would occassionally slap into his open palm to symbolize his toughness. He was almost fired until he was given a second chance and learned to change his habit of bulldozing over anyone and anything that got in the way of what he wanted.[36] Not everyone is this extreme, but we've all known people who bulldoze their way through life. Sometimes it's with aggression and contempt; other times it's more subtle, such as those people who are highly manipulative or get what they want by using veiled threats.

It is critically important to recognize if you have a pattern of running roughshod over others, as this is one of the most dangerous of the killer constraints. Bulldozers alienate everyone, destroy relationships, lose employees, get fired, and create ill will wherever they go. In addition, since they think they're right about everything, it's particularly hard for them to see or admit that they need to change.

One example of a bulldozer who saw the light is Selena Lo. Lo had a reputation as an aggressive, fire-breathing marketing VP who was determined to get her way. She admits that she "left a few dead bodies" behind her. She "always had an answer to almost any question or problem," she says, and her boss would come along behind her and "soothe the people who felt I was steamrolling them." When Lo founded Ruckus Wireless, the yelling and fist pounding to get her way no longer worked. As CEO of Ruckus, she was responsible for all departments and employees, and she realized she was fighting against her own organization. Impatience was her greatest foe, and changing her habit required a huge effort of will, but Lo was able to overcome this potentially fatal flaw. She adopted a group decision-making process that forced her to listen to others. Now, whenever a disagreement arises, she convenes a meeting of disputants and other people affected by the decision to resolve the issue, rather than steamrolling everyone to get her own way.[37]

DISCOVER YOURSELF

Interpret Your Score: Manager Weaknesses (Questionnaire 2)

The scores for questionnaire 2 reflect managerial weaknesses or fatal flaws that can derail a manager's career. In this case, a lower score for each weakness is preferred. Comparative data for the six managerial flaws are: **Never Feeling Good Enough** (Part A): Thirty person Mean score = 11.4, Top Quartile = 13–15; Bottom Quartile = 9–10. **Being a Marshmallow** (Part B): Mean = 10.0, Top Quartile = 11–14; Bottom Quartile = 8–9. **Riding Roughshod over Others** (Part C): Mean = 9.2; Top Quartile = 11–13; Bottom Quartile = 5–7. **Being Mr. Spock** (Part D): Mean = 8.1; Top Quartile = 9–12; Bottom Quartile = 5–7. **Demonstrating Low Self-Control** (Part E): Mean = 8.1, Top Quartile = 9–13; Bottom Quartile = 5–7. **Being Overly Critical** (Part F): Mean = 9.6, Top Quartile = 12–14; Bottom Quartile = 7–7. How do you feel about your weaknesses? What changes would you like to make? CNOW and CourseMate users can access dynamically updated comparative data through www.cengagebrain.com.

© CENGAGE LEARNING 2014

DISCOVER KNOWLEDGE

4. Playing Mr. Spock. In the iconic television series *Star Trek*, Leonard Nimoy plays a character named Spock from the planet Vulcan. Spock is unable to feel emotions or to understand them in others. People who are "playing Mr. Spock" are emotionally tone-deaf. They don't intend to be cold or hard-hearted, they simply don't recognize the role of human feelings and motivations in the organization. People with this killer constraint are typically highly rational and look at problems as objective issues to be solved, devoid of a complex

human component. They come across as highly critical, demanding, and harsh. They usually think they are being insightful and helpful by pointing out flaws and problems. However, unlike marshmallows, who are overly-nurturing, these folks pay absolutely no attention to people's feelings. They rarely show affection, give compliments, or offer help to others. Thus, they end up creating a climate of fault-finding and blame rather than one of working together to solve problems.

5. **Demonstrating Low Self-Control.** Do you make a lot of impulse purchases? How about switching jobs frequently or starting home improvement or crafts projects but never finishing one before you move on to another? If so, you might suffer from this killer constraint. People with this behavior pattern are very easily distracted and lack self-discipline. They can't stay focused on a long-term goal. They get bored easily and crave the variety and excitement of the next thing. Although it is good for managers to value change, change just for the sake of change does nothing but keep everyone off balance and prevent the manager from accomplishing all that he or she could.

6. **Being Overly Critical.** Some managers have an inner critic that is harsh in its view of other people. This person points out what is not working rather than focusing on what is working. When these criticisms are spoken, they come across as highly derogatory and even abusive toward others. Nobody wants to work for a manager who is constantly finding fault and criticizing people and performance. Sometimes the manager just wants to be helpful but unfortunately can see only the negative. Overly critical managers are easily annoyed and pick out shortcomings with every person, plan, report, and hiring decision. They can't see the good side of a report or appreciate the effort and skill that went into the project. Managers who are highly critical often readily admit to the things that annoy them. Examples would include:

- "The thing that sets me off about others is a lack of reason, logic, or planning."
- "I pay too much attention to people's physical appearance. I'm alert to anything I don't like, especially hair, makeup, and fitness."
- "Most people 'beat around the bush' too much and won't just come out and say what they mean. That drives me crazy."

When a manager is thinking so critcially all the time, he or she becomes a fault finder rather than a leader. These managers tear people and projects down rather than build them up. People working for them never get to experience the delightful feelings listed earlier in Exhibit 1.2. There is no optimism, no appreciation, no sensitivity to the contributions of others. People become discouraged and demotivated. Being overly critical rather than seeing things in a balanced way is a sure route to a brief career as a manager.

USE EMOTIONAL INTELLIGENCE TO AVOID THE KILLER CONSTRAINTS

For Mike Krzyzewski, coach of the Duke University Blue Devils basketball team, almost everything about managing a team—or an organization—depends on one element: personal relationships. Although he's a tough man with tough standards, Krzyzewski has been accused of "coaching like a girl" because of his interactive, emotionally charged style. Krzyzewski emphasizes teamwork rather than individual performers, fosters a family feeling among players, and says he coaches "by feel." That is, he gets to know his players as individuals and learns how they can best interact to succeed. He builds such strong positive relationships among players that they communicate constantly and effortlessly on the court, sometimes without saying a word.[38]

We've all seen coaches at both the college and professional level who scream at their players, throw temper tantrums on the sidelines, and make the news because of their frequent outbursts and lack of self-control. Mike Krzyzewski takes a different approach, using emotional intelligence to bring out the best in his players. **Emotional intelligence** refers to a person's abilities to perceive, identify, understand, and successfully manage emotions in self and others. Being emotionally intelligent means being able to effectively manage ourselves and our relationships.[39]

The Components of Emotional Intelligence

The competencies and abilities of emotional intelligence are grouped into four fundamental categories, as illustrated in Exhibit 1.5.[40] It is important to remember that emotional intelligence can be learned and developed.

Exhibit 1.5 Components of Emotional Intelligence

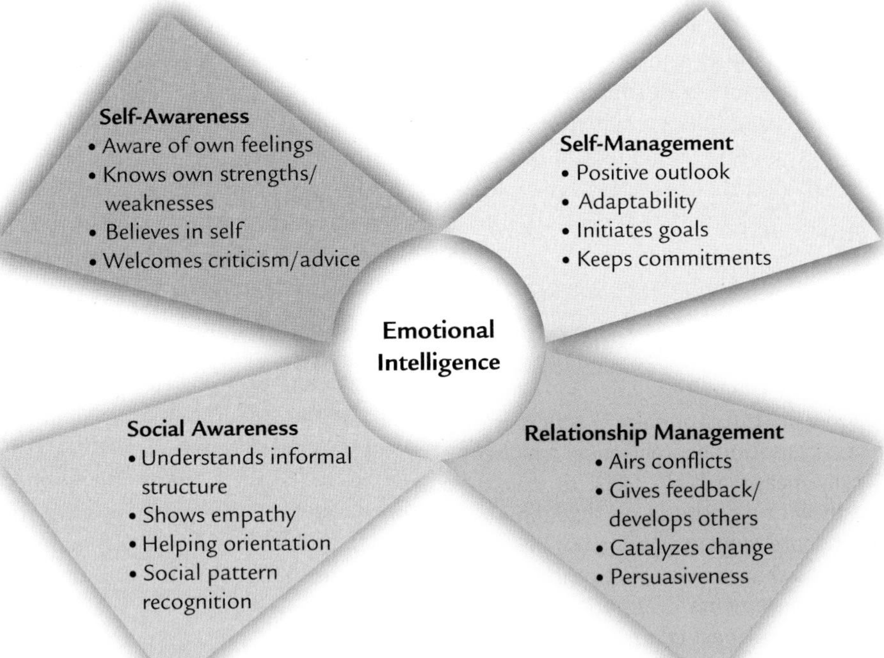

Sources: Based on Laura Guillen Ramo, Willem E. Saris, and Richard E. Sis, "The Impact of Social and Emotional Competencies on Effectiveness of Spanish Executives," *Journal of Management Development* 28, no. 9 (2009): 771–793; Jane V. Wheeler, "The Impact of Social Environments on Emotional, Social, and Cognitive Competency Development," *Journal of Management Development,* 27, no. 1 (2008): 129–145; Margaret M. Hopkins, "Social and Emotional Competencies Predicting Success for Male and Female Executives," *Journal of Management Development,* 27, no. 1 (2008): 13–35; and Daniel Goleman, "Leadership That Gets Results," *Harvard Business Review* (March–April 2000): 78–90.

Anyone can strengthen his or her abilities in these four categories and develop a higher EQ (emotional quotient).

Self-Awareness

Self-awareness is the basis of all the other competencies. Self-awareness includes the ability to recognize and understand your own emotions and how they affect your life and work. People who are in touch with their emotions are better able to guide their own lives. Managers with a high level of self-awareness learn to trust their "gut feelings" and realize that these feelings can provide useful information about difficult decisions. This component also includes the ability to accurately assess your own strengths and limitations, as well as a willingness to accept criticism and advice without getting defensive.

Self-Management

Self-management includes the ability to control disruptive, unproductive, or harmful emotions and desires. An interesting experiment from the 1960s sheds some light on the power of self-management. A group of four-year-olds and five-year-olds were offered a marshmallow, which the researcher placed in front of each child on the desk. Then, the children were told that if they could wait a few minutes while the researcher ran an errand, they would be given two marshmallows. Some children were unable to resist the temptation of a marshmallow "right now" and ate theirs immediately. Others employed all sorts of techniques, from singing or talking to themselves to hiding under the desk, to resist their impulses and earn the reward of two marshmallows instead of one. Researchers then followed the children over a period of 20 years and found some interesting results. As young men and women, the ones who had resisted the desire to eat the marshmallow revealed a much higher ability to handle stress and embrace difficult challenges. They also were more self-confident, trustworthy, dependable, and tenacious in pursuing goals.[41] The children who developed techniques for self-management early in life carried these with them into adulthood.

Other characteristics in this category include a capacity for initiating and pursuing goals, conscientiousness, which means managing and honoring your commitments, and adaptability, which refers to the ability to adjust to changing situations and overcome obstacles.

DISCOVER YOURSELF

Interpret Your Score: Emotional Intelligence (Questionnaire 3)

The four scores for questionnaire 3 reflect the four elements of emotional intelligence. A higher score generally means a higher EQ, that is, a greater sensitivity and aptitude on that dimension. A lower score suggests you probably are not as tuned in to that dimension. Comparative data for the four elements of emotional intelligence are: **Self-Awareness** (Part A): Thirty person Mean score = 13.1, Top Quartile = 15–15; Bottom Quartile = 9–12. **Self-Management** (Part B): Mean = 11.9, Top Quartile = 13–15; Bottom Quartile = 8–10. **Social Awareness** (Part C): Mean = 13.7; Top Quartile = 15–15; Bottom Quartile = 11–13. **Relationship Management** (Part D): Mean = 12.7; Top Quartile = 14–15; Bottom Quartile = 10–11. What do your scores mean to you? What changes would you like to make? CNOW and CourseMate users can access dynamically updated comparative data through www.cengagebrain.com.

© CENGAGE LEARNING 2014

DISCOVER KNOWLEDGE

Social Awareness

Social awareness relates to one's ability to understand others. Socially aware managers practice empathy, which means being able to put yourself in other people's shoes, sense their emotions, and understand their perspectives. Effective management sometimes means pushing people beyond their comfort zone, and socially aware managers are sensitive to the fear or frustration this can engender in employees. They learn to engage in "professional intimacy," which means they can display compassion, concern, and a helpful attitude toward others without becoming so wrapped up in others' emotions that it clouds their judgment.[42] Socially aware managers are also capable of understanding divergent points of view and interacting effectively with many different types of people and emotions. The characteristic of *social pattern recognition* refers to the ability to navigate the currents of organizational life, understand the organization's informal structure, and build networks to accomplish positive results.

Relationship Management

Relationship management refers to the ability to connect with others and build positive relationships. Managers with a high EQ treat others with sensitivity and kindness, and they bring conflicts into the open so they can be resolved.[43] This aspect of emotional intelligence encompasses developing others, learning to listen and communicate clearly and convincingly to persuade others, and using emotional understanding to influence people for positive change. Managers with a high EQ cultivate and maintain a web of relationships both within and outside the organization.

The Emotionally Competent Manager

In one study, two-thirds of the difference between average and top performing managers was due to emotional competence, with only one-third due to technical skills.[44] How is emotional intelligence related to effective management? Taken together, the four components shown in Exhibit 1.5 build a strong base of emotional intelligence that you can use to avoid the six killer constraints discussed in the previous section.

A high level of self-awareness and an ability to manage your own emotions will enable you to display self-confidence, earn respect and trust, and consider the needs of others. Emotionally competent managers are more resilient, more adaptable to ever-changing circumstances, more willing to step outside their comfort zone, and more open to the opinions and ideas of others.[45]

Emotional intelligence is also important because, as a manager, your emotional state impacts the entire team, department, or organization. Most of us recognize that we can "catch" emotions from others. If we're around someone who is smiling and enthusiastic, the positive emotions rub off on us. Conversely, someone in a bad mood can bring us down. This *emotional contagion*[46] means that managers who are able to maintain balance and keep themselves motivated can serve as positive role models to help motivate and inspire those around them. The energy level of the entire team or organization increases when managers are optimistic and hopeful rather than angry or depressed. The ability to empathize with others and to manage interpersonal relationships also contributes to motivation and inspiration because it helps create feelings of unity and team spirit. Perhaps most importantly, emotional intelligence will enable you to recognize and respect subordinates as whole human beings with feelings, opinions, and ideas of their own.

NEED TO KNOW

- You will develop into an effective manager more quickly if you discover your strengths and capabilities and learn how to make the most of them. Everyone has natural talents, and you can turn your natural talents into strengths by supporting and reinforcing them with learned knowledge and skills.
- Ten strengths related to manager performance are self-confidence, emotion control, focus, objectivity, relationship building, initiative, goal-directed mindset, ability to organize, time management, and agility.
- It is equally important for managers to understand limitations and weak points. Some personal weaknesses can be serious enough to constrain effective management and can derail a manager's career.
- Having inadequate people skills is a serious constraint for being an effective manager.
- One survey found that the top two causes of manager failure are poor communication and poor work relationships.
- Six killer constraints, or fatal flaws, are: never feeling good enough, being a marshmallow (being too soft and nurturing), playing Mr. Spock (failing to feel or understand emotions), running roughshod over others, demonstrating low self-control, and being overly critical.
- Managers can develop emotional intelligence to overcome or avoid the six killer constraints. Four components of emotional intelligence are self awareness, self management, social awareness, and relationship management. Emotional intelligence can be learned, and your success as a manager will depend as much or more on your emotional competence as on your technical abilities.

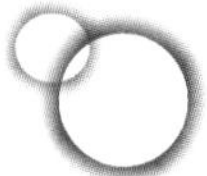

ACTION LEARNING

DELIBERATE PRACTICE EXERCISES

High Performance Strengths[47]

Step 1: Think of two times in your history when you were performing extraordinarily well. This can include a job assignment, volunteer effort, schoolwork, social event, relationship, or a crisis or a project you handled when things really took off and succeeded beyond expectations. Your two choices can be small experiences that were important to you, but not necessarily to the world at large. Complete the table below as you describe these two experiences.

	Successful experience #1	Successful experience #2
What was the experience?		
How did you become aware of and get drawn into the experience?		
How did you get the activity under way (get the ball rolling) for the experience?		
How did you keep the ball rolling? Did you bring others in?		
How did you handle the ups and downs?		
How did you bring the experience to an end?		

(Continued)

Identify the three major strengths you used during the experience.	1. 2. 3.	1. 2. 3.

Step 2: Identify your two top strengths from the table above. Write them here:

1.

2.

Step 3: List two other times that you have used these strengths successfully.

1.

2.

Step 4: What new insights do you have about your strengths?

Step 5 (Optional): Share your insights with a partner, and ask your partner what insights he or she gained.

ACTION LEARNING

Practice Your Strength

ACTION

Step 1: Choose either one of the strengths you identified in the High Performance Strengths exercise above or one from the list of strengths on page 45 that you want to practice this week. For example, you might decide that the strength you will choose is your ability to connect with others. Then you might practice by starting up conversations with strangers in a library or a campus dorm (no place dangerous). You could also decide to give ten authentic compliments a day and make a conscious effort to smile and laugh twice as much as you normally do.

Step 2: Find every chance you can to practice the strength and then write a few sentences on how it felt to use it.

Step 3: Complete the table below about your experiences. It is better to fill it out each time you practice the strength.

What is the strength?	
Give one or two examples when you have used it previously and what effect it had on you and any others around you.	
First time you used it this week: What was the situation and how did you do?	
Second time you practiced it: How different was the situation? How was your use of the strength received?	
Third time: Describe the situation. Are you getting better?	
Fourth time: What was the situation? Is it getting easier and more comfortable?	

Step 4 (Optional): Share your insights with a partner, and ask your partner what insights he or she gained.

Your Killer Constraints

Step 1: Review the "Six Killer Constraints" section in this chapter. Complete the table below to understand your own personal constraints and how to overcome them. Include anything you think is relevant, even if it's not on the list of six killer constraints.

List your constraints below (you can include things in addition to the six killer constraints).	How might each one limit you as a manager?	What might you do about each one to create a more positive outcome?

Step 2: Which is the constraint that gives you the most problems? Write it below.

Step 3: How can you make changes, including restructuring your life, to help you reduce the impact of your constraints?

Step 4 (Optional): Share your insights with a partner, and ask your partner what insights he or she gained.

IN-CLASS TEAM EXERCISES

High Performance Strengths: Another Viewpoint

Step 1: Divide into pairs or small groups as directed by your instructor.

Step 2: Take turns describing your High Performance Strengths stories from the Deliberate Practice Exercise, "High Performance Strengths." Provide enough detail so the others will understand what you did and what you went through. Ask the other person(s) the two questions below and make notes of the answers. Also take your turn providing feedback to the other person(s) about the high-performance strengths that come through in their stories.

What patterns does the person see in how you handled these three situations?	Notes:
What other insights can that person share about you and your strengths?	Notes:

SHUTTERSTOCK #53973379

Strength Impressions

This In-Class Team Exercise is available online at www.cengagebrain.com.

FIELD TEAM EXERCISE

Popular Media and Strengths

Step 1: Divide into small groups as directed by the instructor. As a group, watch one movie that has at least one positive and at least one not-so-positive character.

Step 2: Fill in the table below. Complete column A on your own. Fill in column B as a group. Complete column C on your own after you have spent some time thinking about the movie. (Examples of movies: Any of the *Harry Potter* stories, *Star Wars, Lord of the Rings*, almost any Disney animated film, *Margin Call, Drive, Gone Baby Gone.*)

	A. Your individual response	B. Group responses	C. Your own thoughts (later)
What positive strengths did the "good" hero possess?			
What weaknesses did the "good" hero show?			
What positive strengths did the "bad" hero have?			
What weaknesses did the "bad" hero show?			
What difference did the positive strengths make to the story outcome?			
What difference did the weaknesses make to the story outcome?			
How did this exercise help you understand how strengths and weaknesses work out in real life?			

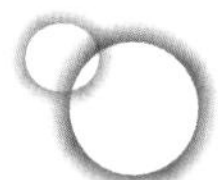

TEST YOUR METTLE

ROLE PLAY SIMULATIONS

Bakery Rivalry

Background: Re-read the written Video Incident at the beginning of the chapter.

Instructions: Your instructor will assign class members to play the roles of Jane Sutton (general manager), Carrie Fishman (director of operations), Jason Wong (sales manager), Heather Carreau (HR director) and Carlos Hernandez (CFO). The setting is the meeting room where the action takes place. Jane has called everyone in to their weekly staff meeting, starting at 10:00 AM. Each person should read only his or her part, below.

Confidential information for Jane: Your job is to run the meeting more effectively. You've been a little frustrated with Carrie, who thinks SHE should be the boss, and with Carlos, who is always disruptive. You've tried firing Carlos, but Jim Honeyman at corporate has his back for some reason or another. You know that if you don't take care of the two items of business today, your job is on the line. Corporate has been after you to submit a budget with a 10-percent, across-the-board cut because sales are sluggish in the stores. You still haven't decided whether to tell everyone at the meeting about the cuts, or if you should tell them individually afterward. You are just going to see how it goes. In addition, you must turn in your response to the new marketing proposal by 5:00 PM; otherwise, corporate will do the big new marketing plan their way.

Confidential information for Carrie: Your job is to let Jane know in an indirect way that Carlos is trying to undermine Jane. You heard this from a sort-of reliable source, so you are hesitant to say it outright, lest Carlos get blamed for something he hasn't actually done. But you feel Jane needs to set proper boundaries with Carlos before it goes too far and Carlos gets too overly confident. You have heard that Carlos is meeting with someone at corporate later this afternoon, but again, this is not certain. You know that Jane really needs your help because she can be a marshmallow at times.

Confidential information for Jason: You've just been hired and after only a few days here, you are wondering what you were thinking when you accepted a job in such a dysfunctional company. No one can keep their mouth shut, especially Carrie, who means well, but is such a Queen Bee. Then there is Carlos, who never listens to anyone. He never seems to get any work done but always knows how other people should do theirs. You are afraid to comment when he says something, lest he come after you the way he did yesterday. Better to keep your head low in the beginning. You have a suspicion that Carlos is running his own business out of the company offices, but you don't feel confident enough to say anything. All you're sure of is that you should stay away from him.

Confidential information for Heather: You think these meetings are a waste of time and human capital. It was so much better in the old days, but now these new people are so disruptive. You'll have to set them straight. At least you and Carlos agree on most things. It's time the rest of the team appreciated you two, especially Jane, who always seems just a little too big for her britches—or skirts.

Confidential information for Carlos: You've been promised a promotion to corporate in six months, if only you can whip everyone in the Madison location into shape. They all seem to be lazy or incompetent. What a challenge. If you don't make sure they straighten up, no promotion for you. That Jane is so wrong for the general manager's job, but you think you can train her to be a decent manager. And Carrie has to start back at square one. Her degree was in marketing. What in the heck does she know about operations? And then this new guy, Jason. Was this some diversity hire, or what? You think if you make it miserable enough for him, he will quit and then you'll have one fewer person to change before you get your own promotion.

After the role play, discuss these questions:

1. Did you agree with how Jane ran the meeting?
2. What would you have done differently?

Your instructor may ask someone else to take on the role of Jane with the same staff members.

Out of Control?

This Role Play Simulation is available online at www.cengagebrain.com.

VIDEO APPLICATION

Strengths and Weaknesses at Modern Shed

Scott Pearl, in charge of sales for Modern Shed's backyard buildings, has some distinctive manager strengths.

Discussion Questions

1. What do you consider Scott Pearl's management strengths? How is Pearl taking advantage of his strengths? Can you detect any management weaknesses? Explain.
2. How would you say Pearl's strengths differ from those of Modern Shed's founder, Ryan Smith? How do you think the two management styles might complement each other?
3. Would you rather work for Smith or Pearl? Why?

CASE INCIDENTS

MacLuren's/Gold Group Salons

Ta'Shauna Westbrook takes pride in her position as salon manager for MacLuren's Salon, one of six local hair salons associated with a large retail store chain located in the Southeast and one of five chain store groups under the Gold Group umbrella. She oversees a staff of 30, including hairdressers, a nail technician, receptionists, shampoo

SHUTTERSTOCK #53973379

assistants, and a custodian. She enjoys a reputation as a manager who works very hard and takes care of her people. Hairdressers want to work for her.

Following salon new-hire policy, Ta'Shauna began as a shampoo assistant and quickly became a top hairdresser in the company through a combination of skill, a large and loyal client base, and long hours at work. In 2007, retiring manager Carla Weems hand-picked Ta'Shauna as her successor and the board quickly approved. Initially the salon, located in a suburban mall, managed a strong, steady increase, holding its position as one of the corporate's top performers. But economic woes hit the area hard, with increases in unemployment, mortgage woes, and foreclosures among current and potential customers. As families sought ways to save, the luxury of regular visits to the hair salon was among the first logical budget cuts. The past year reflected the economic reality and Ta'Shauna's salon saw a sharp decrease in profits.

Ta'Shauna's stomach is in knots as she arrives at the salon on Monday. Scheduled to fly to Atlanta the next morning for a meeting at corporate, she fears potential staffing cuts, but more importantly, she fears the loss of opportunity to secure her dream job, replacing the retiring manager at Riverwood Mall, the top-performing salon located in an upscale area of the city.

Distracted, Ta'Shauna walks past receptionist Marianne who is busily manning the phones. Hanging up the phone, Marianne calls out and informs Ta'Shauna that Holly and Carol Jean, two popular hairdressers, called in sick and she now has to reschedule their clients. Ta'Shauna had denied their earlier request to travel out of town to attend a concert and her irritation is obvious. She orders Marianne to call both and inform each to bring a doctor's statement and a copy of any prescriptions they receive when they return to work. "They had better be sick!" Ta'Shauna shouts as she enters her office, slamming the door more forcefully than she intended. Startled employees and early morning customers could hear the outburst and, after a momentary pause in activity, resumed work and quiet conversation, surprised by the show of managerial anger. Ta'Shauna knows she has let Holly and Carol Jean get away with unwarranted absences before and worries that she will do it again. She needs every head of hair they can style to help the salon's profit.

Ta'Shauna takes a deep breath and sits at her desk, turning on the computer and checking e-mails, including one from the group manager reminding her to send the salon's status report in advance of tomorrow's meeting. She buzzes Marianne on the intercom to request final figures for the report on her desk by 1:00.

Picking up the phone, she calls Sharon, a manager at another MacLuren's salon. "I really lost my cool in front of everyone, but I'm not apologizing," Ta'Shauna admits, adding that she wished she had the guts to fire both stylists. "But this is not the day for that drama. I've got that report hanging over my head. I have no idea how to make things look better than they are, but I have to come up with something. Things look pretty dismal."

Sharon assures her that she did the best she could dealing with two "irresponsible" employees. "What will you do if they show up tomorrow with no doctor's statement?"

"I don't know. I hope I scared them enough so that they'll come in with something."

"I know you're worried about the report and the effect it might have on the Riverwood job," Sharon says. "But everyone knows you cannot control the economy and its effect on the business. Just focus on the positive. You'll be fine."

At 10:30, as Ta'Shauna struggles to put the best possible spin on the report, she is paged to the receptionist desk to speak to an angry customer. "Another interruption," Ta'Shauna fumes to herself. Just then, the door opens and top stylist/assistant manager Victoria Boone pops her head into the office.

"I know you're busy with the report. I'll handle this," she calls enthusiastically.

"Thanks," Ta'Shauna replies.

No sooner had she handed off the irate client to Victoria than she second-guessed the decision. In addition to her talents as a hairdresser, Victoria had experience as manager of a successful salon in another city before moving to the area. Recognizing her organizational and people skills, Ta'Shauna had promoted Victoria to assistant manager soon after her arrival. Now each "I'll handle this" remark by Victoria convinces Ta'Shauna that her assistant manager is positioning herself as a potential rival for the Riverwood job. Ta'Shauna both appreciates her enthusiastic attitude while trying to limit her opportunities to lead or appear too competent before staff, customers, and company officials. Ta'Shauna finds herself wanting to hide Victoria's competence, and she has condescendingly reminded management that Victoria is a "great help to me."

Now, thinking of Victoria's cheerful "I'll handle this," Ta'Shauna rises from her desk and marches to the door. "No, I'll take care of this personally."

Discussion Questions

1. What positive and negative managerial traits does Ta'Shauna possess?
2. How do these traits help or hinder her potential to get the top position at the Riverwood Mall salon?
3. How do you think Ta'Shauna should have handled each of the following scenarios: Marianne? Holly and Carol Jean? Victoria?

100 Days

My name is Michael Collins. Leadership has always fascinated me. Since boyhood, I have studied powerful examples of strategy (Sun Tzu), creativity (Da Vinci), networking (Churchill's "wilderness years"), juggling challenges (FDR), or rebuilding amid devastation (MacArthur in post-war Japan). When I was named southwest regional manager for Creighton Auto Parts, a major parts, sales, and service corporation, I saw the transition period ahead as an exciting new leadership opportunity. I love marketing and this would be a chance to show the company what I could do.

With a degree in automotive engineering and several years' experience in parts manufacturing (design and plant management), I come to the new position with strong industry connections and a keen eye for trends and product innovation. I am aware that the combination of economic factors and the complexity of new automobiles have made do-it-yourself repairs a challenging necessity for some. Nothing so quickly sends a savvy customer out the door as a bumbling parts employee who must first read the back of the box before making a product suggestion. On the other hand, car repair can be a chore on par with going to a neurosurgeon for many customers as they stare, glassy-eyed, at an engine while listening to a mechanic spout technical terms they cannot understand. Both types are my customers.

During the initial stages of the transition, I met with the outgoing regional manager a few times about ongoing business issues, but I was more interested in taking the region in a new direction. While one meeting took place in his office, I wanted to avoid the appearance of depending on "the old man" for guidance, so I scheduled our other meetings offsite. He was focused mainly on employee culture. I doubt if that will be a priority for me. I was mindful of the historical transitioning in American politics of one presidential administration to another and that Congress, the public, and the media give incoming presidents a *honeymoon* period of approximately 100 days to initiate ideas and legislation. I knew my company honeymoon would be limited. I wanted to immerse myself quickly and get on with my vision and my implementation schedule. As a first step, I sent a lengthy e-mail to all key players on my leadership team, both as an introduction and as a prelude to establishing my presence, vision, and transition program.

I traveled around the region meeting with members of my leadership team and held several informal meetings with front-line employees. In so doing, I was surprised to find individuals who were eager to talk openly about their goals, ideas, opinions, and complaints. I questioned them about their length of service, what they liked most about the company, what areas they thought could be improved—things like that. I discovered that, for most of them, this was more than just a job. Many had worked for the company for a long time and felt a great deal of pride in the company as well as a deep sense of responsibility toward their customers. I soon found that I regretted the amount of time spent listening to workers. I wondered if the advance warning of my visit allowed too much time for workers to prep their answers. I wondered how many were genuine in their responses and how many were just trying to hold on to their jobs. Worse, I found myself hostage to those who wanted to rant on about things that displeased them. I tried to be courteous, but I already had my agenda for changes to make in the region. As I proceeded through the onsite visits, I found myself growing impatient, increasingly checking my watch to time the rant or to see how soon I could leave for the next appointment on a packed schedule. I did end up canceling a few store visits to make better use of my time.

More rewarding was the time spent with the marketing staff exploring customer satisfaction levels. I wanted to innovate quickly in areas of new systems and market research. In focusing on customers, I zeroed in on three research areas: customer complaints, area demographics, and the compounding customer—those return customers who generate additional sales among family and friends. Why do customers come? What makes them return? What are their personal "hot buttons"—needs or breaking points in dealing with service industries? Our demographics showed large segments of our population in four areas: under 30, over 60, Hispanics, and women. We also saw an increasing number of unemployed and under-employed do-it-yourself customers trying to keep the family vehicle going just a little longer.

My question for regional sales, service, and marketing was, *"How are we reaching and retaining these segments of the population?"* I soon realized that some of the marketing people might have to be replaced. They didn't seem to understand how powerful the numbers can be for growing the business. Do old-style advertising, Web sites, direct mailing, and coupon campaigns reach the correct demographics? Probably not. For example, are we providing and training Spanish-language sales/service experts and customer information? With large segments of young people, senior citizens, and single moms, wouldn't these populations offer fabulous compounding opportunities with focused marketing and price breaks?

As I take the reins, I am excited about the challenges and opportunities ahead. I am an idea guy, a hands-on manager whose ideal is the Renaissance man capable of doing many things very well. I like to surround myself with similar people. I generate ideas and expect follow-up and accountability. The models of leadership I embrace set the bar high for me and for everyone who works for me. I look forward to injecting a new vision and new standards of excellence in service throughout the region.

Discussion Questions

1. What do you think of Michael Collins' approach to management? How would you characterize his style?
2. What specific strengths and weaknesses can you identify within Collins?
3. What do you forecast about the future success of Collins' region? What is the basis for your forecast?

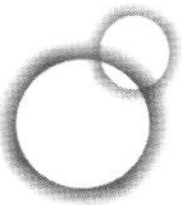

PERSONAL SKILLS LOG

PERSONAL SKILLS LOG

Directions: Fill in the rows below based on what you learned from each part of the chapter that you completed.

	What is my key takeaway or insight from this activity?	What do I personally do well (strength) regarding this activity?	What could I improve (weakness) about myself regarding this activity?	How might I use what I've learned from this activity in the future?
Manager Challenge Incident:				
Discover Yourself Questionnaires:				
Deliberate Practice Exercises:				
In-Class and/or Field Team Exercises:				
Role-Play Exercises:				
Case Incidents:				

REFERENCES

Discover Yourself

1 Based on Chuck Martin, Peg Dawson, and Richard Guare, *Smarts: Are We Hardwired for Success* (New York: AMACOM, 2007); Nicola. S. Schutte and John M. Malouff, *Measuring Emotional Intelligence and Related Constructs* (United Kingdom: Edwin Mellen Press, 1999); and "Personality," Psych-It Web site, http://www.psych-it.com.au/personality.asp (accessed January 11, 2012).

2 Based on Flip Flippen, *The Flip Side: Break Free of the Behaviors that Hold You Back* (New York: Springboard Press, 2007); Schutte and Malouff, *Measuring Emotional Intelligence and Related Constructs*; and "Personality," Psych-It Web site, http://www.psych-it.com.au/personality.asp (accessed January 11, 2012).

3 Based on Hendrie Weisenger, *Emotional Intelligence At Work* (San Francisco: Jossey-Bass, 1998); and N. S. Shutte, et al., "Development and Validation of a Measure of Emotional Intelligence," *Personality and Individual Differences* 25 (1998): 167–177.

Discover Knowledge

4 The strengths questionnaire used by Tami Heim, EVP of Thomas Nelson Publisher, and her management team is at the StrengthsFinder 2.0 Web site. The StrengthsFinder questionnaire requires a code obtained with the purchase of one of the books based on Gallup research (e.g., *Now Discover Your Strengths, StrengthsFinder 2.0, Strengths-Based Leadership*).

5 Marcus Buckingham, *The One Thing You Need to Know . . . About Great Managing, Great Leading, and Sustained Individual Success* (New York: The Free Press, 2005).

6 Marcus Buckingham and Donald O. Clifton, *Now, Discover Your Strengths* (New York: The Free Press, 2001), p. 12.

7 "Special Report: The World's Billionaires; #3 *Warren Buffett*," *Forbes*, March 2010, http://www.forbes.com/lists/2010/10/billionaires-2010_Warren-Buffett_C0R3.html (accessed January 31, 2011).

8 Quoted in Bill George, "The Master Gives It Back," segment in "Special Report: America's Best Leaders," *U.S. News and World Report* (October 30, 2006): 50–87.

9 Richard L. Daft, *The Executive and the Elephant: A Leader's Guild to Building Inner Excellence* (San Francisco: Jossey-Bass, 2010), p. 149.

10 Based on Buckingham and Clifton, *Now, Discover Your Strengths*, pp. 28–61.

11 Richard McDermott, "Why Information Technology Inspired but Cannot Deliver Knowledge Management," *California Management Review* 41, no. 4 (Summer 1999): 103–117.

12 Timothy D. Wilson, *Strangers to Ourselves: Discovering the Adaptive Unconscious* (Cambridge, MA: Belknap Press, 2002).

13 Jonathan Haidt, *The Happiness Hypothesis: Finding Modern Truth in Ancient Wisdom* (New York: Basic Books, 2006), p. 167.

14 This list is from Christopher Peterson, *A Primer in Positive Psychology* (New York: Oxford University Press, 2006), pp. 158–159.

15 Chuck Martin, with Peg Dawson and Richard Guare, *Smarts: Are We Hardwired for Success?* (New York: AMACOM, 2007), p. 31.

16 Lani Hay as told to Liz Welch, "The Way I Work: Lani Hay, Lanmark Technology," *Inc.* (November 2010): 132–136.

17 These executive strengths are from Martin et al., *Smarts*, especially pp. 15–30.

18 Alice Schroeder, *The Snowball: Warren Buffett and the Business of Life* (New York: Bantam Books, 2008).

19 Haidt, *The Happiness Hypothesis*.

20 Jerome Groopman, *How Doctors Think* (New York: Houghton Mifflin, 2007).

21 Marc Gunther, "Is Bob Iger Ready for His Close-Up?" *Fortune* (April 4, 2005): 76–78.

22 Michael Arrington as told to Liz Welch, "The Way I Work: Michael Arrington, TechCrunch," *Inc.* (October 2010): 124–128.

23 Flippen, *The Flip Side: Break Free of the Behaviors That Hold You Back.*

24 Eliyahu M. Goldratt, *What Is This Thing Called Theory of Constraints and How Should It Be Implemented?* (Great Barrington, MA: North River Press, 1990).

25 This discussion is based on Flippen, *The Flip Side.*

26 Timothy D. Wilson, *Stranger to Ourselves: Discovering the Adaptive Unconscious* (Cambridge, MA: Belknap Press, 2002).

27 Morgan W. McCall, Jr. and Michael M. Lombardo, "Off the Track: Why and How Successful Executives Get Derailed" (Technical Report No. 21, Greensboro, NC: Center for Creative Leadership, January 1983); and Carol Hymowitz, "Five Main Reasons Why Managers Fail," *The Wall Street Journal* (May 2, 1988): B1.

28 Ram Charan and Geoffrey Colvin, "Why CEOs Fail," *Fortune* (June 21, 1999): 68–78.

29 Clinton O. Longnecker, Mitchell J. Neubert, and Lawrence S. Fink, "Causes and Consequences of Managerial Failure in Rapidly Changing Organizations," *Business Horizons* 50 (2007): 145–155.

30 *Ibid.*, 149.

31 Reported in Susan G. Hauser, "The Degeneration of Decorum," *Workforce Management* (January 2011): 16–18, 20–21.

32 These limitations and the discussion are based on Flippen, *The Flip Side*; and James Waldroop and Timothy Butler, *Maximum Success: Changing the 12 Behavior Patterns That Keep You From Getting Ahead* (New York: Currency/Doubleday, 2000).

33 Carol Hymowitz, "More CEOs Seek Therapy; Seeing Shrink Helped Their Career, Executives Say," *The Wall Street Journal* (June 22, 2004): B1.

34 Comments from MBA students and practicing managers, reported in Daft, *The Executive and the Elephant*, p. 44.

35 This example is from Waldroop and Butler, *Maximum Success*, pp. 182–183.

36 *Ibid.*

37 Carol Hymowitz, "As Managers Climb, They Have to Learn How to Act the Parts" (In the Lead column), *The Wall Street Journal* (November 14, 2005): B1.

38 Michael Sokolove, "Follow Me," *The New York Times Magazine* (February 2006): 96.

39 Based on Daniel Goleman, *Emotional Intelligence: Why It Can Matter More Than IQ* (New York: Bantam Books, 1995); D. Goleman, "Leadership That Gets Results," *Harvard Business Review* (March–April 2000): 79–90; J. D. Mayer, D.R. Caruso, and P. Salovey, "Emotional Intelligence Meets Traditional Standards for an Intelligence," *Intelligence* 27, no. 4 (1999): 266–298; Neal M. Ashkanasy and Catherine S. Daus, "Emotion in the Workplace: The New Challenge for Managers," *Academy of Management Executive* 16, no. 1 (2002): 76–86; and Hendrie Weisinger, *Emotional Intelligence at Work* (San Francisco: Jossey-Bass, 1998).

40 Based on Goleman, "Leadership That Gets Results"; Laura Guillen Ramo, Willem E. Saris, and Richard E. Sis, "The Impact of Social and Emotional Competencies on Effectiveness of Spanish Executives," *Journal of Management Development* 28, no. 9 (2009): 771–793; Jane V. Wheeler, "The Impact of Social Environments on Emotional, Social, and Cognitive Competency Development," *Journal of Management Development* 27, no. 1 (2008): 129–145; and Margaret M. Hopkins, "Social and Emotional Competencies Predicting Success for Male and Female Executives," *Journal of Management Development* 27, no. 1 (2008): 13–35.

41 Reported in Dave Marcum, Steve Smith, and Mahan Khals, "The Marshmallow Conundrum," *Across the Board* (March–April 2004): 26–30.

42 Peter J. Frost, "Handling the Hurt: A Critical Skill for Leaders," *Ivey Management Journal* (January–February 2004).

43 Rolf W. Habbel, "The Human[e] Factor: Nurturing a Leadership Culture," *Strategy + Business* 26 (First Quarter 2002): 83–89.

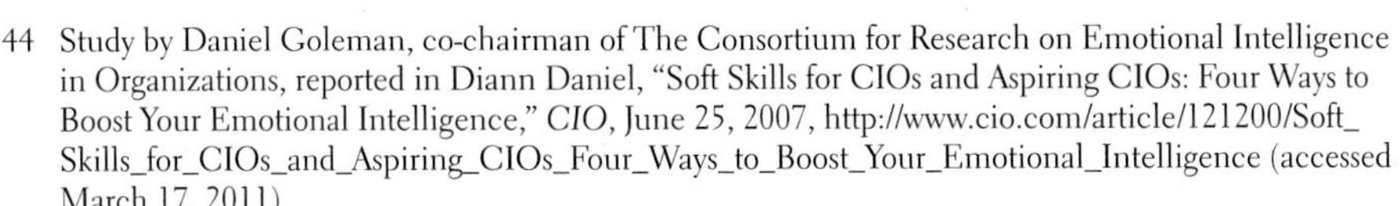

44 Study by Daniel Goleman, co-chairman of The Consortium for Research on Emotional Intelligence in Organizations, reported in Diann Daniel, "Soft Skills for CIOs and Aspiring CIOs: Four Ways to Boost Your Emotional Intelligence," *CIO*, June 25, 2007, http://www.cio.com/article/121200/Soft_Skills_for_CIOs_and_Aspiring_CIOs_Four_Ways_to_Boost_Your_Emotional_Intelligence (accessed March 17, 2011).

45 Stephen Xavier, "Are You at the Top of Your Game? Checklist for Effective Leaders," *Journal of Business Strategy* 26, no. 3 (2005): 35–42.

46 E. Hatfield, J.T. Cacioppo, and R.L. Rapson, *Emotional Contagion* (New York: Cambridge University Press, 1994).

Action Learning

47 Based on Jerry L. Fletcher, *Patterns of High Performance: Discovering the Ways People Work Best* (San Francisco: Berrett-Koehler, 1993).

CHAPTER 2
Learning about Yourself

Chapter Outline

RYAN LASH

MANAGER CHALLENGE

VIDEO INCIDENT: NEVER GOOD ENOUGH

Caffeine and Crullers general manager Jane Sutton is frustrated. Her new director of operations, Carrie Fishman, keeps challenging Jane's decisions. Jane finds it easier to take when it's just the two of them, but in a team meeting the harsh questions can be jarring and off-putting for everyone. On three separate occasions, Jane has talked to Carrie about the matter, but Carrie responds with, "Don't you want us all to make the best decisions possible for the company? I'm just asking tough questions because someone has to. How will we ever meet our numbers unless we're really honest with what we are doing?" At those moments, Jane would agree with Carrie that facing up to their problems was important, and she'd end the meeting by thanking Carrie for being such a responsible watchdog for the team. But later, Jane would get this nagging feeling that something just wasn't right. Recently two other managers, Jason Wong and Carlos Hernandez, have complained to Jane about Carrie's methods.

Initial Thoughts

1. **If you were Jane Sutton, how would you handle this?**

2. **How does self-awareness play a role in this situation?**

Your instructor may ask you to be part of a role play based on the Never Good Enough incident.

DISCOVER YOURSELF

For those students using CourseMate or CengageNOW, you can access the Daft/Marcic Assessment Library to take the questionnaires online and view dynamically updated comparative data.

Questionnaire 1[1]

Instructions: Read each numbered item carefully. Read the statements marked "a" and "b" to determine which statement is most similar to what you would actually do. Assign a point value to the "a" and "b" statements as follows: The total points for "a" and "b" statements together is five (5) depending on the fit of the statement. For example, if the "a" statement is *very* similar to what you would do, you might assign 5 or 4 points to that statement and 0 or 1 point to the "b" statement. Or if the "b" statement is *somewhat* similar to what you would do, you might assign 3 or 4 points to the "b" statement and 1 or 2 points to the "a" statement. The converse is also true. Be sure to assign 5 points total to the "a" and "b" statements for each incident. Answer based on what you would *actually* do rather than what you would want to do.

Part A

1. If a friend in another department had a "personality conflict" with a mutual acquaintance of ours and I thought it was important for them to get along, I would most likely:

   _____ a. Tell my friend that she was somewhat responsible for the problem with the mutual acquaintance and try to let her know how the person was being affected by the conflict.

   _____ b. Not get involved for various reasons.

2. If my relationship with a coworker had been damaged by repeated arguments on an issue important to us both, I would most likely:

   _____ a. Be cautious in future conversations with him so that the issue would not come up again and hurt our relationship.

   _____ b. Explain to him the problems this controversy is causing for our relationship and suggest that we discuss it to get it resolved.

3. If I observed a friend in social and work situations and thought he was doing a number of things that would hurt his relationships, I would most likely:

   _____ a. Take the risk of being seen as a busy-body and tell him what I had observed and my reactions to it.

   _____ b. Keep my opinion to myself rather than interfere in something that is none of my business.

4. If I began to dislike certain behaviors of a coworker to the point that it was interfering with my enjoyment of our working relationship, I would most likely:

   _____ a. Say nothing to her directly, but let her know my feelings by pulling back when the annoying behavior occurred.

   _____ b. Get my feelings out in the open to clear the air so that we could continue our working relationship comfortably and enjoyably.

5. When discussing a performance review with one of my more sensitive direct reports, I would most likely:

_____ a. Avoid mentioning what I see as his personal flaws and weaknesses to avoid hurting his feelings.

_____ b. Focus on what I see as his flaws and weaknesses so he could improve his interpersonal skills.

Total Score Part A ________. (Sum the points you assigned for 1a, 2b, 3a, 4b, and 5b.)

Part B

6. If a friend began to avoid me and act in a distant and withdrawn manner, I would most likely:

   _____ a. Talk to her about her behavior and ask that she tell me what she is feeling toward me.

   _____ b. Accept her withdrawn behavior.

7. If a friend of mine were to tell me that, in his opinion, I was doing things that made me less effective than I might be in work situations, I would most likely:

   _____ a. Ask him to describe what he had observed and suggest changes I might make.

   _____ b. React defensively to his criticism and explain why I behave the way I do.

8. If I felt that one of my friends was being unfair to me, I would most likely:

   _____ a. Wait for her or someone else to bring it up with me.

   _____ b. Ask other friends how they perceive the situation and my perception of it.

9. If I learned that an ugly and embarrassing rumor was being spread about me and suspected that one of my workmates had heard it, I would most likely:

   _____ a. Avoid mentioning the rumor and let it die. He could tell me if he wanted to.

   _____ b. Put him on the spot by asking directly what he knew about the rumor.

10. If I knew a colleague's attitude toward me had been rather negative lately and that I might be assigned an important position in his group, I would most likely:

    _____ a. Approach my colleague to discuss my shortcomings to learn where I could improve.

    _____ b. Try to figure out my own shortcomings so I could improve.

Total Score Part B ________. (Sum the points you assigned for 6a, 7a, 8b, 9b, and 10a.) Go to page 87 to interpret your scores.

Questionnaire 2[2]

Instructions: The following phrases describe various traits and behaviors. Rate how accurately each statement describes you based on whether the statement is clearly true or accurate, clearly false or inaccurate, or in the middle as somewhat true and somewhat false. Describe yourself as you are now, not as you wish to be. There are no right or wrong answers.

Part A	True	Somewhat	False
1. I love large parties.	○	○	○
2. I am talkative.	○	○	○

DISCOVER YOURSELF

	True	Somewhat	False
3. I talk to a lot of different people at parties.	○	○	○
4. I like being the center of attention.	○	○	○
5. I feel comfortable around people.	○	○	○

Total Score Part A ________. (Sum your answers to questions 1–5 as follows: Assign 3 points for each True, 2 points for each Somewhat, and 1 point for each False.)

Part B

	True	Somewhat	False
6. I often feel critical of myself.	○	○	○
7. I am easily bothered by things.	○	○	○
8. I often envy others.	○	○	○
9. I feel tense much of the time.	○	○	○
10. I have a temper.	○	○	○

Total Score Part B ________. (Sum your answers to questions 6–10 as follows: Assign 3 points for each True, 2 points for each Somewhat, and 1 point for each False.)

Part C

	True	Somewhat	False
11. I am kind and sympathetic.	○	○	○
12. I have a good word for everyone.	○	○	○
13. I put others first.	○	○	○
14. I am interested in other people's problems.	○	○	○
15. I never insult people.	○	○	○

Total Score Part C ________. (Sum your answers to questions 11–15 as follows: Assign 3 points for each True, 2 points for each Somewhat, and 1 point for each False.)

Part D

	True	Somewhat	False
16. I have a vivid imagination.	○	○	○
17. I am full of ideas.	○	○	○
18. I typically vote for liberal political candidates.	○	○	○
19. I really like art.	○	○	○
20. I love to learn new things.	○	○	○

Total Score Part D ________. (Sum your answers to questions 16–20 as follows: Assign 3 points for each True, 2 points for each Somewhat, and 1 point for each False.)

Part E

	True	Somewhat	False
21. I am systematic and efficient.	○	○	○
22. I pay attention to details.	○	○	○
23. I get chores done without delay.	○	○	○
24. I am always prepared for class.	○	○	○
25. I put things back where they belong.	○	○	○

Total Score Part E ________. (Sum your answers to questions 21–25 as follows: Assign 3 points for each True, 2 points for each Somewhat, and 1 point for each False.) Go to page 89 to interpret your scores.

Questionnaire 3

Instructions: Circle 12 of the words below that you believe best describe your own cognitive style. Try to be honest and select terms that apply to you as you are, not as you might like to be. There are no right or wrong answers.

A	B	C	D
Analytical	Organized	Friendly	Holistic
Factual	Planned	Receptive	Imaginative
Directive	Controlled	Enthusiastic	Intuitive
Rigorous	Detailed	Understanding	Synthesizing
Realistic	Conservative	Expressive	Curious
Intellectual	Disciplined	Empathetic	Spontaneous
Objective	Practical	Trusting	Flexible
Knowledgeable	Industrious	Sensitive	Open-Minded
Bright	Persistent	Passionate	Conceptual
Clear	Implementer	Humanistic	Adventurous

Scoring: Count the number of words circled in each column and record the totals here:

Column A ______; Column B ______; Column C ______; Column D ______.
Go to page 92 to interpret your scores.

Questionnaire 4[3]

Instructions: For each item below, circle either "a" or "b." In some cases, both "a" and "b" may apply to you. You should decide which is *more* like you, even if it is only slightly more so.

1. I would rather
   a. Solve a new and complicated problem
   b. Work on something that I have done before
2. I like to
   a. Work alone in a quiet place
   b. Be where "the action" is
3. I want a boss who
   a. Establishes and applies criteria in decisions
   b. Considers individual needs and makes exceptions
4. When I work on a project, I
   a. Like to finish it and get some closure
   b. Often leave it open for possible change
5. When making a decision, the most important considerations are
   a. Rational thoughts, ideas, and data
   b. People's feelings and values
6. On a project, I tend to
   a. Think it over and over before deciding how to proceed
   b. Start working on it right away, thinking about it as I go along

7. When working on a project, I prefer to
   a. Maintain as much control as possible
   b. Explore various options
8. In my work, I prefer to
   a. Work on several projects at a time and learn as much as possible about each one
   b. Have one project that is challenging and keeps me busy
9. I often
   a. Make lists and plans whenever I start something and may hate to seriously alter my plans
   b. Avoid plans and just let things progress as I work on them
10. When discussing a problem with colleagues, it is easy for me
    a. To see "the big picture"
    b. To grasp the specifics of the situation
11. When the phone rings in my office or at home, I usually
    a. Consider it an interruption
    b. Don't mind answering it
12. The word that describes me better is
    a. Analytical
    b. Empathetic
13. When I am working on an assignment, I tend to
    a. Work steadily and consistently
    b. Work in bursts of energy with "down time" in between
14. When I listen to someone talk on a subject, I usually try to
    a. Relate it to my own experience and see if it fits
    b. Assess and analyze the message
15. When I come up with new ideas, I generally
    a. "Go for it"
    b. Like to contemplate the ideas some more
16. When working on a project, I prefer to
    a. Narrow the scope so it is clearly defined
    b. Broaden the scope to include related aspects
17. When I read something, I usually
    a. Confine my thoughts to what is written there
    b. Read between the lines and relate the words to other ideas
18. When I have to make a decision in a hurry, I often
    a. Feel uncomfortable and wish I had more information
    b. Am able to do so with available data
19. In a meeting, I tend to
    a. Continue formulating my ideas as I talk about them
    b. Only speak out after I have carefully thought the issue through
20. In work, I prefer spending a great deal of time on issues of
    a. Ideas
    b. People

21. In meetings, I am most often annoyed with people who
    a. Come up with many sketchy ideas
    b. Lengthen the meeting with many practical details
22. I tend to be
    a. A morning person
    b. A night owl
23. My style in preparing for a meeting is
    a. To be willing to go in and be responsive
    b. To be fully prepared and sketch out an outline of the meeting
24. In meetings, I would prefer for people to
    a. Display a fuller range of emotions
    b. Be more task-oriented
25. I would rather work for an organization in which
    a. My job was intellectually stimulating
    b. I was committed to its goals and mission
26. On weekends, I tend to
    a. Plan what I will do
    b. Just see what happens and decide as I go along
27. I am more
    a. Outgoing
    b. Contemplative
28. I would rather work for a boss who is
    a. Full of new ideas
    b. Practical

In the following, choose the word in each pair that appeals to you more:

29. a. Social
    b. Theoretical
30. a. Ingenuity
    b. Practicality
31. a. Organized
    b. Adaptable
32. a. Activity
    b. Concentration

Scoring:

Step 1. Count one point for each item listed below that you circled in the inventory.

Add one point for I: 2a, 6a, 11a, 15b, 19b, 22a, 27b, and 32b. Total I ________.
Add one point for E: 2b, 6b, 11b, 15a, 19a, 22b, 27a, and 32a. Total E ________.
Add one point for S: 1b, 10b, 13a, 16a, 17a, 21a, 28b, and 30b. Total S ________.
Add one point for N: 1a, 10a, 13b, 16b, 17b, 21b, 28a, and 30a. Total N ________.

Circle the total with more points between I and E. *(If tied on I/E, don't count #11.)*
Circle the total with more points between S and N. *(If tied on S/N, don't count #16.)*

Step 2. Count one point for each item listed below that you circled in the inventory.

Add one point for T: 3a, 5a, 12a, 14b, 20a, 24b, 25a, and 29b. Total T ________.

Add one point for F: 3b, 5b, 12b, 14a, 20b, 24a, 25b, and 29a. Total F ________.
Add one point for J: 4a, 7a, 8b, 9a, 18b, 23b, 26a, and 31a. Total J ________.
Add one point for P: 4b, 7b, 8a, 9b, 18a, 23a, 26b, and 31b. Total P ________.

Circle the total with more points between T and F. *(If tied on T/F, don't count #24.)*
Circle the total with more points between J and P. *(If tied on J/P, don't count #23.)*

Your circled score is: I or E ______ S or N ______ T or F ______ J or P ______
Your type is (four letters): ________ (example: INTJ, ESFP, etc.)
Go to pages 93 to interpret your scores.

Questionnaire 5[4]

In each column, rank the 18 values, with 1 being the value that is *most* important to you and 18 being the value that is *least* important to you (you will rank 18 values in the End Values column and 18 values in the Instrumental Values column).

End Values	**Instrumental Values**
A comfortable life ______	Ambition ______
Equality ______	Broad-mindedness ______
An exciting life ______	Capability ______
Family security ______	Cleanliness ______
Freedom ______	Courage ______
Health ______	Forgiveness ______
Inner harmony ______	Helpfulness ______
Mature love ______	Honesty ______
National security ______	Imagination ______
Pleasure ______	Independence ______
Salvation ______	Intellectualism ______
Self-respect ______	Logic ______
A sense of accomplishment ______	Ability to love ______
Social recognition ______	Loyalty ______
True friendship ______	Obedience ______
Wisdom ______	Politeness ______
A world at peace ______	Responsibility ______
A world of beauty ______	Self-control ______

NOTE: The values in each column are listed in alphabetical order and there is no one-to-one relationship between the end values and the instrumental values. Go to page 96 to interpret your scores.

GO ONLINE to find additional questionnaires at www.cengagebrain.com, search for Daft/Marcic Building Management Skills 1e, click on Free Online Resources, click on Additional Self-Assessments.

- Expressed Feelings
- Regulatory Focus

SHUTTERSTOCK #53973379

Chapter 2: Learning about Yourself
DISCOVER KNOWLEDGE

John Bearden sold his real estate business in Canada and went back to his hometown of Nashville, Tennessee, to reflect. He observed that throughout his career, he had often gotten to the finish line "dragging people with him." Bearden recalled when a consultant told him, "*John, you have so much potential, but you're running over everybody . . . you turn people off.*" Bearden decided that now was the time to learn what made him tick.

Before restarting his career, Bearden hired a personal coach. The coach asked him to complete a questionnaire called the Myers–Briggs Type Indicator that revealed his "field marshal" (ENTJ) leadership style. "Field marshals" have essential leadership qualities of vision, drive, and decisiveness. However, the downside is that they also tend to be hasty, insensitive, and overbearing. With these new insights, Bearden accepted an offer to become chief executive of GMAC Home Services. His increased self-awareness enabled him to be less overbearing and to spend more time considering hard data and listening more carefully to colleagues' opinions. At a presentation by his most senior executives, rather than interject his own opinion early to bias the outcome toward what he wanted, he allowed other positions to be articulated and discussed with creative tension. Just sitting and absorbing was a satisfying outcome.[5]

Systematic self-inquiry enabled John Bearden to discover the productive and nonproductive patterns and preferences of which he was not aware. Now he could take advantage of his strengths and change his weaknesses. He saw himself clearly—both the good and the bad. Similarly, learning about yourself will enable you to discover the parts you don't normally see—your blind spots—so that you can either appreciate or fix them. With self-awareness, Bearden redirected himself away from an overbearing attitude to develop his patience and facilitation skills. Do you have abilities and qualities you don't really understand and appreciate? Like John Bearden, are there aspects of yourself that you need to fix?

KNOW YOURSELF

After working tirelessly for a large financial services company for more than a decade, Beth Schneider was growing frustrated. No matter how hard she worked, Beth kept getting passed over for promotion. During her year-end review under a new supervisor, Beth was surprised by his comments about her poor communication skills and tendency to isolate herself from her team. She went home and sulked, complaining to her teenage daughter that the review was unfair. Beth knew she wasn't the most outgoing person, but she also knew she'd made significant contributions to the company's success. After a sleepless night, Beth decided to ask her direct reports and a couple of colleagues for some honest feedback so she could understand why she'd gotten a poor review. Beth was shocked to hear the negative comments from her supervisor echoed by her direct reports and colleagues. One of her longtime employees said, "You're terrific at the details. But you get so immersed in them that you forget to help us understand where you want the department to go and how to help you get there. Sometimes Bob and I will come up with some great ideas over lunch, but you never seem to have time to listen to them."[6]

Many of us, like Beth Schneider, might be surprised to find out what others honestly think about us. You might recall from a psychology course that people have psychological defenses such as repression, reaction formation, scapegoating, denial, and projection. Well-developed defenses will distort reality to protect us from truths that may hurt. Our defenses act like a psychological immune system that defends the mind against unhappiness in the same way the physical immune system defends the body against illness. Unfortunately, this also makes us immune to reality about ourselves.[7]

It is difficult to see one's own characteristics objectively. Most perceptual distortions are in our favor. For example, 94 percent of college professors

DISCOVER KNOWLEDGE

think they do above average work. Ninety percent of drivers consider themselves to be safer than average. Husbands and wives overestimate their personal contribution to housework. The estimates of MBA students' percentage contributions to their team assignments have totaled 139 percent. Concerning athletic prowess, 60 percent of high school students see themselves above average, 6 percent below. Judging their ability to get along with others, 60 percent of people consider themselves to be in the top 10 percent, and 25 percent consider themselves in the top 1 percent. Most people see themselves as having above average intelligence.[8]

Self-awareness is essential to being an effective manager. A survey of 75 members of the Stanford Graduate School of Business's Advisory Council revealed the nearly unanimous answer to a question about the most important capability for leaders to develop: self-awareness.[9] **Self-awareness** means being aware of the internal aspects of one's nature, such as personality traits, beliefs, emotions, values, strengths, and limitations, and appreciating how your patterns affect other people. Self-awareness is achieved by recognizing your needs, traits, patterns, preferences, and limitations, much as John Bearden did in his consultation with an executive coach. With self-awareness, you can put yourself in a position to employ your natural behaviors and enjoy a life of fewer struggles and more satisfaction. If you are a natural at counseling people and dislike math, you are not taking advantage of your talents by pursuing a career as a financial analyst. If you have a knack for math and finance, on the other hand, then working for a bank or investment firm is a natural.

DISCOVER KNOWLEDGE

THE IMPORTANCE OF SELF-AWARENESS

Landon Donovan is considered the best soccer player the United States has ever produced. He's also been considered its greatest disappointment. In the 2006 World Cup, Donovan played so poorly that the United States was eliminated in the first round. He went the entire calendar year without scoring a goal for the national team. Four years later, though, Donovan was a different person and the reigning most valuable player in Major League Soccer. What happened? "I've been on a long journey for the last four years," Donovan said, revealing that he had been attending therapy sessions and spending long hours in introspective conversations with family and friends. Referring to himself at the time of the 2006 competition, Donovan said he was "someone completely unfamiliar." He went on to

What's Your Problem?

Q: I started with my company five years ago, right out of college, working my way up from management trainee to supervisor within a large department. I knew it wouldn't take long for me to move up. Last month, my immediate boss took a job in another firm, and I was certain they'd promote me to her management position, because everyone saw I had much more talent than she ever did. Because I *knew* I'd be getting a substantial raise, I traded my used car for a new one and booked a trip to Tahiti. Then yesterday they announced my boss's replacement and it was someone else. How could they do this to me? All my evaluations have been positive and I've done everything they ever asked. Should I quit and make them pay for their mistake?

A: Don't quit yet. Try to find out what happened first. You say all your evaluations were positive, but did they indicate you had the potential for higher-level positions? There are times when we tend to read or hear feedback with rose-colored glasses, which distorts our self-perception. Take your old boss to lunch, if she's still in the same city, or phone her. Candidly ask her what your potential is as a manager. Don't interrupt when she talks and don't get defensive. Take notes on what she says. Read this feedback over a number of times and try to be honest with yourself about the level you are at and what you need to learn to move ahead. Also consider if your personality type or your values are in sync with everyone else. Ask your new boss or trusted coworkers for feedback about this. Ask in a matter-of-fact way, not sounding accusatory. You really want to know the truth, right? After all the fact-finding, make a list of the changes you can make so you can get that promotion the next time around. Consider this whole situation as a gift—a chance to understand yourself more clearly.

© CENGAGE LEARNING 2014

explain: "Most people don't want to spend time digging deep and finding out why you are the way you are. But I do want to, and I want to embrace it. I want to find the good pieces and leave the bad pieces behind."[10]

Not everyone wants or needs to engage in therapy, as Landon Donovan has done, but each of us can benefit from learning more about ourselves. Almost everyone has heard the maxim "Know thyself," but how many actually apply it? Many of us concentrate on learning all we can about our jobs, college courses, organizations, and even our professors and colleagues, but fail to take the critical step of learning about ourselves. Numerous philosophers and religious thinkers, as well as psychologists and other behavioral scientists, have pointed to the importance of self-knowledge for living a full, rewarding, and successful life. When people understand themselves, they can use their talents to the fullest, work around their limitations, and develop rich, satisfying, and meaningful relationships with others.

Most management experts agree that a primary characteristic of effective leaders is that they know who they are and what they stand for.[11] When managers deeply understand themselves, they remain grounded and constant. People know what to expect from them. As one employee put it, ". . . it's like they have a stick down through the center of them that's rooted in the ground."[12] One study found that people would much rather follow someone they can count on, even when they disagree with that person's viewpoint, than someone who frequently shifts her ideas or position.[13] Effective managers can also change their ways of thinking when appropriate, based on what they learn about themselves and others or because the consequences of their actions indicate change is needed. Thus, knowing who we are and striving to better understand ourselves maximizes our management skills.[14]

Unfortunately, many managers don't take the time to think about who they really are or the effect their patterns of thought and behavior have on others. For example, the CEO of a large asset-management firm couldn't understand why his company's culture continued to be one of blaming and finger-pointing rather than the accountability and teamwork he wanted. When a consultant interviewed people in the firm, asking them what happened when investments they recommended declined in value, he heard countless stories of the CEO's temper tantrums and accusations. The effect of the CEO's emotional outbursts was that people tried to find someone else to blame when things went wrong. Hearing this, the CEO was genuinely surprised. He hadn't realized that his behavior under pressure was sending signals in direct opposition to his speeches about teamwork and accountability.[15]

How to Expand Your Self-Awareness

Typically, there are three ways to enhance your self-awareness: soliciting feedback, self-diagnosis, and self-disclosure.

Soliciting Feedback

When you got ready for school or work this morning, you probably looked in the mirror to shave or fix your hair.[16] Feedback from the mirror made it easier to get your hairstyle the way you wanted it or to avoid cutting yourself as you shaved. Other people can be our mirror. In *The Seven Habits of Highly Effective People*, Stephen Covey talks about the *social mirror*, which refers to the fact that our perceptions of ourselves are shaped partly by how others perceive us.[17] A manager might consider himself to be patient and understanding, but his employees may see that he is easily irritated and unsympathetic. Another might believe that creating order is one of her primary strengths but discover that others see her as disorganized and somewhat absent-minded. We also learn positive things about ourselves from others. You might learn that others consider you exceptionally kind or creative, although you hadn't thought about those aspects of your personality. When we go through life without feedback, we're like the balding man who sweeps thin strands of hair across his scalp and thinks no one notices. Seeking feedback to enhance self-awareness can improve performance and job satisfaction for both managers and employees.[18] Recall the example of Beth Schneider earlier in this chapter. Schneider sincerely sought honest feedback from peers and subordinates about her performance as a manager. With this feedback, Schneider learned to detach from the details with which she was comfortable and start providing more leadership for her team. We all have illusions about ourselves, so we need help from others to accurately assess who we are. When we shut down feedback, we eliminate learning and personal development.

Self-Diagnosis

The second way to increase self-awareness is *self-diagnosis*, which uses self-inquiry and reflection to gain insights into yourself from self-assessment results, such as your scores on assessment instruments in this text. By completing these assessments as honestly as possible, you can analyze your scores and increase your understanding

of various aspects of yourself. Self-diagnosis also means regularly examining yourself objectively. Reflecting on your thoughts and feelings about people, experiences, and events can bring new perspectives and fresh understanding. You can examine the effects of your actions and behavior, looking at the consequences for yourself and others. Some people engage in this kind of structured reflection by writing in a journal; others might talk into a tape recorder or simply set aside a regular time in the evening to reflect on the day's experiences, analyzing what worked and what could have been improved.

Self-Disclosure

The third approach is self-disclosure. Yes, by revealing details about ourselves to others, we learn more about who we are. **Self-disclosure** means sharing your fears, thoughts, emotions, and concepts of yourself with others. Self-disclosure is crucial to enhancing self-awareness because other people mirror back their reaction to what we do and say so we can see ourselves through their eyes. We form opinions of ourselves by observing and interpreting this mirroring. Moreover, people who are willing to open up to others are emotionally healthier and happier, and they are typically more well-liked than low self-disclosers.[19]

For example, a widely disliked assistant director of a social service agency in East Tennessee, Barbara Witham, was called "The Ice Queen" by employees because she never showed any emotion at work and never talked about anything other than work-related matters.[20] Then, she began working with a consultant who advised her to gradually begin opening up about herself at work. Stunned and a bit disconcerted, the director nevertheless agreed to give it a try. The entire agency was abuzz the day The Ice Queen told her secretary that she'd had a difficult weekend because her husband had recently lost his job. It wasn't long before The Ice Queen was being called Barbara by almost everyone, and she became well-liked by most of the staff over the next several years.

DISCOVER KNOWLEDGE

Using the Johari Window to Enhance Self-Awareness

The value of soliciting feedback and self-disclosure for enhancing self-awareness is illustrated by the Johari Window in Exhibit 2.1.[21] Named after the first names of its inventors, Joseph Luft and Harry Ingham, the **Johari Window** is a tool managers can use to move toward greater transparency and alignment with others. The four quadrants of the Johari Window each represent a self-awareness "window."

Exhibit 2.1 The Johari Window

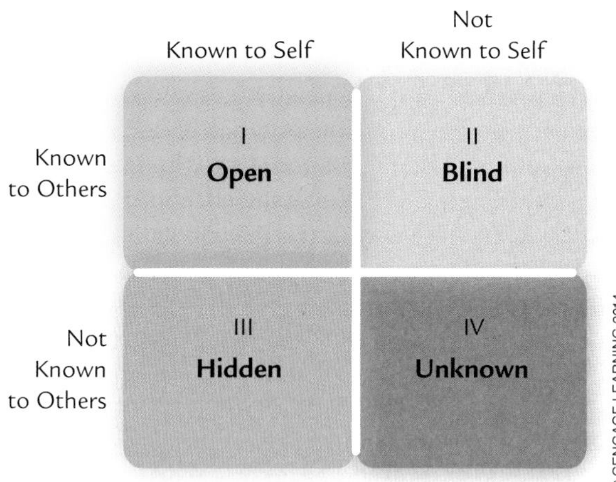

© CENGAGE LEARNING 2014

1. ***The "open" quadrant represents information that is known to the individual and is also known to others.*** For example, I know my name, and so do you if you look at the author's name on this textbook. Consider what happens when a new student team is formed for a class project. When the new team comes together, the open area is typically small because people have little information about one another. They can expand the window by sharing likes and dislikes about team work, their experiences with previous teams, thoughts about the coursework, and personal information about themselves. The goal of the Johari Window technique is to expand the open quadrant of awareness for each individual to help each person and the team be more effective. The open quadrant is where good communication and cooperation happen.

2. ***The "blind" quadrant includes things that are known about an individual by others but are unknown to the individual himself.*** This means you have a blind spot. You may not realize that you interrupt others when they are speaking, but others notice it. If someone asks you to please let them finish their point, then the window shade moves to the right, enlarging the open quadrant's area. That blind spot is removed. As another example, a manager or team leader might fail to make eye contact, which causes employees to question her sincerity. The manager is unaware of this tendency to avoid eye contact. By receiving empathetic feedback from others, the blind area is reduced as she becomes more self-aware.

3. ***The "hidden" quadrant represents things that an individual knows about himself or herself but keeps hidden from others.*** We all keep certain feelings, fears, or desires concealed from others, and it is

natural to want to keep some things private. However, information that affects one's work, performance, or relationships needs to be moved out of the hidden area and into the open. On one work team, for example, a member with a secret fear of flying would get cranky and uncooperative in the days before any scheduled business trip that required flying. As soon as this person told his teammates that he had a deep fear of flying, he moved this bit of information out of the hidden quadrant, enlarging the open quadrant's area. Thus, people had a better understanding of why their normally agreeable and cooperative teammate had turned grumpy and disagreeable. In addition, the teammate learned more about himself from the mirror of others' reactions.

4. ***The "unknown" quadrant represents things that are unknown both to the individual and to others in the group.*** Unknown issues could include things like an unknown illness, repressed or subconscious feelings, undetected abilities or talents, or unconscious values and attitudes. Through a process of self-discovery, people can shrink the unknown quadrant by seeking feedback from others and by disclosing more about themselves. An individual might discover that she has a great talent for organizing events or a great love of public speaking, thus expanding her open area.

DISCOVER YOURSELF

Interpret Your Score: Johari Window (Questionnaire 1)

Your score for Part A reflects self-disclosure (disclosure to others) as described within the chapter for the Johari Window. Your score for Part B reflects the concept of soliciting feedback for the Johari Window. Plot the total for each score on the graph. Record the total from Part B, "Solicits Feedback," along the horizontal axis. Record the total from Part A, "Self-Disclosure," along the vertical axis. Divide the graph into four sections by drawing straight lines from the scores across the empty part of the graph to reveal four quadrants. Which quadrant is biggest for you? This tells where you are on the Johari Window for the ten questions in Questionnaire 1. Interpret your scores based on the text description. What changes would you like to make in your self-disclosure or willingness to solicit feedback? Thirty person comparative data: Thirty person comparative data: **Self-Disclosure** (Part A): Mean score = 12.7, Top Quartile = 16–25; Bottom Quartile = 4–11. **Soliciting Feedback** (Part B): Mean = 15.8, Top Quartile = 20–25; Bottom Quartile = 3–13. CNOW and CourseMate users can access dynamically updated comparative data through www.cengagebrain.com.

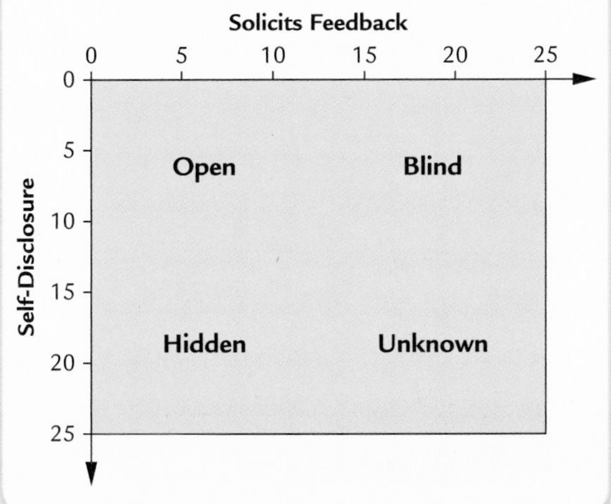

© CENGAGE LEARNING 2014

KEY INDIVIDUAL DIFFERENCES

Mark Zuckerberg's father has characterized him as "strong willed and relentless." Various media reports have referred to the founder and CEO of Facebook as "socially awkward," "self-confident," "arrogant and egotistical," and "shy and self-effacing." Just about the only thing everyone agrees on is that Zuckerberg is smart, rich, and influential. An Internet search will call up thousands of blogs, tweets, and opinion articles talking about the good and the bad sides of Mark Zuckerberg's character. A 2012 *Fast Company* magazine cover story called him the "world's most famous CEO."[22]

Fortunately, most of us aren't in the public eye to have our every move noticed and commented upon. However, like Mark Zuckerberg, each one of us is a unique, diverse, and highly complex jumble of personality traits, values, habits, emotions, needs, attitudes, talents, desires, skills, strengths, weaknesses, and so on. With attention and practice, we can untangle the mystery of ourselves. In the process, we become better able to understand others so we can work with them more effectively. Four areas that encompass important aspects of the self and are strongly related to developing management skills are personality, underlying values and beliefs, thinking style, and ways of dealing

Exhibit 2.2 Four Keys to Self-Awareness

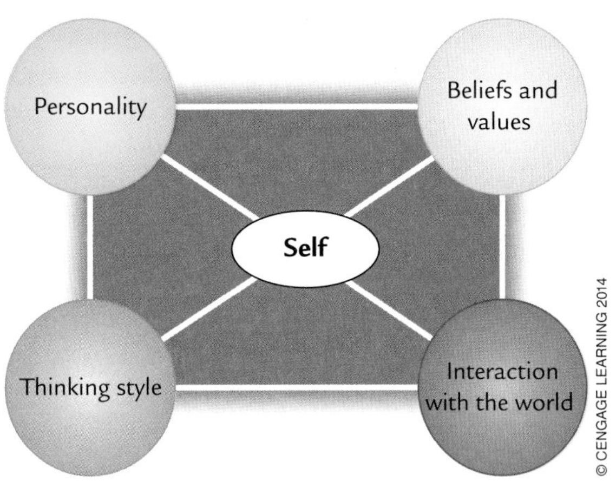

with the world, as shown in Exhibit 2.2. You can significantly enhance your self-awareness by increasing your understanding of yourself in these four areas.

Understanding Personality

Personality is the set of unseen characteristics and thought processes that underlie a relatively stable pattern of behavioral response to people, ideas, and circumstances. We may realize that we are gregarious or shy, happy-go-lucky or cautious, but many of us haven't thought about the collection of personality characteristics that cause us to think and behave in certain ways. We can learn about ourselves by understanding our personality dimensions as reflected in the Big Five model of personality.

The Big Five Model of Personality

Most people think of personality in terms of traits, but although individuals share many traits, each person has a unique personality. Over the past half-century or so, researchers have examined thousands of traits and proposed numerous models of personality. The Big Five model, which groups the myriad personality traits into five key dimensions, is one of the most popular.

Exhibit 2.3 lists the Big Five personality dimensions and some traits associated with each. This model is widely accepted and has enjoyed strong research support.[23] The **Big Five personality dimensions** describe an individual's extraversion, agreeableness, conscientiousness, emotional stability, and openness to experience.

1. **Extraversion** refers to the degree to which a person is outgoing, sociable, assertive, and comfortable meeting and talking to new people. Someone low on extraversion might come across as withdrawn and quiet. This dimension also includes the characteristic of *dominance*. A person with a high degree of dominance likes to be in control and have influence over others. These people often are quite self-confident, seek out positions of authority, and are competitive and assertive. They like to be in charge of

Exhibit 2.3 The Big 5 Personality Factors

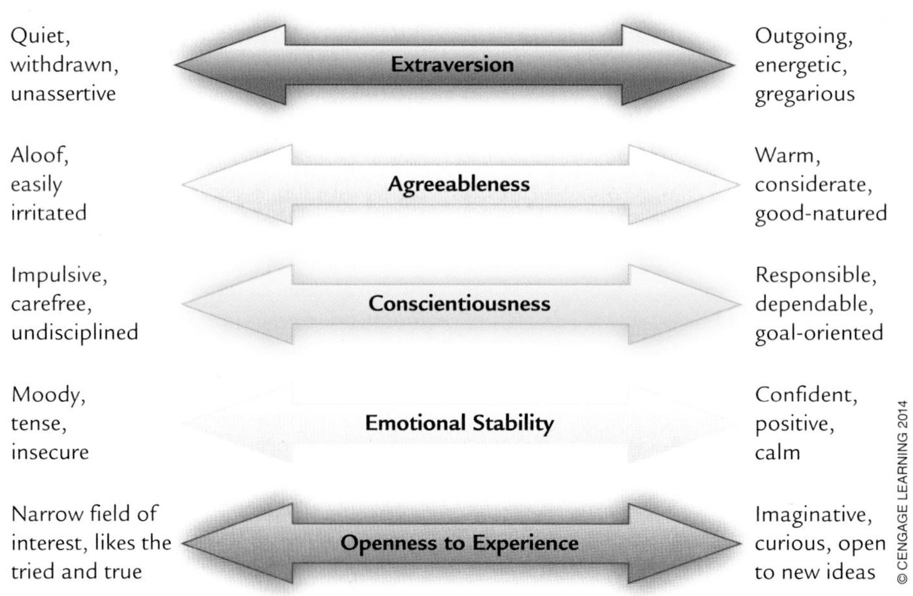

others or have responsibility for others. That is likely why one study found that around 96 percent of managers display extraverted personalities.[24] However, although both dominance and extraversion can be valuable for a manager, not all effective managers necessarily have a high degree of these characteristics. Excessive dominance can even be detrimental to a manager's effectiveness and success. There is some evidence that introverted managers tend to listen more carefully, show greater receptivity to subordinates' ideas and suggestions, and are more likely to make employees feel valued, qualities that are important in today's more collaborative organizations.[25]

2. **Agreeableness** is the degree to which a person is able to get along with others by being good-natured, likable, cooperative, forgiving, understanding, and trusting. People with a high degree of agreeableness seem warm and approachable. They typically make friends easily and often have a large number of friends. Someone low on agreeableness may seem distant, aloof, and insensitive. People low on agreeableness typically establish fewer close relationships.

3. **Conscientiousness** is the degree to which a person is careful, organized, self-disciplined, responsible, dependable, persistent, and achievement oriented. A conscientious person focuses on a few goals and pursues them purposefully and meticulously. A less conscientious person is disorganized, unreliable, impulsive, and easily distracted from goals.

4. **Emotional stability** refers to the degree to which a person is calm, enthusiastic, positive, and self-confident rather than moody, fearful, negative, or insecure. People with a high level of emotional stability handle stress well, can take criticism without being offended or getting emotional, and generally don't take mistakes or failures personally. People with a low degree of emotional stability, on the other hand, tend to be sensitive to criticism, have lower self-confidence, and are more likely to become tense, anxious, or depressed over mistakes and failures.

5. **Openness to experience** means the degree to which a person has a broad range of interests and is curious, imaginative, and willing to consider new ideas. People lower in this dimension tend to have narrower interests and stick to the tried and true way of doing things. They often seem rigid, dogmatic, or narrow-minded.

As illustrated in the exhibit, these factors represent a continuum. That is, a person may have a low, moderate, or high degree of each quality. Having a moderate-to-high degree of each of the Big Five personality factors is considered desirable for a wide range of managers or employees, but this isn't always a key to success. Personality is only one influence on a manager's performance, and many other factors play a part in determining job success. However, some characteristics appear more important for certain types of jobs.[26] Traits associated with agreeableness and extraversion would benefit a sales manager, and those associated with the dimensions of openness to experience and conscientiousness might be particularly beneficial to a research scientist. A high degree of conscientiousness seems to be the one dimension of the Big 5 that is important for success in all types of jobs and careers.[27] In addition, traits of agreeableness are increasingly important for people in today's collaborative organizations.[28] However, there is disagreement regarding even these dimensions. For example, there is some indication that highly conscientious people might be less adaptable to change, which could hinder rather than help their success in some organizations.[29]

DISCOVER YOURSELF

Interpret Your Score: Big Five Personality Dimensions (Questionnaire 2)

Your scores for Parts A–E of Questionnaire 2 represent the Big 5 personality dimensions. Your score for Part A represents your level of **Extraversion**. Thirty student Mean score = 10.9, Top Quartile = 13–14; Bottom Quartile = 6–9. Your score for Part B represents your level of **Emotional Stability** (a low score represents greater emotional stability). Mean = 9.3, Top Quartile = 11–13; Bottom Quartile = 5–7. Your score for Part C represents **Agreeableness**. Mean = 12.6, Top Quartile = 14–15; Bottom Quartile = 9–11. Your score for Part D represents **Openness to New Experiences**. Mean = 12.2, Top Quartile = 13–15; Bottom Quartile = 9–11. And your score for Part E represents your level of **Conscientiousness**. Mean = 12.8, Top Quartile = 14–15; Bottom Quartile = 7–12. Do the scores reflect the way you see yourself? Show your scores to someone who knows you and see if they agree with your scores. CNOW and CourseMate users can access dynamically updated comparative data through www.cengagebrain.com.

© CENGAGE LEARNING 2014

Changing Your Personality

What if you aren't happy with some of your personality characteristics? There is much debate about whether people can change their personalities in terms of the Big 5 dimensions. Research in recent decades suggests that certain aspects of our personalities are determined by the genes we are born with.[30] However, our experiences and the environment, including our families, friends, and other people we closely interact with, also influence our personality.[31] Thus, personality is both genetically and environmentally determined. Nature and nurture work together.

Once an individual's personality is formed, it typically doesn't change very much. However, with conscious effort and attention, people can shift certain thoughts and behaviors that are influenced by their personalities and limit their effectiveness and success. Let's say you are extremely introverted and it is interfering with your ability to network and advance in your career. Managers need to be able to get themselves noticed or they may be overlooked at promotion time. With attention and effort you can learn to be more outgoing, participate more actively in social situations, and network with people to help you accomplish your career goals.

Psychologists have studied the extent to which people are aware of their own thoughts and feelings, and whether they can monitor or shift behavior to fit a new situation. As defined earlier, self-awareness means recognizing internal aspects of one's self, such as thoughts, attitudes, and personality traits that influence your behavior. The ability to adjust behavior relative to the shifting demands of work or social situations is called *self-monitoring*.[32] People who are not aware of their inner world, and who do not change behavior in different situations, typically will not change their personality at all. These individuals have a large blind area regarding themselves. On the other hand, people who see their own thoughts and behaviors can learn to adjust themselves to different situations. A shy person likely will never become an extravert but with awareness can learn to behave in more outgoing and sociable ways to be a more effective salesperson, business consultant, or supervisor. A person with a happy-go-lucky nature might never develop strong traits related to conscientiousness but can learn to act responsibly, be dependable, and follow through on commitments.

Thinking Styles and the Herrmann Whole Brain Model

Another way of looking at how individuals differ is to consider variations in how people perceive, process, interpret, and use information, which affects how they solve problems, make decisions, and relate to others. Understanding that individuals have different *thinking styles* can help you know yourself better and be more effective as a manager. Some managers act as if everyone responds to the same material and behavior in the same way, but this isn't true. Some people prefer facts and figures, whereas others want to know about relationships

DISCOVER KNOWLEDGE

7 STEPS TO... Making Your Natural Personality Work for You

If you're a serious introvert:

1. Practice being friendly and outgoing in less-stressful settings outside of work so you can transfer the new skills to the office.
2. Resist the urge to hibernate in your office; get out and mingle with employees and peers.
3. Remember to smile; a bright countenance reflects confidence in yourself and your abilities.

If you're a raging extravert:

4. Don't bask in the glow of your own personality; learn to hold back and let others sometimes have the limelight.
5. Develop the discipline to talk less and listen more.
6. Don't let your exuberance intimidate others and cause you to miss important facts and ideas.

For both types:

7. Strike the right balance. Whether you're an extravert or an introvert, you can be an effective and successful manager if you learn to emphasize the positive aspects of your natural style and minimize the drawbacks.

Source: Based on Patricia Wallington, "The Ins and Outs of Personality: Whether You're Reserved or Outgoing, Here's How to Emphasize the Positives of Your Natural Style," *CIO* (January 15, 2003): 42, 44.

and patterns. Some people prefer freedom and flexibility, while others crave structure and order.

History of the Concept

In the 1960s and 1970s, scientists discovered that the two distinct hemispheres of the brain influence thinking, which led to an interest in what has been called left-brained versus right-brained thinking patterns. The left hemisphere is associated with logical, analytical thinking and a linear approach to problem-solving, whereas the right hemisphere is associated with creative, intuitive, values-based thought processes.[33] A recent JCPenney television commercial provides a simple illustration. The commercial shows a woman whose right brain is telling her to go out and spend money to buy fun clothes, while the left brain is telling her to be logical and save money. As another simplified example, people who are very good at verbal and written language (which involves a linear thinking process) are using the left brain, while those who prefer to interpret information through visual images are more right-brained.

The Whole Brain Model

Although the concept of right-brained versus left-brained thinking is not entirely accurate physiologically (not all processes associated with left-brained thinking are located in the left hemisphere and vice versa), this concept provided a powerful metaphor for two very different ways of thinking and approaching the world. More recently, these ideas have been broadened to what is called the whole brain concept.[34]

Ned Herrmann began developing his concept of whole brain thinking while he was a manager at General Electric in the late 1970s and has expanded it through many years of research with thousands of individuals and organizations. The **Whole Brain Model** considers not only a person's preference for right-brained versus left-brained thinking, but also for conceptual versus experiential thinking. The model identifies four quadrants of the brain that are related to different thinking styles. Again, while not entirely accurate physiologically, the Whole Brain Model provides an excellent way to understand differences in thinking patterns. Exhibit 2.4 illustrates the model with its four quadrants and some of the mental processes associated with each.

Exhibit 2.4 Herrmann's Whole Brain Model

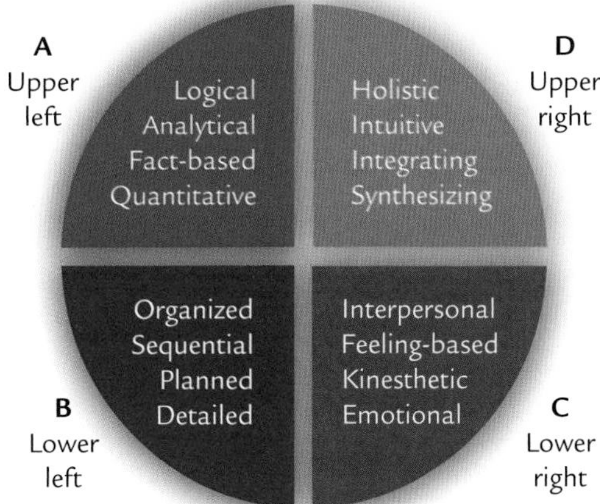

Source: Based on Ned Herrmann, *The Whole Brain Business Book* (New York: McGraw Hill 1996), p. 15.

1. **Quadrant A** is associated with logical thinking, analysis of facts, and processing numbers. A person with a quadrant-A dominance is rational and realistic, thinks critically, and likes to deal with numbers and technical matters. Opinions and feelings are generally not considered as important as facts.

2. **Quadrant B** deals with planning, organizing facts and activities, and careful detailed review. A person who relies heavily on quadrant-B thinking is well-organized, reliable, and neat. These people like to establish plans and procedures and get things done on time.

3. **Quadrant C** is associated with interpersonal relationships and affects intuitive and emotional thought processes. C-quadrant individuals are sensitive to others and enjoy interacting with and teaching others. They are typically emotional and expressive, outgoing, and supportive of others. They are concerned with people's feelings more than with facts and procedures.

4. **Quadrant D** is associated with conceptualizing, synthesizing, and integrating facts and patterns, with seeing the big picture rather than the details. A person with a quadrant-D preference is visionary and imaginative, likes to speculate, break the rules, take risks, and may be impetuous. These people are curious and enjoy experimentation, playfulness, and change.

There is no style that is necessarily better or worse, though any of the styles carried to an extreme can be detrimental. You should remember that every individual, even those with a strong preference in one quadrant, actually has a coalition of preferences from each of the four quadrants. In addition, each of us can learn to use our "whole brain" rather than relying only on one or two quadrants. Although research indicates that few, if any, individuals can be wholly balanced among the four quadrants, we can be aware of our preferences and engage in activities and experiences that help develop the other quadrants.[35]

Managers who reach high levels in organizations often have well-balanced brains. Consider Angela Ahrendts, who applies a balanced thinking style as CEO of Burberry, the $2 billion British fashion empire. Ahrendts has used creative, visionary, big-picture thinking (Quadrant D) to transform Burberry from an outdated brand into a "technologically savvy international fashion powerhouse." Quadrant C characteristics are evident in her emphasis on building positive interpersonal relationships. Ahrendts also demonstrates Quadrant A and Quadrant B thinking in her careful control of the company's finances and her ability to be realistic, analytical, and rational when it comes to making difficult decisions. When the recession hit in 2008, Ahrendts quickly took charge, putting on hold plans for new stores, cutting $78 million in expenses, laying off employees and freezing salaries, and changing company procedures to be more cost-effective.[36] A balanced thinking style is particularly important at higher levels of organizations because managers deal with diverse business functions and a greater variety and complexity of people and issues.[37]

DISCOVER KNOWLEDGE

DISCOVER YOURSELF

Interpret Your Score: Herrmann Whole Brain Model Thinking Styles (Questionnaire 3)

Your score for column A represents Quadrant A in the Herrmann Whole Brain Model in Exhibit 2.4, the Analytical thinking style. Your score for column B represents Quadrant B, the Organizing thinking style. Your score for column C represents Quadrant C, the Feeling style. Your score for column D represents Quadrant D, the Experimental thinking style. The thirty student Mean score for each Quadrant is 3. Your highest scores reflect your thinking preference and style. The four quadrants are evenly balanced for the world at large, but each individual has his or her own configuration. Your thinking style will shape your career interests. Corporate managers, on average, are above average in Quadrant A and below average in Quadrant C, but successful managers can be strong in any quadrant. What is your dominant style according to your scores? Does this reflect your understanding of your thinking style? CNOW and CourseMate users can access dynamically updated comparative data through www.cengagebrain.com.

© CENGAGE LEARNING 2014

Jungian Types for Interacting with the World

Psychologist Carl Jung took still another approach to understanding personality, noting that people's thinking and behavior reflects a relatively stable pattern based on how they prefer to go about gathering and evaluating information, relating to people, and in general interacting with the world.[38] Rather than considering deeply rooted personal traits, as in the Big 5 model, Jung looked at mental preferences.

The Myers–Briggs Type Indicator Assessment

Jung's ideas about psychological types inspired the development of one of the most widely used personality tests in the United States, the **Myers–Briggs Type Indicator (MBTI)** assessment. The MBTI provides a way of measuring differences among individuals in their psychological preferences for how they interact with others and perceive the world.[39] The MBTI assessment of Jungian types has been taken by millions of people and has validity for helping individuals understand themselves. Hallmark Cards, for example, uses the MBTI assessment as a way to help managers gain greater self-understanding and be able to communicate more effectively.[40] The MBTI assessment uses four different pairs of attributes based on Jung's concepts to classify people according to different personality types:

1. **Introversion versus extraversion.** This dimension focuses on where people gain interpersonal strength and mental energy. Extraverts (E) gain energy from being around people and interacting with others, whereas introverts (I) gain energy by being away from people to focus on personal thoughts and feelings. Extraverts are motivated by the outside world, and they tend to speak or act first and think later, while introverts are motivated internally and tend to think first, then act.

2. **Sensing versus intuition.** This identifies how a person absorbs information. Those with a sensing preference (S) gather and absorb information through the five senses, whereas intuitive people (N) rely on less direct perceptions. Sensors, for example, focus on facts, details, and critical analyses for their information. Intuitives, however, look more for patterns, relationships, and hunches that underlie facts.

3. Thinking versus feeling. This dimension relates to how a person makes decisions, especially whether emotions play a role. Feeling types (F) tend to rely more on their values and sense of what is right and wrong, and they consider how a decision will affect other people's feelings. Thinking types (T) tend to rely more on logic as they try to be rational, objective, and impersonal in decision making.

4. Judging versus perceiving. The judging versus perceiving dimension concerns an individual's attitudes toward ambiguity and how quickly a person makes a decision. People with a judging preference like certainty and closure. They enjoy focusing on goals and deadlines and tend to make decisions quickly based on available data to meet deadlines. Perceiving people, on the other hand, enjoy ambiguity and multitasking, will likely miss deadlines, and may change their minds several times before making a final decision. Perceiving types like to gather a large amount of data and information before reaching a decision.

The various combinations of these preferences result in 16 unique personality types, shown in the Interpret Your Score box for Jung Personality Typology. There are a number of exercises available in print and

DISCOVER YOURSELF

Interpret Your Score: Jung Personality Typology (Questionnaire 4)

The scores on this questionnaire measure variables similar to the Myers-Briggs Type Indicator (MBTI) assessment, based on the work of psychologist Carl Jung. The Jung Personality Typology identifies four dimensions and 16 different "types," shown with their dominant characteristics in the following chart. Remember that no one is a pure type; however, each individual does have preferences for introversion versus extraversion, sensing versus intuition, thinking versus feeling, and judging versus perceiving. Based on your scores, read the description of your dimensions and type in the following chart. Do you believe the description fits your personality? CNOW and CourseMate users can access dynamically updated comparative data through www.cengagebrain.com.

Characteristics Associated with Each Dimension

Extraversion: Energized by outer world of people and objects, broad interests, thinks while speaking

Introversion: Energized by inner world of thoughts and ideas, deep interests, thinks before speaking

Sensing: Likes facts, details, and practical solutions

Intuition: Likes meanings, theory, associations among data, and possibilities

Thinking: Makes decisions by analysis, logic, and impersonal criteria

Feeling: Makes decisions based on values, beliefs, and concern for others

Judging: Lives life organized, stable, systematic, and under control

Perceiving: Lets life happen, spontaneous, open-ended, last minute

Characteristics Associated with Each Type

ISTJ: Organizer, trustworthy, responsible, good trustee or inspector.	**ISFJ:** Quiet, conscientious, devoted, handles detail, good conservator.	**INFJ:** Persevere, inspirational, quiet caring for others, good counselor.	**INTJ:** Independent thinker, skeptical, theory, competence, good scientist.
ISTP: Cool, observant, easy-going, good craftsperson.	**ISFP:** Warm, sensitive, team player, avoids conflict, good artist.	**INFP:** Idealistic, strong values, likes learning, good at noble service.	**INTP:** Designer, logical, conceptual, likes challenges, good architect.
ESTP: Spontaneous, gregarious, good at problem solving and promoting.	**ESFP:** Sociable, generous, makes things fun, good as entertainer.	**ENFP:** Imaginative, enthusiastic, starts projects, good champion.	**ENTP:** Resourceful, stimulating, dislikes routine, tests limits, good inventor.
ESTJ: Order, structure, practical, good administrator or supervisor.	**ESFJ:** People skills, harmonizer, popular, does things for people, good host.	**ENFJ:** Charismatic, persuasive, fluent presenter, sociable, active, good teacher.	**ENTJ:** Visionary planner, takes charge, hearty, speaker, natural leader.

© CENGAGE LEARNING 2014

on the Internet that can help people determine their preferences according to the Jung Typology. Individuals develop unique strengths and weaknesses as a result of their preferences for introversion versus extraversion, sensing versus intuition, thinking versus feeling, and judging versus perceiving. As with the whole brain model, Jungian types should not be considered 100 percent fixed and unalterable. People's awareness of their preferences, and new training and life experiences, can cause their preferences to gradually shift over time. Recall John Bearden, the chief executive of GMAC Home Services described at the beginning of this chapter. Bearden took the MBTI assessment of Jungian types and learned that he was an ENTJ. ENTJ types can be dynamic and self-confident as well as overbearing, insensitive, and hasty in their judgments. Bearden said the results of the assessment provided a "quantum leap" in his self-awareness. With determined effort, he learned to listen more carefully to colleagues'opinions.[41]

Research Findings Significant to Managers

Research reveals some interesting, although tentative, findings regarding the significance of the dimensions measured by the Jung typology. For example, although extraversion is often considered an important quality for a manager, many successful top leaders, including Bill Gates, Charles Schwab, and Steven Spielberg, are introverts, people who become drained by social encounters and need time alone to reflect and recharge their batteries. Although introverts make up 30 percent of the population, one study found that four in ten of top executives test out to be introverts.[42] In regard to the sensing versus intuition dimension, data reveal that sensing types are in the majority in fields where the focus is on the immediate and tangible (e.g., construction, banking, manufacturing). However, in areas that involve breaking new ground or long-range planning, intuitive people are in the majority. Thinking (as opposed to feeling) types are more common among managers in business and industry as well as in the realm of science. In addition, thinking types appear to be chosen more often as managers even in organizations that value "feeling," such as counseling centers, because they are objective and organized. Finally, one of the most consistent findings is that judging types are in the majority among the managers studied.

Thus, the two preferences that seem to be most strongly associated with successful management are thinking and judging. However, this doesn't mean that people with other preferences cannot be effective managers. One alternative for managers is to compensate by working with people with complementary strengths. Another alternative is to take advantage of one's own natural preferences. For example, Gertrude Boyle, who took over Columbia Sportswear after the death of her husband, illustrates an extraverted and intuitive style of managing. You might have seen her in one of the company's "Tough Mother" television or print ads. The grandmotherly Boyle actively sought information on what her competitors were doing and decided to try something new to distinguish Columbia. Most sportswear companies advertise their products worn by trim young models, but Boyle decided that starring in the ads herself would make Columbia stand out from the crowd. Boyle believes in continually pushing herself and her company, questioning everything, and trying out new ideas to see what works.[43]

UNDERLYING VALUES

For Esa Heiskanen, some of life's top priorities are spending time with his family, taking good care of his children, and playing football a couple of times a week, both to stay physically fit and to interact with people from different walks of life. Heiskanen is the CEO of Glow Group, a large, global energy company with headquarters in Bangkok. He's a busy man, but he firmly believes in the importance of having a balance between work and personal life. As a manager, Heiskanen leads with authenticity and integrity, values that permeate the organization. Open communication, accountability, commitment, and balance are woven into Glow's corporate culture, as are values of environmental and social responsibility. When asked how to build a healthy corporate culture, Heiskanen says it starts with managers who are self-aware, who understand their own values, and who display those values in their everyday actions. "It's looking inward to ourselves," Heiskanen says. "I mean, people will not take it seriously if the leaders do not present themselves or donate their time to what they start and commit to do."[44]

Esa Heiskanen knows what matters to him in the world, and he incorporates those values into his leadership as CEO of Glow Group. Do you know what matters to you? What is most important to you? What accomplishments are you most proud of? If you won the lottery or inherited a large fortune, what changes would you make in your life and what aspects of your life would you keep the same?[45] The answers to these questions reveal some of your values. Understanding ourselves in the area of *beliefs and values* helps us know what matters to us, understand the choices we make, and realize why we prefer that things be done one way rather than another way. **Values** are fundamental beliefs that an individual considers to be important, that are relatively stable over time, and that influence attitudes, perception, and behavior. They play a vital role in our interpersonal choices, goals, and decision making.[46] Our values and beliefs ultimately shape our lives, as suggested by the following saying attributed to Mahatma Gandhi:

> "Your beliefs become your thoughts,
> Your thoughts become your words,
> Your words become your actions,
> Your actions become your habits,
> Your habits become your values,
> Your values become your destiny."

Instrumental and End Values

Although people may appear to differ significantly in their values, research by Milton Rokeach shows that the total number of values humans possess is relatively modest.[47]

Types of Values

A coherent way to think about values is in terms of Rokeach's 18 instrumental and 18 end values, which are listed in Exhibit 2.5. These values have been found to be more or less universal across time periods and cultures.[48] The exhibit also shows the results of a recent study comparing how individuals (non-managers) from different generations ranked the 18 end values and 18 instrumental values. The study defined "Boomers" as people born in the years 1946 to 1964, "Generation X" as people born in the years 1965 to 1979, and "Generation Y" as adults born in the year 1980 or after.[49]

End values, sometimes called *terminal values*, are beliefs about the kind of goals or outcomes that are worth pursuing. For example, some people value security, a comfortable life, and good health above everything else as the important goals to strive for. Others may place greater value on social recognition, pleasure, and an exciting life. **Instrumental values** are beliefs about the types of behavior that are appropriate for reaching end goals. Instrumental values include such things as being helpful to others, being honest, or exhibiting courage. Although everyone has both instrumental and end values, individuals differ in how they order the values into their life priorities, which accounts for tremendous variation among people.

How Values Differ

Part of the difference in the ordering of values relates to culture. For example, in the United States, independence is highly valued and is reinforced by many institutions, including schools, religious organizations, and businesses. Other cultures place less emphasis on independence and more value on being part of a tightly knit community. Managers also should understand that individual factors, such as family background and personality characteristics, influence a person's values. Values are learned, not inherited, but many values become incorporated into a person's thinking very early in life based on family experiences. Personality characteristics, such as extraversion or introversion, a high or low degree of conscientiousness, and so forth, also influence how people prioritize values.

One area in which individuals may differ significantly is the extent to which their values are self-oriented versus other-oriented. If you study the list of end values in Exhibit 2.5, you will notice that some are personal (for example, pleasure, social recognition), whereas others are social (for example, a world at peace, equality). Values are generally fairly well established by early adulthood, but a person's values do change over time. In terms of end values, for instance, a young man or woman just out of high school might place a high priority on an exciting life; as the person grows older, marries, and has children, that value might decline and the importance of family security might increase in value. An individual's emphasis on instrumental values, or the means used to achieve goals, can also change over time. The data in Exhibit 2.5 reflect interesting differences in values among three generations of non-managers surveyed, but there are some similarities among the generations as well.[50]

Values-Based Management

Why is it important to define the values that guide you as an individual and will one day shape your decisions and actions as a manager? Understanding your

Exhibit 2.5 Non-Manager Rankings of Rokeach's Instrumental and End Values

End Values	Boomers	Gen X	Gen Y	Instrumental Values	Boomers	Gen X	Gen Y
A comfortable life	7	9	1	Ambition	11	8	1
Equality	16	12	15	Broad-mindedness	14	6	10
An exciting life	14	11	10	Capability	9	5	6
Family security	2	5	2	Cleanliness	17	15	7
Freedom	6	8	6	Courage	15	11	12
Health	1	1	3	Forgiveness	6	16	17
Inner harmony	5	7	16	Helpfulness	8	13	14
Mature love	11	13	9	Honesty	1	2	3
National security	15	18	18	Imagination	18	12	18
Pleasure	13	4	12	Independence	4	3	5
Salvation	3	17	13	Intellectualism	10	7	11
Self-respect	4	6	8	Logic	13	1	13
Sense of accomplishment	10	10	7	Ability to love	3	10	2
Social recognition	18	15	14	Loyalty	5	14	9
True friendship	9	3	4	Obedience	16	18	16
Wisdom	8	2	5	Politeness	12	17	15
A world at peace	12	14	11	Responsibility	2	4	4
A world of beauty	17	16	17	Self-control	7	9	8

NOTE: The values are listed in alphabetical order, and there is no one-to-one relationship between the end values and the instrumental values.

Sources: Milton Rokeach, *The Nature of Human Values* (New York: The Free Press, 1973); M. Rokeach, *Understanding Human Values* (New York: The Free Press, 1979); and Edward F. Murphy, Jr., Jane Whitney Gibson, and Regina A. Greenwood, "Analyzing Generational Values Among Managers and Non-Managers for Sustainable Organizational Effectivenss," *SAM Advanced Management Journal* (Winter 2010): 33–55.

DISCOVER YOURSELF

Interpret Your Score: Rokeach's Instrumental and End Values (Questionnaire 5)

End values, according to Rokeach, tend to fall into two categories—personal and social. For example, mature love is a personal end value and equality is a social end value. Analyze your ranking of the end values and determine whether your primary end values tend to be personal or social. What does your order of values mean to you? What does it mean for how you make life decisions? For comparative end value scores from different generations, see Exhibit 2.5. What did you learn about your end values from this exercise? Does your ranking of end values reflect the pattern of your generation?

Instrumental values also tend to fall into two categories—morality and competence. The means people use to achieve their goals might violate moral values (e.g., be dishonest) or violate one's personal sense of competence and capability (e.g., be illogical). Analyze your ranking of the instrumental values and determine whether your primary instrumental values tend to focus on morality or competence. What does your order of instrumental values mean to you? What does it mean for how you will pursue your life goals? For comparative instrumental value scores from different generations, see Exhibit 2.5. What did you learn about your instrumental values from this exercise? Does your ranking of instrumental values reflect the pattern of your generation?

Warning: The two columns of values do *not* represent the full range of instrumental and end values. Your findings would change if a different list of values were provided. This exercise is for discussion and learning purposes only and is not intended to be an accurate assessment of your actual end and instrumental values.

© CENGAGE LEARNING 2014

values is a critical aspect of self-awareness, as well as an essential tool for leading others.[51] Values play a crucial role in how we behave, the decisions we make, and how we perceive the world. As a manager, you will need to understand why one choice seems better than another. You will need to recognize when your values are in conflict with organizational needs or the needs of subordinates. In addition, as a leader of others, you will shape the value system that guides your team, department, or organization. Clarifying your own values is the essential first step toward being a values-based manager.

What Is It?

Although not all managers will have the same values, to be effective, managers integrate their personal values with the needs of the organization, its stakeholders, and the larger society. **Values-based management** means management that provides a shared foundation of ethical values and beliefs that guide individual behavior and organizational actions.[52] These core values help people at all levels know what actions to take in various situations. Recent ethical scandals and financial abuses in both the corporate and government environments underscore the need for shared values that help people make the right decisions. Shared values provide a firm grounding during times of difficulty and rapid change.

Managers find a balance between self-oriented values and community-oriented values to effectively lead organizations that contribute to society.[53] Recall the earlier discussion of self-oriented versus other-oriented values. Managers who hold only self-oriented values as priorities can cause harm to employees, organizations, and the larger society. Think of the now-defunct Bear Stearns, where managers shaped a shared value system that encouraged people to get all they could for themselves without considering the larger impact of their actions. By practicing values-based management, you can empower people throughout the organization to make the right decisions within a framework of ethical values.

Four fundamental values for ethical organizations are honesty, accountability, trust, and caring.[54] *Honesty* means the organization's leaders are open and truthful with employees, customers, shareholders, and the public. *Accountability* means that people accept responsibility for their actions. Managers in ethical organizations place a high value on *trust*. They give people clear goals, provide support, and trust them to carry out tasks appropriately. *Caring* means putting the interests of others ahead of one's own. In ethical

DISCOVER KNOWLEDGE

LEADING WORDS

"He who knows others is wise. He who knows himself is enlightened."

—**Lao Tzu**
philosopher in ancient China; author of *Tao Te Ching*

"Values are the essence of who we are as human beings. Our values get us out of bed every morning, help us select the work we do, the company we keep, the relationships we build, and, ultimately, the groups and organizations we lead."

—**Bob Rue**
senior organizational change specialist for the Joint Surveillance Target Attack Radar System project office, Hanscom Air Force Base

"One of the most sacred relationships among teams of people is that between leaders and followers. This relationship, so central and crucial, depends to an extraordinary degree on the clearly expressed and consistently demonstrated values of the leader as seen through the special lens of followers. That is why leadership and ethics are inextricably woven together."

—**Max DePree**
writer and former CEO of Herman Miller

organizations, people want others to succeed, and they want to take actions that benefit others both inside and outside the organization.

How Do You Do It?

As a manager, you will communicate the values you want to guide employee behavior not just through words, but primarily through your actions. Values-based managers live a life of integrity, and they put their values into practice every day. Jim Hackett, CEO of Steelcase, provides a good example. Hackett wanted to instill organizational values of "unyielding integrity," but his own values were put to the test when the company faced a decision regarding fire-retardant products. Steelcase had great success selling a new line of panels that could be used either for cubicles or to cover floor-to-ceiling walls. The company soon discovered, though, that rules governing walls were stricter than those for cubicles, and the new product might not be up to the higher fire standards in some locations. Some executives (and even some customers) advised Hackett to just ignore the issue since fire codes vary so much from one municipality to another. Hackett knew this was a time to put his values into action. He quietly recalled the panels and replaced them with ones that would meet the strictest fire codes, even though the decision was expensive and time-consuming for the company and caused Hackett and other top managers to lose their annual performance bonuses. The U.S. Department of Defense had some of the Steelcase panels, and after the September 11, 2001, terrorist attack on the Pentagon, leaders there told Hackett the fires likely "would have spread in a far more disastrous outcome" if the new fire-retardant material had not been used.[55]

DISCOVER KNOWLEDGE

USING SELF-AWARENESS TO BUILD MANAGEMENT SKILLS

There are many skills you will use as a manager, many of which are *soft* or *human skills* as described in the introductory chapter. Learning new and effective soft skills, such as communication, teamwork and collaboration, initiative, developing subordinates, and leadership, is a challenge. Learning soft skills is where self-awareness really pays off.

Exhibit 2.6 Self-Awareness Builds Skill Competence

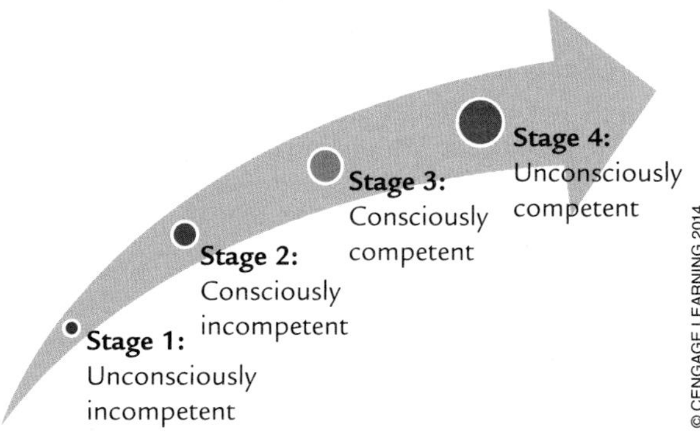

Psychologist Abraham Maslow refers to the mastery of any skill as *unconscious competence*.[56] This is when you are so practiced at doing something well that it occurs correctly without thinking, without special effort. Becoming unconsciously competent typically involves progress through four stages, which are illustrated in Exhibit 2.6. The word *conscious* in Exhibit 2.6 means being self-aware.

The mastery of a new skill, such as driving a car, snow skiing, or a soft skill of management, begins at stage 1 of being unconsciously incompetent. This means that you don't have any competence with the skill, and you aren't even aware that you lack competence. If you've ever played a sport like golf or volleyball, recall the first time you tried it. You likely discovered your incompetence and realized you needed help to move forward. By reading books, watching videos, or taking lessons, you became conscious of what is required to do well at the sport. The same applies to learning to be a good manager. You can learn about what it takes to build a team or how to be an effective communicator. This is stage 2, where you become conscious of what's required to do well but are still personally incompetent.

With practice, your conscious awareness of the correct thing to do will gradually transform into competence. Stage 3 is where the practice of a management skill—or playing a sport such as golf or volleyball—becomes a real pleasure. You receive positive feedback from your skill and are aware of how well you're doing, which sets up the transition to stage 4. In stage 4, the skill becomes an integral part of who you are. It occurs naturally and without conscious thought or effort. If you've been driving a car for awhile, this is how you now drive home from school or work—you drive automatically while your mind might be thinking about other things.

When you achieve unconscious competence in a management skill such as communication, you no longer need to consciously think about how to effectively communicate with a new employee, for example.

It all starts with becoming conscious (self-aware) in stage 2 of Exhibit 2.6. For example, think about the struggles of one executive who kept delaying several new product initiatives because, he said, his direct reports were not capable of assuming more of his duties. The executive was too busy to stay on top of everything needed for developing new products. The problem, he realized later as he became more conscious (self-aware), was within himself. He had failed to focus on coaching and developing his direct reports to handle more responsibility. Once he became conscious of his incompetence, he immediately acted to learn how to develop his people so he could delegate more of his duties and keep those new product initiatives moving.

It is extremely rare for someone undertaking any endeavor to operate in stage 4 without going through the first three stages. Most of us have to struggle with learning about ourselves, learning what it takes to be a good manager, and then becoming competent through practice and experience. Your increase in self-awareness combined with the exercises and chapters in this book are designed to move you up the stairway of both consciousness and competence.

NEED TO KNOW

- Self-awareness is one of the most important capabilities for you to develop as a current or future manager. Self-awareness means being aware of the internal aspects of yourself, such as personality traits, beliefs, emotions, values, strengths, and limitations, and appreciating how your patterns affect other people.
- It is difficult for most people to see themselves objectively, but you can use feedback, self-diagnosis, and self-disclosure to expand your self-awareness and understand yourself better.
- The Johari Window model with its four windows—open, blind, hidden, and unknown—provides a way to understand how feedback and self-disclosure enhance self-awareness. The goal of the Johari Window technique is to expand the open window to help people better understand themselves and others.
- Four key individual differences are personality, thinking style, ways of dealing with the world, and underlying values.
- Personality is the set of unseen characteristics and thought processes that underlie a relatively stable pattern of behavior. The Big Five model of personality groups myriad personality traits into five key dimensions: extraversion, agreeableness, conscientiousness, emotional stability, and openness to experience. Having a moderate to high degree of each of the Big Five dimensions is considered desirable for a manager.
- Personality doesn't change very much once it is formed, but with attention and effort, people can shift certain thoughts and behaviors that are influenced by their personality and might be limiting their effectiveness and success.
- Another area of individual differerences relates to a person's thinking style. The whole brain model explores a person's preferences for right-brained versus left-brained thinking and for conceptual versus experiential thinking. The model provides a powerful metaphor for understanding differences in thinking styles. Individuals can learn to use their "whole brain" rather than relying on one thinking style.
- The Jung Personality Typology, which is similar to the Myers–Briggs Type Indicator (MBTI), measures an individual's preferences for introversion versus extraversion, sensing versus intuition, thinking versus feeling, and judging versus perceiving.
- Values are fundamental beliefs that an individual considers important, that are relatively stable over time, and that influence attitudes, perception, and behavior.
- Everyone has both instrumental and end values, and individuals differ in how they order the values into their life priorities. Although values are fairly well established by early adulthood, many people's values do change over time.

- Values-based management means management that provides a shared foundation of ethical values and beliefs that guide individual behavior and organizational actions, so that people know what decisions to make and how to act in various situations. Managers communicate the values they want to guide employee behavior primarily through their actions.
- Self-awareness is crucial for learning the soft skills of management. Learning any new skill typically passes through four stages: from unconcious incompetence, through conscious incompetence, to conscious competence, and finally to unconscious competence. Unconscious competence means the skill comes naturally and without conscious thought and effort.

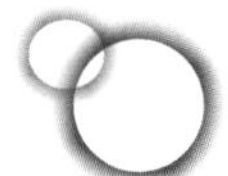

ACTION LEARNING

DELIBERATE PRACTICE EXERCISES

Values in Action

Step 1: Choose the three instrumental values from the list below that are *not* your best strengths. For example, if you are naturally neat and tidy, do not choose "cleanliness," and if you often defer to others, do not choose "obedience." For the next three days, you will practice these three values in your daily actions. Choose one value to purposefully apply throughout the first day, the second value for the second day, and the final one for the third day.

Broad-mindedness ______
Capability ______
Cleanliness ______
Courage ______
Forgiveness ______
Helpfulness ______
Honesty ______
Imagination ______
Independence ______
Intellectualism ______
Logic ______
Ability to love ______
Loyalty ______
Obedience ______
Politeness ______
Responsibility ______
Self-control ______

Step 2: Give some thought to the behaviors that express each of your three selected values and use those behaviors as often as possible during each day.

Step 3: Record in the table below what happened when you used each of the three values.

List the three values below:	How easy or difficult was it to practice the value?	What happened? List outcomes.
1.		
2.		
3.		

Step 4: Answer the following questions:

1. What insights did you gain from practicing values?

2. What are some advantages to living according to values?

Step 5 (Optional): Share your insights with a partner, and ask your partner what insights he or she gained.

Personality Type

Step 1: Consider what you like to do and what you do well, as well as activities you do not like to do and do not do well, and complete the table below. Try to put at least two items in each category.

Like and Do Well Grid	
Things I like and do well:	Things I like but do not do well:
Things I do not like but do well:	Things I do not like and do not do well:

Step 2: What patterns do you notice in the above table?

Step 3: Now, in order to relate what you learned above to your personality type, choose five major characteristics of your personality, using both the Jungian Typology and the Big Five Personality Factors instrument. For example, you might choose Extraversion, Conscientiousness, Feeling, etc. List the five characteristics below:

Your Personality Characteristics
1.
2.
3.
4.
5.

Step 4: Next, choose one activity from each category that you filled out in the Like and Do Well Grid. Put those in column A below.

Column A: Likes and Wells	Column B: Which of your personality characteristics relates to that activity?
Like and do well:	
Like but do not do well:	
Do not like but do well:	
Do not like and do not do well:	

ACTION LEARNING

Step 5: In column B, list one of your personality characteristics that matches with the activity in Column A. For example, you might have listed that you are a good networker and enjoy that, which relates to Extraversion. And then you perhaps wrote down that you do not like clerical work and do not do it well, which relates to you being more "intuitive" rather than "sensing."

Step 6: What did you learn about yourself from this exercise?

Step 7 (Optional): Share your insights with a partner, and ask your partner what insights he or she gained.

IN-CLASS TEAM EXERCISES

Self-Awareness and Feedback

Step 1: Divide into groups of four to six members. Each individual fills out the table below about the other people in the group. Even if you don't know the other people very well, go on your first impressions. Most people make first impressions quickly. Both long-term and first impressions are important feedback we can give one another.

Group members' names	List 2 to 3 unique qualities of each person.
1.	
2.	
3.	
4.	
5.	
6. Yourself	

Step 2: Go around the group, with everyone giving their feedback to one person at a time. For example, Person 1 will listen (without interrupting or defending) to unique qualities that the other group members report. After everyone has given feedback to Person 1, then Person 2 gets feedback, and so on, until all members have received feedback. Each person should write below the feedback that he or she received.

My Unique Qualities—What Group Members Said about Me:

Step 3: Now, in the feedback you wrote in the "My Unique Qualities" box in Step 2, circle the characteristics that you already knew about yourself. Put a check mark next to new information about yourself—characteristics you did not know (whether you agree with it or not). Did you have more circles or checks?

Step 4: Go back to the Johari Window discussion on pages 86–87. Explain how your "open" area just got larger.

Step 5: How can you work to keep increasing your "open" area and reduce your "blind" spots?

ACTION LEARNING

Managerial Values

This In-Class Team exercise is available online at www.cengagebrain.com.

FIELD TEAM EXERCISE

Job Advertisements—Brain Dominance

Step 1: Divide into groups of four to six members. Set up a time for a group meeting.

Step 2: Each person prepares for the meeting by collecting 15 to 20 advertisements for jobs. Try to get varied types of jobs. These can be from postings on various Web sites, in professional journals, in newsletters, and so on.

Step 3: Bring copies of each job announcement with you to the group meeting. Each ad should be on a separate piece of paper.

Step 4: Review as a group the main concepts from the Whole Brain Model, as described on pages 90–92 and in Exhibit 2.4. Your group task will be to divide all the job advertisements into four piles that correspond to the four quadrants of the Whole Brain Model: (a) logical analytical; (b) organizer planner; (c) expressive emotional; and (d) integrating intuitive.

Step 5: Go around the group, one job advertisement at a time. The person who brought in the ad reads it and then gives an assessment of which of the four groups it belongs to. Others comment and the group decides which pile to put it in. Where there is no agreement possible, the originator of that ad places it on one of the piles.

SHUTTERSTOCK #53973379

Step 6: Have a group discussion about what you just did and consider the following questions:

a. Were you surprised at how many jobs there were in a certain category?
b. Were you drawn to jobs that matched your brain dominance?
c. What played a greater role in how you categorized the ads: the nature of the job itself or the way the ad was worded?
d. Is it possible to have an unconscious screening process on jobs before anyone even applies?
e. What did you learn from this exercise?

Step 7: As a group, write the "ideal" job advertisement for each of the four quadrants. Be prepared to turn these in to your instructor.

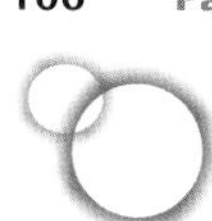

TEST YOUR METTLE

ROLE PLAY SIMULATIONS

Never Good Enough

Background: Re-read the written Video Incident at the beginning of the chapter.

Instructions: Form into groups of two to three. One person will play the role of Jane and one the role of Carrie. If there are three, the third person is an observer. Each person reads only his or her confidential role, but the observer reads both. Spend 10–15 minutes on the role play.

Confidential information for Jane: One of your recent hires is Carrie Fishman, director of operations, who came with stellar recommendations and is a self-described "geek." She loves to develop systems and create more efficiency. Already she's saved the company tens of thousands of dollars by streamlining different processes. But once she began to feel comfortable and achieve some success, she started challenging you in meetings, both just you two and in the team meetings, which has been very disruptive to group solidarity. The problem is, while her approach seems harsh, she is more often right than not. Carrie is really smart, maybe even a genius, so when she is correct, you end up deferring to her. Lately you've seen that this kind of continuous "giving in" to Carrie has confused the team. You've called Carrie in to talk over the problem. This isn't the first time, but rather the fourth time for such a conversation. In previous sessions, Carrie said she understood, but then went and did it again. This time has to be different.

Confidential information for Carrie: Two months ago you joined Caffeine and Crullers as director of operations, a job you really love. Finally, after several years in dead-end jobs, someone recognized your talents. It's not easy being a geek in a world of people who talk *ad nauseum* about strategy and team dynamics and positive feedback. It's all so touchy-feely and a complete waste of time. Why can't they just let you spend all your time streamlining the processes and leave that team stuff to people who actually care? And the problem in meetings is that people are often wrong in their numbers or their assessments. But they want you to shut up. Jane has talked to you several times and it seems she prefers some kind of groupthink to honest communication. But you've learned it is better to just go along when she gets in her complaining mode. Anything to shut her up. But really, if they hired smarter people, you wouldn't have to correct them all the time. You are headed now for another confrontation with Jane. Just keep her happy.

After the role play, discuss these questions:

1. What did Jane do that was effective? What was not effective?
2. What are possible reasons for Carrie's interpersonal problems?
3. How can a manager help someone like Carrie get along more smoothly with other members of the team?

Painful Rumors

This Role Play Simulation is available online at www.cengagebrain.com.

SHUTTERSTOCK #53973379

VIDEO APPLICATION

Becoming Self-Aware at Mitchell Gold + Bob Williams

Manager Kim Clay learns about herself as she moves up the hierarchy.

Discussion Questions

1. What are some of the characteristics that Kim Clay understood about herself? How might knowing something negative about oneself, such as a lack of self-confidence, help a person's management career?
2. What does vice president Dan Gauthreaux mean when he says, "I think you can learn from any job you do and try to make the best of it"?
3. What role did company management play in fostering Kim Clay's self-awareness and personal growth?

CASE INCIDENTS

The Marshall Plan

Marshall Gordon was recognized by associates and competitors as a *man on a mission*. One of four members of the design team for a large chair manufacturing corporation, Marshall's obsession with the creation of comfortable seating dated to a childhood back injury and a lifetime of pain. He recognized, more than most in the industry, the importance of designing chairs that offered some relief to those suffering from debilitating back, hip, and neck pain as well as helping people of all ages to avoid problems with proper posture. In his early days with the company the staff jokingly called his approach *The Marshall Plan*, after America's 1947 initiative (named for Secretary of State George Marshall) to rebuild European economies after the war. Like someone fighting to save the world, Marshall Gordon brought passion and a creative intensity to design meetings as if each drawing, each design tweak would change civilization as we knew it.

Single, and with no apparent family or friendship ties, Marshall was married to his work. He seemed to thrive on 70 hour work weeks, although as a salaried employee, he received no overtime pay. Even his "down time" at meals or on weekends was spent sketching, studying the latest in ergonomics, or reconnoitering each design adjustment by competitors.

"When you visit a furniture store, you fully expect to see Marshall, skulking about in trench coat and hat, checking to see what the competition is offering," says fellow team member John Craddock. "We all laugh about it. The guy brings actually brings chairs to meetings and tears them apart to show us some miniscule *discovery*."

This obsession with chairs and pain and gravity and one-upping the competition, has made Marshall a valuable employee and earned for him a reputation in the industry for creative design. Not since Peter Opsvik's Gravity Balans ergonomic chair of the 1970's has anyone made such an impact on the industry. The effect of his work on company profits is undeniable. The fact that competitors are chomping at the bit to lure him away is also undeniable.

But the Marshall Plan comes at a price. Over the fifteen years he has worked with the company, there has been a constant turnover within the design group as frustrated coworkers leave the company to "get away from Marshall."

"Anything you could learn from this brilliant and dedicated man is destroyed by his cold, calculating attitude," Craddock complains. "I came to this company excited about the chance to work with him. But any knowledge he possesses is carefully guarded. His design ideas are perfect, while ours are picked apart. We all swear he has listening devices scattered around everywhere, because if the rest of the team huddles in some corner of the world to discuss a design idea, *voila!* He walks into the next meeting with *our* idea. Once when he was a few minutes late to a meeting, we thought we had beaten him and quickly presented our idea. Just then, he walks in, and announces, "Ideas must be in the air. I have something very similar," and throws his completed design on screen. Guess who won."

Marshall presents a continuing challenge to company management, having both incredible positive and negative impact on the culture. While his contributions to design and profits far exceed those of other employees, his affect on company and team creativity and morale and his "battle readiness" on all fronts results in the loss of other talented people and a climate of suspicion and discontent. His threat, "I can take my talents elsewhere," hangs over management like a sledge hammer.

Now, Craddock and Leslie Warren, a second talented member of the design team, have approached management with their own ultimatum: *Do something about Marshall or we resign.*"

Discussion Questions

1. If you were a top manager, how would you respond to the ultimatum? Be specific.
2. If you were Marshall's manager, how might you increase Marshall's awareness of the negative impact he is having on other people and guide him toward building a team, sharing his knowledge, and mentoring colleagues?
3. How would you explain Marshall's behavior? Where would Marshall fit in the Johari Window? Where would you place him on each of the Big 5 personality factors? Why?

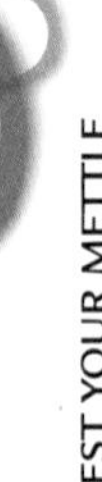

TEST YOUR METTLE

"Giving Back"

"Aren't you Mama Gilman's son?"

That question had followed Reggie all of his life. The youngest of four children, Reggie grew up in the shadow of big-hearted Rose "Mama" Gilman in New Orleans' ninth ward. Mama instilled in each of her children a strong sense of obligation and service to others. With few resources to share, Mama Gilman gave generously of her time and energy to others—soup kitchens, toy drives, clothing drives, and food drives. It all came as easily to her as breathing. Everyone in New Orleans recognized Mama with four children toddling along behind, lending a hand wherever there was a need.

Reggie's older siblings followed Mama's example of service. Brother Isaac, an orthopedic surgeon, works with Doctors Without Borders/Médecins Sans Frontières. His sister Carmelita, a nurse, volunteers with the Catholic Charities operation Healing Hands, while sister Brenda, a teacher, volunteers with a local non-profit group that provides affordable housing for families.

Reggie was a star wide receiver in high school, receiving a football scholarship to Louisiana State University (LSU). Mama died during his freshman year at the

university. An injury in his sophomore season ended his hopes and chances for an NFL career, but Reggie completed a double degree in geology and engineering, followed by an MBA. After graduation, he secured a job with ORI, a top international corporation based in China, which manufactures oil rigging supplies and spare parts. Good pay allowed Reggie the luxury of living in an upscale neighborhood of New Orleans and the opportunity to donate generously to charities in the city. The donation of time, however, was limited by long hours and extensive travel throughout the Gulf Coast.

All of that changed when Hurricane Katrina hit on August 29, 2005. The hurricane and subsequent flooding of the city he loved hurled Reggie into an exhausting schedule, trying to balance work and volunteer efforts. The horrific sights and sounds haunted Reggie and spurred him to action—any action—to aid his New Orleans neighbors. Long after America's attention moved from the city and its trials, Reggie continued helping with relief and rebuilding efforts. In the past, monetary donations had been enough, but with Katrina, he at last felt that he was living up to his mother's ideals while embracing the "people component" that his job in corporate sales did not offer.

When a 7.0 magnitude earthquake struck Haiti in January 2010, Reggie took a three-week leave of absence to travel to his family's ancestral homeland to assist in another disaster. With each image, each life touched, he felt an increasing urge to do more, and at last understood the power of giving that his mother embodied.

Less than three months after Reggie returned to New Orleans, the city and region were again rocked by disaster with the explosion and oil spill from BP's Deepwater Horizon. With an exciting and lucrative career in the oil industry and a lifetime spent in the exquisite beauty of the Gulf Coast, Reggie felt the frustration and pain of locals as well as industry workers and officials. On the one hand, he questioned his career choice, while on the other hand, he believed that working *within* the industry offered opportunities to improve the industry that people around the world depended upon. As Mama Gilman's son and with a growing reputation for helping others, Reggie felt mounting pressure from well-meaning citizens to help out, to sit on boards, and to give more time and money to various causes. Almost daily, he was urged to get out of the oil business. "That's not where Mama Gilman's son belongs."

In May 2011, executives in China began talks with Reggie about a major promotion heading up sales throughout the Western Hemisphere. Based in New York, the position brought a substantial increase in pay and other benefits and offered a chance to gain valuable international experience. Almost simultaneously, Reggie's sister Brenda approached him with a request from the board of her non-profit family housing foundation to take over the reins when the current chairman retired at the end of 2011. The difference in pay for the two jobs was staggering. Reggie was still young and had no family to consider. Each opportunity required a major move—either "up" to the lifestyle he had worked for and dreamed about or "down" from his upscale neighborhood to a more modest apartment in New Orleans, as befitting the chairman of a non-profit. Each job offered valuable new experiences.

As he wrestled with his choices, Reggie felt increasingly isolated. Family, friends, and neighbors pushed him to abandon his career path and take the non-profit position. "Ask yourself what Mama Gilman would advise," was the constant suggestion, keeping at bay any hopes of a serious discussion of options with people he would normally seek out. In his heart, Reggie's various charity efforts had left him feeling used, overwhelmed, and inadequate. His reputation for generous donations of both money and time had drained his enthusiasm for *giving back.*

"There's no end to it. No matter what I do, it doesn't make a dent. I feel this urge to give back as my whole family has done. But I don't even know why I do it anymore,"

Reggie explained to Brad Davis, a business colleague, at the end of a lunch meeting. "I'm torn. I wish Mama was around to offer me some advice." Reggie stopped and looked at Brad. "No, I know exactly what she would advise. It's who she was."

"She knew who *she* was. The question, my friend, is who are *you*?" Brad said as he reached for the check. "The honest answer to *that* will give you the choice that is right for you. Running from one charitable event to another doesn't *make* you a good person if it comes merely from a sense of obligation. Choosing a different career path doesn't *make* you cold and uncaring."

Discussion Questions

1. What does Reggie Gilman need to understand about himself to make the correct decision?
2. How do you think he could figure out who he is in order to make this decision?
3. Which of these opportunities do you think he should take, and which will have the strongest impact on his future? Why?

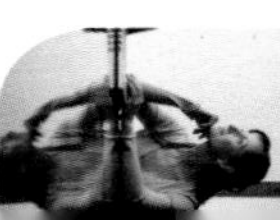

PERSONAL SKILLS LOG

Directions: Fill in the rows below based on what you learned from each part of the chapter that you completed.

	What is my key takeaway or insight from this activity?	What do I personally do well (strength) regarding this activity?	What could I improve (weakness) about myself regarding this activity?	How might I use what I've learned from this activity in the future?
Manager Challenge Incident:				
Discover Yourself Questionnaires:				
Deliberate Practice Exercises:				
In-Class and/or Field Team Exercises:				
Role-Play Exercises:				
Case Incidents:				

PERSONAL SKILLS LOG

REFERENCES

Discover Yourself

1 Questions were drawn from "Johari Window Questionnaire," http://www.austincc.edu/colangelo/1318/johariwindowtest.htm (accessed December 12, 2011) and http://www.indusladies.com/forums/general-discussions/61218-johari-window-questionnaire-included-self.html (accessed December 12, 2011).

2 These questions were adapted from several sources.

3 From MARCIC, Organizational Behavior, 4E. © 1995 Cengage Learning.

4 Based on Robert C. Benfari, *Understanding and Changing Your Management Style* (San Francisco: Jossey-Bass, 1999), pp. 178–183; and M. Rokeach, *Understanding Human Values* (New York: The Free Press, 1979).

Discover Knowledge

5 Coeli Carr, "Executive Life: Redesigning the Management Psyche," *The New York Times*, May 26, 2002, http://www.nytimes.com/2002/05/26/business/executive-life-redesigning-the-management-psyche.html (accessed February 3, 2011).

6 Based on an example in Robert S. Kaplan, "What to Ask the Person in the Mirror," *Harvard Business Review* (January 2007): 86–95.

7 Daniel Gilbert, *Stumbling on Happiness* (New York: Knopf, 2006).

8 These research findings were summarized in Gilbert, *Stumbling on Happiness*, p. 229.

9 William W. George, Peter Sims, Andrew N. MacLean, David Mayer, and Diana Mayer, "Discovering Your Authentic Leadership," *Harvard Business Review* (February 2007): 129–138.

10 Paul Chant, "Is This Guy Mutts Nuts . . . Or a Dog of Awe? Answer June 12, D-Day for Donovan," *The People* (May 30, 2010): 7; Jere Longman, "Donovan Pushes Ahead, Looking Inside," *The New York Times*, May 19, 2010; Nancy Armour, "Top U.S. Soccer Star Finds Peace," *Journal-Gazette*, June 25, 2010; and Des Kelly, "Donovan's Late Show Is a Tear-Jerker as Clinton Joins Party," *Daily Mail*, June 24, 2010.

11 Tricia Bisoux, "What Makes Leaders Great," (interviews with leadership experts), *BizEd* (September–October 2005): 40–45; Warren Bennis, *Why Leaders Can't Lead* (San Francisco: Jossey-Bass, 1989); Daniel Goleman, "What Makes a Leader?" *Harvard Business Review* (November–December 1998): 93ff; and Richard E. Boyatzis, *The Competent Manager: A Model for Effective Performance* (New York: Wiley, 1982).

12 Employee quoted in Stratford Sherman, "How Tomorrow's Best Leaders Are Learning Their Stuff," *Fortune* (November 27, 1995): 90–102.

13 Bennis, *Why Leaders Can't Lead.*

14 This section is based on Scott Williams, "Self-Awareness and Personal Development," *LeaderLetter* Web site, http://www.wright.edu/~scott.williams/LeaderLetter/selfawareness.htm (accessed August 21, 2007); "NHS Leadership Qualities Framework," *National Health Service Institute for Innovation and Improvement*, November 2006, http://www.leadershipqualitiesframework.institute.nhs.uk/portals/0/the_framework.pdf Document1(accessed April 2, 2012); and Richard L. Daft, *The Executive and the Elephant: A Leader's Guide to Building Inner Excellence* (San Francisco: Jossey-Bass, 2010).

15 This example is from Kaplan, "What to Ask the Person in the Mirror."

16 Thanks to Scott Williams, "Self-Awareness and Personal Development," *LeaderLetter* Web site, for this image, http://www.wright.edu/~scott.williams/LeaderLetter/selfawareness.htm (accessed August 21, 2007).

17 Stephen R. Covey, *The Seven Habits of Highly Effective People: Powerful Lessons in Personal Change* (New York: Simon & Schuster, 1989).

18 C. Fletcher and C. Baldry, "A Study of Individual Differences and Self-Awareness in the Context of Multi-Source Feedback," *Journal of Occupational and Organizational Behavior* 73, no. 3 (2000): 303–319.

19 Covey, *The Seven Habits of Highly Effective People*; Robert E. Kelley, *How to Be a Star at Work* (New York: Times Books, 1999); and Daniel Goleman, *Working with Emotional Intelligence* (New York: Bantam Books, 1998).

20 This story is true, but the name has been changed.

21 This discussion is based on Joseph Luft and Harry Ingham, "The Johari Window, A Graphic Model of Interpersonal Awareness," *Proceedings of the Western Training Laboratory in Group Development*, UCLA, 1955; Mike Clayton, "Super Models," *Training Journal* (May 2008): 67; Alan Chapman, "Johari Window," Businessballs Web site, http://www.businessballs.com/johariwindowmodel.htm (accessed May 18, 2009); Duen Hsi Yen, "Johari Window," Noogenesis Web site, http://www.noogenesis.com/game_theory/johari/johari_window.html (accessed May 18, 2009); and Joseph Luft, *Of Human Interaction* (Palo Alto, CA: National Press, 1969).

22 Ellen McGirt, "American Idol: An Intimate Portrait of the World's Most Famous CEO," *Fast Company* (April 2012): 92–100.

23 See J. M. Digman, "Personality Structure: Emergence of the Five-Factor Model," *Annual Review of Psychology* 41 (1990): 417–440; Murray R. Barrick and Michael K. Mount, "The Big Five Personality Dimensions and Job Performance: A Meta-Analysis," *Personnel Psychology* 44, no. 1 (Spring 1991): 1–26; M. R. Barrick and M. K. Mount, "Autonomy as a Moderator of the Relationships Between the Big Five Personality Dimensions and Job Performance," *Journal of Applied Psychology* (February 1993): 111–118; J. S. Wiggins and A. L. Pincus, "Personality: Structure and Assessment," *Annual Review of Psychology* 43 (1992): 473–504; and J. F. Salgado, "The Five-Factor Model of Personality and Job Performance in the European Community," *Journal of Applied Psychology* 82, no. 1 (1997): 30–43.

24 Deniz Ones and Stephan Dilchert, "How Special Are Executives?" *Industrial and Organizational Psychology* (2009), reported in Adam M. Grant, Francesca Gino, and David A. Hoffman, "The Hidden Advantages of Quiet Bosses," *Harvard Business Review* (December 2010): 28ff.

25 Grant et al, "The Hidden Advantages of Quiet Bosses."

26 G. M. Hurtz and J. J. Donovan, "Personality and Job Performance: The Big 5 Revisited," *Journal of Applied Psychology* 85 (2002): 869–879.

27 Barrick and Mount, "The Big Five Personality Dimensions and Job Performance: A Meta-Analysis"; Salgado, "The Five-Factor Model of Personality and Job Performance in the European Community"; and Hurtz and Donovan, "Personality and Job Performance: The Big 5 Revisited."

28 Tim Sanders, *The Likeability Factor* (New York: Three Rivers Press, 2005); Anthony J. Mayo and Nitin Nohria, "Double-Edged Sword," *People Management* (October 27, 2005); and Joseph Nocera, "In Business, Tough Guys Finish Last," *The New York Times* (June 18, 2005).

29 Barbara Griffin and Beryl Hesketh, "Are Conscientious Workers Adaptable?" *Australian Journal of Management* 30, no. 2 (December 2005): 245–259.

30 T. J. Bouchard, "Genetic Influence on Human Psychological Traits: A Survey," *Current Directions in Psychological Science* 13 (2004): 148–151; R. Plomin and D. Daniels, "Why Are Children in the Same Family So Different from One Another?" *Behavioral and Brain Sciences* 10 (1987): 1–60; and G. Marcus, *The Birth of the Mind* (New York: Basic Books, 2004).

31 S. F. Maddi, *Personality Theories: A Comparative Analysis* (Homewood, IL: Richard D. Irwin, 1980); and Marcus, *The Birth of the Mind*.

32 M. Snyder, *Public Appearances, Private Realities: The Psychology of Self-Monitoring* (New York: Freeman, 1987).

33 Henry Mintzberg, "Planning on the Left Side and Managing on the Right," *Harvard Business Review* (July–August 1976): 49–57; Richard Restak, "The Hemispheres of the Brain Have Minds of Their Own," *The New York Times* (January 25, 1976); and Robert Ornstein, *The Psychology of Consciousness* (San Francisco: W. H. Freeman, 1975).

34 This discussion is based on Ned Herrmann, *The Whole Brain Business Book* (New York: McGraw-Hill, 1996).

35 Herrmann, *The Whole Brain Business Book*, p. 179.

36 Nancy Hass, "Earning Her Stripes," *The Wall Street Journal Magazine*, September 9, 2010, http://magazine.wsj.com/features/the-big-interview/earning-her-strips/ (accessed February 10, 2011).

37 Herrmann, *The Whole Brain Business Book*, p. 179.

38 C. G. Jung, *Psychological Types; or The Psychology of Individualism*, trans. H. Godwin Baynes, (New York: Harcourt Brace and Company, 1923).

39 Isabel Briggs Myers with Peter B. Myers, *Gifts Differing: Understanding Personality Type*, (Mountain View, CA: Davies-Black Publishing, 1980); Isabel Briggs Myers, Mary H. McCaulley, Naomi L. Quenk, and Allen L. Hammer, *MBTI Manual: A Guide to the Development and Use of the Myers Briggs Type Indicator*, 3rd ed. (Palo Alto, CA: Consulting Psychologists Press, 1998); Rowan Bayne, *Psychological Types at Work: An MBTI Perspective* (London: Thomson Learning, 2004); Otto Kroeger and Janet M. Thuesen, *Type Talk* (New York: Delacorte Press, 1988); and "Conference Proceedings," The Myers–Briggs Type Indicator and Leadership: An International Research Conference, University of Maryland, College Park, MD (January 12–14, 1994).

40 Jennifer Overbo, "Using Myers–Briggs Personality Type to Create a Culture Adapted to the New Century," *T & D* (February 2010): 70.

41 Carr, "Executive Life: Redesigning the Management Psyche."

42 Del Jones, "Not All Successful CEOs Are Extroverts," *USA Today* (June 6, 2006); and Deniz Ones and Stephan Dilchert, "How Special Are Executives?" *Industrial and Organizational Psychology* (2009), reported in Adam M. Grant, Francesca Gino, and David A. Hoffman, "The Hidden Advantages of Quiet Bosses," *Harvard Business Review* (December 2010).

43 Stephanie Gruner, "Our Company, Ourselves," *Inc.* (April 1998): 127–128.

44 "Self-Awareness a Good Place for Leaders to Start" (an interview with Esa Heiskanen), *The Bangkok Post* (September 14, 2009); and "Glow Group: Our Mission, Vision, and Culture," The Glow Group Web site, http://www.glow.co.th/01-OurMission-Vision-culture.aspx?language=EN (accessed February 15, 2011).

45 These questions are suggested by Kathy Whitmire, "Leading Through Shared Values," *Leader to Leader* (Summer 2005): 48–54.

46 Milton Rokeach, *The Nature of Human Values* (New York: The Free Press, 1973); E. C. Ravlin and B. M. Meglino, "Effects of Values on Perception and Decision Making: A Study of Alternative Work Value Measures," *Journal of Applied Psychology* 72 (1987): 666–673; and Robert C. Benfari, *Understanding and Changing Your Management Style* (San Francisco: Jossey-Bass, 1999).

47 Rokeach, *The Nature of Human Values*.

48 *Ibid.*, and M. Rokeach, *Understanding Human Values* (New York: The Free Press, 1979).

49 Edward F. Murphy, Jr., Jane Whitney Gibson, and Regina A. Greenwood, "Analyzing Generational Values Among Managers and Non-Managers for Sustainable Organizational Effectivenss," *SAM Advanced Management Journal* (Winter 2010): 33–55.

50 *Ibid.*

51 Whitmire, "Leading Through Shared Values"; Michael W. Grojean, Christian J. Resick, Marcus W. Dickson, and D. Brent Smith, "Leaders, Values, and Organizational Climate: Examining Leadership Strategies for Establishing an Organizational Climate Regarding Ethics," *Journal of Business Ethics* 55 (2004): 223–241; and Bob Rue, "Values-Based Leadership," *Program Manager* (July–August 2001): 12–16.

52 James O' Toole, *Leading Change: The Argument for Values-Based Leadership* (New York: Ballantine, 1996); and Susan Smith Kuczmarski and Thomas D. Kuczmarski, *Values-Based Leadership* (Englewood Cliffs, N.J: Prentice Hall, 1995).

53 Whitmire, "Leading Through Shared Values."

54 Based on Rob Lebow and William L. Simon, *Lasting Change; The Shared Values Process That Makes Companies Great* (New York: Van Nostrand Reinhold, 1997), p. 64; and Bob McDonald, "Values-Based Leaders," *Leadership Excellence* (January 2010): 6–7.

55 Noel M. Tichy and Warren G. Bennis, "Managing the Tough Call: Great Leaders Know When Their Values Are on the Line," *Inc.* (November 2007): 36–38.

56 Based on a discussion in Rowena Crosbie, "Learning the Soft Skills of Leadership," *Industrial and Commercial Training* 37, no. 1 (2005): 45–51.

CHAPTER 3

Managing Yourself to Get Things Done

Chapter Outline

RYAN LASH

MANAGER CHALLENGE

VIDEO INCIDENT: WASTED TIME?

Caffeine and Crullers sales manager Jason Wong is ready to explode. He just can't take another meeting where everyone goes on and on and on and nothing gets done. The other managers seem to enjoy talking every single tiny issue to death, looking at every angle and then re-examining each one again and again. Why do they avoid taking action? It's no wonder sales aren't increasing as much as the projections. If only director of operations Carrie Fishman and CFO Carlos Hernandez would agree to move forward on *anything*, it would be a huge improvement. And general manager Jane Sutton seems to enjoy listening to all this verbal rattling. Jason has talked to her three times about this already, but she never does anything about it. He's about to go in to a meeting with her to complain—again.

Initial Thoughts

1. **If you were Jason's boss, Jane Sutton, how would you plan to handle Jason's complaint?**

2. **How do you explain why someone like Jason Wong prefers quick action and others such as Fishman or Hernandez tend to want more discussion and to move forward more slowly?**

Your instructor may ask you to be part of a role play based on the "Wasted Time?" incident.

DISCOVER YOURSELF

For those students using CourseMate or CengageNOW, you can access the Daft/Marcic Assessment Library to take the questionnaires online and view dynamically updated comparative data.

Questionnaire 1[1]

Instructions: Rate how accurately each statement describes you based on whether the statement is clearly true or accurate, clearly false or inaccurate, or in the middle as somewhat true and somewhat false. There are no right or wrong answers, so answer honestly to receive accurate feedback.

Part A

	True	Somewhat	False
1. I always seem to buy gifts at the last minute.	○	○	○
2. I am easily pulled away to other things (e.g. watching TV) before starting on work I have to do.	○	○	○
3. I often say to myself, "I'll do it later."	○	○	○
4. I can almost always find a good reason to put off doing something I don't enjoy.	○	○	○
5. When planning a party or event, I make the arrangements well in advance.	○	○	○

Total Score Part A ________. (Sum questions 1–4, giving 3 points for each True, 2 points for each Somewhat, and 1 point for each False. Reverse the score for question 5, with 1 point for True, 2 for Somewhat, and 3 for False; add it to the total for questions 1–4.)

Part B

	True	Somewhat	False
6. I am very aware of my thoughts.	○	○	○
7. When I am reading, I stop occasionally to think about what it means.	○	○	○
8. When I am working on a topic, I try to see in my mind how it fits with other topics.	○	○	○
9. I ask myself questions about how I am doing something.	○	○	○
10. I think about my assumptions when something is not clear.	○	○	○

Total Score Part B ________. (Sum questions 6–10, giving 3 points for each True, 2 points for each Somewhat, and 1 point for each False.)

Part C

	True	Somewhat	False
11. I often use reminders to help me remember things I need to do.	○	○	○
12. I often mentally rehearse an important task before I actually do it.	○	○	○

	True	Somewhat	False
13. I focus my thinking on the pleasant rather than on the unpleasant things about my work.	○	○	○
14. I visualize images of myself successfully performing a task I don't like.	○	○	○
15. I give myself pep talks to convince myself I can do a difficult task.	○	○	○

Total Score Part C ________. (Sum questions 11–15, giving 3 points for each True, 2 points for each Somewhat, and 1 point for each False.) Go to page 124 to interpret your scores.

Questionnaire 2[2]

Instructions: Think about how you normally handle tasks during a typical day at work or school. Indicate your responses to the statements below based on whether they are True, Somewhat, or False for you. There are no right or wrong answers, so answer honestly.

Part A

	True	Somewhat	False
1. In a typical day, most things I do have a clear purpose.	○	○	○
2. I always do priority tasks first.	○	○	○
3. I am good at planning a daily and weekly schedule.	○	○	○
4. I never lose sight of my longer-term objectives.	○	○	○
5. Many activities I do during the day don't have a specific goal.	○	○	○

Total Score Part A ________. (Sum questions 1–4, giving 3 points for each True, 2 points for each Somewhat, and 1 point for each False. Reverse the score for question 5, with 1 point for True, 2 points for Somewhat, and 3 points for False; add it to the total for questions 1–4.)

Part B

	True	Somewhat	False
6. I frequently take on too many tasks.	○	○	○
7. I spend too much time on enjoyable but unimportant activities.	○	○	○
8. I feel that I am in excellent control of my time.	○	○	○
9. Frequently during the day, I am not sure what to do next.	○	○	○
10. There is little room for improvement in the way I manage my time.	○	○	○

Total Score Part B ________. (Sum questions 6, 7, and 9, giving 3 points for each True, 2 points for each Somewhat, and 1 point for each False. Reverse the score for questions 8 and 10, with 1 point for each True, 2 points for each Somewhat, and 3 points for each False; add this to the total.)

Part C

	True	Somewhat	False
11. I keep a schedule for events, meetings, and deadlines.	○	○	○
12. My workspace and paperwork are well organized.	○	○	○
13. I am good at record keeping.	○	○	○
14. I make good use of waiting time.	○	○	○
15. I am always looking for ways to increase task efficiency.	○	○	○

Total Score Part C ________. (Sum questions 11–15, giving 3 points for each True, 2 points for each Somewhat, and 1 point for each False.) Go to page 130 to interpret your scores.

Questionnaire 3[3]

Instructions: Respond to the 20 statements below based on the specific instructions in each part. There are no right or wrong answers, so answer honestly for accurate feedback.

Part A

Think about how you normally act or feel during a typical day for you, and then respond to the statements below (1–5) based on whether they are True, Somewhat, or False for you.

	True	Somewhat	False
1. I do not like to wait for other people to complete their work before I can proceed with my own.	○	○	○
2. I hate to wait in most lines.	○	○	○
3. It seems like I am always in a rush.	○	○	○
4. I interrupt if someone is slow to get to the point.	○	○	○
5. I am slow and deliberate in my work.	○	○	○

Total Score Part A ________. (Sum questions 1–4, giving 3 points for each True, 2 points for each Somewhat, and 1 point for each False. Reverse the score for question 5, with 1 point for True, 2 points for Somewhat, and 3 points for False; add this to the total.)

Part B

Indicate how well each of the following statements (6–10) describes you:

6. Always rushed.	○	○	○
7. Impatient while waiting.	○	○	○
8. Eat and walk fast.	○	○	○
9. Few outside interests.	○	○	○
10. Feel competitive during sports and games.	○	○	○

Total Score Part B ________. (Sum questions 6–10, giving 3 points for each True, 2 points for each Somewhat, and 1 point for each False.)

Part C

Thinking about a typical day for you *over the last month*, how often was each statement below (11–15) true of your life?

	Seldom	Occasionally	Frequently
11. I felt there was not enough time to complete my daily tasks.	○	○	○
12. I felt pressure from others.	○	○	○
13. I had no time to relax.	○	○	○
14. I felt "stressed out."	○	○	○
15. I had to deal with irritating life hassles.	○	○	○

Total Score Part C ______. (Sum questions 11–15, giving 3 points for each Frequently, 2 points for each Occasionally, and 1 point for each Seldom.)

Part D

In the last month, how often was each statement below (16–20) true of your own life?

	Seldom	Occasionally	Frequently
16. I was able to cope very well with unexpected problems.	○	○	○
17. I felt confident in my ability to handle personal problems.	○	○	○
18. I felt I was on top of things.	○	○	○
19. I could rely on others to help me when things got tough.	○	○	○
20. I could rely on others to share their experiences about concerns similar to mine.	○	○	○

Total Score Part D ______. (Sum questions 16–20, giving 3 points for each Frequently, 2 points for each Occasionally, and 1 point for each Seldom.) Go to page 136 to interpret your scores.

GO ONLINE to find additional questionnaires at www.cengagebrain.com, search for Daft/Marcic Building Management Skills 1e, click on Free Online Resources, click on Additional Self-Assessments.

- Impulsiveness
- Resilience

DISCOVER YOURSELF

SHUTTERSTOCK #53973379

Chapter 3: Managing Yourself to Get Things Done

DISCOVER KNOWLEDGE

Andrew Korba was tired. He knew managers worked long hours, but this was ridiculous—70-plus hours a week and he still couldn't get caught up. He found himself rushing from one task to another and never completing any of them. Andrew became a manager because he really enjoyed leading people and helping them do their best, but his relationships with employees were souring because he never seemed to have time for them anymore. One day an old college mentor suggested over lunch that Andrew track how he managed his time hour-by-hour for a week. "I don't even have time for this lunch," Andrew snapped. "How am I supposed to find time to write down everything I do for a week?" Back at the office, though, Andrew decided anything was worth a try to gain some control over his life.

A week later, as Andrew looked over the results of his time-keeping, he immediately saw how much time he wasted because of disorganization. Moreover, he was shocked to see how much time he was spending on routine matters that could easily be delegated. Andrew began wondering what other ideas might help him make conscious, wise decisions about how to allocate his time.[4]

As a student, you probably notice that on any given day there are multiple demands on your time. How do you decide what to do and when to do it? Do you end the day having accomplished everything you wanted to do? Jeff Immelt, CEO of General Electric, once said "there are 24 hours in a day, and you can use all of them."[5] Indeed, each of us has the same amount of time, but some people accomplish significant results while others never seem to get anything done.

Time is a manager's most valuable resource, and one characteristic that identifies successful managers is that they know how to use time effectively to accomplish the important things first and the less important things later.[6] **Time management** refers to using techniques that enable you to get more done in less time and with better results, be more relaxed, and have more time to enjoy your work and your life. Time management means *managing yourself* so that you are more productive and can accomplish the things you need or want to accomplish. **Self-management** is the ability to engage in self-regulating thoughts and behavior to handle difficult or challenging situations. Yet all of us have patterns of habit and behavior that are hard to change, along with various impulses, desires, and fears that may make it hard to manage ourselves toward more efficient behavior.

We can expect that Andrew Korba, the manager described in the opening example, may have a hard time changing himself into a well-organized person who wastes little time unless he is skilled at self-management. People high in self-management are able to take control of their behaviors and direct themselves to achieve goals.[7]

HIGHER-ORDER THINKING

Early in his management career, Richard Anderson, now CEO of Delta Airlines, would lose his temper when projects weren't moving as fast as he thought they should. He knew losing his temper wasn't a productive way to motivate people, but still he did it, until he taught himself how to be more patient. Similarly, Carol Bartz, former CEO of Yahoo, had a bad habit of interrupting people before they finished a question. Bartz says she "had to be trained to take a breath . . . I have to shut up."[8]

Many managers know the right thing to do but have a hard time doing it. One described it like this: "It was like getting in my car to go east and the car insisted on going west, and I couldn't do anything about it."[9] When one researcher asked 200 CEOs how much time they spent doing the things they knew would bring the best results to their organizations, he found that the average amount of time was only 21 percent.[10] It is not surprising that many of us, like these CEOs, sometimes have trouble doing what we know we should.

Why Can't We Follow Our Good Intentions?

How can you take more control to change or manage yourself when needed? One idea is to engage your "new brain" to manage your "old brain," as shown in Exhibit 3.1.[11] Psychologists and neuroscientists suggest

Exhibit 3.1 Use Your New Brain to Manage the Old Brain

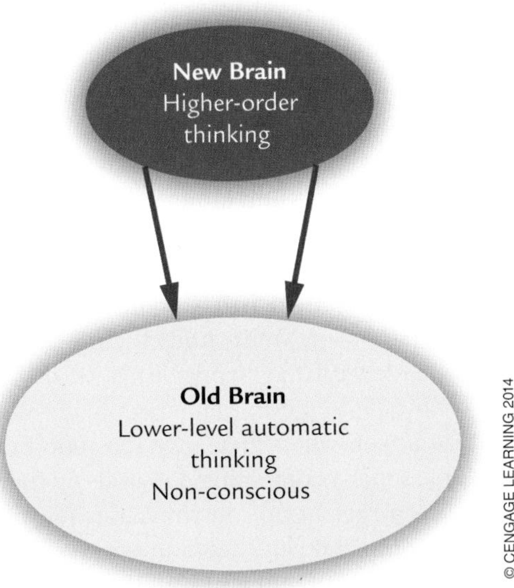

Strengthen Your New Brain: Techniques for building up the new brain to influence old brain behavior can be found in Richard L. Daft, ***The Executive and the Elephant: A Leader's Guide to Building Inner Excellence*** (San Francisco: Jossey-Bass, 2010).

that the brain has two parts, and the two parts are sometimes in conflict.[12] There is a habitual, automatic, stimulus-driven part of the brain, which we refer to as the "old brain" since it is wired into our systems after a lifetime of conditioning. This part of the brain represents our unconscious impulses, fears, emotional drives, and lifelong habits. The other part, the "new brain," represents our intentional, rational, and thoughtful mind. This is the area in which we make a conscious *choice* of how to behave rather than react to a situation out of fear, desire, or other strong emotions.

The old brain is associated with lower-level, automatic thinking. It has evolved as a marvelous internal system that can guide us safely through each day, usually without mishap. It handles memory, language, perception, communication, and other vital information processing. We couldn't live without it. The new brain is associated with higher-order thinking. It can see the big picture and take a conscious and balanced approach to determining the best action. This higher-order thinking process has been called **metacognition**, which is the ability to observe and think about your own thinking and assert some control over your cognitive processes. A well-developed higher-order thinking process provides the self-awareness and self-discipline a manager needs to establish goals, plan and set priorities, see a big picture of how elements fit together, get organized, take initiative, and restrain inappropriate emotions and distractions to persevere and complete a project.

Bring Your Brain into Balance

Psychology has abundant evidence that the vast majority of our thoughts, perceptions, desires, emotions, judgments, and behaviors are the result of unconscious and automatic processes—our "old brain." An automatic thought or behavior reaction to an event or a situation occurs without any conscious intention. One example is the feeling of stage fright that pops up automatically when a person has to give a speech. Another is the annoyance that many people experience when waiting in a slow line or waiting for a Web page to open, or when others behave "improperly." Feelings such as surprise, pleasure, anger, sadness, or fear typically arise within you in automatic response to a specific situation rather than because you consciously force that feeling into existence.

Much of the time, our intentions and our habitual behavior are in alignment. The problem arises when the automatic system is not in alignment with what we intend to do or with what others need and want from us as managers. For example, Barry Ginnetti, now president of GMR Group, a health-care marketing company, used to wonder why he got so little response and participation from coworkers when he led meetings. "People would just hold back and not say anything," Ginnetti recalls, and he would think "'Why are you just sitting there?'" A leadership coach helped Ginnetti realize that his loud, aggressive style was intimidating people. Now, he makes a conscious effort to speak more softly, ask questions, encourage others, and listen. But it isn't easy. Ginnetti grew up in a household where he had to fight for attention—the one who could speak the loudest would be heard. Those patterns of his "old brain" tend to come back unless he intentionally engages the higher-order thinking processes of his "new brain."[13]

When people want to change, their ability to do so largely depends on whether the new brain can gain some control over the automatic habit patterns of the old brain.

For some managers, time management is one area in which the old brain tends to rule. Recall the CEOs who say they spend only 21 percent of their time doing the things that would bring the best results for their companies. "Unfortunately," says the consultant who

DISCOVER KNOWLEDGE

did the survey, "I see CEOs consistently allowing the most important things to fall off their plates and completing all the unnecessary things."[14] Poor time management may indicate poor self-management skills that can sidetrack even the most enthusiastic and competent individual. Fortunately, people can learn to use their higher-order thinking to manage themselves and their time by following some fundamental principles.

DISCOVER YOURSELF

Interpret Your Score: Self-Management (Questionnaire 1)

Your three scores reflect your degree of self-management as described in the chapter. Part A measures procrastination, for which a high score means a lower level of deliberate self-management. Comparative data for **Procrastination** (Part A): Thirty-person Mean score = 10.6; Top Quartile = 12–15; Bottom Quartile = 5–9. Part B reflects the use of metacognition and self-reflection to manage your activities. Comparative data for **Metacognition and Self-Reflection** (Part B): Mean = 12.8; Top Quartile = 15–15; Bottom Quartile = 9–11. Part C measures the extent to which you use the higher consciousness in your "new brain" to intentionally direct your thinking and behavior. Higher scores for Parts B and C are associated with more effective self-management. Comparative data for **Higher Cognition** (Part C): Mean = 12.1; Top Quartile = 14–15; Bottom Quartile = 9–10. How do you feel about your ability to manage yourself? What changes would you like to make? CNOW and CourseMate users can access dynamically updated comparative data through www.cengagebrain.com.

© CENGAGE LEARNING 2014

A BOTTOM-UP APPROACH TO GETTING THINGS UNDER CONTROL

Theresa Daytner owns a successful and busy construction company in Baltimore. She's also a mother of six who lifts weights and mountain bikes, plans surprise parties, and attends a regular book club meeting. Daytner gets so much accomplished on a regular basis that one writer said "I'm jealous that her week beats my month." Daytner was profiled in the book *168 Hours: You Have More Time Than You Think*.[15] The book profiles a number of successful people who seem to have the time management magic bullet. Unfortunately, those people are in the minority, as reflected in the hundreds of books and thousands of articles, blogs, and seminars devoted to the subject of how to manage that crucial, nonrenewable resource—time.

Even the best managers (or the most organized students) can sometimes find themselves feeling overwhelmed, with too many things to do and not enough time to do them. Many people get stuck and can't take action when they have too much on their minds or too many competing demands on their time. How can you "get a grip" on yourself when you have too much to do and can't seem to get any of it done? One approach is to apply a bottom-up strategy that starts by analyzing the details of what you are actually doing right now, and then building a system to manage those activities.

Basic Principles for Self-Management

There are three basic principles[16] that circumscribe how to effectively manage your many big and small commitments so that you can get them accomplished:

- **Clarity of mind.** The first principle is that, if you're carrying too much around in your head, your mind can't be clear. If your mind isn't clear, you can't focus. If you can't focus, you can't get anything done. Thus, anything you consider unfinished needs to be placed in some kind of trusted system *outside* of your head.
- **Clarity of objectives.** Second, you have to be clear about exactly what you need to do and decide the steps to take toward accomplishing it.
- **An organized system.** Third, once you've decided the actions you need to take, you need to keep reminders in a well-organized system.

By building a self-management approach based on these three principles—clarity of mind, clarity of objectives, and a system of organized reminders—you can get unstuck and make measurable progress toward achieving all the things you need to do.

A Step-by-Step Guide to Self-Management

Many people don't realize they waste at least an hour of a typical workday simply because they are unorganized.[17] You can gain better control of your life and the many things you have to do by mastering some simple but powerful steps.[18] Exhibit 3.2 summarizes these five steps, and each is described below.

1. Empty Your Head. If you've ever cleaned out an overstuffed garage, basement, or even a closet, you probably gained control over the mess by separating things into various piles or containers until you could decide what to do with them. The same principle can be applied to organizing the things you have to do. That is, in order to clear your mind, you first have to see all the many things weighing on it. The first step, therefore, is to *collect* all the activities, duties, tasks, or commitments that are demanding part of your attention. The idea is to put everything into a concrete system that is outside of your head—this includes things both personal and work-related, large and small, minor or highly important. It might include letters that need to be answered, magazines or journals that need to be read, birthday presents that need to be bought, reports that need to be written, or work projects that need to be completed.

To capture all this "stuff," imagine putting it into various buckets that can hold it until you have a few moments to decide what to do with it. There are numerous tools that can serve as your buckets, including physical in-baskets for holding mail, journals, memos, and phone slips; notebooks or legal pads for writing down things to do; digital recorders for recording things you need to remember; or various computer and wireless devices for electronic note-taking. Make one bucket a part of your everyday life, such as a notepad or a handheld device, so that anytime, anywhere you can put things into it and out of your mind.

Exhibit 3.2 Follow the Steps to Get Organized

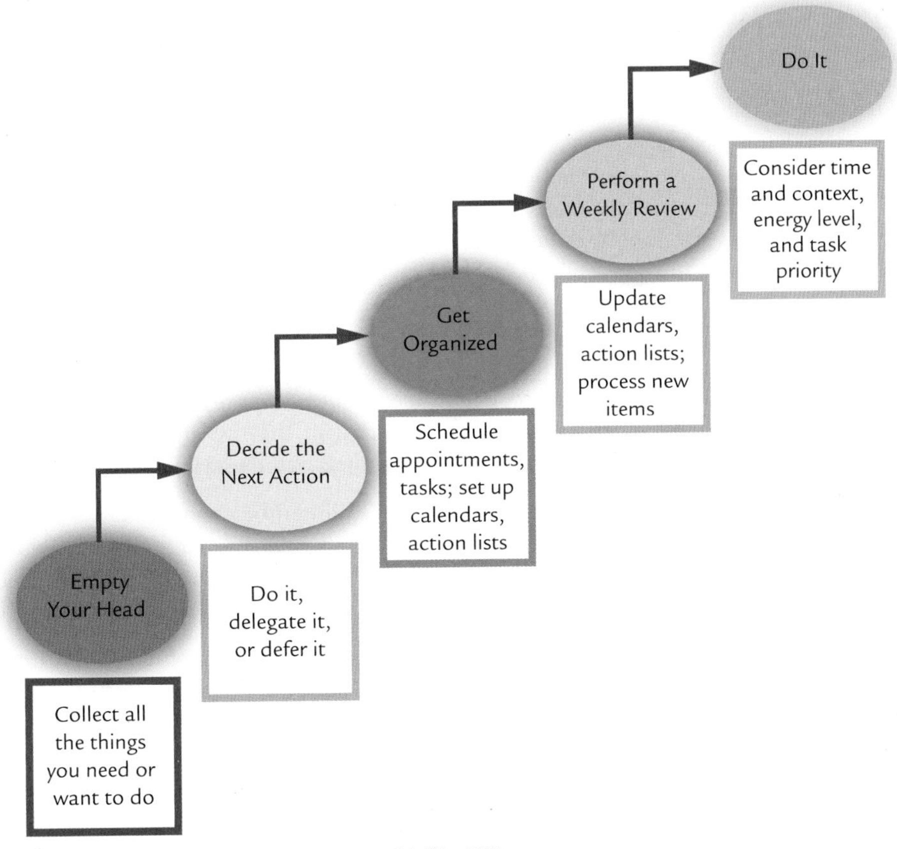

Source: Based on David Allen, *Getting Things Done: The Art of Stress-Free Productivity* (New York: Viking, 2001).

However, remember to keep the number of buckets to a minimum; otherwise, you'll still feel scattered and overwhelmed. You also have to empty the buckets on a regular basis, which leads to the next step.

2. Decide the Next Action. For each item in your bucket, decide the real, specific, physical action you need to take next. For example, if you have a project meeting on Friday, your next action might be to draft thoughts and ideas you want to share with the team. Then, you have three options:

- ***Do It.*** Follow the two-minute rule: If something can be done in less than two minutes, do it now. Immediately trash any items you find in your bucket that require no action and are of no importance. For items that are of potential use in the future, file them in a system for reference material.
- ***Delegate It.*** Ask yourself if you're the right person to handle a task. If something can be done as well by someone else, delegate it.
- ***Defer It.*** If something will take longer than two minutes but cannot be delegated to someone else, you'll have to defer it. These things go into an incubation or tickler file, which you will review regularly and perhaps schedule a specific time for their completion.

3. Get Organized. The third step is to organize all the items you've deferred. At this stage, schedule any appointments you identified as "next actions" and record these on whatever calendar you check daily. Also record on your calendar any items that have to be done on a specific day or time. You can assign yourself a specific date in the future to perform certain tasks that are in your incubation or tickler file.

For all other items, keep a list of "Next Actions," either on paper on in a portable device that you will have with you at all times so that you can take action when and where you have the time to do so. This can be either on a single list or in categories.

4. Perform a Weekly Review. Once a week, review your complete Next Actions list and your calendar for the coming week. Scan the entire list of outstanding projects and actions needed so that you can make efficient choices about using your time. This weekly review is critical, because it keeps your mind from taking back the job of trying to hold and remember everything. The weekly review is also the time to "put your house in order" by collecting, processing, and organizing new items. Thus, during the weekly review, you'll take four actions: (1) collect and process all the new stuff; (2) review your entire system; (3) update your lists; and (4) get clear, up-to-date, and complete about what needs to be done next.

5. Now Do It. Once you have collected, processed, organized, and reviewed your current commitments, you'll have a better sense of what needs to be done, enabling you to make better choices about how to use your time. Your intuition and your understanding of yourself can help you in deciding what to do when.

This bottom-up approach to self-management can help you get a handle on all the various things you have to do and approach them in a systematic way with a clear mind. If you follow it, you'll find yourself getting more accomplished with less stress—and with fewer things falling between the cracks.

SOME TRIED-AND-TRUE TIME MANAGEMENT TECHNIQUES

FedEx drivers know the power of prioritizing. When a *Fortune* magazine writer rode with Nicky Cava to get a glimpse of how FedEx operates, he noticed that Cava seemed to circle the same blocks over and over. It made sense later on, when Cava explained that he carefully calculated his route so that he got the priority packages delivered on time and still had plenty of time to deliver all of his standard packages by the end of the workday. Scheduling and acting based on priorities ensures that FedEx gets all its packages delivered right on time.[19]

Prioritizing tasks is one of many classic techniques that can help you eliminate major time-wasters in your daily routines.[20] You can pick and choose the techniques that work for you, and these can be combined with the overall self-management approaches described in the previous section.

1. Remember Your ABCs. This is a good system for prioritizing tasks or activities. If you have a list of things to do, such your list of "Next Actions" or a daily "To Do" list, rank the items by A, B, C, D, or E:

- An "A" item is something highly important. It *must* be done or you'll face serious consequences. For more than one "A" item, you can further rank them as A-1, A-2, etc. An example of an "A" item would be finishing a report for tonight's board meeting.
- A "B" item is next in importance. This is a *should do*, but consequences will be minor if you don't get it done.

- "C" items are things that would be nice to get done but there are no consequences at all if you don't accomplish them. These items might include things such as having lunch with an old friend or stopping by the Redbox kiosk for some DVDs on the way home.
- "D" items are tasks that you can delegate to someone else. If you haven't already delegated tasks based on the bottom-up system described above, here's the time to identify tasks you can delegate so that you can free up more time for "A"-level tasks that only you can do.
- An "E" task is something that you can eliminate altogether. Many of us still have tasks on our lists that we realize are no longer necessary.

If you use the ABCDE system, you'll be surprised how something so simple can be so effective. Do it on paper or in a computer program so you can physically place a letter ranking by each item on your list. Then, you'll have to discipline yourself to do the "A" tasks first.

2. Follow the 80/20 Rule. Sometimes called Pareto's Law, the 80/20 rule holds that 80 percent of sales come from 20 percent of customers, 80 percent of sick leave is used by 20 percent of employees, 80 percent of revenues come from 20 percent of products or services, and so forth. The ratio may not be exact, but this principle generally holds true.

Entrepreneur and author Timothy Ferriss says learning about Pareto's Law changed his life. Ferriss was working 15-hour days and was always exhausted. That changed when he realized that only five of his 120 customers were generating 95 percent of his revenues. He reorganized his time to focus on those customers, while also striving to build new business.[21] Applying Pareto's Law to time management suggests that 20 percent of your activities and effort produce 80 percent of results. That means, if you have ten items on your "To Do" list, it's likely that two of those items will turn out to produce more value than the other eight put together. If you can identify the 20 percent of your items that will produce the maximum 80 percent of value, you'll know better where to invest your time.

3. Do a Daily Review and Look-Ahead. Management coach Leslie Malin takes 15 minutes at the end of every day to review what she's accomplished and what needs to be done the following day. Malin says it enables her to close the day so she can enjoy her evening and begin the next day productively.[22] This is a powerful

DISCOVER KNOWLEDGE

What's Your Problem?

Q: I got promoted five months ago to a management position, and I can't seem to catch my breath. Every day I fall further and further behind. There is so much work to do. And when I complete one task, to my boss's delight, he piles more on me. Then I get put on one team after another representing my group—more work. Everyone says I have great analytic ability, but these days I can barely think. People tell me to write a list for each day, but I never complete all the items. I don't even have time to go to the gym anymore and I've gained ten pounds. Ugh!

A: First, no one completes all the items on a day's list. You are stressed out not only because you have a lot of work, but your relative inexperience means you are still learning and tasks probably take you longer. Also, you seem to be doing everything as if it were all of the same importance. It's not! Write on your calendar 30 minutes for planning. Close your door, do not answer the phone, do not check the Internet or tweet—no distractions. List everything you have to do in the next week. Put the items into five lists. "A" items are highly important and you will suffer serious consequences if you don't complete them; "B" items are things you *should* do, with minor consequences if they're not done; "C" items are things that no one will notice much; "D" items are things you should delegate; and "E" items are things you can just forget about. Assign as much as you can to your "C," "D," and "E" lists. Then, spend the next three days doing ONLY "A" items or perhaps an occasional "B" but nothing else, except to delegate those "D's." Let yourself relax and flow into your work. You will be surprised how much you get done and how calm you'll be. Keep it up and watch that ten pounds disappear.

© CENGAGE LEARNING 2014

technique for managing yourself and your time. Spend 10 to 15 minutes each evening reviewing the day and then thinking ahead to the next day. Write down the specific items you want to accomplish and the actions that will achieve them. Having a plan enables you to get a jump on your workday. Some experts propose that every minute spent in planning saves ten minutes in execution.[23]

4. Do One Thing at a Time. Multitasking has become the motto of the early 21st century, but too much multitasking is a time waster. Research has shown that multitasking *reduces* rather than enhances productivity. Switching between tasks eats up time, and the more complex the tasks, the more time is wasted. The authors of one study suggest that an inability to focus on one thing at a time could reduce efficiency by 20 to 40 percent.[24] People who multitask get less done than those who focus on one activity at a time. Even for those whose job requires numerous brief activities, the ability to concentrate fully on each one (sometimes called *spotlighting*) saves time. Give each task your full attention and you'll get more done.

5. Keep a To-Do List. If you don't use any other system for keeping track of your responsibilities and commitments, at the very least you should maintain a "To Do" list that identifies all the things you need to do during the day. The more detailed the list, the better it will help keep you on track. Many people use digital organizers or PDAs that automatically sort items so that the current day's tasks float to the top. Others prefer talking into a tape recorder, using pen and paper, or using computer-based organizing programs.

One survey found that 95 percent of business leaders say they keep some type of "To Do" list. However, the majority admitted that they don't accomplish everything on their list each day.[25] Indeed, the nature of management means that new responsibilities and shifting priorities occur frequently. Nevertheless, it's a fact that people accomplish more with a list than without one. In addition, simply marking items off the list brings a sense of accomplishment that can be highly motivating.

WHAT ABOUT PROCRASTINATION?

Robert Fromberg, the editor-in-chief for *Healthcare Financial Management*, admits it: He's a procrastinator. "Not chronically or for long periods, but when faced with a report to write, I find myself with a sudden need for a snack," says Fromberg.[26] Many people, like Robert Fromberg, put off doing highly important tasks and turn their attention instead to matters such as fixing a snack, cleaning off their desks, answering routine e-mails, catching up on filing, or playing computer games. Psychologists who study procrastination estimate that 80 to 95 percent of college students procrastinate at least sometimes and about half do so routinely. An estimated 15 to 20 percent of adults are habitual procrastinators.[27]

Procrastination refers to a delay in starting or completing an intended task or course of action when the delay may have negative consequences. Each of us may have many things needing to be done, and tasks and activities are delayed for many reasons, but when we put off doing something we *intend* to do, and need to do, and feel bad for not doing it, we are procrastinating.[28]

Why Do We Procrastinate?

People procrastinate for a variety of reasons. For one thing, almost everyone tends to put off things that they find unpleasant. We all prefer to do things we enjoy rather than things we don't, and in almost every job there will be times we have to do things we don't particularly enjoy. Our personal characteristics affect the degree to which we procrastinate as well. People who are impulsive, easily distracted, and have low self-control tend to procrastinate more than those who are conscientious and self-disciplined.

Anxiety Holds Us Back

One of the primary reasons people put things off is because of some degree of anxiety associated with the task. We may not always notice the underlying anxiety, but we will notice our avoidance behavior. For example, one salesman was excellent at keeping in touch with current customers, but he tended to put off his "new contacts" list because he disliked cold calling and had a fear of the rejections he might receive. Even a very mild anxiety can cause us to procrastinate, because our minds tend to exaggerate the negative aspects of any situation. Research has shown that perceived negative stimuli have a bigger impact on people's emotions, cognition, and behavior than do stimuli perceived as positive.[29] **Negativity bias** is the term used in psychology to describe how our minds react more quickly and more strongly to perceived bad things than to good things.[30] Therefore, if there are even

Exhibit 3.3 The Time Management Matrix

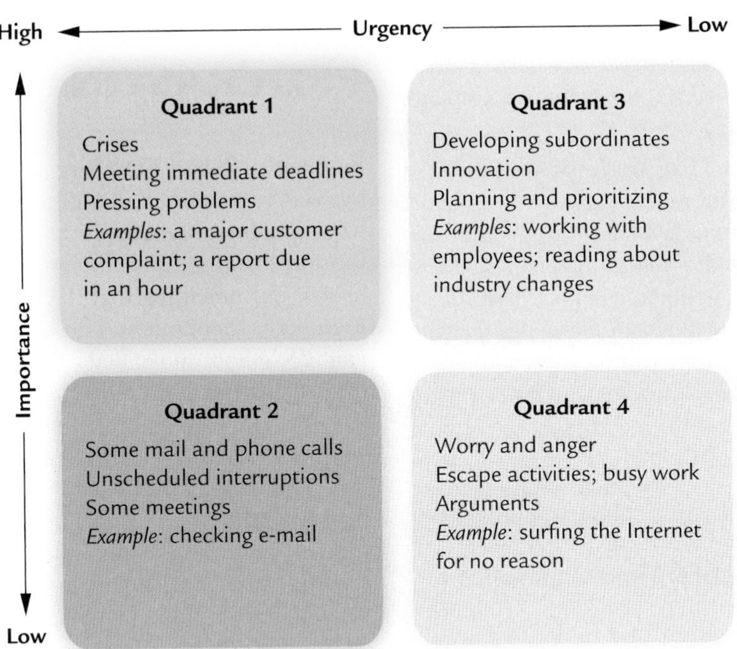

Source: Based on Alan Lakein, *How to Get Control of Your Time and Your Life* (New York: Signet, 1973); Stephen Covey, *The Seven Habits of Highly Effective People* (New York: Simon & Schuster, 1989); and Jeffrey Gitomer, "Difference Between Urgency and Importance," *LI Business News* (December 31, 1999): 21A.

minimal bad feelings associated with a task, your mind will focus on those rather than considering the good feelings that would be associated with getting it done.

We Want to Achieve Perfection

A tendency toward perfectionism can also cause people to procrastinate. A director of an arts agency was invited to write a guest editorial for a prominent newspaper about an issue that was important to him personally and was highly significant to the arts community. He got started on it right away, but he kept procrastinating on finishing it because he wanted it to be "perfect." The director was quite a good writer, but this was his pattern any time he had to write something important. The editorial was never finished, and the issue eventually became old news.

Task Urgency Influences Procrastination

It sounds reasonable that all of us would do our most important tasks first, but that's not what typically happens. We tend to do things that are *urgent* and beg for our immediate attention, whether or not they are *important*.

Exhibit 3.3 illustrates a time management matrix that helps distinguish between what is important and what feels urgent. All of your various tasks and activities can be categorized in terms of their *importance* and their *urgency*.[31] An important activity is one that is tied to your goals, honors your commitments, and accomplishes a significant desired result or achieves a meaningful purpose. An urgent activity is one done in response to something that seems to demand your immediate attention. These activities are typically associated with a need expressed by someone else, or they are related to an uncomfortable problem or situation that requires resolution as soon as possible.

Quadrant 1: Tasks That Are Both Urgent and Important. Some urgent tasks—for example, taking action in response to a fire on the factory floor—are also highly important. Quadrant 1 of Exhibit 3.3 lists examples of these kinds of activities, such as handling crises, responding to pressing problems (a serious customer complaint, for instance), or taking care of a deadline-driven task.

Quadrant 2: Tasks That Are Urgent but Not Important. Many urgent tasks are not really important, such as checking e-mail, responding to routine phone messages, or searching favorite Web sites that may actually distract you from your work. These tasks are shown in Quadrant 2 of the exhibit. The fact is that when something seems to demand our immediate attention, it gets done, even if it interrupts or postpones more important work.

Quadrant 3: Tasks That Are Important but Not Urgent. Many important matters, on the other hand, are not urgent. Quadrant 3 is the crux of the time management problem for many managers because people tend to ignore important matters that do not feel urgent. Things like strategic planning, developing subordinates, improving relationships, and getting organized don't demand immediate attention. Therefore, these matters too easily get shoved aside.

DISCOVER KNOWLEDGE

DISCOVER YOURSELF

Interpret Your Score: Time Management (Questionnaire 2)

Questionnaire 2 pertains to time management. Your score for Part A pertains to purpose. People operating with a clear purpose tend to use time wisely. Comparative data for **Purpose** (Part A): Thirty person Mean score = 12.6; Top Quartile = 14–15; Bottom Quartile = 8–12. Your score for Part B pertains to your perceived control of time. A higher score means you probably take less intentional control over how you spend your time. Comparative data for **Perceived Control of Time** (Part B): Mean = 9.0; Top Quartile = 10–12; Bottom Quartile = 7–8. Part C pertains to some mechanics of good time management. Good physical and mental habits make effective time management much easier. Comparative data for **Mechanics** (Part C): Mean = 13.0; Top Quartile = 15–15; Bottom Quartile = 9–11. How important is good time management to you? How can you specifically improve your time management skills? CNOW and CourseMate users can access dynamically updated comparative data through www.cengagebrain.com.

© CENGAGE LEARNING 2014

Quadrant 4: Tasks That Are Neither Important Nor Urgent. Finally, Quadrant 4 lists activities that are neither urgent nor important. These activities provide little payoff. Everyone needs an escape now and then, but too much time spent in Quadrant 4 is a waste of valuable time.

HOW TO OVERCOME YOUR PROCRASTINATION

Remember Robert Fromberg, the health-care executive who finds himself wanting to fix a snack instead of writing an important report? Fromberg tells the following story to himself and others when faced with an urge to stall on something that needs to be done: One of Fromberg's friends moved from Florida to Chicago for graduate school and ended up staying there. Ten years later, the friend still hadn't gotten his Illinois driver's license. (He would simply renew his Florida license when he visited his mother.) Finally, he decided he had put it off long enough and set off to get the Illinois license he was supposed to get within a few months of a permanent move to the state. Walking to the train station, carrying a black gym bag, he found himself suddenly surrounded by police officers. "Let me see your driver's license," said one. The man handed over the Florida license, but explained that he lived just around the corner. "How long have you lived here?" the officer asked. Blushing and stammering, the man replied, "Um, ten years. I swear I was on my way to get an Illinois license!" The officers, after searching the gym bag, realized this wasn't the man with the black gym bag who had just robbed a local store. Shaking their heads in amusement, they moved on in search of the real perpetrator. The motivating moral of the story, says Fromberg is: "If you procrastinate, the police will surround you and make you feel silly."[32]

Most of us at times need a bit of motivation to avoid procrastinating. Procrastination is a big time waster and can trigger feelings of frustration and self-criticism. You may feel as though there is an invisible barrier that prevents you from doing a project just when you most need to. Understanding how you use your time, and applying the techniques and systems described in this chapter, can help you avoid postponing important matters. This section provides some specific techniques for overcoming procrastination, especially those Quadrant 3 items that are so easy to put off. One powerful approach is mental rehearsal, during which you practice doing the desired task in your mind prior to tackling the task you are avoiding. Exhibit 3.4 illustrates two ways to prepare and rehearse mentally—using visualization and targeted self-talk.[33]

Exhibit 3.4 Two Techniques for Overcoming Procrastination

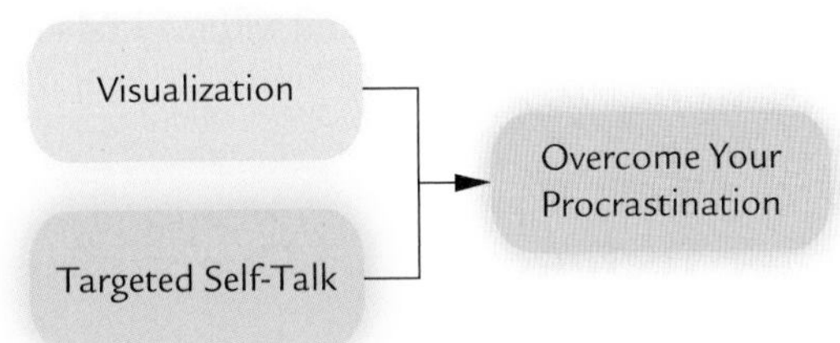

© CENGAGE LEARNING 2014

Visualize Your Intention

Visualization occurs when you create a vivid picture in your mind of the *action* you desire. Visualizing the action steps is called motor imagery in sports, which means imagining the ideal step-by-step sequence of activities that will achieve your goal. You can practice a detailed schema in your mind of the perfect tennis swing that will win the match, or practice a perfect volleyball serve over and over in your mind. For many management activities, such as running a meeting, giving a talk, or confronting a direct report for poor performance, the mental rehearsal pictures a detailed action sequence that will help you handle the situation correctly and give you confidence to do the thing you may be avoiding.

For example, a student who was an officer of a volunteer club was overwhelmed with so many e-mails that he dreaded reading them. It was important to keep in touch with club members, but he found himself procrastinating doing the task. "It was my birthday and I wanted to do something else. Instead, I sat for three minutes and visualized myself quickly and efficiently answering all unread messages. Then I went to my computer and answered all e-mails in record time. I also found that visualizing for other daily tasks kept me focused all day."[34]

The world of sports offers significant examples of using visual images to coach oneself into correct action steps. Most college coaches and athletes practice some form of visual mental rehearsal. In one of the best known visualization studies, Russian scientists assigned Olympic athletes to four groups that were given different training schedules.

- Group 1: 100 percent physical training;
- Group 2: 75 percent physical training with 25 percent mental training;
- Group 3: 50 percent physical training with 50 percent mental training;
- Group 4: 25 percent physical training with 75 percent mental training.

Group 4, with 75 percent of their time devoted to mental training, performed the best.[35] Action pictures in the mind clearly teach the body how to behave.

How are these results possible? Researchers discovered that an intentional thought or visual image creates the same brain signals as the physical act. The electrical activity in the brain is the same whether you are visualizing doing something or actually doing it. This is a powerful thing—your mind's visualization sends signals through the nervous system to the muscles and fibers of your body. EEGs reveal that electrical activity in the brain is the same whether people are doing something or just thinking about doing it. By visualizing an activity, you are sending your body a mental intention to do the activity and your body will listen. Essentially, neurons that fire together wire together.[36] Visualization brings the future into focus exactly as you want it to happen. It is a great way for your metacognition, your new brain, to send a clear intention or instruction to your old brain to adopt a new behavior.

Verbalize Your Intention

Targeted self-talk is a repeated intentional mental statement that is directed toward yourself.[37] The basic idea of targeted self-talk is to seed your mind with a self-instruction for a desired behavior. It is like giving yourself a pep talk when your intention or energy is flagging.

Here's an example of how it works: Abby was a poised young woman, but sometimes in the heat of the moment she became upset, emotional, and irrational. Abby was hard on herself in those moments, with thoughts appearing in her mind such as, "This always happens to me," "I screwed up again," or "I'm so stupid." This negative self-talk did not reestablish her poise. So she tried rehearsing some positive statements beforehand that she could interject in a moment of crisis, including, "I am staying calm," "I am going with the flow," and "I am lightening up." As it happened, her car broke down just before a long drive across country. She was in a fight with the dealership that supposedly had fixed it, and she used her new targeted self-talk to stay calm and poised. "During the ordeal with the dealership, several times I stopped, closed my eyes, took deep breaths, and repeated the new phrases to myself," Abby said later. "I found this very effective! It helped me relax and think rationally, using my intentional thinking rather than my automatic reactions."[38]

Repeating a verbal intention within your mind can be a real help for changing attitudes or behaviors such as procrastination. Experiments in the psychology laboratory, for example, show the clear priming effect of words on a person's behavior. Participants were asked to complete various word problems, such as unscrambling sets of words into a sentence or filling in missing letters to complete the spelling of words. If the words pertained to rudeness, participants who completed the exercise were more likely to interrupt the experimenter when he was busy with other tasks. If the words pertained to politeness, the subjects were more likely to wait patiently for the experimenter to return his attention to them.[39]

For procrastination, people might repeat to themselves something like, "I am flowing into my work more," "I am enjoying my work more," or "I am feeling less resistance to this task."[40] After a few days of repeating a chosen phrase from 40 (20 each morning and evening) to a few hundred times (during pauses such as when driving or exercising) a day, you will likely notice a shift in your thought pattern and behavior.

Remember, *your intentions can come into being through the power of intentional words.* The value of targeted self-talk is to change persistently negative thoughts toward a task into positive, helpful, encouraging thoughts that help you eliminate procrastination. Your body and nonconscious mind will respond to the thoughts of positive volition you insert into your mind with your higher-order thinking.

Other Techniques for Overcoming Procrastination

In addition to using mental rehearsal for tackling projects you're likely to put off, there are several other techniques that can help you limit or avoid procrastination.

1. Maximize Your Prime Time You've probably heard someone say, "I'm a night person" or "I'm a morning person." Each of us has an optimal working time, a time when we are most energetic both mentally and physically. During this time, we think more clearly, have better concentration, are more creative, and feel more physically energetic. It only makes sense to use your high-energy time for accomplishing important, demanding, or dreaded tasks, but many people don't do that. For example, many managers say they are at their best in the morning, but that's the time they tend to use for routine matters like checking e-mail, reading the paper, or scanning through reports. Later, when their energy level drops, they wonder why they find it so difficult to get started on that important project they've been putting off.

2. Just Get Started The big trick when you are feeling anxious and avoiding a necessary task is to "just get started." Sometimes a big, important project seems so formidable that we feel overwhelmed and can't get started. A good way to start is to choose a tiny, tiny piece of the task that is within your comfort zone. Trying to do too much may activate fear in the emotional part of your brain (the "old brain"), which triggers a "flight" response. For example, Arjit aspired to run at least three miles three times a week, but he was not running at all. He ran three miles regularly when he had been employed, but graduate school offered few respites. Arjit decided to start with half a mile. Running a short distance made the task seem easy and

LEADING WORDS

"We are what we repeatedly do; excellence, then, is not an act, but a habit."

—Aristotle
Greek philosopher (384 B.C.–322 B.C.)

"If you really want to manage your time and get stuff done, have a burning life and work purpose that is a beacon for what you do."

—Dean Fuhrman
business consultant

"It's not stress that kills us, it is our reaction to it."

—Hans Selye
Hungarian scientist and stress researcher

"Self-discipline is a form of freedom. Freedom from laziness and lethargy, freedom from the expectations and demands of others, freedom from weakness and fear—and doubt. Self-discipline allows a [person] to feel his individuality, his inner strength, his talent. He is master of, rather than a slave to, his thoughts and emotions."

—H. A. Dorfman
author of *The Mental Game of Baseball*

less time consuming, so he was soon running again. When a job seems too big to deal with, the answer is to "slice and dice"[41] the project into tiny, specific bites that you can do one at a time.

Psychologists call these small steps your *implementation intentions*.[42] Implementation intentions are the specific step-by-step subtasks that will lead to completion of your project. The tiny steps provide a visible and easily doable structure for you to follow. Any time you feel resistance to a task, make a list of subtasks or baby steps needed to complete it. The baby steps are easy to complete, and you will feel satisfaction as you mark off each completed item. The small wins reinforce your forward progress.

3. Use Deadlines A deadline is an effective way to get yourself started on a task you are avoiding. Recall from Exhibit 3.3 that urgent tasks, which include deadline-driven tasks, tend to get done, while tasks low in urgency are put off. One way to turn important tasks into urgent tasks is to create deadlines.

The positive impact of deadlines has been shown repeatedly in the research laboratory.[43] In a course made up of 99 students at the Massachusetts Institute of Technology, one subset of students was given fixed, evenly spaced deadlines for the submission of three short papers, while other students were allowed to set their own deadlines, which could not be changed once they were set.[44] Forty-three of the students chose a late deadline so that they could turn in all three papers during the final week of class; other students set more evenly spaced, intermediate deadlines to complete their papers. At the end of the course, students with evenly spaced deadlines, whether self- or externally imposed, completed the papers earlier and showed higher grades than students who chose to wait until the end of the semester. In addition, grades of the late-deadline students were lower on the final class project, suggesting that they had less time to devote to the project because they were still working on their short papers. Self-imposed deadlines were nearly as effective as externally imposed ones when they were evenly spaced.[45]

MANAGING STRESS

Jeffrey Kindler spent nine years working at Pfizer, the world's biggest pharmaceuticals company, with half that time spent as the company's chief executive. He describes his tenure in the CEO's job as "extremely exciting and rewarding." Yet the job was also extremely demanding, and the ongoing pressures eventually took their toll. Saying the 24-7 nature of the job and the constant burden of meeting multiple goals and requirements had worn him out, Kindler abruptly resigned in December 2010 to recharge his batteries and plan the next stage of his career.[46]

Not every manager's job is as hectic and pressure-packed as that of a CEO for a giant, global drug company, but there are stressful aspects to even a low-level supervisor's job. As a manager at any hierarchical level, you will need excellent time management skills, as well as mechanisms for coping with stress, to keep from being overwhelmed with the duties and responsibilities that come with a management position. Recall from the introductory chapter that a manager's job is diverse, fast-paced, and highly fragmented. In a word, it's stressful. In today's world of heightened competition, instant information, globalization, technological advances, economic uncertainty, and an environment of rapid change, managers' jobs are more nerve-wracking than ever.[47] One study looked at U.S. military research into "combat stress" and found that many of the cognitive and emotional stressors are the same as those people experience in an environment of persistent change. Exhibit 3.5 lists several types of stress that people in organizations experience that are analogous to military combat stress.

Many life events also cause stress. Specific events that have been shown to increase an individual's stress level, in descending order of importance, are as follows:

Death of an immediate family member

Divorce

Major personal injury or illness

Getting married

Losing a job

Gaining a new family member

Major business readjustment (merger, reorganization)

Changing careers

Major change in work responsibility

Major change in living conditions

Troubles with the boss

One type of boss trouble is dealing with a boss who is a bully. Consider that 44 percent of people

Exhibit 3.5 Comparative Stressors—Military Combat Stress versus Organizational Change

Cognitive and Emotional Stressors	Military Combat Stress	Organizational Change
High workloads	X	X
Ambiguous job assignments	X	X
Time pressures	X	X
Conflicting directions or orders	X	X
Inconsistency between rewards and performance	X	X
Inadequate training	X	X
Conflicting values	X	X

Source: Adapted from *U.S. Army Combat Stress Control Handbook*, Department of the Army (2003); and Richard Dool, "Lessons from the Military: A New Framework for Managing Change (C^5)," *Journal of Leadership and Organizational Studies* 17, no. 3 (2010): 253–263.

surveyed by the Employment Law Alliance say they have worked for a manager that they considered an abusive bully.[48] The recent economic slump has triggered an increase in bullying behavior from supervisors, and workplace behavior experts say bullying in general is on the rise as people cope with the stress of today's tough economic environment.[49] You might not even be conscious of the impact that stressful events and people within and outside the organization cause. The wrong kind of stress, however, can add significant wear and tear to your mind and body.

Challenge Stress versus Threat Stress

Formally defined, **stress** is an individual's physiological, mental, and emotional response to external stimuli that place physical or psychological demands on the individual and create uncertainty and lack of personal control when important outcomes are at stake.[50] Stressors are external forces or events, whereas stress itself is the individual's response to them. The stressors listed in Exhibit 3.5 are typically associated with what

7 STEPS TO... Dealing with an Office Bully

1. **Document everything.** Save bullying e-mail messages, keep a diary of incidents, and secure witnesses any time you can.
2. **Confront the bully.** Keep your challenge specific, polite, and firm, such as saying, "I find it demeaning when you undermine me in front of my colleagues. I'd like you to stop, please." Stand tall, maintain eye contact, and keep your nerve.
3. **Seek support.** Don't let youself become isolated. Nurture positive work relationships. Join forces with others you know have been bullied.
4. **Do your job well.** Do everything you can to perform at the top of your game. Don't give a bully any ammunition by slacking off on your performance.
5. **Take care of yourself.** Make an extra effort to eat right, get plenty of rest, and exercise regularly to control your stress level.
6. **Go to the top.** Don't be intimidated by the lines of authority. If your boss is the bully, go to his or her supervisor. Keep climbing until somebody listens.
7. **Don't perpetuate the cycle.** Although it's tempting to find a victim of your own, rise above that motivation. Remember, you need every friend you can get.

Source: Based on "Career Masterclass: Deal with an Office Bully," *Management Today* 15 (November 1, 2010): 15.

we think of as "bad stress," because they produce some combination of frustration (the inability to achieve a goal, such as the inability to meet a deadline because of inadequate training or resources) and anxiety (such as the fear of being disciplined for not meeting deadlines).

However, stress has positive aspects as well. It is not always unhealthy. Stress is helpful when it motivates people to accomplish more. Without a certain amount of stress, we would be complacent and accomplish little. Psychologists have long studied this "dual face of stress," and make a distinction between *challenge stress* and *threat stress*. Challenge stress fires you up, whereas threat stress burns you out.[51] As originally proposed by two Harvard researchers, Robert Yerkes and John Dodson, and illustrated in Exhibit 3.6, stress up to a certain point challenges you and increases your focus, alertness, efficiency, and productivity.[52] After that point, however, things go downhill quickly and stress compromises your job performance, your relationships, and even your health. The point at which things tip over from challenge stress (good) to threat stress (bad) may vary with each individual. Most of us can easily tell when we've gone over the top of the stress curve illustrated in Exhibit 3.6. We stop feeling productive; experience emotions of anxiety, fear, depression, or anger; are easily irritated; and may have trouble making decisions. Many people also have physical symptoms, such as headaches, insomnia, or stomach problems.

Too much stress can cause long-term health problems as well as limit your success and happiness. Another interesting finding is that too much stress inhibits learning and flexibility by causing people to revert to using their old brain, as discussed earlier in this chapter, essentially becoming "victims of habit, operating on autopilot."[53]

Type A and Type B Behavior

One factor used to explain why some people are more vulnerable than others to the ill effects of stress is the distinction between Type A and Type B behavior. Researchers originally categorized people as having behavior patterns called Type A or Type B based on studies of stress-related heart disease.[54] The Type A behavior pattern includes extreme competitiveness, impatience, aggressiveness, and devotion to work. In contrast, people with a Type B behavior pattern exhibit less of these behaviors. They consequently experience less conflict with other people and a more balanced, relaxed lifestyle. Type A people tend to experience more stress-related illness than Type B people.

Most Type A individuals are high-energy people and may seek positions of power and responsibility. By pacing themselves and learning control and

DISCOVER KNOWLEDGE

Exhibit 3.6 The Yerkes-Dodson Stress Curve

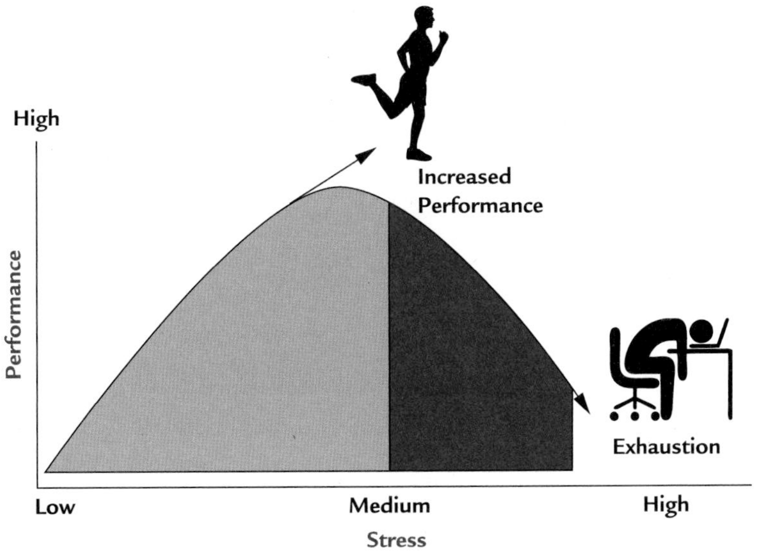

Source: Based on an exhibit by Emeran A. Mayer, M.D., UCLA Center for Neurobiology of Stress.

intelligent use of their natural high-energy tendencies, Type A individuals can be powerful forces for innovation and leadership within their organizations. However, many Type A personalities cause stress-related problems for themselves, and sometimes for those around them. Type B individuals typically live with less stress unless they are in high-stress situations.

Developing Your Stress Management Competencies

Although people with a Type A behavior pattern are particularly susceptible, even Type B individuals can suffer from too much stress. Effective stress management is essential if we are to function at our best. There are a number of techniques for avoiding or alleviating the ill effects of stress.

Seek and Destroy Key Sources of Stress

A recent study found that the most beneficial stress management competency is *prevention*.[55] None of us can eliminate all the potential sources of stress from our lives, but we can avoid some of them and manage others. Experts recommend that you take some time each day to identify stressors in your life and find ways to eliminate or reduce them. Examples of prevention include things such as altering your route to work to avoid traffic jams, replacing a computer or cellphone that is no longer working effectively and is driving you crazy, and scheduling appointments and meetings when you won't be rushed. Being well organized, planning ahead, and using the various time-management techniques we've discussed in this chapter are highly effective ways to manage or prevent stress. People who plan how they will use their time and keep an up-to-date list of things they have to do are less stressed and more productive.

Find Meaning and Support

You are much more likely to experience ill effects of stress if you're working in a job that has no meaning for you and if you feel alone in life without social support. Consider the manager who worked 12-hour days as a computer programming manager for a food company. He had learned programming because he knew he could get a job in the field, but he never enjoyed it. When he found himself struggling to get out of bed in the mornings, hating to walk into the office, and sniping at employees for no reason, he knew it was time to find work that held more meaning for him. He quit his job and founded a boxing school for teenagers and young adults. He loves boxing and will happily climb into the boxing ring with just about anyone. He enjoys meeting new people and likes helping young people learn how to combine their physical and mental energies. He goes to work every day with energy and enthusiasm, which rubs off on his employees and clients. Not all of us can or want to start our own business, but each of us can seek jobs that play to our strengths and provide us with a sense of meaning and connection. When a goal is important to you personally, you will be energized and excited to work toward it rather than feel stressed out and overburdened.

The *buffering hypothesis* says that a perceived high degree of social support from family and friends protects one from the potentially adverse effects of stressful events.[56] That is, if you feel you have a lot of support,

DISCOVER YOURSELF

Interpret Your Score: Stress (Questionnaire 3)

Your four scores on this questionnaire pertain to various aspects of stress described in the chapter. Your score for Part A reflects your sense of time urgency; hence, a low score typically means less internal stress. Comparative data for **Sense of Urgency** (Part A): Thirty person Mean score = 11.5; Top Quartile = 13–14; Bottom Quartile = 9–10. Your score for Part B reflects elements of the Type A personality. A higher score means you are oriented more toward an impatient and tense Type A style than the more placid and relaxed Type B way of being. Comparative data for **Personality Type** (Part B): Mean = 10.3; Top Quartile = 13–13; Bottom Quartile = 7–9. Your Part C score reflects the level of stress you consciously experience. Comparative data for **Conscious Stress Level** (Part C): Mean = 10.6; Top Quartile = 14–15; Bottom Quartile = 5–9. Your score for Part D reflects the amount of personal and social support you have for coping with stress. Comparative data for **Support Level** (Part D): Mean = 12.0; Top Quartile = 14–15; Bottom Quartile = 8–10. Good support can moderate the potentially negative impact of stress on your well-being. How do you feel about your level of stress and support? How do your scores compare to other students? CNOW and CourseMate users can access dynamically updated comparative data through www.cengagebrain.com.

© CENGAGE LEARNING 2014

you're less susceptible to the negative effects of bad stress. People who have interpersonal relationships that provide needed resources (listening, caring) and stability have a better sense of well-being, self-worth, and mental health. If you are embedded in a network of close family and friends, stressful situations are viewed as less demanding and less threatening. Strong relations buffer you from the effects of stressful conditions and events.

Meditate and Manage Your Energy

Meditation is a way to both prevent and alleviate harmful stress responses. Some people meditate every morning or evening as a routine practice. Others find that short breaks to meditate for a few minutes several times a day are just as effective.[57] Anytime during the day when you're feeling overwhelmed, you can close your eyes, focus on an image or a phrase that you find calming, and breathe deeply. If you focus on your breathing and the calming image, pushing all other thoughts away, it will relax both your mind and body within a short period of time. Jurek Gruhn, president of Nova Nordisk US, uses a similar approach. "I saw this comedian who said that a man's brain is filled with boxes, and one of them is empty," Gruhn says. "Well, when the day's really tough in the office, I go to my empty box for 10 or 15 minutes and I do nothing. If I completely switch off for a short period of time, I get my energy back."[58]

A related idea is to treat work as a series of short sprints rather than a marathon. Work intensely for 90 minutes and then take a break to recover. People who work continuously for long hours typically accomplish less than people who take short recovery breaks.[59] Meditation can be an important part of an overall healthy lifestyle that helps you better cope with stress. When you're under pressure, it's especially important to eat right, get enough rest, and exercise regularly. Walking, running, and other forms of exercise relieve physical symptoms of stress and also release chemicals in the brain that make people simply feel better. Many managers appreciate yoga as a form of exercise particularly beneficial for combating stress because it both eases the mind's worries and recharges one's physical energy.[60] One study reported that yoga is as effective as cognitive behavioral therapy for reducing stress.[61]

Get Organized and Manage Your Time

Many of the techniques described earlier in this chapter are effective stress reducers. Procrastinating on an important task or assignment simply adds to your feelings of stress. A period of disorganization in which some responsibilities are overlooked and left undone also increases your stress. The basic principles of self-management and time management are designed to help you reduce the added stress caused by your own misbehavior. Techniques such as emptying your head on pieces of paper, visualization, the daily review and look-ahead, and helping your new brain manage any bad habits of your old brain will help you reduce your feelings of stress.

Find Work-Life Balance

The final technique for managing stress related to the workplace is to balance work with other interests and activities. Managers who handle stress well typically have interests outside of work, such as hobbies and volunteer activities, that help them relieve stress and recharge their batteries. Paul English, co-founder and chief technology officer of travel search engine Kayak, accomplishes a tremendous amount of work and expects the same from his employees. However, English says Kayak's philosophy is to "work really hard for 40 to 45 hours a week, but we believe in people having strong personal lives."[62] English sometimes takes his children on business trips with him so they can have new experiences together. At night, he reads murder mysteries and books about Africa and global health rather than reading about business or technology.

Many organizations offer options such as flexible scheduling and telecommuting to enable people to lead more balanced lives. But you, as an individual, are also responsible for finding your own work-life balance. A survey by the Society for Human Resource Management found that 70 percent of employees surveyed say they work beyond scheduled time and on weekends, but more than half of those admit that it is because of *self-imposed pressure*. When you find your mind telling you that you need to work longer hours, remind yourself that you can actually accomplish more if you take the time to have a balanced life. Regularly participate in activities outside of work that you truly enjoy, which will help refresh your mind and renew your energy. Apply the time-management and self-management skills you've learned in this chapter to enable you to get your work done and still have time for family, friends, and other aspects of life. And, as one manager suggests, remind yourself to "work to live rather than live to work."[63]

NEED TO KNOW

- Managers face multiple demands on their time and need excellent time-management and self-management skills. People high in self-management can control their behaviors and direct themselves to achieve important goals.
- You can improve your self-management by consciously using your "new brain" and higher order thinking to control the impulses and desires of your "old brain" and lower-level thinking.
- Basic principles of self-management include clarity of mind, clarity of objectives, and a system of organized reminders that help you get unstuck and make measurable progress toward accomplishing all the things you need to do.
- Five steps in a system for effective self-management are: Empty your head, decide next actions, get organized, perform a weekly review, and then do what needs to be done.
- Tried and true time-management techniques include prioritizing tasks with an ABCDE system, following the 80/20 rule for identifying tasks that produce the most value, performing a daily review and look-ahead, and keeping a To-Do list.
- Procrastination is a problem for many people. People procrastinate for a variety of reasons, such as anxiety associated with the task, a tendency toward perfectionism, and personal characteristics such as impulsiveness and low self-control.
- Most people tend to do things that seem urgent, even if they are not important. You can use a time-management matrix to classify tasks according to their urgency and their importance so that you do the important things first.
- Two important ways to overcome procrastination are visualizing your intention and verbalizing your intention with targeted self-talk.
- Specific techniques for overcoming procrastination include using your optimal working time for tackling jobs you have been putting off, breaking overwhelming jobs into tiny pieces, and using deadlines to impose a sense of urgency for completing the task.
- Effective time management and self-management can help managers cope with the inevitable stress of their jobs. Stress up to a certain point can be positive because it spurs you to accomplish more, but too much stress hurts your productivity, your relationships, and your health.
- Important stress management competencies include managing the sources of stress, finding meaning and social support, maintaining a healthy lifestyle, meditation, energy management, and finding a balance between work and personal life.

ACTION LEARNING

DELIBERATE PRACTICE EXERCISES

How Do I Allocate My Time—Urgent or Important?

Step 1: Review the time-management matrix in Exhibit 3.3. Complete the table below, listing all the things you do in a typical week (exercise, work, attend class, go to movies, hang out, e-mail, study, make phone calls, watch TV, etc.) in the category you think each activity fits into appropriately. Write beside each activity the number of hours you estimate that you spend on that activity.

Urgent and Important	Not Urgent but Important
Urgent but Not Important	Not Urgent and Not Important

Step 2: Are you spending too much of your time on one category of activities, such as "Not Urgent and Not Important"? Why is that happening?

Step 3: What would you consider a more ideal allocation of your time? What steps might you take to achieve that reallocation?

Step 4 (Optional): Share your insights with a partner, and ask your partner what insights he or she gained.

Mindful Stress Reduction

Perform this exercise three times over two days, each time increasing the length of the period by 2 minutes over the previous period.

Step 1: Sit in a comfortable position in a straight-backed chair with your feet flat on the floor. Arch your lower back slightly forward. Set an alarm for a period of 10–20 minutes so you don't have to keep track of the time.

Step 2: Focus your attention on your breath as it enters and leaves your nostrils.

When a thought grabs your attention, just let it go and refocus back on your breath.

Step 3: When the alarm goes off, pause for a moment to appreciate your quieter mind and relaxed body, and then go about the rest of your day.

Step 4: How do you feel after the Mindful Stress Reduction exercise?

Reducing Stress and Procrastination

Step 1: Your relationship to the activities in your life can be a major factor in your level of stress or procrastination. Think of all the activities you do in a typical week. Fill out Columns A and B in the table below, noting which ones you NEED to do to survive (such as work, pay bills), which ones you SHOULD do (obligations such as attending an event or calling your parents), the ones you LIKE to do (perhaps playing tennis or spending time with friends), and the ones you LOVE to do (maybe a hobby or reading a favorite book).

Column A Activities in my typical week	Column B Percentage of time spent on each	Column C What can I change?
Things I NEED to do:		Less time on NEEDs:
Things I SHOULD do:		Less Time on SHOULDs:
Things I LIKE to do:		More time on LIKEs:
Things I LOVE to do:		More time on LOVEs:
	Total 100%	How many hours per week can I shift?

Step 2: The more time you spend on NEEDs and SHOULDs, the more you will have to force yourself to do things, the more stressed out you will feel, and the more likely you are to procrastinate. If you have a greater percentage of your time spent on LIKEs and LOVEs, you will be more energized and productive. It isn't possible to eliminate all NEEDs and SHOULDs. But think about how you can reduce, by 5 to 10 percent, your NEEDs and SHOULDs, and increase by 5 to 10 percent your LIKEs and LOVEs. At the least, try to shift one hour per week from NEEDs and SHOULDs to activities in the LIKEs and LOVEs categories.

ACTION LEARNING

Step 3: Fill out Column C above, indicating the changes you plan to make.

Step 4: How does finding meaning in what you do reduce the stress level and procrastination in your life?

Step 5 (Optional): Share your insights with a partner, and ask your partner what insights he or she gained.

IN-CLASS TEAM EXERCISE

Time Bandits

Step 1: Form into groups of four to six people. Someone should volunteer to go first. The first person either chooses one item from the "Common Time Bandits" list below or comes up with an original "time bandit" that this person uses frequently. Describe what is done, how the time bandit robs time, and why you do it.

Step 2: The first person looks to the person on the right and asks that person if he or she uses the same time bandit and how and why it is used. The new person then picks another time bandit that he or she uses frequently, describes what is done, how the time bandit robs time, and why he or she uses it.

Step 3: The second person turns to the person on the right and asks if he or she uses the same time bandit and how and why it is used. Keep going around the group in this manner, with each person presenting new time bandits until all members have had a turn.

Step 4: Give anyone a second turn who has a particularly intense time bandit and wants to share.

Step 5: As a group, discuss the following:

1. What were the most common time bandits?
2. Are there times of the day or days of the week that are more high risk for time bandits?
3. How can you reduce your use of time bandits?

Common Time Bandits:

1. Texting
2. Talking on the phone endlessly
3. Surfing the Web endlessly
4. Spending too much time in a grocery or retail store
5. Watching mindless TV, including reality shows
6. Going to useless movies
7. Hanging out endlessly
8. Reading mindless magazines
9. Participating in Web sites such as Twitter or Facebook
10. Gossiping
11. Video or computer games

12. Sports on TV
13. Drinking
14. Yacking
15. Arriving late and having to make up time
16. Someone else is late and you stay longer so he or she can make up time
17. Being disorganized
18. Letting people use you to waste their time (and yours)
19. Not being prepared for an assignment or task
20. Listening to friends' unending drama
21. Making too many lists
22. Over-organizing drawers or closets
23. Oversleeping
24. Undersleeping
25. Running out of food or supplies and having to make last minute trips to the store
26. Cramming for exams or papers
27. Working too long on one project
28. Lacking focus
29. Flitting from one activity to the next
30. Negative self-talk
31. Worrying about what other people will think
32. Not taking breaks when working long stretches

ACTION LEARNING

FIELD TEAM EXERCISE

Who's "Stressed Out" the Most?

Step 1: Divide into groups of four to six and schedule a time for a group meeting.

Step 2: Prepare for your group meeting by having each member identify either a person in the news or from a magazine (perhaps a manager) or a character from fiction or a movie who is under a great deal of stress. Bring in an article about the person, or a picture from the movie, or some description.

Step 3: Take turns going around the group, with each member describing his or her person or character, the stressors the individual experiences, and the coping mechanisms each is employing.

Step 4: As a group, find patterns in the stressors and coping mechanisms.

Decide as a group who is the most stressed out. Why? What additional solutions can you offer to that person or any of the ones presented at the meeting?

Step 5: In what ways did your characters add to their own stress levels? What advice would you give them?

TEST YOUR METTLE

ROLE PLAY SIMULATIONS

Wasted Time?

Background: Reread the written Video Incident at the beginning of the chapter.

Instructions: Form into groups of two or three. One person will play the role of Jason and one the role of Jane. If there are three in the group, the third person is an observer. Each person reads only his or her confidential role; the observer reads both. Spend 10–15 minutes on the role play.

Confidential information for Jane: There are two big marketing campaigns coming up and they both require huge investments of capital. If they fail, it will be a disaster, so it is very important to get the vision and the details right. It won't do any good to look back with, "Oh, we should have considered this or that . . . ." Sales are up from last year, but not as high as everyone wants, so these campaigns are really important. You feel the last few meetings have been really good, because your team is getting at the underlying issues as well as the obvious ones and looking at all aspects. This is what a team should be doing! But your sales manager, Jason Wong, has been pushing to get started with the campaigns. He's expressed his frustrations at the long and continuous meetings on these campaigns. But he, of all people, should be happy that the group is taking such an interest in the sales campaigns. You think it's because Jason is such a "doer" that he gets impatient when the "analyzers" keep wanting to analyze. He's coming in to your office now and you need to set him straight.

Confidential information for Jason: Caffeine and Crullers is in trouble. Sales are not up to the projections, and the other managers don't seem terribly worried about it. They are happy to just yak, yak, yak about the two new sales campaigns, rather than getting in there and doing something. Really, you think the talking is an excuse for not taking action. You are about ready to stop going to the meetings, because they are such a waste of time. Let them talk and talk and talk and you can stay in your office and get some real work done. You've asked for a meeting with general manager Jane Sutton to discuss this with her.

After the role play, discuss these questions:

1. What is the source of the main conflict here?
2. How can the conflict be resolved?
3. How can people learn to appreciate personality differences, rather than seeing them as a personal affront?

The Need to Focus

This Role Play Simulation is available online at www.cengagebrain.com.

SHUTTERSTOCK #53973379

VIDEO APPLICATION

Lost in Translation

After arriving in Tokyo, Japan, Charlotte (Scarlett Johansson) spends quiet time by herself, observing and reflecting on the unfamiliar culture.

Discussion Questions

1. Imagine you are Charlotte. What are you thinking and feeling about what you see?
2. How might taking a break to spend quiet time by yourself, perhaps in a new situation, help you manage yourself? Can this kind of experience make you more effective? Explain.
3. Would you feel any intimidation about exploring a new country alone? How might you influence yourself to move through that feeling of reluctance?

CASE INCIDENTS

Jekyll & Hyde

Manny Goldman opened the office door and peered inside, spotting Louise Jackson as she stood behind her desk, sorting through mail and memos.

"Is it safe to come in?" Manny whispered.

"For the moment; Larry hasn't come in yet," Louise responded.

Manny walked over, opened a plastic container, and reached inside for a brownie. Without looking up, Louise slapped his hand and he jerked it back.

"Those aren't for you," she said.

Manny sat in the desk chair and leaned back. "Should I say something to Larry about his temper?"

"I wouldn't."

"Why not?" he asked.

"He'll kill you. I once casually mentioned anger management classes to him and I thought he was going to jump the desk."

"But yesterday . . . whew," Manny whistled. "Every vein was bulging. I thought the guy was going to have a heart attack. One of these days, he's going to be midway through a fit and drop over dead."

Louise sighed. "At least it will be quiet around here," she said wistfully. Seeing Manny's shocked expression, she shook her head. "Sorry, I shouldn't have said that. But Larry's Jekyll and Hyde act is wearing thin."

"I know. And you have to deal with it more than anyone around here."

"It's just one of the hazards of the job, Manny."

"Do you get *hazard* pay?"

"No."

At the sound of the elevator opening and someone whistling down the hallway, the two exchanged smirking glances.

"Well, this day will *start off* good, anyway," Louise said.

Manny jumped from the chair and headed for a side door. "I'm out of here," he said quietly. "Good luck."

Now all three senior partners had set aside a weekend to meet with Vincent in order to explore ways to address his leadership problems. All agreed he possessed the vision, the talent, and the ability to deliver an amazing product for clients. However, the issues of disorganization, poor time management, weak team cohesion, and poor delegation made the journey to reach that end product a nightmare.

Honesty and critical evaluation were the keys to addressing these issues. Throughout the weekend, the four men explored the situation from several angles. The objective was to allow Vincent to look at options and devise a course of action that best addressed his leadership needs. Among the many possible courses of action were:

Option 1: Was Vincent moved to team leadership too quickly? This option would assign Vincent as a team member for a time under the direction of one of the best organized partners, which could prove beneficial to Vincent by letting him observe the role of team leader and the organization of duties.

Option 2: This option would keep Vincent in the role as team leader, but give him the responsibility to look at the campaign in relation to the strengths and specific skills of various team members who, together with Vincent, would establish a workable timeline with mini-deadlines for the project and the distribution of duties. Vincent would no longer be at the center of all the work for a campaign.

Option 3: A variation of Option 2, this option would temporarily pull Vincent from the pressure of creating a high-profile campaign by allowing him and his team to work on smaller campaigns where there is less pressure and a chance to establish and follow better procedures. While this option could, in the end, build Vincent's confidence as well as team cohesion, there is a concern that team members might view this as a group demotion, removing them from major accounts.

Discussion Questions

1. What do you see as the key underlying problem with Vincent and his team?
2. Which of the three options would you choose? Why?
3. If you were a consultant to the senior partners, what suggestions would you make to help Vincent become more organized and procrastinate less?

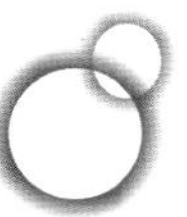

PERSONAL SKILLS LOG

PERSONAL SKILLS LOG

Directions: Fill in the rows below based on what you learned from each part of the chapter that you completed.

	What is my key takeaway or insight from this activity?	What do I personally do well (strength) regarding this activity?	What could I improve (weakness) about myself regarding this activity?	How might I use what I've learned from this activity in the future?
Manager Challenge Incident:				
Discover Yourself Questionnaires:				
Deliberate Practice Exercises:				
In-Class and/or Field Team Exercises:				
Role-Play Exercises:				
Case Incidents:				

REFERENCES

Discover Yourself

1 Based on Joe S. Anderson and Gregory E. Prussia, "The Self-Leadership Questionnaire: Preliminary Assessment of Construct Validity," *The Journal of Leadership Studies* 4, no. 2 (1997): 119–143; Dan J. Neal, and Kate B. Carey, "A Follow-Up Psychometric Analysis of the Self-Regulation Questionnaire," *Psychology of Addictive Behaviors* 19, no. 4 (2005): 414–422; and C. Lay, "At Last, My Research Article on Procrastination," *Journal of Research in Personality* 20 (1986): 474–495.

2 Based on Mark Trueman and James Hartley, "A Comparison Between the Time-Management Skills and Academic Performance of Mature and Traditional-Entry University Students," *Higher Education* 32 (1996): 199–215; M. J. Bond and N. T. Feather, "Some Correlates of Structure and Purpose in the Use of Time," *Journal of Personality and Social Psychology* 55, no. 2 (1988): 321–329; and Therese Hoff Macan, Comila Shahani, Robert L. Dipboye, and Amanda Peek Phillips, "College Students' Time Management: Correlations with Academic Performance and Stress," *Journal of Educational Psychology* 82, no. 4 (1990): 760–768.

3 Based on Joseph L. Fava, Laurie Ruggiero, and Diane M. Grimley, "The Development and Structural Confirmation of the Rhode Island Stress and Coping Inventory," *Journal of Behavioral Medicine* 21, no. 6 (1998): 601–611; Sheldon Cohen, Tom Kamarck, and Robin Mermelstein, "A Global Measure of Perceived Stress," *Journal of Health and Social Behavior* 24 (December 1983): 385–396; S. A. Lawrence, J. Garner, and V. J. Callen, "The Support Appraisal Work Stressors Inventory: Construction and Initial Validation," *Journal of Vocational Behavior* 70 (2007): 172–204; and Jeffrey R. Edwards, "Assessing Your Behavior Pattern," Note UVA-OB-0360, Revised April 2003, Barden Business Publishing, University of Virginia.

Discover Knowledge

4 Based on a story in Robert S. Kaplan, "What to Ask the Person in the Mirror," *Harvard Business Review* (January 2007): 86–95.

5 Quoted in Geoffrey Colvin, "The Bionic Manager," *Fortune* (September 19, 2005): 88–100.

6 A. Garrett, "Buying Time to Do the Things That Really Matter," *Management Today* (July 2000): 75.

7 Indira Pattni and Geoffrey N. Soutar, "The Effectiveness of Self-Management Training in Organizations from Two Culturally Different Countries," *Journal of Management Development*, 28, No. 7 (2009): 633–646.

8 Adam Bryant, "He Wants Subjects, Verbs, and Objects," (Corner Office column, an interview with Richard Anderson), *The New York Times* (April 25, 2009); Adam Bryant, "Imagining a World of No Annual Reviews," (Corner Office column, an interview with Carol Bartz), *The New York Times* (October 18, 2009).

9 Richard L. Daft, *The Executive and the Elephant: A Leader's Guide to Building Inner Excellence* (San Francisco: Jossey-Bass, 2010).

10 Larry G. Linne, "Playing Your Position as a CEO," *Rough Notes* (April 2010): 14–15.

11 This discussion is based on Daft, *The Executive and the Elephant.*

12 Daniel Kahnman, *Thinking Fast and Slow* (New York: Farrar, Straus and Giroux, 2011).

13 Sue Shellenbarger, "To Combat an Office Tyrant, Look at the Roots," *The Wall Street Journal* (April 28, 2010).

14 Linne, "Playing Your Position as a CEO."

15 Jordan Timm, "There Are 168 Hours in a Week. How Many Do You Use Well? *Canadian Business* (July 20 – August 16, 2010): 69; Laura Vanderkam, *168 Hours: You Have More Time Than You Think* (New York: Portfolio/Penguin, 2010).

16 This section on self-management is based heavily on David Allen, *Getting Things Done: The Art of Stress-Free Productivity* (New York: Viking Penguin, 2001).

17 "One of These Days," *The Wall Street Journal* (March 11, 1997).

18 Based on Allen, *Getting Things Done;* and Francis Heylighen and Clément Vidal, "Getting Things Done: The Science Behind Stress-Free Productivity," *Long Range Planning* 41 (2008): 585–605.

19 Daniel Roth, "Trading Places," *Fortune* (January 23, 2006): 120–128.

20 Most of these techniques are described in detail in Pamela Dodd and Doug Sundheim, *The 25 Best Time Management Tools & Techniques* (Ann Arbor, MI: Peak Performance Press, Inc., 2005); and Brian Tracy, *Eat That Frog: 21 Great Ways to Stop Procrastinating and Get More Done in Less Time* (San Francisco: Berrett-Koehler, 2002).

21 Paul R. Brown, "For Entrepreneurs It's All About Time," *The New York Times* (April 1, 2008); and Timothy Ferriss, *The Four-Hour Workweek* (New York: Crown, 2007).

22 Adina Genn, "NFI Research Survey Finds 95% of Business Leaders Keep a To-Do List," *Long Island Business News* (March 18, 2005).

23 Tracy, *Eat That Frog*, p. 14.

24 Joshua S. Rubinstein, David E. Meyer, and Jeffrey E. Evans, "Executive Control of Cognitive Processes in Task Switching," *Journal of Experimental Psychology: Human Perception and Performance* 27, no. 4 (August 2001): 763–797; and Sue Shellenbarger, "Multitasking Makes You Stupid: Studies Show Pitfalls of Doing Too Much at Once," *The Wall Street Journal* (February 27, 2003).

25 Genn, "NFI Research Survey Finds 95% of Business Leaders Keep a To-Do List."

26 Robert Fromberg, "A Cure for Procrastination," *Healthcare Financial Management* (October 2010): 32–33.

27 Reported in Cari Tuna, "How to Put Off Work—Constructively, *The Wall Street Journal* (September 30, 2008).

28 This discussion is based partly on Piers Steel, "The True Meaning of Procrastination," *The Procrastination Equation, Psychology Today* Web site, December 20, 2010, http://www.psychologytoday.com/blog/the-procrastination-equation/201012/the-true-meaning-procrastination (accessed April 3, 2012); and Joseph R. Ferrare, Judith L. Johnson, and William G. McCown, *Procrastination and Task Avoidance: Theory, Research, and Treatment* (New York: Springer Publishing, 1995).

29 Ideas and studies reported in Jared Sandberg, "Some Managers Make It Easy on Themselves with a Ready 'No'" (Cubicle Culture column), *The Wall Street Journal* (October 17, 2006); and Jonathan Haidt, *The Happiness Hypothesis* (New York: Basic Books, 2006), pp. 28–31.

30 R. F. Baumeister, E. Bratlavsky, C. Finenauer, and K. D. Vohs, "Bad Is Stronger Than Good," *Review of General Psychology* 5 (2001): 323–370; and P. Rozin and E. B. Royzman, "Negativity Bias, Negativity Dominance, and Contagion," *Personality and Social Psychology Review* 5 (2001): 296–320.

31 These ideas are discussed in Stephen Covey, *The 7 Habits of Highly Effective People: Powerful Lessons in Personal Change* (New York: Simon & Schuster, 1989); and A. Lakein, *How to Get Control of Your Time and Your Life* (New York: Signet, 1973).

32 Fromberg, "A Cure for Procrastination."

33 Chris P. Neck and Charles C. Manz, "Thought Self-Leadership: The Influence of Self-Talk and Mental Imagery on Performance," *Journal of Organizational Behavior* 13 (1992): 681–699.

34 This example is drawn from Daft, *The Executive and the Elephant*, Chapter 5.

35 Robert Scaglione and William Cummins, "*Karate of Okinawa: Building Warrior Spirit*, (North Clarendon, VT: Total Publishing, 1993); and "Creative Visualization," Wikipedia http://en.wikipedia.org/wiki/Creative_visualization (accessed March 18, 2011).

36 This saying is attributed to neuropsychologist Donald Hebb and is often called Hebb's Law, as reported in Curt Thompson, "Rewiring Your Mind: Insights for Practical Living—'Neurons That Fire Together Wire Together,'" *Being Known Website*, http://www.beingknown.com/2010/07/neurons-that-fire-together-wire-together/ (accessed January 13, 2012), and numerous other sources.

37 James Hardy, "Speaking Clearly: A Critical Review of the Self-Talk Literature," *Psychology of Sport and Exercise* 7 (2006): 81–97.

38 Daft, *The Executive and the Elephant*, Chapter 5.

39 Timothy D. Wilson, *Strangers to Ourselves: Discovering the Adaptive Unconscious* (Cambridge, MA: Belknap Press, 2002), p. 32; and Haidt, *The Happiness Hypothesis*, pp.13–14.

40 Daft, *The Executive and the Elephant*, Chapter 5.

41 Tracy, *Eat That Frog*, p. 93.

42 Peter M. Gollwitzer, "Implementation Intentions: Strong Effects of Simple Plans," *American Psychologist* 54, no. 7 (July 1999): 493–503.

43 See S. J. Karau and J. R. Kelly, "The Effects of Time Scarcity and Time Abundance on Group Performance Quality and Interaction Process," *Journal of Experimental Social Psychology* 28 (1992): 542–571; S. G. Lim and J. K. Murnighan, "Phases, Deadlines, and the Bargaining Process," *Organizational Behavior and Human Decision Processes* 58 (1994): 153–171; and Cornelius J. König and Martin Kleinmann, "Deadline Rush: A Time Management Phenomenon and Its Mathematical Description," *The Journal of Psychology* 139, no. 1 (January 2005): 33ff.

44 Dan Ariely and Klaus Wertenbroch, "Procrastination, Deadlines, and Performance: Self-Control by Precommitment," *Psychological Science* 13, no. 3 (May 2002): 219–224.

45 *Ibid.*

46 Sarah Arnott, "Pfizer Chief Executive in Shock Retirement from 'Demanding' Job," *The Independent* (December 7, 2010): 36; and Jonathan D. Rockoff and Joann S. Lublin, "Citing Fatigue, Pfizer CEO Quits," *The Wall Street Journal* (December 6, 2010).

47 Richard Dool, "Lessons from the Military: A New Framework for Managing Change (C^5)," *Journal of Leadership and Organizational Studies* 17, no. 3 (2010): 253–263; and Joann S. Lublin, "Corporate News: Corner Office Turned Pressure Cooker," *The Wall Street Journal* (December 7, 2010).

48 Reported in Cari Tuna, "Lawyers and Employers Take the Fight to 'Workplace Bullies'" (Theory & Practice column), *The Wall Street Journal* (August 4, 2008).

49 Ed Frauenheim, "Recession Unleashes Boss Bullying," *Workforce Management*, April 2010, http://www.workforce.com/article/20100404/NEWS02/304049990# (accessed January 12, 2012).

50 T. A. Beehr and R. S. Bhagat, *Human Stress and Cognition in Organizations: An Integrated Perspective* (New York: Wiley, 1985); and Bruce Cryer, Rollin McCraty, and Doc Childre, "Pull the Plug on Stress," *Harvard Business Review* (July 2003): 102–107.

51 Discussed in Alice Park, "The Two Faces of Anxiety," *Time* (December 5, 2011): 54–65; and Sue Shellenbarger, "When Stress Is Good for You," *The Wall Street Journal*, January 24, 2012, http://online.wsj.com/article/SB10001424052970204301404577171192704005250.html (accessed April 6, 2012).

52 "Are You Working Too Hard? A Conversation with Mind-Body Researcher Herbert Benson," *Harvard Business Review* (November 2005): 53–58; and R. M. Yerkes and J. D. Dodson, "The Relation of Strength of Stimulus to Rapidity of Habit-Formation. *Journal of Comparative Neurology and Psychology 18* (1908): 459–482.

53 Mathias V. Schmidt and Lars Schwabe, "Splintered by Stress," *Scientific American Mind* (September–October 2011): 22–29.

54 M. Friedman and R. Rosenman, *Type A Behavior and Your Heart* (New York: Knopf, 1974).

55 This section is based on Robert Epstein, "Fight the Frazzled Mind," *Scientific American Mind* (September–October 2011): 30–35.

56 Sheldon Cohen and Thomas Ashby Wills, "Stress, Social Support, and the Buffering Hypothesis," *Psychological Bulletin* 85, no. 2 (1985): 310–357.

57 Eilene Zimmerman, "When Stress Flirts with Burnout," *The New York Times* (January 17, 2010).

58 Quoted in Joanna Barsh, J. Mogelof, and C. Webb, "How Centered Leaders Achieve Extraordinary Results," *The McKinsey Quarterly*, October 2010, http://www.mckinseyquarterly.com/How_centered_leaders_achieve_extraordinary_results_2678 (accessed January 16, 2011).

59 "Being More Productive," *Harvard Business Review* (May 2011): 83–87.

60 Ravi S. Kudesia, "Innovators Love Yoga and You Should Too," *Leader to Leader* (Fall 2010): 11–16.

61 J. Granath, S. Ingvarsson, U. von Thiele, and U. Lundberg, "Stress Management: A Randomized Study of Cognitive Behavioural Therapy and Yoga," *Cognitive Behavioral Therapy* 35, no. 1 (2006): 3–10.

62 "The Way I Work: Paul English, Kayak," *Inc.* (February 2010): 98–101.

63 Hermes Aleman, assistant vice-president, Affinity Bank, Hayward, California, quoted in Michelle Conlin, ed., "How to Get a Life and Do Your Job," *BusinessWeek* (August 25–September 1, 2008): 37–39.

CHAPTER 4
Creative Problem Solving

Chapter Outline

RYAN LASH

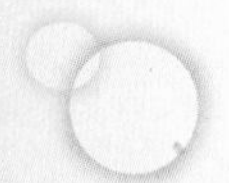

MANAGER CHALLENGE

VIDEO INCIDENT: GO FIGURE!

Caffeine and Crullers general manager Jane Sutton has a problem. Sales at two of C&C's bakery and coffee shops are off 15 percent in the past two months and she needs to find out what is going on. Director of operations Carrie Fishman thinks it is because of road construction. Human resources director Heather Carreau thinks it is because C&C's chief rival, Scone Prone, has started a popular line of gluten-free donuts, cookies, and cupcakes. Jason Wong, sales manager, thinks the stores need more promotions and social media advertising, as Scone Prone has been putting a lot of energy into Twitter lately. CFO Carlos Hernandez thinks it's because of layoffs in the area and says the focus needs to be on streamlining the accounts receivables, as that will help the long-term profit picture. Jane suspects that it is not just one thing causing the decline and that there might be other factors that are being overlooked. She has called everyone together to try to find a solution to the problem.

Initial Thoughts

1. **If you were Jane, what questions would you ask the team?**

2. **What strategies would you suggest for analyzing and solving the problem?**

Your instructor may ask you to be part of a role play based on the "Go Figure!" incident.

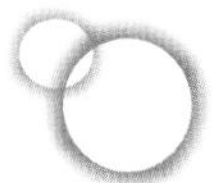

DISCOVER YOURSELF

For those students using CourseMate or CengageNOW, you can access the Daft/Marcic Assessment Library to take the questionnaires online and view dynamically updated comparative data.

Questionnaire 1[1]

Instructions: How do you make important personal decisions? To find out, think about a time when you made an important career decision or made a large purchase or investment. To what extent does each of the words below describe how you reached the final decision? Please check the six words that best describe how you made your final choice.

1. Logic ______	5. Facts ______	9. Reason ______
2. Inner knowing ____	6. Instincts ______	10. Feelings ______
3. Data ______	7. Concepts ______	11. Proof ______
4. Felt sense ______	8. Hunch ______	12. Heartfelt ______

Total Score Questionnaire 1: Number of even numbered words checked ________. Number of odd numbered words checked ________. Go to page 160 to interpret your score.

Questionnaire 2

Instructions: Respond to each of the following statements based on how you have *actually* approached a difficult problem at school or work. Rate how accurately each statement describes you based on whether the statement is clearly true or accurate, clearly false or inaccurate, or in the middle as somewhat true and somewhat false. Describe yourself as you are now, not as you wish to be. There are no right or wrong answers.

	True	Somewhat	False
1. I tried to see the problem in its entirety and see how it affected other people or departments.	○	○	○
2. I started by integrating information from different areas.	○	○	○
3. I enjoyed solving a complex rather than a simple problem.	○	○	○
4. I systematically talked to people who had diverse perspectives on the problem.	○	○	○
5. I certainly attempted to link a solution to an overall strategy or plan.	○	○	○
6. I analyzed root causes of the problem to find leverage points for a solution.	○	○	○
7. My approach was to focus on one part of the problem at a time.	○	○	○
8. I took time to consider the situation from all angles.	○	○	○
9. I studied how different parts of the relevant organization interacted to affect the problem.	○	○	○

Total Score Questionnaire 2 ________. Sum questions 1–6 and 8–9 by giving yourself 3 points for each True, 2 points for each Somewhat, and 1 point for each False; for question 7, scoring should be reversed (3 points for False, 2 points for Somewhat, and 1 point for True). Go to page 162 to interpret your score.

Questionnaire 3[2]

Instructions: In the list below, check each adjective that you believe accurately describes your personality. Be very honest with yourself. Check all the words that you think fit your personality.

1. affected ______	11. honest ______	21. original ______
2. capable ______	12. humorous ______	22. reflective ______
3. cautious ______	13. individualistic ______	23. resourceful ______
4. clever ______	14. informal ______	24. self-confident ______
5. commonplace ______	15. insightful ______	25. sexy ______
6. confident ______	16. intelligent ______	26. snobbish ______
7. conservative ______	17. interests narrow ______	27. sincere ______
8. conventional ______	18. interests wide ______	28. submissive ______
9. egotistical ______	19. inventive ______	29. suspicious ______
10. dissatisfied ______	20. mannerly ______	30. unconventional ______

Total Score Questionnaire 3 ________. Add one point for checking each of the following words: 2, 4, 6, 9, 12, 13, 14, 15, 16, 18, 19, 21, 22, 23, 24, 25, 26, and 30. Subtract one point for checking each of the following words: 1, 3, 5, 7, 8, 10, 11, 17, 20, 27, 28, and 29. The highest possible score is +18 and the lowest possible score is −12. Go to page 166 to interpret your score.

Questionnaire 4[3]

Instructions: For each question below, check A or B, depending on which answer is generally more descriptive of your behavior.

1. When I am working on a task, I tend to
   ______ A. Go along with a consistent level of work.
   ______ B. Work with high energy at some times, and with low energy at other times.

2. If there is a problem, I usually am the one who thinks of
   ______ A. A number of solutions, some of which are unusual.
   ______ B. One or two solutions that are methods other people would generally accept.

3. When keeping records, I tend to
   ______ A. Be very careful about documentation.
   ______ B. Be more haphazard about documentation.

4. In meetings, I am often seen as one who
   ______ A. Keeps the group functioning well and maintains order.
   ______ B. Challenges ideas or authority.

5. My thinking style could be most accurately described as
   _____ A. Linear thinker, going from a to b to c.
   _____ B. Thinking like a grasshopper, going from one idea to another.
6. If I have to run a group or a project, I
   _____ A. Have the general idea and let people figure out how to do the tasks.
   _____ B. Try to figure out goals, time lines, and expected outcomes.
7. If there are rules to follow, I tend to
   _____ A. Generally follow them.
   _____ B. Question whether those rules are meaningful or not.
8. I like to be around people who are
   _____ A. Stable and solid.
   _____ B. Bright, stimulating, and change frequently.
9. In my office or home, things are
   _____ A. Here and there in various piles.
   _____ B. Laid out neatly or at least in a reasonable order.
10. I usually feel the way people have done things in the past
   _____ A. Must have some merit and comes from accumulated wisdom.
   _____ B. Can almost always be improved upon.

Total Score for "I" _______. Give yourself one point for 1B, 2A, 3B, 4B, 5B, 6A, 7B, 8B, 9A, and 10B. **Total Score for "A"** _______. Give yourself one point for 1A, 2B, 3A, 4A, 5A, 6B, 7A, 8A, 9B, and 10A. Go to page 169 to interpret your scores.

GO ONLINE to find additional questionnaires at www.cengagebrain.com, search for Daft/Marcic Building Management Skills 1e, click on Free Online Resources, click on Additional Self-Assessments.

- Intolerance of Ambiguity
- New Manager Decision Making

DISCOVER YOURSELF

SHUTTERSTOCK #53973379

Chapter 4: Creative Problem Solving

DISCOVER KNOWLEDGE

The Atlantic first published the "Battle Hymn of the Republic," provided a public voice for the abolitionist movement, and ushered the first stories of Mark Twain, Henry James, and Ernest Hemingway into print—153 years old and looking like it wouldn't get much older when Justin Smith arrived in 2007 with a mandate to stop the flow of red ink. Smith's problem was to reinvent *The Atlantic*. Smith and editor James Bennet got managers and editorial people together to brainstorm: "What would we do," they asked, "if the goal was to aggressively cannibalize ourselves?" The outcome was that *The Atlantic* became one of the first magazines to assertively combine their print and digital sides. Walls between the print and the digital departments literally and figuratively came crashing down. Advertising salespeople were told it no longer mattered what percentage of their sales were digital or print, a move many magazines are just now making. Young, Web-savvy writers were hired to write blogs and opinion columns, a scary move for a magazine accustomed to producing highly polished, totally fact-checked, error-free articles. To make sure people were reading, managers decided to dismantle the website's subscription paywall so that anyone could freely browse *The Atlantic Online*. Within three years, the company was in the black, and Smith and Bennet were hailed as a marvel in the publishing world because of the decisions they had made to get it there.[4]

At any moment of any day, there are managers engaged in some aspect of problem solving. Some problems are easy, and many are difficult and frustrating, such as the problems faced by managers at *The Atlantic*.

THE PROBLEMS MANAGERS FACE

A fast-food worker doesn't show up for his shift. The computerized customer service system shuts down. A customer complains that sales representatives are disrespectful to her Hispanic employees. A needed shipment of parts is late, threatening to shut down production. Nurses have scheduled a walkout to begin on Monday. Your biggest customer requests a product modification that may alienate other customers. A key team member has been showing up for work late and is not performing up to par. Community residents are complaining about the pollution created by a factory. All of these problems must be solved by managers.

A manager's primary job is to solve problems. Managers solve small problems and big problems, fast ones and ones that may take years to resolve. In the world of a manager, there's always something going wrong that requires a problem-solving response. A **problem** exists whenever a gap exists between actual performance and desired performance—when things are not operating as they should. **Problem solving** basically means the process of taking corrective action to meet objectives and achieve desired results. Any time there's a discrepancy between what you as a manager want to happen and what is actually happening, there is a problem. Your company needs a marketing manager and the current one has just resigned. That's a problem that has to be solved. Your department's goal is to process 500 insurance claims a day but it is routinely processing only 425. Another problem. The company cafeteria runs out of bagels every day but has dozens of muffins that eventually have to be thrown out. Yet another problem a manager has to solve.

Problems take many forms. Simple problems often are instantly clear, and good information is available about how to bring things back in line. Some simple problems occur so frequently that managers can even establish a standard rule or programmed response for solving them.[5] Managers at an insurance company might establish a rule to automatically reorder paper or other office supplies when inventories drop to a certain level, for instance. A hotel banquet manager might solve the problem of staffing a last-minute sit-down function for the local chamber of commerce by relying on a standard rule of calling in one server for every 30 guests.[6] However, managers face many problems that are really difficult to understand and solve. These difficult problems are vague, hard to define, or broad in scope. In some cases, managers disagree over what the real problem is. Managers do the best they can to make a decent judgment based on their best insight. Managers at *The Atlantic*, for example, spent years grappling for a solution to the problem of declining subscriptions and sinking advertising revenues. By the time Justin Smith and James Bennet arrived, managers had already tried various solutions, such as having the magazine's owner personally contact advertisers, printing the magazine on more expensive paper, printing on less expensive paper, increasing the subscription cost, and lowering the subscription cost. For problems that have no clear-cut solution, managers have to rely on research, analysis, creativity, judgment, intuition, experience, trial and error, and some guess work to craft a response. Try solving the problems in Exhibit 4.1 as a metaphor for managerial problem solving. You will get a taste of the difficulties and potential mistakes that await you as a manager.

DISCOVER KNOWLEDGE

Exhibit 4.1 Solve the Following Problems

Answer the questions below before reading the rest of the chapter:

1. A piece of paper is folded in half, in half again, etc. After 100 folds, how thick will it be? Take your best guess: __________. I am 90 percent sure that the correct answer lies between __________ and __________.
2. A compulsive smoker wakes up at 2:00 AM and is out of cigarettes. No stores are open. He searches through the waste paper baskets and ashtrays for butts, knowing that with five butts he can roll a new cigarette. He finds 25 butts, and smokes one cigarette an hour, which is enough to last him until he can buy more. How long did his supply last? The number of hours is __________.
3. Which figure below is most different from the others?

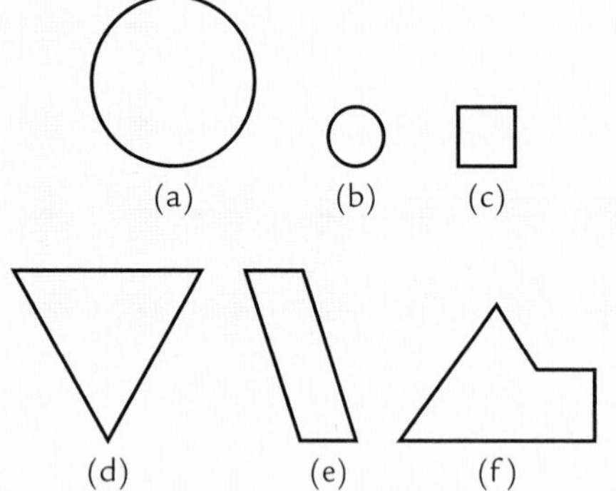

4. As owner and CEO of your company, you decided to invest $100 million to build pilotless drones that cannot be detected by enemy radar. When the project is 90 percent complete, a competing firm begins marketing a completed drone that cannot be detected by radar. In addition, their drone is much faster, smaller, cheaper, and more sophisticated than the drone your company is developing. The question is: Should you invest the last 10 percent of the research funds to finish your drone? Check one of the following answers.

   __________ No—There is no reason to continue spending money on the project.

   __________ Yes—After investing $90 million, we might as well finish the project.
5. Give a quick (five-second) estimate of the following product without actually calculating:

   8 × 7 × 6 × 5 × 4 × 3 × 2 × 1 = __________.
6. How many times does the letter "f" appear in the following sentence?

   These finished files have been developed after years of scientific investigation of administrative phenomena, combined with the fruit of long experience on the part of the two investigators who have come forward with them for our meeting today.

   The letter "f" appears __________ times.
7. Robert is envious, stubborn, critical, impulsive, industrious, and intelligent. In general, how emotional do you think Robert is? (Circle one number.)

   Not emotional at all 1 2 3 4 5 6 7 8 9 Extremely emotional
8. Which would you choose between the two alternatives below?

   __________ Alternative A: A 50 percent chance of gaining $1,000.00

   __________ Alternative B: A sure gain of $500.00

   Which would you choose between the two alternatives below?

   __________ Alternative C: A 50 percent chance of losing $1,000.00

   __________ Alternative D: A sure loss of $500.00
9. An unbiased coin is flipped three times and each time comes up heads. If you had to bet $100.00 on the next toss, which side would you choose?

   __________ Heads

   __________ Tails

   __________ No preference
10. Consider the following problems. Each row of three words has something in common. Just relax and

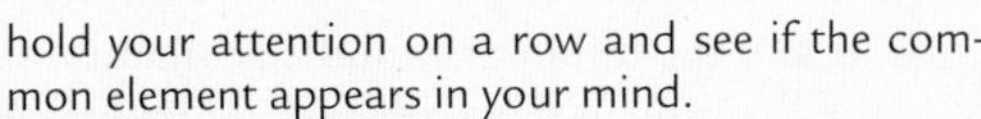

hold your attention on a row and see if the common element appears in your mind.

a. beans	golf	envy
b. blue	rat	cottage
c. April	locker room	bride-to-be
d. fishermen	nuclear reactor	curtain
e. tailor	bowling alley	wrestling match

11. In the following illustration, remove three matches to leave four.

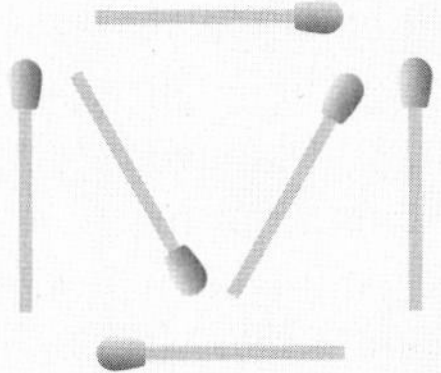

12. Rearrange the matches below to get nothing. You cannot remove, bend, break or overlap any matches.

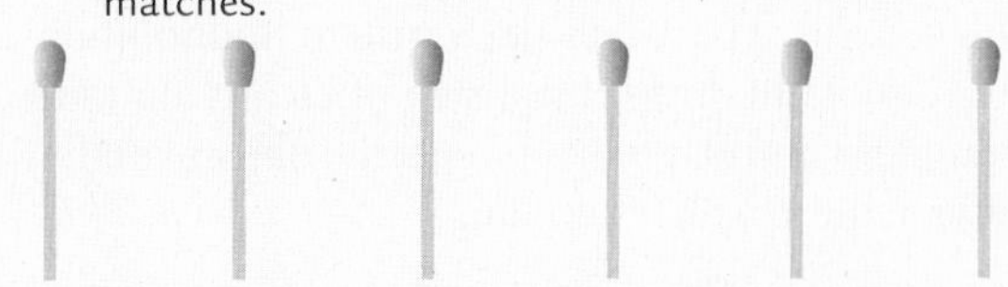

After you have specified an answer to each problem, you will find the answers on pages 183–184.

Sources: Questions 1, 4, 5, 6, 7, 8, and 9 are from research studies reviewed in Scott Plous, *The Psychology of Judgment and Decision Making* (Philadelphia: Temple University Press, 1993); the match puzzles are from Michael Michalko, *Tinkertoys*, 2nd ed. (Berkeley, CA: Ten Speed Press, 2006); question 3 is based on an item in the *Creativity in Action Newsletter* as reported in Arthur B. VanGundy, *Idea Power: Techniques & Resources to Unleash the Creativity in Your Organization* (New York: Amacon, 1992); question 2 is adapted from Eugene Raudsepp with George P. Hough, Jr., *Creative Growth Games* (New York: Perigee Books, 1977).

PROBLEM-SOLVING BASICS

Managers with the Los Angeles Lakers knew that superstar player Kobe Bryant was grumbling to the press about being unhappy with the team.[7] The first step managers needed to take was to clearly define the problem. This would include recognizing that Kobe's grumbling was a genuine problem, not just idle comments, and then determining why he was unhappy. In this case, Kobe felt that the team was not championship material and that managers were doing little to take it to that level. Next, managers had to dig deeper to find out what caused the problem and identify alternative solutions. With a superstar basketball player, there's little time for analysis, so managers sat down face to face with Bryant to figure out what the real issues were. Bryant wanted the Lakers to initiate steps he thought could take the team to the championship level, including obtaining better players and bringing back a former general manager. Finally, managers had to choose what to do about the problem and execute the solutions over the succeeding months as they upgraded the team.

The process LA Lakers managers took follows a classic problem-solving pattern. The model in Exhibit 4.2 shows this straightforward three-stage process for solving problems: Define the problem, select a response, and then execute a solution. This process is sometimes called a *rational* or *analytical* approach to problem solving because it stresses systematic analysis of a problem followed by choice and implementation of solutions in a logical, step-by-step sequence.

Stage 1: Define the Problem

Accurately defining a problem is the first critical step toward solving it. Stage 1 involves defining the problem

Exhibit 4.2 Stages in the Problem-Solving Process

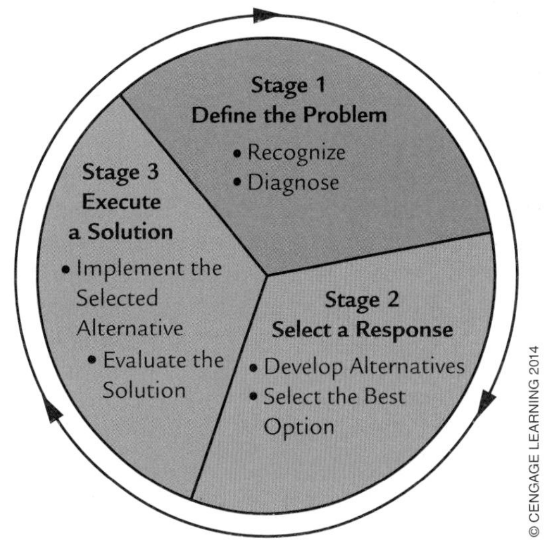

© CENGAGE LEARNING 2014

and getting clear about the goals and outcomes managers desire. Sometimes, managers are so busy with day-to-day activities that they fail to even realize that a problem exists. Then, they often rush to find solutions and overlook the first critical step of clearly defining the problem and clarifying the specific objectives they want to achieve with a solution.

Recognize the Problem

As a manager, you will be responsible for continually monitoring the internal and external organizational environment to detect deviations from planned or acceptable performance.[8] This process resembles the military concept of *gathering intelligence*. Managers scan the relevant world around them to determine whether the organization is satisfactorily progressing. Some people don't want to face bad news, so they stick their heads in the sand and refuse to see problems. To be an effective manager, you won't have that option. When individual or organizational accomplishment is less than desired goals and outcomes, a problem exists—some aspect of performance isn't up to par.

Learn to connect the dots. A radio station manager heard a disk jockey make an unfavorable on-air comment about a community group. Over the course of several months, she also received a written complaint about the DJ, overheard negative comments about him at a local restaurant, and had family members mention hearing unfavorable talk about the DJ. These various tidbits of information alerted the manager to a problem and prompted her to investigate further.[9] Seeing that a problem exists often requires integrating bits and pieces of information in novel ways. It is important to not just see the dots but to connect the dots into a meaningful interpretation. For example, the failure of U.S. intelligence agencies to recognize the imminent threat of Al Qaeda prior to the September 11, 2001 attacks has been attributed partly to a failure to connect the dots. Managers didn't have the systems that could help them put together myriad snippets of information that pointed to a problem.[10]

Use your intuition. Many problems are vague and ill-formed. Managers simply get a gut feeling that something is off kilter. Developing your intuition is an excellent way to pick up on vague problems. **Intuitive problem identification** means using your experience and judgment to recognize problems. Useful intuition is based on years of experience and hands-on practice that is stored in the subconscious mind.[11] Without experience in a job, your intuition may not be grounded in a practical reality. One study of manager problem-finding showed that 30 out of 33 problems were vague and ill-defined.[12] Bits and scraps of unrelated information from informal sources resulted in a pattern in the manager's mind. The manager couldn't prove a problem existed but had a gut feeling that a certain area needed attention.

DISCOVER YOURSELF

Interpret Your Score: Rational versus Intuitive Decision Making
(Questionnaire 1)

The odd-numbered items pertain to a rational decision style and the even-numbered items pertain to an intuitive decision approach. Of the six words you chose, how many represent rationality versus intuition? If all six words are either rational or intuitive, then that is clearly your dominant decision approach. If four words are either rational or intuitive, then that approach would be considered your preference. Comparative data for decision-making styles are: **Rational** (odd-numbered questions) Thirty person Mean score = 2.3, Top Quartile = 3–6; Bottom Quartile = 0–1. **Intuitive** (even-numbered questions) Mean = 3.6, Top Quartile = 5–6; Bottom Quartile = 0–3. CNOW and CourseMate users can access dynamically updated comparative data through www.cengagebrain.com.

© CENGAGE LEARNING 2014

Diagnose the Problem

Diagnosis is the next key step in defining the problem. Managers make a mistake if they jump right into generating alternatives for solving a problem without first exploring what brought about the problem in the first place. Why is the claims department processing only 425 insurance claims rather than the 500 managers have set as a goal? Why are sales of a product in a department store down 20 percent? Why is a formerly punctual employee now late to work every Monday and Thursday?

Grasp the true nature of the problem. Diagnosis involves digging below the surface to analyze underlying causal factors. To get a grasp on the true nature of a problem, you have to take on the role of a detective. Good managers carefully analyze the situation and dig for facts that help them determine the boundaries of the problem they need to address.[13] At one social service agency, managers were concerned with a decrease in the number of the agency's grant proposals being funded, which threatened the ability of the agency to do its work. Some blamed the new grant writer, but careful detective work revealed a more widespread problem.[14] Some program directors were getting their information to the grant writer at the last minute, leaving her little time to double-check facts, seek more information, or proofread proposals. Digging further, the manager-detectives learned that some directors were unaware of the critical importance of meeting proposal deadlines. Their priority was serving clients, not submitting reports to the grant writer. Many of these long-term program directors didn't have much respect for the grant writer, who was a new, young employee in a newly created position. The agency director had failed to make clear the vital need for collaboration and timely submission of information, and he had never reprimanded any of the directors for their failure to cooperate with the grant writer. Only when the problem had been investigated and clarified could managers begin to solve it.

Build consensus. One of the best ways to clarify problems, as well as the goals and outcomes desired from a solution, is to make sure all the people who have a stake in the issue or a perspective on the problem are involved. You will learn that most problems don't affect only you as a single manager. It often takes multiple perspectives to see all sides of a problem clearly. **Problem consensus** refers to the agreement among stakeholders about the nature of a problem and about which goals to pursue. Sometimes, managers agree readily, but in most cases they use discussion, bargaining, and compromise to reach consensus. A good example of problem consensus is when U.S. President Barack Obama delayed the 2009 decision to send additional troops to Afghanistan for several weeks while he built a consensus around diagnosis of the problem. He gathered many diverse and competing perspectives from the military, Department of Defense, State Department, Congress, and his own staff. For example, he learned from General Eikenberry that the Afghan president, Hamid Karzai, would be a weak partner in the counterinsurgency effort. Obama acquired a deep understanding of the problem by looking at it from all angles before he decided on the alternative of sending additional troops.[15]

With consensus problem identification, you identify both your and the other parties' priorities and work together with others to determine what problems to tackle and the options that best meet various sets of needs. An important aspect of collaborative problem solving is devoting time to talking about the outcomes other people want. This outcome or goal aspect of problem identification asks people to think creatively about what is possible. Rather than accepting a problem as given, managers consider what opportunities it might hold.[16] Many times a situation can be framed as an opportunity rather than a burden, which changes the problems managers choose to solve and the priorities they place on them.

Stage 2: Select a Response

In Stage 2 of the problem-solving process illustrated in Exhibit 4.2, managers develop alternatives for solving the problem and select one to implement. In the case of the radio station manager mentioned earlier, options might include talking with the offending DJ to set limits on behavior, issuing a warning, imposing a punishment of some type, or replacing the DJ.

Develop Alternatives

For many problems, managers have to lay out a range of alternatives to address or repair the underlying causes. There are defined approaches to developing alternative solutions.

Search the environment. The first step to developing good options often is to look around in the immediate environment. **Search** means to seek out alternatives within the organization's repertoire of solutions. For example, in the case of correcting a star disc jockey, the manager could ask what the radio station did the last time an announcer broke the rules for on air conduct. To carry out the search, the manager could look into her own memory, talk to other managers, examine formal written policies and procedures, and look at historical documents from previous on-air incidents.[17] The idea is to find what has worked in the past and build on that. If there is no precedent, or if the problem is highly novel so that previous experience has no value, the manager may have to design a custom solution. Forming a custom solution may involve a lot of discussion among managers, who gradually design a solution via trial-and-error. Designing a one-time solution often is an incremental procedure, building the solution brick by brick.

Think systemically. Kepner and Tregoe, who have conducted extensive studies of manager decision making, urge that managers look at the interconnectedness of events and activities.[18] You can't develop an effective solution to a problem if you think too small. Step back and think about the whole system. A **system** is a set of interacting elements that continually affect one another over time and work toward a common purpose.[19] The human body is a system, as is the planet Earth, the city of London, Walmart, and the Pittsburgh Steelers. **Systemic thinking** means to see the synergy of the whole rather than just the separate elements of a system. The point is to learn to develop alternatives with respect to whole system patterns. Sometimes, solving a problem by focusing only on discrete parts actually makes the whole system function less effectively. For example, one small city decided to solve traffic congestion by embarking on a road building program without considering cause-effect relationships in the whole system. With new roads available, people began moving further from the center of the city. The new and widened highways actually increased traffic congestion, delays, and pollution by enabling suburban sprawl.[20]

Organizations are highly complex systems with hundreds of interrelated pieces. It is the *relationship* among the parts that form the whole system that matters. Effective managers learn to look for patterns and interrelationships over time so that they can see how their actions and decisions affect the whole. David McCamus, former chair and CEO of Xerox Canada, calls this the ability to view the organization through a wide angle lens rather than a telephoto lens.[21] When you're confronted with a problem as a manager, you have to ask how changing one thing will affect other things.

DISCOVER KNOWLEDGE

DISCOVER YOURSELF

Interpret Your Score: Systemic Thinking (Questionnaire 2)

Systemic thinking as an approach to problem solving is generally considered to be holistic rather than reductionist, to seek the big picture of how things fit together rather than focus on a specific part. Analytical thinkers, for example, break a problem down into parts whereas a systemic thinker would strive to understand why the parts fit together in a larger context.

If your score is 21 or higher, you probably have a tendency toward systemic thinking. If your score is 15 or less, you probably approach problems by focusing on individual parts of a problem rather than on the interaction of the parts as a whole system. A score of 16–20 implies that you use some elements of systemic thinking some of the time. Comparative data for **systemic thinking:** Thirty person Mean score = 21.6, Top Quartile = 24–25; Bottom Quartile = 14–20. CNOW and CourseMate users can access dynamically updated comparative data through www.cengagebrain.com.

© CENGAGE LEARNING 2014

Select the Best Alternative

For every problem, there comes a time when you have to stop searching, analyzing, and discussing and take the plunge: You have to decide which alternative to try. Some managers can be paralyzed by trying to choose the perfect solution. Others tend to jump on the first alternative that seems reasonable without carefully looking at other options. Managers should strive to find the alternative that offers the most advantages and is least likely to cause problems in other parts of the system.

You sometimes have to "satisfice." **Satisficing** means to accept a satisfactory outcome rather than trying to maximize or achieve an optimal outcome or level of performance. An 80 percent solution now is usually better than a 100 percent solution one year from now. Managers are very busy and most of them approach complex problems with a goal of finding a solution that is "good enough" to solve the problem rather than looking for a "perfect" choice.

Use your judgment. In the case of an ambiguous, difficult problem, intuition and judgment often will be used to pick the better alternative. Intuitive judgment is not arbitrary or irrational because it is based on years of practice and hands-on experience. With long experience, managers develop a gut feeling or hunch about which alternative will solve a problem, speeding the problem-solving process. The value of intuitive judgment is supported by a growing body of research.[22] Managers may walk a fine line when selecting an alternative. They need to conduct adequate study without overreliance on numbers and rational analysis. For example, after Hurricane Katrina hit the Gulf Coast, Valero Energy managers made the intuitive decision to keep everyone on the payroll while other refineries shut down and laid off workers. Valero managers' judgment was that this choice would reflect corporate values of putting employees first. Valero's values-based judgment helped the company rise from number 23 to number 3 on *Fortune* magazine's list of Best Companies to Work For—and enabled Valero to get back to business weeks faster than competitors.[23]

Obtain support. Building consensus among key managers is important for selecting the right alternative just as it was important at the problem identification stage. One part of the organization affects other parts, so a coalition of key department managers is important for smooth implementation of the decision. Effective managers reach broad agreement to support the selection of a desired alternative. A good idea is to consult with everyone who will be affected by the decision, including line departments, staff specialists, and even external groups such as powerful customers, bankers, or union representatives. Particularly for difficult problems, effective problem solving involves a substantial amount of consensus building.

Stage 3: Execute a Solution

The final stage in the problem-solving process in Exhibit 4.2 is to execute a solution. This stage involves action steps and follow-through to bring the solution into reality.

Implement the Selected Alternative

Execution of a solution typically starts with formal or informal *authorization* for the chosen alternative. The decision may be passed up the hierarchy to the responsible hierarchical level, or even to the board of directors. Authorization is often routine because the expertise and knowledge rest with the lower-level managers who identified the problem and developed a solution. However, some solutions might be rejected because of implications not anticipated by lower-level managers.

After authorization, managers use managerial, administrative, and persuasive abilities and give directions to people to ensure that the chosen alternative is put into action. If the alternative is not successfully implemented, it will not solve the problem, no matter how good the chosen alternative might have been. Managers have to get employees to "buy in" to the proposed idea and mobilize the people and resources to put the solution into action, which may be the hardest step in the process.[24] Some people may feel resistance to a new way of doing things, which is why it was important to build consensus in the earlier stages of the process.

Evaluate the Solution

In the evaluation stage, managers follow up by gathering information that tells them how well the alternative was implemented and whether it was effective in solving the problem and achieving desired goals. Feedback is important because problem solving is a continuous, never-ending process. It is not complete when a manager or board of directors votes "yes." Feedback provides managers with information that can precipitate a new decision cycle if things are not working as planned. Implementation may fail, thus generating a new analysis of the problem, new alternatives, and a new choice. A big problem may be solved by trying several alternatives in sequence, each providing modest improvement.

Consider the evaluation and feedback for a new deodorant at Tom's of Maine. Managers at Tom's, known for its all-natural personal hygiene products, discovered a problem when the deodorant worked only half the time, and its all-recyclable plastic dials were prone to breakage. Tom Chappell and other managers diagnosed the underlying cause, which was an incomplete development process that did not test the product properly. Developers did not do stringent testing for a product they loved. Chappell himself helped answer complaints, and the product was recalled, costing the company $400,000 and much negative publicity. This evaluation and feedback effort triggered the establishment of *acorn groups*, cross-departmental teams that supervise a new product from beginning to end. The testing department was part of the acorn groups. Tom's was able to turn a product disaster into an opportunity, thanks to careful evaluation and feedback of the decision outcome. The acorn groups provided a formal organization mechanism for sharing ideas—something the company did not have before.[25]

MAXIMIZE YOUR PROBLEM-SOLVING EFFECTIVENESS

A NASA scientist was taking a shower in a German hotel while pondering how to fix the distorted lenses in the Hubble telescope. He and other engineers had been struggling with the problem of how to fit a corrective mirror into the hard-to-reach space inside the orbiting telescope. Suddenly, he noticed how the European-style showerhead was mounted on adjustable rods. This

LEADING WORDS

"Most people spend more time and energy going around problems than in trying to solve them."
—**Henry Ford, Sr.**
American industrialist, founder of Ford Motor Company

"If you don't ask the right questions, you don't get the right answers. Asking questions is the ABC of diagnosis. Only the inquiring mind solves problems."
—**Edward Hodnett**
American poet (1841–1920)

"It is natural that we make mistakes. The question is, what do we do with these mistakes? Do we repeat the mistakes? Do we learn from them? Do we investigate them and implement a solution?
—**Ori Hadomi**
CEO of Mazor Robotics

"I love to play devil's advocate . . . I always find that you learn more by arguing with someone than by just agreeing with them."
—**Richard D. Fain**
chair and CEO of Royal Caribbean Cruises

© CENGAGE LEARNING 2014

perception connected with the Hubble problem as he realized that corrective mirrors could be extended into the telescope on similar folding arms.[26] This scientist found a new way of thinking about an old problem, which led to a solution.

Using the three-stage model in Exhibit 4.2, beginning with identifying and diagnosing the problem and ending with implementation and evaluation, can help you make better decisions for solving problems. This approach can be used with difficult problems because it helps you think systematically rather than jump to a premature solution. Now let's consider some ideas for maximizing your effectiveness at each of the three stages. Exhibit 4.3 illustrates techniques that can improve your success in applying the three stages of the problem-solving process, and these techniques are discussed in the following sections.

Stage 1: Techniques for Improving Problem Definition

In order to solve a problem, managers need to understand it in both concrete and measurable terms.[27] When faced with a problem, it is tempting for busy managers to rush to a solution before fully understanding what is wrong. Techniques such as *root cause analysis* and the *five whys* can help you avoid moving too hastily.

Root Cause Analysis

Root cause analysis (RCA) is a systematic approach to finding out what the "true" or root cause of a problem is instead of continuing to address symptoms of the problem. For instance, if there is a puddle of oil on the floor, wiping it up fixes the symptom but it does not address the underlying cause of leaking oil. RCA typically involves five steps: defining the problem, understanding the process associated with the problem, identifying possible causes, collecting the data, and analyzing the data.[28] RCA can be time consuming because it involves collecting evidence and carefully identifying cause-and-effect relationships that combine to create a problem. Typically, the root cause of a problem is a result of human behavior or system malfunction. This step-by-step problem-solving method slows things down to find out what has occurred and why it occurred, before considering

Exhibit 4.3 Techniques to Improve Problem Solving

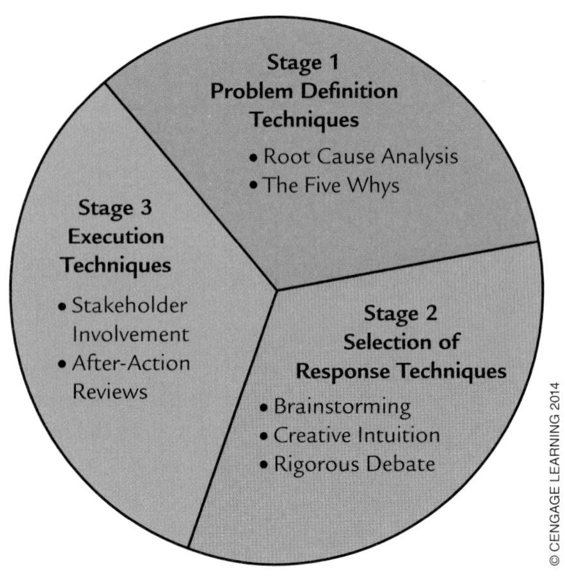

© CENGAGE LEARNING 2014

what, if anything, can be done to fix it. The extra time it takes to uncover the root cause generally fixes the problem and prevents the same or similar problems from reoccuring.

The Five Whys

The **five whys** is similar to root cause analysis in that it is a question-asking approach used to understand cause-effect relationships underlying a problem with an unknown cause. If you have ever been around children then you know they can ask the question "why" often. They will continue to ask why until they have an answer that is sufficiently clear to them. This is the same principle behind the *five whys* method of determining the cause of a recurring problem. The technique primarily involves the simple activity of asking "why" at least five times until the real cause of the problem is discovered.

The steps in the five whys technique are:

1. Describe the problem, preferably in writing, so that both you and others involved are clear about exactly the problem to be solved.
2. Ask "why" the problem has occurred. Keep track of the answers.
3. Keep asking why until the deepest cause of the problem is determined. Ask why at least five times, and more if necessary.
4. From the answers recorded, the cause can be determined. Make sure the team agrees with the outcome before starting to implement a solution.

Joel Spolsky, co-founder and CEO of Fog Software, used the *five whys* technique with the owner and staff of event-planning company Carsonified to get to the bottom of problems he encountered working with the firm to produce a ten-city series of technical conferences. On the second stop on the tour, one problem was an inability to switch video fast enough. Spolsky asked *Why?* The answer was that they were using a cheap switch from a local office supply store. *Why?* Because Carsonified had assumed the venue operators would provide a high-quality switch but they did not. The next *Why?* revealed that the venue didn't have Spolsky's list of audio-visual requirements. *Why?* Because Carsonified hadn't gotten it there in time. *Why?* The successful event-planning company, which had never had anything like this go wrong before, didn't have a standard checklist of procedures to follow for each conference. The five whys revealed the bottom-line cause of the problem, and the company's managers followed up with a solution of improved checklists: what to do one month before an event, one week before, one day before, and so forth.[29]

Stage 2: Techniques for Developing and Selecting Alternatives

Studies show that limiting the search for alternatives is a primary cause of decision failure.[30] When looking for solutions, the more creatively people think, the better. **Creativity** can be defined simply as generating new and potentially useful ideas.[31]

Two first-rate strategies for increasing creativity and generating numerous alternatives for solving a problem are brainstorming and creative intuition. When it comes time to select one alternative to try, rigorous debate can help managers make the best choice. Each of these strategies is described in the following sections.

Use Brainstorming

Brainstorming uses a face-to-face interactive group to spontaneously suggest a wide range of creative ideas. The keys to effective brainstorming are:

- **No criticism.** People shouldn't criticize or evaluate ideas in any way during the spontaneous generation of ideas. All ideas are considered valuable.
- **Freewheeling is welcome.** People should express any idea that comes to mind no matter how weird or fanciful. As a full-time developer of ideas at Intuit said, "It's more important to get the stupidest idea out there and build on it than not to have it in the first place."[32]
- **Quantity desired.** The goal is to generate as many ideas as possible—the more ideas the better. A large quantity of ideas increases the likelihood of finding excellent solutions. Combining ideas is also encouraged. All ideas belong to the group and members should modify and extend ideas whenever possible.[33]

Brainstorming has been found to be highly effective for quickly generating a wide range of creative alternatives. After all the ideas are expressed and recorded, the group can have another session to discuss and evaluate which ideas or combination will best solve the problem.

However, the technique does have some drawbacks.[34] For one thing, people in a group often want to conform to what others are saying. Others may be concerned about pleasing the boss or impressing colleagues. In addition, many creative people simply have social inhibitions that limit their participation in a group session or make it difficult to come up with ideas in a group setting.

One approach that can overcome some of these disadvantages is *brainwriting* or *electronic brainstorming*. Brainwriting brings people together either in person or in an interactive group over a computer network.[35] One member writes an idea, another reads it and adds other ideas, and so on. Studies show that electronic brainstorming generates about 40 percent more ideas than individuals brainstorming alone, and 25 to 200 percent more ideas than regular brainstorming groups, depending on group size.[36] Why? Because the process is anonymous, people feel free to say whatever they want. Also, people can write down their ideas immediately, avoiding the possibility that a good idea might slip away while the person is waiting for a chance to speak in a face-to-face group. Social inhibitions and concerns are avoided, which typically allows for a broader range of participation. Another advantage is that this type of brainstorming can potentially be done with groups made up of employees from around the world, further increasing the diversity of alternatives.

Develop Your Creative Intuition

The creative flash of insight is actually the second stage of creativity. The first stage is data gathering. Your mind is gathering data constantly, especially when you're studying background material on a problem to be solved. Then the creative insight bubbles up as an intuition from the deeper subconscious. It's sometimes difficult to trust that intuitive process because it seems "soft" to many business executives. Yet the subconscious mind remembers all experiences that the conscious mind has forgotten. Intuition has a broader reach than any analytical process focused solely on the problem at hand. Annie Duke, a top professional poker player, relies on her intuition to make decisions and win games. "There are layers upon layers of information [at the poker table]. I can't think of all that consciously, but I'm making instant decisions based on my experience," Duke says.[37]

Where or when do you get your best ideas? The most popular response is "in the shower." Creativity often occurs during a mental pause, a period of mixed tension and relaxation. In the shower, or while exercising, driving, walking, or meditating, the mind reverts to a neutral, somewhat unfocused state in which it is receptive to issues or themes that have not been resolved. A temporary activity that is relatively simple and mindless can provide the moment for a creative flash arising from deep in the subconscious. If the analytical part of the mind is too focused and active, it shuts down the spontaneous part. Thus, the semi-relaxed mental "pause" is like putting the analytical left brain on hold and giving room for the intuitive right brain to find the solution in the subconscious mind.[38] C.S. Lewis, author of *The Chronicles of Narnia*, often went for long walks to facilitate his creative juices. Novelist Stephen King runs several miles most mornings. One university study suggests that a single aerobic workout can kick the brains of college students up a few notches for a couple of hours. Thus, physical exercise may be as effective as the shower for triggering the appropriate relaxed state that enables creative intuition to break through.[39]

Engage in Rigorous Debate

Increasing your own and others' creativity with the techniques just described can help you come up with more alternatives for solving problems. When it comes

DISCOVER YOURSELF

Interpret Your Score: Your Problem-Solving Creativity (Questionnaire 3)

Your score on this questionnaire reflects your creativity. The average score for a set of 256 assessed males on this creativity scale was 3.57, and for 126 females was 4.4. A group of 45 male research scientists and a group of 530 male psychology graduate students both had average scores of 6.0, and 124 male architects received an average score of 5.3. A group of 335 female psychology students had an average score of 3.34. If you received a score above 5.0, your personality would be considered above average in creativity.

To what extent do you think your score reflects your true creativity? Compare your score to others in your class. Comparative data for **Problem-Solving Creativity:** Thirty person Mean score = 4.1, Top Quartile = 8–13; Bottom Quartile = 0–1. CNOW and CourseMate users can access dynamically updated comparative data through www.cengagebrain.com.

© CENGAGE LEARNING 2014

to making better choices among those alternatives, a good approach is to encourage a rigorous debate of the issue at hand.[40] Good managers know that constructive conflict based on divergent points of view can bring a problem into focus, clarify people's ideas, stimulate creative thinking, create a broader understanding of issues and alternatives, and improve solution quality.[41]

There are several ways to stimulate rigorous debate. One way is by ensuring that the group is diverse in terms of age and gender, functional area of expertise, hierarchical level, and experience with the business. Some groups assign a **devil's advocate,** who has the role of challenging the assumptions and assertions made by the group.[42] The devil's advocate may force the group to rethink its approach to the problem and avoid reaching premature conclusions. Jeffrey McKeever, chair and CEO of MicroAge, often plays the devil's advocate, changing his position in the middle of a debate to ensure that other managers don't just go along with his opinions.[43] Another way to encourage constructive conflict is to use a technique called **point-counterpoint,** which breaks a decision-making group into two subgroups and assigns them different, often competing, responsibilities.[44] The groups then develop and exchange proposals and discuss and debate the various options until they arrive at a common set of understandings and recommendations.

Stage 3: Techniques for Executing a Solution

Once an alternative is selected, managers then have to make sure the proposed solution is executed. Managers use communication, motivation, and leadership skills to see that the proposed solution is put into action. For many problems, executing a solution is a slow process that takes place over time.

Moreover, people need to see that managers follow up on their decisions by tracking how effectively the solution addresses the problem. Regular feedback and evaluation is important because solving problems is a continuous, never-ending process. Sometimes solutions fail and managers have to look at the problem from a different perspective. Many big problems are solved by trying several alternatives in sequence, each providing modest improvement. The following sections offer suggestions for effective execution.

Involve Stakeholders

Obtaining multiple perspectives and agreement during the problem identification stage fosters cooperation among affected parties during implementation of the solution. Involvement leads to commitment. Failure to engage stakeholders in the early stages will likely lead to their resistance during implementation. For example, a new professor who wanted to start an academic leadership center in her university's business school talked to several senior professors about how to go about it. Later, when it came time for the faculty to vote on the proposed center, they voted in favor because they had been engaged at the beginning of the project. As another example, before *The New York Times* adopted a pay subscription plan for its online newspaper, internal debates raged for years. Thanks to that broad debate, most of the issues were resolved and internal stakeholders were on board when it came time to implement the decision in 2011.[45]

What's Your Problem?

Q: I'd like to have more guts in the decisions I make. I often think up great ideas and then lack the fortitude to go through with them. I kick myself later when I see that they could have worked. How can I stop worrying and be more of a risk taker?

A: The problem starts with imagination. You've got enough imagination to think up great ideas, and you've also got enough imagination to see the possible drawbacks. It sounds like fear of failure has you obsessing over the snags. No idea is foolproof. You have to detach from the idea and float it out to others. There is no loss if they don't grab it. If someone does grab hold, you can try it out together. Having the idea in the first place is often the easiest part. The next part is to share it with others, and then join them in the grinding work of implementation. You all get credit when it works. If you hold too tightly to your idea, your fear of failure will keep your idea on the ground. Share it with others and let your idea fly.

Source: This problem is based on Jeremy Bullmore, "What's Your Problem?" *Management Today* (March 1, 2008): 79.

Use After-Action Reviews

An excellent mechanism for evaluation and feedback is the after-action review. **After-action reviews** are quick sessions during which managers review the outcome of activities to see what worked, what didn't, and what can be learned from it. The concept of after-action reviews comes from the United States Army. After every identifiable activity—whether in field operations or training simulations—people take 15 minutes to ask four simple questions: What was supposed to happen? What actually happened? What accounts for the difference? What can we learn? Many businesses, including consulting firm Jump Associates, oil giant BP, and Steelcase, Inc., which makes office furniture, also use after-action reviews for feedback and learning.[46]

DISCOVER KNOWLEDGE

PERSONAL APPROACHES TO CREATIVE PROBLEM SOLVING

True Body Products founder Janice Shade recently had to wrestle with the problem of whether or not to grow her company by adding a scented line of soaps to the company's list of all-natural unscented products. Whole Foods requested scented products from the company, and Shade was concerned that saying *no* to the big retailer would hurt True Body's growth. Shade took a big picture approach and thought about whether or not adding a scented line would weaken brand identity, alienate loyal customers, and complicate production and marketing operations for the small company. Shade met with her advisory board to discuss various options for future growth and decided to nix the idea of a scented line. Instead, she would expand True Body into new types of non-scented personal-care products.[47]

Some managers might have decided to test the idea of a scented line with one product and see what happened. Others might have jumped wholeheartedly into providing a full line of scented products because Whole Foods was offering shelf space. Janice Shade, though, took an innovative approach, looking at various alternatives for how the company could grow. Although many managers follow a similar problem-solving process, each individual approaches a problem and its possible solutions differently. Two key types of personal approach to problem solving are the innovator and the adaptor.

Your Creative Problem-Solving Style

Creative approaches to problem solving were studied by Michael J. Kirton, who found that people vary between two primary creative styles for solving problems: innovative and adaptive.[48] Exhibit 4.4 lists some characteristics of innovator versus adaptor styles.

The innovator style likes to challenge basic assumptions to discover new alternatives. This style often starts with a big picture, challenges basic assumptions, may come across as undisciplined and impractical, and may make unusual combinations of symbols, metaphors, or analogies to gain a totally new perspective on a problem. The innovator style is the most likely to develop radical breakthroughs by viewing something from fresh angles. For example, George de Mestral, a Swiss amateur mountaineer, saw the irritating, small prickly burrs stuck to his pants and socks through a truly novel assumption—how could he reproduce the burrs' clinging properties? After ten years of effort, he invented Velcro.

The adaptor style seeks to expand on and improve something that already exists. This style uses creativity to improve a work method or technology already

Exhibit 4.4 Two Key Problem-Solving Styles

Innovator	Adaptor
Disrupts status quo	Works within established framework
Approaches tasks from unexpected angles	Employs a systematic, precise approach
Discovers problems	Concerned with solving rather than finding problems
Questions current assumptions and approaches	Attempts to refine practices within current framework
Has little need for consensus; may be insensitive to others	Is sensitive to group cohesion and cooperation

Sources: Based on Michael J. Kirton, "Adaptors and Innovators: A Description and Measure," *Journal of Applied Psychology* 61, no. 5 (1976): 622-629, and Paul Herbig and Laurence Jacobs, "Creative Problem-Solving Styles in the USA and Japan," *International Marketing Review,* 15, no. 1 (1996): 63–71.

in use. The adaptor approach to creativity works with facts to solve problems and seeks solutions by improving methods that worked in the past. This style may involve fact gathering and trial and error to solve a problem. People using this style tend to be precise and reliable to improve and optimize things already in operation. For example, Levi Strauss found great demand for canvas trousers during the gold rush days of the 1850s. Later he modified his trousers with a fabric called denim and dyed it blue to minimize soil stains. Sales skyrocketed for the improved "blue jeans."

Good managers may use a mix of styles. Most people have a dominant approach to problem solving, but managers may use a different style in solving the varied problems they confront daily. For example, as a manager you might use an adaptor style for solving the problem of revising the look of your company's business cards, yet shift to a more innovative style when handling an interdepartmental conflict. Being aware of your dominant problem-solving style can help you avoid making critical mistakes when your usual style may be inappropriate to the problem at hand.

DISCOVER YOURSELF

Interpret Your Score: Creative Problem-Solving Styles (Questionnaire 4)

If your "A" score is higher, you have an *adaptor* style. If your "I" score is higher, you have an *innovator* style.

Now subtract your I score from your A score to find the absolute value and write it here: ______

If the difference between your A and I scores is 1 or less, you are a **Balanced Innovator/Adaptor** style.

If you are an adaptor and the difference between A and I is 2 to 4, you are a **Moderate Adaptor** style. If you are an Adaptor and the difference between A and I is 5 to 7, you are a **Mid-Range Adaptor** style. If you are an Adaptor and the difference between A and I is 8 to10, you are a **Strong Adaptor** style.

If you are an Innovator and the difference between A and I is 2 to 4, you are a **Moderate Innovator** style. If you are an Innovator and the difference between A and I is 5 to 7, you are a **Mid-Range Innovator** style. If you are an Innovator and the difference between A and I is 8 to 10, you are a **Strong Innovator** style.

Comparative data for creative problem-solving style are: **Innovator** ("I" questions) Thirty person Mean score = 2.9, Top Quartile = 4–6; Bottom Quartile = 1–2. **Adaptor** ("A" questions) Mean = 7.1, Top Quartile = 8–9; Bottom Quartile = 4–6. CNOW and CourseMate users can access dynamically updated comparative data through www.cengagebrain.com.

© CENGAGE LEARNING 2014

COMMON MISTAKES IN PROBLEM SOLVING

For years, General Motors was the world's largest automaker. But by 2009, the storied company was bankrupt and struggling to survive, practically begging people to buy its vehicles. The high cost of offering a multiplicity of brands started to cause problems for GM in the 1970s, largely due to spikes in oil prices and growing competition from foreign automakers. However, managers stuck with their strategic decision to offer a multitude of brands long after there was clear evidence that trying to cover the whole range of the auto market was paving the way to disaster. Only bankruptcy and a forced restructuring finally pushed managers to cut GM's brands from eight down to four.[49]

Solving problems is a large part of a manager's job, but some managers consistently fail in this area because they aren't aware of the cognitive biases that can skew their judgment. Managers at GM, for instance, based their decisions on what had worked in the past rather than carefully analyzing how the auto industry and the market had changed. Researchers have identified several common errors that prevent managers from solving problems effectively.[50]

Getting Trapped in the Status Quo

In a classic *Harvard Business Review* article, researchers Hammond, Keeney, and Raiffa point out that many people who inherit shares of stock they never would have selected themselves don't take the simple

step of selling the shares and putting the money into a different investment. It would be a relatively quick and easy thing to do, but people have a bias toward leaving things as they are.[51]

In organizations, managers frequently solve problems based on what worked in the past rather than exploring new options, digging for additional information, or investigating new technologies, as illustrated by the example of General Motors. As another example, Swiss watchmakers invented quartz technology, but their success in mechanical watches prevented them from recognizing the future path of the watch industry. They essentially gave the new technology away and lost most of the global watch market to U.S. and Japanese companies.[52]

Asking questions such as *What if our strategy is wrong?* or simply *Why not do this?* can help managers avoid the status quo trap. Experts also recommend *over-searching* when considering critical problems, which means digging deeper and looking more widely than you think is necessary.[53] Perpetuating the status quo might not matter so much in small areas, but in situations in which an error in judgment would be highly costly, expand your outlook and actively search for different approaches.

Justifying Previous Solutions

Have you ever been in a relationship that your friends (and even you) could see was bad for you but you kept pouring more and more effort into trying to make it work? If so, you understand the concept of *escalating commitment*. **Escalating commitment** refers to a tendency to continue investing time, money, and energy in something, despite strong evidence that it is not working.[54] For example, in organizations, managers frequently spend a tremendous amount of time and effort trying to improve the performance

7 STEPS TO . . .
Squash Your Creativity

1. **Seek the correct answer.** Formal education teaches us to find the one correct answer to a problem. Creativity is just the opposite, because messy real-life problems have multiple correct answers. The second or third or fifth answer is likely to turn out better than the first.
2. **Be an "expert."** Thinking you know the answer closes your mind to fresh and original thinking. The attitude of beginner's mind is open to new ideas, unlike expert mind.
3. **Always think logically.** Creativity is often illogical to the extreme. Logical thinking helped build society, but forcing everything into a logical sequence pushes away your creativity. Allow your mind to be at play, silly, and contrarian to stimulate your creative juices.
4. **Stay in your comfort zone.** In an era of super-specialization, combining completely unrelated areas of knowledge will spark creative insight. Break your habit pattern of focusing only on the comfort zone of your domain by exploring unusual territory.
5. **Follow the rules.** Arbitrary rules and limits are a destructive force for creativity, especially the rules in your own mind. Often the rebel in you is more creative. Ask *why not* of the perceived limits defining how things "should" be done in your field.
6. **Fear failure.** Great baseball players miss the ball far more often than they hit it. To increase your creativity, stop fearing mistakes. Take more chances and you'll succeed more often. The practice will increase your confidence and fun. See failure as a learning experience.
7. **Think "I'm not creative."** One certain self-fulfilling prophecy is thinking you are not creative. You *are* creative, but you have to strip away your false beliefs to experience that potential. Take baby steps at first, and enjoy the result. When creativity starts bubbling up, that too is self-fulfilling.

Sources: Brian Clark, "Do You Recognize These 10 Mental Blocks to Creative Thinking?" May 17, 2011, http://www.copyblogger.com/mental-blocks-creative-thinking/ (accessed May 21, 2011); Dan Rieck, "8 Bad Habits that Crush Your Creativity and Stifle Your Success," May 18, 2011, http://www.copyblogger.com/creativity-killers/ (accessed May 21, 2011); and Richard L. Daft, *Management*, (Mason, OH: South-Western/Cengage, 2008), p. 280.

Exhibit 4.5 Self-Test of Overconfidence

For each of the following ten items, provide a low and a high estimate, so that you are 90 percent sure the correct answer falls between the two. Your challenge is to be neither too narrow (i.e., overconfident) nor too wide (i.e., underconfident). If you successfully meet this challenge, you should have 10 percent misses—that is, exactly one miss.

	90% Confidence Range LOW	HIGH		90% Confidence Range LOW	HIGH
1. Length of the Amazon River in miles	_____	_____	6. Number of countries on African continent	_____	_____
2. Period in days that a joey (baby) red kangaroo stays in the pouch	_____	_____	7. Thomas Edison's age at death	_____	_____
3. Year of first successful satellite launch into	_____	_____	8. Air distance from Paris to New Delhi	_____	_____
4. Number of Tony Awards given to Rogers and Hammerstein musicals	_____	_____	9. Number of islands in the Hawaiian chain	_____	_____
5. Number of books in the Bible (Old and New testaments)	_____	_____	10. Number of hours first astronauts stayed on the moon's	_____	_____

After you have provided guesses for each item, you will find the answers on page 184.

Source: Based on J. Edward Russo and P. J. H. Schoemaker, *Decision Traps: Ten Barriers to Brilliant Decision Making and How to Overcome Them* (New York: Simon & Schuster, 1989), p. 71.

of a problem employee whom they now realize they should never have hired in the first place or at least fired long ago.

People don't like to make mistakes, so they continue to justify previous choices. In addition, people don't like to lose, whether it be money, love, status, or whatever. Recall our discussion of *negativity bias* from Chapter 3. Our minds tend to accentuate the negative. Therefore, we tend to analyze problems in terms of what we fear losing rather than what we might gain.[55] That's why this bias is sometimes referred to as the *sunk-cost trap*. Managers continue to pour money into a failing project, hoping to turn things around and recover their costs. For example, a major cause of Blockbuster's decline was its huge investment in brick-and-mortar buildings, which its managers couldn't let go of even as Netflix took its customers.

Being Overconfident

Most of us grossly overestimate our ability to predict uncertain outcomes. Evidence of overconfidence is illustrated by cases in which people were so certain of their answer that they assigned odds of 1,000 to 1 of being correct but were in fact correct only about 85 percent of the time. Confidence and optimism are terrific qualities that can enable managers to face trying situations and tough challenges, but overconfidence leads to flawed decisions that often exacerbate rather than solve problems. Test your own confidence level in Exhibit 4.5.

Overconfidence may be the most common trap for successful managers. For example, despite the fact that two-thirds of mergers fail to achieve intended results, overconfident CEOs continue to bet millions of dollars that *this one will be the exception*. When companies experience a long string of success, managers tend to believe that whatever they do will lead to continued success. Consider how overconfidence in blowout preventer technology contributed to the disastrous 2010 BP oil spill off the Gulf Coast of the United States. If the crew of the Deepwater Horizon oil rig lost control of a well and a blowout occurred, a fail-safe device called a blind shear ram was supposed to slice through the drill pipe and seal off the well. But when this disastrous event actually happened, the technology failed. Based on previous incidents, BP and Transocean managers had decided to use just one blind shear ram in the blowout preventer, even though some other rigs were already using two. Overconfidence that they understood and could manage the risks of deep sea drilling caused managers to make numerous poor decisions that led to disaster, and overconfidence meant

that executives weren't prepared to deal with a huge deep sea oil spill.[56]

As a manager, you will solve problems every day. By applying the ideas and techniques discussed in this chapter, you can avoid the mistakes described in the previous section (e.g., fighting for the status quo or being overconfident in your own solutions), prevent strong emotions from getting in the way of making a thoughtful decision, and apply ideas for bringing creativity to the problem-solving process.

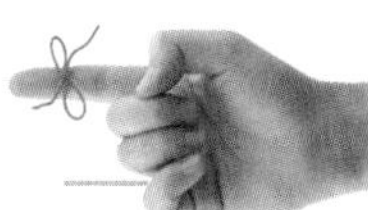

NEED TO KNOW

DISCOVER KNOWLEDGE

- As a manager, you will be a problem solver. A problem exists when there is a discrepancy between what managers want to happen and what is actually happening. Some problems are simple, but many problems managers face are difficult to understand and solve.
- A classic approach to problem solving includes the three stages of defining the problem, selecting a response, and executing a solution. Defining the problem includes recognizing that a problem exists and diagnosing the underlying causes. Selecting a response means generating alternatives and choosing the best option to try to solve the problem. Executing a solution involves implementing the chosen alternative and evaluating how well it addressed the problem.
- Techniques for improving problem definition are to use root cause analysis and a method called the five whys. You can generate better alternatives for problem solving by using brainstorming or brainwriting and creative intuition. Encouraging rigorous debate, using a devil's advocate, and applying the point-counterpoint technique can help managers when it comes time to select the best alternative to try.
- Unless the alternative is effectively executed, the problem cannot be solved. Techniques for effective execution are to involve stakeholders and use after-action reviews for evaluation and feedback.
- Each individual solves problems differently, but most people use either an innovator or an adaptor style. Good managers use a mix of styles to solve varied problems.
- Common mistakes in problem solving include perpetuating the status quo, justifying past decisions, and being overly confident.

ACTION LEARNING

DELIBERATE PRACTICE EXERCISES

The 5 Percent Challenge

According to a story on the *Fast Company* magazine website, if you spend 5 percent of your time on creative activities, you will not take away from how much work you get done.[57] Furthermore, you will find yourself flooded with new ideas and innovative thinking. You can get creative inspiration from activities such as going to an art museum; attending a concert, play, or ballet; visiting an historic landmark, monument, or park; sitting next to a lake or river; painting or potting; attending a lecture by an artist.

Step 1: Plan two or three artistic activities for the next week that will add up to about two hours of your time. That means two hours out of the normal 40-hour workweek, or two hours out of 112 waking hours, which is actually less than 2 percent of your time.

Step 2: Complete the table below.

Artistic activity	When will you do it?	What was it like?
1.		
2.		
3.		

Step 3: Answer the following questions.

1. Did you feel guilty taking time "away"?
2. What was the impact of being in a creative environment?
3. Did you find, as *Fast Company* said, that you suffered no loss of productivity? That is, you got all your work done?
4. How can you sustain this creative endeavor?

Step 4 (Optional): Share your insights with a partner, and ask your partner what insights he or she gained.

Use Your Intuition

There is something in you that knows much better than you know.

—Rochelle Myers

One of the most surprising facts about how managers made the 25 strategic decisions studied is that so few reported using explicit analysis; only in 18 out of 83 choices did managers mention using it.

—Henry Mintzberg

As people move from beginner to expert in a subject area, problem solving moves from fact- and rule-based decision criteria to intuitive judgment. New leaders operate by "sight" (personally see things) and analysis. Experienced leaders operate partly by "feel."

Purpose: This exercise asks you to practice using your intuition. For the following week, you are to practice trusting your experience and intuition above your rational, analytical mind. Try to rely less on your mind's "thinker" or analyzer. To do this, start small. Pay particular attention to your personal life decisions in mundane areas (lunch, driving route, etc.). Each time you have a small decision to make, just ask yourself if it's a "yes" or a "no" to explore the answer within you.

Step 1: Choose four problems or decisions that confront you and use ONLY intuition to solve the problem.

Helpful Tips and Ideas:

Find a way to spend some quiet time alone this week—a useful condition for listening to your intuition. Turn off your radio or iPod. Shut off your phone. Go for a solitary drive. Slow down and wait for the intuitive response.

If your intuition is unclear, flip a coin and assess your feeling about the outcome. Act on the coin flip outcome and see if your intuition tells you that is the right choice.

Step 2: Complete the following table describing the problems and how you used your intuition.

Describe the problem or decision	What might have been your *rational* response?	What did your intuition tell you?	What was the outcome?
1.			
2.			
3.			
4.			

Step 3: How can you find ways to naturally integrate intuition into your life after this week?

ACTION LEARNING

Step 4 (Optional): Share your insights with a partner, and ask your partner what insights he or she gained.

IN-CLASS TEAM EXERCISE

Boyberik: Team Problem Solving[58]

Purpose: To learn how to solve an unusual problem in a group.

Background: The new country of Boyberik has requested help from the World Bank to develop its economic system. One project approved is to develop a reasonable pricing system for its products, in order for Boyberik to compete in the global marketplace. The main industry in Boyberik produces *babkizzes* of high quality. In Boyberik, quantities are measured by bunches and gaggles. Paper currency is called *bani-bani*, and the four types of coins are *groshen*, *mezuma*, *penizay*, and *fluce*.

Team Goal: Your task is to determine the price each *babkiz* should sell for. The instructor will give each group a set of cards with information on each card. You are allowed to tell other group members what your cards say, but you CANNOT show the cards to anyone else.

Step 1: Divide into groups of five to eight members. Each group goes to a different part of the room, after which the instructor gives a set of cards to each group.

Step 2: If desired, one or two members in the group can be assigned to act as observers. One person in the group deals the cards, trying to give an equal amount (or near equal) to each "playing" member (not observers). Members may not show cards to anyone else, but may share information orally among themselves. Cards should not leave their "owners'" hands during playing.

ACTION LEARNING

Step 3: Each group tries to solve the problem of what should be the price of each *babkiz*.

Step 4: The instructor announces the solution to the groups.

Step 5: Observers give feedback. This can be done either within individual groups, after which there is a general discussion, or there can be general feedback given to the class as a whole.

FIELD TEAM EXERCISE

What Does the Future Hold? A Visioning Exercise

Step 1: Each individual prepares for the group exercise by finding at least four articles from newspapers or magazines that talk about changes in technology, economy, climate, social norms, and so on. Read the articles you located and write up a one-paragraph summary of each article. Be prepared to read the summary to your group.

Step 2: Divide into groups of three to six. Your job is to predict the future. You are all members of a strategic planning committee at a huge conglomerate that owns companies doing very diverse types of business. The organization expects to become even more diversified in coming years. The board wants to have a sense of new business opportunities and also current lines of business that may need updating or shutting down.

To stimulate your thinking, consider how much has changed since 1990. We went from:

Climate control to climate change
Hierarchy to "hire me now"
FM to iTunes
VHS to YouTube
Career path to "brand me"
Regular hours to 24/7
One-location to virtual organizations
Two-party cooperation to political stand-off
Some immigrants to lots of immigrants
Dial-up connections to WiFi
Princess phones to smartphones
Empowerment to engagement
Detroit to Japan to Detroit
Those poor nerds to those powerful nerds
"Father of the Bride" to "Bridesmaids"
Job choices to few jobs
Borders to Amazon
JCPenney to Zappos
Check books to debit cards

Step 3: Each individual reads his or her article summaries to the group (Person 1 read one summary, then Person 2 read one summary, and so on, until all summaries have been read). Do not comment until everyone has read their summaries.

Step 4: Spend a few minutes talking within your group about the patterns that emerged from the articles you shared.

Step 5: As a group, prepare a report for the board of directors listing the changes you expect to influence business by 2022. Everyone should more or less agree with the final list you will turn in.

Step 6: Talk about whether your discussion of expected changes has changed the way you look at your own career path. The instructor may choose to have you do this as a class or within your groups.

TEST YOUR METTLE

ROLE PLAY SIMULATIONS

Go Figure!

Background: Re-read the written Video Incident at the beginning of this chapter.

Instructions: Form into groups of five or six. One person will be general manager Jane Sutton, who will run the meeting. One person will be director of operations Carrie Fishman, one CFO Carlos Hernandez, one sales manager Jason Wong, and one HR director Heather Carreau. If there are six, the sixth person will be an observer. Each person reads only his or her confidential role, but the observer reads all. Spend 15 minutes on the role play.

Confidential information for Jane: Caffeine and Crullers corporate office has sent you an urgent message (and followed up with angry phone calls) about the slippage of sales in two of your Madison locations. Sales at the other ten locations are not down, but then again, they are not up to corporate's projections either. You've called your management team together to figure out what is happening. Once you understand what is going wrong, you can devise a plan to reverse the sales decline. You've got to be careful with your people. They can be extreme and sometimes tend to exaggerate, so you know you have to take what they say with a grain of salt.

Confidential information for Jason: Your boss, Jane Sutton, has called a meeting to discuss the sales decline at two C&C locations. Corporate has been on her case. Really, they could have just asked you. Anyone knows that the advertising campaign Corporate endorsed is really lame. Why didn't they ask you for advice? You got your MBA in marketing, after all. They always think they know best, even though they rarely get up to Madison and stay mostly in their executive offices in Milwaukee. Jane wants to know what is going on. Well, she better listen, because you have the answer.

Confidential information for Carrie: Jane Sutton, your boss, has called a meeting so you can all discuss why sales at two of Madison's C&C locations are down. Isn't it obvious? Highway construction right in front of these two places!! They've got orange cones all over the place. What's to discuss? No one wants to face the simple truth. You've seen it over and over again in this dysfunctional company—people prefer to talk about fairy tale reasons rather than accept the obvious answer. The rest of them have their pet answers, the solutions they use for every problem. Why doesn't Jane see this? Really, she is lucky to have you.

Confidential information for Carlos: Oh, another wasted morning. Your boss has called a meeting to discuss declining sales at two locations. You already told her the cause: The Oscar Mayer plant, which is close to both of those locations, had a huge layoff. With fewer plant workers around, that's fewer customers for C&C. Why spend precious time discussing what is already obvious? Oh well, you have to go to the meeting, wasted time or not. At least you can remind everyone how much money can be saved if they give you the resources to focus on accounts receivable. But you intend to make the meeting end as soon as possible, so you can get some REAL work done.

Confidential information for Heather: You're being called in to discuss the problem of declining sales. You are so sick of the fighting that goes on in this group. Why can't people be nice to one another? There just doesn't seem to be any empathy. And anyway, the answer is so obvious. Scone Prone is cleaning up with their new line of gluten-free products. Really, Jane should spend the meeting time having everyone learn to be nice to one another.

After the role play, discuss these questions:

1. How well did the group do in following the problem-solving process? Refer back to Exhibit 4.2 and the text discussion so you can track how well they followed the problem-solving steps.
2. How difficult is it to stay on track with problem solving when everyone has opposing ideas about problem causes and what should be done?
3. What did you learn about problem solving?

The Mess Up

This Role Play Simulation is available online at www.cengagebrain.com.

VIDEO APPLICATION

Solving Problems at Plant Fantasies

Teresa Carleo, owner of Plant Fantasies in New York City, makes decisions and engages in creative problem solving every working day.

Discussion Questions

1. Did Teresa Carleo follow a rational or intuitive decision process to launch Plant Fantasies? Explain.
2. In what ways does Carleo get to use her creativity in solving problems? Have you experienced creative problem solving in a job? Give examples.
3. What did Carleo mean when she said, "The decision to start the business was exciting, but the determination to stay with the business was excruciating." How can one decision be exciting and the other excruciating?

TEST YOUR METTLE

CASE INCIDENTS

Team Players

Krista Acklen was the "golden girl" of a metropolitan government in a large midwestern city. The top graduate of a local high school, she studied in France and interned at *Vogue* in Paris before returning to the States for an MBA and a position with a top New York PR firm. She knew *everyone*, and chatting with or *doing lunch* with the rich and famous was a normal day for Krista.

The only child of a single mom, Krista dropped it all and eagerly returned to her midwestern hometown when her mother's health declined suddenly. She had barely settled in and established home care for her mother when the mayor's office contacted her with a job proposal. Would Krista consider a position developing and directing a public art program for the city? She enthusiastically accepted the job. With her winning connections, drive, and abilities, she quickly expanded her mission to develop a range of arts programs. Donations and grant money poured into programs under her established 501(c) 3 organization developed as a friend's organization for city parks. Headquarters for Acklen and her staff was a comfortable unused third floor space in the city library, which used to hold books and magazines that were now stored digitally.

Acklen was curious to learn why John Mitchell, director of parks and recreation, had summoned her to a meeting "to learn of a decision I have made that will affect your group." Knowing that budget factors recently forced reduction in staff and office space throughout city government, and aware of the importance of dealing carefully with public opinion as well as the feelings of employees and other stakeholders, Acklen felt she was prepared for any decision Mitchell might have reached.

She tried to get comfortable in the chair across from Mitchell, who seemed ill at ease. Avoiding small talk, Mitchell said that he intentionally did not discuss the decision in advance because he believed Acklen would object. He would not accept her objections anyway, he indicated, so the decision was final.

"What is the decision?" queried Acklen.

"The mayor wants half of your group's office space for the Greenways project," Mitchell replied, "and I see no alternative except for you to agree. The mayor's idea makes sense and you must go along."

Acklen felt fury rising within her chest as she stared at Mitchell while thinking to herself, "This people-pleasing, brown-nosing jerk. He will do anything to win the mayor's favor."

The Greenways project, directed by Lisa Todd, had developed a number of beautiful areas throughout the city. In recent years, Greenways had received the bulk of new money and attention from the federal government, and Todd's staff had grown with the additional funding and development projects.

As Acklen regained her composure, she shot back at Mitchell. "Not consulting me on this is unacceptable. I should be part of any decision affecting my staff and program. I could have helped plan a solution that worked for everyone." Mitchell tried to speak, but Acklen kept going. "You have a responsibility to my group as well as to the mayor. I think you are giving us the shaft as an easy way to please her."

The two argued a while longer, but Mitchell wouldn't budge. Finally, Acklen said, "John, since this was your decision, you should be the one to tell my people. You better come over soon before the word gets out."

"No," Mitchell said, "you are their immediate boss. You have to tell them. That's your job. Where is your team spirit, anyway?"

Acklen returned to her office and seethed to Joanne Franklin, her most senior employee. "Oh no," Joanne moaned. "We really need all this space. Our program is growing, too."

Acklen agreed, as she explained Mitchell's support of the suggestion from the mayor's office to make additional office space available to Lisa Todd and her staff. Joanne started brainstorming. "I suppose we could pair up in the offices."

Acklen shook her head. "We *are* team players. But John Mitchell and the mayor need to know that this was not handled in a way that shows respect for our employees." After a pause she continued, "I'm too frazzled to think about it anymore today. Let's talk about this tomorrow."

Discussion Questions

1. What mistakes do you think John Mitchell made with the way he solved the problem of limited office space? Explain.
2. What approach would you have used if you were Mitchell? Why?
3. What are Krista Acklen's options for responding to Mitchell's decision? What should she do now? Why?

Medici Mediterranean Restaurant

Gui-do. Gui-do.

As Alissa Mason drove up the mountain through the rain, she turned up the volume on the radio to clear her mind. However, despite the music, the steady rhythm of the truck's windshield wipers steered her mind back to *the problem.*

Gui-do. Gui-do.

Ten years earlier, Alissa's dream of opening a Mediterranean-style restaurant came true with the launching of Medici. Even now, Alissa smiled, recalling how the once-annoying habit of mispronunciation (*Medi-ki*) by ranchers and townspeople had become yet another endearing quality of owning a business in a small town.

In 2000, a graduation gift from her rancher dad provided Alissa the opportunity to travel throughout the Mediterranean region, culminating in a stint at a cooking school in Tuscany. Upon return to her hometown, and armed with a dream, her MBA, and a box load of ideas for tantalizing meals, Alissa was certain she had the recipe for success. She was right.

The opening of the new restaurant was a triumph, and its popularity and reputation for delicious food spread rapidly, attracting state and regional press coverage. In addition to a strong local customer base, Medici's location on the route from the interstate to several popular mountain resorts offered opportunities to become a favorite stopover for tourists, skiers, and hikers. Within a few years, the amazing success of the business and the constant barrage of suggestions for a second location closer to the resorts encouraged Alissa to consider expansion. The problem was how to manage locations almost an hour apart while maintaining the level of quality and service customers expected.

Guido Bertolli appeared to be the answer to her prayers. A handsome, charming Italian, Guido was a talented chef from a large family of talented chefs. The youngest of four brothers, Guido realized he would not inherit the family restaurant and decided to immigrate to America to build a reputation as a chef away from his dominating father and brothers.

Guido's experience and amazing talents as a chef, his natural ease in attracting staff, and the charm and joy he displayed in his interactions with customers soon convinced Alissa that she had found the perfect person to direct the new restaurant. Looking back, she realized her own enthusiasm for expansion and a starry-eyed impression of the Italian, shared by an adoring public, led to mistakes in her business judgment.

Following a fabulous opening, the new restaurant soared to financial success, far out-pacing its small-town sister location. But by the end of the second year, problems loomed to the point that Medici II could go under financially. Alissa's travels to the resort location became more frequent, cutting into the time needed at the original restaurant. Crowds filled the resort restaurant. ("We *love* Guido." "You're so lucky to have found him.") And patrons waited patiently in lines. However, delivery problems led to frequent changes in popular menu items. Recurring delinquency in the payment of bills and invoices, as well as Guido's increasingly lax attitude regarding his presence on site, led to confrontations. The wait staff were undisciplined, and way too much food was lost or wasted. Realizing his value to the organization, Alissa always accepted Guido's promises to do better. Each time, the problems returned, and staff frustration at both locations increased.

Recently, rumors reached Alissa that Guido was exploring the possibility of opening his own rival Mediterranean restaurant. Alissa was not sure she wanted to keep Guido, but she did not want her popular chef to move and take devoted customers with him. The bottom line—the clientele wanted Guido. Alissa was certain he would be able to obtain financial backing for his venture based on his talents and popularity. She realized she must do something before Guido moved further into the process.

As she drove, Alissa was aware of her growing stress level. The situation with Guido was taking over every aspect of her life. The time for serious discussion loomed. For days she had weighed her options.

The Options

Maintain the Status Quo

Alissa liked Guido and would like to avoid another confrontation. Her own management style was non-confrontational, and she wondered if sitting down with Guido to discuss a more manageable plan for handling office administrative details at his location would be a good solution until she could be certain of his future plans. The thought of hiring someone to assist Guido with the business details occurred to her, but that meant the addition of another full-time employee—a step she was not sure she could take at this time.

Discipline or Fire Guido

With a repeat of the same problems that had been addressed on previous occasions, Alissa felt that disciplinary steps were futile. However, firing Guido set up the very situation—her talented chef as a rival—that she wanted to avoid. Still, with his shaky business skills, there was no guarantee he would be able to create a strong business plan, secure financial backing, and sustain a rival restaurant despite his popularity and talents as a chef. It would not be the first time a great chef failed as an owner.

Focus on Medici II

Alissa wondered if it would be better to move her entire operation to the resort. The original restaurant had her heart, but the resort location had the talented chef and the bulk of the clientele. If she closed the first location and maintained only the resort location, she would take over the business side, relieve Guido of the responsibility for which he was obviously ill-suited, and maintain more control over his work habits.

Offer Guido a Partnership

Rewarding Guido with a partnership might be a way to keep him with Medici and create a stronger sense of loyalty while also fulfilling his desire to run his own business. However, if she offered Guido a minority stake, she would give up a portion of control and increase his role in the direction and day-to-day operations of the business.

Decision Time

As Alissa pulled into the parking lot, the rain ended and Guido stepped out of the doorway and waved. With no clear answer, she walked with Guido to his office.

Discussion Questions

1. Can you think of other options Alissa might consider to solve this problem? Explain.
2. If you were Alissa, do you feel ready to make the decision? What would be your next step? Why?
3. Evaluate each alternative carefully. Which would you choose? Why?

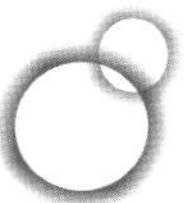

PERSONAL SKILLS LOG

Directions: Fill in the rows below based on what you learned from each part of the chapter that you completed.

	What is my key takeaway or insight from this activity?	What do I personally do well (strength) regarding this activity?	What could I improve (weakness) about myself regarding this activity?	How might I use what I've learned from this activity in the future?
Manager Challenge Incident:				
Discover Yourself Questionnaires:				
Deliberate Practice Exercises:				
In-Class and/or Field Team Exercises:				
Role-Play Exercises:				
Case Incidents:				

Answers to Questions in Exhibit 4.1

1. The answer is unbelievably huge: roughly 800,000,000,000,000 times the distance between the Earth and the sun. Your mind was *anchored* in the thinness of a sheet of paper, thereby leading you to dramatically underestimate the effect of doubling the thickness 100 times. Initial mental anchoring to a low or high point leads to frequent incorrect solutions. How certain did you feel about your answer? This is an example of overconfidence, a major cause of manager mistakes.
2. The answer is six hours. The 25 butts will make five cigarettes that will last five hours. The butts from those five cigarettes will make one additional cigarette to last the sixth hour. If you don't focus carefully on the problem and possible solutions, you may overlook important information.
3. Every figure is different in some way. Figure (a) has the greatest area, (b) has the least area, (c) is the only square, (d) is the only three-sided figure, (e) is most narrow and lopsided, and (f) is least symmetrical and five-sided. Did you stop after finding one correct answer? This would have prevented you from finding the ultimate correct answer.
4. If you checked "yes," you felt the desire to continue investing in a previous decision even when it was failing, which is called escalating commitment. This is a mistake many managers make because they are emotionally attached to a previous decision, even one as hopeless as this inadequate drone.
5. The median estimate from students is 2,250. When the numbers are given in reverse order starting with 1 × 2, etc., the median estimate is 512. The correct answer is 40,320. The order in which information is presented makes a difference to a person's solution, and acting quickly produces an answer that is far from correct.
6. The correct answer is 11. Many people answer 7. Native English speakers pronounce the word *of* with a "v" sound, hence the f does not register in their minds. A manager's conditioning can blind him or her to important information for solving a problem.
7. When judging people, early information has more impact than later information, called the primacy effect. Reversing the word sequence so that "intelligent" and "industrious" come first creates a more favorable impression. Respondents rate Robert more or less emotional depending on the order of the descriptive words.
8. Although the options are numerically equivalent, most people choose alternatives B and C. People hate losing more than they enjoy winning, and hence about 80 percent choose a sure small gain (B), and 70 percent will take more risk in the hope of avoiding a loss (C). A manager's solutions may be asymmetrical when they involve financial gains and losses.
9. The correct answer here is "no preference." The human mind has a tendency to see a pattern where none exists, which may lead to an incorrect solution. Each flip of the coin is completely random, and previous heads or tails have no bearing on the next flip.
10. For the word sets, the correct answers are (a) green, (b) cheese, (c) shower, (d) rods, and (e) pins. The answer that appeared in your mind is an example of creative intuition. A steady relaxed focus allows it to emerge. You can improve creative intuition with practice.

11. The answer depends on expanding your interpretation of the word "four." If you can break from your pattern of thinking "4," you may see the "IV" by removing the top, bottom, and right-hand matches.
12. This answer depends on expanding your definition of "nothing." Can you visualize a broader concept of nothing? The six matches can be organized into a "zero" (0) or formed into the word "NIL." Creativity benefits from looking at things from different angles and breaking free from habitual thought patterns.

Answers to Questions in Exhibit 4.5

1. 3977 miles
2. 270 days
3. 1957
4. 34
5. 66
6. 47
7. 84 years
8. 5,300 miles
9. 137
10. 21.5 hours

REFERENCES

Discover Yourself

1 Reprinted with permission of Academy of Management, from "Understanding and Measuring Linear-Nonlinear Thinking Style for Enhanced Management Education and Professional Practice" *Academy of Management Learning & Education*, by Charles M. Vance, Kevin S. Groves, Yongsun Paik, and Herb Kindler, Vol. 6, no. 2 (2007): 167–185; permission conveyed through Copyright Clearance Center.

2 Adapted from Harrison G. Gough, "A Creative Personality Scale for the Adjective Check List," *Journal of Personality and Social Psychology* 37, no. 8 (1979): 1398–1405.

3 Dorothy Marcic, "Adaptors and Innovators," in *Organizational Behavior: Experiences and Cases*, 4th ed. (St. Paul, MN: West Publishing, 1995), pp. 378–381.

Discover Knowledge

4 Jeremy W. Peters, "Web Focus Helps Revitalize *The Atlantic*," *The New York Times*, December 13, 2010; and "A History of *The Atlantic Monthly*," from a presentation given in 1994 by Cullen Murphy, *The Atlantic Online*, http://www.theatlantic.com/past/docs/about/atlhistf.htm (accessed February 25, 2011).

5 Herbert A. Simon, *The New Science of Management Decision* (Englewood Cliffs, NJ: Prentice Hall, 1977).

6 Paul J. H. Schoemaker and J. Edward Russo, "A Pyramid of Decision Approaches," *California Management Review* (Fall 1993): 9–31.

7 Based on Edward Chuang, "Communicating with a Corporate Superstar: Lessons from Kobe Bryant," *CIO*, August 8, 2007, http://www.cio.com/article/print/128802 (accessed October 18, 2007).

8 Marjorie A. Lyles and Howard Thomas, "Strategic Problem Formulation: Biases and Assumptions Embedded in Alternative Decision-Making Models," *Journal of Management Studies* 25 (1988): 131–145; and Susan E. Jackson and Jane E. Dutton, "Discerning Threats and Opportunities," *Administrative Science Quarterly* 33 (1988): 370–387.

9 This example is based on Henry Mintzberg, Duru Raisinghani, and André Théorêt, "The Structure of 'Unstructured' Decision Processes," *Administrative Science Quarterly* 21 (1976): 246–275.

10 Jena McGregor, "Gospels of Failure," *Fast Company* (February 2005): 62–67.

11 Eduardo Salas, Michael A. Rosen, and Deborah DiazGranados, "Expertise-Based Intuition and Decision Making in Organizations," *Journal of Management* 36, no. 4 (July 2010): 941–973; Herbert A. Simon, "Making Management Decisions: The Role of Intuition and Emotion," *Academy of Management Executive* 1 (February 1987): 57–64; and Daniel J. Eisenberg, "How Senior Managers Think," *Harvard Business Review* 62 (November–December 1984): 80–90.

12 Marjorie A. Lyles, "Defining Strategic Problems: Subjective Criteria of Executives," *Organizational Studies* 8 (1987): 263–280; and Marjorie A. Lyles and Ian I. Mitroff, "Organizational Problem Formulation: An Empirical Study," *Administrative Science Quarterly* 25 (1980): 102–119.

13 Jeffrey Pfeffer and Robert I. Sutton, "Why Managing by Facts Works," *Strategy + Business*, Issue 42, Spring 2006, http://www.strategy-business.com/article/06114?gko=fbd4e (accessed March 23, 2011).

14 This example is from Joyce S. Osland, David A. Kolb, Irwin M. Rubin, and Marlene E. Turner, *Organizational Behavior: An Experiential Approach*, 8th ed. (Upper Saddle River, NJ: Pearson Prentice Hall, 2007), Chapter 11.

15 Peter Baker, "How Obama Came to Plan for 'Surge' in Afghanistan," *The New York Times*, December 6, 2009; and Mark Landler and Jeff Zeleny, "Among Obama Aides, Debate Intensifies on Troop Levels," *The New York Times*, November 12, 2009, http://www.nytimes.com/2009/11/13/world/asia/13eikenberry.html?scp=2&sq=karl+w.+eikenberry&st=nyt (accessed November 12, 2009).

16 Osland et al., *Organizational Behavior*, Chapter 11.

17 Mintzberg et al., "The Structure of 'Unstructured' Decision Processes."

18 C. Kepner and B. Tregoe, *The Rational Manager* (New York: McGraw-Hill, 1965).

19 This section is based on Peter M. Senge, *The Fifth Discipline: The Art and Practice of the Learning Organization* (New York: Doubleday, 1990); John D. Sterman, "Systems Dynamics Modeling: Tools for Learning in a Complex World," *California Management Review* 43, no. 4 (Summer 2001): 8–25; and Rom Zemke, "Systems Thinking," *Training* (February 2001): 40–46.

20 Sterman, "Systems Dynamics Modeling."

21 Peter M. Senge, Charlotte Roberts, Richard B. Ross, Bryan J. Smith, and Art Kleiner, *The Fifth Discipline Fieldbook* (New York: Currency/Doubleday, 1994), p. 87.

22 Kurt Matzler, Franz Bailom, and Todd A. Mooradian, "Intuitive Decision Making," *MIT Sloan Management Review* 49, no. 1 (Fall 2007): 13–15; Eric Dain and Michael G. Pratt, "Exploring Intuition and Its Role in Managerial Decision Making," *Academy of Management* Review 32, no. 1 (2007): 33–54; and Gary Klein, *Intuition at Work: Why Developing Your Gut Instincts Will Make You Better at What You Do* (New York: Doubleday, 2002).

23 Janet Guyon, "The Soul of a Money-Making Machine," *Fortune* (October 3, 2005): 113–120; and Robert Levering and Milton Moscowitz, "And the Winners Are… (The 100 Best Companies to Work For)," *Fortune* (January 23, 2006): 89–108.

24 John P. Kotter, interviewed by Jeff Kehoe, "Managing Yourself: How to Save Good Ideas," *Harvard Business Review* (October 2010): 129–132.

25 Jenny C. McCune, "Making Lemonade," *Management Review* (June 1997): 49–53; and Douglas S. Barasch, "God and Toothpaste," *The New York Times*, December 22, 1996.

26 Francine Russo, "The Hidden Secrets of the Creative Mind," *Time* (January 16, 2006): 89–90.

27 Joshua Klayman, Richard P. Larrick, and Chip Heath, "Organizational Repairs," *Across the Board* (February 2000): 26–31.

28 For more information on root cause analysis, see Duke Okes, *Root Cause Analysis; The Core of Problem Solving and Corrective Action* (Milwaukee, WI: ASQ Quality Press, 2009); Robert J. Latino, "What Does Root-Cause Analysis Mean to You?" *Fabricating & Metalwork* (November–December 2007): 66–69; and S. C. Sweitzer and M. P. Silver, "Learning from Unexpected Events: A Root Cause Analysis Training Program," *Journal of Healthcare Quality* 27, no. 5 (September–October 2005): 11–19.

29 Joel Spolsky, "How Hard Could It Be? When and How to Micromanage," *Inc.* (December 2009–January 2010): 33–34.

30 Paul C. Nutt, "Expanding the Search for Alternatives During Strategic Decision Making," *Academy of Management Executive* 18, no. 4 (2004): 13–28; and P. C. Nutt, "Surprising But True: Half the Decisions in Organizations Fail," *Academy of Management Executive* 13, no. 4 (1999): 75–90.

31 Carol Kinsey Goman, *Creativity in Business: A Practical Guide for Creative Thinking* (Menlo Park, CA: Crisp Publications, 2000), p. 46; and Dorothy A. Leonard and Walter C. Swap, *When Sparks Fly: Igniting Creativity in Groups* (Boston: Harvard Business School Press, 1999), pp. 6–8.

32 David Kirkpatrick, "Throw It at the Wall and See if It Sticks," *Fortune* (December 12, 2005): 142–150.

33 Leigh Thompson, "Improving the Creativity of Organizational Work Groups," *Academy of Management Executive* 17 (2003): 96–109; and Bruce Nussbaum, "The Power of Design," *BusinessWeek* (May 17, 2004): 86–94.

34 ChiChi Madu, "Brainstorm: Group Free-for-Alls Can Stifle Creativity," *Psychology Today* (January–February 2010): 28; Karen Girotra, Christian Terwiesch, and Karl T. Ulrich, "Idea Generation and the Quality of the Best Idea," *Management Science* 56, no. 4 (April 2010): 591–605; and Robert C. Litchfield, "Brainstorming Reconsidered: A Goal-Based View," *Academy of Management Review* 33, no. 3 (2008): 649–668.

35 Madu, "Brainstorm: Group Free-for-Alls Can Stifle Creativity"; R. B. Gallupe, W. H. Cooper, M. L. Grise, and L. M. Bastianutti, "Blocking Electronic Brainstorms," *Journal of Applied Psychology* 79 (1994): 77–86; R. B. Gallupe and W. H. Cooper, "Brainstorming Electronically," *Sloan Management Review* (Fall 1993): 27–36; and Alison Stein Wellner, "A Perfect Brainstorm," *Inc.* (October 2003): 31–35.

36 Wellner, "A Perfect Brainstorm"; Gallupe and Cooper, "Brainstorming Electronically."

37 Carlin Flora, "Final Analysis: Annie Duke on Gut Instincts," *Psychology Today* (May–June 2007): 112.

38 R. Donald Gamache and Robert Lawrence Kuhn, *The Creativity Infusion: How Managers Can Start and Sustain Creativity and Innovation* (New York: Harper& Row, 1989); Alison Stein Wellner, "Cleaning Up," *Inc.* (October 2003): 35; and Roger von Oech, *A Kick in the Seat of the Pants* (New York, Harper & Row, 1986).

39 Richard A. Lovett, "Jog Your Brain," *Psychology Today* (May/June 2006): 55–56; Mary Carmichael, "Stronger, Faster, Smarter," *Newsweek* (March 26, 2007): 38–46.

40 Michael A. Roberto, "Making Difficult Decisions in Turbulent Times," *Ivey Business Journal* (January–February 2002): 14–20.

41 Kathleen M. Eisenhardt, "Strategy As Strategic Decision Making," *Sloan Management Review* (Spring 1999): 65–72; and David A. Garvin and Michael A. Roberto, "What You Don't Know About Making Decisions," *Harvard Business Review* (September 2001): 108–116.

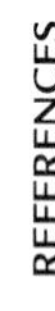

42 David M. Schweiger and William R. Sandberg, "The Utilization of Individual Capabilities in Group Approaches to Strategic Decision-Making," *Strategic Management Journal* 10 (1989): 31–43; and "The Devil's Advocate," *Small Business Report* (December 1987): 38–41.

43 George T. Doran and Jack Gunn, "Decision Making in High-Tech Firms: Perspectives of Three Executives," *Business Horizons* (November–December 2002): 7–16.

44 Garvin and Roberto, "What You Don't Know About Making Decisions."

45 Jeremy W. Peters, "Times's Online Pay Model Was Years in the Making," *The New York Times*, March 20, 2011.

46 Thomas E. Ricks, "Army Devises System to Decide What Does, Does Not, Work," *The Wall Street Journal*, May 23, 1997; John O'Shea, "Army: The Leader as Learner-in-Chief," *The Officer* (June 2003): 31; Thomas A. Stewart, "Listen Up, Maggots! You *Will* Deploy a More Humane and Effective Managerial Style," *Ecompany* (July 2001): 95; and Dan Heath and Chip Heath, "Made to Stick: Watch the Game Film," *Fast Company*, June 1, 2010, http://www.fastcompany.com/magazine/146/made-to-stick-watch-the-game-film.html (accessed March 2, 2011).

47 Adriana Gardella, "Yes, You Can Say No to Whole Foods," *The New York Times*, June 4, 2010, http://boss.blogs.nytimes.com/2010/06/04/yes-you-can-say-no-to-whole-foods/ (accessed April 9, 2012).

48 Michael J. Kirton, "Adaptors and Innovators: A Description and Measure," *Journal of Applied Psychology* 61, no. 5 (1976): 622–629.

49 Micheline Maynard, "With Eye on Profits, G.M. Began Missing on Innovation," *The New York Times*, December 6, 2008; John D. Stoll, Kevin Helliker, and Neal E. Boudette, "A Saga of Decline and Denial," *The Wall Street Journal*, June 2, 2009; David Welch, "GM: His Way or the Highway," *BusinessWeek* (October 5, 2009): 62ff; Sharon Terlep, "Corporate News: Girsky Takes Corporate-Strategy Role at GM," *The Wall Street Journal*, February 23, 2010; and General Motors Reinvention Web site, http://www.gmreinvention.com/?evar24=Reinvent_Sitelet (accessed March 31, 2010).

50 The discussion of these biases is based on Max Bazerman, *Judgment in Managerial Decision Making*, 5th ed. (New York: John Wiley & Sons, 2002); John Hammond, Ralph L. Keeney, and Howard Raiffa, "The Hidden Traps in Decision Making," *Harvard Business Review* (September–October 1998): 47–58; John S. Hammond, Ralph L. Keeney, and Howard Raiffa, *Smart Choices: A Practical Guide to Making Better Decisions* (Boston: Harvard Business School Press, 1999); Max H. Bazerman and Dolly Chugh, "Decisions without Blinders," *Harvard Business Review* (January 2006): 88–97; Oren Harari, "The Thomas Lawson Syndrome," *Management Review* (February 1994): 58–61; Dan Ariely, "Q&A: Why Good CIOs Make Bad Decisions," *CIO* (May 1, 2003): 83–87; and Leigh Buchanan, "How to Take Risks in a Time of Anxiety," *Inc.* (May 2003): 76–81.

51 Hammond et al., "The Hidden Traps in Decision Making."

52 Kris Frieswick, "The Turning Point: What Options Do Companies Have When Their Industries Are Dying?" *CFO Magazine*, April 2005, http://www.cfo.com/article.cfm/3786531/c_3805512 (accessed March 18, 2011); and Bazerman and Chugh, "Decisions without Blinders."

53 "How Can You Increase Your Awareness?" sidebar in Bazerman and Chugh, "Decisions without Blinders"; and Barry Nalebuff and Ian Ayres, *Why Not? How to Use Everyday Ingenuity to Solve Problems Big and Small* (Boston, MA: Harvard Business School Press, 2003).

54 Barry M. Staw, "The Escalation of Commitment to a Course of Action," *Academy of Management Review* 6 (March–April 1981): 577–587; Joel Brockner, "The Escalation of Commitment to a Failing Course of Action: Toward Theoretical Progress," *Academy of Management Review* 17 (1992): 39–61.

55 Daniel Kahneman and Amos Tversky, "Prospect Theory: An Analysis of Decision Under Risk," *Econometrica* 47 (1979): 263–292; Daniel Kahneman, Dan Lovallo, and Olivier Sibony, "Before You Make That Big Decision . . . ," *Harvard Business Review* (June 2011): 50–60; James Krohe Jr., "Money Changes Everything," *The Conference Review Board* (November–December 2007): 48–53.

56 Ben Casselman and Guy Chazan, "Disaster Plans Lacking at Deep Rigs," *The Wall Street Journal*, May 18, 2010; and David Barstow, Laura Dodd, James Glanz, Stephanie Saul, and Ian Urbina, "Regulators Failed to Address Risks in Oil Rig Fail-Safe Device," *The New York Times*, June 20, 2010, http://www.nytimes.com/2010/06/21/us/21blowout.html?scp=2&sq=bp%20bop&st=cse (accessed July 7, 2010).

Action Learning

57 Based on Josh Linkner, "The 5% Creativity Challenge, *Fast Company*, April 18, 2011, http://www.fastcompany.com/1748184/the-5-creativity-challenge (accessed March 19, 2012).

58 By Dorothy Marcic and Gedaliahu Harel, from Dorothy Marcic and Joseph Seltzer, *Organizational Behavior: Experiences and Cases*, 5th ed. (Cincinnati, OH: South-Western College Publishing, 1998), pp. 291–292.

CHAPTER 5
How Managers Communicate

Chapter Outline

RYAN LASH

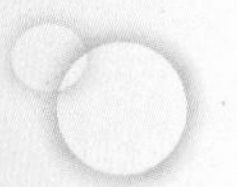

MANAGER CHALLENGE

VIDEO INCIDENT: GET ON BOARD!

Caffeine and Crullers needs a communication makeover. Human resources director Heather Carreau just came back from a conference on "redesigning your communications" that looked at a new approach for determining when it's best to phone, when to Skype, when to e-mail, and when to talk face-to-face. The evidence is showing that this new way of choosing how to communicate can have a positive impact on an organization's productivity. With great enthusiasm Heather presented her ideas for employee training sessions at the weekly managers meeting. Sales manager Jason Wong, who usually embraces new ideas, thought it was a good thing but said he's not sure if the timing is right. Still, he said he'd go along with the group's decision. But CFO Carlos Hernandez couldn't stop talking about costs and budget gaps and fiscal responsibility. Director of operations Carrie Fishman thinks it is a good idea and will smooth operations.

Initial Thoughts

1. If you were Heather, what would you do?

2. How would you persuade other managers to take on this new method?

Your instructor may ask you to be part of a role play based on the "Get On Board!" incident.

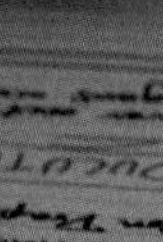

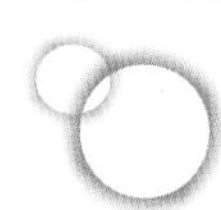

DISCOVER YOURSELF

For those students using CourseMate or CengageNOW, you can access the Daft/Marcic Assessment Library to take the questionnaires online and view dynamically updated comparative data.

Questionnaire 1[1]

Instructions: Respond to the statements below based on how you communicate with others concerning your work. Rate how accurately each statement describes you based on whether the statement is clearly true or accurate, clearly false or inaccurate, or in the middle as somewhat true and somewhat false. Describe yourself as you are now, not as you wish to be. There are no right or wrong answers.

	True	Somewhat	False
1. When giving a talk, I speak clearly and distinctly.	○	○	○
2. I frequently explain the bigger picture to others for what I am doing.	○	○	○
3. When I explain something, it tends to be well organized.	○	○	○
4. I regularly explain my understanding of issues and events.	○	○	○
5. When introducing myself, I fully and concisely let others know who I am.	○	○	○
6. I am very open with others about things I am doing.	○	○	○
7. I openly express my feelings and thoughts.	○	○	○
8. When I speak with others, my ideas are clearly and concisely presented.	○	○	○

Total Score ________. (Sum questions 1–8, giving 3 points for each True, 2 points for each Somewhat, and 1 point for each False.) Go to page 196 to interpret your score.

Questionnaire 2[2]

Instructions: Think about how you communicate during a typical day at work or school. Respond to the statements below based on whether they are True, Somewhat, or False for you. There are no right or wrong answers, so answer honestly.

	True	Somewhat	False
1. I feel tense and nervous speaking up in a group discussion.	○	○	○
2. My thoughts become confused and jumbled when talking to a group.	○	○	○
3. I am very calm and relaxed participating in group discussions.	○	○	○

	True	Somewhat	False
4. I feel tense and nervous about giving a speech.	○	○	○
5. I dislike giving presentations.	○	○	○
6. I anticipate giving a speech with great confidence.	○	○	○
7. I feel tense and nervous expressing myself at large meetings.	○	○	○
8. I tense up if called upon during a department or class meeting.	○	○	○
9. My thoughts become confused and jumbled if called upon in a large meeting.	○	○	○
10. I frequently have some nervous mannerisms in my speech.	○	○	○
11. I am a very relaxed communicator in all situations.	○	○	○
12. I am an excellent communicator in all situations.	○	○	○

Total Score ________. (Sum questions 1, 2, 4, 5, and 7–10 with 3 points for each True, 2 points for each Somewhat, and 1 point for each False. Reverse score questions 3, 6, 11, and 12 with 1 point for each True, 2 points for each Somewhat, and 3 points for each False. Add this to the total.) Go to page 198 to interpret your score.

Questionnaire 3[3]

Instructions: Think about how you communicate during a typical day at work or school. Respond to the statements below based on whether they are True, Somewhat, or False for you. There are no right or wrong answers, so answer honestly.

Part A

	True	Somewhat	False
1. I often ask people to clarify what they mean.	○	○	○
2. I ask questions in every conversation.	○	○	○
3. In conversations, I am genuinely curious about what other people think.	○	○	○
4. During a conversation, I frequently probe for deeper information.	○	○	○
5. I inquire about others' points of view on topics.	○	○	○

Total Score Part A ________. (Sum questions 1–5 with 3 points for each True, 2 points for each Somewhat, and 1 point for each False.)

Part B

	True	Somewhat	False
6. I am extremely attentive to what others say.	○	○	○
7. I deliberately show people that I am listening to them.	○	○	○
8. I really enjoy listening very carefully to people.	○	○	○
9. My mind does not wander when someone is talking.	○	○	○

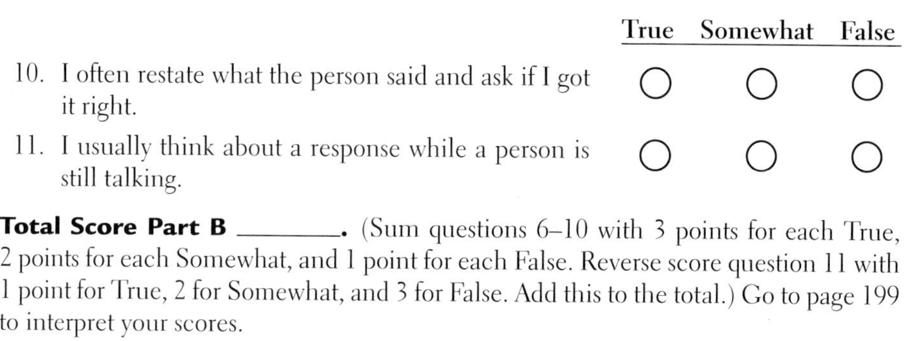

	True	Somewhat	False
10. I often restate what the person said and ask if I got it right.	○	○	○
11. I usually think about a response while a person is still talking.	○	○	○

Total Score Part B ________. (Sum questions 6–10 with 3 points for each True, 2 points for each Somewhat, and 1 point for each False. Reverse score question 11 with 1 point for True, 2 for Somewhat, and 3 for False. Add this to the total.) Go to page 199 to interpret your scores.

Questionnaire 4

Instructions: Respond to the statements below based on how you speak to others during personal or work conversations. Answer whether each statement is True, Somewhat, or False for you. There are no right or wrong answers, so answer honestly.

	True	Somewhat	False
1. I say exactly what I think to people.	○	○	○
2. I never hesitate to hurt people's feelings by telling the truth.	○	○	○
3. I like to be strictly candid about what I say.	○	○	○
4. I am very straightforward when giving feedback.	○	○	○
5. I present evidence for my opinions.	○	○	○
6. I am an extremely frank communicator.	○	○	○

Total Score ________. (Sum questions 1–6, giving 3 points for each True, 2 points for each Somewhat, and 1 point for each False.) Go to page 203 to interpret your score.

Questionnaire 5[4]

Instructions: Respond to the following statements about how you make a persuasive speech or presentation. Indicate whether each statement is True, Somewhat, or False for you.

Part A

When making a formal presentation, I:

1. Use energetic body movements to act out the idea.
2. Show animated facial expressions.
3. Use a lot of gestures.
4. Talk with varied tone and pitch.
5. Dramatize my excitement.

Total Score Part A ________. (Sum questions 1–5 with 3 points for each True, 2 points for each Somewhat, and 1 point for each False.)

Part B

When making a formal presentation, I:

6. Explicitly point out the relationship between the topic and its broader context.
7. Make sure my content has real substance.
8. Confirm that the presentation is coherent and logical.
9. Make certain the presentation is thoughtful and in-depth.
10. Cite facts and examples to support my points and arguments.

Total Score Part B ________. (Sum questions 6–10 with 3 points for each True, 2 points for each Somewhat, and 1 point for each False.) Go to page 208 to interpret your scores.

GO ONLINE to find additional questionnaires at www.cengagebrain.com, search for Daft/Marcic Building Management Skills 1e, click on Free Online Resources, click on Additional Self-Assessments.

- Personal Voice

SHUTTERSTOCK #53973379

Chapter 5: How Managers Communicate

DISCOVER KNOWLEDGE

Bob and Stan Lee, the founders of Corrugated Replacements Inc. (CRI), are worried. CRI, which makes parts for machines that produce cardboard boxes, has been successful since the day the brothers started it in their family's barn 25 years ago, but things are changing fast in the industry, and CRI is having a hard time keeping pace. The Lees have made some technological changes to meet recent challenges, but they need help defining a new strategic direction. Now this! Rather than helping them with strategy, the consultants they hired have told them they have a *morale problem.* Employees don't seem to care whether the company succeeds or not, they say. Bob and Stan are shocked when they hear some of the comments from staffers and plant workers. "In the time I've worked here, the owner has said maybe two words to me," lamented one employee. Another laughed when asked how the company might develop new markets, then joked that it seemed like Bob and Stan Lee were afraid sales might actually increase if they listened to their staff.[5]

Bob and Stan Lee are facing a strategic crisis, but their biggest problem is a breakdown in communication. Employees feel like the owners of CRI don't care about them, so they don't care about the company. People have thoughts about how CRI can meet new challenges, but no one is asking for their help or listening to their ideas.

It is impossible to overstate the importance of effective communication for managers. Good communication doesn't just mean giving speeches, issuing orders, or talking with consultants. It involves asking questions, listening, and paying attention to people's nonverbal behavior. As a manager, you will likely spend at least 80 percent of your time directly communicating with others. Think about it. That's 48 minutes of every hour spent in meetings, on the telephone, reading and writing e-mails, or talking informally with people inside or outside the organization.[6] If this communication is ineffective, significant problems can result, including poor employee morale, lack of innovation, decreased performance, and a failure to meet goals.

YOUR SUCCESS AS A MANAGER DEPENDS ON GOOD COMMUNICATION

Harvard researcher John P. Kotter looked at great leaders of the twentieth century and found that one characteristic most of them had in common was an ability to communicate in simple, clear ways.[7] Your effectiveness as a manager—and your career success—depends greatly on your communication skills, because communication permeates every aspect of management.

What Is Manager Communication?

Most of us think of spoken or written language when we think about communication, but words are only a tiny part of human communication. As a manager, you will be watched by employees, so it's important to remember that everything you do or don't do and say or don't say will communicate something. In addition, communication is a two-way street that includes asking questions, seeking feedback, paying attention to the nonverbal communication of others, and actively listening. **Manager communication** is the process by which information is exchanged and understood by two or more people, usually with the intent to influence or motivate behavior.

Surveys of managers reveal that they consider communication their most critical skill and one of their top responsibilities.[8] Yet Bob and Stan Lee, described in our opening example, are by no means the only managers who are weak in this vital skill. One survey found that fewer than half of responding managers bothered to tailor their messages to employees, customers, or suppliers. Even fewer managers seek feedback from employees or customers because they fear hearing bad news. Without feedback, though, managers can't adequately respond to problems or opportunities, and their plans and decisions may be out of alignment with employee perceptions and interests.[9]

A Model of Communication

Being a good communicator starts with appreciating how complex communication is and understanding the key elements of the communication process, as illustrated in Exhibit 5.1.

Many people think communication is simple and natural. After all, we communicate every day without even thinking about it. In reality, though, human communication is quite complex and fraught with opportunities for misunderstanding. Communication is not just sending information but sharing information in a planned way. A manager who has the ability to deliver rousing speeches or write brilliant commentary, but who doesn't know how to listen, is not an effective communicator. Honoring this distinction between *sharing* and *proclaiming* is crucial for successful management.

Knowing what communication entails helps you appreciate the complexity of communication. As shown in Exhibit 5.1, a manager who wants to communicate with an employee *encodes* a thought or idea by selecting symbols (such as words) with which to compose and transmit a message. The *message* is the tangible formulation of the thought or idea sent to the employee, and the *channel* is the medium by which

Exhibit 5.1 A Model of Communication

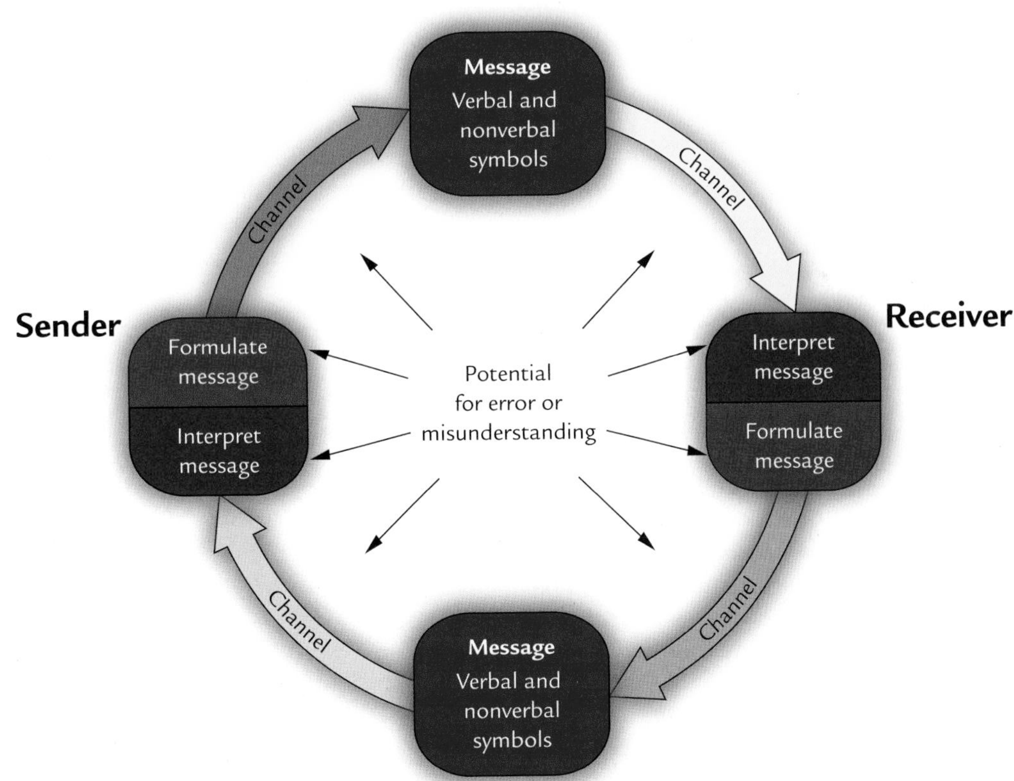

Sources: Based on Gabriela Moise, "Communication Models Used in the Online Learning Environment," *The 3rd International Conference on Virtual Learning 2008,* ICVL (http://www.icvl.eu/2008), pp. 247–254; and Wilbur Schramm, *The Process and Effects of Mass Communication,* 6th ed. (Urbana, IL: University of Illinois Press, 1965).

the message is sent. The channel might be a telephone call, for example, or an e-mail message, formal report, or face-to-face conversation. The employee *decodes* the symbols to interpret the meaning of the message. *Feedback* occurs when the employee responds to a manager's communication with a return message. As illustrated in the exhibit, the nature of effective communication is cyclical, in that a sender and receiver may exchange messages several times to achieve a mutual understanding.

Encoding and decoding can sometimes cause communication errors. Have you ever heard someone say "But that's not what I meant!" or wasted time and energy on misunderstood instructions? Individual differences, knowledge, values, attitudes, and background act as filters and may create "noise" when translating from symbols to meaning. We've all likely experienced communication breakdowns, because people can easily misinterpret a message.

Feedback enables a manager to determine whether the employee correctly interpreted the message. The potential for communication errors is why feedback is so important. Without feedback, the communication cycle is incomplete. Effective communication involves both the transference and the *mutual understanding* of information.[10]

THE MANAGER'S BIGGEST JOB

In April 2010, a Transocean oil rig digging a deep sea well for BP exploded in the Gulf of Mexico, killing 11 workers and spewing oil into the sea for months. Managers at both Transocean and BP were in a harsh spotlight for their companies' roles in the disaster. Although there was plenty of blame to go around, investigations uncovered poor communication as one distinct problem. A survey commissioned by Transocean found that some workers on the rig had concerns about safety but hadn't reported mistakes, problems, or risky behavior for fear of reprisals. Most said they felt free to raise concerns that could be immediately addressed on the rig, but they hesitated to bring up issues that had to be passed up the hierarchy. Some workers even admitted that they entered false data into Transocean's system for tracking safety issues; thus, top managers at Transocean had a distorted perception of maintenance and safety on the rig.[11]

The BP Transocean disaster is a painful example of the dangers of poor organizational communication. No one likes to hear bad news, but managers have to know about problems or they cannot solve them. When people are afraid to speak up, don't care enough to speak up, or find that no one is listening, the organization and everyone associated with it will eventually suffer. As a manager, you will define your team or organization's communication climate, whether things are discussed openly or suppressed. In addition, you will have a tremendous responsibility for directing, coordinating, motivating, and developing employees, which requires that you communicate effectively.

Managers Are Sensegivers

Managers are responsible for shaping how people think about their work and the organization, including the values that guide decisions and behavior. *Sensegiving* refers to the process of influencing how others construct meaning and make sense of their environment.[12] Good managers use communication to inspire people with a vision and shape the values that are necessary for achieving it, and they help people understand the larger purpose of their work and see how they fit in the

DISCOVER YOURSELF

Interpret Your Score: Sensegiving (Questionnaire 1)

Your score on this questionnaire pertains to the manager's role as *sensegiver*. It reflects communication competency. A higher score means that you have the potential ability to explain things clearly, give a bigger picture, are open, and can help people understand their role. A lower score means that you may need to work on your communication competency for playing the manager's sensegiving role. Comparative data for **Sensegiving:** Thirty person Mean score = 20.4, Top Quartile = 23–24; Bottom Quartile = 11–20. CNOW and CourseMate users can access dynamically updated comparative data through www.cengagebrain.com.

© CENGAGE LEARNING 2014

organization. Whether they walk around asking questions or thoughtfully listen to a subordinate's ideas or problems, the everyday actions of effective managers convey a deep commitment to communication and sensegiving. Communication isn't just about occasional meetings, formal speeches, or presentations. As a manager, you will actively communicate through both words and actions every day. Ongoing effective communication is essential for building personal relationships with followers and motivating people toward accomplishing goals.

The Manager as Communication Champion

To act as sensegivers, managers are communication champions. A **communication champion** is philosophically grounded in the belief that good communication is essential to building trust, gaining commitment, and inspiring and uniting people to work together to accomplish a common purpose. Communication champions visibly and symbolically engage in a variety of communication-based activities. Exhibit 5.2 shows the manager-as-communication-champion model. By creating an open communication climate, asking questions, and actively listening, you can engage people in conversations that help move the team, department, and organization forward. Effective manager communication is *purpose-directed*, in that it directs people's attention toward the vision, values, and desired outcomes of the team or organization and persuades people to act in ways to achieve important goals. You can use a number of communication methods, including selecting rich channels of communication, paying attention to symbolic and nonverbal communication, and making effective presentations.

Exhibit 5.2 The Manager as Communication Champion

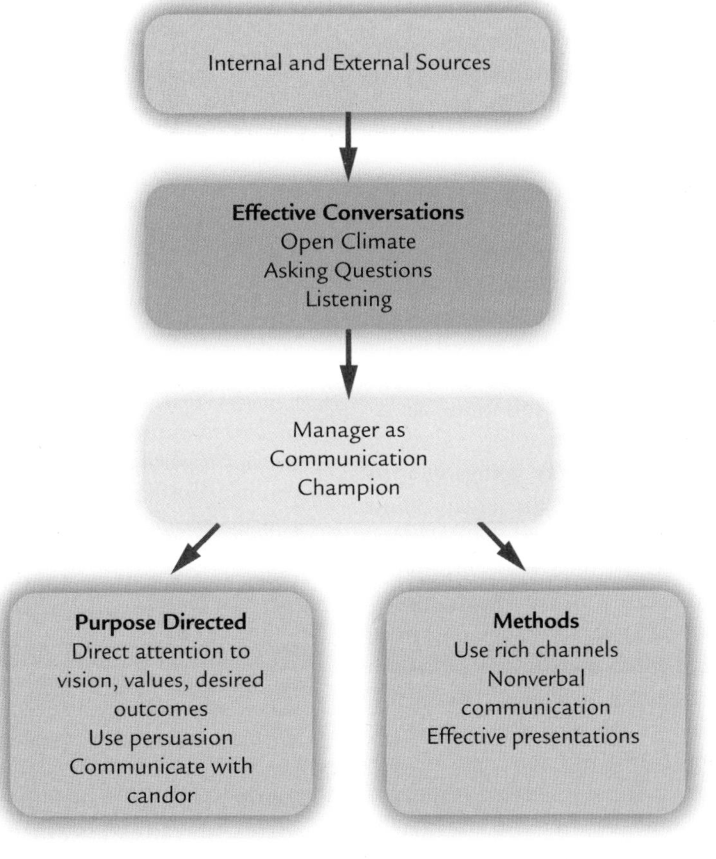

© CENGAGE LEARNING 2014

LEADING EFFECTIVE CONVERSATIONS

Many top managers admit their performance as communication champions likely fell short during the worst of the recent economic crisis as they spent more time trying to make sure the financial status of their companies remained sound. Yet, as soon as the worst was over, Quicken Loans CEO Bill Emerson got back out among Quicken's 3,000 employees to reinforce his commitment to open communication. Emerson holds two-hour lunch meetings with groups of 15 employees at a time. He fills them in on what is happening with the company and the mortgage industry, asks about their problems and concerns, and solicits ideas and opinions about how the company operates. Emerson depended heavily on middle and lower-level managers for maintaining a strong communication climate while he wrestled with business problems, but he knows his visible commitment is essential to keep effective organizational conversations going.[13]

The elements outlined in Exhibit 5.2 comprise the factors necessary for effective conversations to occur. These elements include an open communication climate, asking questions, and active listening.

Creating an Open Communication Climate

A survey of U.S. employees reveals that people genuinely want open and honest communication from their managers, including the bad news as well as the good.[14] **Open communication** means sharing all types of information throughout the organization, across functional and hierarchical boundaries.

Employees need to know what's going on with the company. People throughout the organization need to see the big picture, understand the decisions managers make, and know how their work contributes to the success of the company. Particularly in times of change, if people don't hear what's happening from managers, they rely on rumors and will often assume the worst.[15] In an open communication environment, people know where they stand and what rules they need to play by. Open communication helps people accept, understand, and commit to goals. People can see how their actions interact with and affect others in the organization. When people have access to complete information, they are more likely to come up with creative solutions to problems and make decisions that are good for the company.

Good managers want communication to flow in all directions. Unfortunately, when the employees in the survey mentioned above were asked to evaluate how well their managers were doing in providing open and honest communication, the average score on a scale of zero to 100 was 69.[16] You can build an open communication climate by breaking down conventional hierarchical and departmental boundaries that may be barriers to communication. You can take care to communicate honestly with subordinates, keep people posted when things change in either a positive or negative direction, and help people see the financial impact of their decisions and actions. Just as importantly, you can show that you want to hear what employees have to say and be willing to answer tough questions about your own actions.[17]

Here are some examples of open communication in action. One General Motors plant manager holds "rap sessions" to encourage people to tell him what's on their minds, even though he sometimes hears things he'd rather not. "You have to make yourself vulnerable," he says. "You have to be willing to let people tell you you're wrong."[18] Managers at IBM hold forums on the intranet where employees from around the world can join in online discussions. Many

DISCOVER YOURSELF

Interpret Your Score: **Communication Apprehension** (Questionnaire 2)

Your score is an indication of how much apprehension (fear or anxiety) you feel in various types of communication situations. Apprehension is the opposite of confidence. If your score is high, you may not have sufficient confidence to be an effective *communication champion*. You should work to overcome communication anxiety by learning and practicing communication in a variety of settings. Look at your answers to specific questions and see whether your apprehension is greater during group discussions, in larger formal meetings, or when giving a speech. Comparative data for **Communication Apprehension:** Thirty person Mean score = 20.3, Top Quartile = 22–29; Bottom Quartile = 15–19. CNOW and CourseMate users can access dynamically updated comparative data through www.cengagebrain.com.

© CENGAGE LEARNING 2014

of today's CEOs have open e-mail policies, encouraging workers to send them messages and reading each one personally. Open communication plays a critical role in building trust between managers and employees and inspires commitment and collaboration to achieve a common purpose.[19]

Asking Questions

As very young children, we're typically full of questions, but we may be discouraged from asking them. We may be told that questioning adults is rude or disrepectful. As students, we're expected to hold up our hands in class to give the right answer, and we're often chastised for an incorrect response. No wonder we believe we're supposed to have all the answers when we become managers. We assume that if someone comes to us with a problem, our job is to solve it with the correct answer.[20] We fear that not having an answer means employees will lose respect for us or see us as ineffective. Most managers do 80 percent telling and 20 percent asking, while it should be the other way around. Asking questions can benefit both managers and employees in numerous ways.[21]

Asking questions builds critical thinking skills. Searching for an answer comes naturally to most managers, but answers can create blockages in thinking rather than opening up new avenues for exploration, learning, and creativity. In other words, questions make people think, whereas an answer typically puts a full stop to thinking.[22] In one survey, 99 percent of top managers said critical thinking skills at all levels are crucial to the success of their organizations.[23] Asking questions stimulates critical, independent thinking, encourages people to use their creativity, and leads to deeper, more lasting learning.

Asking questions shows people that you're interested in who they are and what they think. Anyone who's ever been on a first date with someone who talks only about him or herself and never asks a question understands this. If someone never asks what you think or how you feel, you get the idea pretty quickly that your thoughts and feelings don't matter, that this person is concerned only about him or herself. For managers, that's a sure route to failure; people don't willingly follow someone they think doesn't care about them. Asking questions shows that you value the knowledge of others and are open to new ideas, which helps to build trusting, respectful relationships.

Questions stimulate the mind and give people a chance to make a difference. When you ask a question of someone, you put them on alert in a way that making a statement does not; they have to think in order to respond.[24] If a plant foreman says, "We have to increase production to fill this order for an important customer," workers can listen to him or not and try to speed things up or continue working as they have been. If, instead, the foreman asks employees, "What can we do to make sure we fill this order on time?" people can't ignore him; they have to start looking for solutions. Thus, asking questions gets people to accept responsibility for solving their own problems.

Active Listening

Dr. Robert Buckman is a cancer specialist who teaches other doctors how to break bad news. His number one tip? *Listen.* "The trust that you build just by letting people say what they feel is incredible," Buckman says.[25]

There are few things as maddening as not being listened to. Whether we're talking to a doctor, a parent, a sales clerk, a spouse, or a supervisor, if we feel that the person is listening to our needs, we simply feel better, even if the communication doesn't produce the result we desire. Good customer service reps

DISCOVER YOURSELF

Interpret Your Score: Asking Questions, Listening (Questionnaire 3)

A high score for Part A reflects your habit of inquiry, which means asking questions to learn more about something or to confirm your understanding. Asking questions is an important part of an effective manager's communication repertoire. Comparative data for **Asking Questions** (Part A): Thirty person Mean score = 12.1, Top Quartile = 13–16; Bottom Quartile = 8–11. Your score for Part B reflects your listening habits. Comparative data for **Listening Habits** (Part B): Thirty person Mean score = 13.1, Top Quartile = 15–17; Bottom Quartile = 7–11. Managers face many distractions, which makes it hard to pay attention when someone is speaking. A higher score means you listen attentively, which can prevent many communication mistakes. If your score is low, what can you do to be a better listener? CNOW and CourseMate users can access dynamically updated comparative data through www.cengagebrain.com.

© CENGAGE LEARNING 2014

understand this and use listening to soothe irate patrons. Yet many people do not know how to listen effectively. They let their minds wander, concentrate on what they want to say next, or strive to make their point without first hearing what the other person is saying. Although about 75 percent of effective communication is listening, most people spend only about 30 to 40 percent of their time really listening.[26] Moreover, our listening efficiency, as measured by the amount of material understood and remembered by subjects 48 hours after listening to a ten-minute message, is on average no better than 25 percent.[27]

We hear with our ears, but we listen with our minds and hearts. **Listening** refers to consciously striving to grasp and interpret a message's genuine meaning. This involves paying attention not only to facts but also to feelings, which means observing facial expressions and body language as well as hearing the words that are being spoken. To be effective as a manager, you have to be an active listener. Active listening is engaged listening; it requires concentration, interaction, thinking, and questioning. Active listening is also supportive listening, in that the listener genuinely strives to understand the other person's point of view and uses listening as a way to build and enhance positive interpersonal relationships. Good managers work hard at listening, because they know it is a key to building good relationships, understanding what motivates people, identifying employees' expectations and needs, and learning new ways to approach organizational problems.

Managers who are perceived as good listeners are promoted more often than those who don't have effective listening skills.[28] Managers who fail to listen to employees send the message, "You don't matter." Active listening expands a manager's credibility in the eyes of others and enhances the manager's influence, effectiveness, and success.

DISCOVER KNOWLEDGE

7 STEPS TO...
Supportive Listening

1. **Show genuine interest.** Don't assume the topic is boring or unimportant; look for opportunities to learn something new.
2. **Listen actively.** Look at the speaker, and use both verbal and nonverbal signals to demonstrate that you're paying attention to what is being said. Nod your head, ask questions, use facial expressions, and paraphrase to make sure you understand.
3. **Use supportive statements.** Encourage the speaker by making appropriately placed supportive comments, such as "That's interesting," "I hear you," or "I see what you're saying."
4. **Avoid distractions.** Concentrate fully on what the speaker is saying. Strive to make the person feel as if what he or she has to say is the most important thing in the world to you at that moment.
5. **Don't prejudge.** When we prejudge someone as shallow or ill-informed, or hear everything in the context of our own beliefs, we stop listening. Keep an open mind and don't jump to conclusions before hearing what the other person has to say.
6. **Listen with empathy.** Listen for feelings as well as content. Don't interrupt with your own ideas or make light of a situation the speaker is distressed about. And don't jump in with advice or answers, which can prevent you from reading emotions and deeply listening to the other person.
7. **Pay attention to nonverbal signals.** Be aware of your own and the other person's facial expressions, tone of voice, and body language. In English, as much as 90 percent of emotional information is transmitted by body language and tone of voice rather than by words.

Sources: Based on Philip Morgan and Kent Baker, "Building a Professional Image: Improving Listening Behavior," *Supervisory Management* (November 1985): 34–38; Tony Alessandra, "Look of Leadership: Listen, Speak, and Project Image," *Leadership Excellence* (October 2010): 13; and Sherman K. Okun, "How to Be a Better Listener," *Nation's Business* (August 1975): 62.

COMMUNICATING TO PERSUADE

Karen Tse was just 37 years old when she founded an organization that would change the lives of thousands of prisoners in places like China, Cambodia, and Vietnam. Her organization, International Bridges to Justice, trains public defenders and raises awareness of human rights abuses in these countries. Tse persuades by connecting emotionally to people, whether it be a businessman she's asking for a donation or a prison guard she's encouraging to allow prisoners daily exercise. Rather than fighting against the "bad," Tse says she tries to find the good in each person and work with that part of them to make changes. One Cambodian prison director who initially told Tse he would beat prisoners down "like rats" eventually worked with her to improve the prison's dark, dank cells, build a garden, and implement exercise classes for prisoners and guards.[29]

As a manager, you will need to communicate not only to convey information, but also to influence and persuade others to behave in ways that accomplish desired goals.

The Art of Persuasion

The ability to persuade others is more critical today than ever before. The command-and-control mindset of managers telling workers what to do and how to do it is gone. Key points for practicing the art of persuasion include:[30]

- **Establish credibility.** Your credibility is based on your knowledge and expertise as well as how you relate to others. By demonstrating that you make well-informed, sound decisions, you increase others' confidence in your knowledge and expertise.
- **Build goals on common ground.** To be persuasive, you should describe how what you are requesting will benefit others as well as yourself. An example is the manager who wanted to persuade fast food franchisees to support new pricing discounts desired by headquarters. The manager didn't just explain that headquarters wanted the policies implemented; he cited research showing that the revised pricing would increase franchisees' profits.[31] When the franchisees saw how they would personally benefit, they were eager to adopt the new policies. If you can't find common advantages, this is typically a good sign that you need to adjust your goals and plans.
- **Make your position compelling to others.** It is important to appeal to people on an emotional level by using symbols, metaphors, and stories to express your messages, rather than relying on facts and figures alone.
- **Connect emotionally.** The most effective managers learn to sense others' emotions and adjust their approach to match the audience's ability to receive their message. In addition, by looking at how people have interpreted and responded to past events, you can get a better grasp on how they might react to new ideas and proposals you want to persuade them to adopt.

Persuasion requires listening, learning from and understanding others, and frequently negotiating or compromising to find win-win solutions. Managers often fail at their attempts to persuade because they think of persuasion as aggressively convincing others to see things their way. Exhibit 5.3 takes a light-hearted look at four ways *not* to persuade.

Communicating with Candor

To influence and persuade, managers also have to be frank and straightforward about what they want and need from others. Communicating with candor means being direct, honest, and clear about what employees need to do to meet objectives, while also expressing respect for others and not making people feel slighted, controlled, or exploited. Unfortunately, communicating with candor is a problem for many managers. Jack Welch, speaker, author, and former CEO of General Electric, says when he asks groups of managers how many of them have received candid performance appraisals, only about 10 percent of people raise their hands. When he asks how many have given candid appraisals to their employees, the results aren't much better.[32]

Communicating with candor is a confident, positive approach that lets others know exactly where you stand and what you're asking of them. The appropriate use of candid communication acknowledges the other person's perspective and opinion, yet is very specific about what you want and why. Some valuable techniques for communicating with candor include:[33]

- **Use "I statements."** To effectively communicate with candor, you should keep the focus on the

Exhibit 5.3 How to Fail Miserably at Persuasion

1. **Take the John Wayne Approach.** Ineffective managers strongly state their position and then use persistence, logic, and enthusiasm to try to push it on others. This hard-sell approach almost always backfires. Stating a strong position up front gives potential opponents a clear target to fight against.
2. **Refuse to Compromise.** This guarantees that others will dig in their heels and refuse to budge in return. Ineffective managers see compromise as surrender. Effective persuasion is a give-and-take process that incorporates and responds to the ideas and needs of others.
3. **Rely on a Killer Argument.** Sure, great arguments matter when you're trying to get people to change their minds, but there are other factors that are equally important. Effective persuasion depends not just on a killer argument, but on the manager's credibility, ability to connect emotionally with others, and knack for framing a position so that others see the benefits.
4. **Assume Persuasion Is a One-Shot Effort.** You'll never be good at persuading if you don't have patience. Considering that persuasion takes listening and give-and-take, it's almost never possible to arrive at a shared solution on the first try. Rather than being a one-time event, persuasion is a slow and frequently difficult process.

Source: Based on Jay A. Conger, "The Necessary Art of Persuasion," *Harvard Business Review* (May–June 1998): 84–95.

specific perception you have, how it makes you feel, and the effect it is having on you, rather than accusing or blaming the other person. Suppose you share office space with a sloppy colleague. Rather than saying, "You drive me crazy by leaving food wrappers scattered all over the place," you might say, "I'm finding it really hard to get our work done with all this clutter on the work table."

- **Stick to facts rather than judgments.** Don't tell your colleague she's a disgusting slob; just let her know that the clutter she's leaving on the table is interfering with your ability to do your work.
- **Be clear, specific, and direct in your requests.** Say "I'd like for you to keep the work table clean since we both have to use it to get our jobs done," rather than "Why don't you clean up the mess you leave around here?"

Communicating with candor is an important part of creating an open communication climate. When managers communicate with candor, they encourage others to do the same. In an organization where candid communication is the norm, everything works faster and better.[34] When everyone feels free to open up and speak frankly, more people get involved in organizational conversations, which leads to more ideas and faster learning. In addition, candor means that ideas get debated, adapted, and acted upon more quickly. Candid communication leads to genuine ongoing conversations and limits common problems such as meaningless meetings, workplace incivility, or rancorous silence.

What's Your Problem?

Q: I pride myself on communicating exactly what I think, and I've had lots of people tell me they admire me for this. But in the last two jobs I've had, people don't seem to appreciate this communication skill. When I point out that what they are saying is inaccurate or how their understandings are off the mark, I get a lot of dirty looks. Several of my coworkers have told me I'm the one who is wrong, but that's obviously just a way for them to stay in denial. Should I look for another job and try to find some place that appreciates my honesty?

A: It's hard to tell from your letter whether the way you see things is more in line with reality than that of your coworkers, but I feel pretty confident in pointing out that the major problem here seems to be your *belief* that you are always right. It probably comes across as self-righteousness, which is generally not an attractive quality or one that other people are drawn to. Asserting your view as correct is the same as saying everyone else is wrong. Rather, communicate your ideas as just your personal view, not as the correct view. Also, start asking more questions. Approach other viewpoints with true curiosity. Try to understand *why* other people have come to their conclusions. What is their evidence? How did they reason it out? Try hard to put yourself in their shoes. You will learn a lot and will likely find yourself in better relationships with others.

© CENGAGE LEARNING 2014

DISCOVER YOURSELF

Interpret Your Score: Candor
(Questionnaire 4)

Your score on this questionnaire reflects the level of candor with which you communicate. Many people have a hard time giving straightforward opinions and feedback because they don't want to hurt a person's feelings or don't want people to dislike them. Hence, the sharing of honest observations is limited. A higher score on this scale reflects a habit of candor, which will add to your managerial effectiveness. A low score means you may have a hard time speaking straight and you may want to practice to improve your candor. Comparative data for **Candor:** Thirty person Mean score = 11.8, Top Quartile = 13–16; Bottom Quartile = 8–11. CNOW and CourseMate users can access dynamically updated comparative data through www.cengagebrain.com.

© CENGAGE LEARNING 2014

USING THE CORRECT CHANNEL

Randy Hanson was eager to get his vacation underway. Ten days in Hawaii was all he'd had on his mind for most of the day. One more task and he was done. As he left the plant, Randy tacked a letter on the bulletin board:

> Dear Team,
>
> I've recently been informed that we will be making significant changes in how we operate to meet stringent new corporate quality goals. This will affect everyone in the department over the next few months as new procedures are implemented, equipment is upgraded, and we all get training to enable us to meet tougher standards. The VP of operations wants things to get rolling right away, and Tom will be handling the changes until I get back. It's been a tough year for all of us, and I know more change is not welcome news. But we can do this together! You're the best!
>
> Randy

What was he thinking? Randy Hanson knew the upcoming changes were going to be difficult for employees and would likely encounter some resistance. As a manager, he also needed the insight to realize that telling them about it in a letter would spark even greater anger and resentment.

An important part of effective communication is using the right **communication channel**, which is the medium by which a message is carried from one person to another. You have a choice of many channels through which to communicate with employees. You can discuss a problem face-to-face, use the telephone, give a speech, write a memo or letter, use e-mail, send a text message, communicate through a blog or Web page, or put an item in a newsletter, depending on the nature of the message.

The Continuum of Channel Richness

Research has looked at how managers select communication channels to enhance communication effectiveness.[35] Channels differ in their capacity to convey information and can be classified into a continuum based on information richness. **Channel richness** is the amount of information that can be transmitted during a communication episode. Exhibit 5.4 illustrates the continuum of channel richness.

What Influences Channel Richness?

The richness of an information channel is influenced by three characteristics: (1) the ability to handle multiple cues simultaneously; (2) the ability to facilitate rapid, two-way feedback; and (3) the ability to establish a personal focus for the communication. Face-to-face discussion is the richest medium, because it permits direct experience, multiple information cues, immediate feedback, and personal focus. Face-to-face discussions facilitate the assimilation of broad cues and deep, emotional understanding of the situation. Sociologist David Stark studied the work of financial traders and found that those who work in close proximity do better because of the rich stream of information all around them. Things such as tone of voice and stress level of others in the room enable traders to make better decisions.[36]

Telephone conversations are next in the richness hierarchy. Although eye contact, gaze, posture, and other body language cues are missing, the human voice still carries a tremendous amount of emotional information. E-mail, instant messaging, and text messaging, which lack both visual and verbal cues, are increasingly being

Exhibit 5.4 A Continuum of Channel Richness

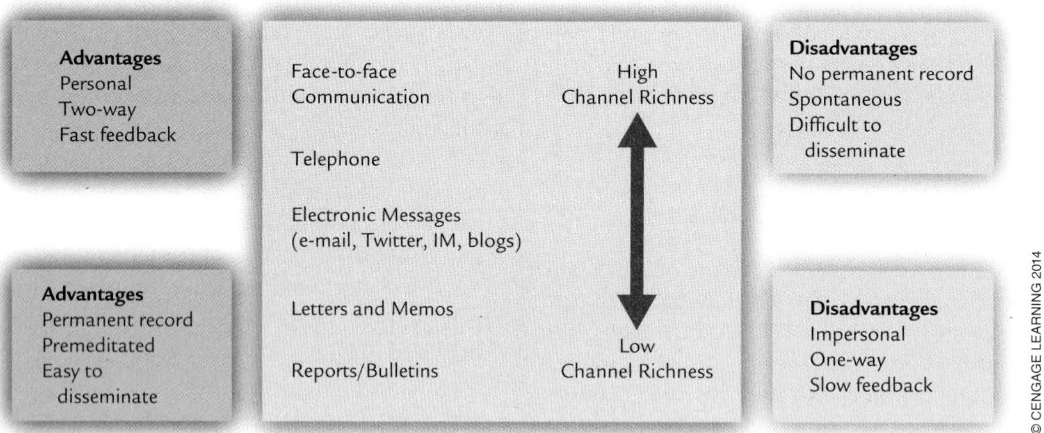

used for communications that were once handled over the telephone, yet research has confirmed that good managers still use the telephone or face-to-face conversations for expressing affection, giving advice, or communicating difficult news.[37] Electronic communication can enable reasonably rich communication if the technology is used appropriately.[38]

A lower level of richness is offered by the Internet and company intranets, but these have opened new avenues for keeping in touch with employees and customers. A blog on the intranet, for example, enables managers to disseminate certain types of information to a huge number of employees simultaneously, such as a traditional company newsletter might, and in addition, it allows for rapid feedback. Some managers use Twitter to keep in close touch with employees about everyday matters.

Written media such as notes and letters can be personalized, but they convey only the cues written on paper and are slow to provide feedback. Impersonal written media, including fliers, bulletins, nonpersonalized letters, and standard computer reports, are the lowest in richness. These channels are not focused on a single receiver, use limited information cues, and do not permit feedback.

How to Select a Channel

The importance of understanding channel richness is that each communication channel has advantages and disadvantages, and each can be an effective means of communication in the appropriate circumstances.[39] To be most effective, select a communication channel based on whether the message you need to convey is routine or nonroutine. *Routine communications* are simple, straightforward, and noncontroversial, such as a product price change. Routine messages convey data or statistics or simply put into words what people already understand and agree on. These messages can be efficiently communicated through a channel lower in richness, such as a memo.[40] On the other hand, *nonroutine communications* typically concern issues of change, conflict, or complexity that have great potential for misunderstanding or controversy. Nonroutine messages often are characterized by time pressure and surprise, such as the earlier example of the changes needed in Randy's production department. In that example, the manager inappropriately used a channel low in richness, a letter to the department, to convey a message that was potentially highly volatile. You can effectively communicate nonroutine messages only by selecting a rich channel.

Much manager communication by its very nature consists of nonroutine messages. E-mail and memos can be efficient, but don't let anything substitute for the rich face-to-face channel when important issues are at stake.

Using Electronic Channels

The increased use of e-mail in business communications is one reason top executives are paying more attention to their managers' writing skills. If you cannot communicate well in writing, you will limit your opportunities for advancement.[41] "Writing is both a 'marker' of high-skill, high-wage, professional work and a 'gatekeeper' with clear equity implications," says Bob Kerrey, president of New School University in New York and chair of the National Commission on Writing.[42]

Electronic communication is a fact of life in today's organizations and has many advantages, but there are disadvantages as well. For one thing, electronic methods increase the potential for communication errors. You can easily come across as sounding cold, arrogant, or insensitive if you attempt to discuss delicate issues via e-mail, for example. Things that might be handled smoothly in a face-to-face conversation or over the phone turn into massive problems by fostering resentment, bitterness, and hard feelings.[43] Here are some guidelines for effectively using electronic communication in the workplace:

- **Combine high-tech and high-touch.** Never allow electronic communication to take the place of human connections. As a manager, get to know your employees on a face-to-face basis. Don't rely on electronic communication for building relationships.
- **Consider the circumstances.** People who know one another well and have worked together a long time can typically communicate about more complex issues via e-mail or text messaging than can people who have a new working relationship.[44] In addition, when all parties involved have a good grasp of the issues being discussed, e-mail can be used effectively.
- **Mind your manners.** In general, business e-mails should open with a salutation and close with a sign-off. Formal e-mails might use a salutation such as "Dear Ms. Johansen" and close with "Yours sincerely," but it is acceptable to use "Hi Emma" and "Take care" or "Kind regards" if you know the person well. Avoid the use of sarcasm, which can be misinterpreted without the cues of body language and tone of voice, and never, ever use profanity in a work-related electronic message.
- **Read twice before you hit "Send."** Citigroup recently sent a memo to employees reminding them to "think before writing, read before sending."[45] The memo was partly in reaction to careless and profanity-laced electronic messages that came back to haunt Goldman Sachs in 2010 congressional hearings. In all cases, you need to check your messages for spelling, grammar, and clarity, as well as make sure you are minding your manners.
- **Know what's off limits.** Never send an electronic message when you are angry or upset. This is a situation that definitely calls for a richer communication channel. Select richer channels of communication as well for important, complex, or sensitive messages. Layoffs, firings, and reprimands should *always* be given face-to-face, or at least via telephone. In addition, never use electronic messaging to complain about or ridicule your boss, colleagues, or subordinates. One manager at CNN wrote a nasty message about her boss, intending to send it to a friend. Only too late did she realize she sent it to the boss instead![46]
- **Get a second opinion.** When the communciation is highly important, such as a department-wide announcement, ask someone to read it before you send it to learn how it comes across. Don't be too proud to take advice.

In addition to these guidelines, Exhibit 5.5 lists some specific tips for writing a good e-mail message. A former manager of communication services at consulting firm Arthur D. Little Inc. estimates that around

LEADING WORDS

"I often ask one question, whether I'm interviewing a senior-level executive or a campus person: Tell me your story. It's the best way to get to know the entire human being."

—John Berisford
head of human resources at *Pepsi Beverages*

"With the fast pace of today's electronic communications, one might think that the value of fundamental writing skills has diminished in the workplace. Actually, the need to write clearly and quickly has never been more important."

—Joseph M. Tucci
president and CEO of *EMC Corporation*

"The right word may be effective, but no word was ever as effective as a rightly timed pause."

—Mark Twain
American humorist, author of *The Adventures of Huckleberry Finn*

"Courage is what it takes to stand up and speak. Courage is also what it takes to sit down and listen."

—Winston Churchill
British Prime Minister, 1940–1945 and 1951–1955

© CENGAGE LEARNING 2014

Exhibit 5.5 How to Write a Good E-mail Message

Here are some step-by-step tips to make your e-mail messages stand out above the crowd.

1. **Write a meaningful subject line.** Use a subject line that accurately describes what the message is about. Many people get hundreds of e-mail messages a day and will easily overlook one that doesn't have a subject line or doesn't seem to require their attention.
2. **Focus on a single topic.** People find it difficult to keep track of different issues when they're all jumbled together. If you need to write to your boss about several different issues, put them in separate messages.
3. **Get straight to the point.** You're not writing an essay, so don't waste time with a long introductory paragraph.
4. **Keep it short.** Use short (but complete) sentences and break the message into several short paragraphs. Consider using bullet points for extra clarity, such as if you are:
    - listing several questions for the recipient to answer
    - suggesting a number of alternative options
    - explaining your next action steps
5. **Say It Clearly.** As with all good writing, avoid the use of jargon and pretentious vocabulary.
6. **Make Follow-Up Easy.** Include your name, e-mail address, phone number, and postal address (if appropriate) as part of your e-mail signature to make it easy for the recipient to get in touch with you. Of course, you should follow your organization's procedures and guidelines.

Sources: Based on Ali Hale, "Email Etiquette," Daily Writing Tips Web site, http://www.dailywritingtips.com/email-etiquette/ (accessed January 20, 2011); Dennis G. Jerz and Jessica Bauer, "Writing Effective E-Mail: Top 10 Tips," Seton Hill University—Jerz's Literacy Weblog, March 4, 2010, http://jerz.setonhill.edu/writing/etext/e-mail.htm (accessed January 20, 2011); and Diana Middleton, "Students Struggle for Words; Business Schools Put More Emphasis on Writing Amid Employer Complaints," *The Wall Street Journal* (March 3, 2011).

30 percent of all business memos and e-mail messages are written simply to get clarification about an earlier written communication that didn't make sense to the reader.[47] These tips can help you get your point across the first time.

NONVERBAL COMMUNICATION

Effective managers don't just communicate in words. They also send important messages by the way they live their lives and what they seek to inspire in others.[48] Managers are watched, and their appearance, behavior, actions, and attitudes are symbolic to others. Indeed, **nonverbal communication**—messages transmitted through action and behavior—accounts for at least half of the entire message received in a personal encounter.[49]

Employees will notice the extent to which your actions correspond with your words. If you talk about customer service but spend no time with customers, for example, your subordinates will likely place little value on service. Research suggests that if there is a discrepancy between a person's verbal and nonverbal communication, the nonverbal is granted more weight by the interpreter.[50]

Consider how one plant manager used nonverbal communication to symbolize the importance of cost-cutting when he took over at a struggling factory. He noticed that when most of the management team had to travel, they flew first class. Rather than issuing a directive that first-class travel was not allowed, the plant manager always flew coach. Soon, everyone throughout the company was flying coach.[51] In a similar fashion, the CEO of a book publisher did not send a memo when he decided that people no longer needed to dress up at work. He just stopped wearing ties, and soon everyone was dressing less formally. Leaders use actions to symbolize their vision and draw attention to specific values and ideas.

The method of communication and where you choose to carry out a communication can be symbolic. In other words, people attach meaning to a manager's choices. Reports and memos typically convey formality and legitimize a message. Calling an employee into your office can emphasize hierarachy and your status as manager. Personal visits from a manager are interpreted as a sign of teamwork and caring.[52] At Diebold, a Canton, Ohio, maker of automated teller machines, CEO Thomas Swidarski wants everyone to feel like they are an important part of the team. Swidarski personally drops by employees' desks to ask about their work or invites them to lunch to see what's on their minds.[53]

You are communicating all the time, without saying a word. Many people don't realize they are always communicating by their facial expressions, body language, and behavior.[54] The regional manager of a national insurance company said that he felt like a

"24-hour television station" because people watched everything he did all the time. As a manager, be aware of what you signal to others in addition to your verbal messages. People will interpret your actions as symbols, just as they attach meaning to your words.

MAKING PRESENTATIONS

A manager of the state program for the National Endowment for the Humanities spent several months each year traveling around the state of Tennessee giving talks at community groups, universities, and other organizations. His presentations were always successful, and he gained a reputation as an excellent speaker who laced his talks with humor and kept people interested and involved. No one would ever have believed he was the same person who literally passed out when giving his first public speech. Telling the story of that humiliating experience later, the manager recalls that he fainted after a series of thoughts like this ran through his mind: *Oh, geez, they can hear my voice quivering … they can see my hands shaking … wonder if they notice my knees are starting to wobble….* Interestingly, he later learned from several audience members that they were interested in what he was saying and hadn't even noticed he was uncomfortable until he suddenly stopped talking, started shaking all over, and slid down behind the podium. The audience was there to get something out of what he said—not to judge his performance.[55]

As a manager, you will be called upon many times to speak publicly, whether to explain your ideas at a departmental meeting, present a proposal to a potential client, speak at an industry meeting, or make a report to the board of directors. Many people have a fear of public speaking, even when speaking to a small group of colleagues, but by focusing on *communication* rather than *performance* you can relieve some of the anxiety associated with giving a presentation. You can be more relaxed and effective by paying attention to five aspects of making a presentation, outlined in Exhibit 5.6 as the Five Ps for Effective Presentations. Each of these is described in the following sections.[56]

Prepare

Your goal in making any presentation is to communicate something, so you have to know what that "something" is and be well prepared if you want to get your point across.

Exhibit 5.6 The Five Ps for Effective Presentations

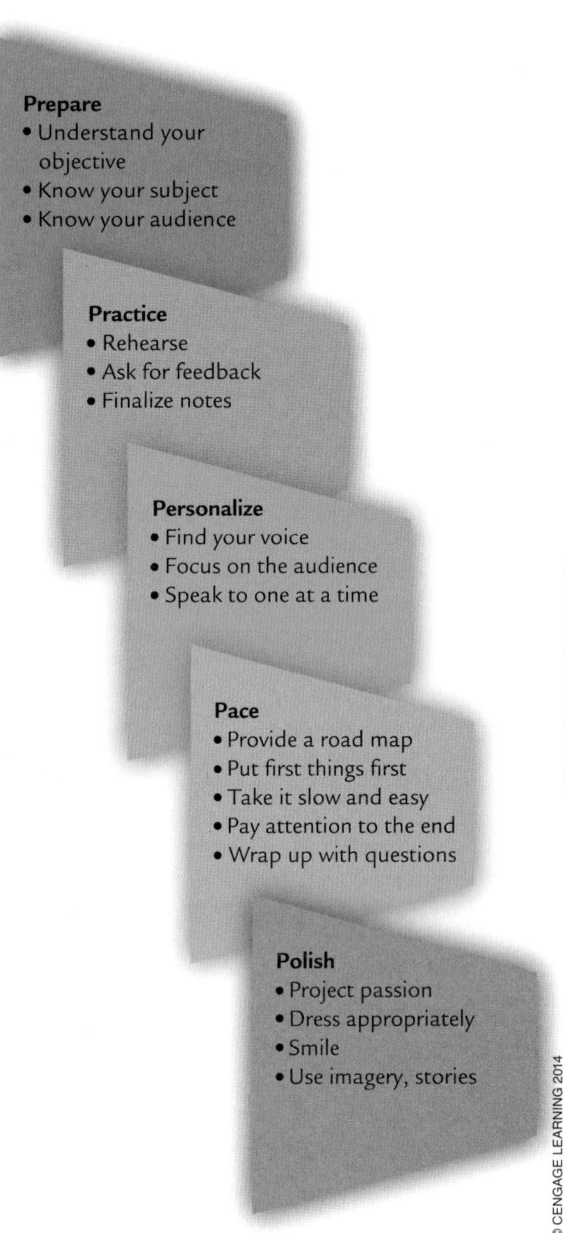

© CENGAGE LEARNING 2014

DISCOVER KNOWLEDGE

- **Clearly understand your objective.** What do you want the audience to know, understand, or believe following your talk? Everything else should flow from the answer to that question. Focus on one clear objective and ideally limit the presentation to two or three main points.
- **Know your subject backwards and forwards.** Prepare your talk by breaking the subject into main points and gathering the information, examples,

and statistics you need to support each point. Prepare an outline or notes, but keep it simple.

- **Understand your audience.** Effective presentations are tailored to the audience, which means you have to understand their previous knowledge of the topic and their expectations for your presentation. Approach the audience on their terms and try to see the presentation from their perspective.

DISCOVER YOURSELF

Interpret Your Score: Perceived Presentation Passion (Questionnaire 5)

This questionnaire was developed to measure the persuasiveness of presentations made by entrepreneurs seeking to obtain investment money from venture capitalists. Comparative data for **Presentation Passion** (Part A): Thirty person Mean score = 11.1, Top Quartile = 13–15; Bottom Quartile = 5–9. Comparative data for **Presentation Preparedness** (Part B): Mean = 13.2, Top Quartile = 15–15; Bottom Quartile = 9–12. The research showed consistently that preparedness, not passion, had the most positive impact on venture capitalists' decisions to invest money with entrepreneurs. Thus, a higher score on Part B is more important for an effective presenter than is a high score on Part A. CNOW and CourseMate users can access dynamically updated comparative data through www.cengagebrain.com.

© CENGAGE LEARNING 2014

DISCOVER KNOWLEDGE

Practice—and Then Practice Again

Practice can make the difference between a great presentation and a ho-hum one. Don't aim for perfection, but use practice as a way to thoroughly know and refine your presentation.

- **Time yourself.** You might find that you're spending so much time on the first point that you won't have time to cover the other two.
- **Ask for advice and feedback.** Once you've practiced on your own, ask a few trusted colleagues to give you candid feedback.
- **Finalize your outline and notes.** Don't memorize your speech or read it word for word. If you know your subject well and have clear notes, you will be able to speak conversationally rather than like a wind-up doll.

Personalize

To personalize the presentation means two primary things: putting yourself into the presentation and making each audience member feel like he or she is important to you.

- **Find your own voice.** Don't try to give a presentation like your boss does–even if she's the best speaker you've ever heard. Be your authentic self rather than trying to emulate someone else's presentation style.
- **Make it more about them and less about you.** The best presentations are audience centered. Connect with the audience early on and pay attention and respond to people's reactions.
- **Use eye contact and speak to one person at a time.** Move on to another after 10 to 15 seconds. If you're nervous, find an open, friendly face and start your presentation by speaking directly to that person. Whenever you start to feel anxious, go back to the friendly face.

Pace

When you give a presentation, you're taking the audience on a journey. By pace, we're referring to the movement, rhythm, and speed of the trip itself.

- **Provide a road map.** Start by telling people what the purpose of the presentation is, giving a brief overview of where you will be taking them, and how long it's going to take to get there.
- **Put first things first.** People are more likely to remember opening and closing comments rather than what comes in the middle. In most cases, it is best to present your key points first, and then follow up with elaboration and supporting details.
- **Take it slow and easy.** Slow down your speech, and pause occasionally to take a breath and review your notes. People who are nervous about public speaking are often unaccountably afraid of pauses, but a pause helps both you and the audience.
- **Pay attention to the ending.** The end is as important as the beginning. Use it to summarize your best thoughts, ideas, and images for the audience.
- **Wrap up with questions.** For most presentations, it is a good idea to give people a chance to ask questions at the end. Try to anticipate the toughest questions people might ask and plan how you will answer them.

Polish

The polish is the shiny part of the presentation. This is where you think about the impression you will make.

- **Project passion.** If you care about the subject, you will make others care about it. When you're talking about something that you genuinely want to share with others, your presentation will sparkle with that enthusiasm.
- **Dress for success and don't forget to smile.** You want to dress in such a way that you feel comfortable and confident. In addition, a smile projects self-assurance and interest in your audience.
- **Don't forget to use imagery.** To leave a lasting impression, don't rely too heavily on data. Be sure you have a few examples, images, or stories to make the presentation come alive and contribute to deeper understanding.
- **Don't panic if your mind goes blank.** If you forget what you were going to say, think of it as a good time for a pause. Don't start giggling, apologizing, or stammering. The audience doesn't have any idea what you were going to say next, so they won't even notice that you've lost your way. Take a drink of water and a deep breath, look at your notes, and then go on.

NEED TO KNOW

- Manager communication is the process by which information is exchanged and understood by two or more people. Communication involves the components of encoding, formulating a message, selecting a communication channel, decoding, and feedback.
- Managers act as sensegivers by shaping how people think about their work and the organization, including the values that guide decisions and behavior. This requires that managers be communication champions who build an open communication climate, ask questions, actively listen, and engage in purpose-directed conversations.
- Open communication means sharing all types of information across departmental and hierarchical boundaries. Asking questions develops critical thinking skills, stimulates new ideas, gives people a chance to make a difference, and lets people know you care about them and what they think.
- Listening is a vital part of communication. You can learn to be an active listener by paying attention not only to words and facts but also to emotions, facial expressions, and body language.
- Managers must communicate to influence people and persuade them to behave in ways to accomplish goals. The art of persuasion involves establishing credibility, building goals on common ground, making your position compelling to others, and connecting to others on an emotional as well as a rational level. Communicating with candor is also important for influencing and persuading people to do what you want and need them to do.
- The selection of a communication channel is often just as important as the message itself. Managers need to understand the hierarchy of channel richness and select rich channels, such as face-to-face talk, for difficult, sensitive, or complex communications. Electronic channels can effectively be used for many routine communications, but managers should learn how to avoid potential pitfalls with electronic communications. The frequent use of e-mail means that writing well in electronic communications has become a critical manager skill.
- Effective managers pay attention to their own and others' actions, facial expressions, tone of voice, and behavior. Nonverbal communication accounts for at least half of a message received in a personal encounter.
- Managers are frequently called upon to make presentations. You can be more effective if you pay attention to these five Ps: prepare, practice, personalize, pace, and polish. You'll be less nervous if you remember to make the presentation more about the audience and less about yourself.

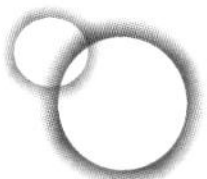

ACTION LEARNING

DELIBERATE PRACTICE EXERCISES

Asking Questions

Step 1: During the next few days, engage in your normal conversations by asking more questions. On the first day, ask three questions in each of three conversations.

On days two and three, ask five questions in each of three conversations. Be careful not to pull attention to yourself with your questions, but rather keep the focus on the other person.

Follow these rules for asking questions:

1. Make sure the question is thoughtful and that you do not know the answer; don't ask a question that ultimately would show you as the expert.
2. Try to figure out the underlying meaning of the other person's statements.
3. See if you can helpfully ask, "Why?"
4. Ask out of a genuine sense of curiosity.
5. Don't go overboard. It can take the focus off the speaker and on to you.
6. Be sincere.
7. Avoid giving an opinion. When you feel the urge to do so, replace that urge with the question to the speaker: "Why?"

Step 2: Answer the following questions.

1. What difficulty did you experience asking the questions?
2. What impact did your question asking have on the quality of the conversations?

Step 3 (Optional): Share your insights with a partner, and ask your partner what insights he or she gained.

Channel Richness

Step 1: Recall communications you've had during the past week using different media, such as face-to-face, Skype, phone, letter, e-mail or text, etc.

Step 2: Complete the table on the next page to examine the different types of media or channels you used for the various communications. You should include at least two communication instances in which you were the recipient. Refer to the continuum of channel richness in Exhibit 5.4 for more information.

What was the channel used?	What was the purpose of the communication?	Was the communication routine or nonroutine (complex, emotional)?	Was the channel the best fit for that purpose?	What other channels might you have used and how would that have worked?
1.				
2.				
3.				
4.				
5.				

Step 3: What advice would you give a new manager on choosing the best channel for a particular communication?

Step 4 (Optional): Share your insights with a partner, and ask your partner what insights he or she gained.

IN-CLASS TEAM EXERCISE

Listening (or Not) Skills

One of the most serious blocks to communication is lack of listening. This is an exercise to help you become aware of listening problems and to learn skills to become a better listener.

Step 1: Form into groups of four or five.

Step 2: Have one person at a time *talk about some current problem* he or she is having (something the person feels comfortable sharing with the group). Each person gets three minutes to explain the situation. No matter what happens, the speaker should attempt to finish the story.

During the first part of the exercise, the rest of the group will use some familiar "not listening" tactics. In the final round, members will actively listen. The table at the end of this exercise will help you follow the rounds.

Round 1A: Person #1 talking. During this person's talk, the other members of the group should interrupt with **unsolicited advice**.

Round 1B: Person #1 debriefs what it was like to try to talk with all the advice coming. Then, the person should describe whether the advice was helpful or not.

Round 2A: Person #2 talking. While this person talks, other members introduce **self-excursional comments**. This means you bring up something that is somewhat related but that is about your own point. For example, if Person #2 says, "I was trying to figure out whether to eat at McDonald's or not," you might butt in with, "My favorite at McDonald's are their wraps. And, you know, they are really healthier than the Big Mac . . . "

Round 2B: Person # 2 debriefs what it was like trying to finish the story.

Round 3A: Person #3 talking. During this person's talk, other members jump in with **negative comments** about what Person #3 is saying, such as, "I don't like so and so" or "That was stupid."

Round 3B: Person #3 debriefs what it was like to talk with all the negativity.

Round 4A: Person #4 talks while others interrupt with **interrogative responses**. So, if Person #4 says, "We left on our vacation last month," others jump in with questions such as "Where did you go?" What was the weather?" "What made you decide to go there?" etc. The idea here is not to be so interested in what the other person is saying, but to ask questions to draw the attention to your interest.

Round 4B: Person #4 debriefs the experience of trying to talk with constant questioning.

Round 5A: Person #5 talks while the other members of the group *listen like a professional therapist or psychologist would listen*. Notice your body language, pay attention to what the person is saying, and only rarely interrupt with a pertinent question.

Round 5B: Everyone talks about the experience of talking and listening during this round.

You may use the table below to help you follow the rounds.

Round number	Who speaks	What the rest of group does
1A	Person 1 talks	Unsolicited advice
1B	Person 1 debriefs	
2A	Person 2 talks	Self-excursional comments
2B	Person 2 debriefs	
3A	Person 3 talks	Negative comments
3B	Person 3 debriefs	
4A	Person 4 talks	Interrogative responses
4B	Person 4 debriefs	
5A	Person 5 talks	Listen like professionals
5B	Person 5 debriefs	Debrief also

Step 3: How many of the "Not Listening" tactics felt familiar to you? How will you practice being a better listener?

FIELD TEAM EXERCISE

Presentation Skills

Step 1: Divide into groups of four to six. Schedule a time for a group meeting at which each member will give one short presentation and everyone will give feedback to each speaker.

Step 2: Before your meeting, each individual should read "On Presentations" below and review the text discussion related to "Communicating to Persuade" on pages 201–203 and "Making Presentations" on pages 207–209.

Step 3: Before your meeting, each individual prepares a 45-second presentation that would persuade your audience about something. (You choose the topic to persuade.) Practice it.

On Presentations

Individuals typically form first impressions within the first two to four minutes. First, people tend to focus on what they can see, such as appearance, facial expressions, personal space, eye contact, and touch—and these "what you look like" components make up an astonishing 55 percent of the meaning. And you haven't yet opened your mouth.

Next, people focus on what they can hear, including rate of speech, volume, pitch, tone, and articulation. Your voice—not including your actual words—may transmit as much as 38 percent of the meaning in face-to-face conversations. Last, and certainly least in terms of those first few moments, the other person gets around to your words, which contribute a mere 7 percent to the meaning.

It's not that your words are unimportant. But if others do not like what they see, or if they get past your body language only to be stopped by something in your voice, they may not care at all about what you say. Their minds may already be made up, their first impressions indelibly formed. First impressions are also important because they can be lasting. In the initial two to four minutes, others will make a positive or negative evaluation. If that impression is positive, studies say you will be granted higher credibility and trust than if the first impression is negative.

Step 4: Meet as a group and choose someone to be the time-keeper. That person gives the go-ahead for Person #1 to start his or her 45-second presentation. The time-keeper holds a hand up when there are 10 seconds left and both hands when time is up. The presenter may finish only the current sentence at that time.

Step 5: After the presentation, allow a minute or two to fill out the Feedback Checklist below. Then, the group gives oral feedback to that particular speaker for up to three minutes. Go through each speaker in the group in this manner.

Step 6: After everyone has had a chance to speak and receive feedback, discuss as a group what is important in public speaking. How can you continue to improve? What specifically will you work on?

Feedback Checklist—How Did the Presenter Do in Terms of:

Characteristic	Person 1	Person 2	Person 3	Person 4	Person 5	Person 6
Visual Appeal						
Appearance						
Facial expression						
Eye contact						
Movement						
Personal space						
Touch						
Voice						
Voice—speed						
Voice—pitch						
Voice—volume						
Voice—quality						
Voice—articulation						
Objective						
Right approach						
Grabbing interest						
Concise						
Listener's level						
Asking questions						
Visualization						
Overall First Impression						

TEST YOUR METTLE

ROLE PLAY SIMULATIONS

Get on Board!

Background: Re-read the written Video Incident at the beginning of the chapter.

Instructions: Divide into groups of five or six. Assign group members to play Jane, Jason, Carlos, Carrie, and Heather. The sixth person, if present, will be an observer. Each person reads only his or her confidential role; the observer reads all roles. Spend 15 minutes on the role play.

Confidential information for Heather: You are so psyched to share this new communications methodology with the team. The conference you attended was so energizing, with dynamic speakers who gave lots of data on how this new technique will help reduce overlaps and redundancies in your communications, both written and oral. Preliminary findings show it can improve productivity up to 15 percent. And these days, with sluggish sales at the stores, your company needs all the help it can get. You know Jane will probably go along with this, as she always likes new ideas, but the others might need convincing. Ultimately, though, you know they'll go along, because you really need something new and effective right now. This is your first chance to present a new idea—all by yourself—and you can't wait!

Confidential information for Jason: Your boss, Jane Sutton, has called a meeting to go over a new communication technique Heather learned at a conference. Usually Jane has good ideas, and you like working in a place that is more innovative. But this is not a good time. Corporate has just started a new marketing program, and you are trying your best to get the stores to come on board with this new vision. It's not the time to be bringing *another* new idea. Just wait a while. But if they push it, you might as well go along, because it's not worth the energy to fight it.

Confidential information for Carlos: Jane is always coming up with one crazy idea after another. Sales are down now, and everyone just needs to keep their nose to the grindstone. You have to watch the bottom line, and getting people distracted is not the best course of action now. Jane should know better. She got her MBA, after all.

Confidential information for Carrie: Your boss, Jane Sutton, is letting Heather present a new idea. Even though you think, from what you've heard, the idea is good, you're not sure if Heather is the right one to lead this venture. Shouldn't it be you, as the COO? You've got to show them that you are the logical and most capable one to take this project on.

Confidential information for Jane: You are pleased that Heather has come up with a new idea, and you think it has merit. The company's sales are down, so any help with productivity will be good. But you aren't sure Heather has the skills to present this well, so she might need some help.

After the role play, discuss what happened and answer these questions:

1. What gets in the way of looking at new ideas?
2. What are effective ways to persuade? Ineffective ways?

3. Think of some recent examples from the news or personal experience of someone trying to persuade others. How similar or different were those from your role play?

What's Going On?

This Role Play Simulation is available online at www.cengagebrain.com.

VIDEO APPLICATION

Communication Choices at Plant Fantasies

Owner Teresa Carleo and sales director Steve Martucci have clear preferences for effective communication.

Discussion Questions

1. Why do you think Martucci prefers face-to-face for communicating with employees and clients?
2. Why do you think Carleo is sending personal handwritten notes to clients when she has digital communication technologies at her disposal?
3. What role does candor play in communications at Plant Fantasies? Do you think gender might influence the communication choices of Carleo and Martucci?

CASE INCIDENTS

TEST YOUR METTLE

Toy-Gate

Toys are associated with the world of play, imagination, and the innocence of childhood. Walk through a toy store or flea market and the glimpse of a simple toy—a bag of tiny green soldiers, a rack of Barbie clothes, the inviting knobs of an Etch-a-Sketch, the plush softness of a teddy bear, or the outstretched arms of a Raggedy Ann doll—stirs the senses and unleashes a flood of memories.

However, those whose career and livelihood rest upon the success or failure of the next toy trend can attest to the fact that they are involved in a rough industry. It can be as cut-throat as any pirate adventure. *Yo-ho-ho!* Snooping, corporate espionage, and efforts to keep emerging ideas under wraps are all part of life in the toy industry. A certain level of managerial paranoia is to be expected.

But when the private e-mail of an industry CEO was discovered and began making the rounds, it unleashed a firestorm, and the resulting *Toy-Gate* brought unwanted media attention and public embarrassment, resulting in disastrous drops in company morale and stock prices.

On the wall of his office, Howard Tannenbaum, long-time CEO of a major toy company, has a framed print of *Decatur Boarding the Tripolitan Gunboat* by Dennis

SHUTTERSTOCK #53973379

Malone Carter, with its chaotic depiction of battle against Barbary pirates. It is a favorite possession, and the topic of conversation with new employees or visitors to the office. Tannenbaum offers the scene as a visual reminder of the need to protect innovative ideas (and market share) "against all comers."

Over the past few years, the company worked to develop a new product line that all concerned believed would be a blockbuster. The brain-child of Tannenbaum, the new line of toys was so top secret that portions of the line were created and produced, piece-meal, among the various divisions. In the beginning, it was all very hush-hush. But as the line moved closer to completion and the expected Christmas season launch date more than a year away, press and industry rumors gained momentum. Then a reporter from a trade magazine called Tannenbaum's office to confirm details of the new toy line that his magazine was about to print.

At 8:00 AM the next day, managers at all levels across the company opened their e-mail and found a flagged message from Howard:

> TO ALL MANAGERS:
>
> We have a disaster in the making. Our security on the new toy line has been breached. Product design information on the new line, information that should have been under the HIGHEST SECURITY, has been breached and is about to appear in *Toy Weekly*. At this point, YOU are suspect. EVERYONE is suspect. Needless to say, I am FURIOUS! When I find out who it is—and it could be anyone—believe me, heads will roll!!! Let me make it clear that each of you is responsible for investigating your department and finding the source of the leak. Please be thorough in your investigation and TOTALLY HONEST with me in presenting your findings in this matter. THIS IS A PRIORITY!
>
> Howard Tannenbaum, CEO

Every recipient of the e-mail felt personally attacked and threatened. Before the day's end, e-mails, phone calls, and rumors were flying. By the following day, Tannenbaum felt pressured into trying to defuse the anger by issuing a second, apologetic, e-mail. However, events were already spiraling out of hand, as somehow the contents of the original e-mail began to circulate to employees and at least one member of the press, who dubbed the debacle *Toy-Gate*. The perception of a CEO and a company out of control spread through the industry and even the stock price took a substantial hit.

"The e-mail left me stunned," one long-time manager said. "When I saw Howard's e-mail and the level of contempt he showed for all of us, making us *all* appear incompetent and dishonest—that, for me, was the last straw. Even if I stay, it has destroyed the relationship with Howard forever."

Now Tannenbaum sat, head in hands, in his office, talking to his most senior VP and longtime friend. "Barry, I was simply trying to find the truth."

Barry Paine walked over to a bookshelf and pulled an old, well-used volume. "Do you remember your Sophocles from school, Howard? In one Greek tragedy, Oedipus the King in his persistent search for truth in the murder of his predecessor, King Laius, followed a path that abandoned reason and led to his own undoing. My friend, in your case, it's not the search for truth, but it's the path you take—what you say, how you say it, and to whom you say it—that is important."

"Okay," Tannenbaum said, "What are the next steps?"

Discussion Questions

1. What is the underlying problem in this case? Why do you think Howard Tannenbaum sent that e-mail?
2. Revise the CEO's e-mail to reflect what you would say in that situation. To whom would you send the e-mail?
3. What should Tannenbaum do now to try to recover from the negative impact of his e-mail? Suggest specific steps.

Loose Cannon

Mike Arnold had a reputation as a tough, no-nonsense manager able to clean up, transform, or scuttle and totally rebuild an organization. When he was brought in from west Texas to "fix" the city's poorly managed Department of Public Works, there was a collective sigh of relief. Aside from a handful of reporters, no one questioned his reading of a prepared statement at the press conference announcing his appointment as Director of Public Works. In the presence of cameras, public works employees, and the mayor, Arnold spoke of quality of life and the unsung heroes who fill the potholes. He vowed to organize and transform the department to reflect the quality of the men and women serving the city and to restore the reputation of the city as one of beauty, cleanliness, and hospitality.

Public Works managed nearly 6,000 travel-lane miles, over 300 bridges, and 800 linear miles of sidewalk in addition to a dozen recycle drop-off sites and the collection of approximately one million pounds of home refuse each year. In addition, traffic lights and signs, brush pickup, alley and dump site cleanup, roadside cleanup, mowing, and landscaping fell under the department's long list of responsibilities. Over the years, lax record keeping, budget overruns, poor supervision, and personnel cuts had resulted in low employee morale and a barrage of criticism from citizens and the press.

Mike Arnold enthusiastically took over and began calling the shots and holding accountable those responsible for creating "this mess." Arnold had good communication skills, often speaking to employees about public works activities, sharing helpful information, and inspiring people with the larger mission. Ignoring the long-held tradition of avoiding criticism of previous administrators, sneering disapproval of his predecessor and references to comments such as, "What was he thinking?" would sometimes creep into Arnold's talks, initially delighting employees and citizens. Arnold enjoyed press conferences, in which every statement was grabbed up and relayed to an adoring public.

"Old Mike really tells it like it is," was the general consensus.

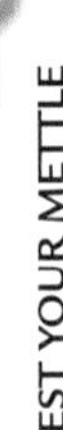

The changes in public works were impressive. Within a few years, projects were coming in under budget. Increased community service and volunteer workers supplemented staff reductions to provide an army for cleanup projects, saving thousands of dollars each month in labor costs. College students, in particular, appreciated the expansion of the city's bike lanes and shared routes. Corporations were enticed to provide gift cards and other incentives to volunteers as well as participants in the recycling programs.

Along the way, though, Arnold's *telling it like it is* lost much of its appeal. While it had been considered fine to criticize politicians with colorful remarks ("These rats can join other vermin we've removed from our fair city"), it was not fine to loudly rake employees over the coals or to make disparaging remarks about the citizenry. During one spontaneous visit to a neighborhood that had joined the recycling effort, Arnold noted that the presence of recycling bins along the street was great, adding sarcastically, "Now why don't these folks clean up their yards; mow some grass. Let's wake up here, people." When a group of women secured air time on a local newscast to complain about the

need for a traffic light at one neighborhood intersection, Arnold's repeated on-camera references to the women as "the little ladies" drew fire.

Despite the public apologies, each remark was just one more shot from what many people now considered a "loose cannon." The city's PR director cringed each time Mike Arnold opened his mouth. As social network comments, tweets, and editorials demonstrated, Arnold retained a large number of supporters who firmly believed his remarks were honest outpourings of what others thought but would not say for fear of being criticized. The press still covered every comment but, increasingly, both press and public fascination focused on new reasons to hate this guy.

Now the city administration faced a mounting chorus of calls to replace Mike Arnold as head of Public Works, creating a dilemma for the mayor. Arnold's improvements to the department and the city while working within budget restrictions were undeniable. No other department matched his numbers. What's more, each program, each improvement he made was *visible.* City council members as well as the mayor's office agreed, "He's the last guy we would want to lose." But the question persisted: "In light of the polarizing love-hate relationship he has with the citizens of our community, how do we handle our 'loose cannon'?"

Discussion Questions

1. What is going on with Mike Arnold? What do you see as the underlying cause of his communication problems?
2. If you were the mayor, would you keep Arnold despite his issues or let him go? If you keep him, how would you rein in his comments?
3. What other options can you think of for consideration by the mayor and council to handle Arnold's communication improprieties? Which option would you adopt? Why?

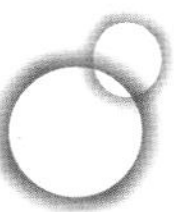

PERSONAL SKILLS LOG

PERSONAL SKILLS LOG

Directions: Fill in the rows below based on what you learned from each part of the chapter that you completed.

	What is my key takeaway or insight from this activity?	What do I personally do well (strength) regarding this activity?	What could I improve (weakness) about myself regarding this activity?	How might I use what I've learned from this activity in the future?
Manager Challenge Incident:				
Discover Yourself Questionnaires:				
Deliberate Practice Exercises:				
In-Class and/or Field Team Exercises:				
Role-Play Exercises:				
Case Incidents:				

REFERENCES

Discover Yourself

1 Based on Rebecca B. Rubin, "The Validity of the Communication Competency Assessment Instrument," *Communication Monographs* 52 (June 1985): 173–185.

2 Based on Dennis Bline, Dana R. Lowe, Wilda F. Meixner, and Hossein Nouri, "Measurement Data on Commonly Used Scales to Measure Oral Communication and Writing Apprehensions," *The Journal of Business Communications* 40, no. 4 (October 2003): 266–288; and J. C. McCrosky and V. P. Richmond, "Validity of the PRCA as an Index of Oral Communication Apprehension," *Communication Monographs* 45 (1978): 152–203.

3 Partially based on William B. Snavely and John D. McNeill, "Communicator Style and Social Style: Testing a Theoretical Interface," *Journal of Leadership and Organizational Studies* 14, no. 1 (February 2008): 219–232.

4 Based on Xiao-Ping Chen, Xin Yao, and Suresh Kotha, "Entrepreneur Passion and Preparedness in Business Plan Presentations: A Persuasion Analysis of Venture Capitalists' Funding Decisions," *Academy of Management Journal* 52, no. 1 (2009): 199–214.

Discover Knowledge

5 Ron Stodghill, "Boxed Out," *Forbes Small Business* (April 2005): 69–72.

6 Henry Mintzberg, *The Nature of Managerial Work* (New York: Harper & Row, 1973); and Henry Mintzberg, *Managing* (San Francisco: Berrett-Koehler Publishers, 2009).

7 John P. Kotter, interviewed by Jeff Kehoe, "Managing Yourself: How to Save Good Ideas," *Harvard Business Review* (October 2010): 129–132.

8 Eric Berkman, "Skills," *CIO* (March 1, 2002): 78–82; Louise van der Does and Stephen J. Caldeira, "Effective Leaders Champion Communication Skills," *Nation's Restaurant News* (March 27, 2006): 20; and Byron Reimus, "Ready, Aim, Communicate," *Management Review* (July 1996).

9 Reimus, "Ready, Aim, Communicate"; and Dennis Tourish, "Critical Upward Communication: Ten Commandments for Improving Strategy and Decision Making," *Long Range Planning* 38 (2005): 485–503.

10 Bernard M. Bass, *Bass & Stogdill's Handbook of Leadership*, 3rd ed. (New York: The Free Press, 1990).

11 Ian Urbina, "Workers on Doomed Rig Voiced Concern about Safety," *The New York Times* (July 22, 2010).

12 This discussion is based on Dennis A. Gioia and Kumar Chittipeddi, "Sensemaking and Sensegiving in Strategic Change Initiation," *Strategic Management Journal* 12, no. 6 (September 1991): 433–448; and Anne D. Smith, Donde Ashmos Plowman, and Dennis Duchon, "Everyday Sensegiving: A Closer Look at Successful Plant Managers," *The Journal of Applied Behavioral Science* 46, no. 2 (June 2010): 220–244.

13 Dana Mattioli, "CEOs Welcome Recovery to Look After Staff," *The Wall Street Journal* (April 5, 2010).

14 Reported in van der Does and Caldeira, "Effective Leaders Champion Communication Skills."

15 Quint Studer, "Case for Transparency," *Leadership Excellence* (April 2010): 19.

16 van der Does and Caldeira, "Effective Leaders Champion Communication Skills."

17 Studer, "Case for Transparency."

18 Harvey Thomas, a General Motors plant manager in Spring Hill, Tennessee, quoted in Kelley Holland, "Under New Management: The Silent May Have Something to Say," *The New York Times* (December 4, 2006).

19 "What Is Trust?" results of a survey by Manchester Consulting, reported in Jenny C. McCune, "That Elusive Thing Called Trust," *Management Review* (July–August 1998): 10–16; and Mirta M. Martin, "Trust Leadership," *The Journal of Leadership Studies* 5, no. 3 (1998): 41–49.

20 "The Power of Questions," *Leader to Leader* (Spring 2005): 59–60.

21 Many of these benefits are based on "The Power of Questions" *Leader to Leader* (Spring 2005): 59–60; Quinn Spitzer and Ron Evans, "The New Business Leader: Socrates with a Baton," *Strategy & Leadership* (September–October 1997): 32–38; and Gary B. Cohen, "Just Ask Leadership: Why Great Managers Always Ask the Right Questions," *Ivey Business Journal*, July–August 2010, http://www.iveybusinessjournal.com/topics/leadership/just-ask-leadership-why-great-managers-always-ask-the-right-questions (accessed March 7, 2011).

22 J. T. Dillon, "The Use of Questions in Organizational Consulting," *The Journal of Applied Behavioral Science* 39, no. 4 (December 2003): 438–452.

23 Reported in Spitzer and Evans, "The New Business Leader: Socrates with a Baton."

24 Dorothy Leeds, *Smart Questions: The Essential Strategy for Successful Managers* (New York: Berkley Books, 1988).

25 Reported in Curtis Sittenfeld, "Good Ways to Deliver Bad News," *Fast Company* (April 1999): 58, 60.

26 M. P. Nichols, *The Lost Art of Listening* (New York: Guilford Publishing, 1995).

27 Gerald M. Goldhaber, *Organizational Communication*, 4th ed. (Dubuque, IA: Wm. C. Brown, 1980), p. 189.

28 Study reported in Peter Meyer, "So You Want the President's Job?" *Business Horizons* (January–February 1998): 2–6.

29 Elizabeth Weiss Green, "The Power of Persuasion," *U.S. News and World Report* (August 7, 2006): 60, 62.

30 This section is based heavily on Jay A. Conger, "The Necessary Art of Persuasion," *Harvard Business Review* (May–June 1998): 84–95.

31 Conger, "The Necessary Art of Persuasion."

32 This discussion is based in part on Jack Welch with Suzy Welch, *Winning* (New York: HarperBusiness, 2005), Chapter 2.

33 These are based on E. Raudsepp, "Are You Properly Assertive?" *Supervision* (June 1992); M. J. Smith, *When I Say No, I Feel Guilty* (New York: Bantam Books, 1975).

34 Based on Welch, *Winning*, Chapter 2.

35 Robert H. Lengel and Richard L. Daft, "The Selection of Communication Media as an Executive Skill," *Academy of Management Executive* 2 (August 1988): 225–232; and Richard L. Daft and Robert H. Lengel, "Organizational Information Requirements, Media Richness, and Structural Design," *Managerial Science* 32 (May 1986): 554–572.

36 Reported in Anya Kamenetz, "The Laws of Urban Energy," *Psychology Today* (July–August 2007): 81–87.

37 Studies reported in "E-mail Can't Mimic Phone Calls," *Johnson City Press* (September 17, 2000): 31.

38 John R. Carlson and Robert W. Zmud, "Channel Expansion Theory and the Experiential Nature of Media Richness Perceptions," *Academy of Management Journal* 42, no. 2 (1999): 153–170; and R. Rice and G. Love, "Electronic Emotion," *Communication Research* 14 (1987): 85–108.

39 Ronald E. Rice, "Task Analyzability, Use of New Media, and Effectiveness: A Multi-Site Exploration of Media Richness," *Organizational Science* 3, no. 4 (November 1994): 502–527.

40 Richard L. Daft, Robert H. Lengel, and Linda Klebe Treviño, "Message Equivocality, Media Selection and Manager Performance: Implications for Information Systems," *MIS Quarterly* 11 (1987): 355–368.

41 Diana Middleton, "Students Struggle for Words; Business Schools Put More Emphasis on Writing Amid Employer Complaints," *The Wall Street Journal* (March 3, 2011).

42 National Commission on Writing, "Writing Skills Necessary for Employment, Says Big Business," *Writing Commission*, September 14, 2004, http://www.writingcommission.org/pr/writing_for_employ.html (accessed April 8, 2008).

43 Edward M. Hallowell, "The Human Moment at Work" *Harvard Business Review* (January–February 1999): 58–66; and Andrea C. Poe, "Don't Touch That 'Send' Button!" *HR Magazine* (July 2003): 74–80.

44 Carlson and Zmud, "Channel Expansion Theory and the Experiential Nature of Media Richness Perceptions."

45 Cassell Bryan-Low and Aaron Lucchetti, "George Carlin Never Would've Cut It at the New Goldman Sachs—Firms Ban Naughty Words in Emails; An 'Unlearnable Lesson' on Wall Street?" *The Wall Street Journal* (July 29, 2010).

46 Jared Sandberg, "Workplace E-Mail Can Turn Radioactive in Clumsy Hands," *The Wall Street Journal* (February 12, 2003).

47 Mary Anne Donovan, "E-Mail Exposes the Literacy Gap," *Workforce* (November 2002): 15

48 Howard Gardner, *Leading Minds: An Anatomy of Leadership* (New York: Basic Books, 1995).

49 Albert Mehrabian, *Silent Messages* (Belmont, CA: Wadsworth, 1971); Albert Mehrabian, "Communicating Without Words," *Psychology Today* (September 1968): 53–55.

50 I. Thomas Sheppard, "Silent Signals," *Supervisory Management* (March 1986): 31–33.

51 Linda Klebe Treviño, Laura Pincus Hartman, and Michael Brown, "Moral Person and Moral Manager: How Executives Develop a Reputation for Ethical Leadership," *California Management Review* 42, no. 4 (Summer 2000): 128–142.

52 Jane Webster and Linda Klebe Treviño, "Rational and Social Theories as Complementary Explanations of Communication Media Choices: Two Policy Capturing Studies," *Academy of Management Journal* (December 1995): 1544–1572.

53 Carol Hymowitz, "How to Lead After Sudden Rise," *The Wall Street Journal* (May 8, 2006).

54 Mac Fulfer, "Nonverbal Communication: How to Read What's Plain As the Nose . . . or Eyelid . . . or Chin . . . on Their Faces," *Journal of Organizational Excellence* (Spring, 2001): 19–27.

55 Based on a personal story and ideas from Michael T. Motley, "Taking the Terror Out of Talk," *Psychology Today* (January 1988): 46–49.

56 The tips for making effective presentations are based on "Tips for Speakers," sidebar in Michael T. Motley, "Taking the Terror Out of Talk," *Psychology Today* (January, 1988): 46–49; Tony Alessandra, "Look of Leadership: Listen, Speak, and Project Image," *Leadership Excellence* (October 2010): 13; "How to Make a Speech or Presentation," Learning for Life Web site, http://www.learningforlife.org/exploring-resources/99-720/y10.pdf (accessed March 11, 2011); "The SSSAP Approach to Effective Presentations," as described in R. E. Quinn, S. R. Faerman, M. P. Thompson, M. R. McGrath, and L. S. St. Clair, *Becoming a Master Manager; A Competing Values Approach*, 5th ed. (Hoboken, NJ: John Wiley & Sons, Inc., 2011), pp. 273–283; and Mellody Hobson, interviewed by Beth Kowitt, "Make Your Next Presentation a Home Run," *Fortune* (March 22, 2010): 44.

CHAPTER 6

Becoming an Ethical Manager

Chapter Outline

RYAN LASH

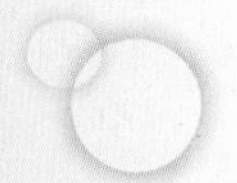

MANAGER CHALLENGE

VIDEO INCIDENT: IS IT A SECRET OR IS IT ESPIONAGE?

Jane Sutton, general manager of Caffeine and Crullers, is worried about declining sales. Much of the decline is due to a hot new competitor, Scone Prone, that recently opened in Madison. Jane's staff has been working for weeks trying to keep one step ahead of Scone Prone on marketing and new product development. Sales manager Jason Wong just walked into Jane's office and told her he has valuable information about Scone's plans and new products. After answering a lot of difficult questions, Jason finally admitted that he met Scone's COO, Allison Jamison, at a party. He pretended to be an Internet entrepreneur to woo her, taking her on several dates and making all kinds of personal promises, so Allison would give him important insights—which she did. Jason is really proud of himself. What he learned can help C & C succeed, instead of possibly being trampled by Scone Prone. Jane is thinking Jason's behavior may be legal, but it seems unethical to her. She wants an ethical climate, but she also doesn't want her employees to suffer decline and layoffs.

Initial Thoughts

1. If you were Jane, what would you do?

2. To what extent do you think Jason's behavior was unethical? Why?

Your instructor may ask you to be part of a role play based on the "Is It a Secret or Is It Espionage?" incident.

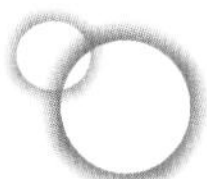

DISCOVER YOURSELF

For those students using CourseMate or CengageNOW, you can access the Daft/Marcic Assessment Library to take the questionnaires online and view dynamically updated comparative data.

Questionnaire 1[1]

Instructions: Please respond to the following statements based on your view of the tactics for getting things done through others. Rate how accurately each statement describes your thinking, based on whether the statement is clearly true or accurate, clearly false or inaccurate, or in the middle as somewhat true and somewhat false.

	True	Somewhat	False
1. It is hard to get to the top without sometimes cutting corners.	○	○	○
2. Accumulating wealth is an important goal for me.	○	○	○
3. A good way to handle people is to tell them what they want to hear.	○	○	○
4. It makes sense to flatter important people.	○	○	○
5. I am willing to interfere with the efforts of other people if they threaten my success.	○	○	○
6. I would cheat if there was little chance of getting caught.	○	○	○
7. I believe that small lies are necessary to maintain a competitive advantage over others.	○	○	○
8. The best reason to talk to others is to get information that I can use for my benefit.	○	○	○
9. If you trust somebody completely, you are asking for trouble.	○	○	○
10. I want to be rich and powerful someday.	○	○	○

Total Score ________. (Sum your answers 1–10, with 3 points for each True, 2 points for each Somewhat, and 1 point for each False.) Go to page 230 to interpret your score.

Questionnaire 2[2]

Instructions: When responding to the statements below, try to answer in terms of how you behave in real situations, not as you would prefer to behave.

	True	Somewhat	False
1. If I have made a mistake or failed at something, I promptly admit it to myself and others.	○	○	○
2. When I have made a mistake or failed at something, I quickly forgive myself and move on.	○	○	○

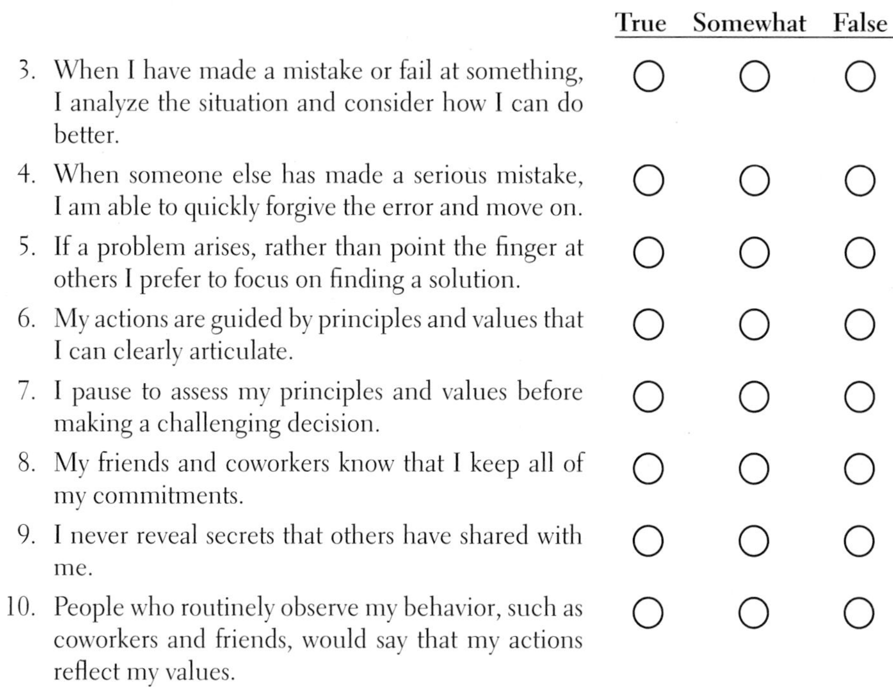

	True	Somewhat	False
3. When I have made a mistake or fail at something, I analyze the situation and consider how I can do better.	○	○	○
4. When someone else has made a serious mistake, I am able to quickly forgive the error and move on.	○	○	○
5. If a problem arises, rather than point the finger at others I prefer to focus on finding a solution.	○	○	○
6. My actions are guided by principles and values that I can clearly articulate.	○	○	○
7. I pause to assess my principles and values before making a challenging decision.	○	○	○
8. My friends and coworkers know that I keep all of my commitments.	○	○	○
9. I never reveal secrets that others have shared with me.	○	○	○
10. People who routinely observe my behavior, such as coworkers and friends, would say that my actions reflect my values.	○	○	○

Total Score ________. (Sum your answers 1–10, with 3 points for each True, 2 points for each Somewhat, and 1 point for each False.) Go to page 233 to interpret your score.

Questionnaire 3[3]

Instructions: Think about how you typically behave and make decisions and respond to the statements below. Answer as you actually behave, not as you would want to behave.

	True	Somewhat	False
1. I often find myself worrying about something.	○	○	○
2. At times I am so restless that I cannot sit still for very long.	○	○	○
3. My feelings are hurt more easily than other people's.	○	○	○
4. I am more self-conscious than other people.	○	○	○
5. I take things hard.	○	○	○
6. I often compromise in situations to avoid conflict.	○	○	○
7. When I make a decision, I may second-guess it later.	○	○	○
8. I feel self-conscious when a significant person compliments me.	○	○	○
9. Instead of wanting to celebrate, I feel a "let down" after completing an important project.	○	○	○
10. When I play a game and people are watching. I am very aware of their presence.	○	○	○

Total Score ________. (Sum your answers 1–10, with 3 points for each True, 2 points for each Somewhat, and 1 point for each False.) Go to page 240 to interpret your score.

Questionnaire 4

Instructions: Think about how you typically handle issues that arise at work or school. Respond to the statements below based on whether they are True, Somewhat, or False for you. Answer as honestly as you can.

	True	Somewhat	False
1. I risk substantial personal loss to achieve my vision.	○	○	○
2. I easily resist the social pressure to conform.	○	○	○
3. I take personal risks to make and defend my proposals.	○	○	○
4. I can tell someone "No" even if I have a lot to lose.	○	○	○
5. I confront someone if I see them doing something that isn't right.	○	○	○
6. I frequently make clear statements about what I prefer.	○	○	○
7. I promptly speak out against organizational injustices.	○	○	○
8. I act according to my conscience even if it means I lose status and approval.	○	○	○
9. When hesitant, I put my fear aside and do what needs to be done.	○	○	○
10. I seek out challenging opportunities that are beyond my skill and ability.	○	○	○

Total Score ________. (Sum your answers 1–10 with 3 points for each True, 2 points for each Somewhat, and 1 point for each False.) Go to page 242 to interpret your score.

GO ONLINE to find additional questionnaires at www.cengagebrain.com, search for Daft/Marcic Building Management Skills 1e, click on Free Online Resources, click on Additional Self-Assessments.

- Ethical Leadership at Work
- Workplace Deviance

DISCOVER YOURSELF

SHUTTERSTOCK #53973379

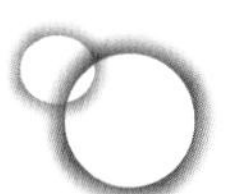

Chapter 6: Becoming an Ethical Manager

DISCOVER KNOWLEDGE

Becky McClain was working as a scientist at Pfizer when she began to suspect that a genetically engineered virus at the company laboratory was responsible for her ill health. McClain tried to get information about the genetic content of the virus and complained about desks being located next to where biological experiments were done. She says the company was uncooperative and eventually fired her in retaliation. Pfizer's position is that McClain was fired because she didn't return to work for 11 months—not because she spoke out about concerns regarding worker safety. A federal court didn't agree, with a jury awarding McClain $1.37 million from Pfizer. The case has opened the discussion concerning employee safety in biological labs and can potentially improve federal safeguards for people who are exposed to new biological materials being developed in the competitive pharmaceutical and biotechnology industries.[4]

Being courageous in a business setting can be risky. It can lead to losing one's job, losing the support of colleagues, feeling like a failure, and experiencing a setback in reaching personal and professional goals. However, courageous acts can often save lives, improve working conditions for fellow employees, and make organizations accountable for their misdeeds. Becky McClain's fight is still not over. Pfizer is expected to ask the judge to overturn the award, and McClain, who suffers from a potassium deficiency that causes sporadic, temporary paralysis, is still seeking punitive damages. She had the courage to go against a major pharmaceutical company because she believed people are being endangered at Pfizer and perhaps other companies. Jeremy Gruber, president of the Council for Responsible Genetics, applauded her courage and the jury's award. "I personally believe [she] is really the canary in the coal mine," he said. "[Federal regulations] have not kept pace with the explosion of research."[5]

As a manager, you will need courage for many reasons. One of the biggest reasons is that courage is necessary for practicing ethical behavior. Most managers think they are ethical. However, a closer examination of many managers' behavior leaves a question as to how ethical they really are in the decisions they make and the actions they display. This chapter describes the difficulty in being ethical when it goes against the grain, breaks social norms, affects profits, and tests one's personal will to act in a way that is the opposite of one's own value and belief system.

WHAT MANAGERS DO TO MAKE THINGS GO WRONG

The word ethics originates from the Greek word, *ethos*. In a general sense, ethics is the code of moral principles and values that governs the behaviors of a person or group with respect to what is right or wrong. Ethics define standards as to what is good or bad in conduct and decision making.[6]

Managers set the ethical tone for the organization. Managers signal what matters through their behavior, and when managers operate from principles of selfishness and greed, many employees come to see that type of behavior as okay. For example, at the now-defunct Bear Stearns, senior executives were openly arrogant and ambitious for personal successes, and they built a "sharp-elbowed, opportunistic culture" in which rules and basic standards of fairness and honor could be bent for the sake of achieving personal gain. One former Bear Stearns CEO said he "looked for managers with *PSD* degrees—poor, smart, with a deep desire to get rich."[7]

Some executives are preoccupied with their own importance. These managers take every opportunity to feed their greed or nourish their egos. They focus on having a huge salary, a big office, and other symbols of status rather than on what is good for the organization. These managers typically pay more attention to gaining benefits for themselves rather than for the company or the larger society. For example, top managers at AIG spent $400,000 on a corporate retreat at a lavish California beach resort just weeks after receiving an $85 billion rescue loan from the U.S. government. At Washington Mutual, the process of setting top executive bonuses was revised so that steep losses related to the housing crisis wouldn't affect their pay.[8] Managers

who expect big salaries, bonuses, and perks at the same time the company is struggling, clients and customers are hurting, and employees are losing their jobs are not likely to create an environment of trust and integrity.

Unethical managers frequently treat people unfairly. Managers make things go wrong when they treat people inequitably. They may give special favors or privileges to followers who flatter their egos, or promote people based on favoritism rather than concrete business results.

Unethical managers focus on their own needs and goals. Whereas ethical managers serve others and try to help others grow, unethical managers are concerned only with their own needs. These managers take all the credit for successes but blame others when things go wrong. By taking credit for followers' accomplishments, failing to allow others to have meaningful participation in decision making, and generally treating people with discourtesy and disrespect, they diminish the dignity of others. They see followers as a means to an end, and they show little concern for treating people as individuals or helping followers develop their potential.

Unethical managers fail to speak up against acts they believe are wrong. A manager who holds his tongue in order to "fit in with the guys" when colleagues are telling sexually offensive jokes is essentially giving his support for that type of behavior. A manager who knows someone is being treated unfairly by a colleague and does nothing is setting a precedent for others to behave unfairly as well. Peers and subordinates with lax ethical standards feel free to act as they choose. It is often hard to stand up for what is right, but this is a primary way in which managers create an environment of integrity.

DISCOVER YOURSELF

Interpret Your Score: Machiavellian Management (Questionnaire 1)

These items were drawn from the works of Niccolo Machiavelli, an Italian political philosopher who wrote *The Prince* in 1513 to describe how a prince can retain control of his kingdom. Successful political intrigue at the time of Machiavelli was believed to require behaviors that are somewhat ego centered and manipulative, which is almost the opposite of ethical leadership. A high Mach score suggests that a manager may be vulnerable to ego-centered behaviors that produce negative outcomes for self and organization as described in the chapter. Comparative data for **Machiavellian Management:** Thirty person Mean score = 14.8, Top Quartile = 17–25; Bottom Quartile = 10–12. CNOW and CourseMate users can access dynamically updated comparative data through www.cengagebrain.com.

© CENGAGE LEARNING 2014

WHAT DOES AN ETHICAL MANAGER DO?

Warren Buffett and Berkshire Hathaway did not escape the fallout from the economic crisis of 2008. Buffett had his worst business year in four decades. His holding company reported a 62 percent drop in net income. In his early 2009 letter to shareholders, Buffett accepted the blame for some of the decline but also pointed a finger at unnamed and unethical CEOs who left the credit and stock markets in shambles. Despite the heavy losses, Berkshire still had about $25 billion of cash on hand and was shopping for bargains while share prices of many companies were sliding. But what makes Buffett one of corporate America's best managers is not his investing ability, but his ethical leadership. The two are, in a sense, tied together. Buffett always looks at a company's "intrinsic business value" rather than just at the stock price. He is known for his commitment to sound ethics and transparency in disclosing mistakes or failures. As for bending the rules, his advice to employees of Salomon Brothers when it was embroiled in a scandal with the U.S. Treasury Department seems apt for today's climate: "You don't need to play outside the lines," Buffett said. "You can make a lot of money hitting the ball down the middle."[9]

When managers forget that business is about values and not just economic performance, organizations and the broader society suffer. Top managers in companies that get into trouble typically make quarterly earnings and the share price their primary purpose of business and the most important measure of individual and organizational success.[10] To be an ethical manager doesn't mean you ignore profit and loss, share price, production costs, and other hard, measurable data, but it does require that you recognize and adhere to ethical values and acknowledge the importance of human meaning, quality, and higher purpose.[11]

Ethical managers make a conscious and visible commitment to ethics. Despite the corporate realities of greed, competition, and the drive to achieve goals and profits, you can act based on ethical standards and encourage others to develop and use ethical values in the workplace. The single most important factor in ethical decision making in organizations is whether managers show a commitment to ethics in their talk and especially their behavior.[12] Employees learn about the values that are important in the organization by watching managers.

Ethical managers build an environment that encourages others to behave themselves. Exhibit 6.1 lists some specific ways managers act to build an environment that allows and encourages people to behave ethically. Managers create organizational systems and policies that support ethical behavior, such as creating open-door policies that encourage people to talk about anything without fear, establishing clear ethics codes, rewarding ethical conduct, and showing zero tolerance for violations.

Many companies have hired high-level chief compliance officers to police managers and employees. Most companies have established codes of ethics to guide employee behavior. However, an ethics code alone is not enough. Most importantly, managers must articulate and uphold high ethical standards, and then behave ethically even if they think no one is looking. If managers cut corners or bend the rules when they think they won't get caught, they and their organizations will ultimately suffer the consequences.

Ethical managers realize that what they do in their personal lives carries over to the professional arena. Consider Mike Price, who was fired as the University of Alabama's football coach before he ever coached a game. While in Florida participating in a golf tournament, Price spent hundreds of dollars on drinks and tips for exotic dancers, spent the night with a woman other than his wife, and ran up a $1,000 room-service bill. The university administration fired Price as a clear signal that the "boys-will-be-boys" mindset in the athletic department would no longer be tolerated.[13] A visible management position entails the responsibility for conducting both your personal and professional life in an ethical manner.

Ethical managers demonstrate the importance of serving people and society. For ethical managers, serving others is just as important as winning football games, increasing business profits, or making money for themselves. For example, Warren Buffett, described in the earlier example, stunned the world in 2006 by assigning most of his $40 billion fortune to charity, with the majority committed to the Bill and Melinda Gates Foundation, which funds programs in global health, education, and financial services for the poor. As for himself, Buffett lives a modest lifestyle. He lives in the same house he bought for $31,500 in 1956, drives an old car, and eats simple meals at inexpensive restaurants.[14]

Exhibit 6.1 How to Be an Ethical Manager

1. Articulate and uphold high ethical principles.
2. Focus on what is right for the organization as well as all the people involved.
3. Set the example you want others to live by.
4. Be honest with yourself and others.
5. Drive out fear and eliminate undiscussables.
6. Establish and communicate ethics policies.
7. Develop a backbone—show zero tolerance for ethical violations.
8. Reward ethical conduct.
9. Treat everyone with fairness, dignity, and respect, from the lowest to the highest level of the organization.
10. Do the right thing in both your private and professional life—even if no one is looking.

Sources: Based on Linda Klebe Treviño, Laura Pincus Hartman, and Michael Brown, "Moral Person and Moral Manager: How Executives Develop a Reputation for Ethical Leadership," *California Management Review* 42, no. 4 (Summer 2000): 128–142; Christopher Hoenig, "Brave Hearts," *CIO* (November 1, 2000): 72–74; and Patricia Wallington, "Honestly?!" *CIO* (March 15, 2003): 41–42.

WHAT IS YOUR LEVEL OF MORAL DEVELOPMENT?

Viktor Frankl was in one of the death camps in Nazi Germany. Writing about his experience in 1959, Frankl recalled the difficult choices that had to be made, and the courageous and ethical individuals who made the right ones:

> "We who lived in concentration camps can remember the men who walked through the huts comforting the others, giving away their last piece of bread. They may have been few in number, but

they offer sufficient proof that everything can be taken from a man but one thing: the last of the human freedoms—to choose one's attitude in any given set of circumstances. To choose one's own way.

And there were always choices to make. Every day, every hour, offered the opportunity to make a decision, a decision which determined whether you would or would not submit to those powers which threatened to rob you of your very self, your inner freedom…."[15]

Most of us will never face the kind of harrowing situation Viktor Frankl lived through, but each of us face decisions every day that test our ability to do the right thing. As a manager, you will have great influence and some degree of control over many people. It is important to remember that management is not merely a set of practices without an association with right or wrong. All management practices can be used for good or evil, and thus have a moral dimension. You can choose whether to act from selfishness and greed to diminish others or to behave in ways that will serve others and motivate people to expand their potential as employees and as human beings.[16]

Moral leadership is about distinguishing right from wrong and doing right, seeking the just, the honest, the good, and the right conduct in achieving goals and fulfilling purpose. Moral leadership gives life to others, enhances the lives of others, and uplifts people, enabling them to be better than they were without the leader. Immoral leadership takes away from others in order to enhance oneself.[17] A manager's capacity to make moral choices is related to the individual's level of moral development.

The Moral Development Scale

Lawrence Kohlberg, an American psychologist, expanded on the original moral judgment theory developed by Swiss psychologist Jean Piaget. Kohlberg's theory is an approach frequently used to understand the stages of moral development and values maturity.[18] A manager's level of moral maturity and ethical reasoning may contribute to decision-making behavior. However, organizational policies, higher management pressures, and situational circumstances sometimes make a manager's ultimate decision not reflective of his or her personal level of moral development. Exhibit 6.2 illustrates the three major levels of moral development. Within each level, there are two stages a person must pass through to reach the next level. These stages are sequential, so, for example, the person must pass through stage 1 first before passing through stage 2. An individual's morals evolve as the person travels from childhood to adulthood and develops from level one to level three. However, not everyone reaches level three.

Exhibit 6.2 Kohlberg's Levels and Stages of Moral Development

Level 1: Preconventional	Level 2: Conventional	Level 3: Postconventional
Follows rules to avoid punishment. Acts in own interest. Blind obedience to authority for its own sake. **Stage 1** - Obedience & Punishment **Stage 2** - Instrumental Orientation	Lives up to expectations of others. Fulfills duties and obligations of social system. Upholds laws. **Stage 3** - Interpersonal **Stage 4** - Duty	Follows internalized universal principles of justice and right. Balances concern for self with concern for others and the common good. Acts in an independent and ethical manner regardless of expectations of others. **Stage 5** - Individual Rights **Stage 6** - Universal
Self-Interest	**Societal Expectations**	**Internal Values**

Sources: Based on Lawrence Kohlberg, "Moral Stages and Moralization: The Cognitive-Developmental Approach," in *Moral Development and Behavior: Theory, Research, and Social Issues*, ed. Thomas Likona (Austin, TX: Holt, Rinehart and Winston, 1976), pp. 31–53; and Jill W. Graham, "Leadership, Moral Development, and Citizenship Behavior," *Business Ethics Quarterly* 5, no. 1 (January 1995): 43–54.

Preconventional Level

At the first level, individuals are ego-centered and concerned with receiving external rewards and avoiding punishments. This level includes the stages of *obedience & punishment* and *instrumental orientation (individualism)*. At stage 1, individuals have a fear of punishment so they obey authority and follow rules to avoid detrimental personal consequences. For example, a person at this stage has the motivation to pay state and federal income taxes because it's required by law and not doing so will lead to punishment. The second stage, instrumental orientation, means people want to satisfy their immediate self-interests. The instrumental orientation toward the world is one of taking what one can get. A manager with this orientation would tend to be autocratic toward others and use the position for personal advancement.

Conventional Level

At level two, the conventional level, people learn to conform to the expectations of good behavior as defined by their superiors, colleagues, family, friends, and society. There are the *interpersonal* and *duty* (*law and order*) stages within this level. Interpersonal means to be a "good boy or good girl," with an emphasis on being nice. Duty means that an individual's moral reasoning encourages him or her to respect authority, maintain the social order, and live up to the rules, norms, and values in the corporate culture. People at the conventional level adhere to the norms of the larger social system, such as paying income taxes because it is one's duty as a citizen and is expected by the larger social system. In organizations, if the rules are to not steal, cheat, make false promises, or violate regulatory laws, people at this level will attempt to obey. If the social system says it is okay to inflate bills to the government or make achieving the bottom line more important than honesty and integrity, they will usually go along with that norm also. When organizations do something illegal, many managers and employees are simply going along with the system.[19]

Postconventional Level

At the postconventional level, sometimes called the principled level, people are guided by an internalized set of principles universally recognized as just and right. Continuing our income tax example, people at this level might pay taxes based on a higher principle of supporting society, sharing wealth, and helping others. Warren Buffett, for instance, publicly disagrees with rich people such as himself paying less in federal taxes as a percentage of their income, and he believes the wealthy should serve society and help others by paying increased taxes.[20] This level includes the *individual rights* and *universal* stages. Stage 5 (individual rights) adherents basically believe that a good society is composed of different values and beliefs and people agree on society's standards. Each individual has a social contract with society. Employees are expected to follow the company's rules but can bend them if circumstances conflict with social values. At stage 6 of this level, internalized universal values become more important than the expectations of other people in the organization or community. Individuals may even disobey what they see as unjust rules or laws that violate universal ethical principles. In Israel, for example, staff members and volunteers at Rabbis for Human Rights serve as human shields to protect Palestinians from harm, even though it means they might be arrested or beaten.[21] A manager at this level is visionary, empowering, and committed to serving others and a higher cause. This is the most mature level of moral values.

DISCOVER YOURSELF

Interpret Your Score: Ethical Maturity (Questionnaire 2)

Your score for this questionnaire reflects your ethical maturity and indicates whether you are near Level 3 in Exhibit 6.2. The postconventional level of moral development means that you consider principles and values, take personal responsibility, and do not blame others. A high score suggests that you have a highly developed moral sense. A lower score suggests that you may be at the conventional or even pre-conventional level. Comparative data for **Ethical Maturity:** Thirty person Mean score = 26.2, Top Quartile = 28–33; Bottom Quartile = 21–25. Reflect on what your score means to you. CNOW and CourseMate users can access dynamically updated comparative data through www.cengagebrain.com.

© CENGAGE LEARNING 2014

Where Are You on the Moral Development Scale?

Most adults operate at level two of moral development, and some have not advanced beyond level one. Only about 20 percent of American adults reach the third,

postconventional level of moral development, although most of us have the capacity to do so.[22] People at level three are able to act in an independent, ethical manner regardless of expectations from others inside or outside the organization, and despite the risk to their own reputation or safety. During the Civil Rights movement of the 1960s, for example, many people followed a value system higher than the duty to obey laws when they intentionally broke what they considered unjust laws that discriminated against African Americans.

Applying universal standards to resolve ethical conflicts balances self-interest with a concern for others and for the common good. Research has consistently found a direct relationship between higher levels of moral development and more ethical behavior on the job, including less cheating, a tendency toward helpfulness to others, and the reporting of unethical or illegal acts, known as *whistleblowing*.[23]

The method Kohlberg used to understand the levels of moral maturity was to present a series of dilemma stories to children 16 years old and younger. All of the subjects were male, and Kohlberg's research has been criticized for emphasizing the male value of "justice" over the female value of "caring" during one's moral development; however, there is little empirical evidence to show that moral development differs between men and women.[24] During Kohlberg's research interviews, subjects were asked questions that related to the story. The responses were evaluated to understand the moral reasoning behind the answer and determine the stage of moral maturity of the participant. The following is one of the stories used in the study.

> ***Heinz Steals the Drug***
>
> *In Europe, a woman was near death from a special kind of cancer. Doctors thought there was one drug that might save her. It was a form of radium that a druggist in the same town had recently discovered. The drug was expensive to make, but the druggist was charging ten times what the drug cost to make. He paid $200 for radium and charged $2,000 for a small dose of the drug. The sick woman's husband, Heinz, went to everyone he knew to borrow the money, but he could only get half of what it cost. He told the druggist that his wife was dying and begged him to sell the drug at a lower price or let him pay him later. But the druggist said, "No, I discovered the drug and I'm going to make money from it." So Heinz grew desperate and broke into the store to steal the drug for his wife.*[25]

Before reading on, use the space below to write down your answer to this question: Should the husband have stolen the drug? Also write down your reasoning for your answer.

The reasoning behind a participant's response was the main concern for Kohlberg, not whether the participant answered "yes" or "no" to whether Heinz should have stolen the drug. Following are examples of some of Kohlberg's interpretations of the arguments that interview subjects gave for their decisions. Compare your reasoning to the reasons given below.[26]

Preconventional Level

Stage 1 (Obedience & Punishment Orientation): Reasoning at this stage is that Heinz should not steal the drug because stealing is against the law. If you steal you will get punished, go to jail, and be a bad person.

Stage 2 (Instrumental Orientation): The focal point at this stage is self-interest, so Heinz will decide according to what would be best for him. Reasoning might be that Heinz should steal the drug because it will make him happy to save his wife, and she can take care of the children at home. On the other hand, if Heinz wants to marry someone else, he likely would not steal the drug.

Conventional Level

Stage 3 (Interpersonal): The reasoning at this stage could be that Heinz should steal the drug to be a good husband and good person. Also, he could steal the drug because he loves his wife. His intentions are good and the druggist is a bad person.

Stage 4 (Duty): Reasoning at this stage might go the other way: Heinz should not steal because it is against the law. He should respect authority, obey the laws, and perform his duty to society so that social order is maintained.

Postconventional Level

Stage 5 (Individual Rights): Reasoning at this stage is more abstract and complex. Respondents believe that a good society is where people freely work for the benefit of all. Different social groups have different values, and people are not in favor of breaking laws, but in this

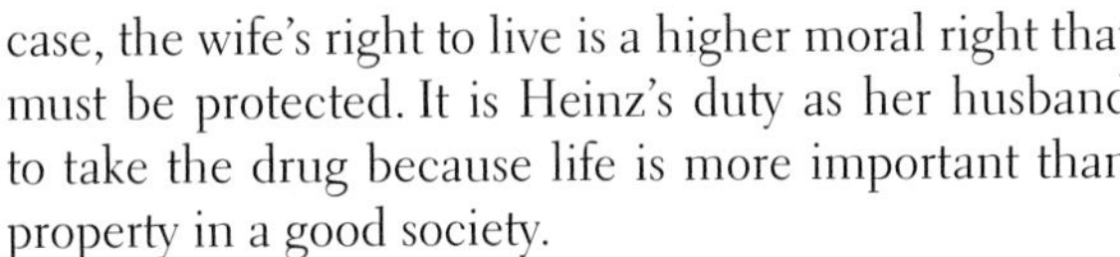

case, the wife's right to live is a higher moral right that must be protected. It is Heinz's duty as her husband to take the drug because life is more important than property in a good society.

Stage 6 (Universal): Universal principles of justice influence reasoning at this stage. A universal principle is that society must protect and respect the basic dignity of all people in an impartial manner, so any human life must be saved if possible. Heinz should steal the drug because of a universal principle that a human life is valued more highly than another person's personal property.

WHAT MAKES ETHICAL DECISIONS SO DIFFICULT?

Green Project Inc., a small ink-cartridge reseller, has filed suit against Seiko Epson, saying managers at the larger company sent an investigator pretending to be a customer to snoop around Green Project's operations. Green Project says the trick constitutes trespassing and theft of trade secrets. Even some managers who don't think the tactic is against the law say it is highly unethical. The laws regarding information gathering aren't clear cut, and neither are opinions regarding the ethics of such tactics. What do you think? Whereas some people think any form of corporate spying is wrong, others think it is an acceptable way of learning about the competition.[27]

The reason ethics presents a problem is that the situations we face as managers are seldom clear cut, with an obvious answer as to what is best for everyone concerned. Managers frequently encounter situations in which it is difficult to determine what is right. Many problems have fuzzy areas that make them difficult and sometimes impossible to resolve with satisfactory results. People have different world views (based on life experiences, education, family background, religious and political affiliations, perceptions, values, and so forth) that they bring into the decision-making process, which causes individuals to see and interpret situations in different ways.[28] In addition, as a manager you will likely encounter some situations in which any choice you make has potentially negative as well as potentially positive consequences.

Ethical Dilemmas

Being ethical is always about making decisions, and some issues are tough to resolve. Because ethical standards are not codified, disagreements and dilemmas about proper behavior often occur. An **ethical dilemma** arises in a situation concerning right or wrong when values are in conflict.[29] Right and wrong cannot be clearly identified. Managers face an ethical dilemma, for example, when they must choose between their own interests and the interests of someone else or some other group. People with an interest in the outcome of the decision are referred to as *stakeholders*. As a manager in an organization, it is up to you to consider the needs and interests of all key stakeholders—the employees, customers, suppliers, and shareholders who are affected by the decision—in addition to yourself. Decisions you make reflect not only your values but also the values of the organization you represent. Decisions you make on behalf of your organization carry consequences for the company's reputation and success in the community.[30]

The individual who must make an ethical choice in an organization is the *moral agent*.[31] Here are some dilemmas that a manager in an organization might face. Think about how you would handle them:

1. Your company requires a terrorist watch list screening for all new customers, which takes approximately 24 hours from the time an order is placed. You can close a lucrative deal with a potential long-term customer if you agree to ship the products overnight, even though that means the required watch list screening will have to be done after the fact.[32]
2. As a sales manager for a major pharmaceuticals company, you've been asked to promote a new drug that costs $2,500 per dose. You've read the reports saying the drug is only 1 percent more effective than an alternate drug that costs less than $625 per dose. The VP of sales wants you to aggressively promote the $2,500 per dose drug. He reminds you that, if you don't, lives could be lost that might have been saved with that 1 percent increase in the drug's effectiveness.
3. Your company is hoping to build a new overseas manufacturing plant. You could save about $5 million by not installing standard pollution control equipment that is required in the

United States. The plant will employ many local workers in a poor country where jobs are scarce. Your research shows that pollutants from the factory could potentially damage the local fishing industry. Yet building the factory with the pollution control equipment will likely make the plant too expensive to build.[33]

4. You have been collaborating with a fellow manager on an important project. One afternoon, you walk into his office a bit earlier than scheduled and see sexually explicit images on his computer screen. The company has a zero-tolerance sexual harassment policy, as well as strict guidelines regarding personal use of the Internet. However, your colleague was in his own office and not bothering anyone else.[34]

Varying Ethical Intensity

The perception of an ethical dilemma can be changed by the degree to which ethical importance is given to an issue. Variation in perceived ethical importance is known as *ethical intensity* on the decision maker. Greater ethical intensity can mean greater ambiguity about the correct action for an ethical issue or dilemma. Intensity is related to six factors identified by researcher Thomas Jones, as illustrated in Exhibit 6.3.[35]

Exhibit 6.3 Six Factors Determining Ethical Intensity

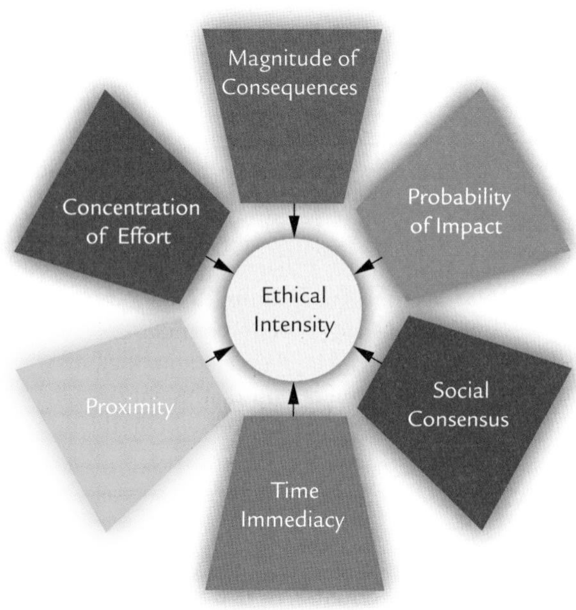

© CENGAGE LEARNING 2014

1. **Magnitude of Consequences.** This is the amount of harm or benefit accruing to the individuals affected by a decision or behavior. An act that causes 2,000 people to suffer an injury has greater consequences than an act that causes one person to suffer the same injury. A decision that causes the death of a human being is perceived as having greater consequence than one that causes a broken leg.

2. **Probability of Impact.** This is the likelihood that if a decision is carried out, it will lead to the harm or benefit predicted. The production of an automobile dangerous to occupants during normal driving has greater probability of harm than the production of a NASCAR racecar that endangers the driver if curves are taken at great speeds. The sale of a gun to a known armed robber has a greater probability of harm than the sale of a gun to a law-abiding citizen.

3. **Social Consensus.** This is the degree of public agreement that a suggested decision is either right or wrong, good or evil. Actively discriminating against minority job candidates is considered worse than not making an effort to seek out minority job candidates. Bribing a customs official in the United States or Canada evokes greater public condemnation than bribing a customs official in a country where such behavior is an accepted way of doing business. Managers and employees have difficulty deciding what is and isn't ethical if they aren't guided by a reasonable amount of public agreement or if the organization's ethical culture is weak.

4. **Time Immediacy.** This refers to the length of time that elapses between making a decision and when the consequences of that decision occur. A shorter length of time implies greater immediacy. Assume Merck releases a drug that causes 1 percent of the people who take it to have acute nervous reactions within one week. This has greater time immediacy than releasing a drug that will cause 1 percent of those who take it to develop nervous disorders after 25 years of use. A reduction in the retirement benefit of current retirees at UPS has greater time immediacy than a reduction in the future retirement benefits of employees who are currently 24 years of age.

5. **Proximity.** This is the feeling of closeness (psychological or physical) that the decision maker has for those who will be affected by the decision. Here's an illustration: Recently, Citigroup cut 53,000 jobs, and more layoffs were anticipated. This action likely had a greater impact on supervisors and managers who had

to hand out pink slips to their employees than it had on top executives who did not personally know the people who were losing their jobs. As another example, it is typically more difficult for a soldier who has to kill an enemy face-to-face than for a military leader to order the launch of a missile that will kill hundreds or thousands of people.

6. **Concentration of Effect.** This is determined by the magnitude of the action or the number of people affected by a decision. A change in an insurance policy denying coverage to 40 people with claims of $50,000 each has a more concentrated effect than a change denying coverage to 4,000 people with claims of $500 each. Cheating an individual or small group of individuals out of $10,000 has a more concentrated effect than cheating an organization, such as the IRS, out of the same sum of money.

The six factors of ethical intensity influence the perceived characteristics of an ethical decision, especially when there is a dilemma with competing options. Ethical intensity may become more severe with increases in one or more of the factors and decline with reductions in one or more of the factors. Moreover, each individual may rate the ethical intensity of the same decision differently. People place different weights on the various factors when making decisions.

HOW TO MAKE ETHICAL CHOICES

A recent survey revealed that more than half of American employees have observed at least one type of ethical misconduct (theft, lying, etc.) per year in their organization. Patricia Harned, president of The Ethics Resource Center, the organization that conducted the survey, reminds managers of their everyday responsibility for managing ethics: "We know formal programs are critical and work well initially, but we must now focus greater attention on building the right culture in which ethics programs operate. The data show . . . that leaders need to behave by example to set an ethical culture throughout the whole organization."[36]

As a manager, you will carry a tremendous responsibility for setting the ethical climate for your

7 STEPS TO... Ethical Difficulty

Moral justification is the process of reinterpreting your own bad behavior. You may alleviate your conscience by self-justifying your poor behavior, but try as you will, other people are likely to see through your favorite excuses. Here are some justifications that can get you into ethical trouble:

1. **It's someone else's fault.** This is the "blame others" approach. You can blame the boss, the organization, or anyone else for your unethical behavior.
2. **Everyone else does it.** This allows you to think it is okay for you to cheat, steal, or lie if you think others are doing it too.
3. **They owe me.** This lets you feel entitled to take office supplies, enjoy long lunches, use work time and computers for personal business, or pad your expense report.
4. **I didn't get any benefit.** You can ignore the fact that colleagues, employees, shareholders, suppliers, customers, or society may suffer when you practice unethical behavior.
5. **It was legal.** Sometimes you can justify something as narrowly legal even when it is ethically the wrong kind of behavior to practice.
6. **It's for a good cause.** This lets you think the ideal outcome you desire justifies the unethical means you use to get there.
7. **Two wrongs make a right.** If "they" did something wrong that broke the rules and hurt you, you think it's okay to do the same to them.

Sources: Based in part on Robert N. Lussier, *Human Relations in Organizations: Application and Skill Building,* 7th ed. (New York: McGraw-Hill/Irwin, 2006), p. 95; and "Ethics Scoreboard: Rule Book," ProEthics, Ltd. Web site, http://www.ethicsscoreboard.com/rb_fallacies.html (accessed March 28, 2011).

Exhibit 6.4 Rotary International's Four-Way Test

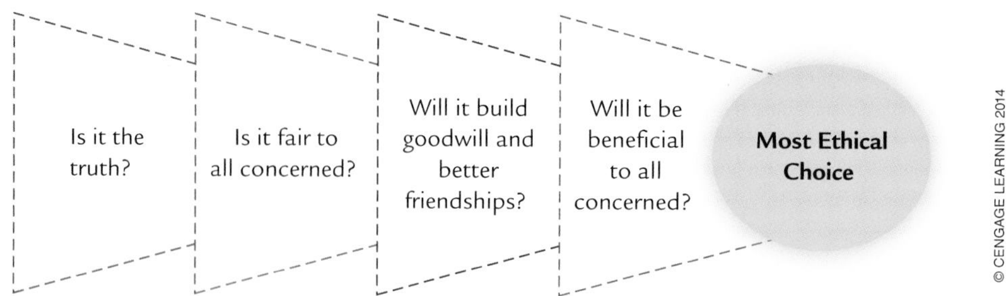

© CENGAGE LEARNING 2014

team and organization and serving as a role model for others.[37] Making ethical decisions is one of the best ways you can influence an ethical organization. Yet, as discussed earlier in this chapter, ethical issues aren't always clear cut. As a manager, you can use techniques to help resolve difficult ethical questions.

Use Rotary International's Four-Way Test

One technique that can guide you in making ethical decisions and helping others work through ethical issues is Rotary International's Four-Way Test, illustrated in Exhibit 6.4. When considering an action, ask yourself four simple questions:

1. Is it the truth?
2. Is it fair to all concerned?
3. Will it build goodwill and better friendships?
4. Will it be beneficial to all concerned?[38]

An example of failing the Four-Way Test happened at Toyota. Executives at Toyota Motor Corporation will probably think twice when they hide decisions regarding information about defects on their vehicles. The automaker was fined $16.375 million, the maximum fine allowed, because they failed to promptly notify

What's Your Problem?

Q: I've got a good job and have been getting high ratings on my reviews, so I know I must be doing something right. But lately I've been hearing rumors that "Jack," a colleague from another department with whom I've been teamed, has said I am a slacker and unreliable, that I don't follow through, etc. He posted something negative on Facebook, and I can't get access to it. Now I've noticed a few of my coworkers won't look me in the eye anymore. What should I do?

A: Your first reaction might be to start spreading negative stories about Jack, or to march into his office and demand an apology. But these behaviors might only make things worse. Instead, get the facts. Write down what you have heard from people. No need to go back and get details from anyone—that would only give the rumors more energy. It would be helpful, however, if you can find out exactly what is on his Facebook page. Then, casually go into Jack's office, taking your notes with you. Make a little polite conversation and then ask if he has any concerns about your work, because you've been hearing from people that he has. Keep your voice calm and even. If, and only if, he asks for more information on what you've heard, take out your notes and share one or two items. If Jack denies saying anything, respond with, "Well, that's a relief that you are not saying negative things about me." Passive-aggressive people often backbite because they do not have the courage to confront directly. Once Jack knows you are onto him, he will probably back off. If, however, Jack doesn't stop, have another, more sobering and explicit conversation with all the facts. Let Jack know that if this continues, you will be taking your notes to the boss. And then do it.

© CENGAGE LEARNING 2014

the U.S. Transportation Department of a dangerous and sticky accelerator pedal. Transportation Secretary Ray LaHood stated, "We now have proof that Toyota failed to live up to its legal obligations. Worse yet, they knowingly hid a dangerous defect for months from U.S. officials and did not take action to protect millions of drivers and their families."[39] An investigation by the Department's National Highway Traffic Safety Administration concluded that Toyota knew of the problem in September 2009 but did not inform U.S. regulators until January 2010.

Other Approaches to Guide Ethical Decision Making

Here are some additional tests you can use as a reference point to choose an ethical approach when making a decision:

- **The front-page test:** Would I be embarrassed if my decision became a headline in the local newspaper?
- **The personal gain test:** Would I make the same decision if the outcome did not benefit me in any way?
- **The good night's sleep test:** Whether or not anyone else knows about my action, will it allow me to have a good night's sleep?[40]

If, after trying these tests, you still have doubts about whether the pending decision or action is ethical, you can consult a person you consider to be ethical in their decisions and behaviors. This person may not tell you what you want to hear, but it is better to hear the truth from an ethical colleague, friend, or family member rather than make an error in ethical judgment.[41]

COURAGE DRIVES ETHICS

Doing the right thing is not always easy. Managers sometimes have to reach deep within themselves to find the strength and courage to resist temptations or to stand up for ethical principles when others may ridicule them or when they may suffer financially or emotionally for their actions. Managerial courage requires that you set aside your own selfish interests and personal goals for the benefit of the organization or a good cause.

Can ethical management exist without courage? For many managers, particularly those working in large organizations, the role of courage is easily obscured. The natural tendency is to get along, fit in, and do whatever it takes to get promotions and pay raises. Ethics and courage go hand in hand, but fear often gets in the way. The fear of rejection, fear of losing one's job, or fear of legal ramifications may discourage managers from asserting ethical behavior. That's when courage is needed most.

What Is Courage?

Courage is both a moral and a practical matter for managers. As John McCain, the U.S. Senator from Arizona and former candidate for President in 2008, puts it, "the lack of courage is what allows greed and self-interest to overcome concern for the common good."[42] The defining characteristic of courage is the ability to step forward through fear. **Courage** doesn't mean the absence of doubt or fear, but the ability to act in spite of them.

In fact, if there were no fear or doubt, courage would not be needed. To feel fear when real risk is involved is natural. Risks such as losing your life, your job, the acceptance of peers, love, or your reputation will naturally make you stop and think before acting. Many fears are learned and have a way of preventing us from doing what we really want in life. True managers step through these learned fears to accept responsibility, take risks, make changes, speak their minds, and fight for what they believe. Poet Maya Angelou said: "One isn't necessarily born with courage, but one is born with potential. Without courage we cannot practice any other virtue with consistency. We can't be kind, true, merciful, generous, or honest."[43]

Courage means accepting responsibility. Managers make a real difference in the world when they are willing to step up and take personal responsibility. Courageous managers create opportunities to make a difference in the lives of those they manage, in their organizations, and in their local communities. One societal example is Barbara Johns, an ordinary 16-year-old who made an extraordinary difference during the Civil Rights movement in the South. Johns led students of her segregated high school on a two-week strike after a bus full of white students refused to pick her up. The NAACP stepped in and helped the young people sue for an integrated school. The Johns family home was burned the same year.

DISCOVER YOURSELF

Interpret Your Score: Avoidance
(Questionnaire 3)

Your responses to these statements indicate your general level of anxiety or fear that would cause you to act cautiously and to avoid difficult situations that require courage. A high score means that you likely feel fears that would have to be overcome in order to act courageously. A low score means that feelings of fear and avoidance are lower and would be more easily transcended to act courageously. Comparative data for **Avoidance:** Thirty person Mean score = 19.7; Top Quartile = 23–28; Bottom Quartile = 13–17. CNOW and CourseMate users can access dynamically updated comparative data through www.cengagebrain.com.

© CENGAGE LEARNING 2014

Other young people took a stand too, with some as young as grade school being jailed for protesting the segregation of lunch counters, community centers, or sports leagues.[44]

Managers also demonstrate courage by openly taking responsibility for their failures and mistakes, rather than avoiding blame or shifting it to others. The acceptance of responsibility in many of today's large organizations seems non-existent. For example, at Lehman Brothers, CEO Richard Fuld refused to admit mistakes as Lehman teetered on the brink of collapse. After the firm went bankrupt following a shocking $4 billion quarterly loss and the breakdown of buyout negotiations with Bank of America, Fuld blamed Lehman's failure on inaction on the part of government and a general loss of confidence in the financial markets. Testifying before a congressional committee, Fuld calmly stated that he took all "prudent and appropriate" measures to fulfill his fiduciary duties.[45]

Courage means going against the grain, breaking traditions, reducing boundaries, and initiating change. Going against the status quo can be difficult. It's often easier to stay with what is familiar, even if it will lead to certain failure, than to initiate bold change. Many managers hurt their organizations and their careers by sticking with the status quo rather than facing the difficulty of change. Fast-paced business environments need managers able to read the signs of potential problems and take action to prevent losses and disasters. Oftentimes, change requires action and taking risks. But taking chances means making mistakes, enduring mockery or scorn, being outvoted, and sometimes failing miserably.

Take the example of Tory Burch, the co-founder and creative director of the Tory Burch fashion label. When Burch started her company, many said she shouldn't launch it as a retail concept. She was encouraged to start as a wholesaler because that was the traditional way. Yet, with encouragement from her mentor, Glen Senk, the CEO of Urban Outfitters, she decided to follow her instincts, take the risk, and create a new way of looking at retail. Drawing upon her experience working at Ralph Lauren, she built a company that is "an extension" of herself, in which the products, marketing, store visuals, and more are tightly integrated into a cohesive vision that feels very personal, as if customers "were in my home."[46] Her courageous risk taking paid off. Burch launched her line in 2004 and it was an immediate success. In 2005 her fashions were endorsed by several celebrities, including Oprah Winfrey.

To improve things, you have to push beyond your comfort zone. People encounter an internal "wall of fear" when they go beyond their comfort zone. People may encounter the internal wall of fear when about to ask someone out on a date, confront the boss, end a relationship, launch an expensive project, or change careers. Needless to say, facing that wall is when courage is needed most.

Courageous managers ask for what they want and say what they think. Managers have to speak out to influence others. However, the desire to please others—especially the boss—can sometimes block the truth. Everyone wants approval, so it is difficult to say things when you think others will disagree, disapprove, or retaliate. Author and scholar Jerry Harvey tells a story of how members of his extended family in Texas decided to drive 40 miles to Abilene for dinner on a hot day when the car air conditioning did not work. They were all miserable. Talking about it afterward, each person admitted they had not wanted to go but went along to please others. Harvey uses the title "The Abilene Paradox" to describe the tendency of people to not voice their true thoughts because they want to please others.[47] Courage means speaking your mind even when you know others may disagree with you and may even deride you. Courage also means asking for what you want and setting boundaries. It is the ability to say no to unreasonable demands from others, as well as the ability to ask for want you need to achieve the vision.

"For a long time people believed that the only purpose of industry was to make a profit. They are wrong. Its purpose is to serve the general welfare."
—**Henry Ford, Sr.**
Industrialist and entrepreneur, founder of Ford Motor Company

"It is curious—curious that physical courage should be so common in the world, and moral courage so rare."
—**Mark Twain**
American humorist, author of *The Adventures of Huckleberry Finn*

"Relativity applies to physics, not ethics."
—**Albert Einstein**
German theoretical physicist; developed the *Theory of Relativity*

"Just saying you're ethical isn't very useful. You have to earn trust by what you do every day."
—**Charles O. Holliday**
chairman, *Bank of America Corporation*

© CENGAGE LEARNING 2014

Courage means fighting for valued outcomes that benefit the whole. Leaders take risks, but they do so for a higher purpose. Courage doesn't mean doing battle to destroy the weak, feed one's ego, or harm others. It means doing what you believe is right, even when this goes against the status quo and possibly opens you to failure and personal sacrifice.

Nelson Mandela was given a life sentence and imprisoned for his stand against apartheid in South Africa. Even while incarcerated, he consistently refused to compromise his political position in order to be released. He was eventually released from prison in 1990 and went on to be the first democratically elected president of South Africa. Mandela continued the work he started in the 1950s and has been known to emphasize that "courage is not the absence of fear, but the triumph over it; the brave man is not he who does not feel afraid, but he who conquers that fear."

The Need for Personal Moral Courage

Recall the example of Becky McClain at the beginning of this chapter. McClain had the courage to go against a large pharmaceutical company because she believed people were being hurt by certain decisions and actions. **Whistleblowing** means employee disclosure of illegal, immoral, or unethical practices in the organization.[48] Whistleblowing has become more widespread in recent years, but it is still highly risky for employees, who may lose their jobs, be ostracized by coworkers, or be transferred to undesirable positions. Most whistleblowers realize they may suffer financially and emotionally, but they act courageously to do what they think is right. Whistleblowers such as Becky McClain take extraordinary risks, jeopardizing their jobs and future career prospects. "A whistleblower is considered a sacred cow but treated like the office pariah."[49]

To practice ethical management, managers have to know themselves, understand their strengths and weaknesses, know what they stand for, and often be nonconformists. An honest self-analysis can be painful, and acknowledging one's limitations in order to recognize the superior abilities of others takes personal strength of character. In addition, ethical management means building relationships, which requires listening, having significant personal experiences with others, and making oneself vulnerable—qualities that frighten many people.

How does a manager find the courage to step through fear, to overcome doubt and confusion, and to act despite the risks involved? All of us have the potential to live and act courageously, if we can push through our own fears.

DEVELOP YOUR BACKBONE

When Daniel Lynch took the job as CEO of ImClone, things were about as bad as they could get. Founder Sam Waksal had been hauled off in handcuffs for alleged insider trading, the financial state of the company was in shambles, and the company's application for FDA approval of a key cancer drug had just been rejected. Over a two-year period, Lynch led a remarkable turnaround by focusing on getting the financial house in order, restoring trust among employees, and getting approval for the new cancer drug. Lynch was brave enough to tell people he needed their help, and managers and employees rose to the challenge. According to chief financial officer Michael Howerton, the camaraderie that emerged as people struggled through the difficulties together gave them the courage to keep putting one foot in front of the other, no matter how bad things looked.[50]

People at ImClone found courage by banding together and leaning on each other. Similarly, you can strengthen your backbone for doing the right thing by drawing upon various sources of courage. Most of us have been conditioned to follow the rules, to not rock the boat, to go along with things we feel are wrong so others will like and accept us. Yet, by drawing on some sources of strength, you can unlock the courage that lies within you.

DISCOVER KNOWLEDGE

DISCOVER YOURSELF

Interpret Your Score: Courage (Questionnaire 4)

Each question pertains to some aspect of displaying courage in a group situation. A high score indicates a high degree of moral courage and a postconventional level of development when you are faced with ethical issues. You are able to stand up for what you believe is right in the face of social pressure to do otherwise. A high courage score indicates a willingness to take risks, overcome fear, and to behave at a higher level of moral development. How might you increase your courage? Comparative data for **Courage:** Thirty person Mean score = 22.1; Top Quartile = 24–28; Bottom Quartile = 15–20. CNOW and CourseMate users can access dynamically updated comparative data through www.cengagebrain.com.

© CENGAGE LEARNING 2014

Believe in a Higher Purpose

Courageous management often springs from a true sense of vision and a commitment to that vision that transcends the inevitable roller coaster ride of a manager's career. The vision acts as fuel to fight through fear toward action. Courage comes more easily when we fight for something we really believe in. A business example comes from Lawrence Fish, who retired as chairman, president, and CEO of Citizens Financial Group in 2009. Fish built Citizens into a banking powerhouse, but he said, "If we just make money, we'll fail." Fish is known for his volunteer efforts and commitment to the community, as well as his unconventional approach to operating a bank efficiently but with heart. Throughout his career, Fish has experienced both tremendous success and downright failure, but he has maintained the courage to pursue a vision that business is as much about doing good in the world as it is about making money.[51]

Draw Strength from Others

Caring about others and having support from others is a potent source of courage in a topsy-turvy world. Managers who genuinely care about the people they work with will take risks to help those people grow and succeed. Having the support of others is also a source of courage, and the best managers aren't afraid to lean on others when they need to. People who feel alone in the world take fewer risks because they have more to lose.[52] Being part of an organizational team that is supportive and caring, or having a loving and supportive family at home, can reduce the fear of failure and help people take risks they otherwise wouldn't take.

Harness Frustration and Anger

If you have ever been really angry about something, you know that it can cause you to forget about the fear of failure, the fear of embarrassment, or the fear that others won't like you. In organizations, we can also see the power of frustration and anger. After he was paralyzed in a motorcycle accident, Glenn McIntyre got angry every time he stayed at a hotel. His anger over how poorly hotels served disabled guests gave him the courage to stop feeling sorry for himself and start a new business, Access Designs, that helps hotels redesign their space to be more usable for disabled travelers.[53]

Managers can harness their anger to deal with difficult situations and make changes for the better. When someone has to be fired for just cause, a supervisor may put it off until some incident makes the supervisor angry enough to step through the fear and act. Sometimes, outrage over a perceived injustice can give a mild-mannered person the courage to confront the boss head on.[54] Anger, in moderate amounts, is a healthy emotion that provides energy and the impetus to move forward. The challenge is to harness anger and use it appropriately.

Start Small

Although harnessing frustration and anger can be useful for finding courage, "flying off the handle" is typically not beneficial for achieving positive outcomes. In most cases within organizations, finding courage is a deliberate act rather than an instantaneous response.[55] You can develop courage-type skills step-by-step. Start with courageous acts in small situations to strengthen yourself for bigger challenges that lie ahead. Courageous managers are not reckless and foolhardy; they typically are people who have developed the skills and resources they need to take a difficult stand or pursue a tough course of action. In addition, courageous managers can develop courageous followers by modeling courage and by helping people practice courage. Courage can be thought of as a decision-making skill that is developed through conscious thought and practice.

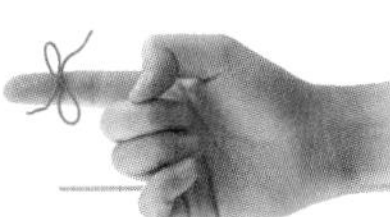

NEED TO KNOW

- Most managers think they are ethical, but many behave unethically because they lack courage. Managers make things go wrong in their organizations when they are preoccupied with their own importance, when they treat people unfairly, when they focus on their own needs and goals rather than what is good for the whole, and when they fail to speak up against actions they believe are unethical.
- Ethical managers make a visible commitment to ethics, build an environment that encourages others to behave themselves, behave ethically in both their personal and professional lives, and demonstrate the importance of serving others.
- A manager's capacity to make ethical choices is related to the individual's level of moral development. Three levels of moral development are preconventional, conventional, and postconventional. Most managers operate at the conventional level, meaning they conform to the expectations of good behavior as defined by their superiors, colleagues, family, friends, and society.
- Ethical situations are rarely clear cut, and you will likely face ethical dilemmas as a manager. Greater ethical intensity may increase your uncertainty about the correct action. Six factors that influence ethical intensity are magnitude of consequences, probability of impact, social consensus, time immediacy, proximity, and concentration of effect.
- Courage and ethics go hand in hand. You can unlock the courage within you by believing in a higher purpose, drawing strength from others, harnessing frustration and anger, and developing courage as a skill.

ACTION LEARNING

DELIBERATE PRACTICE EXERCISES

The Courage to Ask "Dumb" Questions

"Dumb" questions are those questions we don't ask because we think the answer must be obvious, or we'll look silly, or we're supposed to know, or we're trying to control and manipulate rather than increase our awareness and creativity. In fact, dumb questions ignore or are "dumb to" the surface aspects of the situation and are brilliant in going for the deeper conditions in which the creative possibilities are hidden, particularly in groups. They are the sort of naïve questions full of wonder ("wonder-full") that children aren't afraid to ask.

Do you remember the story of the Emperor's new clothes?

> *A vain emperor is convinced that a weaver has made him a stunning suit of gorgeous lightweight clothes—so light, in fact, that he feels as if he's wearing nothing at all. Not wanting to look stupid, he doesn't admit he can't see these clothes, and he parades proudly around town to show them off. Everyone "Oohs" and "Ahs" at the emperor's marvelous new clothes. No one dares look dumb by admitting they don't see them.*
>
> *A little child, however, pipes up, "How come the Emperor isn't wearing any clothes?" A very dumb question, because of course everyone "knows" he's wearing a suit of the most expensive fine fabric.*
>
> *This "dumb" question shatters the masquerade and brings the truth to light.*

Step 1: For the next three days, make a conscious effort to ask a minimum of three dumb questions each day. Try to ask enough dumb questions that it becomes easy for you. It might be a question to get clarification of a point made in a meeting or a lecture, or it might be about something commonplace but curious, like asking the grocery store cashier why he doesn't get to sit down while scanning grocery items.

Rules of the game:

- Only ask questions you are sincerely curious about.
- Observe the reaction of the person you ask and of others who hear the question.
- Listen to the actual content of the response.
- Note your feelings and other reactions.

Step 2: Complete the table below at the end of each day.

	Day 1	Day 2	Day 3
List the dumb questions you asked:			
How did you feel?			
How did people respond?			

Step 3: How did courage play a role in asking your dumb questions?

Step 4: Describe how your attitude toward "dumb" questions changed after you completed this assignment.

Step 5 (Optional): Share your insights with a partner, and ask your partner what insights he or she gained.

Practice Humility

This Deliberate Practice Exercise is available online at www.cengagebrain.com.

My Own Four-Way Test

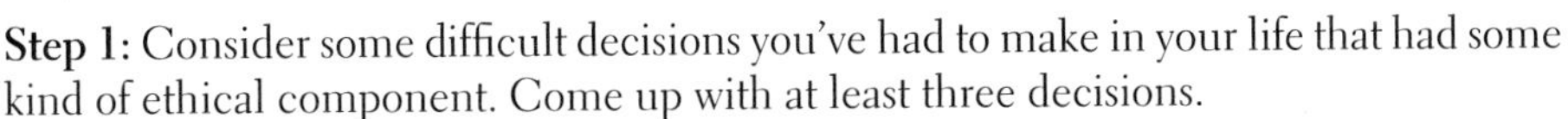

Step 1: Consider some difficult decisions you've had to make in your life that had some kind of ethical component. Come up with at least three decisions.

Step 2: Fill out the table below to examine each of these decisions according to the Rotary International Four-Way Test, as described in the chapter and illustrated in Exhibit 6.4.

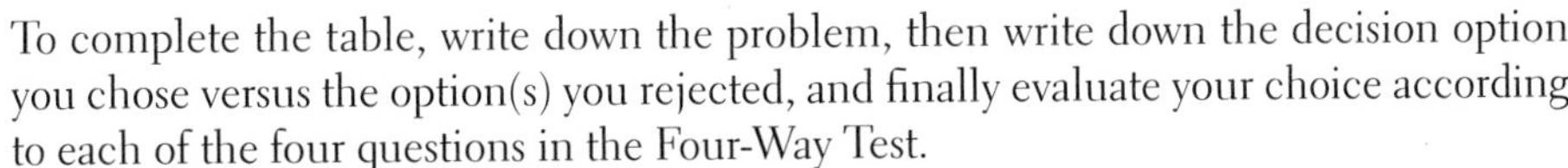

To complete the table, write down the problem, then write down the decision option you chose versus the option(s) you rejected, and finally evaluate your choice according to each of the four questions in the Four-Way Test.

Problem	Decision alternatives and choices	Was it the truth?	Was it fair to all concerned?	Did it build goodwill and better friendships?	Was it beneficial to all concerned?
Problem 1	The decision option you selected: Options you rejected:				
Problem 2	The decision option you selected: Options you rejected:				
Problem 3	The decision option you selected: Options you rejected:				

ACTION LEARNING

SHUTTERSTOCK #53973379

Step 3: Which of the three decisions do you now think you made correctly and which ones might you go back and redo if you could? Why?

Step 4 (Optional): Share your insights with a partner, and ask your partner what insights he or she gained.

IN-CLASS TEAM EXERCISE

Social Values

Step 1: Form into groups of four to six members. Before the group discussion, each individual ranks the social values below in terms of which are the most desirable for him or her and for what he or she would consider an orderly society. Complete the first column, "Your individual ranking," with 1 as most important and 14 as least important.

Social Value	Your individual ranking (1–14)	Group ranking (1–14)	Ideal Characteristics
Personal freedom			
A world at peace			
A comfortable life			
Stable economy			
Low taxes			
Good transportation system			
Good defense system			
Freedom from diseases			
Spiritual/religious fulfillment			
Efficient businesses/entrepreneurial opportunities			
Environmental well-being/climate control			
Equal opportunity for everyone			
Elimination of poverty			
Freedom from corruption and crime			

Step 2: In your group, develop a group ranking of the social values and list that ranking in the "Group ranking" column. Work toward consensus, try to state reasons for your individual ranking, and listen to others members' explanations.

Step 3: Now consider the rank ordering your group considers "ideal." What are the top three and bottom three values?

What are your top three values?	1. 2. 3.
What are your bottom three values?	1. 2. 3.

Step 4: Now consider what kind of society you have just developed. This is rather like your own "SimCity." What would this type of society look like? Fill out the last column in the table with the characteristics that your group would expect to be present in this "ideal" society.

Step 5: As a group, talk about whether you'd want to live in an environment like this and discuss the following questions:

1. What would the ethical climate be?
2. What development level on Kohlberg's model (Exhibit 6.2) do you think most people would operate from?
3. What other qualities, besides an emphasis on efficient business, are needed to keep a business community vibrant?

FIELD TEAM EXERCISE

Ethical Working Conditions

Step 1: Divide into groups of four or five and set up a time for a group meeting. Before the group meeting, each individual will prepare by doing some research on one of the following two categories. As a group, make sure both categories are covered. You can divide up the work if you want.

Category I: Manufacturing in Shenzhen, China

Find out:

What kinds of products are made there?

For which companies?

How many workers are employed?

What are the working conditions?

What problems have there been with worker accidents or deaths?

Look at information made public by the foreign (American or other) companies who use these factories—what do they say about working conditions; do they have any rationalizations?

What do they say about pollution?

Category II: Conditions of Off-shore Manufacturing of U.S. Clothing

Look at Adidas, Nike, and others and find out:

What are the working conditions?

What kind of wages are paid?

How are worker concerns addressed?

How much pollution is generated, and what is done with it?

What is the "public face" of U.S. companies regarding these conditions?

Step 2: Come to your group meeting with your individual research completed. As a group, discuss the following questions:

1. What are the justifications for continuing the poor working conditions in China and other countries? Does it make a difference that without these "sweatshops," potential employees might be forced to dig through garbage, steal, and so on?
2. What is it about western countries that demands cheap labor?
3. What about the pollution? Is it fair that another country lives with the pollution for products that U.S. customers consume?

Step 3: Refer to Exhibit 6.3, Six Factors Determining Ethical Intensity, to discuss the situation your group researched. As a group, discuss and evaluate western perceptions of that situation according to the six factors. Complete the table below.

Ethical Intensity Factor	Rate the situation from 1 (low) to 5 (high)
1. Magnitude of consequences	
2. Probability of impact	
3. Social consensus	
4. Time immediacy	
5. Proximity	
6. Concentration of effect	

Step 4: Discuss the following question as a group. If you were the CEO of a company that was involved in the situation you researched and your salary increases and bonuses—and perhaps even your job (and the jobs of tens of thousands of others)—depended on keeping the working conditions as they were, what would you do?

TEST YOUR METTLE

ROLE PLAY SIMULATIONS

Is It a Secret or Is It Espionage?

Background: Re-read the written Video Incident at the beginning of the chapter.

Instructions: Form into groups of two or three. One person will play the role of Jane and one the role of Jason. If there are three people in the group, the third person is an observer. Each person reads only his or her confidential role, but the observer reads both. Spend 10–15 minutes on the role play.

Confidential information for Jason: Your company, Caffeine and Crullers, has been pretty successful and you have a great job, which you love. But a new competitor in Madison, Wisconsin, has threatened your company's profitability and maybe even its existence. Everyone at work has been trying to figure out what to do to catch up with Scone Prone. Serendipitously, you met Scone's COO at a party two weeks ago. As you are both single and she seemed attracted, you decided to go with the flow and before you knew it, you two were an item. So, maybe you always saw her as a way "in" to Scone Prone. And maybe you made her a few promises, but that's no different from what lots of guys do. And could you help it if she left out, in plain sight, the company's strategic plan and documents with their operational plans as well? She *knows* you work for Caffeine and Crullers, so she must not have felt it was all that private. And could you help it that her all-in-one printer was right there just begging for copies to be made while she ran out to the grocery store? You're just about to go in to your boss's office to surprise her with the news. She'll be so grateful that you, Jason Wong, are saving the company.

Confidential information for Jane: Your company was doing well financially until a new competitor, Scone Prone, swept into town. Sales have declined. You've called in your staff for meetings and have tried to take on Scone, but they always seem to be one step ahead. You've got to think of something extraordinary, or the company will be in dire circumstances. Just this morning you were alerted by one of your staff that sales manager Jason Wong is on his way in with some news he gathered from Scone Prone via corporate espionage. You think the word "espionage" might have been an exaggeration, but you'll wait to see what Jason says. You've always tried really hard to do the right thing, to take the ethical high road, and you want to keep doing so. You also feel the pressure to stop the decline before you have to start issuing layoffs.

After the role play, discuss these questions:

1. Is any piece of information you find about competitors "fair game," as they say?
2. Does ethics matter in information gathering?
3. How can you tell the difference between getting some useful information on your competitors and stepping over the line to corporate espionage?

Your instructor may lead a class discussion of ethics in small business.

What's the Big Deal?

This Role Play Simulation is available online at www.cengagebrain.com.

VIDEO APPLICATION

Social Responsibility at Theo Chocolate

Owner Joe Whinney sets a high standard for serving the environment, suppliers, and customers with organic and fair trade practices. Theo Chocolate uses an enlightened approach and still makes a profit.

Discussion Questions

1. At which of the three levels is Joe Whinney on the personal moral development scale? Explain.
2. What does vice president Debra Music mean when she says that Theo Chocolate is a "triple bottom line" company? How is that different from any other company?
3. Theo Chocolate wants every person it deals with to succeed. Is that ethical standard realistic in today's business environment? Might Theo become a force for changing other companies in the industry? Why?

CASE INCIDENTS

The Way It's Done

The sudden heart attack of his predecessor, Bill Andrews, propelled Russell Hart into a temporary top management assignment for Kresk International in the company's new Middle East Division in Riyadh, Saudi Arabia. Kresk management had targeted Saudi Arabia as a must-have division and was enthusiastic about the expansion.

After six months of a one-year assignment in Riyadh with travel throughout the Middle East, Russell was making a brief trip to Dallas to report at the semi-annual board meeting before returning to Saudi. He understood that in addition to his assessment of the company's situation in the region, a portion of the board meeting would focus on the improved health condition of Andrews and, based on that, a determination would be made as to whether he or Bill Andrews would have the permanent assignment at the end of the year. The two were close friends and had corresponded regularly over the past months, and Russell looked forward to Bill's full recovery and return to work. However, single and adventurous by nature, Russell enjoyed the top assignment in Saudi Arabia and hoped to impress management at the meeting so that he would be named director of the Middle East Division.

"Here's where my personal ambitions and my personal ethics collide," Russell admitted to his assistant, Christopher Dunn, as the Kresk corporate jet left Riyadh. "I mean, look at all of this. It's a dream job. It's *my* dream job, and I can do this. If anyone had told me back in high school in Nebraska that I would be on a corporate jet flying from Saudi Arabia, I'd have laughed them out of Sydney."

"Excuse me, Russell, would you and Christopher care for anything to drink?" the cabin attendant asked.

"Yes, a *Jameson,*" Russell said.

"Same here," Christopher added.

As the attendant walked away, Russell leaned over, speaking quietly. "Corporate is *so* enthusiastic about this region. They are expecting nothing short of a glowing report that basically says, 'Wow, we really hit the jackpot with this move.' And that's what we've put together here over the past few weeks. It looks fantastic! But my little man in here," he said, pointing to his stomach, "keeps nagging me—do I give them, 'Wow, we hit the jackpot' and become the darling of the company, or do I give them the truth—that we have some potentially serious problems with this division …"

"… and hand the job to Bill," Christopher finished for him as the drinks arrived.

"Exactly. By the end of the year, their numbers may look great and they may meet our performance standards, but I have serious problems with the management here. I realize that we're working with a different culture and I can make allowances. I have no problem pacing my day around their prayer obligations. I know to avoid any business during Ramadan or around the two Eids.* I've become comfortable meeting a Sheikh or *Sayyid*† and I've even lost my sense of self-consciousness when a businessman holds my hand to lead me into a room. I can deal with all these things. But there is a level of hostility here within the organization that bothers me and that I think would bother most managers at headquarters, and *that's* what I struggle with in this report. Should I be honest?"

"Well, you know—honesty is the best …," Christopher began.

"Don't say it. This is my career we're talking about."

"Okay, what do you want to add—or *not* add?"

"The major problem here is Youssef Said," Russell said.

"I know. But I think I would stay away from mentioning that. The company loves the guy. Bill Andrews has been his champion because of excellent results, at least in the short run."

"I don't agree. And I think they won't when they see him in action. I don't understand why Bill supports him."

"They've *seen* him in action," Christopher said.

"Oh, they've seen what he *wants* them to see. You and I have seen his interaction with staff and employees on a daily basis. His mistreatment of people is appalling. I see a total disregard for the opinions of others, and he seems to take considerable pleasure in humiliating people. He screams at them! A few have quit. I've questioned him about it a couple of times and all he says is, 'I know. Please understand …'"

"… 'It is the way it is done here,'" Christopher said, completing the phrase the two heard on a regular basis.

"I *don't* believe it is the way it's done here. It's not our cultural values that are the problem, at least not in the United States and Europe. I think this has always been *his* way. I wonder about the effects on morale, and I worry that the people who work here will believe we're in agreement with him and that this is our policy. How does that reflect on our company here in the region?" Russell asked. "Youssef has that little inner circle of family and friends that he trusts and really nothing beyond that. To me, it seems he's always working a deal, bending a rule. I know that Arabs love to trade and love to negotiate, but there are too many favors, too many unspoken agreements and payments, and I wonder if we should intervene. I wonder if international laws or the company's own ethics are being set aside. I have serious doubts that this guy is going to work with the Kresk culture and our company ethics. But do I need to include my concerns in this initial report?"

*the major festivals of *Eid al-Fitr* and *Eid al-Adha*

†descendant of the Prophet Muhammad

"Or will you just be busting the board's bubble, and raise doubts about Bill?" Christopher joined in. "Or perhaps they will doubt you, and you risk your shot at the job you want."

"On the other hand," Russell said, "if I'm seeing what I consider severe long-term problems and say nothing now in this report, and the problems show up later, will *I* be guilty of breaking a code of ethics?" He paused. "So, Christopher, what do I say tomorrow at the board meeting?"

Discussion Questions

1. What do you think Russell Hart should include in his report about Youssef Said? Why? What would you do in his position?
2. What amount or kind of courage will be required for Russell to disclose everything honestly? How would you advise him to acquire that courage?
3. At which stage of Kohlberg's moral development scale would you place Youssef Said, Russell Hart, and Christopher Dunn? Why?

Worth It?

John Worth had considered himself blessed after he landed a sales job with Olivia Medical Group. Now he wondered if the job was a blessing or a curse.

Unemployed for over a year following the downsizing of his previous employer, Worth, married and father of five, credited family and faith for his ability to make it through those tough times before getting the sales job. With Olivia's solid reputation and rapid growth, he felt that the new job would enable him to bring financial security and long-term stability to his family. But over the past four months with the company, he found himself facing a different kind of struggle. His dilemma involved the company's premier product, Protair, and the culture surrounding its promotion.

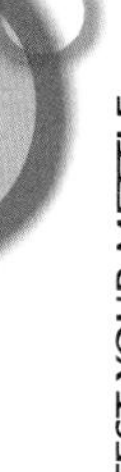

A protein used to promote lung health following treatment for cancer, the product initially received rave reviews in medical journals and quick FDA approval. Clinical trials showed an acceptable rate of side effects. With increased or longer-term use, that rate increased slightly. However, expanded "off-label" use related to other medical problems associated with breathing spurred a dramatic increase in side effects by 20 to 40 percent. These side effects included the sudden swelling and closing of air passages, and in several instances, the shutdown of the lungs and death. So far, that number remained small and was barely a blip on the media and public radars.

Salespeople at Olivia continued to aggressively push Protair, and Worth found doctors receptive and eager to use the product. Despite growing personal misgivings about product safety, Worth worked hard to increase his sales. However, product safety was only one of his growing concerns. He was expected to reconnoiter and recruit influential, high-profile physicians to whom royalty payments and consulting fees could be made for a variety of services including trials, journal articles, and physician training in support of Protair.

"So, we're basically *bribing* doctors to support this product and not raise questions," he complained to Connie Shackleford, another member of the sales team.

"Well, yes and no," she said. "It's an expansion of tradition within the field. We have to have the trials, the articles, the endorsements in order to increase our market. We can't expect busy physicians to do this for nothing."

"But it seems to me it is way beyond *expansion* when we're paying these doctors to agree to something that can be harmful."

"Any medicine is harmful to a certain percentage of patients under certain circumstances," Connie said.

"It's shutting down lungs!"

"In off-label use, in a small percentage of the patients..."

"Shouldn't the trials and articles we're paying for say that?" asked Worth.

"Our job is to sell the product," Shackleford argued. "There are risks with the product, but that is not our area of expertise."

"So can I reconnoiter and recruit high profile physicians who will honestly assess the product?" John asked.

Connie raised her eyebrows and peered over her reading glasses at him. "I wouldn't."

Several weeks passed following the conversation. One day, John was stopped in the hall by sales manager, Fred Thomas. When Thomas walked away, John headed straight for Connie Shackleford's office.

"Hey, John, what's up?" Connie asked, and glanced up at his face. "Oh, God, what happened?"

"Tomorrow night, I've been assigned to take a really important physician to dinner to complete an agreement for consulting on Protair," John said.

"Great!"

"... And then to a strip club."

"What did you tell Fred? You're going, right?"

"I didn't say anything. I just nodded and came here."

"Have a seat, John, and let me explain something to you," Connie said. "When an important person is going to put his name out there to promote your product, he expects something in return. It may be a trip or an exciting night on the town . . . whatever. On several occasions, I have turned down opportunities and guess what—I'm no longer asked to work with the top clients. Those go to someone else. It's not a level playing field. So you have to make a choice here. I made my choice and now I'm stuck, and with the job market the way it is, I can't even move somewhere else. Before you turn this down, think about it."

"I don't know what to do," Worth moaned. "I can't do this. It goes against everything I believe as a Mormon."

"Did you explain to Fred that this goes against your religion?"

"No. I couldn't think of anything to say. I just stood there. He was going on about what a great job I had been doing and how this was just the beginning and I had a great future and blah, blah, blah."

"So what do you do?" Connie asked. "Since the beginning, you've had a lot of questions about what you're asked to do. And now this."

"I don't know. How much of this is legal? How much of this is ethical? And even if it is, do I drop my own sense of ethics? I went for a solid year with no job. I can't lose this job. I have a wife and five kids."

Discussion Questions

1. Try to imagine yourself in John Worth's position. What do you think you would do about attending the strip club?
2. Identify each ethical dilemma you find in the above case. How do you think each one should be resolved?
3. How hard should the company work to prevent off-label applications of a drug if it is an important source of income and profit? What actions might the company take to prevent its off-label use?
4. Is it ethically sound for someone to claim "That is not our area of expertise" for potential drug side effects? Why?

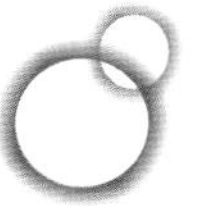

PERSONAL SKILLS LOG

PERSONAL SKILLS LOG

Directions: Fill in the rows below based on what you learned from each part of the chapter that you completed.

	What is my key takeaway or insight from this activity?	What do I personally do well (strength) regarding this activity?	What could I improve (weakness) about myself regarding this activity?	How might I use what I've learned from this activity in the future?
Manager Challenge Incident:				
Discover Yourself Questionnaires:				
Deliberate Practice Exercises:				
In-Class and/or Field Team Exercises:				
Role-Play Exercises:				
Case Incidents:				

REFERENCES

Discover Yourself

1 Based on R. Christie and F. L. Gels, *Studies in Machiavellianism* (New York: Academic Press, 1970); and Jason J. Dahling, Brian G. Whitaker, and Paul E. Levy, "The Development and Validation of a New Machiavellianism Scale," *Journal of Management* 35 no. 2 (April 2009): 219–257.

2 Adapted from Doug Lennick and Fred Kiel, *Moral Intelligence: Enhancing Business Performance and Leadership Success* (Upper Saddle River, NJ: Cordon School Publications, 2005), pp. 251–263.

3 Based on Janet A. Taylor, "A Personality Scale of Manifest Anxiety," *The Journal of Abnormal and Social Psychology* 48, no. 2 (1953): 285–290; and Donnah Canavan-Gumpert, Katherine Garner, and Peter Gumpert, *The Success-Fearing Personality: Theory and Research with Implications for the Social Psychology of Achievement* (Lexington, MA: Lexington Books, 1978).

Discover Knowledge

4 Andrew Pollack and Duff Wilson, "A Pfizer Whistle-Blower Is Awarded $1.4 Million," *The New York Times*, April 2, 2010, http://www.nytimes.com/2010/04/03/business/03pfizer.html (accessed March 23, 2011).

5 *Ibid.*

6 Gordon F. Shea, *Practical Ethics* (New York: American Management Association, 1988); and Linda K. Treviño, "Ethical Decision Making in Organizations: A Person-Situation Interactionist Model," *Academy of Management Review* 11 (1986): 601–617.

7 Michiko Kakutani, "The Tsunami That Buried a Wall Street Giant," *The New York Times* (March 10, 2009).

8 James Bandler with Doris Burke, "What Cuomo Wants from Wall Street," *Fortune* (December 8, 2008): 103–110; and Valerie Bauerlein and Ruth Simon, "WaMu Board Shields Executives' Bonuses," *The Wall Street Journal* (March 5, 2008).

9 Bill George, "The Master Gives It Back" and "Truly Authentic Leadership" segments in "Special Report: America's Best Leaders," *U.S. News & World Report* (October 30, 2006): 50–87; and David Segal, "In Letter, Buffett Accepts Blame and Faults Others," *The New York Times* (March 1, 2009).

10 Carly Fiorina, "Corporate Leadership and the Crisis," *The Wall Street Journal* (December 12, 2008).

11 Al Gini, "Moral Leadership and Business Ethics," *The Journal of Leadership Studies* 4, no. 4 (Fall 1997): 64–81.

12 Michael E. Brown and Linda K. Treviño, "Ethical Leadership: A Review and Future Directions," *The Leadership Quarterly* 17 (2006): 595–616; Darin W. White and Emily Lean, "The Impact of Perceived Leader Integrity on Subordinates in a Work Team Environment," *Journal of Business Ethics* 81 (2008): 767–778; Gary R. Weaver, Linda K. Treviño, and Bradley Agle, "'Somebody I Look Up To': Ethical Role Models in Organizations," *Organizational Dynamics* 34, no. 4 (2005): 313–330; and Joseph L. Badaracco, Jr., and Allen P. Webb, "Business Ethics: A View from the Trenches," *California Management Review* 37, no. 2 (Winter 1995): 8–28.

13 Jere Longman, "Alabama Fires Coach for Off-Field Indiscretions," *The New York Times* (May 4, 2003).

14 Bill George, "The Master Gives It Back" and "Truly Authentic Leadership."

15 Viktor E. Frankl, *Man's Search for Meaning* (New York: Pocket Books, 1959), p. 104.

16 Donald G. Zauderer, "Integrity: An Essential Executive Quality," *Business Forum* (Fall 1992): 12–16.

17 James M. Kouzes and Barry Z. Posner, *Credibility: How Leaders Gain and Lose It, Why People Demand It* (San Francisco: Jossey-Bass, 1993), p. 255.

18 Lawrence Kohlberg, "Moral Stages and Moralization: The Cognitive Development Approach," in Thomas Likona, ed., *Moral Development and Behavior: Theory, Research, and Social Issues* (Austin, TX: Holt, Rinehart and Winston, 1976), pp. 31–53; Linda K. Treviño, Gary R. Weaver, and Scott J. Reynolds, "Behavioral Ethics in Organizations: A Review," *Journal of Management* 32, no. 6 (December 2006): 951–990; Jill W. Graham, "Leadership Moral Development, and Citizenship Behavior," *Business Ethics Quarterly* 5, no. 1 (January 1995): 43–54; James Weber, "Exploring the Relationship Between Personal Values and Moral Reasoning," *Human Relations* 46, no. 4

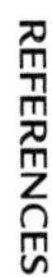

(April 1993): 435–463; and Duane M. Covrig, "The Organizational Context of Moral Dilemmas: The Role of Moral Leadership in Administration in Making and Breaking Dilemmas," *The Journal of Leadership Studies* 7, no. 1 (2000): 40–59.

19 Tom Morris, *If Aristotle Ran General Motors* (New York: Henry Hold, 1997).

20 "Obama Seeks 'Buffett Rule'—A New Tax," *Chicago Sun Times*, September 18, 2011.

21 Nicholas D. Kristof, "In Israel, the Nobel vs. the Ugly," *The New York Times*, July 7, 2010, http://www.nytimes.com/2010/07/08/opinion/08kristof.html (accessed March 24, 2011).

22 J. R. Rest, D. Narvaez, M. J. Bebeau, and S. J. Thoma, *Postconventional Moral Thinking: A Neo-Kohlbergian Approach* (Mahwah, NJ: Lawrence Erlbaum, 1999).

23 James Weber, "Exploring the Relationship Between Personal Values and Moral Reasoning," *Human Relations* 46, no. 4 (April 1993): 435–463.

24 Carol Gilligan, "In a Different Voice: Women's Conceptions of Self and Morality," *Harvard Educational Review* 47, no. 4 (1982): 481–517, and Christina Hoff Sommers, *The War Against Boys* (New York: Simon and Schuster, 2000).

25 David A. Whetten and Kim S. Cameron, *Developing Management Skills*, 8th ed. (Upper Saddle River, NJ: Prentice Hall, 2010), p. 71.

26 These are discussed in W. C. Crain, *Theories of Development* (Upper Saddle River, NJ: Prentice Hall, 1985), pp. 118–136.

27 Justin Scheck, "Accusations of Snooping in Ink-Cartridge Dispute," *The Wall Street Journal Online*, August 11, 2009, http://online.wsj.com/article/SB124995836273921661.html?KEYWORDS=%22Accusations+of+Snooping+in+Ink-Cartridge+Dispute%22 (accessed August 14, 2009).

28 Suzanne C. DeJanasz, Karen O. Dowd, and Beth Z. Schneider, *Interpersonal Skills in Organizations*, 2nd ed. (New York: McGraw-Hill Irwin, 2006), p. 53.

29 Linda K. Treviño and Katherine A. Nelson, *Managing Business Ethics: Straight Talk About How to Do It Right* (New York: John Wiley & Sons, Inc. 1995), p. 4.

30 DeJanasz et al., *Interpersonal Skills in Organizations*, pp. 53–54.

31 Thomas M. Jones, "Ethical Decision Making by Individuals in Organizations: An Issue-Contingent Model," *Academy of Management Review* 16 (1991): 366–395.

32 Based on a question from the General Electric employee ethics guide, reported in Kathyrn Kranhold, "U.S. Firms Raise Ethics Focus," *The Wall Street Journal* (November 28, 2005).

33 Based on information in Constance E. Bagley, "The Ethical Leader's Decision Tree," *Harvard Business Review* (February 2003): 18–19.

34 Based on information in Vadim Liberman, "Scoring on the Job," *Across the Board* (November–December 2003): 46–50.

35 Thomas M. Jones, "Ethical Decision Making by Individuals in Organizations: An Issue-Contingent Model"; and Joan M. McMahon and Robert J. Harvey, "The Effect of Moral Intensity on Ethical Judgment," *Journal of Business Ethics* 72, no. 4 (June 2007): 335–357

36 Reported in Don Hellriegel and John W. Slocum Jr., *Organizational Behavior*, 13th ed., (Mason, OH: South-Western Cengage Learning, 2011), p. 37.

37 Gary R. Weaver, Linda K. Treviño, and Bradley Agle, "'Somebody I Look Up To'."

38 Donald C. Mosley, Leon C. Megginson, and Paul H. Pietri, *Supervisory Management: The Art of Empowering and Developing People*, 5th ed. (Mason, OH: South-Western Cengage Learning, 2000), p. 113.

39 Micheline Maynard, "U.S. Is Seeking a Fine of $16.4 Million Against Toyota" *The New York Times*, April 5, 2010, www.nytimes.com/2010/04/06/business/06toyota.html (accessed April 6, 2010).

40 David A. Whetten and Kim S. Cameron, *Developing Management Skills*, 8th ed. (Upper Saddle River, NJ: Prentice Hall, 2010), p. 73–74.

41 Robert N. Lussier, *Human Relations in Organizations: Applications and Skill Building*, 7th ed. (New York: McGraw-Hill/Irwin, 2006), p.96.

42 John McCain, "In Search of Courage," *Fast Company* (September 2004): 53–56.

43 As reported in Lance Secretan, "Moral Courage: It's the Hallmark of Leadership," *Leadership Excellence* (January 2009): 18.

44 Jeffrey Zaslow, "Kids on the Bus: The Overlooked Role of Teenagers in the Civil-Rights Era," *The Wall Street Journal* (November 11, 2005).

45 Walter Kirn, "The Age of Neo-Remorse," *The New York Times Magazine* (January 25, 2009): 9–10; Christian Plumb and Dan Wilchins, "Lehman CEO Fuld's Hubris Contributed to Meltdown," *Reuters.com*, http://www.reuters.com/article/2008/09/14/us-lehman-backstory-idUSN1341059120080914 (accessed March 28, 2011); and "Former Lehman Brothers CEO Subpoenaed," *CNNMoney.com*, http://money.cnn.com/2008/10/17/news/companies/lehman_subpoena/ (accessed March 28, 2011).

46 "Trust Your Instincts," *Fortune*, (July 6, 2006): 45.

47 Jerry B. Harvey, "The Abilene Paradox: The Management of Agreement," *Organizational Dynamics* (Summer 1988): 17–43.

48 Janet P. Near and Marcia P. Miceli, "Effective Whistle-Blowing," *Academy of Management Review* 20, no. 3 (1995): 679–708.

49 Steven L. Schooner, "Badge of Courage," *Government Executive* (August 2002): 65.

50 Linda Tischler, "The Trials of ImClone," *Fast Company* (September 2004): 88–89.

51 Joseph Rebello, "Radical Ways of Its CEO Are a Boon to Bank," *The Wall Street Journal* (March 20, 1995); and Michael S. Hopkins, "Bad Banking. Good Ethics. Discuss," *MIT Sloan Management Review* 51, no 2 (Winter 2010): 96.

52 James M. Kouzes and Barry Z. Posner, *The Leadership Challenge: How to Get Extraordinary Things Done in Organizations* (San Francisco: Jossey-Bass, 1988).

53 Michael Warshaw, ed., "Great Comebacks," *Success* (July/August 1995): 33–46.

54 Ira Cheleff, *The Courageous Follower: Standing Up to and for Our Leaders* (San Francisco: Berrett-Koehler, 1995).

55 Kathleen K. Reardon, "Courage As a Skill," *Harvard Business Review* (January 2007): 58–64.

PART 2

Managing Relationships

© CLOVER/A.COLLECTIONRF/AMANA IMAGES INC./ALAMY

Chapter Outline

CHAPTER 7

Motivating for Performance

RYAN LASH

MANAGER CHALLENGE

VIDEO INCIDENT: EQUALITY OR NOT?

Two of the top four managers at Caffeine and Crullers are relatively new. General manager Jane Sutton found that she had to give these new managers higher salaries than the other two top managers, despite the fact that they had no experience with C&C, in order to match what they were making at their previous jobs. Jane felt uneasy about it at the time, but she discovered that this pattern seemed to be the norm across industries. Now the two longer-term employees, CFO Carlos Hernandez and HR director Heather Carreau, have each talked to her separately because they are aware of the higher salaries given to the new managers. Carlos and Heather are not happy. They haven't said so directly, but Jane thinks they might be looking for jobs and leave to work for competitors. This would be a serious problem, because the other two executives, sales manager Jason Wong and director of operations Carrie Fishman, have only been in place a short time. In addition, hiring new, inexperienced people would mean having to pay them higher salaries anyway. Even so, Jane's boss, Edmund Daniels at corporate, has vetoed any salary increases for the next year. Jane is meeting with both Carlos and Heather to talk about how to keep them on board and keep them motivated for the next year without a pay raise. She is going to start with Heather.

Initial Thoughts

1. If you were Jane, what would you try to accomplish, and how would you start your conversation with Heather?

2. Why do you think the salary difference caused the CFO and HR director to become less motivated?

Your instructor may ask you to be part of a role play based on the "Equality or Not?" incident.

DISCOVER YOURSELF

For those students using CourseMate or CengageNOW, you can access the Daft/Marcic Assessment Library to take the questionnaires online and view dynamically updated comparative data.

Questionnaire 1

Instructions: Think of a specific activity you recently performed at work or school. How important were each of the following as a reason for doing that activity? Rate how accurately each statement describes you based on whether the statement is clearly true or accurate, clearly false or inaccurate, or in the middle as somewhat true and somewhat false.

Part A

	True	Somewhat	False
1. I got rewarded for doing it.	○	○	○
2. I was supposed to do the activity.	○	○	○
3. It was something I felt that I had to do.	○	○	○
4. I avoided the negative consequences that would result if I didn't do it.	○	○	○

Total Score Part A ________. (Sum your answers to items 1–4, with 3 points for each True, 2 points for each Somewhat, and 1 point for each False.)

Part B

	True	Somewhat	False
5. I thought the activity was interesting.	○	○	○
6. I enjoyed doing this activity.	○	○	○
7. I acquired new knowledge or skill.	○	○	○
8. I became fully immersed in the activity.	○	○	○

Total Score Part B ________. (Sum your answers to items 5–8, with 3 points for each True, 2 points for each Somewhat, and 1 point for each False.) Go to page 270 to interpret your scores.

Questionnaire 2[1]

Instructions: Think of a specific job (current or previous) you have held. If you are a full-time student, think of your classes and study activities as your job. Please respond to the statements below about those work activities. Indicate whether each item is True, Somewhat, or False.

Part A

	True	Somewhat	False
1. I feel physically safe at work.	○	○	○
2. I have good health benefits.	○	○	○

Total Score Part A ________. (Sum your answers to items 1–2, with 3 points for each True, 2 points for each Somewhat, and 1 point for each False.)

Part B	True	Somewhat	False
3. I am satisfied with what I'm getting paid for my work.	○	○	○
4. I feel that my job is secure as long as I want it.	○	○	○

Total Score Part B ________. (Sum your answers to items 3–4, with 3 points for each True, 2 points for each Somewhat, and 1 point for each False.)

Part C	True	Somewhat	False
5. I have good friends at work.	○	○	○
6. I have enough time away from my work to enjoy other things in life.	○	○	○

Total Score Part C ________. (Sum your answers to items 5–6, with 3 points for each True, 2 points for each Somewhat, and 1 point for each False.)

Part D	True	Somewhat	False
7. I feel appreciated at work.	○	○	○
8. People at my workplace respect me as a professional and expert in my field.	○	○	○

Total Score Part D ________. (Sum your answers to items 7–8, with 3 points for each True, 2 points for each Somewhat, and 1 point for each False.)

Part E	True	Somewhat	False
9. I feel that my job allows me to realize my full potential.	○	○	○
10. I feel that I am realizing my potential as an expert in my line of work.	○	○	○
11. I feel I'm always learning new things that help me to do my work better.	○	○	○
12. There is a lot of creativity involved in my work.	○	○	○

Total Score Part E ________. (Sum your answers to items 9–12, with 3 points for each True, 2 points for each Somewhat, and 1 point for each False.) Go to page 273 to interpret your scores.

Questionnaire 3[2]

Instructions: Think about situations in which you were in a student group or organization. To respond to the statements below, think about your informal approach to motivating others as a leader or fellow member. Indicate whether each item is True, Somewhat, or False.

Part A	True	Somewhat	False
1. I ask the other person what rewards he or she values for high performance.	○	○	○
2. I find out if the person has the ability to do what needs to be done.	○	○	○

	True	Somewhat	False
3. I explain exactly what needs to be done for the person I'm trying to motivate.	○	○	○
4. Before giving somebody a reward, I find out what would appeal to that person.	○	○	○

Total Score Part A ______. (Sum your answers to items 1–4, with 3 points for each True, 2 points for each Somewhat, and 1 point for each False.)

Part B

	True	Somewhat	False
5. I promptly commend others when they do a better-than-average job.	○	○	○
6. I only reward people if their performance is up to standard.	○	○	○
7. I use a variety of rewards (treats, recognition) to reinforce exceptional performance.	○	○	○
8. I generously and publicly praise people who perform well.	○	○	○

Total Score Part B ______. (Sum your answers to items 5–8, with 3 points for each True, 2 points for each Somewhat, and 1 point for each False.) Go to page 277 to interpret your scores.

Questionnaire 4[3]

Instructions: Think about organizations you have worked for, and for each statement below, allocate 10 points between the two choices based on how much each choice describes you. Give the *most* points to the choice that is *most* like you and the *fewest* points to the choice that is least like you (for example, 10 to A and 0 to B, 4 to A and 6 to B, 2 to A and 8 to B, etc.).

1. I work hard for the organization but receive less from the organization than I give.
   _____ a. Okay with me to give more to the organization.
   _____ b. Not okay with me to give more to the organization.

2. My responsibilities and contributions are equal to my peers, but I receive less recognition/appreciation.
   _____ a. Okay with me to receive less recognition.
   _____ b. Not okay with me to receive less recognition.

3. My responsibilities and contributions are equal to peers, but my income is less.
   _____ a. Okay with me to receive less income.
   _____ b. Not okay with me to receive less income.

4. I am satisfied with my income, but I receive less satisfying work than others.
   _____ a. Okay with me to have less satisfying work.
   _____ b. Not okay with me to have less satisfying work.

5. As a general rule of working for an organization:
   _____ a. I would rather give than receive.
   _____ b. I have to watch out to get what I deserve.

Total Score Questionnaire 4: _______. (Sum your responses for 1a, 2a, 3a, 4a, and 5a.) Go to page 279 to interpret your score.

Questionnaire 5[4]

Instructions: Think of a specific job—either a current or previous job—that was important to you, and then respond to the items below with respect to the managers above you in that job. Indicate whether each item was True, Somewhat, or False.

In general, my manager and organization:

	True	Somewhat	False
1. Gave me the support I needed to do my job well.	○	○	○
2. Gave me the performance information I needed to do my job well.	○	○	○
3. Explained top management's strategy and vision for the organization.	○	○	○
4. Gave me many responsibilities.	○	○	○
5. Trusted me.	○	○	○
6. Allowed me to set my own goals.	○	○	○
7. Encouraged me to take control of my own work.	○	○	○
8. Used my ideas and suggestions when making decisions.	○	○	○
9. Made me responsible for what I did.	○	○	○
10. Encouraged me to figure out the causes and solutions to problems.	○	○	○

Total Score Questionnaire 5: _______. (Sum your answers to items 1–10, with 3 points for each True, 2 points for each Somewhat, and 1 point for each False.) Go to page 281 to interpret your score.

GO ONLINE to find additional questionnaires at www.cengagebrain.com, search for Daft/Marcic Building Management Skills 1e, click on Free Online Resources, click on Additional Self-Assessments.

- Employee Engagement
- Need for Achievement, Affiliation, and Power

SHUTTERSTOCK #53973379

Chapter 7: Motivating for Performance

DISCOVER KNOWLEDGE

Roy Pelaez is in charge of an Aramark service operation in the northeastern United States where most employees are non-English speaking immigrants working for little more than minimum wage. They spend their days cleaning airplanes for Delta and Southwest in all kinds of weather. It's not the place you might expect to find satisfied, committed, and motivated employees, yet Pelaez has created an environment in which, as one observer put it, "people will do anything in the world for him."

Across the country, the De La Salle Spartans, a team of high-school football players who were once derided as "undersized and untalented," are looking forward to their next big win. The Spartans never had a winning season until Bob LaDouceur took over as head coach. Under his leadership, the once-demoralized team amassed an amazing 151 consecutive wins that spanned 13 years and inspired a full-length documentary titled *"1": The Story Behind the Longest Winning Streak in Football History.*[5]

Roy Pelaez and Bob LaDouceur don't have a magic potion; they've just learned how to motivate and inspire people to high performance. An early twentieth-century management thinker defined management as "the art of getting things done through people."[6] Whether a manager is supervising a group of service workers, coaching a football team, managing a manufacturing department, or leading a political campaign, a key requirement is the ability to motivate others to accomplish goals.

Knowing how to motivate people is a challenge for managers. Motivation arises from within individuals and typically differs for each person. In reality, there are many different ways to develop the kind of commitment and motivation that Roy Pelaez and Bob LaDouceur built at Aramark and in the De La Salle Spartans. However, there are basic concepts and ideas that you can understand and apply to create highly motivated and productive employees. The following sections examine these basic ideas and look at how to apply them in organizations.

ESTABLISH GOALS FOR HIGH PERFORMANCE

When Advanced Circuits of Aurora, Colorado, was having trouble with frequent stops and restarts on its production line, costing the company about $50,000 a month, former CEO Ron Huston came up with a plan. He bought a junk car, placed it in the parking lot, and told employees they could take a sledgehammer to the car every day the production line didn't have a restart. Employees set a goal of flattening the car in 90 days. Everybody had fun, and they met the 90-day goal by solving production line problems, which was the whole point of the exercise for Huston. Huston realized how motivating it could be for people to have a clear goal, especially if achieving it was fun. Huston began setting goals for other aspects of the business and rewarding people when the goals were met. He dramatically improved performance by setting extremely high goals, then defining exactly what it would take to reach them. He also steered performance toward goals by giving everyone ongoing numerical feedback about every aspect of the business.

LEADING WORDS

"Give me a stock clerk with a goal and I'll give you a man who will make history. Give me a man with no goals and I'll give you a stock clerk."

—James Cash Penney

American entrepreneur; founded the J.C. Penney Company in 1902

"Pleasure in the job puts perfection in the work."

—Aristotle (384 BC–322 BC)

Greek philosopher

"Motivation is the art of getting people to do what you want them to do because they want to do it."

—Dwight D. Eisenhower

34th President of the United States

"Forty-six percent of those who quit their jobs last year did so because they felt unappreciated."

—U.S. Department of Labor report

© CENGAGE LEARNING 2014

People began checking the data throughout the day to track their progress toward goals. "The more goals we get, the better it is for us," said employee Barb Frevert.[7]

Numerous studies have shown that people are more motivated when they have specific objectives and targets to work toward.[8] You might have noticed in your own life that you feel more motivated when you have a definite target in mind, such as losing ten pounds before spring break or earning enough money during the summer to buy a used car. Thus, the first step in building an effective motivation program is to establish clear, specific, and appropriate goals.

Applying Goal Setting Theory

Goal setting for motivation means setting specific, challenging goals that are accepted as valid by employees, and then helping people track their progress toward goals by providing timely feedback. A large amount of research literature boils down to four key points[9] to remember for setting goals:

- **Clarity.** Clarity means providing goals that are specific and measurable. Asking people to "do their best" is not as motivating as giving them a concrete, unambiguous target, such as "Sell $1,000 worth of parts this week" or "Recruit three new campaign volunteers by the end of the month."
- **Challenge.** This means asking people to stretch their abilities. Most people aren't motivated by easy goals that provide little challenge and ask for little increased effort. Goals are motivating when people believe the goal can be accomplished, but only by putting forth their best effort, such as the motivation the De La Salle Spartans felt to keep winning football games against bigger schools and tougher players. A related concept is the idea of **stretch goals**, which are highly ambitious goals that are so clear, compelling, and imaginative that they get people fired up about meeting the challenge. On the other hand, keep in mind that unrealistic goals can be demoralizing and lead to failure.[10]
- **Commitment.** The best way to gain commitment is to let people participate in setting goals. People have to "buy into" the goals and be committed to them. It isn't always possible or desirable to involve everyone in goal-setting, but you should involve people to the extent possible. For example, a specific project and deadline might be set by higher executives and passed down the hierarchy. As team leader, you could then engage people by allowing them to break the job into manageable chunks and establish their own smaller goals to meet the major project goal.
- **Feedback.** Provide regular feedback. People need to know how well they're progressing toward goal achievement. If employees feel uncertainty and anxiety about how effectively they're moving toward the goal, their motivation and performance will suffer. You can increase motivation by providing ongoing communication about how well—or how poorly—people are doing, thus enabling them to adjust and improve their performance. In addition, there is evidence that *self-feedback*, where people are able to monitor their own progress toward a goal, is an even stronger motivator than external feedback.[11]

The Impact of Goal Setting

How does goal setting increase motivation? Exhibit 7.1 illustrates the motivational aspects of goal setting. *Clarity*, which means providing a clear, specific goal, enables people to focus their energies in the right direction. Employees know what to work toward, so they can direct their efforts toward the most important activities to accomplish the goal. The *challenge* of the goal energizes people and compels them to develop ideas, plans, and strategies for achieving the objective.

Commitment to the goals occurs when people participate in setting goals so they feel a sense of control over their own work, have a better understanding of the goals they are striving toward, and feel more committed to achieving the goals. For example, at Aluminio del Caroni, a state-owned aluminum company in southeastern Venezuela, plant workers felt a renewed sense of commitment when top leaders implemented a co-management initiative that had managers and lower-level employees working together to set budgets, determine goals, and make decisions. "The managers and the workers are running this business together," said one employee who spends his days shoveling molten aluminum down a channel from an industrial oven to a cast. "It gives us the motivation to work hard."[12]

Finally, *feedback* is an important motivator because the manager provides guidance, support, redirection, and recognition. One aspect of feedback is related to the rewards that managers offer people for

Exhibit 7.1 Motivational Aspects of Goal Setting

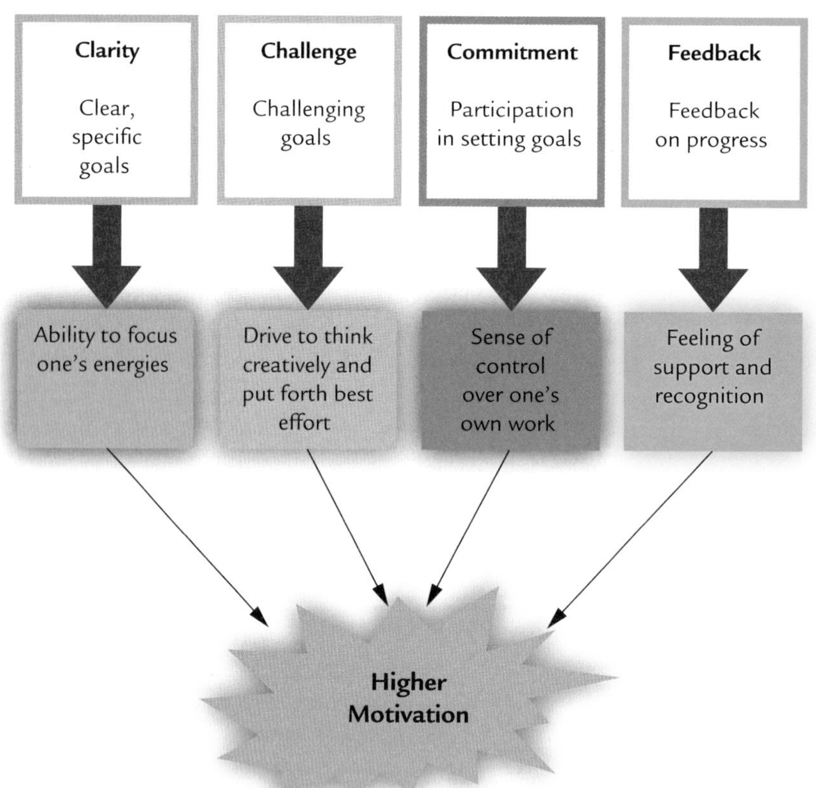

© CENGAGE LEARNING 2014

DISCOVER KNOWLEDGE

accomplishing goals. Providing rewards of some type is essential for motivation, but rewards can differ widely. Managers often find that people are motivated by different types of rewards. This is partly because people have different needs, and understanding the link between individual needs and individual motivation is a critical skill for managers.

THE FOUNDATIONS OF MOTIVATION: RECOGNIZING HUMAN NEEDS

Santa Castillo works in one of the world's most unusual garment factories. Alta Gracia, a factory in the Dominican Republic owned by Knights Apparel of Spartanburg, South Carolina, pays workers three times the average pay of the country's apparel workers, and it doesn't fight against allowing employees to join a union. For Castillo and the other 120 or so employees at Alta Gracia, the high pay is a powerful motivator. "We never had the opportunity to make wages like this before," she says, pointing out that the pay is enabling her family to build a new house with an indoor bathroom and move from the small wooden shack they now inhabit. Another employee is enthusiastic because she can now send her daughter to college, and still another is simply happy that she can pay off a $300 debt.[13]

Employees at the Alta Gracia factory in the Dominican Republic are motivated by the high pay the company provides because they need money to support their families and can't make nearly as much anywhere else. Many motivational ideas rest on a foundation of understanding the *needs* that motivate people. People have basic needs, such as for economic security, friendship and affection, recognition, or achievement, that are translated into an internal tension that motivates specific behaviors to try to fulfill the need. To the extent that the behavior is successful,

the person is rewarded in the sense that the need is satisfied. The reward also lets the person know that the behavior was appropriate and can be used again to achieve rewards and meet needs.

The Link between Individual Needs and Motivation

An individual's needs are like a hidden catalog of the things he or she wants and will work to get. It is important to remember that people have a range of needs, some of which are called *lower-level needs*, such as the need for economic security, food and water, decent housing, and safety, and some are called *higher-level needs*, such as the need for friendship, recognition, and accomplishment. Your job as a manager is to recognize differing needs so that you can design reward systems that meet people's needs and direct their energies toward attaining the organization's goals. For example, the employees at the Alta Gracia factory were motivated by money, considered a lower-level need, because they had little money to meet their basic requirements for living.

People Are Driven to Act by Various Motives

You can be a better motivator if you understand the type of motives that compel people to alter or continue a desired behavior. Exhibit 7.2 illustrates four categories of motives based on two criteria.[14] The horizontal dimension contrasts motives that are driven by fear or pain versus those driven by growth or pleasure. The vertical dimension contrasts motives that are triggered from within the individual (intrinsic) versus those triggered from outside the individual (extrinsic), such as by a manager. The four quadrants represent four differing approaches for motivating people.

Exhibit 7.2 Four Categories of Motives Managers Can Use

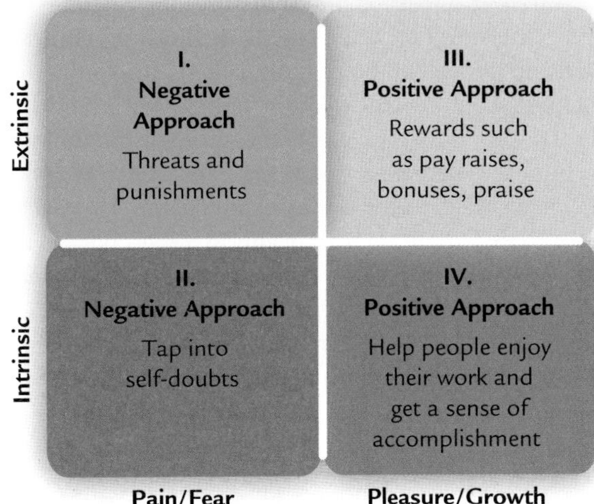

Source: Based on Bruce H. Jackson, "Influence Behavior: Become a Master Motivator," *Leadership Excellence* (April 2010): 14.

DISCOVER KNOWLEDGE

What's Your Problem?

Q: I'm a new manager (four months) in a company that makes hair care products. I supervise the accounting department where we have eleven employees, some salaried and some hourly. I've noticed in the past two months that five of them have been slacking off. Maybe they think I'm too nice or something, because I granted a lot of the requests they made. So I had to make them realize they can't just push me here and there. In the past two weeks, I've told them "no" to almost everything they asked, plus I warned them that with the economy so bad, we might have to make cutbacks, so they better work harder. Problem is, it hasn't helped. The harder-working employees seem nervous now, and the slackers must be looking for other jobs online while at work, because I don't see an uptick in their productivity. What should I do?

A: No more threats! You are using a negative approach to motivation, which did not have the outcome you wanted. You need a new approach. Talk to each employee individually to learn what people want and expect from their jobs. Also tell them how important their work is and the goals you'd like to accomplish in the near future. Evidently the negative messages have de-motivated everyone, so you need to work on positive messages and rewards. However, you are probably right that you seemed like a pushover. Be more reasoned and thoughtful with employee requests—not too many "yeses" but also not too many "nos." Good luck!

© CENGAGE LEARNING 2014

Avoid Relying on Negative Motives

Quadrants I and II are both negative approaches to motivating. Quadrant I uses negative, extrinsic methods, such as threats or punishments, to get people to perform as desired. Quadrant II methods attempt to motivate people by tapping into their self-doubts or anxieties, such as motivating people to work hard by emphasizing the weak economy and high unemployment rate. Quadrant I and II methods can indeed be effective, as fear is a powerful motivator. However, using fear to motivate people almost always has negative consequences for employee development and long-term performance. In the real world, almost every manager sometimes has to impose some form of punishment, but good managers avoid the use of fear tactics.

Provide Both Extrinsic and Intrinsic Rewards

Quadrant III motivational methods attempt to influence behavior by using extrinsic rewards that create pleasure. **Extrinsic rewards** are things such as pay increases, bonuses, promotions, and praise that are controlled by someone outside the person, such as a manager. This positive motivational approach is useful but limited. External rewards lose their power as motivational tools over time.

The most effective managers emphasize a Quadrant IV motivational approach. Quadrant IV techniques tap into deep-seated employee energy and commitment by helping people get intrinsic rewards from their work. **Intrinsic rewards** are experienced by an employee as a result of the work itself. Intrinsic rewards include such things as a feeling of accomplishment, self-esteem, and personal or professional growth.

Extrinsic rewards (Quadrant III) are targeted primarily toward meeting people's lower-level needs, whereas intrinsic rewards (Quadrant IV) meet higher-level needs. Extrinsic rewards are important, but good managers don't rely on them as their primary motivational tool. Instead, they also strive to help people find meaning and joy in their work.

For example, managers at Tasty Catering in Elk Grove Village, Illinois, provide extrinsic rewards of competitive pay and good benefits, but they also motivate people by giving them opportunities to learn, grow, and contribute. CEO Thomas Walter turned strategic decision making over to teams of front-line employees from all across the company—chefs and accountants, clerical workers and drivers, supervisors and servers. "It puts all of us on an even playing field," said Anna Wollin, an account executive. "I had been with the company less than a year, and my opinion was as important as an owner's opinion."[15]

DISCOVER KNOWLEDGE

> **DISCOVER YOURSELF**
>
> **Interpret Your Score: Intrinsic or Extrinsic Motivation** (Questionnaire 1)
>
> Your total score for Part A reflects your *extrinsic* motivation and your score for Part B indicates your *intrinsic* motivation for that activity. Comparative data for **Extrinsic Motivation** (Part A): Thirty person Mean score = 10.1; Top Quartile = 12–12; Bottom Quartile = 7–9. Comparative data for **Intrinsic Motivation** (Part B): Thirty person Mean score = 9.3; Top Quartile = 11–12; Bottom Quartile = 4–8. As described in the chapter, managers and organizations often use extrinsic motivation techniques, but intrinsic motivation is more satisfying for most people. Which score was higher for you? Do you prefer intrinsic or extrinsic rewards in your career? CNOW and CourseMate users can access dynamically updated comparative data through www.cengagebrain.com.

© CENGAGE LEARNING 2014

Most People Are Not Motivated Primarily by Money

Some managers think money is the most important tool for motivation. In reality, many people consider factors other than pay to be more important. Nelson Motivation Inc. conducted a survey of 750 employees across various industries to assess the value they placed on various rewards. Cash and other monetary awards came in dead last. The most valued rewards involved praise and manager support and involvement.[16] A global online survey by Accenture found that "interesting work" was the top desire for 60 percent of job seekers, and "regular recognition and rewards" ranked higher than a good salary.[17] An interest in money actually declined for many employees during the recent recession. A 2010 survey by the Society for Human Resource Management found that people valued job security and benefits most, followed by the opportunity to use their skills and interesting work. Compensation was ranked last.[18] And a small study of workers in Los Angeles found that good relationships and positive interactions were considered more important than money during challenging economic times.[19] The point is, as a manager you should recognize that any

Exhibit 7.3 What Employees Want, Ranked by Employees and Supervisors

Job Factors	Employees	Supervisors
Being informed and included	3	10
Respectful feedback and discipline	9	9
An expression of appreciation	2	8
Reciprocal loyalty with employees	8	7
Intellectually stimulating work	1	5
Understanding/ allowance of personal problems	10	6
Opportunities for training and development	6	3
Healthy working conditions	7	4
Job security	4	2
Competitive, fair pay	5	1

Source: Based on Kenneth A. Kovach, "What Motivates Employees? Workers and Supervisors Give Different Answers," *Business Horizons* (September–October 1987): 58–65.

group of people will reflect a wide diversity of needs and desires and will thus value different rewards.

Another survey some years ago confirms that many managers fail to understand what truly motivates employees. Exhibit 7.3 reflects this disparity between what managers think people want and what really matters to employees. The exhibit lists ten job factors. The first column indicates how the ten factors were actually ranked by a group of 1,000 employees, which included people in both blue-collar and white-collar, skilled and unskilled, jobs. The second column shows how supervisors predicted employees would rank the factors. Note that managers predicted *competitive pay* would be the most important factor to employees, whereas the employees actually ranked it fifth. The two most important factors for employees were *intellectually stimulating work* and *being appreciated* for doing a good job, but the managers placed these factors relatively low on the scale of importance. A different group of employees and managers would, of course, rank these same criteria differently. However, the results of this and other surveys indicate that the discrepancy between what workers truly value and what managers think they value can be quite wide.[20]

The Hierarchy of Needs

One of the best-known models of human needs was developed by psychologist Abraham Maslow, who proposed that people are motivated by multiple needs that exist in a hierarchical order, as illustrated in Exhibit 7.4.[21] This **hierarchy of needs** indicates that people are motivated by five general types of needs: *physiological, safety, belongingness, esteem,* and *self-actualization.* The hierarchy suggests that lower-level needs take priority. As each level of needs is satisfied, it declines in importance and the next higher level of needs is activated. As physiological needs are met, safety needs are

Exhibit 7.4 Maslow's Hierarchy of Needs

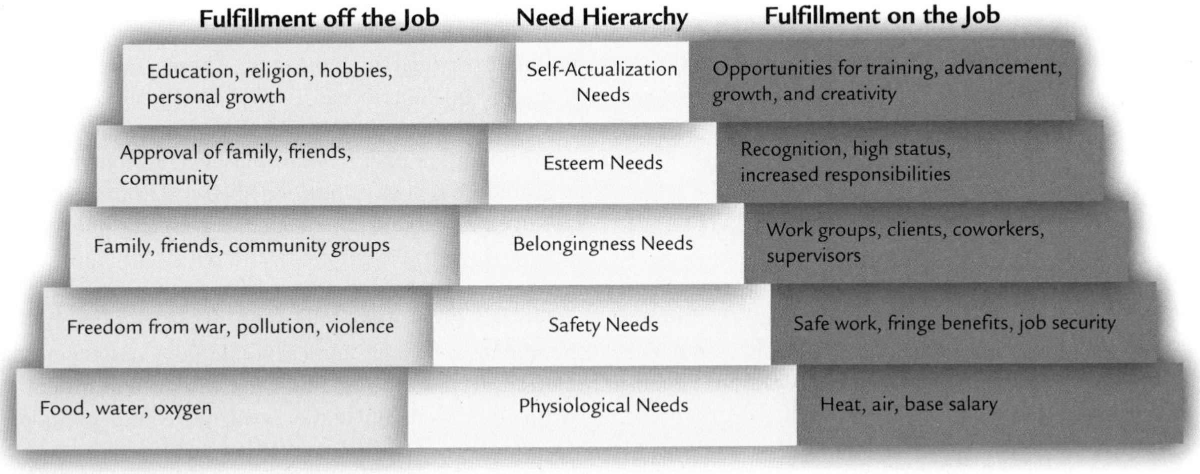

Fulfillment off the Job	Need Hierarchy	Fulfillment on the Job
Education, religion, hobbies, personal growth	Self-Actualization Needs	Opportunities for training, advancement, growth, and creativity
Approval of family, friends, community	Esteem Needs	Recognition, high status, increased responsibilities
Family, friends, community groups	Belongingness Needs	Work groups, clients, coworkers, supervisors
Freedom from war, pollution, violence	Safety Needs	Safe work, fringe benefits, job security
Food, water, oxygen	Physiological Needs	Heat, air, base salary

Exhibit 7.5 Herzberg's Two-Factor Theory

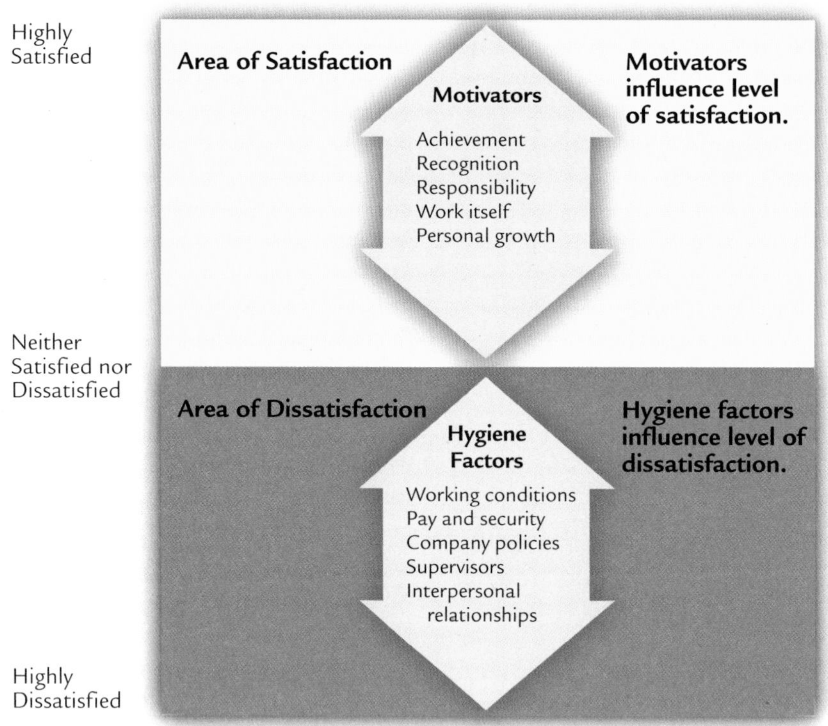

activated; as safety needs are met, belongingness needs become more important; and so on. For example, a person who is desperate for a job and an adequate salary to support himself and his family *(physiological needs)* will not be concerned about being recognized for his contributions at work *(esteem needs)* or about high-level training programs that offer an opportunity to expand his potential (*self-actualization needs*). The job is all this person needs for motivation in the beginning. Once the lower-level needs are satisfied, however, the next level of needs kicks in and the employee will no longer be highly motivated simply by the fact of having a job and getting a paycheck.

Motivate by Meeting Higher-Level Needs

An alternative approach to understanding human needs as motivators was developed by Frederick Herzberg.[22] Herzberg interviewed hundreds of employees about times when they were highly motivated to work and other times when they were dissatisfied and unmotivated. His findings suggest that the work characteristics associated with dissatisfaction and low motivation are quite different from those pertaining to satisfaction and high motivation, which prompted the **two-factor theory** of motivation.

Exhibit 7.5 illustrates the two factors and how they are related to motivation. The first, **hygiene factors**, refers to characteristics that influence job *dissatisfaction*, such as working conditions, pay, company policies, and interpersonal relationships. These factors focus primarily on employees' lower-level needs. When hygiene factors are poor—such as low pay, a noisy work environment, or poor relationships with a supervisor—an employee is likely to be dissatisfied and unmotivated. However, improving these factors typically does not increase the employee's motivation; it simply removes the dissatisfaction.

To increase satisfaction, motivation, and commitment, managers have to incorporate the second factor, referred to as *motivators*, into the work environment. **Motivators** focus on higher-level needs and include elements such as achievement, challenging work, recognition, responsibility, and opportunity for growth and personal development. Indeed, a study by the Families and Work Institute found that U.S. businesses that incorporate attributes such as job flexibility, learning and skill development, and involving employees in decision making are much more effective at engaging workers, increasing job satisfaction, and boosting employee retention.[23]

This indicates the importance of a two-pronged approach to enhance motivation. First, managers improve hygiene factors by providing adequate pay and a positive work environment. This removes the dissatisfaction. Next, they use motivators to meet higher-level needs and propel employees toward higher motivation and better performance. For example, when David Bryce was hired to improve customer service at Rackspace, a San Antonio-based Web hosting service, he found a group of employees who already enjoyed positive hygiene factors. His challenge was to find motivators that would encourage a group of techies to focus on providing "fanatical customer support." He found the key by meeting the higher-level needs of employees for responsibility, recognition, and achievement. Employees are now organized into teams, each of which is treated as its own separate business, serving a specific group of customers and with responsibility for its own profit and loss. Employees can earn bonuses based on how well the team meets financial and customer service goals. The bonuses are a serious incentive, but just as important for motivation is the public recognition of achievement. Customer compliments are posted on the walls and "Fanatic" signs hang above the desks of people who have gone above and beyond the call of duty.[24]

DISCOVER YOURSELF

Interpret Your Score: Need Motivation (Questionnaire 2)

Your scores for Parts A–E reflect how you see your needs being met in the specific work situation. The five scores represent Maslow's hierarchy of needs. A higher score means that need is met for you. Comparative data for self-management scores are: **Physiological** (Part A): Thirty person Mean score = 5.7; Top Quartile = 6–6; Bottom Quartile = 4–5. **Safety** (Part B): Mean = 4.1; Top Quartile = 5–5; Bottom Quartile = 2–4. **Belongingness** (Part C): Mean = 5.3; Top Quartile = 6–6; Bottom Quartile = 2–5. **Esteem** (Part D): Mean = 4.5; Top Quartile = 6–6; Bottom Quartile = 2–3. **Self-Actualization** (Part E): Mean = 8.4; Top Quartile = 10–12; Bottom Quartile = 4–7. Many people find that their scores for lower-level needs are higher than for higher-level needs. Is that true for you? What do your five scores say about the degree of need satisfaction in your job? In developed countries, lower needs are often taken for granted, and work motivation is based on the opportunity to meet higher needs.

Re-read the 12 questions again. The first four questions (Parts A and B) are comparable to hygiene factors in Herzberg's Two-Factor Theory and the last eight questions (Parts C-E) reflect Herzberg's motivators. To compare your scores for *hygiene factors* vs. *motivators*, first add your scores for Parts A and B and then double that number for the *hygiene factors* total: _____. Then calculate your score for *motivators* by adding your scores for Parts C, D, and E for the total: _____. Which motivates you more—hygiene factors or motivators? What do you interpret from your scores on these two factors? CNOW and CourseMate users can access dynamically updated comparative data through www.cengagebrain.com.

© CENGAGE LEARNING 2014

SHAPING BEHAVIOR TOWARD HIGH PERFORMANCE: DESIGN MOTIVATING JOBS

"It would be nice to be an electrician," says James Ault. "You can take pride in what you've accomplished." Ault recently visited a park where he worked in maintenance during college. He can still see some of the signs he painted, the electrical jobs he wired, and the trees he planted. Now Ault spends his days working on state energy policy, where he invests countless hours researching and debating issues. He might never see concrete results of his work. Consequently, Ault sometimes finds it difficult to get gratification from his job. Like Ault, many employees work in jobs where they can't immediately see the results of their efforts, which

makes the manager's task of keeping motivation high even tougher.[25]

Recall our discussion of intrinsic and extrinsic rewards earlier in this chapter. Managers can shower an employee with extrinsic rewards and still have an unmotivated employee if the person finds the job boring or unfulfilling. One way to help people get more intrinsic rewards from their work, thus increasing their motivation, is to design jobs that meet employees' needs and direct their behavior toward high performance.

Job design refers to structuring jobs in a way to meet higher level needs and increase motivation toward the accomplishment of goals. Managers can strive to find a good **person-job fit**, which means matching job characteristics to an employee's interests, personality, and abilities, so that work is done by people who are well-suited to it. This requires being clear about the various tasks that need to be accomplished and the type of people who would succeed at various assignments.

Sometimes, however, enhancing motivation requires that jobs be redesigned to incorporate more high-level motivators. **Work redesign** involves altering jobs to increase both the quality of employees' work experience and their productivity. One model, called the **job characteristics model**, proposes that certain core job dimensions create positive psychological

DISCOVER KNOWLEDGE

7 STEPS TO...
Using Rewards Effectively

1. **Don't make it all about the money.** People should be paid well and paid fairly, but managers should emphasize other types of rewards too. A study of *Fortune* magazine's "most admired companies" found that these companies pay about 5 percent *less* in base pay for managers and professional positions.
2. **Make people feel valued.** Sincerely thanking people for their efforts can provide a tremendous motivational boost. A thank you can be verbal, a handwritten note, or a gift card, just as long as you do it often. One administrative assistant said her biggest motivator was a personal "thank you" from her immediate supervisor at the end of every day.
3. **Give people opportunities to learn and grow.** Good managers have regular one-on-one meetings to help each employee achieve personal and professional development goals. Simply receiving individual, positive attention from a supervisor makes people feel important, too.
4. **Make it fun.** When people have fun at work, they want to be there. Managers influence whether people develop positive relationships and are able to have moments of levity and joy during the work day.
5. **Feed people once in a while.** One consultant says free food comes up every time she asks people what creates a motivating work environment. It can be a pizza for lunch, afternoon snacks, or a trip to a fancy restaurant.
6. **Be aware of the nonverbal signals you send.** Some managers say that nonfinancial rewards are important for employees, yet they still reward *themselves* with huge salaries and bonuses. This hurts motivation by signaling that managers think they are more important than employees.
7. **Promote a "total rewards" philosophy.** Find ways to help people know the value of the rewards they get from the organization, including benefits and intangible rewards. Many people switch jobs to get a slightly higher salary, only to realize they're actually receiving *less* when other rewards are considered.

Sources: Based on Tom McMullen, Mel Stark, and Mark Royal, "Finding the Right Combination: How the Most Admired Companies Unlock Reward Effectiveness," Hay Group (2009), http://www.haygroup.com/downloads/ie/Finding_the_right_combination.pdf (accessed March 16, 2011); Martin Dewhurst, Matthew Guthridge, and Elizabeth Mohr, "Motivating People: Getting Beyond Money," *McKinsey Quarterly*, Issue 1 (2010): 12–15; and Regina M. Clark, "Are We Having Fun Yet? Creating a Motivating Work Environment," *Industrial and Commercial Training* 41, no.1 (2009): 43–46.

Exhibit 7.6 The Job Characteristics Model

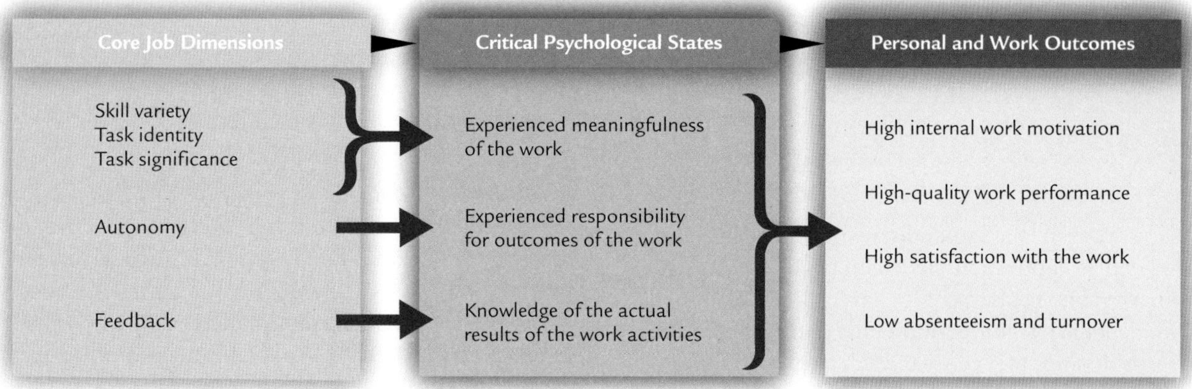

Source: Adapted from J. Richard Hackman and G. R. Oldham, "Motivation through the Design of Work: Test of a Theory," *Organizational Behavior and Human Performance* 16 (1976): 256.

reactions within employees that lead to higher motivation and better performance.[26] The core job dimensions, related psychological reactions, and outcomes are illustrated in Exhibit 7.6.

As a manager, you can make alterations in five dimensions of jobs to increase the job's motivational potential:

1. *Increase skill variety.* Jobs with a variety of activities that require a diversity of skills are more motivating.
2. *Structure jobs so that an employee can perform a complete task from beginning to end.* The job characteristics model refers to this as *task identity*, which means the job has a recognizable beginning and ending.
3. *Incorporate task significance into the job.* When people feel that they are performing a job that is important and that influences customers and the company's success, they are more motivated.
4. *Give people autonomy for choosing how and when to perform specific tasks.* People are typically more motivated when they have freedom, discretion, and self-determination in planning and carrying out tasks. To illustrate this point, consider the motivating power of *flexible work schedules*. Options such as flexible work hours, telecommuting, and job sharing are highly valued by employees because this enables them to balance their work and personal responsibilities.
5. *To the extent possible, design jobs to provide feedback and let employees see the outcomes of their efforts.* In cases where the job itself does not provide timely feedback, such as the job described in the example of James Ault working on state energy policy, managers have to work harder at giving people specific manager feedback and helping them see how the job contributes to the organization's success.

The more these five characteristics can be designed into the job, the higher employees' motivation will be, and the higher will be their performance. As illustrated in Exhibit 7.6, these dimensions cause individuals to experience three positive psychological reactions. The first three dimensions—higher skill variety, task identity, and task significance—enable the employee to see the job as meaningful and significant (*experienced meaningfulness of work*), which makes the job intrinsically satisfying. Greater autonomy in a job leads to a feeling of increased responsibility for the success or failure of task outcomes (*experienced responsibility for outcomes of the work*), thus increasing commitment. The final dimension, feedback, provides the employee with *knowledge of the actual results of work activities*. Thus, the employee knows how he or she is doing and can adjust work performance to increase desired outcomes.

These positive psychological reactions in turn lead to greater intrinsic satisfaction, higher motivation, better work performance, and lower absenteeism and turnover, as illustrated in the exhibit.

SHAPING BEHAVIOR TOWARD HIGH PERFORMANCE: USE REWARDS APPROPRIATELY

Now we turn to a deeper discussion of how rewards are related to motivation. To channel motivation toward appropriate goals, people have to understand that their behavior and performance is directly related to the outcomes they receive (such as monetary rewards, positive recognition, reprimands, or promotions). In addition, they need to believe that their efforts can lead to positive outcomes.

Use Rewards to Reinforce Desirable Behavior

When people get positive feedback and reinforcement for their actions, they're likely to continue that behavior. Anyone who has been unable to resist laughing at a four-year-old's use of a dirty word understands the power of reinforcement. The child likes the positive response and is likely to say the word again to evoke more laughter.

Managers use reinforcement as a motivational tool by positively reinforcing behaviors and actions that lead to goal accomplishment, and negatively reinforcing undesirable behaviors. **Reinforcement** refers to anything that causes a certain behavior to be repeated or inhibited. The four types of reinforcement—positive reinforcement, avoidance learning, punishment, and extinction—are described in Exhibit 7.7.

Positive reinforcement helps to improve performance. By linking rewards to performance, managers can strengthen employees' high-performance behaviors and increase the frequency of desired actions. Moreover, nonfinancial reinforcers, such as positive feedback, social recognition, and attention, are just as effective as financial rewards.[27] At many companies today, employees are doing more work for less money because of the tough economic environment. Managers are finding inexpensive ways, including gift cards and thank you notes, to let people know they're appreciated. People are more motivated simply by "the fact that someone walked up to them and said, 'Thank you. You did a good job,'" says Steve Nieuwsma, a Rockwell Collins division vice president.[28]

The timing of reinforcement influences motivation and behavior. Continuous reinforcement, in which every occurrence of the desired behavior is positively reinforced, is highly effective for helping people learn new behaviors. When one manager wanted to

Exhibit 7.7 Changing Behavior with Reinforcement

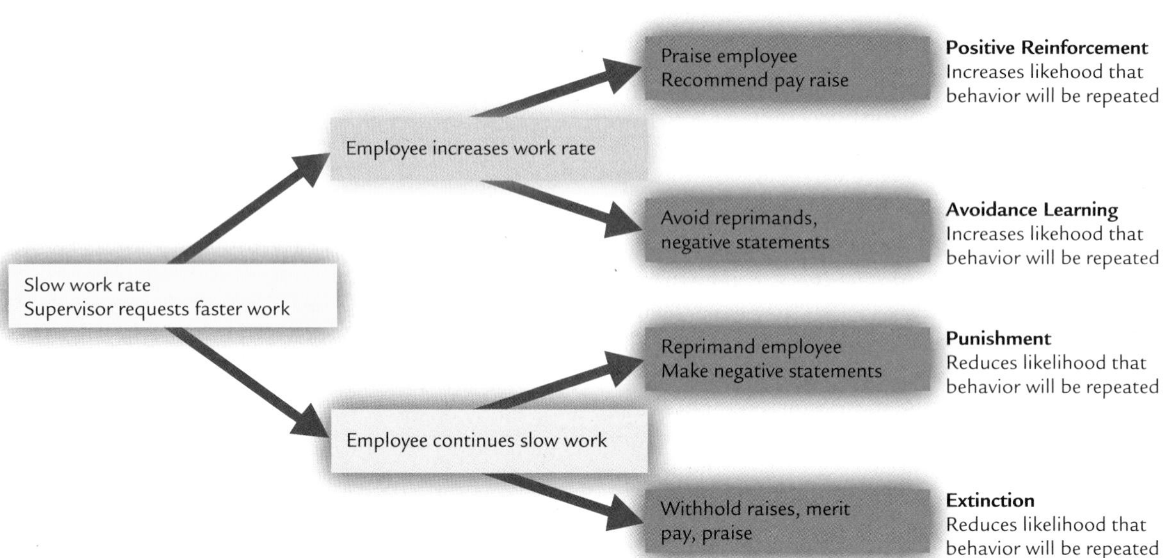

Source: Based on Richard L. Daft and Richard M. Steers, *Organizations: A Micro/Macro Approach* (Glenview, IL: Scott, Foresman, 1986), p. 109.

boost daily sales from $28,000 to $30,000, he offered each member of the sales team a $50 bill for every week they had a daily average above $30,000. They achieved the goal the first week, and the manager kept up the continuous positive reinforcement for several months until the new behavior of more aggressive selling was learned. Even after the incentive was discontinued, sales never dropped to their previous level.[29]

Partial reinforcement, in which the manager gives positive reinforcement only after some occurrences of the correct behavior, is more effective for maintaining appropriate behaviors and actions over the long term.[30] If a person receives positive reinforcement every time he or she performs a desired action, the reward ceases to have significance and thus loses its motivating power. Boeing implemented a rewards initiative called Pride@Boeing, which encourages managers to give fun tokens of appreciation, such as movie tickets and other small items, to employees on the spur of the moment. "Recognition should be fun and spontaneous," says Boeing's Lynne Eskil. "If it's expected to happen at a certain time every quarter, it really loses its value."[31]

DISCOVER YOURSELF

Interpret Your Score: Expectancy/Reinforcement Theory (Questionnaire 3)

These two scores represent how you apply the motivational concepts of expectancy and reinforcement in your role as an informal leader. A high score on using *expectancy theory* (Part A)means you motivate people by managing expectations. You understand how a person's effort leads to performance and make sure that high performance leads to valued rewards. Comparative data for **Expectancy Theory** (Part A): Thirty person Mean score = 10.0, Top Quartile = 12–12; Bottom Quartile = 6–9. A high score for *reinforcement theory* (Part B) means that you attempt to modify people's behavior in a positive direction with frequent and prompt positive reinforcement. Comparative data for **Reinforcement Theory** (Part B): Thirty person Mean score = 10.7, Top Quartile = 12–12; Bottom Quartile = 7–10. New managers often learn to use reinforcements first, and as they gain more experience are able to apply expectancy theory. CNOW and CourseMate users can access dynamically updated comparative data through www.cengagebrain.com.

© CENGAGE LEARNING 2014

DISCOVER KNOWLEDGE

Help People Perform to Achieve Rewards

Another important skill for managers is to understand how an employee's perceptions regarding his or her abilities, the potential for rewards, and the desirability of rewards affect motivation.

You can apply principles of expectancy theory to motivate. **Expectancy theory** suggests that high motivation depends on an individual's belief, or expectation, that he or she has the ability to perform tasks and receive desired awards.[32] The manager's job is to understand each individual's expectancies. If a salesperson has a strong desire to reach the level of sales needed to earn the reward of an all-expenses-paid vacation to Hawaii, her motivation will be influenced by: (1) the belief that extra effort will enable her to increase sales to the desired level, and (2) the belief that reaching the desired sales level will result in being rewarded with the vacation. If the salesperson believes she cannot achieve the high level of sales, or that achieving that level will not result in receiving the reward, she will not be highly motivated.

Consider effort, performance, and the desirability of outcomes. The three elements of expectancy theory—the individual's effort, the individual's performance, and the desirability of available outcomes—are illustrated in Exhibit 7.8. The exhibit also defines the necessary relationships among these elements. For high motivation, the individual must first believe that he or she has the ability, previous experience, necessary resources, and opportunity to perform well. One interesting study of expectancy theory looked at patrol officer drug arrests in the midwestern United States. The research found that officers who made the most arrests were those who received specialized training to hone their skills and perceived that they had sufficient time and resources to properly investigate suspected drug activity.[33] Next, the employee has to believe that successful performance will lead to a specified outcome, such as a pay raise, recognition, or other reward. Finally, the outcomes that are available from high effort and good performance must be valued by the employee for motivation to be high. If the reward available for high sales, for instance, is a publicly presented company award, an employee with a desire or need for recognition and achievement would

Exhibit 7.8 Major Elements of Expectancy Theory

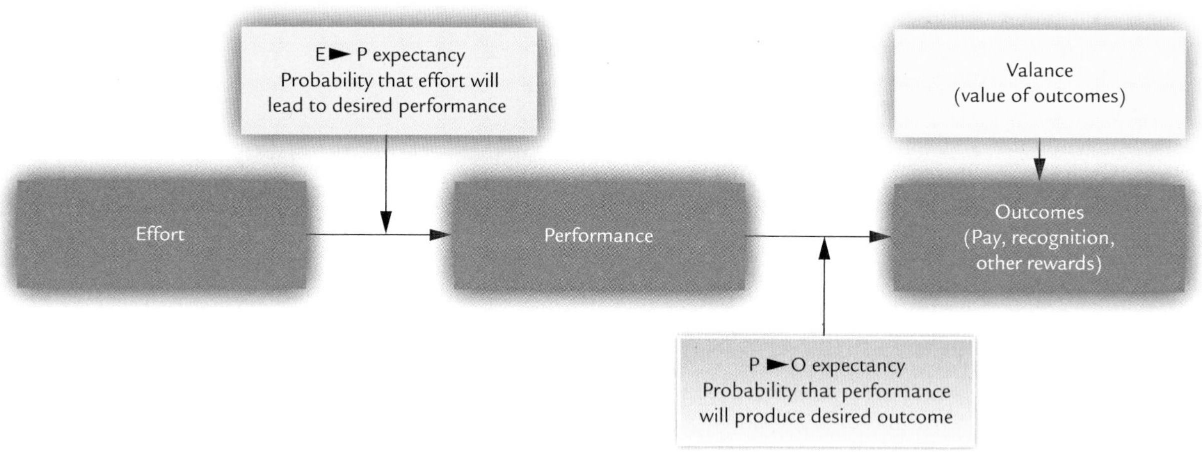

© CENGAGE LEARNING 2014

be highly motivated, whereas someone with no interest in achieving this sort of recognition would be less motivated.

You can help people meet their needs and at the same time attain organizational goals. Doing so means trying to find a match between an employee's skills and abilities and the demands of the job, then designing rewards that are desired by the employee. To increase motivation, you can clarify what the employee needs and wants, clarify the goals, define the outcomes available for achieving goals, and make sure the employee has the training, support, and resources needed to perform well and attain the rewards. Don Mayer, CEO of Small Dog Electronics in Waitsfield, Vermont, says designing the right incentives is the most important part of his job. He knows that people are motivated only when the rewards they can receive from their hard work are things they really want. "My job is to figure out how to create a workplace so exciting and rewarding that people can't wait to get up in the morning and come to work," Mayer says.[34]

Treat People Fairly: The Concept of Equity

Among the many needs that people want to have satisfied in the workplace, one that is shared by most people is a desire to feel that they are treated fairly.

When people feel that they are treated fairly, they are more motivated. **Equity theory** proposes that people are motivated to seek social equity in the rewards they receive for performance; that is, they want to feel that they are receiving fair compensation for their contributions as compared to others.[35] The idea of equity suggests that people evaluate equity by a ratio of inputs to outcomes. They look at what they put into a job, including their education, experience, effort, and ability (inputs), and consider what they get out of the job, such as pay rate, recognition, benefits, and promotions (outcomes). Then they compare their input-to-outcome ratio to others in the organization. If a person feels that the ratio of their outcomes to inputs equals the ratio of others, the person typically will feel treated fairly.

Treating people inequitably can have a devastating effect on motivation. Exhibit 7.9 illustrates what happens when ratios are out of balance. Resentment grows, teamwork suffers, and motivation and morale plummet. In one small company, managers found themselves having to hire new people very quickly to meet growing demand, and they often had to pay these people salaries higher than those of the company's long-time employees in order to match what they were making elsewhere. Moreover, in their effort to bring fresh thinking into the company, managers tended to pay more attention to the ideas and suggestions of the newcomers. These steps had a damaging effect on the performance of long-time employees, who felt slighted and soon began putting less effort and energy into their jobs. The perceived state of inequity decreased their motivation.[36]

Perceived inequity works in the opposite direction too. Studies of the brain by researchers at the California

Exhibit 7.9 Inequity Hurts Motivation

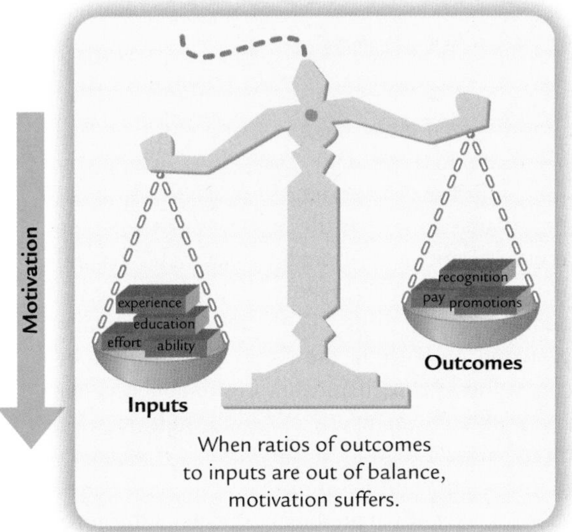

© CENGAGE LEARNING 2014

Institute of Technology and Trinity College suggest that we are "hardwired" to dislike inequality, even when it is in our favor.[37] In experiments using magnetic resonance imaging, the part of the brain associated with reward processing reacted strongly to perceptions of inequality for almost all research subjects. Thus, if an employee discovers that she is making more money than other people who contribute the same inputs to the company, she might experience anxiety and tension that is detrimental to her performance. Most people don't feel as good about themselves—and thus are less satisfied, committed, and motivated at work—when they believe they are getting more rewards than they should compared to others. The part of the brain associated with reward processing and pleasure is more stimulated and active when people have to work to accomplish a reward than if they simply have the reward given to them.

The importance of these ideas is to recognize that people do indeed evaluate the perceived equity of their rewards compared to others. As a manager, strive to keep feelings of equity in balance to maintain a motivating atmosphere.

DISCOVER YOURSELF

Interpret Your Score: Equity Sensitivity (Questionnaire 4)

A score above 25 for these questions represents Benevolence, which means that you are willing to provide more inputs to the organization than you would need to take in outputs. A score below 25 is considered Equity Sensitive, indicating that you are sensitive about giving more to the organization than you want to receive. A score of about 25 is considered Balanced in that you would like an equal balance between your inputs and outcomes compared to others. Comparative data for **Equity Sensitivity:** Thirty-person Mean score = 19.8; Top Quartile = 25–32; Bottom Quartile = 0–17. CNOW and CourseMate users can access dynamically updated comparative data through www.cengagebrain.com.

© CENGAGE LEARNING 2014

MOTIVATE BY EMPOWERING PEOPLE

DISCOVER KNOWLEDGE

When Meetup.com went through a period of rapid expansion, top executives implemented a command-and-control structure as a way to regulate and monitor performance. The trouble was, "productivity went through the floor," says chief technology officer Greg Whalin. So, managers decided to go in the opposite direction. Now, Meetup's employees have almost total freedom to select the projects they work on and how and when they accomplish them. With the new self-management approach, many people began working harder than ever before. "We got more done in six weeks than in six months last year," said CEO Scott Heiferman.[38]

One significant way managers meet higher motivational needs is to shift power down from the top of the organization and share it with employees to enable them to achieve goals. **Empowerment** is power sharing, the delegation of power or authority to subordinates in an organization. Increasing employee power heightens motivation for task accomplishment because people improve their own effectiveness, choosing how to do a task and using their creativity.[39] Empowering employees involves giving them four elements that enable them to act more freely to accomplish their jobs: information, knowledge, power, and rewards.[40]

1. **Employees receive information about company performance.** In companies where employees are fully empowered, all employees have access to all financial and operational

information, and they are educated about how their work contributes to financial success.

2. **Employees have knowledge and skills to contribute to company goals.** Companies use training programs and other development tools to help people acquire the knowledge and skills they need to contribute to organizational performance.
3. **Employees have the power to make substantive decisions.** Empowered employees have the authority to directly influence work procedures and organizational performance, such as through quality circles or self-directed work teams.
4. **Employees are rewarded based on company performance.** Organizations that empower workers often reward them based on the results shown in the company's bottom line.

Current approaches to empowerment can be classified based on two dimensions: (1) the extent to which employees are involved in defining desired outcomes; and (2) the extent to which they participate in determining how to achieve outcomes. Exhibit 7.10 shows that empowerment efforts range from a situation in which front-line employees have almost no discretion, such as on a traditional assembly line, to full empowerment, where workers even participate in formulating organizational strategy. When employees are fully empowered, they are involved in defining mission and goals as well as in determining how to achieve them.

Exhibit 7.10 Degrees of Empowerment

© CENGAGE LEARNING 2014

DISCOVER KNOWLEDGE

GIVE MEANING TO WORK THROUGH ENGAGEMENT

How do you motivate people who perform menial jobs? Morrison Management Specialists, which provides food, nutrition, and dining services to the healthcare and senior living industries, does it by providing people a sense of meaning through engagement. Several years ago, executives made employee engagement a top management priority. They started by making sure everyone understood the company's mission and five core values of trust, teamwork, customer focus, learning, and profit. The company's Web site address and ending for corporate e-mail addresses is *iammorrison.com*, which reinforces that every employee *is* the company. Each year, top executives present an update of the company's direction and accomplishments to managers, who in turn hold conversations with employees throughout the organization to disseminate information about where the company stands and where it wants to go. Training sessions for hourly associates are organized under the title "Our Great Partnership" and strive to help people see how their everyday jobs tie in with the larger mission. A "People First" recognition program gives employees a chance to recognize one another for exceptional service.[41]

Employee **engagement** means that people enjoy their jobs and are satisfied with their work conditions, contribute enthusiastically to meeting team and organizational goals, and feel a sense of belonging and commitment to the organization. Engagement means being emotionally engaged at a personal level. Fully engaged employees care deeply about the organization and actively seek ways to serve the mission.[42] As a manager, you can encourage engagement by organizing the workplace in such a way that employees experience a sense of meaningfulness, connection, and growth.[43]

Good managers help people understand the purpose of their work and experience a sense of meaningfulness. When people have purpose, they have pride and dignity. Most employees aren't enthusiastic about just enriching shareholders; they need work with meaning and purpose. Zappos.com, for example, states its purpose as "delivering happiness to customers and employees through a great experience."[44] People have a sense of meaningfulness when they believe

Interpret Your Score: Empowerment (Questionnaire 5)

These ten questions represent aspects of empowerment—autonomy, impact, information, resources, and meaning—that an employee may experience in a job. If your score is high, you felt empowered in the job for which you answered the questions. If your score was low, you probably did not feel empowered. Comparative data for **Empowerment:** Thirty person Mean score = 24.9, Top Quartile = 28–30; Bottom Quartile = 17–23. Did you feel highly motivated in that job, and was your motivation related to your level of empowerment? What factors explained your level of empowerment? CNOW and CourseMate users can access dynamically updated comparative data through www.cengagebrain.com.

© CENGAGE LEARNING 2014

they are working toward something of importance and have a chance to accomplish something that provides real value to the world.

Engaged employees feel connected to the company, to one another, and to their managers. In a survey asking people what factors contributed to their engagement, 79 percent of people said "good relationships with coworkers" drove engagement to a high or very high extent. Even more, 91 percent, pointed to good relationships with their immediate supervisor as highly important.[45] It is the behavior of managers that makes the biggest difference in whether people feel engaged at work.[46] Managers promote engagement when they listen to employees, genuinely care about their concerns, and help them develop positive relationships with colleagues. People love working at Zappos, for example, because managers have created "a lifestyle company and a company lifestyle where people want to hang out with each other."[47]

To be engaged, people need to feel competent to handle what is asked of them and feel that they have the chance to learn, grow, and advance. Good managers help employees understand their own unique set of talents, skills, interests, attitudes, and needs; put people in jobs where they can make their best contribution and receive intrinsic rewards every day; and make sure people have what they need to perform well.[48] In addition, they give people the chance to work on challenging projects, participate in high-quality training and learning programs, and provide opportunities for advancement within the organization. At Zappos, employees get hundreds of hours of training and can choose which and how many of 25 skill sets they want to learn. People are encouraged to try new things and be creative in serving customers. Everyone has a chance to build new skills and stretch their abilities.[49]

Studies suggest that organizations with engaged employees have less turnover, are more productive and profitable, and enjoy greater employee and customer loyalty.[50] Alarmingly, recent surveys reflect low levels of engagement, particularly among Gen Y employees. A survey of 7,500 workers found that 25 percent of Gen Y employees in North America, 30 percent in the United Kingdom and Ireland, and 35 percent in Southeast Asia are disengaged.[51] Another survey found that a whopping 73 percent of U.S. workers surveyed in 2009 described themselves as "disengaged."[52] As a manager, you can help reverse the slide toward disengagement by enabling people to find meaning, connection, and challenge at work.

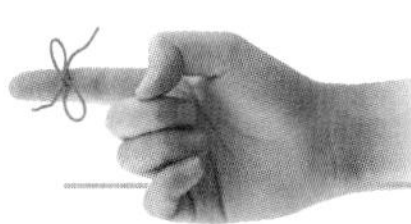

NEED TO KNOW

- One way to motivate people toward high performance is with goal setting. Four guidelines for using goal setting for motivation include: making goals specific and measurable, setting goals that stretch people's abilities, letting employees participate in setting goals, and providing regular feedback.
- People are driven to act by various motives. Good managers focus on providing people with motivation based on pleasure and growth rather than fear and pain. Intrinsic rewards are rewards that are experienced by an employee as a result of the work itself, such as a feeling of accomplishment or self-esteem. Extrinsic rewards are provided by a manager, such as a bonus or note of thanks.
- Many motivational ideas are based on understanding human needs. Maslow's hierarchy of needs proposes that people are motivated by five general

types of needs—physiological, safety, belongingness, esteem, and self-actualization—that exist in a hierarchical order. Physiological and safety would be considered lower-level needs and belongingness, esteem, and self-actualization higher-level needs.

- Herzberg proposed a two-factor theory. The term hygiene factors refers to characteristics such as working conditions, pay, and company policies that meet employees' lower-level needs. Good hygiene factors keep people from being dissatisfied, but they don't increase motivation. Herzberg uses the term motivators to refer to factors that focus on higher-level needs and increase motivation, such as achievement, challenging work, and recognition.
- Jobs can be designed to increase motivation. The job characteristics model proposes that motivation will be higher when jobs are designed to have greater skill variety, task identity, importance, autonomy, and feedback.
- Reinforcement is anything that causes a certain behavior to be repeated or inhibited. Managers use positive reinforcement as a motivational tool by linking rewards to performance, thus increasing the frequency of desired actions. Nonfinancial reinforcers such as positive feedback and manager attention can be just as effective as financial rewards.
- Expectancy theory suggests that high motivation depends on an individual's belief that he or she has the ability to perform the requested task and receive desired rewards. Equity theory reminds managers that people want to feel that they are treated fairly in the workplace.
- Empowerment, the delegation of power or authority to subordinates, is a great way to meet higher motivational needs. Managers empower people by giving them information, knowledge, skills, power to make decisions, and rewards based on performance.
- The most motivated employees are *engaged* employees. When people are engaged, they enjoy their jobs and are satisfied with their work conditions, contribute enthusiastically to meeting team and organizational goals, and feel a sense of belonging and commitment to the organization. Managers promote engagement by helping people find a sense of meaningfulness, a sense of connectedness, and a sense of competence and growth.

ACTION LEARNING

DELIBERATE PRACTICE EXERCISES

Positive Reinforcement

Step 1: For the next three days, practice giving positive feedback in the form of compliments and statements of appreciation to others. Be authentic. Try to give at least four compliments each day.

Step 2: Fill out the table below.

Positive feedback given	Who did you give the positive feedback to?	What was it for?	How did the person react?
First Day			
#1			
#2			
#3			
#4			
Second Day			
#1			
#2			
#3			
#4			
Third Day			
#1			
#2			
#3			
#4			

Step 3: Which were the easiest compliments to give? The most difficult? Why?

Step 4: What long-terms effects do you think might result from giving positive feedback to people?

Step 5 (Optional): Share your insights with a partner, and ask your partner what insights he or she gained.

Job Characteristics

Step 1: Think about a job you have had that you consider to be your "best job" ever. This can be a job you have now or one you've had in the past. What was the title of the job and what did you do in that job?

Step 2: Now think of the "worst job" you've ever had and write down what you did in that job.

Step 3: Review the job characteristics model as illustrated in Exhibit 7.6. Fill out the table below, indicating how well these jobs suited you in terms of the four dimensions of the job characteristics model. Score "5" if your needs were fully met on that dimension, all the way down to "1" if they were not met at all.

ACTION LEARNING

Job Characteristic	Best Job (5 is high; 1 is low)	Worst Job (5 is high; 1 is low)
1. Enough skill variety		
2. Structured so you could experience tasks from beginning to end		
3. You felt task significance		
4. You had autonomy for choosing how and when to perform specific tasks		
Total score for each job		

Step 4: What were the major differences between your best job and the worst job?

Step 5: Use the job characteristics model to indicate what you can do to make your current job better.

Step 6 (Optional): Share your insights with a partner, and ask your partner what insights he or she gained.

IN-CLASS TEAM EXERCISES

Work vs. Play[53]

Step 1: Form into groups of three or four members.

Step 2: Each individual answers these questions: What drives you to expend energy on a play (leisure) activity? Why do you choose the leisure activities you do? (Don't discuss the particular activities, but rather *why* you choose them.)

Step 3: Each individual completes the table below.

Question	Your answer
What play activities do you engage in?	
What do you get out of them?	
Does anybody pressure you to do these activities?	

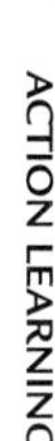

ACTION LEARNING

Step 4: Now look more closely at what you get out of each activity and complete the following table as a group. Then look for the major themes that explain what your group members get from play activities.

What is the play activity?	What do you get out of this activity?
Example: video games	Mental challenge, fun, emotional stimulation, etc.

Step 5: Each group presents its list of activities and major themes (outcomes) to the class.

Step 6: Discuss the following questions in class:

1. How can you build some of these motivations for play into a work environment?
2. What prevents you from making work more intrinsically motivating, as play is?
3. Which motivation theories are relevant here?

The Impact of Positive and Negative Reinforcement

This In-Class Team Exercise is available online at www.cengagebrain.com.

FIELD TEAM EXERCISE

Another Day at the Office[54]

Step 1: Form into groups of four or five and meet to make the following decisions:

1. Which of these TV shows will you study for examples of motivation issues?
   The Office
   Parks and Recreation
   30 Rock
   Any other show approved by the instructor
2. Find three characters in your chosen show that have motivation problems. The group should agree on which three characters to study.

Step 2: Someone from the group volunteers to research episodes, choosing three shows from your selected series to watch. These should be episodes in which your three characters are shown having motivation problems.

Step 3: Watch the three shows as a group, taking notes on how expectancy theory works with your three characters. Review Exhibit 7.8 to refresh your memory about expectancy theory.

Step 4: Fill out the table below.

ACTION LEARNING

	Character #1:	Character #2:	Character #3:
Name of the character			
Describe the motivation problem			
E-P Expectancy: Does this person believe that if effort is exerted, the task can be performed successfully? Explain.			
P-O Expectancy: Does the character perceive that outcomes are likely to be obtained if performance is successful?			
Valence: Does the person desire the outcomes that could result from successful performance?			

Step 5: What insights about expectancy theory and motivation can you get from analyzing your characters?

Your instructor may ask you to make a presentation to the class.

SHUTTERSTOCK #53973379

TEST YOUR METTLE

ROLE PLAY SIMULATIONS

Equality or Not?

Background: Reread the written Video Incident at the beginning of this chapter. General manager Jane Sutton's challenge is how to help her HR director Heather Carreau maintain a higher level of motivation.

Instructions: Form into groups of two or three. One person will play the role of Jane and one the role of Heather. If there are three in the group, the third person is an observer. Each person reads only his or her confidential role; the observer reads both. Spend 10–15 minutes on the role play.

Confidential information for Jane: You've got a capable team of four managers who all work hard and have made important contributions. Two of them are newer and earn more money because it was necessary to hire them at the "market" rate, which was higher than what the longer-term employees get. This happens a lot in business. It seems that people who hop jobs can keep their salaries moving upward. Because of a leak, the other two managers, Carlos Hernandez and Heather Carreau, found out their pay is about $10,000 less than the new hires, who are doing work at the same level and have little experience with the company. Both have come to you to complain. You've noticed during the past couple of weeks that they don't seem as focused in meetings, and they aren't coming up with solutions as often as before. But until they both confronted you, the reason for this behavior change was not clear. You think they deserve to earn as much, or close to as much, as the newer hires, but your boss has vetoed any salary increases for one year. He seems to care only about the bottom line—forget about employees feeling valued or what their motivation is. But you worry that if you don't give Carlos and Heather the raise, their productivity will continue to erode. You've decided to talk to both of them, starting with Heather, and try to get them to stay, as well as discussing how to get their motivation back up.

Confidential information for Heather: You've put in six good years at C&C and have always gotten good reviews from Jane and the previous boss. And you like your work. But you recently found out that the two new managers on the team are earning way more money, simply because they are new. It's not fair, because they do the same level of work, and they are both younger and have less experience than you and Carlos. In the past month, you've gotten distracted because of this information. You've been looking around at other job opportunities and there are some real possibilities, but you'd stay in a heartbeat if C&C would give you a raise, even half of the $10,000 extra those two get. In a big corporation like this, surely $5,000 won't break the bank. Now Jane wants to talk to you. Maybe she found the money!

After the role play, discuss the following questions:

1. How effective do you think Jane was in handling this situation, and what advice would you give her?
2. How can an understanding of equity theory help in a situation like this?

Who Wants to Be Empowered?

This Role Play Simulation is available online at www.cengagebrain.com.

VIDEO APPLICATION

LivingSocial Escapes

Maia Josebachvili started the social adventure company Urban Escapes and soon took on a partner, Bram Levy. After some success, the company was acquired by LivingSocial. Josebachvili and Levy have clear ideas about how to motivate employees.

Discussion Questions

1. Levy states, "When people are excited about something, they'll do virtually anything." Some employees were willing to accept low salaries because they were having fun. What theories of motivation would explain this?
2. Josebachvili believes that things like autonomy and respecting the people you work with are important motivators. Do you agree? Why?
3. Maia Josebachvili and Bram Levy had experience on Wall Street and with a consulting firm, yet they left to join a risky start-up. What do you think motivates each of them?

CASE INCIDENTS

Balancing Act

DeMarco's Department Store manager Lauren Brewster's "wow" moment came when she saw a Chicago restaurant staff's gushing treatment of an international celebrity.

"Everyone dreams of that kind of star treatment, like being Oprah," Lauren told her assistant, Jack Klein. "Think about it. People brag about their bank or the local bar where 'everybody knows your name,' or enjoy showing off a favorite restaurant where the hostess always remembers their favorite table."

DeMarco's, like other upscale department stores, suffered the double whammy of a slumping economy and increased competition from discount retailers and online shopping. How could the store, the "box," compete, retain its old customers, and build a strong future customer base?

"We've always known that it's all about customer service," Jack responded. "What's so great about grabbing a giant plastic shopping cart and slogging through some giant warehouse in your shorts and flip-flops, and then joining the herd at the check-out? That is not a shopping *experience*."

"I know that you are too young for this, but I can remember my mother dressing up in a lovely suit and hat and gloves and going downtown to have lunch with her friends and shop all afternoon. She would come home with shopping bags and hat boxes. When she shopped, she was a queen and I thought it was fabulous!" Lauren said.

SHUTTERSTOCK #53973379

"We've lost that. But that sort of customer experience can be recaptured—here—at DeMarco's."

Lauren's formal proposal to senior management was that store customers receive that personal, upscale, "you're somebody special in here" treatment. Sales associates would raise their own professional level, regard customers as worthy of personalized service, and build their own clientele. As an incentive, the entire DeMarco sales team would be changed over from hourly pay to straight commission. The idea intrigued corporate, which approved a two-year experiment. "Your pay is built through your own initiative and individualized service that makes customers return to you again and again," Lauren told the sales force at the outset of the experiment.

As expected, the new plan created a minor exodus among those who wanted the assurance of a "regular paycheck." But as the program moved through its first year, both store and corporate management was pleased with the overall numeric results. Marketing pushed the new image of elite, personalized customer service and phrases such as "Katherine at DeMarco's helped me select this outfit," or "Damien always lets me know when something new arrives at DeMarco's that he thinks is perfect for me" became a typical boast of savvy shoppers.

Now, two years into the experiment, corporate has urged Lauren to submit a full assessment of the program as a potential model for implementation throughout the department store chain. Sales numbers vouched for the overall success, particularly over the last two quarters of the second year. Certain associates, including Katherine Knowles in designer dresses and Damien Fotopolous in women's shoes, showed significant gains in sales and pay as a result of straight commissions. Overall, most sales associates and customers responded favorably and urged a continuation of the program. Reliance on commissions inspired most sales associates to treat their individual department as if it were their own small business, becoming experts on nuances of merchandise, exploring designs and trends, finding ways to promote their expertise, and building an impressive number of loyal customers.

The satisfaction level of customers was apparent in the numbers—not only sales numbers, but in repeat business, customer referrals to friends, and customer comment cards, all of which had been tracked since the beginning of the program.

The downside of the experiment—and there was a downside—was that while some associates soared, others either veered toward an aggressive, pushy sales style or became intimidated by coworkers and teetered, monthly, on the verge of replacement by not making enough sales. The previous high level of cooperation among sales staff was, in many instances, eaten away by relentless competition. Behind the scenes, staff fought over new customers. Work assignments away from the sales floor that contributed to the store in general were ignored or resented. No one wanted to straighten up merchandise, retag items for a sale, handle returns, do stock work, or ring up small customers. In addition, the managers and sales associates of certain departments such as women's accessories complained of lower wages because, as one associate pointed out, "My commission on a $50 belt is nothing compared to Katherine's commission on a $2,800 designer dress." Resentment was high among those who witnessed the extravagant wages of a few.

"If we change this program, if we keep straight commission for some and return to hourly pay for others, how does that fit with our new image?" Lauren said to Jack. "How does it deal with the difference in pay scale? How does it assure us that the attitudes of

our sales team and the culture of this store will not return to what we were before—just another store?"

Discussion Questions

1. What kind of incentive system do you suggest DeMarco's use for sales associates? Why?
2. Do you think the complaints of lower paid sales associates are legitimate? Why? How do you suggest Lauren respond to these complaints, such as the gripe that the system offers few opportunities for large commissions in some departments?
3. Have the successes of sales associates such as Katherine or Damien created a situation in which loyalty to customers is stronger than loyalty to the store? Is that the best culture for a store like DeMarco's? For example, if a successful associate leaves DeMarco's, might the customer leave also?

Sun Spots

SunDax CEO Dax Hollandsworth turned his leather desk chair from the blinding sunlight streaming through the large office window and leaned back, facing Mark Roberts, the company CFO.

"You know, Mark, on the surface this seems impossible. We look at the numbers, we look at energy trends, we look at tax breaks and the grants and loans poured into this effort, and . . . " his voice trails off as he raises his hands in a gesture of surrender.

"I dread the quarterly meeting and video feed," Mark says. "Everyone has been working really hard and they've come to expect the year-end bonus. Hell, they plan for it and their families budget for it."

"I realize this will come as a huge disappointment, but I really don't think it will come as a big shock to them. Do you want some of these?" Dax asks, taking a handful of jelly beans and extending the jar to Mark, who takes a few. "They're working their tails off, but I've detected a decline in overall morale. Everyone here keeps a close eye on the industry and on the mood and efforts at the federal level. They deal every day with the competition from the Chinese, and they see this big trend toward mergers and acquisitions. They may not want to admit it any more than we want to say it, but I think they know the bonus pool is empty and they wonder what the future holds."

The question hanging over offices throughout the U.S. solar industry echoes that of California-based SunDax: "*How could this happen?*"

To the outsider, things appear great for solar power. The numbers are staggering, with an overall increase of more than 60 percent from the previous year. And American home and commercial construction shows the rising popularity of solar energy as a viable power alternative. Like the electric automobile, it is the wave of the future. But the public sees only the sun; industry insiders are looking at the sun spots.

Private funding was, from the start, a problem for the industry. Few investors were willing to take a chance on solar over fossil fuel until more evidence was forthcoming. Of those who took the leap, most of those private funding sources dried up with the recession. The solar industry faced a mounting crisis until the federal government stepped in to offer tax credits, loan guarantees from the Department of Energy, and federal stimulus money. Recharged, solar companies such as SunDax moved quickly with increased inventory and expanded sales worldwide. Boom time brought U.S. Treasury grants to the tune of several hundred million dollars and as sales increased,

so did employee bonuses, many of which equaled up to a third of an employee's salary—money for a child's college tuition, a down-payment on a home, a special trip, or other luxuries.

Now, amid shaky global economic conditions, SunDax and other companies see a decline in European solar energy incentives while Chinese competitors undercut costs, providing an inventory glut for many U.S. producers. In this climate, there is reluctance on the part of Congress to renew mini-grants or to extend tax credits. The stimulus packages upon which so many companies depended to jumpstart market expansion are a thing of the past. And unemployed Americans, as well as those sitting on the employment "bubble," cringe at the notion that companies that accepted stimulus money could offer extravagant bonuses to employees.

"I'm afraid employees will believe we are bending to public pressure in withholding their bonuses, or think we are holding onto financial assets in order to look stronger for a potential merger or acquisition," Dax tells Mark.

"Mergers and acquisitions are the trend right now, and some big names have given in. If we are acquired, they can share in the gains," Mark reminds Dax.

"We're not there yet," Dax says. "Our challenge is to shore up faith in our future among employees while dealing with the realities of the market. But if you say 'look at all of these challenges' and, 'oh, by the way, don't expect a year-end bonus,' what can we offer to shore up that faith and restore enthusiasm?"

Discussion Questions

1. What options can you think of for Dax and Mark to mitigate the damage from unfulfilled expectations for the annual bonus?
2. What specific steps would you take if you were a senior manager in this situation? Explain why for each step.
3. Do you consider it motivational and equitable when a substantial part of an employee's pay is a bonus based on company results in an uncertain environment? Why or why not?

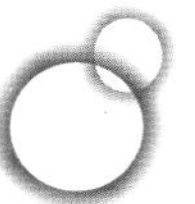

PERSONAL SKILLS LOG

PERSONAL SKILLS LOG

Directions: Fill in the rows below based on what you learned from each part of the chapter that you completed.

	What is my key takeaway or insight from this activity?	What do I personally do well (strength) regarding this activity?	What could I improve (weakness) about myself regarding this activity?	How might I use what I've learned from this activity in the future?
Manager Challenge Incident:				
Discover Yourself Questionnaires:				
Deliberate Practice Exercises:				
In-Class and/or Field Team Exercises:				
Role-Play Exercises:				
Case Incidents:				

REFERENCES

Discover Yourself

1 These questions are taken from M. Joseph Sirgy, David Efraty, Phillip Siegel, and Dong-Jin Lee, "A New Measure of Quality of Work Life (QWL) Based on Need Satisfaction and Spillover Theories," *Social Indicators Research* 55 (2001): 241–302. Reprinted with kind permission of Kluwer Academic Publishers.

2 These questions are based on D. Whetten and K. Cameron, "Diagnosing Poor Performance and Enhancing Motivation," *Developing Management Skills*, 5th ed. (Upper Saddle River, NJ: Prentice-Hall, 2002), pp. 302–303; and P. M. Podsakoff, S. B. Mackenzie, R. H. Moorman, and R. Fetter, "Transformational Leader Behaviors and Their Effects on Followers' Trust in Leader, Satisfaction, and Organizational Citizenship Behaviors," *Leadership Quarterly* 1, no. 2 (1990): 107–142.

3 Based on Wesley C. King, Jr. and Edward W. Miles, "The Measurement of Equity Sensitivity," *Journal of Occupational and Organizational Psychology* 67 (1994): 133–142; and Roy Thomas Dobson, Rein Lepnurm, and Elmer Struening, "Developing a Scale for Measuring Professional Equity Among Canadian Physicians," *Social Science & Medicine* 61 (2005): 263–266.

4 These questions were adapted from Bradley L. Kirkman and Benson Rosen, "Beyond Self-Management: Antecedents and Consequences of Team Empowerment," *Academy of Management Journal* 42, no. 1 (February 1999): 58–74; and Gretchen M. Spreitzer, "Psychological Empowerment in the Workplace: Dimensions, Measurements, and Validation," *Academy of Management Journal* 38, no. 5 (October 1995): 1442–1465.

Discover Knowledge

5 George Brymer, "Building Pride," *Vital Integrities Blog*, December 22, 2010, http://allsquareinc.blogspot.com/2010/12/building-pride.html (accessed March 13, 2011); John A. Byrne, "How to Lead Now: Getting Extraordinary Performance When You Can't Pay for It," *Fast Company* (August 2003): 62–70; Don Wallace, "The Soul of a Sports Machine," *Fast Company* (October 2003): 100–102, and Neil Hayes, *When the Game Stands Tall. The Story of the De La Salle Spartans and Football's Longest Winning Streak* (Berkeley, CA: Frog, Ltd/North Atlantic Books, 2005).

6 Mary Parker Follett, quoted in James A. F. Stoner and R. Edward Freeman, *Management* 4th ed. (Englewood Cliffs, N.J.: Prentice Hall, 1989).

7 Julie Sloane, "The Number Cruncher," in Ellyn Spragins, "The Best Bosses," *Fortune Small Business* (October 2004): 39–57; and Maggie Rauch, "Great Expectations," *Incentive* (December 2004):18–19.

8 Edwin A. Locke and Gary P. Latham, "Building a Practically Useful Theory of Goal Setting and Task Motivation: A 35-Year Odyssey," *The American Psychologist* 57, no. 9 (September 2002): 705–717; G. P. Latham, "The Motivational Benefits of Goal-Setting," *Academy of Management Executive* 18, no. 4 (2004): 126–129; G. P. Latham and E. A. Locke, "Self-Regulation through Goal Setting," *Organizational Behavior and Human Decision Processes* 50, no. 2 (1991): 212–247; G. P. Latham and G. H. Sejits, "The Effects of Proximal and Distal Goals on Performance of a Moderately Complex Task," *Journal of Organizational Behavior* 20, no. 4 (1999): 421ff; P. C. Early, T. Connolly, and G. Ekegren, "Goals, Strategy Development, and Task Performance: Some Limits on the Efficacy of Goal Setting," *Journal of Applied Psychology* 74 (1989): 24–33; E. A. Locke, "Toward a Theory of Task Motivation and Incentives," *Organizational Behavior and Human Performance* 3 (1968): 157–189; and G. H. Seijts, R. M. Meertens, and G. Kok, "The Effects of Task Importance and Publicness on the Relation Between Goal Difficulty and Performance," *Canadian Journal of Behavioural Science* 29, no. 1 (1997): 54ff.

9 Locke and Latham, "Building a Practically Useful Theory of Goal Setting and Task Motivation."

10 S. Kerr and S. Laundauer, "Using Stretch Goals to Promote Organizational Effectiveness and Personal Growth: General Electric and Goldman Sachs," *Academy of Management Executive* 18, no. 4 (2004):134–138; and K. R. Thompson, W. A. Hockwarter, and N. J. Mathys, "Stretch Targets: What Makes Them Effective? *Academy of Management Executive* 11, no. 3 (1997): 48–60.

11 Latham and Locke, "Self-Regulation through Goal Setting"; and J. M. Ivanecevich and J. T. McMahon, "The Effects of Goal Setting, External Feedback, and Self-Generated Feedback on Outcome Variables: A Field Experiment," *Academy of Management Journal* (June 1982): 359ff.

12 Brian Ellsworth, "Making a Place for Blue Collars in the Boardroom," *The New York Times* (August 3, 2005).

13 Steven Greenhouse, "A Factory Defies Stereotypes, But Can It Thrive?" *The New York Times* (July 18, 2010).

14 This discussion is based on Bruce H. Jackson, "Influence Behavior: Become a Master Motivator," *Leadership Excellence* (April 2010):14.

15 "A Company of 'Level 5' Leaders," *Inc.* (June 2010): 87.

16 Reported in Charlotte Garvey, "Meaningful Tokens of Appreciation," *HR Magazine* (August 2004): 101–105.

17 Accenture Survey, reported in Donna M. Airoldi, "What Workers Want," *Incentive* (October 2006): 11.

18 "2010 Employee Satisfaction Survey: Exploring What Matters Most to Employees," Society of Human Resource Management, as reported in Barbara J. Bowes, "More Than Money: Make Your Employees Feel Secure, Satisfied in Job," *Winnipeg Free Press* (July 24, 2010).

19 Joan Marques, "Spiritual Considerations for Managers: What Matters Most to Workforce Members in Challenging Times," *Journal of Business Ethics* 97 (2010): 381–390.

20 Surveys reported in Kenneth A. Kovach, "What Motivates Employees? Workers and Supervisors Give Different Answers," *Business Horizons* (September–October 1987): 58–65.

21 Abraham Maslow, "A Theory of Human Motivation," *Psychological Review* 50 (1942): 370–396.

22 Frederick Herzberg, "One More Time: How Do You Motivate Employees?" Best of HBR, *Harvard Business Review* (January 2003): 87–96.

23 *When Work Works*, Families and Work Institute (April 2004), as reported in Mark Henricks, "Flextime Revisited," *Southwest Airlines Spirit* (August 2004): 52–56.

24 Alison Overholt, "Cuckoo for Customers," *Fast Company* (June 2004): 86–87.

25 Jared Sandberg, "A Modern Conundrum: When Work's Invisible, So Are Its Satisfactions," *The Wall Street Journal* (February 19, 2008).

26 J. R. Hackman and G. R. Oldham, *Work Redesign* (Reading, MA: Addison-Wesley, 1980); and J.R. Hackman and G. R. Oldham, "Motivation through the Design of Work: Test of a Theory," *Organizational Behavior and Human Performance* 16 (1976): 250–279.

27 Alexander D. Stajkovic and Fred Luthans, "A Meta-Analysis of the Effects of Organizational Behavior Modification on Task Performance, 1975–1995," *Academy of Management Journal* (October 1997): 1122–1149; and F. Luthans and A. D. Stajkovic, "Reinforce for Performance: The Need to Go Beyond Pay and Even Rewards," *Academy of Management Executive* 13, no. 2 (1999): 49–57.

28 Dana Mattioli, "Theory & Practice: Rewards for Extra Work Come Cheap in Lean Times; With Raises and Promotions Scarce, Managers are Generous with Low-Cost Incentives Like Thank-You Notes, Gift Cards," *The Wall Street Journal* (January 4, 2010).

29 Example reported in Ellyn Spragins, "The Best Bosses." *Fortune Small Business* (October 2004): 39–57.

30 R. D. Pritchard, J. Hollenback, and P. J. DeLeo, "The Effects of Continuous and Partial Schedules of Reinforcement on Effort, Performance, and Satisfaction," *Organizational Behavior and Human Performance* 25 (1980): 336–353; and L. M. Saari and G. P. Latham, "Employee Reactions to Continuous and Variable Ratio Reinforcement Schedules Involving a Monetary Incentive," *Journal of Applied Psychology* 67 (1982): 506–508.

31 Garvey, "Meaningful Tokens of Appreciation."

32 Victor H. Vroom, *Work and Motivation* (New York: Wiley, 1964); B. S. Gorgopoulos, G. M. Mahoney, and N. Jones, "A Path-Goal Approach to Productivity," *Journal of Applied Psychology* 41 (1957): 345–353; and E. F. Lawler III, *Pay and Organizational Effectiveness: A Psychological View* (New York: McGraw Hill, 1981).

33 Richard R. Johnson, "Explaining Patrol Officer Drug Arrest Activity Through Expectancy Theory," *Policing: An International Journal of Police Strategies & Management* 32, no. 1 (2009): 6–20.

34 Spragins, "The Best Bosses."

35 J. Stacy Adams, "Injustice in Social Exchanges," in *Advances in Experimental Social Psychology*, 2nd ed., ed. L. Berkowitz (New York: Academic Press,1965); and J. Stacy Adams, "Toward an Understanding of Inequity," *Journal of Abnormal and Social Psychology* (November 1963): 422–436.

36 John Peterman, "The Rise and Fall of the J. Peterman Company," *Harvard Business Review* (September–October 1999): 59–66.

37 Reported in Elizabeth Weise, "Our Brains Dislike Inequality, Even When It's in Our Favor," *USA Today*, February 25, 2010, http://content.usatoday.com/communities/sciencefair/post/2010/02/our-brains-dont-like-inequality-even-when-its-in-our-favor/1 (accessed March 21, 2011).

38 Chris Taylor, "Democracy Works," *Fortune Small Business* (May 2009): 40; and Heather Green, "How Meetup Tore Up the Rule Book," *BusinessWeek* (June 16, 2008): 88–89.

39 Edwin P. Hollander and Lynn R. Offermann, "Power and Leadership in Organizations," *American Psychologist* 45 (February 1990): 179–189; Jay A. Conger and Rabindra N. Kanungo, "The Empowerment Process: Integrating Theory and Practice," *Academy of Management Review* 13 (1988): 471–482; and Robert C. Ford and Myron D. Fottler, "Empowerment: A Matter of Degree," *Academy of Management Executive* 9, no. 3 (1995): 21–31.

40 David E. Bowen and Edward E. Lawler III, "The Empowerment of Service Workers: What, Why, How, and When," *Sloan Management Review* (Spring 1992): 31–39; and Ray W. Coye and James A. Belohav, "An Exploratory Analysis of Employee Participation," *Group and Organization Management* 20, no. 1 (March 1995): 4–17.

41 This example is from Maureen Soyars and Justin Brusino, "Essentials of Engagement: Contributions, Connections, Growth," *T&D* (March 2009): 62–65.

42 This definition is based on Mercer Human Resource Consulting's Employee Engagement Model, as described in Paul Sanchez and Dan McCauley, "Measuring and Managing Engagement in a Cross-Cultural Workforce: New Insights for Global Companies," *Global Business and Organizational Excellence* (November–December 2006): 41–50.

43 The following discussion is based on Soyars and Brusino, "Essentials of Engagement"; Kenneth W. Thomas, "The Four Intrinsic Rewards That Drive Employee Engagement," *Ivey Business Journal*, November–December 2009, http://www.iveybusinessjournal.com/topics/the-workplace/the-four-intrinsic-rewards-that-drive-employee-engagement (accessed November 24, 2009); and Cristina de Mello e Souza Wildermuth and Patrick David Pauken, "A Perfect Match: Decoding Employee Engagement—Part II: Engaging Jobs and Individuals," *Industrial and Commercial Training* 40, no. 4 (2008): 206–210.

44 Anne Perschel, "Work-Life Flow: How Individuals, Zappos, and Other Innovative Companies Achieve High Engagement," *Global Business and Organizational Excellence* (July–August, 2010): 17–30.

45 Survey results reported in Soyars and Brusino, "Essentials of Engagement."

46 Theresa M. Welbourne, "Employee Engagement: Beyond the Fad and Into the Executive Suite," *Leader to Leader* (Spring 2007): 45–51.

47 Perschel, "Work-Life Flow."

48 Brian Brim and Jim Asplund, "Driving Engagement by Focusing on Strengths," *Gallup Management Journal*, November 12, 2009, http://gmj.gallup.com/content/124214/driving-engagement-focusing-strengths.aspx (accessed March 16, 2011).

49 Perschel, "Work-Life Flow."

50 See J. K. Harter, F. L. Schmidt, and T. L. Hayes, "Business-Unit-Level Relationship Between Employee Satisfaction, Employee Engagement, and Business Outcomes: A Meta-Analysis," *Journal of Applied Psychology* 87, no. 2 (2002): 268–279; C. Coffman and G. Gonzalez-Molina, *Follow This Path: How the World's Greatest Organizations Drive Growth by Unleashing Human Potential* (New York: Warner Books, 2002); Kate Rockwood, "The Employee Whisperer," *Fast Company* (November 2008): 72–73; and A. M. Saks, "Antecedents and Consequences of Employee Engagement," *Journal of Managerial Psychology* 21, no. 7 (2006): 600–619.

51 "New Global Report Finds Gen Y Employees Least Engaged," BlessingWhite press release, August 7, 2008, http://www.blessingwhite.com/docDescription.asp?id=254&pid=6&sid=1 (accessed April 19, 2012).

52 Zogby poll, reported in Chris Taylor, "Democracy Works," *Fortune Small Business* (May 2009): 40.

Action Learning

53 Adapted from an idea by Phil Anderson, University of St. Thomas, Minneapolis, MN.

54 Adapted from an idea by Lynne E. Miller and Richard M. Weiss.

Chapter Outline

CHAPTER 8

Getting Things Done through Networks, Relationships, and Soft Power

RYAN LASH

MANAGER CHALLENGE

VIDEO INCIDENT: CLIQUES

Jane Sutton, general manager of Caffeine and Crullers, has noticed that her group of managers is not as united as it used to be. In fact, it has broken down into two subgroups, Jason Wong and Carrie Fishman in one group and Carlos Hernandez and Heather Carreau in the other. At meetings, the two sides tend to snipe at each other and discount what is said by the other group's members. Jane has asked them to stop, but they just look at her with a blank stare and keep saying there are no cliques, that everybody is the same. Jane sees it differently. And she knows until she can break down this subgroup friction, she won't get the productivity the management group is capable of.

Initial Thoughts

1. If you were Jane, what would you do?

2. What factors do you think might cause two subgroups to form on Jane's management team?

Your instructor may ask you to be part of a role play based on the "Cliques" incident.

DISCOVER YOURSELF

For those students using CourseMate or CengageNOW, you can access the Daft/Marcic Assessment Library to take the questionnaires online and view dynamically updated comparative data.

Questionnaire 1[1]

Instructions: Think about your life in general and respond to the following statements. Rate how accurately each statement describes you based on whether the statement is clearly true or accurate, clearly false or inaccurate, or in the middle as somewhat true and somewhat false.

	True	Somewhat	False
1. I feel isolated some of the time.	○	○	○
2. Friends and family mainly get in the way of accomplishing my goals.	○	○	○
3. I have family and friends who visit and support me, no matter what.	○	○	○
4. I have many friends from whom I get major help when I need it.	○	○	○
5. I am involved and know many people in local social organizations.	○	○	○
6. I am an important part of my local community.	○	○	○
7. I know most of the people in the area in which I live.	○	○	○
8. I feel that people around me care about each other.	○	○	○
9. When I go out, I frequently run into friends and acquaintances.	○	○	○
10. I can do just about anything because I have great support from those close to me.	○	○	○

Total Score ________. (Sum your answers to items 3–10, with 3 points for each True, 2 points for each Somewhat, and 1 point for each False. Reverse score questions 1–2, with 3 points for each False, 2 points for each Somewhat, and 1 point for each True; add this to the total.) Go to page 302 to interpret your score.

Questionnaire 2

Instructions: Think about your relationships with other people and indicate whether each of the following statements is True, Somewhat, or False.

	True	Somewhat	False
1. I actively build networking relationships.	○	○	○
2. I network as much to do things for other people as to help myself.	○	○	○
3. I am fascinated by other people and what they do.	○	○	○

	True	Somewhat	False
4. I frequently use lunches to meet and network with new people.	○	○	○
5. I regularly participate in charitable causes.	○	○	○
6. I maintain a long list of friends and colleagues to whom I reach out annually.	○	○	○
7. I maintain contact with people from previous organizations and school groups.	○	○	○
8. I actively send new information to peers and my boss.	○	○	○
9. I make it a point to attend trade shows and company events.	○	○	○
10. I make it a point to know and talk with peers in other work units.	○	○	○

Total Score ________. (Give yourself 3 points for each True, 2 points for each Somewhat, and 1 point for each False.) Go to page 303 to interpret your score.

Questionnaire 3[2]

Instructions: Respond to each statement below based on your behavior as an employee or student. Mark whether each statement is True, Somewhat, or False for you.

Part A

	True	Somewhat	False
1. I seem to have a larger network of contacts than most people I know.	○	○	○
2. People in my network frequently find me a source of helpful advice.	○	○	○
3. I learn early on about changes going on in the organization and how they might affect things.	○	○	○
4. Colleagues often depend on me for essential information.	○	○	○
5. People seek my judgment about key matters at work (or school).	○	○	○

Total Score Part A ________. (Give yourself 3 points for each True, 2 points for each Somewhat, and 1 point for each False.)

Part B

	True	Somewhat	False
6. I act as a bridge from my work group to other groups.	○	○	○
7. I often introduce like-minded individuals in my network to each other.	○	○	○
8. I like to coordinate the people required to complete a task.	○	○	○

DISCOVER YOURSELF

	True	Somewhat	False
9. I like learning about connections among all the people I know.	○	○	○
10. I am a matchmaker between people who have mutual interests.	○	○	○

Total Score Part B ________. (Give yourself 3 points for each True, 2 points for each Somewhat, and 1 point for each False.)

Part C

	True	Somewhat	False
11. I lose touch with people whom I do not see often.	○	○	○
12. I am comfortable with a small network of people.	○	○	○
13. I seldom reach out informally to people in other work units.	○	○	○
14. I think of non-task-related talk at work as a waste of time.	○	○	○
15. I do not try to form alliances with people in other parts of my organization.	○	○	○

Total Score Part C ________. (Give yourself 3 points for each True, 2 points for each Somewhat, and 1 point for each False.) Go to page 306 to interpret your scores.

DISCOVER YOURSELF

Questionnaire 4[3]

Instructions: Respond to each statement below based on how you relate to people you want to influence. Mark whether each statement is True, Somewhat, or False.

	True	Somewhat	False
1. I instinctively know the right thing to say or do to influence others.	○	○	○
2. I am good at using my people connections to make things happen.	○	○	○
3. I try to develop a good rapport with people.	○	○	○
4. I describe a clear vision of what a proposed project would accomplish.	○	○	○
5. I stress higher ideals and values when proposing a new idea.	○	○	○
6. I consult with several people to get their ideas about a proposed activity.	○	○	○
7. I encourage people to express any concerns about a proposed change.	○	○	○
8. I help people understand how a proposed change will benefit them.	○	○	○
9. I appeal to our friendship when asking someone to do something.	○	○	○
10. I ask for someone's help as a personal favor.	○	○	○

	True	Somewhat	False
11. I offer to do a favor in exchange for someone's support.	○	○	○
12. I give something a person wants in return for help on a project.	○	○	○
13. I am very direct in asking people for what I want.	○	○	○
14. I often praise people's skill or knowledge when asking them to do something.	○	○	○
15. I help people understand the benefits to them from doing a task.	○	○	○

Total Score ________. (Give yourself 3 points for each True, 2 points for each Somewhat, and 1 point for each False.) Go to page 315 to interpret your score.

GO ONLINE to find additional questionnaires at www.cengagebrain.com, search for Daft/Marcic Building Management Skills 1e, click on Free Online Resources, click on Additional Self-Assessments.

- Social Competence
- Four Frames of Reference

DISCOVER YOURSELF

SHUTTERSTOCK #53973379

Chapter 8: Getting Things Done through Networks, Relationships, and Soft Power

DISCOVER KNOWLEDGE

What do George Clooney, Bill and Melinda Gates, Ashley Judd, Rick Santorum, Pope John Paul II, Jordan's Queen Noor, former Secretary of State Condoleeza Rice, Presidents Bill Clinton and George W. Bush, and countless other celebrities, politicians, and world leaders have in common? They all consider Bono, the rock superstar and lead singer of U2, a friend. You could call Bono the consummate networker. Bono knows he needs help to engineer the big social changes that he champions. He has used his fame to develop a network of folks whom he knows can wield their influence to help him fight world hunger, HIV/AIDs, and other social and economic ills. Bono has learned through experience that the way to accomplish his mission in life is to know the right people and convince them to use their influence and decision-making power to assist him. For example, Bono does not have the power to convince governments to forgive the huge debt of African countries, but he knows the people who do.[4]

You might never have the type of high-powered connections Bono has developed, but as a manager, your ability to network will similarly determine your effectiveness and success. The introductory chapter of this book described the reality of a manager's job. It is less about formal control and mostly about relationships, including building networks, influencing others, and persuading people to behave as needed to accomplish goals. Managers must thrive amid multiple relationships, which makes interpersonal and relationship-building skills essential keys to your success.

RELATIONSHIPS 101

The manager's role is to influence others to get things done, energize and persuade others, and demonstrate the wherewithal to pull together a team. As a manager, you will work through others to perform diverse tasks and must hold these individuals accountable while maintaining positive affiliations.[5]

Networking is one of the most obvious and sometimes dreaded challenges aspiring managers face. Networking means creating a fabric of personal contacts that will provide support, feedback, insight, resources, and information. Discomfort about networking is understandable for introverts or specialized individual performers. Managers typically rise through the ranks because of strong technical expertise and a focus on accomplishing their own objectives. New managers may be reluctant to move away from the technical prowess that got them to where they are, and they may not understand that building a network is not a distraction but a key part of the job. The development of relationships is at the heart of any manager's duties.[6]

Managers need a high level of social capital. The role of formal education is to develop your *human capital*. Education, prior work history, technical and task-related knowledge, skills, and abilities are examples of the human capital that make each of us of value in the workplace. Building human capital is the investment we make in ourselves to make us marketable.

DISCOVER YOURSELF

Interpret Your Score: Social Capital (Questionnaire 1)

Your score for Questionnaire 1 pertains to your level of social capital, which means the resources available to you as a consequence of your personal relationships. It reflects your social bonds and sense of community. A higher score means that you have a strong sense of social community, which is supposedly becoming rarer in a fragmented world. A lower score means that you may want to develop stronger relationships that will support your endeavors. Comparative data for **Social Capital Level:** Thirty person Mean score = 22.8; Top Quartile = 27–30; Bottom Quartile = 15–19. CNOW and CourseMate users can access dynamically updated comparative data through www.cengagebrain.com.

© CENGAGE LEARNING 2014

However, to succeed as a manager, you have to develop *social capital* as well. Social capital includes the resources available to an individual as a consequence of his or her personal relationships. Human capital is about the task, which is the key to success for individual performers. Social capital is about relationships, and it is essential to the effectiveness and success of a manager. Networking is the primary skill used to increase an individual's social capital.[7]

NETWORKING

Tim Ayers, the director of global services marketing for Tellabs Inc., a telecommunications-technology company in Naperville, Illinois, devotes about five minutes a day to networking. This means he calls or e-mails colleagues, vendors, and other contacts from his 900-name database. Ayers faithfully does this first thing in the morning, or in the evening if he wants to catch overseas contacts. "My schedule may have no more than a few open blocks and even then, people might be queued up waiting to talk with me," he says, "but I just make the time." The system works. In 2002, Ayers lost his job in Chicago but soon found a new one through a networking contact. Talking with others regularly also helps him stay informed about trends and potential job candidates for Tellabs.[8]

Tim Ayers is a busy global executive, yet he knows how important it is to take the time to maintain his network. If you aren't making the time to network, ask yourself: Are you really so busy that you can't spare five minutes on something so beneficial? **Networking** is defined as proactive attempts by individuals to develop and maintain personal and professional relationships with others for the purpose of mutual benefit in their work or career.[9] The benefits of a network for you are that these contacts can provide you with information, access to diverse skill sets, and expanded influence.[10] Networking is important because relationships with others are the source of new ideas, job opportunities, business leads, influence, and social support. Today, individuals are responsible for their own career growth, and as the world economy goes through ups and downs, keeping in contact with a network of people has clear benefits. Many career opportunities are found via knowing people who are aware of openings that are not advertised. You have to make a concerted effort to network, just as you have to make an effort to exercise your body or learn new skills. Networking relationships are built on trust, cooperation, collaboration, and the willingness to give and receive help.[11]

Types of Personal Networks

"Listen my children and you shall hear
Of the midnight ride of Paul Revere."

Many of us who went to school in the United States likely recall reading and reciting parts of Henry Wadsworth Longfellow's poem commemorating the efforts of American patriot Paul Revere on April 18, 1775. How did Paul Revere reach so many people so quickly? He was successful because he targeted well-connected people with his message that the British were coming, and those people communicated the message to others so that word spread widely and quickly.[12]

DISCOVER YOURSELF

Interpret Your Score: Networking (Questionnaire 2)

Your score on this questionnaire is an indication of your networking capability. Networking is the active process of building and managing productive relationships that facilitate mutual support. A higher score means active network building, which is associated with more effective managers and broader influence in an organization. A lower score indicates that you may want to become more proactive in developing connections that will support your managerial or professional endeavors. Comparative data for **Networking Ability:** Thirty person Mean score = 22.1; Top Quartile = 25–30; Bottom Quartile = 12–19. CNOW and CourseMate users can access dynamically updated comparative data through www.cengagebrain.com.

© CENGAGE LEARNING 2014

As a manager, you won't need to share information about Redcoats, but you might think of sharing information about a new product or innovation. Microsoft founder and chair Bill Gates provides a business example. One distinctive person in his network was his mother, Mary Gates. She sat on the board of the United Way with John Akers, who was a high-level executive at IBM. At that time, Akers was leading IBM into the desktop computer business. Bill's mother spoke with

Akers about the new breed of small companies in the computer industry, which she felt were unappreciated. IBM typically partnered with large firms, but after his conversation with Mary Gates, Akers began looking more closely at proposals from small companies. One of those companies was Microsoft, which went on to win the contract for the first DOS operating system for personal computers. Microsoft became the largest and most powerful software company and Bill Gates one of the richest people in the world.[13] Now that is the power of a network.

A **professional network** is the set of relationships critical to one's ability to get things done, get ahead, and develop personally and professionally. There are three types of professional networks important for managers: work, social, and career networks.[14] Exhibit 8.1 provides a visual summary of these three types of networks. Managers who think they are adept at networking are often operating at a work level. Effective managers can also learn to employ networks for career or strategic purposes.

Work Network

The work network is made up of people who are beneficial in making a manager's job more effective and efficient. The size of a work network can be small or large, depending on the manager, the nature of the organization, and the tasks required by the position. Many of the people in a work network are not personally chosen by a manager but end up in the network by default because they play a necessary role in completing the work for which the manager is responsible. Your work network will include internal employees such as supervisors, direct reports, peers, and people from other departments. In addition, some outsiders such as vendors, customers, board members, regulators, and distributors are included because they also contribute to the work process.

The level of rapport and trust you develop with these people gives the work network its power. Consider Rose Ann Scanlon, who started her career as a private practice lawyer and then joined the legal team at AstraZeneca. Scanlon soon realized what she really loved was leading and motivating people, not just dealing with legal issues. When she took a job as regional director of the company's North Atlantic Oncology Sales division, people were skeptical. Morale was low, communication across the division was poor, and performance had declined. How could a lawyer with no field sales experience manage these challenges? As it turns out, she was just what the division needed. Scanlon "quickly made connections with people," said the national sales director. "No one had experienced anything like her style." Scanlon got to know every member of the team on an individual basis, investing time with them up front and building trust. Her approach to strengthening the work network caused others to interact with her and with each other in ways that created synergies and dramatically improved performance. A year and a half after Scanlon took over the division, it was awarded one of AstraZeneca's most prestigious awards, the Circle of Excellence.[15]

Exhibit 8.1 Types of Professional Networks

Type	Key Activities
Work Network	Building strong, trusting work relationships
Social Network	Reaching out to a broad range of people who can make referrals
Career Network	Creating links across boundaries, both inside and outside the organization; leveraging contacts for strategic purposes

Source: Based on Herminia Ibarra and Mark Hunter, "How Leaders Create and Use Networks," *Harvard Business Review* (January 2007): 40–47.

Social Network

Some people dislike the idea of spending their personal time developing a social network. However, it is through gatherings, interest groups, and events outside of everyday work that managers can get new perspectives on their careers and establish a wide variety of contacts, mentors, and coaches. There is power in the social network because of the potential referrals you may receive that will help you do your job, advance your career, or give you information of value. Think of the boost Mary Gates gave to her son's career because of her connection to John Akers at IBM. Through useful social contacts and referrals, you can save valuable time and effort by readily getting to a key source via introductions through a network contact. Typically, a social network is made up of friends with common interests who are not necessarily in the same line of work. They can be mutual sports enthusiasts, members of a charitable organization, or people who live in the same neighborhood. This diverse set of contacts can offer ideas, leads, suppliers, customers, and suggestions on how to solve problems.

Career Network

One thing that differentiates highly successful managers from less successful ones is the ability to figure out how to enlist the help of people and groups to get where they want to go in their careers. Being able to line up allies and sympathizers, find a senior person to be a mentor, understand the political landscape, and coordinate efforts with unconnected parties is how the most effective managers get things done and advance their careers.[16] Building the network takes effort, resolve, and purpose, but it is important for promotions and job changes. Whether you are a manager in business, a nonprofit, a government agency, the military, or another field, you won't get ahead without a network of relationships with people who know you and will help you realize your career goals.

You can assess the effectiveness of your network by evaluating the results from using it. When you are able to direct information, support, and resources from one sector of the network to achieve results in another, your networking efforts have paid off. Successful networkers use their convincing, negotiating, and motivating skills to positively influence people in their network to act in a way that ultimately benefits the careers, business goals, and social aspirations of both parties.

Roles in a Network

Unlike the positions on a formal organization chart, roles in a network are hard to see. Network roles make up the *informal structure* of an organization, which is the regular pattern of interactions among employees. The *formal structure* describes how things are supposed to work and who reports to whom. The informal network is how things really work day-to-day and who communicates with whom to get things done. Do you understand your role in your organization's informal structure? A senior vice president of marketing and sales had an organization chart that showed her formal responsibility over six departments. But informally, she spent time overlooking only four departments. The head of the fifth department spent time overlooking two departments, which he had been doing for 25 years. The informal network pattern was very different from the formal chart.

There are three kinds of network roles or patterns of relationships that are seen over and over in all types of organizations. As illustrated in Exhibit 8.2, these

DISCOVER KNOWLEDGE

Exhibit 8.2 Roles in an Organizational Network

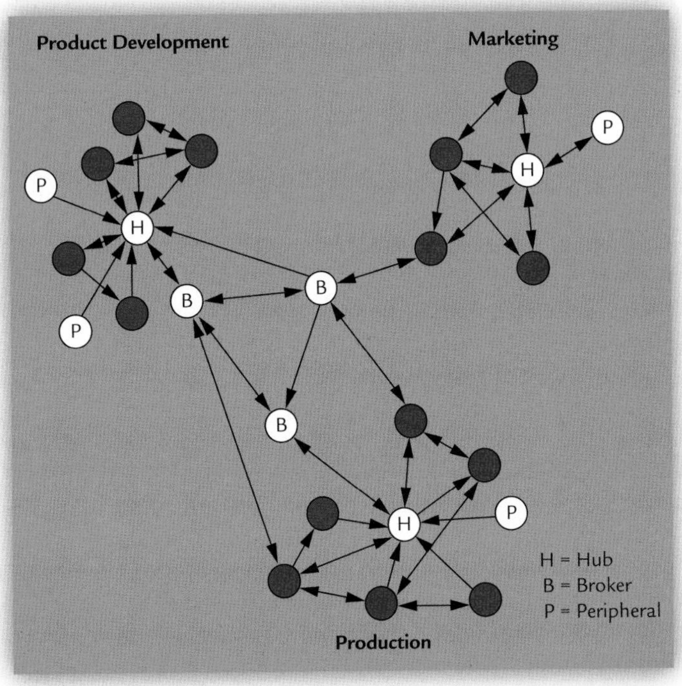

© CENGAGE LEARNING 2014

are known as the *hub*, the *broker*, and the *peripheral player*.[17] Organizations can be stronger and more effective when the formal hierarchy and informal networks complement each other.

Hub

Individuals who play the role of central connectors are the "hubs" of a network. Hubs are sought out for their information. They typically have technical expertise and organizational memory, as well as a set of relationships that helps others get information (or other resources) to accomplish their jobs. Hub individuals readily give and receive information and resources to help others work effectively, which saves time and money for the organization. Alison Pincus, co-founder of One Kings Lane, an online business that offers private sales on high-end home décor, says, "I am a connector by nature and I love connecting industry luminaries with One Kings Lane. I'm constantly looking for interesting people to collaborate with, including lifestyle icons, up-and-coming designers, and experts."[18]

These central connectors are the "go to" people in the organization. If they don't know the answer, they will know where to find it. Within organizations, a frequent purpose of a hub is to socialize newcomers to the culture and networks. Hubs help the new employee learn the culture, the accepted way of doing things, and who the key people are for various resources. For example, a new sales representative can "shadow" a seasoned representative to observe the decision-making process, make vital contacts, and learn how to behave with customers.

Broker

The role of the "broker" is to provide links across subgroups and to use these connections to integrate the larger network. A broad knowledge of how the organization operates gives the broker an ability to recognize opportunities based on diversified knowledge. Brokers within companies connect the specialized pools of knowledge by linking independent clusters together. This gives every member of a cluster better access to other parts of the company-wide network.[19] For example, a well-known investment bank won the business of a major account from a rival bank thanks to Dan, a manager who played a broker role. The client had been with the rival bank for years. However, Dan had connections to different product and service groups within his bank that the executive at the rival bank didn't have within his firm. Dan served as a link across his bank's groups and introduced the client to them, which enabled his bank to create a more targeted and customized financial solution that met the client's unique needs.[20]

High-performing managers often occupy broker network positions that bridge disconnected groups. Research has found that "broker" managers are more likely to be in the top 20 percent based on performance reviews, and they are promoted more rapidly.[21] Even though brokers may have a limited number of connections, they are able to mobilize and coordinate different groups to pursue opportunities. They serve as translators between groups because of their technical expertise and knowledge of specialized terminology within different subgroups. Brokers tend to be well-tenured, highly credible, effective translators, and skilled negotiators. Employees with these skills can be groomed to assume the role of broker within an organization.

DISCOVER YOURSELF

Interpret Your Score: Networking Roles: Hub, Broker, Peripheral (Questionnaire 3)

These questions pertain to the role you play in a network. Comparative data for the three roles: **Hub,** or central node of a network (Part A) Thirty person Mean score = 11.5; Top Quartile = 13–15; Bottom Quartile = 6–10. **Broker,** or linking pin between people and groups (Part B) Mean = 10.7; Top Quartile = 13–15; Bottom Quartile = 5–9. **Peripheral,** a less active role of someone who is more isolated (Part C) Mean = 9.3; Top Quartile = 10–15; Bottom Quartile = 5–8. Which role do you primarily play? How does your network role prepare you to be a manager? CNOW and CourseMate users can access dynamically updated comparative data through www.cengagebrain.com.

© CENGAGE LEARNING 2014

Peripheral

Peripheral employees have the fewest number of connections and tend to work on the boundaries of a network. Because of their distance, they are often seen as marginal players in a network. However, they still play an important role. Peripherals have niche expertise that is not needed on a daily basis but may be useful during a crisis or for specialized knowledge. In addition, they often have valuable outside contacts that can be beneficial to the organization. For example, an

expert researcher at a pharmaceutical company was encouraged to bring in outside guests to speak on different topics at workshops in order to bring new ideas, perspectives, and current discoveries into the company. This person's outside network provided employees with fresh technical information and external contacts.

Peripherals often have valuable insights when drawn into a conversation. They may need to be engaged in activities and processes that connect them to others so their expertise can be used by others and they can feel more a part of the company. Linking brokers to peripheral players can provide benefits to both. Brokers can serve as network mentors and peripherals can provide specialized knowledge and insight.

LEARN TO NETWORK

Reed Thompson quit his job as controller for a medical software company to start his own company, Thompson & Associates, a financial advisory firm in Wakefield, Massachusetts. He needed to build his client list so he went to his first networking event sponsored by the Winchester, Massachusetts, Chamber of Commerce at an exclusive country club. It was a prime opportunity to meet wealthy businesspeople, but when Thompson opened the door to the event, he froze. Within ten minutes he was out of the building and heading for his car. "I found it incredibly difficult to break through the psychological barriers," he says. "I didn't have a plan." Thompson knew he needed to meet potential clients if his business was to succeed, but attending networking events made him ill, and he came away with no leads. He eventually worked with a networking coach for a few months to get over his anxiety. Ten years after his networking makeover, Thompson's firm has over 200 clients. He met more than half of them at events, parties, and even on airplanes. This once shy business owner now hosts his own events at restaurants in Boston and encourages his clients to recommend his services. Thompson no longer dreads events put on by the Winchester Chamber of Commerce because he is now one of the organization's directors.[22]

Many people think business owners are outgoing, confident, and born to network, but that isn't the case with introverted individuals like Reed Thompson. Some people are naturals at networking, but others feel "network anxiety" and hate the thought of networking. It is never too late to develop your networking muscles. Don't wait until you need a job or need to find new customers to start networking—experts say to "make it a way of life."[23]

Just Get Started

A good way to get started on networking is to attend a few networking events, whether related to professional or personal interests.[24] If you would rather go to the dentist than attend a networking event, then begin by getting involved in activities you truly enjoy and let nature take its course. If you like skiing, join a local ski club. If you prefer fishing or boating, join a fishing or boating club. These activities will introduce you to people with a common interest. The other members are likely from other industries or disciplines, so it is an opportunity to compare notes with people not in your usual circle. Consider joining professional associations affiliated with your business or the business you want to be in. Don't forget that there are networking opportunities at the health club, your alumni association, and at charitable causes in which you participate.[25]

After getting your feet wet with less stressful networking ventures, you can make a strategic effort to attend events specifically for the purpose of making professional contacts. One tip Reed Thompson offers to the skittish networker is to show up early for an event. This way the cliques haven't formed yet and you can break the ice slowly as people enter the room. In addition, networking experts suggest several strategies, discussed in the following sections, that can help you be a confident and successful networker.

Dig the Well Before You Are Thirsty

Perhaps the top tip for networking is to build the network before you need it. The author of two books on networking, Keith Ferrazzi is an expert in professional relationship development. One of his networking techniques is to keep a list of people he *already knows* and more importantly, a list of people he *wants to know*. Slowly but surely he has been able to transfer the names of people such as Bill Clinton and Michael Milliken off of his *wants* list onto his *knows* list.[26] In 1999 Ferrazzi left Deloitte Consulting, where he had become the youngest partner at the firm, and went to Starwood Hotels. His goal was to become CEO, but things weren't working out because his relationship with his boss was strained. While at Starwood, Ferrazzi's typical day began with making about 40 phone calls to people on his network list. On his last day at Starwood, one of the calls was

to Sandy Climan, a well-connected Hollywood investor and businessman. Many of the individuals Ferrazzi called that day used to be on his *wants* list. Thanks to his lifelong networking, three months after being let go from Starwood, Ferrazzi had five job offers.[27]

Take Names

When you meet a new person, ask for a business card. Later, make a note on the back of the card about where you met the individual and how he or she can play a role in your network. As you get more serious about developing your contact list, keep track of individuals you meet and those you may want to get to know in some type of database. Using online networks will be discussed later in this chapter.

You can develop a habit of reading the business sections of local and national newspapers to see what is happening in your function and industry. You might save notices of people and organizations that appear beneficial to your career now or in the future. Many newspapers have a section about promotions and new hires in managerial and executive positions. To get attention in a world of e-mails and tweets, send a handwritten note of congratulations to people you might want to add to your network. When lists for the "best places to work," "the top entrepreneurs of the year," "the top CEOs," and "the year's up-and-coming businesses" come out, put copies in your networking files. If you see a good list of names on a Web site, save it. Keep these lists and incorporate the relevant names into your networking database.

Never Eat Alone

No matter how busy you are, do not eat lunch alone in your office when you are at work. Make it to the cafeteria or restaurant with other colleagues two or three times a week. On other days, make lunch appointments with contacts, vendors, customers, and friends. Keep your social calendar full. Be visible. Being seen in the company of others gives you the appearance of being someone worth knowing. Some managers think eating lunch at their desk is a way to prove how hard they work, but this typically backfires. For example, Carrie Hussan was a hard-working and conscientious mid-level manager at a large consulting firm. Her department colleagues went to lunch together every day, while Carrie stayed at her desk working and eating a lunch she brought from home. When there was talk of a sales decline and possible layoffs, Carrie was not aware of what was going on. Her colleagues exchanged the latest information while eating together. When it came time for the downsizing, Carrie was unprepared. Managers didn't know her, so she was let go. Her search for a new job went slowly. She had not built a network, so she did not have many people to call for leads.

Have Something to Give

Remember, networking is a type of relationship that needs to benefit both parties. Make yourself available to help others just as your contacts have helped you. You are in someone's networking database and they hope to contact you someday if they need help, so make it a point to give something whenever you can. Giving makes networking a positive experience, not just a one-sided opportunity to use other people for favors or information that benefit you. Networking is about people helping each other move forward in their careers and personal lives.[28] Anne Baber is the co-founder of Contacts Count, a networking training company based in Silver Springs, Maryland. Baber defines networking as "the deliberate process of making connections for mutual benefit." When you're building your network, instead of thinking "What can I get out of this?" think, "What can I give to this?" Reciprocity is essential to successful networking.[29]

Everyone needs help at one point or another in the fast-moving global economy, so sharing what you have is part of the networking code of ethics. Networking isn't just about you; it's about laying the groundwork for long-term, mutually beneficial relationships.[30]

Find a Kingpin

A *kingpin* is someone who has more information about what is going on than anyone else. Rock star and social activist Bono, described in the chapter opening example, developed relationships with kingpins worldwide and became a kingpin himself. Kingpins are not necessarily the CEOs or the people in charge. Their influence is high because they are trusted by people within the group or organization. Consider what George W. Bush says about Bono in his book, *Decision Points*: "Bono bounded into the Oval Office with his high-voltage personality and signature shades. He quickly dispelled the notion that he was a self-promoter. He knew our budgets, understood the facts, and had well-informed views about the challenges in Africa." Bush says his trust and respect for Bono grew over time as he learned more about the rock star's knowledge and commitment. "His only motive was his passion for the cause we shared," Bush writes.[31]

Bono illustrates some of the personality traits that seem to be associated with a kingpin. These traits include being bold, assertive, and self-assured. Kingpins tend to be central players in connecting critical individuals who can get things done. Most of us are not kingpins, so it is important that you learn to identify and build relationships with the people who are. One final suggestion as you learn to network: Always assume that anyone you meet today might be a kingpin in the future. You never know where someone will end up in his or her career. It makes sense to treat everyone with respect. Some industries are very small, and people's careers take them to different organizations for new opportunities. So, the low-level accountant who irritated you at your previous employer might end up working with you in your current job. Who knows? That accountant might even end up being your next boss.[32]

NEW MEDIA NETWORKS

Nick Kellet quit his job to publish a new board game called GiftTRAP, but he wasn't sure how to get the game manufactured and marketed. He learned that a former coworker, whom he kept in touch with through LinkedIn, was teaching Chinese to the inventors of the popular board game Cranium. Kellet was intrigued. His friend told him the Cranium inventors wanted to be able to work more effectively with their contract manufacturer in Shanghai. Eventually, Kellet's former coworker used her contacts and language skills to introduce Kellet to the owners of the Shanghai facility, and he got GiftTRAP into production. Through other online networking contacts, Kellet found buyers at Walmart and Toys "R" Us. He also connected with influential players at BoardGameGeek.com, who got the new game into the hands of reviewers. His networking efforts paid off. *Games Magazine* named GiftTRAP the best party game of 2008. The game has been translated into eight languages and an online version and is popular around the world.[33]

Many managers, like Nick Kellet, have dramatically expanded their networking efforts by going online with networking sites such as LinkedIn and Facebook, or focused online communities such as Meet the Boss (for finance executives), Epernicus (for scientists), or Graduate Junction, a peer-support network for Master's, PhD, and postdoctoral researchers. Saverio Gentile, a visiting fellow at the National Institute of Environmental Health Sciences working on a project concerning nicotine receptors, connected with two researchers who were working on the same issue on Within3.com, a social network for doctors. Interestingly, all three doctors were working in the same building! "Without the social network," Gentile says, "we would have never known we were all working on this."[34]

The slump in the economy has led to an increase in the use of online networking. The dramatic power of online networking was demonstrated by the Obama for President campaign in the United States, which took an obscure senator from Illinois to the White House in 2008.[35] Campaign managers used social networking, including a dedicated site (www.my.barackobama.com), to raise money, spread the word, organize volunteers, fight bad publicity, and get people—especially the young—out to vote. Recognizing the power of online networking, people from all walks of life began tapping into social networks to navigate through a tough economy. By early 2009, LinkedIn was adding a million new members every two weeks.[36] An online networking presence is becoming vital to one's career, but aspiring managers need to learn some guidelines to effectively use this networking tool.

Make it Personal

As a manager, you should use online networking tools to complement your real-world networking, rather than to substitute for it. As easy as it is to post on someone's Facebook wall or send a tweet or text message, if you want to build a deep connection based on mutual trust, it's still better to make a phone call every now and then. Your voice conveys tone and personality, and LOL cannot substitute for real laughter when it comes to establishing a connection. In addition, there is still much to be said for networking in person. Body language, eye contact, and gestures can't be duplicated in a written message or even a video. A photo on your LinkedIn profile can't substitute for a warm smile and a friendly handshake.

Anthropologists say human beings can maintain stable social relationships with only about 150 people, but online networking allows people to have many more "weak ties," which can be highly beneficial for advancing one's career. In their book, *Throwing Sheep in the Boardroom: How Online Social Networking Will Transform Your Life, Work and World*, Matthew Fraser and Soumitra Dutta talk about "the kindness of strangers," observing the remarkable fact that people will openly share information, influence, and referrals

online for people they don't know at all in the real world.[37] However, they also note that expanding the online network too far strains deeper social relationships that are important for effective networking.

Online networking is here to stay, but you should make a conscious effort to mix some telephone and face-to-face contact with your online networking.

Keep It Appropriate

Job seekers beware. Do you think the pictures you posted of yourself drunk at last weekend's bash won't affect your job search? Think again. On the Internet, you can come across as a party-animal rock star or as a professional employee. The image you present online defines you to many different audiences, so post wisely. Prospective employers sometimes use social networking sites to screen out job candidates and learn about the private lives of current employees. For example, managers hiring for law enforcement agencies dig deep into the social media accounts. Some agencies have asked job candidates to sign waivers and even to provide user IDs and passwords so investigators can access their Facebook, MySpace, YouTube, Twitter, and other online activities.[38] The practice of employers asking for user names and passwords has come under attack, with lawmakers drawing up a "password protection bill" and urging the U.S. Department of Justice and the Equal Employment Opportunity Commission to investigate the legality of the practice. The State of Maryland became the first state to ban employers from asking for user names and passwords.[39]

However, companies will still have ways to investigate employees and prospective employees online, so

DISCOVER KNOWLEDGE

7 STEPS TO . . . Using Online Networks Professionally

1. **Use the right network.** Facebook and LinkedIn are currently the biggest names in online networking, but they might not be the right ones for you. Depending on your goals, using a more targeted network may be more effective.
2. **Make it about sharing, not about selling.** Shameless self-promotion isn't appreciated any more online than it is at a cocktail party or business conference. Approach online networking as a giver, not a taker, and gradually build relationships according to reciprocated favors.
3. **Create the right profile.** Take the time to fill out your profile completely so people can get to know you on both a personal and professional level. Use words that a recruiter or others might use to search for specific talents, expertise, or accomplishments.
4. **Remember that everyone is watching.** Let your personality shine through, but always keep it appropriate. Project the image you want your professional colleagues, bosses, subordinates, and potential employers to see.
5. **Understand and use privacy settings.** Online networks inevitably mix work and fun. Most sites have privacy settings that allow you to control (to some extent) who sees what. Learn to use them.
6. **Interact regularly.** Your goal is to build a network of *relationships*, which means you have to take the time to get to know people and let them get to know you. By regularly sharing your ideas, information, and influence, you build social capital.
7. **Focus for best results.** Most sites have groups targeted to particular interests or disciplines. This is a great way to focus your networking efforts and get noticed by others who share your interests or will appreciate your knowledge.

Sources: Bonnie Jo Davis, "5 Crucial Tips for Using Social Networking to Build Your Business," *BusinessKnowHow.com Web site*, 2010, http://www.businessknowhow.com/internet/socialtips.htm (accessed March 29, 2011); David La Gesse, "Turning Social Networking into a Job Offer," *U.S. News and World Report* (May 2009): 44–45; Charles Hamilton, "Use Social Networks Effectively," *Gigaom.com Web site*, July 9, 2009, http://gigaom.com/collaboration/use-social-networks-effectively/ (accessed March 29, 2011); and Stephanie Chandler, "How to Use Facebook for Business: Social Networking 101 for Entrepreneurs, Authors, and Speakers," *Social Media and Your Business Web site*, April 1, 2009, http://socialmediaandyourbusiness.blogspot.com/2009/04/how-to-use-facebook-for-business-social.html (accessed March 29, 2011).

it only makes sense to present the image you want your professional colleagues to see. As Jim Pasco, executive director of the International Association of Chiefs of Police, said, "If you post something on Facebook it should be something you wouldn't mind seeing in the newspaper."[40] With high unemployment and fierce competition for jobs, employers in all fields, not just law enforcement, can be very choosy. Not only are employers conducting drug screens, criminal background checks, and reviewing credit history, they are now able to find out about your personal likes, dislikes, and lifestyle before they even consider you for an interview. If you post unsavory personal information and photos about yourself, it could come back to haunt you. Decide what your goal is when using social networking sites. Do you want to move forward in your career, find a date, or have the most online friends? If you are concerned about your career, then post prudently to support the image you want.[41]

HOW MANAGERS USE NETWORKS FOR SOFT POWER AND POLITICAL INFLUENCE

Former U.S. Deputy Secretary of Defense Paul Wolfowitz jumped at the chance to be the new president of World Bank. But he doomed his career at that organization from the start. Most World Bank leaders had been in their positions for many years when Wolfowitz arrived, and they were accustomed to "promoting each other's interests and scratching each other's backs," as one board member put it. Wolfowitz came in and tried to assert his own ideas, goals, and formal authority without considering the interests, ideas, and goals of others. He quickly alienated much of the World Bank leadership team and board by adopting a single-minded position on key issues and refusing to consider alternative views. Rather than attempting to persuade others to his way of thinking, Wolfowitz issued directives to senior bank officers, either personally or through his handpicked managers. Several high-level officers resigned following disputes with the new president. Eventually, the board asked for Wolfowitz's resignation.[42]

The fundamental challenge of management is to figure out how to get things done with and through other people. Paul Wolfowitz failed because he tried to wield power without building the necessary relationships he needed to assert influence. Being in a position of authority justifies a boss to use the power and formal authority attached to his or her position. However, that isn't typically the best way to get people to do what you want. Jeffrey Immelt, CEO of General Electric, considers himself a failure if he exercises his formal authority more than seven or eight times a year. The rest of the time, Immelt uses softer means to persuade and influence others and to resolve conflicting ideas and opinions.[43]

Exhibit 8.3 illustrates five types of manager power, categorized as either *hard power* or *soft power*. Hard power is power that stems largely from a person's position of authority. Hard power includes legitimate, reward, and coercive power, which are defined largely by the organization's policies and procedures. How

DISCOVER KNOWLEDGE

What's Your Problem?

Q: I work in a software company as an engineer. In my five years there, I've seen how other people get listened to more than I do. Often my ideas for a new product, a software improvement, or even just a way to get our work done more efficiently—well, no one seems to notice. But then there's Jason, the wonder boy, who spends time talking people up. The boss always listens to him, even when he makes no sense. What do I do?

A: I suspect Jason has better networking skills than you do. He probably understands the power of helping people to like him, helping people out, and so on. You've heard the saying, "If you continue to do what you've done, you'll continue to get what you got." So, try some new behaviors. Reach out to your boss, ask for advice, listen, go to lunch with coworkers. Develop alliances with people. Be interested in their ideas, their lives. You will likely find, then, that your ideas begin to carry more weight with them.

© CENGAGE LEARNING 2014

Exhibit 8.3 Soft and Hard Manager Power

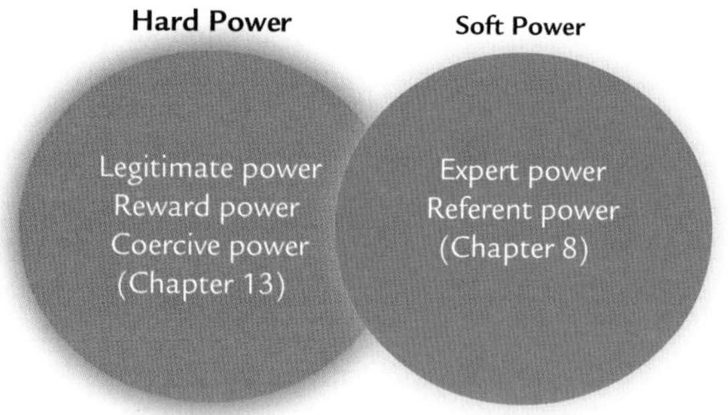

© CENGAGE LEARNING 2014

to appropriately use hard power will be discussed in Chapter 13. Effective managers don't rely solely on the hard power of their formal position to influence others, but instead frequently use softer means of persuasion.

What Is Soft Power?

The majority of work in organizations is accomplished through soft power rather than hard power. **Soft power** is based on building positive relationships and personal credibility. Managers can use social or political influence, for example, to gain agreement for a new initiative, secure a consensus for a change in strategy, or win concessions from a difficult vendor.[44] A few charismatic individuals seem naturally able to convince, sell, influence, and persuade any audience, whether they hold a formal position of authority or not. Most managers, though, have to learn the basic principles of social influence and how to use soft power. As illustrated in Exhibit 8.3, soft power includes expert power and referent power, which are based on personal characteristics and interpersonal relationships more than on a position of authority.

Referent Power

This kind of power comes from a manager's personality characteristics that command others' identification, respect, and admiration so much so that people want to emulate the manager. When employees admire a supervisor because of the way he or she deals with them, the influence is based on referent power. This type of power depends on the manager's personal characteristics, not on a formal title or position. For example, Steve Jobs clearly had strong position power during his tenure as the CEO of Apple, but it was referent and expert power that made him one of the most famous and powerful leaders in the world.[45]

Expert Power

Power resulting from a manager's special knowledge or skill regarding tasks performed by followers is called expert power. When a manager is a true expert, people go along with recommendations because of the manager's superior knowledge and credibility. For example, in a manufacturing setting, managers at supervisory levels often have experience in the production process that gets them promoted to management. At more senior levels of management, though, executives may lack expert power because they were appointed to their position because of education or management experience in business. Subordinates often know more about technical details than they do. People throughout the organization with expertise and knowledge can use it to influence or place limits on decisions made by people above them who are less technically astute.

The Value of Soft Power

Soft power, more than ever, is the influence tool of effective managers. Even the United States military stresses the importance of building relationships rather than using brute force. Former Defense Secretary Robert Gates, for instance, said that in the battle for hearts and minds abroad, the United States has to be "good at listening to others" rather than just good at kicking down doors, and the Army's revised stability operations field manual openly talks about the value of soft power.[46] Wesley Clark, former supreme commander of NATO who led the mission against Serbian President Slobodan Milosevic, suggests that, for leaders in businesses as well as nations, building a community of shared interests should be the first choice, rather than using threats, intimidation, and raw hard power.[47]

Build Your Soft Power for Social and Political Influence

As a manager you will be well served by remembering one point: Successful change results from a *coalition* of people rather than the actions of a single individual. Building coalitions is the domain of political influence and soft power, which are often seen as the same. *Soft-power management* or *political influence* involves assembling a coalition of people who support the manager's goals and who help influence others to implement the manager's decisions and objectives.[48]

Soft-power managers build alliances and partnerships via positive relationships both within and outside the organization. These managers spend time learning others' views and establishing mutually beneficial associations. Soft-power managers often use three actions, discussed in the following sections, to build effective coalitions that will support major changes in organizational strategy, structure, or business processes.

Soft-power managers conduct lots of interviews. To build a political coalition for change, managers conduct informal interviews with stakeholders from across the organization to gather information and get a clear sense of the challenges and opportunities they face. Asking open-ended questions and listening to others enables the manager to learn about the needs and goals of others, find out who believes in and supports the change, who might be opposed and why, and who has ideas, opinions, and expertise that can contribute to accomplishing the desired goals. In addition to interviews, managers talk informally with people whenever they get a chance.

For example, Jim Goetz, CIO of ServiceMaster, wanted to develop an Internet-based system for collecting, reporting, and sharing information and delivering Six Sigma improvements to customers. Goetz understood that some managers in the branches and divisions, who were accustomed to initiating and implementing their own projects, wouldn't be happy about a centralized information technology (IT) system. So, after a grueling ten-hour day of meetings to discuss the new Six Sigma initiative, Goetz headed for the hotel lobby rather than his room. He approached people from all divisions and talked with them over a beer or a coffee, probing for their feelings about the Six Sigma initiative, their goals and interests, and their expectations for how IT could help them meet their own department's objectives. Several hours later, as Goetz finally settled in his room, he understood the major challenges he faced. More importantly, he also now had a good idea of who were his allies and who was strongly opposed. He was already formulating ideas for how he could bring other people into a coalition by aligning the project with their specific interests.[49]

Soft-power managers develop a map of stakeholder buy-in. Managers typically find that some people strongly support their goals and plans, some people adamantly oppose them, and a large percentage are in the middle. As illustrated in Exhibit 8.4, when mapping the level of buy-in for any significant change, about 10 percent of people can typically be classified as *advocates*. These stakeholders inside and outside the organization are strong supporters and will help lead the change effort. Another 10 percent might be considered *partners*, people who support and encourage the change but will not actively lead it. Twenty percent are typically strongly opposed to the change. These *resisters* might even disrupt or sabotage change efforts. The remaining 60 percent are classified as *observers* because they have a neutral attitude toward the proposed ideas and changes. By knowing who is in each category, a manager knows where to focus his or her energy for a new initiative.

Soft-power managers break down barriers and promote cross-silo cooperation. The final critical step in using soft power to build coalitions is to break down barriers and promote cooperation and collaboration across departments, divisions, and levels. For example, when Colin Powell was U.S. Chairman of the Joint Chiefs of Staff, he regularly brought together the heads of the Army, Air Force, Navy, and Marines so they could understand

LEADING WORDS

"A genuine leader is not a searcher for consensus but a molder of consensus."

—Martin Luther King, Jr.

Baptist minister and leader of the Civil Rights movement in the United States

"More business decisions occur over lunch and dinner than at any other time, yet no MBA courses are given on the subject."

—Peter Drucker

highly influential management scholar, consultant, author, and teacher

"The successful networkers I know, the ones receiving tons of referrals and feeling truly happy about themselves, continually put the other person's needs ahead of their own."

—Bob Burg

motivational speaker and author of *It's Not About You*

"I destroy my enemy by making him my friend."

—Abraham Lincoln

16th President of the United States

© CENGAGE LEARNING 2014

Exhibit 8.4 Mapping Stakeholder Buy-In

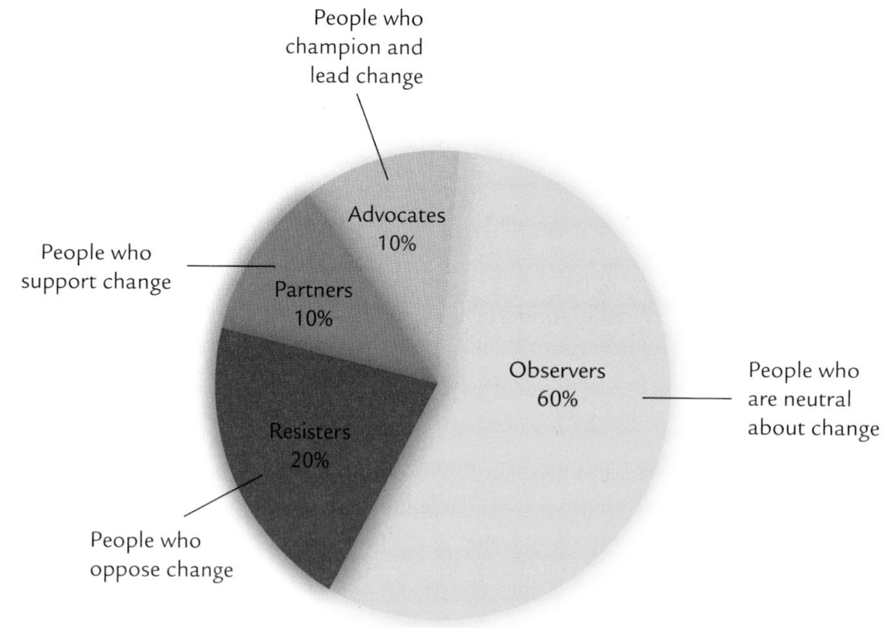

Source: Data are adapted from materials supplied by ExperiencePoint, Inc., in conjunction with the GlobalTech simulation, 2007.

one another's viewpoints.[50] Cross-enterprise understanding and cooperation is essential to achieving a larger vision.

Techniques for Applying Soft Power and Political Influence

Mellody Hobson, the president of mutual fund company Ariel Investments, started at the company as a student intern and joined full time after college graduation. She immediately started networking, making friends and supporters that she's kept to this day. Even when she was a 25-year-old new employee, Hobson was able to influence Ariel founder John Rogers and board members regarding a critical strategic decision—to strengthen Ariel as a brand focused on value investing by separating it from the Calvert Group, which focused on social investing (the two firms were involved in a joint venture). Rogers was initially taken aback by Hobson's boldness, but Hobson used information, networking, and personal persuasion to convince him it was the right decision. "She went out and did a lot of heavy lifting and convinced our board and myself it was the right thing to do," Rogers says.[51]

Mellody Hobson had little formal power as a young Ariel employee, but she already understood how to use political influence to get things done. As a manager, it is critical that you understand basic principles of influence that can cause people to change their attitudes or behaviors. Exhibit 8.5 illustrates six principles that rely on the use of soft power for asserting influence.

Tie Your Request to a Higher Purpose

One effective way to motivate people to enact new behaviors or make significant changes is to frame the request in a way that emphasizes the mission or higher purpose of the change.[52] Change is often painful and difficult, so providing people with *meaning* can help them see the effort as worthwhile. For example, Matt VanVranken, president of Spectrum Health Systems, needed a way to influence 10,000 overworked, stressed-out health-care professionals to go beyond their basic job descriptions and provide exceptional patient service. One key approach VanVranken uses to influence people to make the right decision rather than the expedient decision is to connect what they do to individual patients. Every so often, VanVranken brings groups of employees together to hear former patients talk about their experiences and how the actions of individual workers affected their health and well-being.[53]

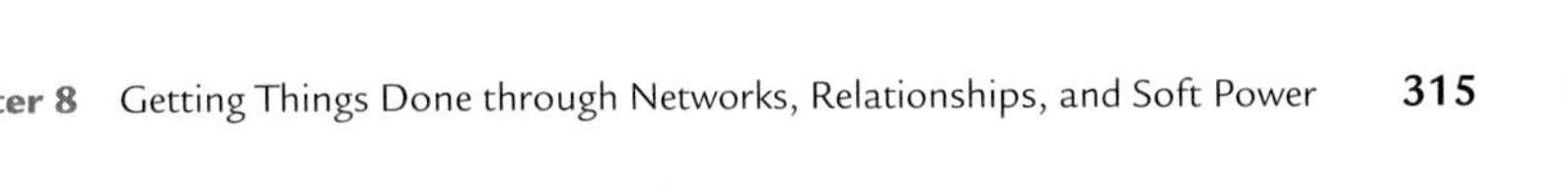

Exhibit 8.5 Six Principles for Asserting Influence

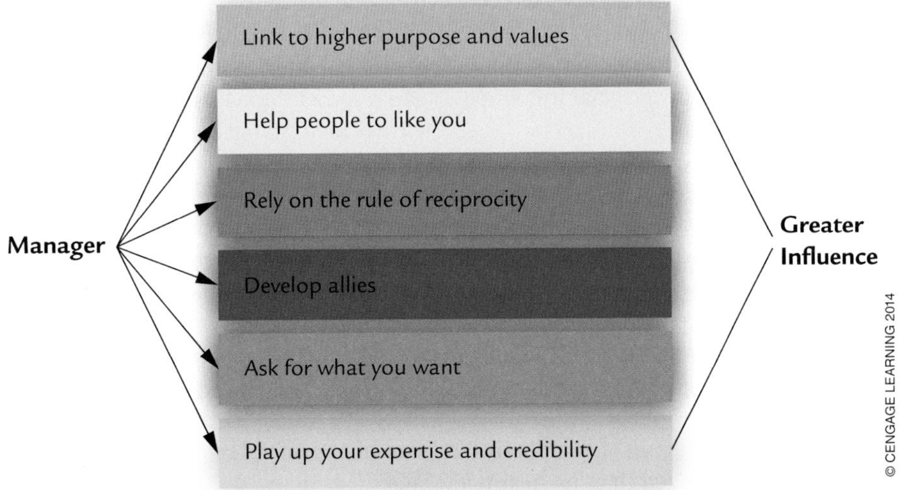

© CENGAGE LEARNING 2014

Help People to Like You

We all know it's easier to say yes to someone we like than to someone we don't like. It's important to create a bond with those you work with to promote goodwill and cooperation. Take, for instance, the "Tupperware phenomenon." Many women are familiar with being invited by a friend, coworker, or relative to a party selling cookware, lingerie, toys, or cosmetics. This type of demonstration party is where a hostess displays an array of products and distributes catalogs in an effort to sell as much product as possible to receive points or free products. In the *Journal of Consumer Research*, researchers reported that the guests' affinity for their hostess weighed twice as heavily in their purchase decisions as their fondness for the products they bought. This means that party attendees purchase items not just to please themselves but primarily to please their hostess.[54]

> **DISCOVER YOURSELF**
>
> **Interpret Your Score: Soft Power** (Questionnaire 4)
>
> Your score reflects your use of *soft power* to influence others. Soft power or political influence can be more effective than hard power for many managers. Soft power approaches include instinct (Question 1), consulting with others and building a coalition for support (Questions 2, 6, 7), using friendships (Questions 9,10), helping people like you (Questions 3,14), showing benefits (Question 15), making an inspirational appeal (Questions 4, 5), offering something in exchange (Questions 11,12), and being assertive (Question13). Comparative data for the **Use of Soft Power:** Thirty person Mean score = 35.4; Top Quartile = 39–52; Bottom Quartile = 22–32.
>
> If you scored high on soft power, which tactics do you use most? If you scored low, which approaches would you like to use more? CNOW and CourseMate users can access dynamically updated comparative data through www.cengagebrain.com.

© CENGAGE LEARNING 2014

Rely on the Rule of Reciprocity

A primary way to gain social influence is to share what you have—whether it is time, resources, services, or emotional support. There is much research indicating that most people feel a sense of obligation to give something back in return for favors others do for them.[55] This is one reason why organizations like Northrup Grumman, Kraft Foods, and Pfizer make donations to the favorite charities of House and Senate members. Corporate executives attempt to curry favor with lawmakers by doing well for them and hoping to receive legislative consideration in return that will benefit their business.[56] The "unwritten law of reciprocity" means that managers who are generous toward others can expect others to do favors for them in return. Soft-power managers elicit the cooperative

and sharing behavior they want from others by demonstrating it with their own actions. By setting an example of trust, cooperation, or grace, a manager sets the pace for office behavior.[57] Some researchers argue that the concept of exchange—giving something of value for what you want—is the basis of all social influence tactics.[58]

Develop Allies

Allies are people who speak up and actively help the manager accomplish his or her goals. You can develop allies by taking the time to talk with people outside of formal meetings to explain your point of view and understand other people's needs and concerns.[59] Managers can expand their network of allies by also reaching out to establish contact with new people. When employees hear a peer speak up in support of an initiative, they are more likely to be persuaded than by hearing another pitch from the boss.[60]

One study found that political skill, particularly the ability to develop allies, has a positive impact on both followers' perceptions of the manager's abilities as well as on the actual, objective performance of the work unit.[61] Sheila Bair, former chairman of the Federal Deposit Insurance Corporation (FDIC), is an expert at developing allies. Bair enhanced both her reputation and the power of the FDIC by courting people to support her views on how to fix the troubled U.S. financial system. Bair was one of the first in Washington, D.C., to propose helping distressed homeowners with loan modifications, and she stood her ground against intense criticism. "She very likely will be the only agency head to come out of this crisis with an enhanced reputation," said Carmen Fine, president and chief executive of the Independent Community Bankers of America. *Forbes* magazine ranked Bair the second-most powerful woman in the world, behind only German Chancellor Angela Merkel. People who have negotiated with her say she is always willing to listen. "We don't always agree," said Carmen Fine, "but her door has always been open and she consults with everyone."[62]

Ask for What You Want

If you "hem and haw" as if afraid to ask for exactly what you want, you are not building soft power. Sheila Bair employs this straightforward technique for influencing people, which is to be clear about what you want and openly ask for it. Even opponents praise her knack for being forceful at the right times in order to achieve her goals. Bair obtained greater power for the FDIC (and for herself) partly because she clearly asked for it. If managers do not ask, they seldom receive. Political activity is effective only when the manager's vision, goals, and desired changes are made explicit so others can respond. Managers can use their courage to be assertive, saying what they believe to persuade others. An explicit request may be accepted simply because other people have no better alternatives. Also, an explicit request for change or for a specific decision will often receive favorable treatment because other options are less well defined. Effective social and political influence requires sufficient forcefulness and risk-taking to at least ask for your desired outcome.[63]

Play Up Your Expertise and Credibility

The final principle for asserting influence is the manager's legitimacy in the organization. A key source of soft power influence is to be knowledgeable, credible, and trustworthy. Managers who become known for their expertise, who are honest and straightforward with others, who know what they are doing, and who inspire trust can exert greater influence than those who are not seen as credible.[64] But don't assume your expertise is self-evident. As a manager, you should make the effort to show your expertise *before* you need to exert influence so people will defer to you when the time comes. Consider that when a television news program or newspaper article presents an acknowledged expert's views on a topic, the effect on public opinion is dramatic. According to a study described in the *Public Opinion Quarterly*, a single expert-opinion news story published in *The New York Times* is associated with a 2 percent shift in public opinion nationwide. Previously, researchers reported that when an expert's view was aired widely on television there was as much as a 4 percent shift in public opinion.[65] Effective soft-power managers realize that influence depends heavily on their perceived credibility and legitimacy.

Good managers use their understanding of soft-power tactics to assert influence and get things done. When managers ignore social and political influence, they may find themselves failing to accomplish goals without understanding why, as Paul Wolfowitz did at World Bank. Do you want to be like Paul Wolfowitz? Or would you rather be as influential in your organization as Bono, Mellody Hobson, or Sheila Bair are in their endeavors? Learn to network and use soft power, and you are well on your way to success as an influential manager.

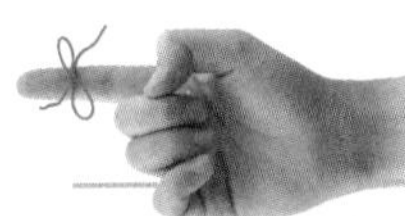

NEED TO KNOW

- Networking builds social capital and provides you with information, access to diverse skills, and expanded influence. If you want to succeed as a manager, you must learn to network. Three types of networks found in organizations are work, social, and career. You might be a hub, a broker, or a peripheral player, three distinct network roles. Many highly successful managers play the broker role.
- If you're uncomfortable with networking, start slowly by participating in low-stress activities and events that give you opportunities to meet new people. You can be an effective networker by remembering these tips: Build a network before you need it; create a list of contacts and people you want to add to your network; never eat lunch alone; help others as you expect them to help you; and find a kingpin.
- Many people have expanded their networks dramatically by using online networking sites such as Facebook or LinkedIn. Online networking should supplement, rather than replace, your real-world networking. In addition, when networking online, remember to make it personal and to keep it appropriate and professional.
- Managers use networks to influence people with soft power rather than hard power. Soft power includes expert power and referent power. Six influence tactics that use soft power are to tie your requests to a higher mission and values; help people to like you; rely on the rule of reciprocity; develop allies; ask for what you want; and play up your expertise and credibility.

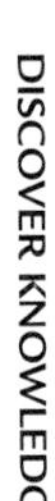

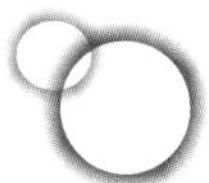

ACTION LEARNING

DELIBERATE PRACTICE EXERCISES

Soft Power Influence

Understanding how people influence you and how you influence others can make you more effective in your relationships. This exercise will help you gain greater awareness and give you a chance to practice some influence skills.

Step 1: During the next few days, notice when others try to influence you, or you try to influence others. What tactics are used?

Step 2: Intentionally try to influence another person by using a tactic you *typically use*. The situation can be as simple as influencing where to go for lunch or what route to take in a car. Push harder with your influence tactic than normal. What happened?

Step 3: Intentionally attempt to influence another person by using an influence tactic you *typically do not use*. What happened? Did it work? What were you thinking and feeling?

Step 4: Fill out the tables below based on the information you gathered.

When Others Tried to Influence You

Incident	What was the situation?	What tactics were used?	What was the outcome?
1			
2			
3			
4			
5			

When You Tried to Influence Others

Incident	What was the situation?	What tactics did you use?	What was the outcome?
1			
2			
3			
4			
5			

Step 5: How did you feel about others trying to influence you?

Step 6 (Optional): Share your insights with a partner, and ask your partner what insights he or she gained.

Learn to Network Better

This Deliberate Practice exercise is available online at www.cengagebrain.com.

My Networks

Step 1: Fill out the table below to see the extent of your network. Refer to the text discussion of types of networks on pages 303–305 for more information. Put at least one name in each frame if possible. If you have more than one name, include others as well.

Type of network	Names of people in your network
Work network	
Social network	
Career network	

Step 2: If you had blank spaces, why is that?

How can you make sure you have at least three people in each category? Develop some steps you can take to do so.

Circles of Influence

This Deliberate Practice exercise is available online at www.cengagebrain.com.

ACTION LEARNING

IN-CLASS TEAM EXERCISE

SHUTTERSTOCK #53973379

Power Dynamics[66]

This is an exercise in which you will learn to use your powers of persuasion in a situation that may feel familiar to you.

Step 1: Your instructor will divide you into three groups.

Step 2: Each person gives a dollar bill to the instructor. Two-thirds of the money will go to the "top" group and the other one-third to the middle group.

Group Tasks

Top Group: To be responsible for the overall effectiveness of the organization and learning from the simulation, and to decide how to use its money.

Middle Group: To assist the Top Group in providing for the overall welfare of the organization, and to decide how to use its money.

Bottom Group: To identify its resources and to decide how best to assist in the overall effectiveness of the organization.

For Everyone: Use your time to figure out how your group will best complete its task.

Step 3: Instructor assigns each group to its "space." Everyone reads the rules for the simulation exercise.

Rules

1. Members of the top group are free to enter the space of either of the other groups and to communicate whatever they wish, whenever they wish, with anyone.
2. Members of the middle group may enter the space of the bottom group whenever they wish but must request permission to enter the top group's space (which the top group can refuse).
3. The bottom group has the right to "knock on the door" of the middle group and request permission to communicate with them. (This can also be refused.)
4. Members of the top group have the authority to make any changes in the rules they wish, at any time, with or without notice.

Step 4: Conduct the simulation as directed by the instructor.

Step 5: Afterwards, each group chooses two representatives who will go to the front of the class and discuss the following with the instructor:

1. What happened?
2. What did you learn about persuasiveness and power?
3. What seemed familiar to you?
4. What did people do to gain more power?

FIELD TEAM EXERCISE

Developing Trust and Relationships

This is an exercise to demonstrate how you can develop deeper relationships with people, and how trust and authenticity play an important part in this development.

Step 1: Divide into groups of two. Set up a time to meet in a relatively quiet place.

Step 2: Person #1 asks a question from the list at the end of this exercise that Person #2 answers. Then Person #2 asks a question that Person #1 answers. Keep rotating with the asking of questions for about an hour.

Guidelines

You must both agree to follow these guidelines:

1. Anything said must be held in confidence.
2. You do not have to answer every question.
3. Do not ask a question of your partner that you would not be willing to answer yourself.
4. Do not write down answers to the questions, but rather give answers back in conversation.

Step 3: After you've finished asking and answering the questions to one another, talk about the exercise. What was it like to share? What did you learn about relationship building?

Questions

Choose any questions from this list.

1. Who is the most important person in your life?
2. Why did you want to study your major?
3. As a child, what did you want to be when you grew up?
4. Are you proud of your grades?
5. What was the most successful experience you've had?
6. How do you have fun?
7. How do you cope with stress?
8. Describe your parents.
9. Do you have or want children?
10. Who is your best friend?
11. Has anyone betrayed your trust?
12. If you could be anything you wanted, what would it be?
13. What are you most proud of in your work life?
14. What are you most proud of in your personal life?
15. What do you value most?
16. What has been your favorite course? The worst?
17. Where would you really like to live?
18. What do you want to be doing ten years from now?
19. What makes you angry or annoyed?
20. What is difficult for you?
21. What kinds of people do you like best?
22. Are you a religious person?
23. Are you always truthful?
24. Do you have a romantic relationship?
25. Are there situations where men are better than women? Or women better than men?
26. Do you usually show your feelings or hide them?
27. What is your best personal quality?
28. Is acquiring money an important goal for you?
29. Describe a unique communication problem you have had.
30. Do you believe in professor-student dating?
31. Are you a leader or a follower?
32. Do you want to be like your parents?
33. Who was your best boss? Your worst?
34. What fascinates you?
35. What bores you?
36. What would an ideal life be like for you?
37. What do you think of me?
38. Do you like yourself?
39. What's your favorite music?
40. Whom do you admire most?
41. What do you think the other students think of you?

TEST YOUR METTLE

ROLE PLAY SIMULATIONS

Cliques

Background: Re-read the written Video Incident at the beginning of the chapter.

Instructions: Divide into groups of five or six. One person will be Jane, one will be Jason, one Heather, one Carlos, and one Carrie. If there are six people in the group, the sixth will be an observer. Each person reads only his or her confidential role, but the observer reads all. Spend 15 minutes on the role play.

Confidential information for Jane: You've got to get this group feeling and acting as one, not as two parts. This subgroup sniping is hurting productivity and morale is down. But none of the group members wants to admit they have a problem. You need to help these people see how harmful their behaviors are, how the sniping is hurting the company, and how much better things would be if they felt unified as one group. You've called a meeting to bring them all together and try to make the situation more positive.

Confidential information for Jason: You don't know why Jane is always harping about the group—all you want is for her to just leave you alone and let you get your work done. These meetings are such a waste of time, especially because Carlos and Heather keep making such stupid comments. If they would just restrain themselves from talking all the time, everyone could get back to their offices sooner. Thank goodness Carrie is there, at least, because she makes sense.

Confidential information for Heather: You agree with Jane that it's important for groups to function well, but you think this group is great. It's all those other employees in the restaurants that Jane needs to focus on, not your group. Carlos, whom you've worked with for several years, really helps keep the group on task and always has good ideas. You realize Carrie and Jason are relatively new, so that's why they are always saying inappropriate things. They'll learn over time—you hope.

Confidential information for Carlos: Why do these managers keep spending so much time on this "soft" stuff? Such an absolute waste of time. No one has ever proved that it helps the bottom line, so what's the point? And you've just about had enough of newbies Jason and Carrie spouting off about this and that. They don't know what they are talking about, so why can't they just keep quiet so you can get back to the REAL work? At least Heather knows better. She's head of HR, so she should. And you can't figure out why the others don't listen to her more.

Confidential information for Carrie: You've had several really good jobs before this and you were so looking forward to this one. Mostly it's good. But so much time is wasted on these meetings. People just go on and on, especially Heather and Carlos. They think because they've been here longer they are the experts. Problem is, they are just more stuck in a bad routine. What is needed is some new analysis of the work system in the restaurants. At least Jason gets it.

After the role play, discuss these questions:

1. How well do you think Jane did in handling this situation?
2. What else would you recommend Jane do?
3. What did you learn about cliques in the workplace?

Soft Power

This Role Play Simulation is available online at www.cengagebrain.com.

VIDEO APPLICATION

The Personal Touch at Camp Bow Wow

Heidi Ganahl, founder of Camp Bow Wow, used a highly personal style to grow her business to 2,000 employees.

Discussion Questions

1. What role does the founder's personal approach to problems play in the success of Camp Bow Wow?
2. Heidi Ganahl says there is a fine line between personal and business because she has hired friends as franchise owners. How do you think Ganahl uses soft power to maintain business accountability and brand consistency across 200 franchises?
3. As Camp Bow Wow gets bigger, how do you think Ganahl might maintain her networks and her personal touch with franchisees? Should she even try? Why?

CASE INCIDENTS

Sweating the "Suarez Effect"

Pat Talley stood and watched, with grudging admiration, as Carmelita Suarez worked the room. Sharp, charming, and armed with a personality that left an indelible memory, Carmelita at one moment had the ear of CEO Chris Blount and the next could be observed smiling and studying something on her electronic notebook with the executive assistant of a major board member.

"She's amazing," Kent Schlain whispered to Pat as he gave him a cocktail. "I like to observe and learn. She's a real education in office politics."

"We're not in politics," Pat answered somewhat defensively. "We're in IT."

"Come on, Pat." Kent teased. "Tell me she doesn't worry you. Everyone knows she's your main competition for the CIO job."

Pat smirked, took a sip from his scotch and water and said sarcastically, "I'm *worried.* Satisfied?"

As he walked away from Kent's mischievous goading, Pat's usual confidence suffered a fleeting twinge of fear. *No. I'm OK. I'm OK,* he thought.

SHUTTERSTOCK #53973379

After weeks of speculation, interviews, onsite visits by top execs, and endless waiting, a decision on the new CIO was to be made and announced by CEO Blount this week during the annual meeting. Although Mansfield, Inc. boasted an extraordinarily talented IT group, company insiders and industry watchers agreed that the decision would come down to a choice between Carmelita Suarez and Pat Talley.

To this point, Pat carried the confidence of a sterling 20-year record with Mansfield. Technically gifted, he was one of the team members that designed and implemented the company's original IT system and had been a major player throughout the years in guiding its growth and expansion. Task oriented, almost to a fault, Pat built a reputation as a guy who relentlessly analyzed needs and then charged ahead until the job was completed—usually under budget. His special strength lay in the twin areas of electronic security and risk management.

Pat considered technical expertise and competence to be *the* qualifications for the position as CIO, as he explained during a recent interview with executives and board members. "Our work and reputation should be the *only* considerations," Pat emphasized. "My job is not to schmooze and glad hand. I'm not running for public office. I'm running an IT division."

Over the years, Pat maintained strictly defined areas of work and friendship and, in fact, could count on one hand the number of casual, work-related friendships he had developed over 20 years. He was proud of his ability to compartmentalize these areas so that personal relationships had no bearing on management decisions. He considered this an important part of his reputation as a fair but tough leader. He demanded excellence and could be unforgiving in his attitude toward those with less technology interest or expertise.

The word *politics* was odious to Pat Talley, and he considered office politics a waste of time. However, at company gatherings such as this, he also carried a slight chip on his shoulder, aware that, despite his importance to the company, he was only on the periphery of this group–not *excluded*, but not really *included* either. The significance of this particular meeting—and now watching Suarez put on a clinic in office politics—only increased those feelings for Pat, making him defensive and uncharacteristically concerned about his future.

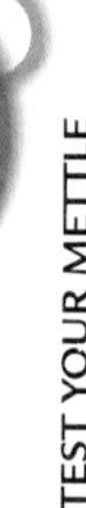

Could office politics really be the deciding factor, he suddenly wondered. *Carmelita knows her stuff. She does her research and stays on top of the latest trends and products in IT. She can handle any situation, particularly those sticky problems that arise within teams or with suppliers.* Pat smiled ruefully. *Heck, I've even brought her in a time or two.*

Now, as he stood and observed the activity in the room, he watched as his rival moved effortlessly among individuals and various groups. *I feel like I'm watching* Survivor. *Does the guy who trusts his own abilities win or is it the one who builds coalitions and alliances?* He shook his head as if to shake off the imagery. *That was stupid. This is not a reality television show. This is corporate America. Do your job. I've built my reputation on that and I'll stand by that.*

His attention snapped back as Carmelita handed him a fresh scotch and water. "You could use a fresh one," she said, smiling and pointing to his empty glass. "I guess tomorrow's the big day and I wanted to come by and wish you well. These are exciting days for the company and for IT and, whichever way it goes tomorrow, I look forward to working together. Cheers."

"Same here," he answered. Their glasses clinked together in a toast. *Dang, she's good*, Pat thought.

Discussion Questions

1. Who do you think the CEO should appoint as CIO? Why?
2. Is Pat sabotaging his career by thinking of relationship building as "office politics" that takes the focus away from day-to-day work? What advice would you give Pat, who is not a natural networker, about how to network more effectively?
3. What roles do Pat and Carmelita play in the company network—hub, broker, or peripheral player? Explain.

Outside the Loop

Nearing the end of a brief meeting with his CEO, Everett Saltzman, marketing director David Grossman heard an e-mail beep and glanced to see a message from team member Curt Bennett.

Since we didn't get to have our traditional marketing planning retreat to Brandy's cabin, some of us are going up there this weekend. Would you and Katy like to join us?

David sighed and turned back to the conversation.

"Problem?" Everett asked.

"No. Well, yeah . . . . No. No," David replied.

"Yes or no?"

"That was Curt, inviting me to join some team members at Brandy's cabin this weekend."

"And that's a problem?" asked Everett. "Brandy and Steve have a fabulous place in the mountains, although I would *hardly* call it a cabin."

"Well, I think it's a veiled reference to the fact that we had to move the planning session to another location this time to accommodate Chad's wheelchair. It was not a popular move with the team," said David.

Everett chuckled. "They survived. You would have thought they were teenagers being denied their winter break getaway, for Pete's sake. There was no way Chad could have gotten around those grounds or up all those steps leading to the porch."

"With my bad knees, *I* can barely get around up there," David said. "Tell me, Everett. What do you think about Chad?"

"He's a fine man. I admire his accomplishments, which is why we wanted him here. That résumé would be impressive for anyone, but it's more so when you realize all the things he's had to overcome to reach this level. The guy comes early; stays late. He's always working at his desk."

"Yeah, always at his desk," David repeated thoughtfully.

"Is that a problem?" asked Everett.

"I don't know. Maybe he just needs more time. He's great. He's just not fitting in. I'm not sure what to do about it."

"Do you think the reason is his disability?"

"I think folks are having trouble *relating* to Chad, in part, because of the disability," David remarked. "Initially, there was some low-level grousing when we had to readjust their cubicles in order to add space to his area to accommodate the wheelchair and a wider entry."

"Now, they all know we have to make accommodations to meet ADA requirements," Everett said.

"Yeah, they know that. I don't want it to sound like they were whining, but space is tight here. I believe they admire him. When he first came to work, Hailey, in particular,

really made an effort to make him feel like part of the team. The first few weeks she would even go down with him to the cafeteria to assist him through the buffet line. Apparently, the buffet, condiment station, and drink center are too high for Chad to reach from the chair."

"Hmmm. I didn't realize that. We'll check to see about making adjustments."

"Well, I noticed that Hailey quit going down there with him. I don't know if she just got tired of doing it or whatever, but she started making herself scarce around lunch time. He's started eating at his desk. But that just separates him once again from the group."

"What do you think needs to be done?" Everett asked.

"I'm not sure. I stop by and talk to him whenever I can. I was in there with him the other day and Trevor buzzed him and said, 'Could you come down . . . Oh, forget it, I'll come down there.' I'm sure he didn't mean it to sound that way, but it's those kinds of little incidents that reinforce my feeling that Chad is being kept out of the loop. He doesn't mention it, but he must feel somewhat isolated."

"Does he contribute at meetings?"

"He has some good ideas and he's willing to pull his weight. Like I said, I think they admire him, but I don't know that they respect his opinion to the point that they're willing to give him full participation as a member of the team. Chad did mention during a recent work review that he felt like people didn't really listen to what he said. He thinks his ideas have no impact."

"So, what do we need to do here?" Everett asked. "I hate to see that talent wasted and I certainly would not like to lose Chad. On the other hand, these people are all professionals and members of a long-standing team with a solid reputation, so we can hardly have some sort of 'You kids play nice with the new guy' conversation."

"Well. Let's move on it," Everett said, rising from his chair. "Something should be done to ensure that Chad is a full member of this team. We shouldn't be wasting more time or his talent while we try to get him *in* the loop."

Discussion Questions

1. What do you think are some reasons that Chad feels peripheral to the team? How might Grossman have prepared coworkers for the changes necessary to accommodate Chad's arrival in the company?
2. What steps might Grossman take at this point to help Chad become more included as a team member?
3. What might Chad do to build his soft power and influence with the team? Be specific.

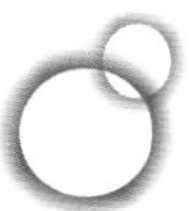

PERSONAL SKILLS LOG

Directions: Fill in the rows below based on what you learned from each part of the chapter that you completed.

	What is my key takeaway or insight from this activity?	What do I personally do well (strength) regarding this activity?	What could I improve (weakness) about myself regarding this activity?	How might I use what I've learned from this activity in the future?
Manager Challenge Incident:				
Discover Yourself Questionnaires:				
Deliberate Practice Exercises:				
In-Class and/or Field Team Exercises:				
Role-Play Exercises:				
Case Incidents:				

REFERENCES

Discover Yourself

1 Adapted from Doreen Anne Rosenthal, Jean Russell, and Garry Thomson, "Social Connectedness among International Students at an Australian University," *Social Indicators Research* 84 (2007): 71–82; Jenny Onyx and Paul Bullen, "Measuring Social Capital in Five Communities," *The Journal of Applied Behavioral Science* 36, no. 1 (March 2000): 23–42; and Alfred P. Rovai, "Development of an Instrument to Measure Classroom Community," *Internet and Higher Education* 5 (2002):197–211.

2 Based on N. Anand, "Diagnosing Your Network," unpublished paper, London Business School (June 8, 2004); and James Michael and Gary Yukl, "Managerial Level and Subunit Function as Determinants of Networking Behavior in Organizations," *Group & Organization Management* 16, no. 3 (September 1993): 328–351.

3 Adapted from Caesar Douglas and Anthony P. Ammeter, "An Examination of Leader Political Skill and Its Effect on Ratings of Leader Effectiveness," *The Leadership Quarterly* 15 (2004): 537–550; and Yair Berson and John J. Sosik, "The Relationship between Self-Other Rating Agreement and Influence Tactics and Organizational Processes," *Group & Organization Management* 32, no. 6 (December 2007): 675–698.

Discover Knowledge

4 James Traub, "The Statesman," *The New York Times Magazine* (September 18, 2005): 80–89, 96–97, 113, 120, 180, and 187.

5 Linda A. Hill, *Becoming a Manager: Mastery of a New Identity*, 2nd ed. (Boston, MA: Harvard Business School Press, 2003).

6 Herminia Ibarra and Mark Hunter, "How Leaders Create and Use Networks," *Harvard Business Review* (January 2007): 40–47.

7 Suzanne C. De Janasz and Monica L. Forret, "Learning the Art of Networking: A Critical Skill for Enhancing Social Capital and Career Success," *Journal of Management Education* 32, no. 5 (October 2008): 629–650.

8 Perri Capell, "Let Networking Come Naturally, No Trade-Show Duty Required," *The Wall Street Journal* (June 28, 2005).

9 Monica L. Forret and T. W. Dougherty, "Correlates of Networking Behavior for Managerial and Professional Employees," *Group & Organization Management* 26 (2001): 283–311.

10 Brian Uzzi and Shannon Dunlap, "How to Build Your Network," *Harvard Business Review* (December 2005): 53–60.

11 De Janasz and Forret, "Learning the Art of Networking."

12 As described in Malcolm Gladwell, *The Tipping Point* (New York: Little Brown and Company, 2000); and Uzzi and Dunlap, "How to Build Your Network."

13 Uzzi and Dunlap, "How to Build Your Network."

14 This discussion is based on Ibarra and Hunter, "How Leaders Create and Use Networks."

15 Jean L. Hurd, "The Profile of a Successful Midlevel Manager at AstraZeneca Proves That Great Leaders Aren't Only in the C-Suite," *Global Business and Organizational Excellence* (July–August 2010): 52–63.

16 Ibarra and Hunter, "How Leaders Create and Use Networks."

17 Salvatore Parise, Rob Cross, and Thomas H. Davenport, "Strategies for Preventing a Knowledge-Loss Crisis," *MIT Sloan Management Review* 47, no. 4 (Summer 2006): 31–38.

18 Alison Pincus, as told to Liz Welch, "Alison Pincus: The Way I Work," *Inc.* (July–August 2011): 112–116.

19 Uzzi and Dunlap, "How to Build Your Network."

20 This example is from Rob Cross and Robert J. Thomas, "How Top Talent Uses Networks and Where Rising Stars Get Trapped," *Organizational Dynamics* 37, no. 2 (2008): 165–180.

21 Cross and Thomas, "How Top Talent Uses Networks."

22 Mike Spinney, "Learning to Love Networking: How a Shy Guy Became a Master Glad-Hander," *Inc.* (August 2006): 38–39.

23 Cheryl Dahle, "When Networking Is a Way of Life," *The New York Times* (October 3, 2004); and Cross and Thomas, "How Top Talent Uses Networks."

24 Dahle, "When Networking Is a Way of Life."

25 Phyllis Korkki, "You May Not Like It, but Learn to Network," *The New York Times* (December 21, 2008).

26 Tahl Raz, "The 10 Secrets of a Master Networker," *Inc.* (January 2003): 90–98.

27 "About Keith," *Keith Ferrazzi Web site*, www.keithferrazzi.com/about/keiths-bio/ (accessed April 2, 2011).

28 William C. Byham, "Start Networking Right Away (Even If You Hate It)," *Harvard Business Review Web site*, January 2009, http://hbr.org/2009/01/start-networking-right-away-even-if-you-hate-it/ar/1 (accessed April 1, 2011).

29 Korkki, "You May Not Like It, but Learn to Network."

30 Dahle, "When Networking Is a Way of Life."

31 Excerpt from George W. Bush, *Decision Points* (New York: Crown Publishers, 2010), pp. 348–350.

32 N. Anand and Jay A. Conger, "Capabilities of the Consummate Networker," *Organizational Dynamics* 36, no. 1(2007): 13–27.

33 Jake Swearingen, "Social Networking for Business," *Bnet.com Web site*, September 5, 2008, http://www.bnet.com/article/social-networking-for-business/219914 (accessed March 29, 2011).

34 *Ibid.*

35 David Talbot, "How Obama Really Did It," *Technology Review Web site*, September–October 2008, https://www.technologyreview.com/web/21222/ (accessed March 29, 2011); and David Carr, "How Obama Tapped into Social Networks' Power," *The New York Times* (November 10, 2008).

36 David LaGesse, "Turning Social Networking into a Job Offer," *U.S. News and World Report* (May 2009): 44–45.

37 Soumitra Dutta and Matthew Fraser, "When Job Seekers Invade Facebook," *McKinsey Quarterly* Issue 3 (2009): 16–17; and S. Dutta and M. Fraser, *Throwing Sheep in the Boardroom* (Chichester, West Sussex: John Wiley & Sons, 2008).

38 Kevin Johnson, "Police Recruits Screened for Digital Dirt on Facebook, Etc.," *USAToday Web site*, November 12, 2010, http://www.usatoday.com/tech/news/2010-11-12-1Afacebookcops12_ST_N.htm (accessed April 1, 2011).

39 Judy Greenwald, "Employer Requests for Applicants' Online Access Gets Lawmakers' Attention," *Workforce.com Web site*, March 27, 2012, http://www.workforce.com/article/20120327/NEWS01/120329967 (accessed April 20, 2012); and Helen A. S. Popkin, "Maryland Is First State to Ban Employers from Asking for Facebook Passwords," *MSNBC.com Web site*, April 10, 2012, http://www.technolog.msnbc.msn.com/technology/technolog/maryland-first-state-ban-employers-asking-facebook-passwords-700452 (accessed April 23, 2012).

40 Quoted in Johnson, "Police Recruits Screened for Digital Dirt."

41 Riva Richmond, "On Networking Sites, Learning How Not to Share," *The New York Times* (January 29, 2009); Julia Angwin, "Putting Your Best Faces Forward," *The Wall Street Journal* (March 28, 2009); and Robert Angel and Joseph Sexsmith, "Social Networking: The View from the C-Suite," *Ivey Business Journal Web site*, July–August 2009, http://www.iveybusinessjournal.com/topics/strategy/social-networking-the-view-from-the-c-suite (accessed April 1, 2011).

42 Steven R. Weisman, "How Battles at Bank Ended 'Second Chance' at a Career," *The New York Times* (May 18, 2007).

43 Reported in Vadim Liberman, "Mario Moussa Wants You to Win Your Next Argument" ("Questioning Authority" column), *Conference Board Review* (November–December, 2007): 25–26.

44 Robert B. Cialdini, "Harnessing the Science of Persuasion," *Harvard Business Review* (October 2001): 72–79.

45 Steve Moore, "Not Bad for a Hippie Dropout," *Management Today* (March 2009): 27; and Connie Guglielmo, "What Makes Steve Jobs Run?" *National Post* (May 17, 2008).

46 Anna Mulrine, "Harnessing the Brute Force of Soft Power," *U. S. News & World Report* (December 1–December 8, 2008): 47.

47 Wesley Clark, "The Potency of Persuasion," *Fortune* (November 12, 2007): 48.

48 This discussion is based on Stephen Friedman and James K. Sebenius, "Organizational Transformation: The Quiet Role of Coalitional Leadership," *Ivey Business Journal Web site*, January–February 2009, http://www.iveybusinessjournal.com/topics/leadership/organizational-transformation-the-quiet-role-of-coalitional-leadership (accessed January 27, 2012); Gerald R. Ferris, Darren C. Treadway, Pamela L. Perrewé, Robyn L. Brouer, Ceasar Douglas, and Sean Lux, "Political Skill in Organizations," *Journal of Management* (June 2007): 290–320; Vadim Liberman, "Mario Moussa Wants You to Win Your Next Argument," *Conference Board Review* (November–December, 2007): 25–26; Samuel B. Bacharach, "Politically Proactive," *Fast Company* (May 2005): 93; and Lauren Keller Johnson, "Debriefing Jay Conger: Exerting Influence without Authority," *Harvard Management Update* (December 2003): 3–4.

49 Meridith Levinson, "The Art of the Schmooze," *CIO* (April 15, 2002): 99–104.

50 Friedman and Sebenius, "Organizational Transformation."

51 Jennifer Reingold, "The Unsinkable Mellody Hobson," *Fortune* (October 27, 2008): 148–157.

52 This is based on Joseph Grenny, David Maxfield, and Andrew Shimberg, "How to Have Influence," *MIT Sloan Management Review* (Fall 2008): 47–52.

53 *Ibid.*

54 Cialdini, "Harnessing the Science of Persuasion."

55 Robert B. Cialdini, *Influence: Science and Practice*, 4th ed. (Boston, MA: Allyn & Bacon, 2001); Cialdini, "Harnessing the Science of Persuasion"; Allan R. Cohen and David L. Bradford, "The Influence Model: Using Reciprocity and Exchange to Get What You Need," *Journal of Organizational Excellence* (Winter 2005): 57–80; Jared Sandberg, "People Can't Resist Doing a Big Favor—Or Asking for One," ("Cubicle Culture" column), *The Wall Street Journal* (December 18, 2007).

56 Raymond Hernandez and David W. Chen, "Keeping Lawmakers Happy through Gifts to Pet Charities," *The New York Times* (October 19, 2008).

57 Cialdini, "Harnessing the Science of Persuasion."

58 Cohen and Bradford, "The Influence Model."

59 Jeffrey Pfeffer, *Power in Organizations* (Marshfield, MA: Pitman Publishing, 1981), p. 70; and V. Dallas Merrell, *Huddling: The Informal Way to Management Success* (New York: AMACON, 1979).

60 Cialdini, "Harnessing the Science of Persuasion."

61 Ceasar Douglas and Anthony P. Ammeter, "An Examination of Leader Political Skill and Its Effect on Ratings of Leader Effectiveness," *Leadership Quarterly* 15 (2004): 537–550.

62 Mark DeCambre, "Bair Breaks Rank—FDIC Chief Challenges Geithner, Treasury Plan," *The New York Post* (March 20, 2009); Alan Zibel, "FDIC Chairman Sheila Bair Finds Friends in Obama Administration," *The Ledger* (February 9, 2009); Joanna Chung, "Bair Lobbies for Stronger Position," *Financial Times* (June 12, 2009); and Michael Crittenden, "Top Women to Watch," *The Wall Street Journal Europe* (November 10, 2008).

63 Richard L. Daft, *Organization Theory and Design*, 10th ed. (Mason, OH: Cengage South-Western, 2010), pp. 516–517.

64 Cialdini, *Influence: Science and Practice*.

65 Reported in Cialdini, "Harnessing the Science of Persuasion."

Action Learning

66 Lee Bolman and Terrence Deal, "A Simple—But Powerful—Power Simulation," *Exchange* 4, no. 3 (Summer 1979): 38–42.

CHAPTER 9

Developing People with Coaching, Delegation, and Deliberate Practice

Chapter Outline

RYAN LASH

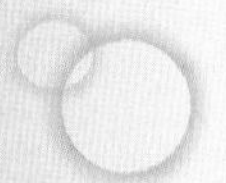

MANAGER CHALLENGE

VIDEO INCIDENT: ROUGH AT THE EDGES

Caffeine and Crullers has hired two new managers in recent months. General manager Jane Sutton has spent some time helping them get acclimated, but she is not happy with the progress of Carrie Fishman, director of operations. Carrie isn't as good a "team player" as Jane expected, but she does get her work done and has come up with some astounding new ideas. The biggest problem is that, in meetings, Carrie always wants to have the last word, to be "right," and she'll keep pushing until the rest of the group agrees to do something her way. Jane can see that Carrie's behavior is starting to take a toll on the team's morale, so she has to decide how to handle this.

Initial Thoughts

1. **If you were Jane, how would you intervene and handle this situation with Carrie?**

2. **What do you think are some possible causes of Carrie's behavior? Might anyone other than Jane be expected to intervene to improve the team's interpersonal dynamics?**

Your instructor may ask you to be part of a role play based on the "Rough at the Edges" incident.

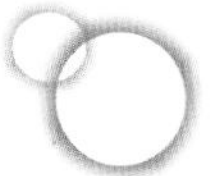

DISCOVER YOURSELF

For those students using CourseMate or CengageNOW, you can access the Daft/Marcic Assessment Library to take the questionnaires online and view dynamically updated comparative data.

Questionnaire 1[1]

Instructions: Think about your attitude toward personal growth and answer the following questions with Yes, Maybe, or No.

	Yes	Maybe	No
1. Do I have a strong desire to improve myself?	◯	◯	◯
2. Am I open to new ways of behaving?	◯	◯	◯
3. Can I be really honest with myself about my strengths and weaknesses?	◯	◯	◯
4. Do I welcome negative feedback?	◯	◯	◯
5. Do I follow through on commitments to change myself?	◯	◯	◯

Total Score ________. (Give yourself 3 points for each Yes, 2 points for each Maybe, and 1 point for each No.) Go to page 339 to interpret your score.

Questionnaire 2

Instructions: Think about your approach to helping others improve themselves and rate how accurately each statement describes you based on whether the statement is clearly true or accurate, clearly false or inaccurate, or in the middle as somewhat true and somewhat false.

	True	Somewhat	False
1. I am at ease coaching another person.	◯	◯	◯
2. I am skillful at guiding others toward personal improvement.	◯	◯	◯
3. I have a positive vision for how people can be effective.	◯	◯	◯
4. I am skillful at helping a person work through difficult situations and personal concerns.	◯	◯	◯
5. I can understand other people as if I am in their place.	◯	◯	◯
6. I comfort and calm others during periods of stress.	◯	◯	◯
7. I take the time to learn about a person's personal needs.	◯	◯	◯
8. I provide emotional support to people.	◯	◯	◯
9. I willingly take responsibility for the personal growth and development of people.	◯	◯	◯
10. I encourage people to act on their personal values and beliefs.	◯	◯	◯

Total Score ________. (Sum answers 1–10 by giving yourself 3 points for each True, 2 points for each Somewhat, and 1 point for each False.) Go to page 340 to interpret your score.

Questionnaire 3

Instructions: Think about how you give feedback or performance information to group members, friends, or colleagues, and indicate whether each of the following statements is True, Somewhat, or False for you.

	True	Somewhat	False
1. I always tell people when they are doing a good job.	○	○	○
2. I am very comfortable providing honest feedback to others.	○	○	○
3. I immediately point out performance problems before they become serious.	○	○	○
4. I explicitly communicate the negative consequences of poor performance to people.	○	○	○
5. I confront poor performance in a way to maintain a person's dignity.	○	○	○
6. When a conflict occurs, I clarify what the person is saying to better understand his or her concerns.	○	○	○
7. I let people know when they make a mistake.	○	○	○
8. I thank people for completed jobs.	○	○	○
9. I directly disclose my feelings about poor performance.	○	○	○
10. I provide a good balance of negative feedback with positive feedback.	○	○	○

Total Score ________. (Sum answers 1–10 by giving yourself 3 points for each True, 2 points for each Somewhat, and 1 point for each False.) Go to page 344 to interpret your score.

Questionnaire 4

Instructions: Consider how you relate to others in school or work activities such as performing group assignments for class. Indicate whether each of the following statements is True, Somewhat, or False.

Part A

	True	Somewhat	False
1. I freely delegate tasks for which I am responsible.	○	○	○
2. I completely trust other people to do good work.	○	○	○
3. I know and follow a procedure when delegating tasks to others.	○	○	○
4. I give assignments by patiently explaining the rationale and desired outcomes.	○	○	○
5. I genuinely believe that others can do a job as well as I can.	○	○	○
6. I leave people alone after I delegate a task to them.	○	○	○

	True	Somewhat	False
7. I am better at managing work of others than actually doing it.	○	○	○

Total Score Part A ________. (Sum answers 1–7, with 3 points for each True, 2 points for each Somewhat, and 1 point for each False.)

Part B

	True	Somewhat	False
8. I try to do the work better than anyone else.	○	○	○
9. I have high expectations for myself and others.	○	○	○
10. I am hardly ever satisfied with my performance.	○	○	○
11. I set very high standards for myself.	○	○	○
12. I have a strong need to strive for excellence.	○	○	○

Total Score Part B ________. (Sum answers 8–12, with 3 points for each True, 2 points for each Somewhat, and 1 point for each False.) Go to page 350 to interpret your scores.

Questionnaire 5[2]

Instructions: Respond to each of the following statements regarding your study habits.

	True	Somewhat	False
1. I create and use a schedule to keep my studies on track.	○	○	○
2. I am able to stay focused for long periods when I am studying.	○	○	○
3. When dealing with a subject or topic that is new or hard to understand, I devote extra effort.	○	○	○
4. I am motivated to achieve more and get higher grades than other students.	○	○	○
5. People have told me I have high expectations of myself.	○	○	○
6. Time management comes easily to me, so I am able to balance my study time with other commitments.	○	○	○
7. I typically study early in the day, when I'm refreshed and able to learn.	○	○	○
8. I continue studying even when I get tired.	○	○	○
9. I like to evaluate and strengthen my weak areas.	○	○	○
10. To help me evaluate my performance, I ask my instructors and fellow students for feedback.	○	○	○

Total Score ________. (Give yourself 3 points for each True, 2 points for each Somewhat, and 1 point for each False.) Go to page 351 to interpret your score.

GO ONLINE to find additional questionnaires at www.cengagebrain.com, search for Daft/Marcic Building Management Skills 1e, click on Free Online Resources, click on Additional Self-Assessments.

- Receiving Feedback

SHUTTERSTOCK #53973379

Chapter 9: Developing People with Coaching, Delegation, and Deliberate Practice

DISCOVER KNOWLEDGE

Zack was appointed sales manager on your recommendation. You saw Zack as a fast learner who worked well with other people. He had an excellent sales record and had been a sales trainer for two years. Zack was an effective champion for customer interests while also understanding company goals. You felt certain that he would succeed as a sales manager. Now, after less than a year, you have been hearing negative comments about Zack's performance. Salespeople are complaining about his overly cautious approach, the increase in paperwork, and how he slows the sales process. Zack is asking people to document every stage of a sale, and he wants to approve every decision. He comes across as overbearing with salespeople, insisting they do things his way. For one lost sale, Zack reportedly blamed a salesperson publicly for sloppy work when part of the reason may have been his own delay. In his role as a sales manager, something in Zack's style has emerged that you had not seen before. As vice president of sales, you wonder what action to take.

After reading about the problem with Zach, what thoughts come into your mind about how to proceed? If what you are hearing about Zach is true, then a change in Zack's behavior is probably called for. Is your first thought that you made a mistake and should look for someone to replace Zack? Is your thought to send Zack to a course that would teach him about delegation? Perhaps you thought to ask someone from human resources to consult with Zack about his management style. Maybe you considered transferring Zack to another position where he could learn manager skills while doing less damage to the sales mission. Or perhaps you thought you should personally intervene and teach Zack how to be an effective sales manager.

If you are willing to personally intervene and help Zach toward more effective behavior, you are thinking like a coach.

Executive development consultants Michael Lombardo and Robert Eichinger did a study to see what typical managers and executives are *worst* at doing. Which answer in the following list do you think is correct?

1. Managing conflicts
2. Confronting direct reports
3. Motivating others
4. Developing direct reports and others
5. Managing and measuring work.[3]

If you said number 4, "Developing direct reports and others," you are correct. Managers have many pressing responsibilities, and the opportunity to develop people often gets pushed aside in the pressure to complete other urgent work. Many managers do not see themselves as coaches, nor do they take personal responsibility for developing their people.

An often overlooked responsibility of managers is to foster the growth and progress of people's talents and

LEADING WORDS

"Of all the things successful people do to accelerate their trip down the path of success, participating in some kind of coaching program is at the top of the list."
—**Jack Canfield**
motivational speaker, coach, and author of *The Success Principles*

"The conventional definition of management is getting work done through people, but real management is developing people through work."
—**Agha Hasan Abedi**
Pakistani businessman

"An ounce of practice is worth more than tons of preaching."
—**Mohandas Gandhi**
leader of the Indian nationalist movement against British rule; advocate of nonviolent protest

"Surround yourself with the best people you can find, delegate authority, and don't interfere."
—**Ronald Reagan**
40th President of the United States

© CENGAGE LEARNING 2014

skills so they make a bigger contribution to the organization, qualify for promotion, and enjoy successful careers. McKinsey & Company conducted a survey of management development techniques. There are various tactics for developing people, and the McKinsey survey showed that candid, insightful feedback and personal coaching were by far the most beneficial to manager development compared to, say, classroom training.[4] This chapter will discuss personal coaching, delegation, and deliberate practice as ways to develop people. By the end of the chapter, you will know which approach you would use to help someone like Zach achieve his potential as a sales manager.

WHAT IS MANAGERIAL COACHING?

"Coaching is the art of facilitating the performance, learning, and development of another."[5] **Coaching** is a one-on-one interaction between a manager (the coach) and a person being coached, which we refer to as the *coachee*, for the purpose of helping the individual improve and enhance his or her organizational contribution and career.

A Crucial Skill for Manager Performance

Managerial coaching is an important skill for managers who take seriously the responsibility of enhancing the skills, performance, and career options of their direct reports.

Improving the performance of individuals directly improves the effectiveness and efficiency of the organization. Managerial coaching can correct many performance problems, resolve a behavior that is inappropriate, help the employee learn new skills, and encourage the employee to develop new capabilities so he or she can accept new responsibilities. Some employees might need more time and attention, but even individuals who are stellar performers can benefit from this one-on-one relationship and form of communication with their supervisors.

Here are some of the types of issues and goals[6] that can be addressed in a coaching relationship:

- Correct poor manager behavior, such as micromanagement, tactless remarks, not listening, always finding fault, or emotional overreaction.
- Encourage newly promoted managers and ensure their success.
- Increase self-awareness and self-confidence.
- Help managers deal with difficult people.
- Encourage growth by helping individuals accept more responsibility.
- Increase leadership skills of technically oriented employees.
- Improve communication and delegation skills.

The coaching process can determine which skills are more important in each employee's job to help the individual develop appropriately. Many of today's top executives have been coached at one time or another in their careers and can attribute some of their success to this process.

The coach's role is to actively listen, observe, question, and provide feedback. This helps the employee reflect on and improve work performance. Feedback is a critical tool used to facilitate change in an employee's performance. The coach's role is not to criticize or tell an employee exactly what to do, but rather to give the person relevant feedback and the time to understand and change his or her actions and reactions. The coach should avoid negative judgments, threatening comments, and ultimatums about the employee's behavior so the employee has the opportunity to learn and improve. The coach and the coachee together develop solutions to problems and action plans for the employee to follow.

Just like sports coaches, managerial coaches develop players and the team as a whole to win. Both sports coaches and managerial coaches have to bring out the best in others rather than do the job themselves. Meridee A. Moore, founder of Watershed Asset Management, a $2 billion hedge fund business based in San Francisco, says she learned this from a coach early in her career. "When I started managing people, when something would go wrong I would tend to go in and try to fix it myself . . . ," Moore says. "Now I realize that, just like coaching a basketball game, if your player misses the free throw, you're not allowed to go out there and take the second one yourself. You have to sit on the bench and yell: 'Bend your knees! You've got this one!'"[7]

What People Want

All employees and organizations can benefit from the process of coaching. It is a training tool used to develop

Interpret Your Score: Ready for Coaching (Questionnaire 1)

The attitude of the coachee is equally important to that of the coach for a successful relationship. Your score for this questionnaire pertains to your readiness to receive coaching from another person. If your score is average or above, you probably have the correct mindset for a coachee, and hence you would know the mindset to look for in someone you might coach. If your score is below average, you may not be receptive to coaching. Comparative data for **Readiness for Coaching:** Thirty person Mean score = 13.0; Top Quartile = 14–20; Bottom Quartile = 10–12. If you are not open to receiving coaching for yourself, do you think you would be a good coach to others? Would you like to change your coaching mindset? What is the first step you might take? CNOW and CourseMate users can access dynamically updated comparative data through www.cengagebrain.com.

© CENGAGE LEARNING 2014

an individual so the person can reach his or her fullest potential. Exhibit 9.1 shows the results of a survey about what people want from their relationship with a coach. People being coached want the benefits from clarity about performance, honest feedback, learning their own strengths and weaknesses, having a positive working relationship, and feeling supported in trying to solve work problems.[8]

Managers doing the coaching benefit because they improve their interpersonal and coaching skills, have the opportunity to work with more motivated and productive employees, and often are able to delegate some of their daily tasks to make space for new responsibilities. As the bond develops between a coach and coachee, a positive work culture is created where all employees improve their contributions to the employer. The overall organization benefits because there is greater communication between employees and managers, a higher level of creative problem solving emerges, top employees are more likely to stay with the organization, and workflow is more efficient, leading to greater productivity.

THE COACHING-FRIENDLY MINDSET

David Wolfskehl started a business at age 24. He quickly found that being top leader of his own company presented a real challenge. Feeling that he had to gain the respect of his small group of employees, Wolfskehl acted like an alpha male who had all the answers. He'd stand before his employees at weekly staff meetings expounding on what needed to be done and how to do it. But after a few years of not getting results, Wolfskehl decided to take a different approach. Despite his fear of what might happen, he went into the staff meeting one morning and did something simple yet remarkable: He asked a question! With that

Exhibit 9.1 What Do People Want from a Coach?*

1. Clarify what results and performance outcomes are needed	82.2%
2. Provide honest, ongoing, balanced performance feedback	77.8%
3. Communicate feedback based on an accurate assessment of performance	71.1%
4. Know the junior manager's strengths and weaknesses	68.9%
5. Offer expert counsel on performance improvement	64.4%
6. Develop a working relationship based on mutual benefit and trust	60.0%
7. Understand the context, pressures, and demands of the junior manager's job	57.8%
8. Support the junior manager in solving work problems	53.3%
9. Help the junior manager prioritize and stay focused	46.7%
10. Create accountability for performance improvement	44.4%

*The top ten desired coaching behaviors, based on a survey of 225 managers in 45 focus groups.

Source: Reprinted from Business Horizons 48, no. 6, Clinton O. Longenecker and Mitchell J. Neubert, "The Practices of Effective Managerial Coaches," pp. 493–500, Copyright 2005, with permission from Elsevier.

one act, Wolfskehl started his company on a transformation that accelerated the growth of his small business, Action Fast Print. "I was worried that everyone was going to tell me all the things I was doing wrong," he says now. "Once I started asking how I could help, amazing things started happening."[9]

DISCOVER YOURSELF

Interpret Your Score: Coaching-Friendly Mindset (Questionnaire 2)

A coaching-friendly mindset is the foundation for being a successful coach. Your score for Questionnaire 2 is an indication of your coaching mindset. A higher score means that you are more facilitative than controlling, more interested in developing people than in controlling them, more non-directive than directive. A low score means that you may think like a traditional manager rather than like a coaching manager. The personal relationship of coaching others may not be for you. How does your score compare to others in your group or class? Comparative data for a **Coaching-Friendly Mindset:** Thirty person Mean score = 26.0; Top Quartile = 29–30; Bottom Quartile = 18–23. CNOW and CourseMate users can access dynamically updated comparative data through www.cengagebrain.com.

DISCOVER KNOWLEDGE

David Wolfskehl learned to think like a coach rather than take the traditional approach of a manager telling everyone else what to do. A coach's thinking is that most people want to do a good job, meet high standards, and learn how to improve, so the coach adopts an attitude of helpfulness. One key rule of coaching, though, is: *Don't try to fix people.* If you're trying to fix people, you're assuming they are broken. Instead, a coach focuses on trying to improve outcomes. Coaching has a different orientation than a traditional approach to management.

Coaching versus Traditional Managing

To understand what it means to be a coach, consider the difference in mindset and behavior[10] required for managing versus coaching:

Managing	Coaching
Telling	Empowering
Judging	Facilitating
Controlling	Developing
Directing	Supporting; removing obstacles
Immediate needs	Long-term development
Authority	Partnership

Traditional management evolved as the person in charge telling followers what to do, directing and controlling their behavior, judging their performance, and acting as an authority figure to meet immediate task needs. Coaching, by contrast, empowers followers to explore, helps them to understand and learn, supports their efforts, removes obstacles that stand in the way, and partners with followers for long-term development of their skills so they can grow and excel.

Directive versus Consultative Coaching

There are two differing approaches to coaching, as summarized in Exhibit 9.2 and described in the following paragraphs.[11]

Directive coaching often fails because it is active for the coach and passive for the employee. The manager is the expert and the employee is the student. As

Exhibit 9.2 Two Approaches to Managerial Coaching

Directive Coaching

- A push to solve someone's problem by directing, instructing, advising, suggesting
- Often fails; use only when necessary, combined with non-directive coaching

Non-Directive Coaching

- A pull to draw out someone's own solution by listening, understanding, reflecting, summarizing, asking questions
- Best approach to encourage learning; also called consultative coaching

Source: Based on Myles Downey, *Effective Coaching: Lessons from the Coach's Coach,* 2nd ed. (Cincinnati, OH: Thomson Texere, 2003), p. 23.

© CENGAGE LEARNING 2014

the one with the experience, know-how, and answers, the manager tells the employee, in a direct approach, what to do. The manager observes the employee, figures out what the person is doing wrong, and corrects the employee with statements and directives. The directive approach may work if the individuals being critiqued can be motivated to improve, especially if they respect and value the manager's expertise and position.

Non-directive coaching, sometimes called consultative coaching, involves the employee in finding the answers. A non-directive coach encourages people to learn for themselves in order to improve performance and correct any weaknesses that prohibit them from becoming outstanding employees. The primary approach used by the consultative coach is to ask key questions, listen, and observe the employee's behavior. The individual being coached has the freedom to think through the dynamics of the problem and come up with his or her own answers in a supportive environment. This is how most learning and growth takes place. Over time, the coachee becomes less dependent on the coach for instruction and direction.

In reality, coaching is often a combination of the two styles. Both forms of coaching have their proper place in management. Invariably, there will be times when the employee is stuck and unable to think through a problem. If the solution is simple and clear and the coach has the answer, it is often best to offer it rather than allow the employee to flounder indefinitely. Also, if the employee is asked to use a new technology, an upgraded system, or a complex piece of equipment, then it makes sense to give direct instructions to properly train the employee. Also, when time is of the essence, directive coaching is often appropriate. However, when problems and solutions are multi-faceted and employees are required to make difficult judgment calls, then a non-directive, consultative coaching approach is fitting. Also, if the same problem keeps reappearing, and there is less urgency to respond, non-directive coaching makes sense. The employee has time to figure things out rather than having the coach give instructions on what to do.

THE COACHING MODEL

Al Rodriguez had been a relatively successful partner with his law firm for more than ten years when his performance and attitude began to decline. Al wasn't happy, and neither were his partners. When it became clear to him things needed to change or he would lose his job, Al sought the help of a coach. The two began by talking about what Al wanted from the coaching and exploring the roots of his decline in performance. Al realized his attitude had gotten worse and worse ever since he had felt slighted in the bonus program. He had begun to take everything personally and grew more and more angry and frustrated. The coach helped Al focus on his own behavior and develop a specific plan for how he would behave when he encountered situations that caused him to feel defensive or frustrated. They came up with specific action steps to shift his behavior. Al is still going through the coaching process, practicing his new behaviors on the job, and meeting regularly with his coach to discuss progress and next steps. One of his partners noted that his performance has improved significantly since he began working with a coach. The coach has helped Al replace frustration and negativity with positive action steps that are enhancing his career.[12]

Depending on the individual and the problems involved, coaching can be a long-term commitment, as with Al Rodriguez, or a short-term process that helps a person overcome a specific obstacle. In either case, successful managerial coaching encompasses eight steps within the three stages shown in Exhibit 9.3. Stage 1 is *planning*, which includes mental preparation, discussion and agreement with the employee (the coachee) to proceed, and setting broad goals. Stage 2

Exhibit 9.3 The Coaching Process

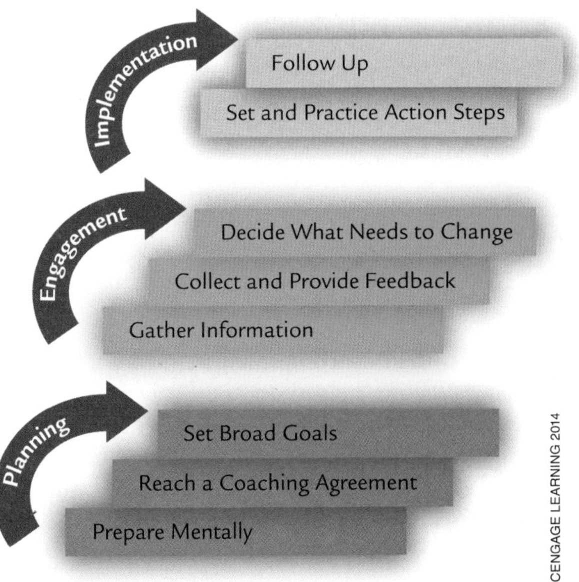

© CENGAGE LEARNING 2014

DISCOVER KNOWLEDGE

is *engagement*, during which the coach gathers data about the coachee's behavior, provides explicit feedback, and decides together with the coachee exactly what needs to change and how success will be measured. Stage 3 is *implementation*, during which the coachee's specific action steps are selected, new behavior is practiced, and the coach follows up by checking and reinforcing progress while looking for the next learning opportunities. Each of the eight coaching steps illustrated in Exhibit 9.3 is described in the following sections.

Step 1: Prepare Mentally

If, as a manager, you decide to become a coach to one or more direct reports, you will need to change your mindset from being a "doer" to being a person who "helps others do." Coaching requires a different frame of mind from previous day-to-day work behavior. Mental preparation is essential, because a change in behavior requires mental intention and practice. As a coach, you become a teacher and facilitator to help another person grow, rather than thinking of yourself as the person in charge whose job is to "tell and sell." Coaching means setting aside your own agenda to care about another person and help that individual achieve his or her goals. Many managers find this mental transition difficult, and some are not able to make the transition at all.

What should you focus on to get in the right frame of mind for coaching? When asked "What did your coach do that was helpful?" respondents said:

- "My coach seems to genuinely want to help."
- "My coach listened; she didn't impose her own agenda."
- "My coach asked me what I was trying to accomplish."
- "My coach helped me think the problem through for myself."
- "My coach told me about my strengths as well as my weaknesses."[13]

The correct coaching mindset is one that leaves coachees feeling helped and uplifted by the experience. Even when a successful coach takes a tough-minded approach, that toughness is expressed in a way that the coachee sees as helpful and motivating. An additional bonus for adopting the right mindset is that learning to facilitate the growth and improvement of another person often provides unanticipated personal growth to the coach as well.

DISCOVER KNOWLEDGE

Step 2: Reach a Coaching Agreement

Ask permission to coach. A big mistake is to start coaching an employee without discussing it first. For example, at one company employees resented the department head who suggested last minute changes to a client presentation about a $100 million dollar investment because there had been no agreement that he would be involved in the preparations. Unexpected advice typically will be confusing and cause the recipient to wonder why he or she has been singled out for criticism and instruction.

As a manager, you should raise the idea of coaching with an employee well beforehand so there is time to reflect and reach a coaching agreement. If both sides believe that working together through the coaching process will lead to improved performance, you and the employee will agree to form a coaching relationship. Effective coaching requires mutual agreement. The employee *must* want to do better and *must* welcome a coach's help.[14] This initial agreement represents a commitment from both parties.

The coaching agreement will help the person being coached understand that he or she can talk to you about a problem or performance goal without being criticized. The coachee will also understand that you will not solve a problem but will listen, ask questions, and draw out the coachee's solution to the issue. The initial agreement may also provide for putting the coachee into a different job, task, or project to facilitate learning and feedback. The coachee will expect to be observed and to receive feedback on performance.[15] This preliminary agreement is critical because it sets the scope and tone for the coaching relationship. It increases the probability of success. In some cases, the person being coached may not express wholehearted agreement, but as he or she sees improvement, the level of enthusiasm will increase.

Step 3: Set Broad Goals

After reaching agreement, the coach and coachee need to make a plan. Discuss with the employee his or her goals and expectations of coaching prior to beginning. During this conversation, it may be possible to identify examples of specific situations that did not go well or that illustrate specific behaviors that the coachee would like to improve. This information gives both you and the employee an opportunity to make sure you are on the same page regarding the improvements that need to take place. Broad goals may also include a timeline for goal accomplishment and a discussion of how success will be measured. For example, if one of the coaching goals is to help the employee move from a technical role in the organization to a leadership position, then both parties have an opportunity to present their thoughts on the ideal characteristics and challenges of someone in leadership. This kind of discussion and broad goal setting establishes the framework for the coaching work to be completed.[16]

Step 4: Gather Information

There are various ways you as a manager can gather information about an employee's behavior and performance. These are: making observations, asking open-ended questions, listening, collecting feedback from other people who observe the coachee, and using assessment tools. This is the first step in the *engagement* stage of the coaching process. It can be time consuming but provides accurate and timely information about an employee's work habits and behaviors, without which the manager is not able to initiate the coaching relationship with substantive understanding.

Observe

The best first step for gathering information is to directly observe the employee's work performance to get a better understanding of current skills, strengths, and weaknesses. As a coaching manager, you are looking for learning and coaching opportunities. You can sit in on meetings where the coachee handles people-management processes, such as giving a talk, running an informational meeting, giving a performance review or development review to subordinates, goal-setting meetings, team problem-solving sessions, and team performance reviews. Through direct observation, you can diagnose the coachee's assets and liabilities and discuss them with the employee. Then, together, you and the coachee develop a plan.[17] Effective feedback is possible only when it is based on *accurate observation or other kinds of objective data.*[18]

Ask Questions

Recall our discussion of the power of manager questioning in Chapter 5. If you want to get to know what a person really thinks, you have to ask the right kind of questions. Open-ended questions require that the person answering give comprehensive and thoughtful responses. Open-ended questions promote deeper reflection, and the answers are likely to be more creative, thought-provoking, and insightful. Closed-ended questions usually require only a *yes* or *no* answer. This saves time, but it limits how well you can get to know an employee, interpret how the person thinks, and understand why he or she handled a situation in a particular way. Naturally, an occasional closed-ended question is necessary, but a good coach emphasizes the use of open-ended questions to promote learning.

Mastering the use of open-ended questions is a challenge for many managers. It helps to practice different types of open-ended questions that can be useful for coaching. Here are some examples:

- What were your reasons for doing that? Why is that important to you?
- What do you see as the major issues with this project?
- What would be the implications if you did X rather than Y?
- How do you feel about your progress to date?
- What are your feelings about _______?
- Do you have any additional thoughts about this?[19]

Once you ask a question, *remember to keep quiet and wait for the answer.* Novice coaches are often afraid of silences and will quickly jump in with another question. Yet, without some quiet spaces, the employee loses valuable reflection time. Silence truly is golden in coaching.[20]

Listen

Listening was also described in Chapter 5 as an important manager skill. When you act as a coach, active listening is essential. Being effective as a coach means being selfless and "tuned in" to the other person, paying complete attention to what the other person is saying. Being impatient or interrupting will send the message that you are not interested in the employee. Review the tips for supportive listening in Chapter 5.

Step 5: Collect and Provide Helpful Feedback

Coaching feedback can be defined as information about work or personal performance that enables a person to change his or her behavior.[21] To help people improve, coaching managers gather feedback from other people and provide it to the coachee. To get a bigger picture of the employee's capabilities, strengths, weaknesses, and problems, collect feedback

from other people. One effective feedback source is 360-degree feedback.

360-Degree Feedback

The performance appraisal method known as 360-degree feedback gathers data from the supervisors, colleagues, subordinates, and customers of the employee you are coaching. With 360-degree feedback, employees evaluate their own performance, too. Gathering 360-degree observations is a key tool you can use as a coaching manager to help an employee understand how he or she comes across to other people.[22] Remember, we all have blind spots about ourselves and each of us is actually two people—the one we think we are and the one other people think we are. For example, when he was CEO of Dell, Kevin Rollins learned that other people saw him quite differently than he saw himself. Rollins was upset with Dell's management culture, so he asked all Dell managers to submit periodic evaluations by their subordinates and other people with whom they worked, and Rollins did the same. One senior vice president proclaimed that Rollins was "aloof, a poor listener, and a leader who at times could seem unapproachable." Another executive said, "He could be so supercilious and icy cold that his personality should be stored in a meat locker."[23] With that feedback, Rollins immediately set out to change his leadership style.

DISCOVER KNOWLEDGE

360-degree feedback is valuable because a manager has to be aware of the specific details of an employee's performance in order to help the individual improve. Stories and examples of behavior from other employees, peers, customers, other managers, and performance metrics are specific enough to create true "Aha" moments for both the coach and coachee.[24]

Take the example of Samantha, an R&D manager who was still operating like a hands-on bench scientist. According to the director of human resources, Sam wasn't delegating, was taking credit for her direct reports' work, and had a "closed-door" policy. This previously "nice guy" scientist promoted to manager had her direct reports frustrated and de-motivated. Sam's peers viewed her as rigid, opinionated, and defensive. Sam entered into a coaching relationship with the HR manager because her own immediate superior also had poor management skills. At their first meeting, the HR manager presented Sam with observations and examples from her direct reports and peers. Sam was stunned when she heard how she came across to others. Both she and the coach discovered that Sam just wasn't aware of the expectations for her new role as a manager. She had received no guidance. She didn't understand what a management role meant for her own behavior and actions. This was Samantha's "Aha" moment. She was open and eager for more feedback. She wanted to start learning to apply some of the management concepts she had heard in a training course a few years before, and to learn tools and techniques to improve her communication and leadership skills.[25]

Overcome Your Reluctance

Once you have gathered information by observing, asking, listening, and collecting feedback from others, it's time to provide the valuable feedback to the coachee. Many managers have a hard time giving feedback. For example, Declan is a talented market researcher. His statistical and data analysis skills are marvelous, but his interpersonal and organizational skills are weak. Declan spends time on his computer and avoids meetings with product designers and market planners. His valuable insights are not often included in product plans, and his career is going nowhere. However, Indira, Declan's boss, says his introverted nature cannot be changed, and she is content with the status quo because his superb quantitative skills are needed. She does not want to confront Declan about changing his behavior to enhance his career development.

DISCOVER YOURSELF

Interpret Your Score: Giving Feedback (Questionnaire 3)

Some people have a hard time giving feedback, an essential component of coaching. A high score on this questionnaire indicates that you may already have an orientation toward giving feedback, so the other aspects of coaching may be easy for you to embrace. A low score suggests that giving feedback is not natural for you, and this is an aspect of coaching that you will have to develop. Comparative data for **Giving Feedback:** Thirty person Mean score = 24.8; Top Quartile = 27–30; Bottom Quartile = 16–23. What techniques can you adopt to improve your ability to give feedback? CNOW and CourseMate users can access dynamically updated comparative data through www.cengagebrain.com.

© CENGAGE LEARNING 2014

Many managers, like Indira, are reluctant to engage in a feedback dialogue with their employees. Always remember that feedback is the lynchpin that allows a person to learn and change. Without feedback, growth is stymied. Yet reluctant managers hesitate because they think, "I don't know how he will react," "I don't want to hurt her feelings," or "I don't want to get into a conflict." These managers have a point, because giving helpful feedback requires some practice and skill. If feedback is given clumsily, little benefit will result.

Feedback is vital for someone like Declan to learn from his shortcomings. His manager should push through her fear; otherwise, Declan will continue to think his behavior is effective and perhaps not realize that his dislike of meetings shortchanges the company's product design as well as hinders his career success.

Exhibit 9.4 illustrates the **adaptive learning cycle** that all living organisms share, starting with action to feedback to synthesis and then to a new action.[26] People sense the environment, take action, and then correct themselves as feedback and synthesis indicate whether previous actions were effective or ineffective. When feedback causes a change in behavior, learning has occurred. In simple terms, a puppy might learn not to urinate in the house because of a reprimand, or a child might learn not to touch a hot stove by being burned. *Your job as coach is to provide the feedback that enables learning.* Only if the coach provides feedback can coachees learn whether their behavior is working or not working. Without feedback, people can't learn.

Exhibit 9.4 The Adaptive Learning Cycle

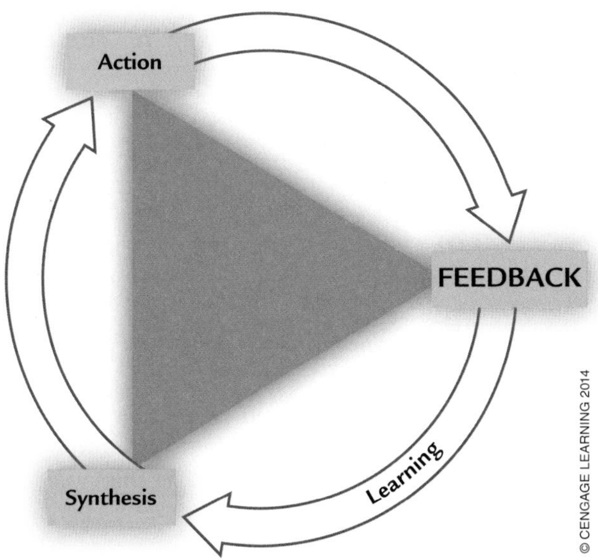

© CENGAGE LEARNING 2014

Giving Useful Feedback

For employees to change and improve, coaches must provide specific, timely, and ongoing feedback about their performance. A pat on the back for a job well done is not enough to stimulate change. Feedback needs to be both positive and negative for coaching to work. Allocating some of your coaching time—say, 10 percent—to building on an employee's strengths will help maintain and improve them. But your real coaching value will come from helping people with their blind spots and big weaknesses.[27]

When offering feedback, be honest, straightforward, and supportive. Avoid being critical and judgmental and don't make assumptions about the employee's motives. Just state facts and direct observations and let the employee interpret meaning and motivations. Communicating in a respectful, supportive, and objective way helps create a professional and helpful environment in which the employee knows you are on his or her side.

However, as a manager, you will learn that it is just as difficult to give feedback as it can be to receive it. Sometimes after people receive feedback they might be feeling wounded, angry, embarrassed, or unsure about their position in the organization. This is human nature, so make allowances for some negative reaction. Exhibit 9.5 offers suggestions for giving feedback in a way that limits people's defensiveness and negative reactions. You should also make certain your relationship is intact before the coaching session comes to an end by engaging in some light banter and discussing something positive. Give the employee time to digest what has been said and connect with the person again in a few days to provide reassurance and learn how things are going.

Step 6: Define Together What Needs to Change

An employee is more likely to change once the ineffective behavior is clearly specified. Some behaviors, such as making a poor verbal presentation, always being late for meetings, constantly interrupting presentations, or not participating at all, are pretty obvious to an employee when pointed out by the coach. Agreement about what needs to change will be reached quickly. Other behaviors, such as the tendency to be headstrong with others, inflexible opinions, or impulsively finding fault, are unconscious habit patterns that may be a little harder for an individual to see in himself or herself. Some discussion

Exhibit 9.5 Some Feedback Dos and Don'ts

Do Say It This Way	Don't Say It This Way
In your monthly reports I've noticed you are making errors in your spelling.	Are you too lazy to use spell check?
I need for you to be at your desk and ready to work at 8:30 A.M.	You must not know how to use an alarm clock yet.
You interrupted Jared three times during the staff meeting, making him lose his train of thought.	How rude and domineering can you be?
You have exceeded your sales goal for the last three months, and this is a department record!	You're the best!
I noticed a coffee stain on your weekly progress notes.	You are such a slob.
This problem with the customer is serious. How can I help?	You better get this straightened out or else.
The data show that your advertising strategy did not increase sales.	You don't have a clue about marketing.
I notice that you spend an hour at the end of the day doing record keeping. Is this something to delegate to your assistant?	It is obvious that you're terrible at delegation and will never be promoted.
During the next staff meeting, I would like for you to speak up about your ideas for how to increase efficiency on the line.	You must be afraid of your own shadow.
The schedule you proposed has not produced the results we had hoped for, so let's go back to the old routine.	What an idiotic idea *that* was.

Sources: Based on James E. Lukaszewski, "Mastering the Art of Giving Advice," *Leader To Leader* (Fall 2008): 45–50; Judith Sills, "Criticism: Taking the Hit," *Psychology Today* (July–August, 2006): 61–62; and Meryl Runion and Jenelle Brittain, "And, Besides That, You're Lazy," *The Conference Board Review* (March–April 2007): 13.

DISCOVER KNOWLEDGE

7 STEPS TO . . .
Valuable Feedback

1. **Don't delay.** The right moment for giving feedback is soon after the event. The right place is private. The right timing is to give it often.
2. **Focus on behavior.** Do not comment on someone's character, attitude, or personality. Make it your intention to help the employee improve behavior.
3. **Avoid attacks.** Avoid critical or judgmental language, because the person will become defensive and not hear you. Use "I" statements ("I felt *x* when I saw you do *y*.") rather than "You" statements ("You are wrong.") that could be perceived as critical or attacking.
4. **Be objective.** Be as specific and objective as possible. Feedback should be backed by impersonal facts and data or direct observation.
5. **Be realistic.** Do not offer corrective feedback that is out of the control of the employee.
6. **Remember the positive.** For every corrective statement, partner it with a positive comment. The employee needs to know when she has done something right so she can repeat that behavior.
7. **Move to the future.** After feedback is shared, move the discussion toward better results in the future. Ask the employee how he could do things differently the next time. Offer your own ideas if suitable only after the employee finishes making suggestions.

© CENGAGE LEARNING 2014

will be required for the coach and coachee to agree on what needs to change.

As a coach, remember that things are not always what they seem. Prematurely jumping to a conclusion about the cause of a person's behavior is a common mistake made by new coaches. Open dialogue can bring out more information. In some cases, it may be necessary for a coach and coachee to dig beneath the surface to co-discover the real reasons behind a behavior by forming hypotheses about what is going on and then seeking confirming or disconfirming information. Sometimes, people can change their behavior when they see that it is ineffective. Other times, people may need to understand the root causes of an ineffective behavior before they can change. In coaching, you have discovered the real need when the employee becomes self-aware about why she behaves as she does. This may take some time, probing with the right questions, and giving the employee an opportunity to express inner feelings. Consider the following example of a coaching incident and dialogue.

Marwan was part of a team of middle managers in a top advertising agency. He had been with the organization for three years and was considered a rising star. Steve, his manager and the senior vice president of marketing, had started coaching Marwan nine months ago to help him polish his organizational leadership skills. The sessions were going well and Marwan had reached just about all of his coaching goals. It was anticipated that he would be promoted to a vice president position by the end of the year. Out of the blue, though, Marwan started to act erratically. He started to show an impatient side during team meetings and his colleagues began complaining about his behavior. Then, during a one-on-one meeting with a coworker, he started yelling and stormed out of the meeting. Everyone was surprised and concerned by the changes in his behavior. Marwan had always been well-liked and cool-headed. Fortunately, there was a coaching session scheduled the day after Marwan stormed out of the meeting, so Steve explored what was going on. The coach started by asking some general questions about how things were going. Marwan seemed distant but responded that things were fine. Steve probed into the upsetting incident at the meeting:

Steve: *Marwan, can you tell me why you stormed out of the meeting yesterday?*

Marwan: *I was annoyed by the comments Sarah was making about my performance on the team, and I didn't want to hear anymore.*

Steve: *From my observations you're typically very patient and low key. What made you react so strongly?*

Marwan: *She was pushing my hot buttons, and she told me before the meeting that I was acting insane. I didn't appreciate her comments in the meeting, so I told her off. She has no right to interfere in my personal life.*

Steve: *How was she interfering in your personal life?*

Marwan: *I'd rather not talk about it. It isn't related to work. I can still do my job. Can't I?*

Steve: *Sometimes our personal lives interfere with our work lives. That's pretty normal. But in the three years I've known you, I have never seen you blow up at anyone. I'm not a therapist but have you found yourself becoming impatient and angry lately for some reason?*

Marwan: *Maybe a little.*

Steve: *Can you elaborate?*

Marwan: *Well, I might as well tell you. My father died three weeks ago.*

Steve: *I am so sorry. I didn't know. This must be a rough time for you. I am very sorry for your loss. Why haven't you ever spoken of him before?*

(After a few moments of silence Marwan began to speak).

Marwan: *My father was in a hospital for people with emotional problems and I didn't want people here to know. I figured they would think I had emotional problems too, and it would limit my career growth. When he died, I thought I'd be relieved because he suffered a lot the last five years, but I just feel guilty.*

Steve: *Guilty? Why?*

Marwan: *I was ashamed of him and never let my son meet him. This was a mistake and I regret it now. I guess this is why I've been so reactive and angry lately. Then when Sarah said in the meeting that my comment sounded insane, I just lost it. I've been afraid I would lose my chance for promotion if people found out about my father's emotional illness.*

Steve: *Now I understand. It's a big deal to lose your father and particularly to a long-term illness. But you aren't going to lose your job, and I don't think any differently of you. You're a valued part of the team and I'm glad you shared this with me. Our coaching relationship is about trust, and when something is bothering you, I want you to talk with me about it. Like I said before, I'm not a therapist but sometimes we just have to get things off of our chests. I'm here to listen.*

Marwan: *I now realize I've been walking on eggshells thinking I would be judged and penalized for my father's illness but now I see that isn't the case. I feel better.*

Steve: *All families have situations and circumstances that are not easy. So, I want you to take a few days and spend them with your family. You have time coming and we'll pick up where we left off when you return.*

If Steve had been a novice coach he might have jumped to the wrong conclusion about Marwan's behavior. Instead, he probed and listened and helped Marwan open up. Steve was able to further build trust and get to the root of Marwan's overreaction. Storming out of a meeting was just the symptom of his fear about being labeled "insane" as his father had been. A coach needs to be empathetic and ask skilled questions so the employee can arrive at an awareness of his or her own problem. When people have a foundation of self-awareness, understanding who they are and why they behave ineffectively, they can more easily achieve their goals.

Step 7: Together Set Action Steps for Change

In organizations, there are many different types of goals being set. There are the sales goals, the financial goals, and the people goals. When it comes to people, there are outcome goals and development goals. An employee's development goals should relate in a meaningful way to both the needs of the employee and the needs of the organization.[28] Typically, a goal that results in a more effective employee will advance the goals of the organization. To be an effective managerial coach, you should understand the organization's short-term and long-term goals so you can direct the performance improvements of coachees toward outcomes that will benefit the organization as well as advance their careers.

Set Goals

Coachees are more likely to succeed at reaching their improvement goals when they are motivated and enthusiastic about what is expected. The probability of reaching goals is higher with just a few realistic goals. If too many goals are established, the coachee can lose focus and motivation and not reach any. For each goal, take the time with the coachee to think about the following questions[29] and clarify the coachee's understanding of what each goal will require:

1. How will my work group and the organization as a whole benefit?
2. What will I gain personally by reaching this goal and participating in the process?
3. What will I have to give up?
4. What obstacles might I encounter and how will I manage them?

It is important for the coachee to assume ownership of the goals and believe the goals are important; otherwise, there will be little incentive to reach them. The best coaching approach is to let the coachee set the goals and then discuss the goal and the organizational implications with the coach.

Define Action Steps

Once goals are agreed upon, the coach and coachee can develop action steps. The action steps should include the following components:

- A written action plan that is mutually agreed upon.
- A schedule of events and activities for the employee; these activities should be specific and spelled out in detail.
- Clear benchmarks. Periodic measurement and check-ins will evaluate progress, allow for necessary adjustments, and determine if the coachee is on the right course. There will be times that changes need to be made to the action plan. It is through monitoring the benchmarks that progress can be determined and alternate action steps considered as needed.
- A deadline for the goal to be attained. The deadline gives it priority. Having intermediate and ending dates offers a clear structure and measurable outcomes.

Step 8: Follow Up

After the coachee reaches a goal, you as the coach need to follow up and monitor that the goal is having a positive impact on the organization and the individual. Meeting for a follow-up discussion after a goal is reached allows the employee time to practice new skills and behaviors. A follow-up meeting also shows that you care about the progress of the employee and the relationship you have established. There are times when circumstances change and adjustments have to be made to goals or action steps. For example, if a coachee's goal was to learn a new software package, but after a few weeks the organization changed software vendors, then coach and coachee can re-visit the goal. During a follow-up discussion, it might be determined that the coachee needs to work on making additional changes in behavior, learn new skills, and

What's Your Problem?

Q: I was recently promoted to manager and find myself supervising people who previously were my colleagues. It's been an adjustment for all of us, but I'm finally in a good place with them—with one exception. Robin, who was a fairly close friend, is not performing at the same level as the others. Because the previous manager gave everyone "excellent" ratings, I am not sure if Robin is sliding because of our friendship, or if there were problems before I became manager. All I know is, this cannot continue. It's not fair to the others. What should I do?

A: In some sense, the reason for Robin's slacking doesn't matter. The most important information is that her work is not up to par. You need to have a feedback session with Robin and be supportive, but direct, making sure you take charge as the boss. Let Robin know about the poor quality of her work and be very factual and specific. Then, offer to coach Robin, which means setting goals for new behaviors and helping her figure out how to attain them, with periodic follow-up and assessment sessions. Always be professional in these sessions, but that doesn't mean you have to be cold. Just define careful boundaries between work and friendship. Give Robin a chance to improve. Good luck!

© CENGAGE LEARNING 2014

accept new responsibilities. Then the pair can pick up where they left off and begin the coaching process over again.

LEARN TO DEVELOP PEOPLE WITH DELEGATION

Mark Pincus, founder and CEO of Zynga, a provider of online social games, has firsthand understanding of the power of delegation for helping people learn and grow. He recalls the story of a young, smart receptionist, who began working for the company when it was small. Zynga expanded rapidly, and as the company grew, it constantly needed bigger and better phone systems. Pincus put the receptionist in charge of researching and buying each new phone system. He notes, "She was so motivated by that. I think that was a big lesson for me because what I realized was that if you give people really big jobs to the point that they're scared, they have way more fun and they improve their game much faster." Eventually, she was promoted to office manager.[30]

When managers like Mark Pincus are able to delegate work, they give their subordinates the opportunity to grow, stretch, and learn new skills. If a manager doesn't delegate, he or she is holding onto an important potential means of developing employees.

As mentioned earlier in this chapter, being a coach requires being selfless and sincerely wanting to help others. The same applies to being good at delegating. The ability to delegate is a sign of leadership but it can be difficult, especially for new managers. "Learning how to delegate, learning how to let go and still make sure everything happened, was a very important lesson in my first role in management," says Tachi Yamada, an M.D. and president of the Bill & Melinda Gates Foundation's Global Health Program. Yamada believes "the most difficult transition for anybody from being a worker bee to a manager is this issue of delegation. What do you give up? How can you have the team do what you would do yourself without you doing it?"[31]

What does it mean to delegate effectively? When delegating work as a method to develop employees, it is important to help subordinates be successful by offering the right mix of support, guidance, and resources. The outcome of the work being delegated is on the shoulder of the one who is doing the delegating. When delegating, communicate with the employee upfront about his or her responsibility, agree on an overall goal or outcome, and create benchmarks to monitor progress. The employee must be held accountable for the tasks to be completed, and the manager should not jump in at the first sign of difficulty or take over the work. Give employees enough authority to carry out the task, which means giving them the necessary resources and arranging cooperation from others. Make sure you give people autonomy and don't interfere.

DISCOVER YOURSELF

Interpret Your Score: Delegation, Perfectionism (Questionnaire 4)

Delegation and perfectionism are opposite sides of the same coin. Your score for Part A reflects your attitude toward delegation, which is a key factor in developing direct reports. Your score for Part B reflects your level of perfectionism, which prevents delegation. A perfectionist individual wants to do everything him or herself so it is just exactly the way the individual wants it. A high score for Part B probably means that delegation will not come easily for you. Comparative data for **Delegation** (Part A): Thirty person Mean score = 14.9; Top Quartile = 16–22; Bottom Quartile = 10–14. Comparative data for **Perfectionism** (Part B): Mean = 12.9; Top Quartile = 14–15; Bottom Quartile = 9–12. How does your delegation score compare to your perfectionism score? What would you need to change about yourself to be a better delegator? CNOW and CourseMate users can access dynamically updated comparative data through www.cengagebrain.com.

© CENGAGE LEARNING 2014

When you delegate effectively, everyone benefits. The employee gets to learn new skills and assume additional responsibility, and your time is freed up to do what you get paid to do—manage. Delegation can be in the form of a one-time assignment or turning over a responsibility on an ongoing basis, making it a part of the employee's job description. The following are key points to consider when you are first starting to delegate or want to hone your delegation skills:

- Decide what to let go of. What are some of the tasks and projects you are holding on to?
- Know your people and pick the right person to take on the work. Ask yourself if this is an appropriate assignment for the individual you are considering.
- Think about the outcome you want as the result. The outcome should be described to the employee, as when Mark Pincus described the outcome of a new phone system.
- Delegate the complete task to the employee and let him or her figure it out. Learning happens when people are pushed beyond what they think they can accomplish and end up succeeding.
- Encourage questions, discussion, and participation from the employee.
- Provide needed material resources and personal support. Ask people what they need.
- Figure out with the employee a way to measure results so you both will know when the desired outcome is achieved.
- Determine and agree on a deadline. Do not leave the completion date open-ended.
- Pay attention to how things are going by periodically checking in.
- Don't be critical. Don't give advice. Answer questions but do not jump in and take over the work at the first sign the employee is having difficulty.
- Schedule a meeting on the deadline date to follow up and hold the employee accountable.
- After the work is completed, whether on time or not, debrief what worked and didn't work regarding the delegation of the assignment. Offer appreciation and acknowledgement to the employee for the work accomplished, and review areas for improvement.

LEARN TO USE THE POWER OF DELIBERATE PRACTICE

How do you become a great manager or help others excel? No one is a "born manager," just as no one is a born classical musician or world-class athlete. Jack Welch, the former CEO of General Electric, showed no particular talent for business management when he graduated with a PhD in chemical engineering and began interviewing for various types of jobs. Yet he was later named by *Fortune* magazine as the twentieth century's "manager of the century." Jeffrey Immelt, Welch's successor as CEO at GE, and Stephen Ballmer, CEO of Microsoft, were rather bumbling young managers sharing a cubicle at Procter & Gamble in the late 1970s. "We were voted the two guys probably least likely to succeed," one of the two said later, recalling the afternoons of playing waste-bin basketball. Yet, by the age of 50, both Immelt and Ballmer had succeeded in reaching the top-level position at major corporations.[32] How did they get there?

It is likely that Welch, Immelt, and Ballmer all have some natural abilities and intelligence that have aided in their success. However, research shows that natural talent has little to do with achieving great success in any endeavor, whether it is golfing, scientific research, or management.[33] The way to coach someone to greatness, or to become a great manager yourself, is to focus on something called *deliberate practice*. People achieve greatness not because they were born lucky but through many years of hard work. Sure, some people are born with a natural gift for music, science, sports, or managing people, but without a great amount of work, these gifts are never developed into greatness.

Evidence shows that people need around ten years of hard, focused work before reaching the level of world-class performance. Bobby Fischer, who became a chess grandmaster at the age of 16, had nine years of intensive study before reaching this accomplishment. Tiger Woods already had 15 years of intensive golfing practice under his belt by the time he became the youngest person ever to win the U.S. Amateur Championship at the age of 18. Learning and improving any skill requires conscious, diligent, continuous practice, or what researchers refer to as deliberate practice, as outlined in Exhibit 9.6.[34]

Deliberate practice is designed specifically to improve performance. Especially in the early stages, it is important to have an expert, such as a coach or teacher, design the tasks and activities that can help you improve.

Exhibit 9.6 The Five Elements of Deliberate Practice

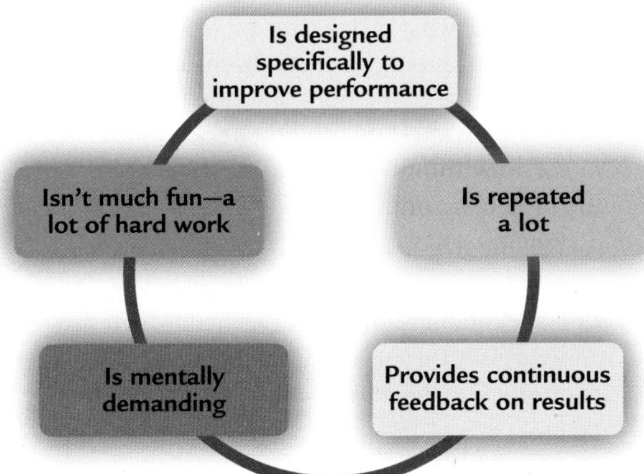

Sources: Based on Geoff Colvin, *Talent Is Overrated: What Really Separates World-Class Performers from Everybody Else* (New York: Penguin Portfolio, 2008); Geoff Colvin, "What It Takes to Be Great," *Fortune* (October 30, 2006): 88–95; and K. Anders Ericsson, Ralf T. Krampe, and Clemens Tesch-Römer, "The Role of Deliberate Practice in the Acquisition of Expert Performance," *Psychological Review* 100, no. 3 (July 1993): 363–406.

After all, if you go out and practice hitting golf balls the same way you've always done it, you aren't likely to make any breakthroughs. The same applies to improving performance as a manager. In addition, a coach can help provide a clear, honest assessment of your performance and identify specific elements that need improvement.[35] Then, to engage in deliberate practice, you tackle each task or activity *with the explicit goal of getting much better at it*. Research indicates that this difference in mental approach is vital to improvement.

DISCOVER YOURSELF

Interpret Your Score: Deliberate Practice (Questionnaire 5)

Deliberate practice is effective for mastering academic coursework just as it is for mastering athletics, music, art, and management. Comparative data for **Deliberate Practice Habits:** Thirty person Mean score = 22.3; Top Quartile = 25–30; Bottom Quartile = 10–21. These ten statements were correlated with effective academic mastery in a group of undergraduate majors in pre-medicine. If your score is high, you know deliberate practice in your studies that you can apply to other areas of your life. If your score is low, you might think about how to change your habits, or in what field you could apply deliberate practice in order to excel. CNOW and CourseMate users can access dynamically updated comparative data through www.cengagebrain.com.

DISCOVER KNOWLEDGE

© CENGAGE LEARNING 2014

Deliberate practice means repeating an activity over and over and over and over. Repetition of specific targeted tasks or activities identified with the coach is essential. Ted Williams, baseball's greatest hitter, practiced hitting balls until his hands bled. Activities have to be clear and focused enough that they can be repeated *a lot*. It is important to pinpoint the specific behaviors you are trying to improve rather than trying to learn too many things at once.[36]

Continuous feedback promotes motivation and improvement. As discussed earlier in this chapter, feedback is essential for learning. When people don't get feedback, they don't improve and they lose interest and motivation. If you are the coach, remember to give feedback often. If you're the coachee, seek it out and use the feedback your coach offers.

Deliberate practice is mentally demanding. By focusing wholeheartedly on improving a precise task, you are paying attention to *what* you are doing, *why* you are doing it, and the *way* you are improving the task. That means it can be mentally exhausting, similar to the concentration required to learn to speak a foreign language. Many top-level musicians, for example, say four to five hours of deliberate practice, split into two or three sessions, is the upper limit of what they can do.[37]

"Deliberate practice is hard. It hurts. But it works."[38] Let's just face it: This doesn't sound like very much fun—and it isn't. It is fun to do things we already know how to do well, but that doesn't improve us or advance us in our careers. Deliberate practice means identifying those things you're really *bad* at, determining difficult activities that can make you better, and then doing those activities over and over. It means continually seeking out feedback and perhaps having to do the most painful activities to the point of exhaustion. Why do it? Because it works. If it were easy, everyone would do it; because it's hard, only the best stick with it.

There is evidence that deliberate practice is powerful. Professor K. Anders Ericsson of Florida State University and his colleagues looked at 20-year-old violinists and found that the best performers averaged 10,000 hours of deliberate practice over their lives; the next-best averaged 7,500 hours; and the next, 5,000 hours. Ericsson has studied world-class performers in a variety of fields and seen the same pattern.[39]

Remember: It is not just about repeating a task over and over again. Rather, deliberate practice involves stretching yourself with specific activities and goals, obtaining immediate feedback, and concentrating as much on technique as on outcome.[40] As you engage in deliberate practice, you should continually be building and expanding your mental understanding of what it takes to be a good manager and to achieve success as a manager. You should remember also that *occassional* practice does not work. Professor Ericsson emphasizes the importance of consistency: "Elite performers in many diverse domains have been found to practice, on the average, roughly the same amount every day, including weekends."[41]

There are no shortcuts for developing management skills, but with hard work and deliberate practice, effective management skills can become like second nature. If you are motivated and committed, over ten years or so you can make the transition to the highest level of management competence, where you will make it look easy. You will perform as if you were born knowing exactly how to be a great manager.

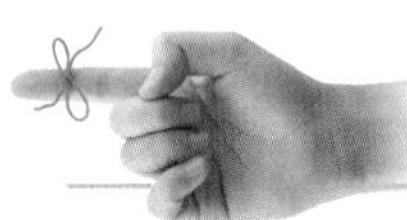

NEED TO KNOW

- Managerial coaching means working one-on-one with a subordinate or other employee (the coachee) to help the individual improve, learn new skills, enhance contributions to the organization, and advance his or her career.
- Coaching follows eight steps in three stages. The planning stage includes mental preparation, discussion and agreement with the employee, and setting broad goals. During the engagement stage, the coach gathers data about the coachee's behavior, provides explicit feedback, and decides together with the coachee exactly what needs to change and how success will be measured. In the implementation stage, the coachee's specific action steps are decided, and the coach follows up by checking and reinforcing progress as the coachee practices new behaviors.
- Another important way to help people grow and improve is through delegation. You can follow some guidelines to improve delegation effectiveness: decide what to delegate; pick the right person; specify the desired outcome; delegate the complete task; encourage questions but don't take over the project; provide support and check in periodically to see how things are going; and follow up when the project is completed.
- A powerful way to coach someone—and to become a great manager yourself—is to use a technique called deliberate practice. Deliberate practice focuses on specific, clearly defined tasks and activities rather than trying to learn a lot of things all at once.
- Deliberate practice is designed specifically to improve performance of a key task, is repeated a lot, provides regular feedback, is mentally demanding, and isn't much fun because it asks people to stretch themselves and focus on the things that are the hardest for them. Yet research shows that it really works and can turn an average manager into a great one.

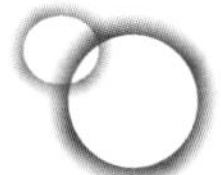

ACTION LEARNING

DELIBERATE PRACTICE EXERCISES

Coaching Practice

The purpose of this exercise is to help you gain more self-awareness and some understanding and expansion of your own coaching skills.

Step 1: During a typical day, count how many times you give advice to people. Fill in the boxes below. If you did not give advice on that day, then continue on subsequent days until you do give some advice.

Number of times you gave unsolicited advice:	Number of times you gave solicited advice:

Step 2: Then, on the following day (or days), ask open-ended questions of people instead of giving advice. Refer to the text discussion on page 343 for ideas on types of questions to ask. List the questions you asked, and indicate, in the following table, how people responded.

What question did you ask?	How did the person respond? Did the individual appreciate your question?
1.	
2.	
3.	
4.	

Step 3: What differences in people's responses did you notice between giving advice and asking questions?

Step 4: How can you remind yourself to ask more questions of others?

Step 5: What did you learn about yourself from this exercise? What did you learn about coaching others?

Step 6 (Optional): Share your insights with a partner, and ask your partner what insights he or she gained.

My Best Coach Ever

Step 1: Think of people who have tried to help you solve a problem or develop a plan. This could include friends, parents, teachers, counselors, sports coaches, bosses, and so on. Who was the most effective and the least effective? Fill out the table below.

Behaviors of the Person	Best Coach	Worst Coach
What did the person do?		
What kind of interaction was there with you?		
How did you feel toward that person?		
What made the individual the best or worst coach?		
What lesson did you learn from the interaction with this person?		

Step 2: Based on what you learned by thinking about your best and worst coaches, what advice would you give to someone who wants to be a coach?

Step 3 (Optional): Share your insights with a partner, and ask your partner what insights he or she gained.

ACTION LEARNING

Directing versus Coaching

This Deliberate Practice Exercise is available online at www.cengagebrain.com

How Do You Delegate?

This Deliberate Practice Exercise is available online at www.cengagebrain.com

IN-CLASS TEAM EXERCISE

Non-Directive Listening versus Advising

Part of the coaching process involves the coach helping an individual find his or her own answers, with the coach being more of a facilitator than a counselor. This exercise will help you see the difference between advice-giving and non-directive listening, which means reflecting back what the person is saying and feeling.

Step 1: Divide into groups of three to four people.

Step 2: Using the table below, take one problem situation at a time. (The first two rows of the table provide examples.) Each person writes down the "advice" answer and also the "non-directive" response. Then discuss that item as a group before you move on to the next item.

The statement made	An advising response	A non-directive or facilitative response
I know I'm supposed to work with Manny, but he's such a pain. Sure, he's smart and he never lets me forget it. Can't you put us on separate projects?	Example: Come on, Luis, don't be so critical. You can work with him if you try harder.	Example: You feel frustrated when you have to work with Manny.
This project is turning out to be a mess. Why can't those other three quit fighting with each other?	Example: Mind your own business.	Example: You feel angry when you watch them in conflict.
I'm tired of having you interrupt me whenever I talk. Can't I get a word in edgewise with you?		
The boss just called me on the carpet for something that wasn't my fault. How can I squeal on someone else?		
I want to go for that senior management position, but I really don't have a chance. After all, no one from my minority group has ever held one before. But, I guess I'll try anyway.		
I'm supposed to be working with four people from the other department on this new project. But they never listen to my ideas and hardly seem to know I'm there.		
It ticks me off because our group is always expected to work harder, and on more difficult tasks. Then at evaluation time, we all get the same raise. Unfair!		
Hey, this idea is really good. Who are you to question it? I've worked on it for four years, and nobody knows it better than I do.		

SHUTTERSTOCK #53973379

Step 3: When you have finished with the problem situations, talk as a group about the differences between advising and being non-directive. When have you experienced each of these approaches?

FIELD TEAM EXERCISE

Analyzing and Practicing Feedback

Giving effective feedback is essential in good coaching. This exercise will help you analyze feedback and then practice feedback in your group. In organizations, managers sometimes need to coach in a group setting.

Part I. Analyze Coaching Styles

Step 1: Divide into groups of four to six. It is preferable that groups be made up of people who have worked together before.

Step 2: Watch one or two episodes of *Friday Night Lights* (the TV show) together. Your focus will be on (a) Coach Eric Taylor and how he coaches and gives feedback; and(b) Tammy Taylor, Coach's wife, who works as a guidance counselor or principal (depending on the episode), and how she gives feedback to students and teachers.

Step 3: Compare Eric and Tammy's styles to the coaching models in the chapter. What do Eric and Tammy do effectively, and what could they do better?

Step 4: Discuss which parts of Eric and Tammy's styles you would like to emulate.

Part II. Giving Feedback

Step 1: Go around the group, one person at a time, with each person choosing one of the feedback statements/questions (see below) to share or ask. You do not have to cover every item and individuals may skip back and forth over the items (that is, you do not have to go in any particular order with the statements/questions). Follow these ground rules:

1. Keep confidential whatever is said in the group. Whatever people say must stay within this group.
2. You don't have to answer any particular question. But if you ask a certain question, you must be ready to also answer it, if asked of you.

Go through at least one complete round, with each person taking a turn sharing feedback or asking a question. If there is enough time, it would be good to do at least two rounds.

Step 2: At the end, discuss as a group how this exercise affected your group dynamics. Did it make you feel differently about the group? How?

Feedback Statements/Questions

You do not have to write the answers down. Give your response to the feedback or ask your questions in the group.

1. The things I like most about this group are:
2. In this group, I have the most difficulty discussing the following topics:

3. With these people, it is easy for me to talk about:
4. It bothers me when group members do the following things:
5. In this group, I would like to change:
6. I wish ____________________ (group member's name) would:
7. If I could, I'd like to tell ____________________:
8. In this group, the person with whom I have the strongest relationship is ____________________:
9. The strong relationship exists because:
10. I would like to ask ____________________ how he/she sees me.
11. I would like to ask if ____________________ is angry or upset with me.
12. I would like to ask ____________________ what my best contribution to the group is.
13. I would like to ask ____________________ what my best quality as a person is.
14. I would like to ask ____________________ if I have seemed to change since entering the group.
15. I would like to ask ____________________ if there is anything confusing about me.
16. I would like to ask the group what you like most about me.
17. What I like most about ____________________ (group member's name) is:

TEST YOUR METTLE

ROLE PLAY SIMULATIONS

Rough at the Edges

Background: Re-read the written Video Incident at the beginning of this chapter.

Instructions: Form into groups of two to three. One person will be Carrie and one Jane. If there are three, the third person is an observer. Each person reads only his or her confidential role, but the observer reads both. Spend ten minutes on the role play.

Confidential information for Carrie: You've been in this job at Caffeine and Crullers for just a few months and already you've been whipping this place into shape. If only your boss, Jane, would notice and appreciate all you are doing for C&C. Occasionally she'll remark on your outstanding work, but mostly she seems to want to harp on you personally. "Change this! Do that! Be more this way!" It's really starting to get on your nerves. And now she's called you in for a meeting. Another way to waste your time!

Confidential information for Jane: Some of the other employees are coming to you to complain about Carrie, especially the managers, who are tired of her always having to be the smarty-pants in the meetings. What you are trying to build is a high-performance team, so you don't want individual stars, but people who can make the group better. You've got to get Carrie to understand this and show her the new behaviors she needs to help accomplish the goal of building a high-performance management team. You've called her in for a meeting in a few minutes.

After the role play, discuss these questions:

1. How well do you think Jane did in convincing Carrie to be more of a team player? Is Carrie a good candidate for coaching?
2. If you were Jane, what metrics would you use to help motivate and focus Carrie on team performance?

Delegation Dilemma

This Role Play Simulation is available online at www.cengagebrain.com.

VIDEO APPLICATION

Welcome Home, Roscoe Jenkins

Roscoe Jenkins (Martin Lawrence), a successful Hollywood talk-show host, visits his brother, Sheriff Otis Jenkins (Michael Clarke Duncan), in their hometown and the brothers' differences emerge.

SHUTTERSTOCK #53973379

Discussion Questions

1. How would you describe the life values and philosophies of the two brothers? What feedback would you give to Roscoe Jenkins and Sheriff Otis Jenkins to change their individual behavior in order to improve their relationship?
2. Which brother needs to change more to make the relationship work? How would you "define together" what that brother needs to change?
3. What specific deliberate practice activity would you suggest one of the brothers engage in to change his behavior in a positive direction? Explain.

CASE INCIDENTS

Rookie

Evan Wardine was clearly uncomfortable sitting across the desk from HR director Shelly Wilcox. "I feel like some middle school kid sitting in the principal's office and ratting on another kid," Evan said.

"No," Shelly remarked. "You're an adult who is addressing a concern about your workplace." She motioned for him to continue.

"Thanks. Okay. I didn't ask for this, but almost from day one, Larry has taken it upon himself to 'coach' me. I've got my MBA. I've worked in Atlanta, which is a bigger market, and yet he thinks I'm clueless about everything."

"Well, Larry has been around here . . . " started Shelly.

"For 40 years," Evan cut in. "I know. He reminds me constantly. I think that's one of the reasons he insists on coaching me. He even calls me 'Rookie,' which I find very annoying and a bit demeaning."

Shelly smiled slightly. "Okay. Tell me what's happening."

"I realize that when you join the sales department of a long-established company, there is a period of adjustment—a time when you're learning how things are done, meeting and establishing relationships with clients, becoming familiar with things such as deadlines, turn-around times, and how to fine-tune reports. That's fine. But Larry's devotion to coaching me has gone way beyond what's practical or comfortable, and I have to say that I resent it."

"Do you think he's interfering with your work?"

"How much work could you do if every time you look up, there's Larry—'Just checking on you, Rookie.'? He's asking clients, sometimes in front of me, how I'm doing. He's practically grabbing my sales reports out of my hands—'Oh, let's have a look at these,'" Evan mocked. "'You're coming along, Rookie,' he says." Evan rose from his chair in frustration and marched to the window.

"Do you think he respects your opinion?" Shelly asked.

Evan turned and looked at Shelly. "My opinion? He doesn't want *my* opinion. He asks Bill and Terry *their* opinions. But when I start to speak up at meetings, he raises his hand," Evan demonstrates. "As if to cut me off, and then he says something like, 'Let's just keep this train of thought going and we'll talk later.' *We* never talk. *He* talks. I listen. I have a lot to offer. He might actually learn something from me, but, hey—he's the coach and I'm the rookie."

Shelly motioned to Evan to sit down again. "I know you're talented, and I understand that you are really frustrated right now. I've also known Larry for many years, and for some reason, he seems to believe there is a problem."

"I think the problem is that he resents the fact that I have a business degree while he and the others worked their way up through the company. He's always mentioning the 'ivy walls of higher learning.' My university didn't even have stupid ivy walls."

The remark broke the tension in the room and they both chuckled.

"I'm sure he means well with his coaching," Shelly assured Evan. "He may just be going about it the wrong way or he may be reluctant to release you to stand on your own. Let me talk to him and see what's up. He may be unaware that his coaching is overbearing."

The following day, Larry dropped by Shelly's office to leave some paperwork.

"Oh, Larry, this is great. I've been hoping to catch you." She rose from her chair, walked around to the front of her desk and leaned against it casually. "I haven't had a chance to talk to you since we hired Evan. I was wondering how that is working out."

Larry chuckled. "You mean the rookie?"

"Oh, Larry, that's what you call him?"

"Yeah. You know—'coach,' 'rookie'—like in football."

"I know. I know. I hope you don't call him that to his face."

"Sometimes. I don't mean anything," Larry said, helping himself to a handful of jelly beans from the bowl on Shelly's desk. "It's like a friendly nickname."

"I still think it's more professional to just call him Evan."

"Yeah, I guess. He still has a lot of the qualities of a rookie. I don't think we've ever had to spend so much time developing all of that talent."

"So, you believe he has talent."

"Oh, yeah. The kid's got lots of potential. We have to kick a little of that *by the book* nonsense out of him and help him to appreciate things from a practical standpoint, but I think he'll be great."

"So you like him?"

"Sure, he's fine. Got any more of these jelly beans?"

TEST YOUR METTLE

Shelly refilled the bowl and Larry's outstretched hand. "Do the two of you ever have the opportunity to discuss any of the business approaches he learned from his MBA program?"

"No. He's got to get this stuff down first. You know—get with *our* program. But he's . . . um . . . he's improving."

"Do you think you're spending more time coaching and developing Evan than you did for, say, Terry?"

Larry nodded. "Yeah! Terry had more common sense. It seemed easier to fit Terry into the system and fit him with the clients. Evan will get there. It just takes time and a little one-on-one. You know—the rookie and the coach." Larry looked at his watch. "Oh, I've got to go. It was great talking to you, Shelly." He grabbed another handful of candy and bolted toward the door.

Shelly heaved a sigh of exasperation as the office door closed behind him. "Now what?" she whispered to herself. "This is going to be a challenge and I will have to do some *serious* intervention."

Discussion Questions

1. Why do you think Larry is using this approach to coaching Evan? Is his approach effective? Why or why not?

2. Do you think Evan needs coaching? What steps might Evan take to redefine his relationship with Larry?
3. What steps should Shelly take for resolving the situation between Evan and Larry?

"This Isn't the Wild West, Son"

"I was watching an old western last night," sales director Miguel Garcia told his CEO, Dale Branson. "A big ranch owner had been ruthless in fighting for his land. He had become his own law and used his gun to fight off Comanches, bandits, and small ranchers. And over time, he built a ranching empire and gained respect. But times changed and now he couldn't convince his son that the gun was no longer the code to live by."

Dale leaned back in his chair and looked confused. "And, what, exactly, is your point?"

"You're the rancher," Miguel said. "And the new hot-shot salesman, Ryan Carter, is the kid."

The background to this unusual conversation began 40 years ago when Dale Branson dropped out of Rutgers University and moved west, eventually tapping into the environmental trend and founding a solar energy company. In the early days, Branson gained a reputation for hard work, innovative sales tactics, and, quite frankly, a cut-throat style that left competitors dazed and trying to make up lost ground. Over the years he became a much-admired and much-maligned corporate leader. The stories about him were legendary.

Fast forward to the present: Now a mellow 60 years old, Branson controls a business empire that stretches across the west and has a reputation as both maverick and corporate icon. Ryan Carter, a Rutgers grad and grandnephew of Dale Branson, grew up in awe of the legendary Branson and saw himself as the modern version of the founder. Ambitious and willing to put in incredibly long hours, Ryan eagerly joined the Branson sales force and set his sights on establishing unprecedented sales records for the company. *He* would capture the attention of the maverick, walk in his footsteps, and eventually secure a top management position. His goals were obvious to those around him. Everyone joked that Ryan had his sights on Miguel Garcia's corner office.

"Are you *worried* about the kid, Miguel?" Branson teased.

Garcia refused to take the bait. "Not as far as my corner office is concerned. No, my concern is the effect his sales tactics are having on the entire sales force. I know how impressive his sales have been. But Dale, I believe he is potentially toxic to the organization."

"Well, he's number one in sales month after month," Branson remarked. He's blowing our own staff out of the water as well as the competition. He really does remind me of myself in the early days. I realize I'm blowing my own horn, here, but I think that is something to encourage."

"It's not *what* he's doing. It's the way he's doing it," Garcia explained. "This is neither the old days nor the old west. Employees don't make their own laws. Ryan routinely violates company policy and makes his own agreements with clients in the field. He never checks with anyone about pricing or delivery schedules. He is very popular with his clients because they know that they are his priority. But we can't have someone making up the rules as he goes, making his own agreements, and then strong-arming the folks in manufacturing to meet *his* deadlines. He doesn't see the hidden costs of

stopping the line to squeeze in his orders. The manufacturing folks don't resist too hard because they know Ryan is your relative."

"Wow. Have you talked to him?"

"Of course. I've even pulled him from the field for a few days, but some major clients complained and so I put him back out. Now other salesmen are complaining. If he can make his own deals, why can't they? Shop supervisors are complaining about his aggressive behavior. Schedulers are hiding when they see him coming. Who isn't upset about his disruptions?"

"Are you exaggerating? How big has this problem become, really?"

"It's not overwhelming—yet. He's not doing this with every sale, but it's becoming all too frequent on major sales to win new clients," Garcia said. "He is not hearing what I say about respecting the needs of other departments. I'm sorry to say this, but he seems terribly self-centered, interested only in getting his way. And it is working—for him."

"I see," Branson murmured.

"Dale, I can understand and certainly you can understand his drive and his desire to give his clients priority," Garcia continued. "He's a fabulous and talented salesman and really has a bright future with this company—up to and probably including my corner office." Both laughed. "But we have to find a way to develop his talent without setting a bad precedent for the entire sales force and wrecking the rest of the company. If he weren't your relative, I would have let him go by now."

"I agree," Branson said, slapping his hand on the desk. "It's time to tame our young maverick."

Discussion Questions

1. If you were Miguel Garcia, what approach would you take to turn around this high performing individual who is creating lots of problems? Be specific. Why do you think your approach would have success with Ryan Carter?
2. Is Miguel Garcia the right coach for Ryan in this case? How about Dale Branson? Who do you think should be Carter's coach? Why?
3. What part should Dale Branson play in the development of an employee who idolizes and copies his original working style?

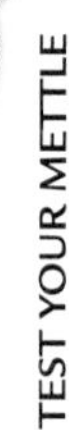

PERSONAL SKILLS LOG

Directions: Fill in the rows below based on what you learned from each part of the chapter that you completed.

	What is my key takeaway or insight from this activity?	**What do I personally do well (strength) regarding this activity?**	**What could I improve (weakness) about myself regarding this activity?**	**How might I use what I've learned from this activity in the future?**
Manager Challenge Incident:				
Discover Yourself Questionnaires:				
Deliberate Practice Exercises:				
In-Class and/or Field Team Exercises:				
Role-Play Exercises:				
Case Incidents:				

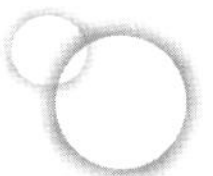

REFERENCES

Discover Yourself

1 Based on Susan Battley, *Coached to Lead: How to Achieve Extraordinary Results with an Executive Coach* (San Francisco: Jossey-Bass, 2006), pp. 20–40.

2 Based on Véronique Moulaert, Maarten G. M. Verwijnen, Remy Rikers, and Albert J. J. A. Scherpbier, "The Effects of Deliberate Practice in Undergraduate Medical Education," *Medical Education* 38, no. 10 (2004): 1044–1052.

Discover Knowledge

3 Survey results reported in Michael M. Lombardo and Robert W. Eichinger, "HR's Role in Building Competitive Edge Leaders," *Human Resource Management* 36, no. 1 (Spring 1997): 141–146; and Robert N. Llewellyn, "The Power in Being a People Developer: Who Is the Best People Developer in Your Organization? Why Isn't It You?" *HR Magazine* (July 2002): 85–87.

4 Reported in Mark D. Cannon and Robert Witherspoon, "Actionable Feedback: Unlocking the Power of Learning and Performance Improvement," *Academy of Management Executive* 19, no. 2 (May 2005): 120–134.

5 Myles Downey, *Effective Coaching: Lessons from the Coach's Coach*, 2nd ed. (New York: Thomson Texere, 2003), p. 21.

6 Adapted from James M. Hunt and Joseph R. Weintraub, *The Coaching Manager: Developing Top Talent in Business* (Thousand Oaks, CA: Sage, 2002).

7 Adam Bryant, "An Office: She'll Pass on That" (Corner Office column), *The New York Times*, March 5, 2010, http://dealbook.nytimes.com/2010/03/08/an-office-shell-pass-on-that/ (accessed April 7, 2011).

8 Based on Clinton O. Longenecker and Mitchell J. Neubert, "The Practices of Effective Managerial Coaches," *Business Horizons* 48, no. 6 (November–December 2005): 493–500.

9 Leigh Buchanan, "In Praise of Selflessness: Why the Best Leaders Are Servants," *Inc.* (May 2007): 33–35.

10 This list and the discussion are based on Andrea D. Ellinger and Robert P. Bostrom, "An Examination of Managers' Beliefs About Their Roles as Facilitators of Learning," *Management Learning* 33, no. 2 (2002): 147–179.

11 This discussion is based on Downey, *Effective Coaching*.

12 Jim Struck, "A Different Kind of Coach," *Collector* 73, no. 3 (October 2007): 30–33. This is a true story, but the name and some details have been changed.

13 Hunt and Weintraub, *The Coaching Manager*, p. 23.

14 "Appraisal and Coaching: Improving Results with Feedback," in *Manager's Toolkit: The 13 Skills Managers Need to Succeed*, Harvard Business Essentials series (Boston: Harvard Business School Press, 2006), pp. 10–11.

15 Hunt and Weintraub, *The Coaching Manager*, pp. 20–21.

16 Jean L. Hurd, "Development Coaching: Helping Scientific and Technical Professionals Make the Leap into Leadership" *Global Business and Organizational Excellence* 28, no. 5 (July–August, 2009): 39–51.

17 *Coaching and Mentoring: How to Develop Top Talent and Achieve Stronger Performance*, Harvard Business Essentials series (Boston: Harvard Business School Press, 2004), p. 67.

18 Hunt and Weintraub, *The Coaching Manager*, p.124.

19 *Ibid.*, p. 101; and Terry R. Bacon and Karen I. Spear, *Adaptive Coaching: The Art and Practice of a Client-Centered Approach to Performance Improvement* (Palo Alto, CA: Davies-Black Publishing, 2003), pp. 166–174.

20 Downey, *Effective Coaching*, pp. 67–68.

21 A. C. Daniels and J. E. Daniels, *Performance Management: Changing Behavior That Drives Organizational Effectiveness*, 4th ed., (Tucker, GA: Performance Management Publications, 2004).

22 Mary Carson, "Saying It Like It Isn't: The Pros and Cons of 360-Degree Feedback," *Business Horizons* 49, no. 5 (September–October 2006): 395–402.

23 Gary Rivlin, "He Naps, He Sings. And He Isn't Michael Dell," *The New York Times*, September 11, 2005.

24 Longenecker and Neubert, "The Practices of Effective Managerial Coaches."

25 From a story in Hurd, "Development Coaching: Helping Scientific and Technical Professionals Make the Leap into Leadership."

26 This discussion is based on Thomas Petzinger, Jr., *The New Pioneers: The Men and Women Who Are Transforming the Workplace and Marketplace* (New York: Simon & Schuster, 1999), pp. 30–42; and Stefan H. Haeckel, *Adaptive Enterprise: Creating and Leading Sense and Respond Organizations* (Boston: Harvard Business School Press, 1999), pp. 75–92.

27 Brad Smart and Geoff Smart, *Topgrading: How to Hire, Coach and Keep A Players* (Dallas, TX: Pritchett, 2005), p. 50.

28 Hunt and Weintraub, *The Coaching Manager*, p. 173.

29 Hurd, "Development Coaching," p. 46.

30 Adam Bryant, "Are You a C.E.O. of Something?" (Corner Office column), *The New York Times*, January 31, 2010.

31 Adam Bryant, "Talk to Me. I'll Turn Off My Phone" (Corner Office column), *The New York Times*, February 28, 2010.

32 Geoff Colvin, "Why Talent Is Overrated," *Fortune* (October 27, 2008):137ff.

33 This discussion is based on information in Geoff Colvin, *Talent Is Overrated: What Really Separates World-Class Performers from Everybody Else* (New York: Portfolio, 2008); Geoff Colvin, "Why Talent is Overrated"; and Geoff Colvin, "What It Takes to Be Great," *Fortune* (October 30, 2006): 88–95.

34 The discussion of these five elements of deliberate practice is based heavily on Colvin, *Talent Is Overrated.*

35 Colvin, *Talent Is Overrated.*

36 Albert Bandura, *Social Learning Theory* (New York: General Learning, 1977); and A. Bandura, *Social Foundations of Thought and Action* (Englewood Cliffs, NJ: Prentice Hall, 1986).

37 Reported in Colvin, "Why Talent Is Overrated."

38 Colvin, *Talent Is Overrated.*

39 Reported in Colvin, "What It Takes to Be Great."

40 Timothy T. Baldwin, William H. Bommer, and Robert S. Rubin, *Developing Management Skills: What Great Managers Know and Do* (New York: McGraw-Hill Irwin, 2008), p. 10.

41 K. Anders Ericsson, quoted in Colvin, "What It Takes to Be Great."

CHAPTER 10

Handling Difficult Conversations, Conflict, and Negotiation

Chapter Outline

RYAN LASH

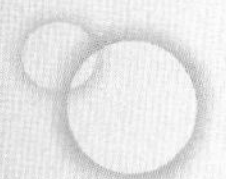

MANAGER CHALLENGE

VIDEO INCIDENT: APPRAISAL INFLATION

Caffeine and Crullers general manager Jane Sutton noticed that some six-month personnel review ratings were disproportionately high. The ratings seemed especially high in the accounting department. In recent months, she had seen mistakes in reports and incorrect balance sheets, so she knew there were accountability problems. She wondered why CFO Carlos Hernandez was not giving people proper feedback. She called Carlos in to talk it over with him. "We have some problems here. You are rating your people too generously," Sutton said to him.

Hernandez responded immediately, "Are you saying I'm not telling the truth?"

Jane pulled back and remarked, "I'm not saying anything like that."

Carlos continued, "But you have to be nice to people, you know, otherwise they won't work hard."

"Yes, that is true," Jane said, knowing she had a problem that had to be solved; otherwise, it could cause morale problems in the other departments.

Initial Thoughts

1. If you were Jane, how would you have handled this differently?

2. Where did the conversation get off track? Why do you think the conversation failed?

Your instructor may ask you to be part of a role play based on the Appraisal Inflation incident.

DISCOVER YOURSELF

For those students using CourseMate or CengageNOW, you can access the Daft/Marcic Assessment Library to take the questionnaires online and view dynamically updated comparative data.

Questionnaire 1

Instructions: When participating in a team discussion, how do you communicate? For each statement below, rate how accurately each statement describes you based on whether the statement is clearly true or accurate, clearly false or inaccurate, or in the middle as somewhat true and somewhat false.

	True	Somewhat	False
1. Often, I am thinking about what I want to say rather than listening intensely.	○	○	○
2. If someone disagrees with me, I get excited and try to prove my point is correct.	○	○	○
3. If I get negative feedback, I try to explain why the person did not see the situation correctly.	○	○	○
4. I express an opposing viewpoint so well that the group knows I understand, even if I don't agree.	○	○	○
5. I never hesitate to fully share my own perspective.	○	○	○
6. I automatically accept that two people can disagree yet both be right and still get along.	○	○	○
7. I make lots of inquiries, especially when the discussion is difficult.	○	○	○
8. When a point of view opposes mine, I never react adversely.	○	○	○
9. I actively facilitate people to express diverse opinions.	○	○	○
10. Team members will say that I share my opinions without being offensive.	○	○	○

Total Score ________. (For questions 4–10, sum 3 points for each True, 2 points for each Somewhat, and 1 point for each False. For questions 1–3, reverse the scores with 1 point for each True, 2 points for each Somewhat, and 3 points for each False and add to the total.) Go to page 374 to interpret your score.

Questionnaire 2

Instructions: Think about how you behave when confronting someone with whom you have a very serious difference of opinion that will be difficult to discuss. Indicate your response to each of the statements below as True, Somewhat, or False.

Part A

	True	Somewhat	False
1. I would typically express my point of view first.	○	○	○
2. I admit that I probably assume the problem is the other person's fault.	○	○	○

	True	Somewhat	False
3. I like to jump into solving the problem fairly quickly.	○	○	○
4. If the conversation becomes heated, I would probably feel blame toward the other person.	○	○	○
5. I would try to keep things rational and avoid feelings and emotions if possible.	○	○	○
6. I am likely to think that I am right and the other person is wrong.	○	○	○
7. If I get upset I am likely to get defensive or vent.	○	○	○

Total Score Part A ________. (Sum questions 1–7: 3 points for each True, 2 points for each Somewhat, and 1 point for each False.)

Part B

	True	Somewhat	False
8. I would rehearse my procedure out loud beforehand.	○	○	○
9. Early on I would explicitly describe the gap between our perspectives.	○	○	○
10. I would definitely acknowledge that I understand the other person's point of view.	○	○	○
11. I would intentionally wait to solve the problem until we both fully expressed our views.	○	○	○
12. I know specific techniques to make the conversation successful.	○	○	○
13. My initial task would be to find out the other person's point of view.	○	○	○
14. I believe that underlying feelings must be expressed.	○	○	○

Total Score Part B ________. (Sum questions 8–14: 3 points for each True, 2 points for Somewhat, and 1 point for each False.) Go to page 378 to interpret your scores.

Questionnaire 3

Instructions: Think about how you typically handle a dispute with a team member, friend, or coworker, and then respond to the statements below based on whether they are True, Somewhat, or False for you. There are no right or wrong answers, so answer honestly.

Part A

	True	Somewhat	False
1. I feel that differences are not worth arguing about.	○	○	○
2. I would avoid a person who wants to discuss a disagreement.	○	○	○
3. I would rather keep my views to myself than argue.	○	○	○
4. I typically avoid taking positions that create a dispute.	○	○	○

Total Score Part A ________. (Sum questions 1–4: 3 points for each True, 2 points for each Somewhat, and 1 point for each False.)

Part B

	True	Somewhat	False
5. I try hard to win my position.	◯	◯	◯
6. I strongly assert my opinion in a disagreement.	◯	◯	◯
7. I raise my voice to get other people to accept my position.	◯	◯	◯
8. I stand firm in expressing my viewpoint.	◯	◯	◯

Total Score Part B ________. (Sum questions 5–8: 3 points for each True, 2 points for each Somewhat, and 1 point for each False.)

Part C

9. I give in a little if other people do the same.	◯	◯	◯
10. I will split the difference to reach an agreement.	◯	◯	◯
11. I offer trade-offs to reach a solution.	◯	◯	◯
12. I give up some points in exchange for others.	◯	◯	◯

Total Score Part C ________. (Sum questions 9–12: 3 points for each True, 2 points for each Somewhat, and 1 point for each False.)

Part D

13. I don't want to hurt others' feelings.	◯	◯	◯
14. I am quick to agree when someone I am arguing with makes a good point.	◯	◯	◯
15. I try to smooth over disagreements by minimizing their seriousness.	◯	◯	◯
16. I want to be considerate of other people's emotions.	◯	◯	◯

Total Score Part D ________. (Sum questions 13–16: 3 points for each True, 2 points for each Somewhat, and 1 point for each False.)

Part E

17. I suggest a solution that includes the other person's point of view.	◯	◯	◯
18. I combine arguments into a new solution from ideas raised in the dispute.	◯	◯	◯
19. I try to include the other person's ideas to create a solution he or she will accept.	◯	◯	◯
20. I assess the merits of other viewpoints as equal to my own.	◯	◯	◯

Total Score Part E ________. (Sum questions 17–20: 3 points for each True, 2 points for each Somewhat, and 1 point for each False.) Go to page 383 to interpret your scores.

DISCOVER YOURSELF

Questionnaire 4[1]

Instructions: If you are in a serious business negotiation for an outcome of great value to your business, which of the following tactics would you be willing to use? Indicate your response to each item below with Yes, Maybe, or No.

Part A

	Yes	Maybe	No
1. Gain information about an opponent's position by asking among your friends and associates.	○	○	○
2. Make an opening demand that is far greater than what you hope to achieve.	○	○	○
3. Hide your real goal from your opponent.	○	○	○
4. Give the impression that you are in absolutely no hurry to reach an agreement.	○	○	○
5. Lead the other person to believe he or she can get what they want only by negotiating with you.	○	○	○

Total Score Part A ________. (Sum questions 1–5: 3 points for each Yes, 2 points for each Maybe, and 1 point for each No.)

Part B

	Yes	Maybe	No
6. Threaten to make your opponent look foolish to that opponent's superiors.	○	○	○
7. Promise good things to your opponent beyond what you can or will deliver.	○	○	○
8. Gain evidence about your opponent's negotiating position by trying to hire someone who knows key information.	○	○	○
9. Misrepresent factual information to your opponent to support your position.	○	○	○
10. Threaten severe consequences to your opponent if you don't get what you want.	○	○	○

Total Score Part B ________. (Sum questions 6–10: 3 points for each Yes, 2 points for each Maybe, and 1 point for each No.) Go to page 386 to interpret your scores.

GO ONLINE to find additional questionnaires at www.cengagebrain.com, search for Daft/Marcic Building Management Skills 1e, click on Free Online Resources, click on Additional Self-Assessments.

- Social Rapport

DISCOVER YOURSELF

SHUTTERSTOCK #53973379

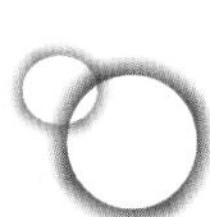

Chapter 10: Handling Difficult Conversations, Conflict, and Negotiation

DISCOVER KNOWLEDGE

Bill Gates and Steve Ballmer met at Harvard University in the mid-1970s, where they played poker and pushed their intellectual limits. Once they skipped an entire semester of a graduate economics class, and then crammed a few days before the final exam to learn all the material. Test results showed that Gates got a 99 and Ballmer a 97. Competition and hard work defined their early relationship—and it later defined the culture of Microsoft. In the early days, Gates served as CEO and focused on technology and business strategy while Ballmer handled most other matters. By the late 1990s, their centralized management style broke down in the midst of competitive and government challenges. Gates and Ballmer decided to switch roles. Ballmer became CEO and Gates was named "chief software architect." The result of this significant swap was indecision, lack of agreement, and personal clashes that threatened Microsoft's future. Gates' sarcastic side reared its ugly head during meetings, which undermined Ballmer's ability to execute his leadership role. The board of directors encouraged the two to resolve their differences. Gates and Ballmer met privately to talk through their disparities. Gates admitted that his behavior was not reinforcing teamwork to reach mutual goals. He changed his behavior to promote Ballmer as the number one executive with the authority to run and restructure the company.[2]

The success of a company such as Microsoft often depends on the quality of communication among managers, especially at the middle and upper levels. The ability of managers to sort out problems inherent in work relationships makes the critical difference in whether things get done or get stalled due to conflicts. Several of the chapters in this book are designed to build skills for managing relationships. The harsh reality is that major forces work against positive relationships in organizations. Busyness, distractions, the rush to get work done, fear of conflict, fear of difficult conversations, and personal resistance to "rocking the boat" by bringing up negative issues are all factors that make talking about relationships the last thing most managers want to do.[3] Difficulties and disagreements always arise in work relationships; a crucial skill for managers is the ability to work out difficulties, just as Bill Gates and Steve Ballmer worked out their differences at Microsoft.

Effective managers learn to surface rather than avoid or suppress personal differences. Managers have options that can be learned to manage the various interpersonal problems and conflicts that arise. By the end of this chapter, you will be well on your way toward acquiring the skills necessary to handle difficult conversations, resolve conflicts, and negotiate issues for mutual gain.

LEADING WORDS

"What you cannot talk about, you cannot resolve."
—**Loretta Malandro**
consultant and author of *Say It Right the First Time*

"If we try to listen we find it extraordinarily difficult, because we are always projecting our opinions and ideas, our prejudices, our background, our inclinations, our impulses; when they dominate, we hardly listen at all to what is being said."
—**Jiddu Krishnamurti**
Indian spiritual teacher and leader

"The most difficult thing in any negotiation, almost, is making sure that you strip it of the emotion and deal with the facts."
—**Howard Baker**
politician and former U.S. ambassador to Japan

"He who has learned to disagree without being disagreeable has discovered the most valuable secret of a diplomat."
—**Robert Estabrook**
former editor of *The Washington Post* editorial page

USE ROBUST DIALOGUE FOR TEAM ISSUES

In the late 1990s, NECX Global Exchange was a hot online marketplace for computer hardware and peripherals. After NECX was acquired by another company and went through a period of rapid growth, serious internal tensions arose that threatened the company's success. Henry Bertolon, cofounder and CEO, introduced the idea of robust dialogue to improve communication. "We'd have meetings that just melted down," he said. "Everyone would scream at each other and then leave." Bertolon hired Wil Calmas, a psychologist with an MBA, to lead a series of programs to get people talking—and listening—to one another on a deeper, authentic level. In the sessions, Calmas encouraged people to express fear, hostility, frustration, secret wishes—whatever feelings were affecting their lives and work. The dialogue sessions created a safe environment for people to honestly reveal their feelings, explore ideas, and build common ground. Bertolon also believed the sessions helped employees be more flexible and open to new ideas—ready to respond to the rapid changes taking place all around them.[4]

Many teams and organizations, like NECX, have communication meltdowns because of the strains of growth, merging with another company, rapid internal changes, or competitive pressures. Communication in some companies is poor even when things seem to be going smoothly. Henry Bertolon discovered the way to fix team communication at NECX was by using robust dialogue. There are numerous reasons a manager might want to use the dialogue technique. In meetings, some people want to fight for their point of view rather than listen to others. Other people think managers should make the tough decisions rather than ask a group to struggle with disagreement. The fear of disapproval, desire to avoid conflict, and a hectic work pace can combine to hinder open and effective communication among team members.

Is Team Dialogue Really Needed?

Is it safe to assume that competition, fear, and individualism that may impede communication prevail in most organizations? Yes, it is. Meetings too often include unstated agendas and blaming, insinuations, and power plays such as what happened at NECX. Or, people keep quiet to achieve the appearance of agreement. Small groups of individuals may have behind-the-scenes conversations about the causes and solutions to problems, but in formal meetings they soften their comments, or they don't speak at all. These bad habits of team communication are common.

The Abilene Paradox, as described in Chapter 6, partly explains the inability of groups to manage differences and achieve genuine agreement. Recall that the idea of the Abilene Paradox was born when a family decided to take a long drive to Abilene for a meal on a hot, dusty, miserable day. No one wanted to go, but no one would express his or her true opinion. Thus, they all did something no one wanted to do because no one spoke up. The theory states that individuals are not willing to act contrary to what they believe other members of the group are thinking or doing. Individuals do not want to openly voice their true feelings for fear of disagreement. These false assumptions limit the potential for good decisions based on honest information from divergent viewpoints. The frustration for managers is that valuable insights are hidden from view. Indeed, during meetings people may express the opposite of their true opinion or share inaccurate information just so they fit in and gain perceived approval from the group.[5]

How Does Robust Dialogue Work?

Travis, the manager of a plant that repaired and remanufactured jet aircraft engines, enjoyed the role of key decision maker. He might talk to one or two individuals and would usually end up making decisions without the involvement of most of his people. Travis wanted to grow as a manager and was coached by a consultant to try robust dialogue. This new method came in handy when a crisis arose at the plant about a failed engine repair. He brought together all the people who had information about the failed engine. The conference room was too small so they sat in a circle on the shop floor. They used a "shop stick," which was passed from person to person. When a person's turn came to hold the stick, that individual presented his or her full observation on the cause of

DISCOVER YOURSELF

Interpret Your Score: **Robust Dialogue** (Questionnaire 1)

Is your team communication style appropriate for a "robust dialogue"? Effective dialogue includes both disclosure and inquiry by participants. If you have a high score, you probably have the right communication mindset to succeed with team dialogue as described in the chapter. If your score is low, you may need to develop new communication habits to achieve better dialogue in teams you lead. Comparative data for **Robust Dialogue:** Thirty person Mean score = 22.2; Top Quartile = 25–27; Bottom Quartile = 16–19. Why is robust dialogue so important for resolving team issues? How can you improve your dialogue skills? CNOW and CourseMate users can access dynamically updated comparative data through www.cengagebrain.com.

© CENGAGE LEARNING 2014

the problem. Anyone not holding the stick could only listen. After everyone spoke and the full picture of the problem emerged, the stick was sent around for a second time so people could comment on what they had heard from others and suggest possible solutions. By the end of this robust dialogue, everyone had full information and agreed on proposed solutions. Participants broke into smaller groups to solve a part of the problem that had been clarified and coordinated during the dialogue. Travis was thrilled with the speed at which the complex problem was resolved.

The reason for Travis's success is illustrated in Exhibit 10.1. Most conversations look like the straight line in part A. People in a meeting want a straight line to the outcome because they would rather be elsewhere doing "important" work. Travis, however, led a conversation that looked like part B in Exhibit 10.1. The dialogue started by engaging divergent thinking and diverse perspectives, allowing the team to struggle through the listening and integration of widely different views to reach a decision point. Travis was smart enough to design a dialogue that would foster a solution when the problem was complicated. Although the dialogue took longer than a normal meeting, the problem was totally solved and implemented in less time than normal. The divergent stage of a dialogue draws out multiple perspectives, opinions, and insights. The convergent stage follows, in which information is integrated into a common interpretation, enabling the best solution.

As a manager, you can engage people in a dialogue by keeping some simple pointers[6] in mind:

- Have people sit in a circle or around a table so they have face-to-face connection with all present.
- Begin by spending a few minutes discussing the purpose of dialogue and agreeing on simple ground rules, such as showing respect to one another.
- Initially, give each person a chance to speak about the topic without interruption. There is no back-and-forth conversation until everyone has had a chance to speak and voice his or her perspective at least once.
- Some groups use a talking stick or talking ball to direct traffic. As one dialogue facilitator said, "This ball has the power. If you are holding the ball, you are empowered to speak until finished. If you don't have the ball, you are empowered to shut up and listen."[7]
- Each participant has the responsibility of *disclosure*. Disclosure, sometimes called advocating, during a dialogue means that everyone must be willing to say what is really on their minds about the subject.[8] Each participant must bring himself or herself fully into the conversation to help realize the truth. However, disclosure does not mean insistence upon your own opinion. When people insist that their view is "right," the truth remains hidden. All participants are expected to freely express their own thoughts as well as refrain from belittling the thoughts of others.
- Each participant has the responsibility of *inquiry*. Inquiry during a robust dialogue means to ask questions to deepen one's understanding about what something means. Inquiry also means to explore assumptions, both your own and those of other people. Inquiry means listening deeply and without defensiveness. Inquiry means that even when ideas are contrary to your own beliefs and values, you listen to understand how it makes sense to the speaker and to the group. This is in contrast to conventional listening, which is a period of waiting to talk while our ears are tuned to uncover errors and flaws as we plan our rebuttals.[9]
- At the end, allow ten minutes or more to collect and agree on key learning points from the dialogue.

Exhibit 10.1 The Dynamics of Robust Dialogue

Part A: Typical Group Decision Making

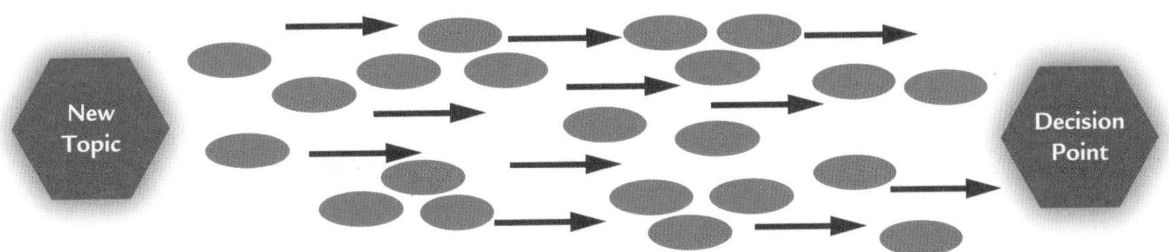

Part B: Robust Dialogue

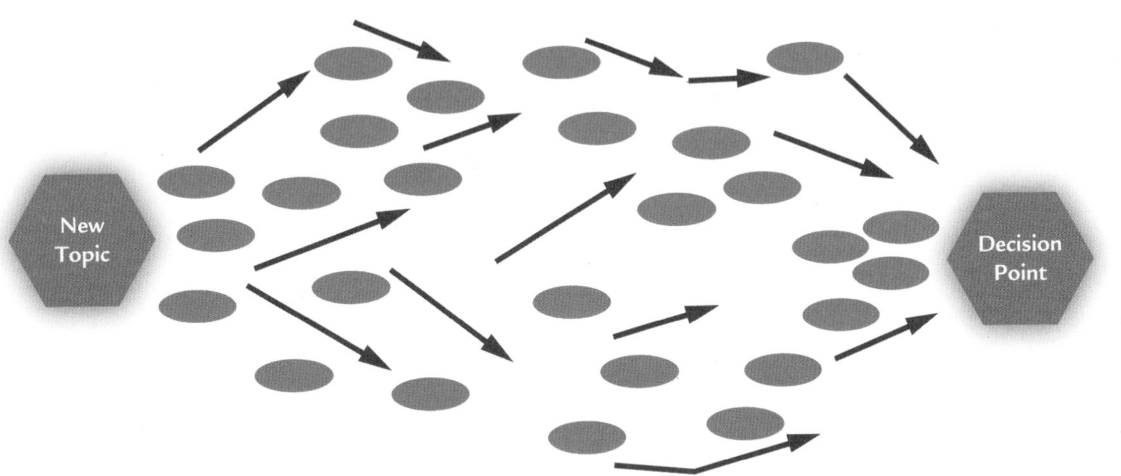

© CENGAGE LEARNING 2014

The Foundation of Dialogue

Improving communication through the use of dialogue can improve the entire organization.[10] Dialogue can harness the collective intelligence of the people around you.

A good way to understand the distinctive quality of dialogue is to contrast it with the debate or discussion we often use to communicate, as illustrated in Exhibit 10.2.[11] Typically, the intent of debate is to present one's own point of view and persuade others in the group to adopt it. A debate is often resolved by logic or by "beating down" opposing viewpoints. **Dialogue,** on the other hand, requires that participants suspend their attachment to a particular point of view so that a deeper level of listening, synthesis, and meaning can emerge from the group. A dialogue's focus is to reveal feelings and build common ground, with the emphasis on inquiry rather than argument.

HANDLING DIFFICULT CONVERSATIONS

Claudia Casselman, the vice president for an architectural firm, has just assigned a project to her newest hire. When Ayman, an experienced architect already on board, found out about the assignment to the new employee, he protested vehemently. "How come you overlooked me on this new project?" Ayman

Exhibit 10.2 Dialogue versus Discussion

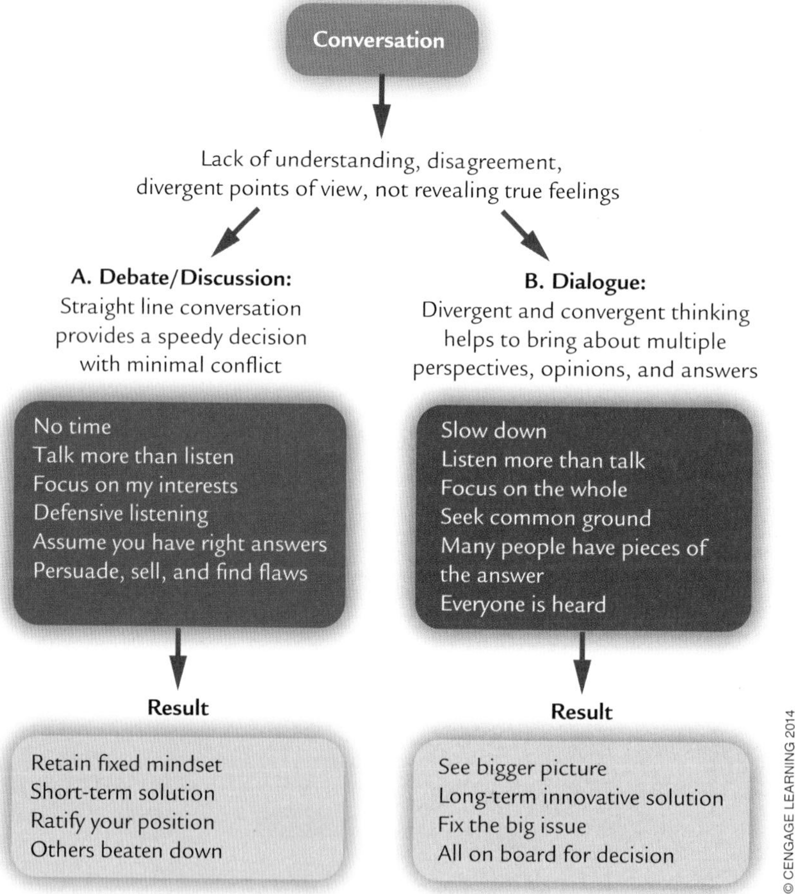

© CENGAGE LEARNING 2014

challenged. "You knew when I originally came to the firm that this is the type of work I was dying to do." Claudia was a bit surprised, because Ayman tended to grumble whenever she gave him extra work. She knows the assignment went to the correct person, but she realizes now she should have spoken with Ayman about his negative comments and grumbling long ago. His chronic complaints about how overworked he is bother others in the group and they too are afraid to ask for his help. This was a lesson for Claudia. She should have cleared up the conflict months ago instead of avoiding it and hoping it would go away.

Claudia had hidden her head in the sand to avoid a difficult conversation, which happens to many managers. The avoided conversation frequently comes back to haunt them. The good news is that handling a difficult conversation is a skill you can learn. The previous section was about conversations in a group or team setting. This section is about one-on-one difficult conversations.

A **difficult conversation** can be defined as a discussion between two or more people where (a) outcomes are important, (b) viewpoints differ, and (c) emotions run high. These three common threads make difficult conversations easy for us to put off because we don't want to deal with them.[12] Here are some practical examples that would be considered difficult conversations:

- Confronting an associate who behaves offensively or makes suggestive or inappropriate comments
- Giving the boss comments about his or her behavior

- Approaching a department head who is breaking his own quality policies
- Talking to a team member who isn't meeting obligations or carrying her share of the work
- Laying off or dismissing an employee
- Talking to a colleague who is hoarding information or resources
- Giving unfavorable feedback to a direct report[13]

The goal in each of these situations is to have a successful conversation that enables the free flow of information. The aim is for both participants to openly and candidly express their opinions, share their feelings, and articulate their theories, even when they are controversial or unpopular.

A GUIDE FOR CONDUCTING DIFFICULT CONVERSATIONS

One behavioral characteristic of an effective manager is the ability to have a successful conversation about a difficult topic. This is a skill that can be learned. To handle a difficult conversation, think about both the preparation and the process, as illustrated in Exhibit 10.3.

Prepare Your Mind: Learning versus Combat

When you anticipate you will be engaging in a difficult conversation, the first thing to do is step back to get yourself into the right frame of mind. Open your mind to the big picture and to learning as much as you can about the other person's point of view. One critical skill when confronted with a risky, controversial, and emotional conversation is the free and honest sharing of thoughts, theories, views, and feelings that will lead to a successful outcome.[14]

However, if you are rushed, anxious, frustrated, or confused about the situation you will not have the right frame of mind to accomplish the purpose of the conversation. If you don't prepare, there is a good chance that you will tighten up mentally, feel anxious, retreat into yourself, and adopt a *combat* mentality, probably without realizing it. In the combat mindset, you want to win and you want the other person to lose, so the conversation becomes a battlefield. If a combat mentality takes over, the conversation can easily deteriorate into verbal attacks, retaliation, or trying to get even.

For example, Derek, an executive at a pharmaceuticals company, invited Laura Chen, a middle manager, to sit in on the meetings of a companywide sustainability taskforce. Laura was remarkably silent during the meetings. Derek was frustrated and concluded that Laura was too busy to participate and had little to offer the task force. He decided to talk to her about it. One frame of mind he could take would be to encourage Laura to resign because she wasn't participating the way he expected. Another frame of mind would be to ask himself why she didn't say much on the committee. He could prepare himself to learn about her work and career plans and how the committee fit those plans. In the first frame of mind, Derek would go into the conversation with the small view that he needed to get Laura off the committee. In the second frame, Derek's mindset would be much bigger—he would approach Laura, wanting to learn as much as he could about her and the role of the task force in her career goals.[15]

Exhibit 10.3 Handling a Difficult Conversation

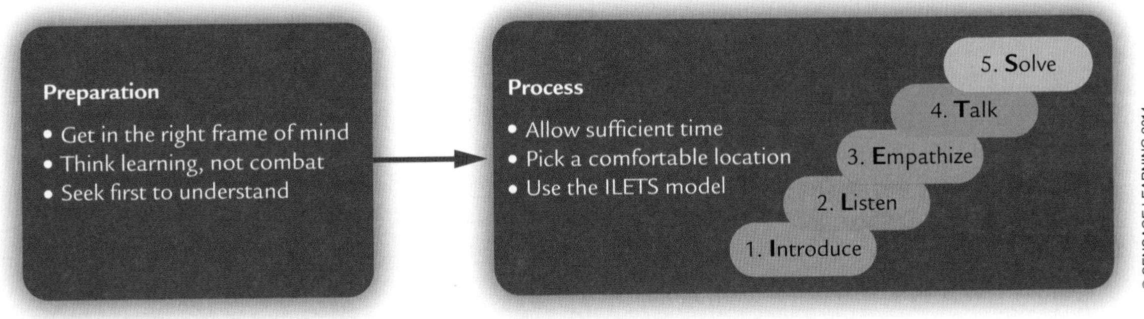

© CENGAGE LEARNING 2014

The First Rule for Any Difficult Conversation

The most important step of a difficult conversation is for each person to truly hear the other. How can you get another person to hear and understand you, especially when he or she may be upset or agitated? Here is a Zen story that illustrates the correct approach: The Zen master instructed a student to bring him some tea. The student dutifully went to the kitchen and prepared the tea. Soon the student returned with a teapot and a cup and saucer on a tray. The master picked up the teapot and poured some tea into the cup. Soon the cup was full, but the master kept pouring. The tea spilled onto the saucer, then onto the tray, and then onto the floor. "Master, Master, what are you doing? You're spilling the tea." The master responded, "Yes, so I am. What is the lesson?" The confused student stammered that he did not know. "Okay, then. Return the tea to the kitchen and clean up this mess. Then I will give you the lesson." The student returned and sat cross-legged before the master. Soon the master provided his lesson: "A full cup will hold no more tea."

Here is the lesson for you as a manager: When involved in a conversation and you keep talking and talking to make a point, it is like pouring tea into a cup. The head of the person receiving all your talk is like a full teacup, so it can't accept any more tea. All the words and points of view are being wasted, because the person with whom you are talking is filled with beliefs, opinions, skepticism, worry, fear, defensiveness, and things to do, along with distrust and distraction. And your talk is not helping. If you really want that person to hear what you have to say, stop talking. You have to let people "empty their cup" before you speak. When you allow someone to first empty his or her cup on the topic without interruption, there will then be space in the cup for the person to hear what you think. So, to be heard, listen first. When the person has finished, then you can speak. Indeed, you will find that most people, after emptying their cup, will *want* to hear what you have to say.[16] The bottom line is: "To be understood, first seek to understand the other person."[17]

DISCOVER KNOWLEDGE

> **DISCOVER YOURSELF**
>
> **Interpret Your Score: Difficult Conversations** (Questionnaire 2)
>
> The ability to handle a difficult conversation is the mark of a successful communicator. Your score for Part A reflects a combative or defensive one-on-one communication style; hence, a low score is better. Comparative data for **Combative Style** (Part A): Thirty person Mean score = 14.6; Top Quartile = 16–18; Bottom Quartile = 11–13. Your score for Part B reflects a non-defensive communication style, for which a high score is better. Comparative data for **Non-Defensive Style** (Part B): Thirty person Mean score = 17.0; Top Quartile = 19–21; Bottom Quartile = 13–15. How do your Part A and Part B scores compare to others in your group or class? CNOW and CourseMate users can access dynamically updated comparative data through www.cengagebrain.com.

© CENGAGE LEARNING 2014

Use the ILETS Model

When leading a crucial conversation you can use a step-by-step technique called the **ILETS model**, which is illustrated in Exhibit 10.3.[18]

1. **I=Introduce the topic.** This statement tells the other person the subject that you would like to discuss. This introduction should be concrete and factual rather than theoretical or judgmental.

2. **L=Listen to the other person.** Let the other person empty his or her cup. For difficult conversations, you must be sincere in inviting others to share their stories, what's on their minds, and their perceptions of the issue. Listen actively and supportively. Ask questions and paraphrase what is said to clarify your understanding. Hear and understand the other person so that he or she will want to hear and understand you.

3. **E=Empathize. Empathy** means being able to put yourself in other people's shoes, sense their emotions, and understand their perspective. Let the other person know you care and that you respect his or her feelings and opinions. Effective communicators learn the skill of *professional intimacy*, which means they show compassion and concern for others without getting caught up in the emotions of the conversation.[19] When you acknowledge another's story, you validate its importance but you don't necessarily give up your own opinions, ideas, or perspectives.

4. **T=Talk.** Now is your turn to talk and tell your story or perspective. Be calm and convey facts in an

objective manner. If you are speaking to a subordinate, a calm tone can help the individual feel comfortable and not threatened by the conversation. The subordinate may have spent hours or even days dreading this meeting. You might reassure the employee that he or she is not in trouble. When you're having a difficult conversation, emphasize that you want to understand the other person's viewpoint and solve the problem together.

5. S=Solve the problem. Now that both parties have told their stories and all the facts and viewpoints are in the open, it is feasible to work toward a solution. When both parties know what the other party wants and needs, it is easier to brainstorm options to meet the needs of both sides.

The ILETS approach will work well for most difficult conversations. Hear the concrete facts and interpretations from both sides, but start with the other person speaking first. Ask questions to get the full story. Listen deeply so that you understand the impact of events on the person. Acknowledge the other person's emotions of pain, anger, embarrassment, ridicule, or sadness that the events might have triggered. Here's how one manager handled a difficult conversation with a new employee who was yelling at teammates and blaming them when things went wrong. She introduces the topic, listens first, gives her view second, and then moves to problem solving.[20]

Adrianne: *Hi Sue. I wanted to talk with you about how things have been going for you over the last couple of months. I've had some complaints from other team members that you've said they are slow and sloppy in their work.*

Sue: *I get frustrated with how long it takes people to get me the information I need. We lost a client because Roberto got his part of the proposal to me late and it contained errors. I knew it was going to happen because no one else seems to care about doing things right. The harder I try to get people to work faster and better, the more they seem to drag their feet and goof off. I'm really determined to succeed in this job, but I'm getting roadblocks thrown up by the people who are supposed to be helping me win new business.*

Adrianne: *I understand your frustration, Sue. I know you worked hard to win this job and that you feel your performance is being undermined by circumstances out of your control. But everyone has been working really long, hard hours just to keep up with the work recently. People felt really bad when you blamed them and told them they were slow and sloppy, after they had worked overtime and even taken work home on weekends. It's easy for us to get frustrated about a lot of things, but we can't take it out on others in the group. We're a team and we need to work together on projects and respect one another. The other members of the team know you work hard, but they work hard too. They want you to succeed in this job, but they become frustrated and demoralized when you accuse them of not caring about the work.*

Sue: *I didn't mean to offend anyone. I guess I overreacted after we lost that client. It just seems to me that we could do things faster if we eliminated some of the steps that seem redundant.*

Adrianne: *Other firms face the same kind of constraints we do, but maybe we can review our procedures and see if there are some steps that can be eliminated. Have you talked with other team members about this?*

Sue: *No. I guess I should do that. They've all been here longer than I have.*

Adrianne: *That's a good observation, and they can help you if you ask. And maybe you can keep track of situations where things seem to move too slowly and talk with me about them. Maybe we need to add some support staff or review workloads. The important thing to remember, though, is that you will succeed as part of a team here, not as an individual.*

Sue: *You're right. I was told that when I was hired. I guess I need to apologize for my behavior and see if the team will give me another chance.*

Additional Tools for Difficult Conversations

At one point or another, every manager will be required to participate in or initiate a difficult conversation. It is not possible to alleviate the apprehension of these exchanges, but it is possible to remove the emotion so that each person can be heard. You may be tempted to avoid a difficult conversation, believing it will stir up feelings such as fear, confusion, embarrassment, anger, or distress. Taking the ILETS approach will make these conversations less stressful. Also, consider the following tips when you plan your next difficult conversation:[21]

- **Plan the best time and place.** Don't have a difficult conversation on the run or when there

isn't sufficient time allotted to complete the conversation. If you think it can be held in your office, fine. However, a neutral location may put the other person at ease.

- **Invite a third person.** Ask a third person to observe if you are concerned that the participant will fly off the handle, create a scene, or distort what happened.
- **Rehearse beforehand.** Rehearse a difficult conversation with a friend, colleague, or family member. Practice listening and staying even-keeled in the conversation. You can also ask your practice partner to observe your body language and make suggestions so you won't be grimacing or making unpleasant expressions out of nervousness.
- **Avoid conversation killers.** You will kill the other person's interest if you are thinking, "You are the problem," "It's your fault," or "I'm right and you are wrong." Speaking your opinion as "truth" instead of just your perception creates tension. Another killer is not listening and showing it with your body language: not making eye contact, fidgeting like you want to be elsewhere, or staring into space like you aren't paying attention.

How to Deliver Bad News

When delivering bad news (firing, layoff, death, or catastrophe), use extra care in preparing for this conversation. Reverse the procedure of the ILETS model by speaking first and listening second. The ITELS model is:

I=Introduce. Set the stage by introducing the topic.

T=Talk. Put the bad news out there first. Say it straight. Don't beat around the bush.

E=Empathize. Understand how the other person is feeling—accept the raw emotion this news might cause.

L=Listen. Let the other person spill his or her emotions. Listen carefully and supportively to help the person get the emotions out.

S=Solve. Offer to be of help. If you can be of assistance, make sure you follow up on commitments made during the conversation.

For example, let's say your neighbor's dog is run over in the street and killed. It would not make sense to introduce the topic of her dog and listen first to the

DISCOVER KNOWLEDGE

What's Your Problem?

Q: I share an office with Jay, who is a pretty decent guy and gets his work done. But he does one thing that really annoys me. He talks to me too much. Sometimes it is work related, but he goes on and on. Other times he brings up office gossip, which I feel is a big waste of time. We don't punch a clock, which means I have to stay late if I don't get my work done by 5 P.M. Most of the time Jay is yakking away, I am thinking about all the work I have to do. The thing is, I really like Jay, as do others. So I don't want to alienate him. And since we share an office, I don't want there to be tension. And I would rather not quit my job, but I can hardly take it anymore. So, what can I do?

A: If you quit your job, you can be pretty much guaranteed there will be a new "Jay" at that place, too. Some statistics say that up to 30 percent of employees have annoying behaviors, so good luck finding a place where everyone is tic-free. What you can do is try to understand the reason why Jay behaves this way. Thinking hard about how his habit came to be will go a long way toward accepting Jay. Then list Jay's good qualities, so you can focus on one of those when you get frustrated. If none of that works, have a "difficult conversation" with Jay. Start by matter-of-factly bringing up the subject of your joint talking. Try to draw out how he feels about it. Then be quiet and just listen to what he says. Only after he is finished should you give your point of view, remaining as calm as possible. When both of you hear both sides, there is potential for a shift in understanding and behavior. You might also suggest a solution, such as a specific time for talking. Rather than view Jay's excessive talking as a personal affront, try to see this as a business issue to solve. Good luck!

© CENGAGE LEARNING 2014

neighbor speak about her beloved pet. In a case of bad news, you speak first, "I have terrible news. Your dog was just run over in the street." Then you can listen carefully to help your neighbor cope with the tragedy.

Your job is to deliver bad news clearly and compassionately. You may want to prepare in advance, just as with other kinds of difficult conversations. If the information you are giving is final, such as dismissal of an employee, make sure the person does not have a false hope that the decision can be reversed. Be empathetic, but don't compromise. You can measure your success by the other person's understanding.[22]

WHAT IS YOUR CONFLICT HANDLING STYLE?

Why are skills for team dialogue and difficult conversations among individuals so important for managers? Because conflicts that have to be managed exist within every organization. Each individual has his or her own approach to conflict, and effective conflict management has a positive impact on team cohesiveness, employee motivation, and performance. Conflict can arise among members within a team or between teams.

Conflict refers to antagonistic interaction in which one party, in order to achieve its goals, will prevent or block the intentions or goals of another.[23] Whenever people work together, some conflict is inevitable. Teams or individuals may find themselves in competition over resources, such as money or supplies. Differences in goals, such as growth versus profitability, short-term versus long-term priorities, or the importance of centralization versus decentralization, are natural in organizations. Individual salespeople's targets may put them in conflict with one another or with the sales manager. Moreover the sales department's goals of rapid delivery may conflict with the manufacturing department's goals of producing high quality products.

Types of Conflict

Two basic types of conflict that occur in organizations are task conflict and relationship conflict.[24] **Task conflict** refers to disagreements among people about the goals to be achieved or the tasks to be performed. For example, two shop supervisors might disagree over whether to replace a valve in a machine or let it run despite the unusual noise it is making. **Relationship conflict** refers to interpersonal incompatibility that creates tension and personal animosity among people. In one team at a children's furniture manufacturer, some team members who needed peace and quiet were irked at those who wanted music playing in the background. Compulsively neat team members found it impossible to work with those who liked working among lots of clutter.[25] As a manager, you will likely encounter these kinds of task and relationship conflicts many times.

Research suggests that mild to moderate task conflict can be beneficial because it leads to better decision making and problem solving. Different viewpoints and moderate disagreement during a team dialogue, for example, help the team reach a better solution. On the other hand, relationship conflict is typically associated with negative consequences for team effectiveness. One study of top management teams found that task conflict was associated with higher decision quality, commitment, and decision acceptance, whereas the presence of relationship conflict significantly reduced those same outcomes.[26]

A healthy level of task conflict prevents the Abilene Paradox, described earlier in this chapter, in which people are reluctant to express contrary opinions. People need to express differences of opinion and opposing ideas to find real agreement and the best solution. However, conflict that is too strong, or conflict that is focused on personal rather than work issues, is typically damaging to a team's morale and productivity. Too much conflict can be destructive; too little conflict prevents a healthy exchange of viewpoints. The challenge for you as a manager is to find the right balance between conflict and cooperation.

Styles to Handle Conflict

Exhibit 10.4 illustrates five styles for handling conflict. How an individual approaches conflict is measured along two dimensions: *assertiveness* and *cooperation*. The extent to which you want to satisfy your own concerns determines the degree to which you are assertive or unassertive. The extent to which you want to satisfy the concerns of others determines the degree to which you are cooperative or uncooperative. Although you may relate to one or two of the styles shown in Exhibit 10.4, as a manager you will end up adopting aspects of all of these styles, depending on the type of conflict you find yourself involved in. Effective

Exhibit 10.4 Interpersonal Conflict Handling Styles

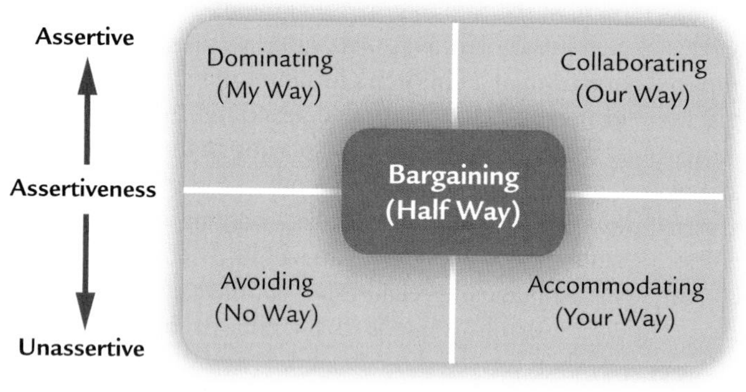

Sources: Adapted from Kenneth Thomas, "Conflict and Conflict Management," in *Handbook of Industrial and Organizational Behavior*, ed. M. D. Dunnette (New York: John Wiley, 1976), p. 900; and Nan Peck, "Conflict 101: Styles of Fighting," North Virginia Community College Web site, September 20, 2005, http://www.nvcc.edu/home/npeck/conflicthome/conflict/Conflict101/conflictstyles.htm (accessed April 13, 2011).

managers vary their style to fit a specific situation, as each style is appropriate in certain circumstances.[27]

1. *Dominating Style (my way)*. **Aspects:** This style reflects a high degree of assertiveness. The desire is to get one's own way and fulfill one's self-interest. **When to use:** The dominating style should be used when quick, decisive action is vital on important issues or unpopular actions, such as during emergencies or urgent cost-cutting. This is a "fight to the finish" style in which the person intends to win without concern for others or the relationship. There is no concession on any point. With a dominating style, you may win the battle but damage the relationship. **Attitude:** "I like to speak my mind and what I say goes."

2. *Avoiding Style (no way)*. **Aspects:** This style reflects neither assertiveness nor cooperativeness, which means that conflict is avoided if possible. **When to use:** Avoiding is appropriate when an issue is trivial, when there is no chance of winning, when a delay to gather more information is needed, or when a disruption would be costly. One can pretend a conflict doesn't exist or not want to engage with another because an argument is inevitable, so withdrawing is the preferred behavior. **Attitude:** "I usually don't express opinions that will create a controversy."

3. *Bargaining Style (half way)*. **Aspects:** This style reflects a moderate amount of both assertiveness and cooperativeness. **When to use:** Bargaining is appropriate when the goals on both sides are equally important, when opponents have equal power and both sides want to split the difference, or when people need to arrive at temporary or expedient solutions under time pressure. Both parties are partially satisfied because common ground was found through a give-and-take process. **Attitude:** "After failing to get my way, I seek a fair compromise of gains and losses for everyone."

4. *Accommodating Style (your way)*. **Aspects:** This style reflects a high degree of cooperativeness and a desire to oblige others. **When to use:** This style works best when people realize that they are wrong, when an issue is more important to others than to oneself, when building social credits for use in later discussions, or when maintaining positive relationships is especially important. The accommodator makes peace to get past the issues, but if this is done on a regular basis the accommodator might begin to resent the other party. Managers who use this style too often may also be perceived as martyrs, too weak, or submissive. **Attitude:** "If it makes other people happy, I'm all for it."

5. *Collaborating Style (our way)*. **Aspects:** This style reflects a high degree of both assertiveness and cooperativeness. **When to use:** This style is popular because it enables both parties to win, although it may require substantial dialogue. The parties talk and listen to each other so they can discuss and clarify goals and areas of agreement. The collaborating style is especially valuable when both sets of concerns are too important to be compromised, when insights from different people need to be merged into an overall solution, or when the commitment of both sides is needed for a consensus. Collaboration requires courage, consideration, and the willingness of the parties to understand and acknowledge each other's positions. **Attitude:** "I tell others my ideas, actively seek out their ideas, and search for a mutually beneficial solution."

Each approach can be successful, depending on the people involved and the situation.[28] As a general rule, managers who use a collaborating approach are believed to be more successful conflict handlers who generate positive feelings toward themselves. On the other hand, the avoiding and dominating styles are believed to often create negative feelings among others. The bargaining style usually produces positive feelings. The accommodating style tends to create

Interpret Your Score: Handling Conflict (Questionnaire 3)

Five categories of conflict-handling strategies described in the chapter are measured by these 20 questions. Comparative data for **Avoiding** (Part A): Thirty person Mean score = 7.1; Top Quartile = 9–11; Bottom Quartile = 4–5. **Dominating** (Part B): Thirty person Mean score = 8.4; Top Quartile = 10–12; Bottom Quartile = 4–7. **Bargaining** (Part C): Thirty person Mean score = 10.1; Top Quartile = 12–12; Bottom Quartile = 4–8. **Accommodating** (Part D): Thirty person Mean score = 10.5; Top Quartile = 11–12; Bottom Quartile = 8–10. **Collaborating** (Part E): Thirty person Mean score = 10.5; Top Quartile = 12–12; Bottom Quartile = 8–9. The higher your score for a strategy, the more likely that is your preferred conflict-handling approach. A lower score suggests you probably do not use that approach. How do you feel about your approach to handling conflict? What changes would you like to make? CNOW and CourseMate users can access dynamically updated comparative data through www.cengagebrain.com.

© CENGAGE LEARNING 2014

positive feelings but the manager is seen as not strong in his or her performance and abilities. Your typical conflict handling style will have a lot to do with how you negotiate personal and business agreements.

NEGOTIATION STRATEGIES FOR REACHING AGREEMENTS

Alex, an executive with a *Fortune* 500 firm, is known as an excellent negotiator. Alex's company negotiated with a small European firm to buy an ingredient for a health care product. The two sides quickly settled on volume (one million pounds annually) and price ($18 per pound). But they could not agree on exclusivity, which the U.S. firm wanted and the European firm refused to give. This made no sense to Alex because his company would take all the ingredient the firm could produce. He started probing beneath the surface with questions, and flatly asked: "What are your reasons for not giving us an exclusive deal?" The answer surprised the U.S. team: A relative of the European firm's owner used 200 pounds of the ingredient a year. With that information out on the table, the two sides quickly agreed to carve out an exception for the owner's relative to purchase the product she needed, and all other sales would go exclusively to Alex's firm.[29]

Alex had the negotiating skills to dig below the surface, find the reason for a stalled negotiation, and get talks back on track. Managers often use a formal negotiation process to reach business agreements and contracts. Negotiators engage in give-and-take discussions to consider various alternatives and reach a joint decision that is acceptable to both parties. **Negotiation** is a formal process of discussion used to reach an agreement between parties in conflict, such as negotiating a contract between a union and management or when a business is to be bought or sold. Differences between the parties are resolved by systematic negotiation.

Many people don't realize that they are involved in informal negotiations all the time. For example, you may negotiate with another student when buying a used textbook, or with friends when you decide which movie to see, or with your life partner about where to go on vacation or which car to purchase. If you decide to remodel your kitchen, you will likely negotiate with the contractor and perhaps the appliance store. With negotiation, there are two key parts: the planning and the actual negotiation.

Planning the Negotiation

Planning is the key step to achieve a successful outcome.[30] Whether negotiating royalties on a book contract, buying a home, becoming a vendor for Walmart, or negotiating with all the people involved in putting on a wedding, planning is an essential aspect of negotiating. It is important not to get lazy and just "show up" and start talking without thinking through the various issues at hand. Most experts agree that the outcome of a negotiation has less to do with how forcefully you argue in the negotiation and more to do with how well you prepare in advance. It feels great to uncover nuggets of information that will help you do better in the negotiation. Information and preparation will also give you confidence. There are valuable techniques to use in the actual negotiation, but your best weapon is to be thoroughly prepared for the challenges you will face.

Know Your Priorities

The first thing you need to do is decide what is most important to you. Begin the negotiation preparation, whether it is business or personal, by getting clear about the issues at stake for your side and determining your top priorities. Write down the key issues on paper in order of their importance. Also, think about what you will need in order to achieve your priorities. What type of information, documents, licenses, or financial backing will you need prior to attending the first session of a specific negotiation? Prepare any documents or financing arrangements in advance, if possible. The more professional and in control of the details you are as you go into a negotiation, the more likely you are to achieve your goals and priorities.

Search for Standards that May Apply

Learn if any standards exist that are relevant to the issue you are negotiating. Taking this search a step further—try to find standards that are favorable to a successful outcome for you. For example, the online *Kelley Blue Book* reports prices for used cars, so when you set the price for selling your ten-year-old Ford Taurus, you have an industry standard to point to as fair market value. Standards can be researched in advance as part of the planning and will help support your position.[31]

Know Your Alternatives

What will you do if the negotiation fails? Think through your next best alternative.[32] Facing and defining precisely what you will do helps you put a value on your options and reach a bottom line figure beyond which you will walk away. The next best option is called the **best alternative to a negotiated agreement (BATNA).** Roger Fisher and William Ury, the authors who coined the BATNA term in their bestselling book, *Getting to Yes*, point out: "The more easily and happily you can walk away from a negotiation, the greater your capacity to affect its outcome."[33]

Importance of the Relationship versus the Outcome

Is the person you are negotiating with your boss? Your cousin? Or someone you will never see again and don't care about at all? The role of the other party in your life may affect your strategy for the negotiation. If it is a one-shot deal where the financial outcome is all important, and you will never see the person again, you may fight harder for the outcome you want. But if you care about preserving an ongoing relationship, you may settle for less. It may be better to compromise now to enhance the relationship. American managers have learned the importance of compromise to enhance relationships when doing business in other countries. However, it is essential that managers aren't too eager to compromise, says negotiation expert Jim Camp. If you enter a negotiation with compromise on your mind, then that probably will be your outcome.[34]

Conducting the Negotiation

If you've prepared and planned carefully, you'll be much more comfortable and confident when it comes time for the actual negotiation. Experience is the best way to improve negotiation skills, but even a novice negotiator can do better by taking a valid approach and following some simple guidelines, as described in the following sections.

Integrative or Distributive Approach?

A negotiation is typically categorized as using either an *integrative* or a *distributive* approach.[35] Exhibit 10.5 provides a comparison of the two approaches. The **integrative approach** tries to combine the needs of both

Exhibit 10.5 Integrative versus Distributive Negotiation

	Integrative Approach	Distributive Approach
Mindset	Cooperation	Playing hardball
Goal	Joint gain	Own gain
Information	Share	Conceal
Understanding	What other side needs/wants	Own demands/interests
Assumption	Grow the pie for all	Get bigger share of fixed pie
Tactic	Use reason and principle	Apply pressure and emotion
Solution	Help all sides	Block others

Source: Based on La Piana Associates, "The Negotiation Process: The Difference between Integrative and Distributive Negotiation." www.lapiana.org (July 2007).

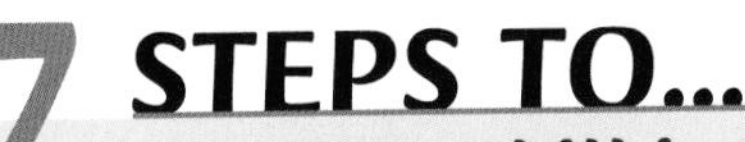

More Skill in Negotiations

1. **Allow silence.** Most people feel uncomfortable with silence. Experts say this negotiating technique can often get the other side to make concessions or agree to points they had no intention of accepting.
2. **Arrange the seating.** Where you sit and whom you sit near during a negotiation matters. If you sit across from someone, you may signal a competitive or combative mode. Sitting at one corner of the table with your counterpart to your side signals a collaborative approach.
3. **Don't accept the first offer.** Even if the offer meets all your needs, don't accept a first offer because the other party will leave dissatisfied, thinking they could have done better in the negotiation. Make a counteroffer that forces some small concession in your direction.
4. **Have other offers pending.** Having offers from other parties strengthens your position to negotiate for better terms. Basically, your counterpart will be competing with other bidders rather than competing with you. The other party will want to beat the pending deals you already have.
5. **Exaggerate things you don't care about.** Making a fuss about conceding things you don't really care about can sometimes encourage a concession from the other party. A little theatrics can keep the other party guessing about what really matters to you.
6. **Try good cop, bad cop.** In negotiating, one person on a team can act tough while the other acts mild and sympathetic, which may cause the other party to reveal information to the "good guy" when the "bad guy" is out of the room.
7. **Be Prepared for the Other Side's Tactics.** The other party probably knows some negotiating ploys too, so don't let their tactics rattle you. If someone uses silence on you, for example, simply ask, "Did I miss something that needs to be addressed?" This will require an answer and get things moving. If the other party tries seating tricks, such as sitting higher than you, suggest rearranging the chairs.

Sources: Based on Robert Adler, Benson Rosen, and Elliot Silverstein, "Thrust and Parry: The Art of Tough Negotiating," *Training & Development* (March 1996): 43–47; Rob Walker, "Take It Or Leave It: The Only Guide to Negotiating You Will Ever Need," *Inc.* (August 2003): 74–82; and Robb Mandelbaum, "How to Negotiate Effectively," *Inc.*, November 1, 2010, http://www.inc.com/magazine/20101101/how-to-negotiate-effectively.html (accessed April 12, 2011).

sides and is based on a win-win assumption that tries for a creative solution to benefit both parties. Those involved in integrative negotiations want everyone to walk away with a gain and a positive feeling. Participants look at the conflict from different angles, consider trade-offs, and try to "expand the pie" for everyone instead of fighting over how to divide it. This is a good style to use when the relationship is important to you. The philosophy behind integrative negotiation is an attitude of plenty to go around and you benefit from compromise and cooperation because long-term results foster trust and harmony.

The other type of negotiation is a distributive one, which means the outcomes will be dispersed and you had better get your full share. This **distributive approach** assumes a win-lose negotiation. With distributive negotiation, one party gets something he or she wants only if the other gives up something they have. The outcome likely won't have the feel of an equitable deal. One party will believe he or she lost out, and the other party will feel as if he or she got the better deal. This type of negotiation isn't good if you want to build lasting relationships, but it may work if you want to get the best price regardless of damage to the other party. When the economy is weak, people with extra cash might use a distributive approach to buy houses at rock bottom prices from people who have lost their jobs, for example. Distributive negotiations take place when financially strapped individuals need to quickly sell cars, boats, or other personal belongings in order to raise cash. The other party can offer prices well below fair market price to take advantage of a desperate situation.

A good example that illustrates the two types of negotiation is the story about the last orange in the fruit bowl. Two sisters both wanted the orange and argued

over who was going to get it. This was a distributive negotiation because one sibling would win so the other would lose. Then their mother walked in and wanted to know what they were arguing over. The mother, after hearing their arguments, asked each of her daughters why she wanted the orange. One said she was hungry and wanted to eat the orange; the other said she wanted to use the rind in an art project she was working on. Voilà! The mother used an integrative approach and was able to give them both what they wanted.[36] Although the integrative style is preferred, realistically there will be times when a negotiation needs to be distributive because of cost considerations and a fixed pie.

Who Makes the First Offer?

It is generally best to let the other party go first when it is time to consider offers.[37] Many negotiators think whichever side puts their price on the table first may lose out if they set the price range too high or low. In some cases, you may want to go first in order to inflate your offer, because it is easier to go down in price than to go up. The inflated first offer raises the bar of the perceived value of the item being negotiated. The other party may make a counter-offer that is more attractive than expected.

DISCOVER KNOWLEDGE

> **DISCOVER YOURSELF**
>
> **Interpret Your Score: Negotiation Strategies** (Questionnaire 4)
>
> Which techniques are considered legitimate in a serious negotiation, and which techniques cross the line into unethical territory? Your score for Part A should be fairly high because these five techniques are considered to be legitimate forms of concealment and bluffing in a business negotiation. Your score for Part B is probably lower, because these five techniques are considered by most business students to be inappropriate. On a seven-point scale of ethical appropriateness, the first five techniques received scores of 6.10, 5.84, 5.75, 5.37, and 4.28 respectively by a sample of business students, and the second five techniques received scores of 2.35, 2.20, 2.00, 1.99, and 1.87. Other comparative data for **Legitimate Negotiating** (Part A): Thirty person Mean score = 9.8; Top Quartile = 12–15; Bottom Quartile = 6–8. For **Inappropriate Negotiating** (Part B): Thirty person Mean score = 5.6; Top Quartile = 6–9; Bottom Quartile = 5–5. Are you willing to use "inappropriate" techniques to win a negotiation? Are you unwilling to use any of the "appropriate" techniques? What do your scores mean to you? CNOW and CourseMate users can access dynamically updated comparative data through www.cengagebrain.com.

© CENGAGE LEARNING 2014

Focus on Underlying Interests

It is always better to concentrate on your and the other party's underlying interests, and not on stated positions.[38] That is, don't just focus on what the other side says it wants (i.e., price, amount, characteristics) from the negotiation, but find out *why* they want it. Positions appear as concrete, specific, and inflexible statements. Interests go deeper and reflect the party's underlying needs, wants, and concerns. It is easy to assume you know the underlying need when you don't. Stated positions are demands that create yes-or-no obstacles during a negotiation, whereas underlying interests present problems that can be solved creatively. In an integrative negotiation, it is possible to invent options for mutual gain.

An electronics company called Barker Industries was coming out with a new device that would revolutionize television remote controls. Competitors were working in the same area, and Barker wanted to be first to market. Managers were in negotiations with a manufacturer in China for a rush order. The manufacturer was able to make and ship the product in four months for $20 million. Barker wanted the products sooner and for a lower price. Eventually the two sides reached a tentative agreement of $18 million with delivery in three months. The negotiator for Barker was still not satisfied and asked, "Why can't you make them any faster?" The counter-part explained that manufacturing was not the problem: "We can make them in two months but the shipping costs are prohibitive." After some more questions, Barker's negotiator proposed a solution: "We ship all over the world and have negotiated very reasonable rates because of our volume. Let us have our shipper transport the goods at our price, and you pay for the shipping." The Chinese manufacturer was thrilled. The final deal was delivery in two and a half months at a cost of $17.5 million. Everyone was happy.[39]

Listen and Ask Questions

A good strategy for most negotiations is to listen and ask questions.[40] You can learn more about your opponent's position, their constraints, and their needs by being quiet or asking questions. Smart negotiators want to learn the other side's constraints so they can help overcome them. Don't dismiss the opposing party's limitation as unreasonable or think "that's their problem." You can take it on as your own problem and try to come up with a solution for your opponent so you can get closer to an agreement. Recall our earlier example of Alex, the negotiator from the *Fortune* 500 company who dug into the reasons why the European company wouldn't provide an exclusive contract. Asking questions enabled Alex to solve the constraint by allowing 200 pounds of the product to be sold to the owner's relative. Experts agree you can gain more by listening and questioning than by being forceful and arrogant. Don't respond to overbearing behavior with your own version of being overbearing. Instead, ask questions and listen as you work toward a solution.

Hold Your Ground

When a negotiator is inexperienced or feels intimidated by the other side, he or she tends to over-compromise. We overestimate the importance of relationships and want approval from others, so it's easy to compromise too much in order to keep the peace, establish goodwill, and preserve a positive working relationship. A good point to remember is that, even when people are angry and upset during a negotiation, they typically get over it quickly. There will be times when you have to risk damaging the relationship in order to hold your ground in an important negotiation.

NEED TO KNOW

- Robust dialogue is a technique to improve communication in teams. Dialogue requires people to suspend their attachment to a particular point of view so that a deeper level of listening, synthesis, and meaning can emerge from the group.
- Managers often have to carry out difficult conversations with individuals, such as giving unfavorable performance feedback or confronting a colleague or superior about inappropriate behavior. A difficult conversation is one in which outcomes are highly important, viewpoints differ, and emotions run high.
- You can use the ILETS model to guide a difficult conversation: introduce the subject; listen to the other person's opinion and views; empathize with the other person; talk and tell your side; then solve the problem together. *Always listen first* and strive to understand the other person's side of the story. However, when delivering bad news, reverse this order. After introducing the topic, go ahead and put the bad news out there (talk); then empathize, listen, and solve by offering to help (ITELS).
- Conflict is inevitable when people work together. Conflict refers to antagonistic interaction in which one party wants to achieve its goals and will prevent or block the intentions or goals of another. Two basic types of conflict in organizations are task conflict and relationship conflict. Five manager styles for handling conflict are dominating, collaborating, avoiding, accommodating, and bargaining. Each individual has a preferred style, but good managers use a mix of styles, as each approach is appropriate in certain circumstances.
- When conflicts or differences are formalized, managers use negotiation to reach an agreement. Planning is essential for obtaining a successful outcome of negotiation.
- Two types of negotiation are integrative (win–win) and distributive (win–lose). Good managers try to focus on integrative negotiation, but distributive negotiation is sometimes necessary. When you negotiate, it is important to focus on interests rather than stated positions or demands. As with all forms of communication, listening and asking questions are crucial to being a good negotiator.

TATIANA POPOVA/ISTOCKPHOTO.COM

ACTION LEARNING

DELIBERATE PRACTICE EXERCISES

The ILETS Model: Easy Conversations

Step 1: Refer to the description of the ILETS model on page 377–381.

Step 2: Arrange three conversations during the next three days that follow the ILETS model by drawing out the other person before you speak your point of view. Empty the other person's cup before you say what you want to say.

Step 3: After your conversations, answer the following questions.

1. How did it feel to listen first?

2. How did listening add to or detract from the quality of the conversations?

The ILETS Model: A Difficult Conversation

Step 1: Consider an issue or difference of opinion you are feeling with someone right now. It should not be with a significant other, which can be too emotionally charged. Arrange a meeting with the person with whom you have the difference.

Step 2: Use the ILETS model by introducing the topic and then drawing out the perspective of the other person before you give your opinions. Follow these guidelines:

- Listen actively.
- If the person gets emotional, stay calm. Accept the emotion without reacting.
- When the other person finishes, ask questions or paraphrase to clarify your understanding in a supportive manner.
- Then it is your turn to talk.
- When both points of view are expressed, now both of you can throw out ideas for a solution.

Step 3: After your conversation, answer the following questions.

1. What was most difficult about conducting this difficult conversation?

2. What new skills did this exercise require from you?

Step 4: Try this process with some friends so that you can keep practicing your skills.

Observe Your Communication Behavior

This Deliberate Practice Exercise is available online at www.cengagebrain.com.

Conflict Styles

REFLECTION

Step 1: Think of two conflicts you have experienced over the last few weeks. Describe them in a few words below.

1.
2.

Step 2: What conflict handling style did you use in each case? Refer back to page 382 to review the dominating, avoiding, bargaining, accommodating, and collaborating styles. List the style you used for each conflict below.

1.
2.

Step 3: How effective was the style for you in resolving the conflict for each situation?

1.
2.

Step 4 (Optional): Share your insights with a partner, and ask your partner what insights he or she gained.

ACTION LEARNING

IN-CLASS TEAM EXERCISE

Dialogue Circle

Step 1: Form into groups of six to eight. Put your chairs in a circle if you can. Otherwise, sit as close to being in a circle as possible.

Step 2: Choose some object to be your "talking stick." This can be a large stick, a tennis ball, even a pen. One person should be appointed to be time-keeper, someone who can count seconds and minutes on a device.

SHUTTERSTOCK #53973379

Step 3: One person starts by holding the talking stick. The rest of the group practices listening skills and no one comments or asks questions. After the person finishes or time runs out, the next person has a turn with the talking stick, and so on, until everyone has had a turn to talk. Follow the rounds below:

Round 1: Each person is to talk for a maximum of two minutes on the following topic: *Who was the one person who positively influenced you most as a younger person? What qualities did that person have? How has the influence made you the person you are today?*

Round 2: Each person is to talk for a maximum of one minute. For this round, each person answers the following questions:

1. What did you hear during the first round?
2. What were the themes or common characteristics that you heard?

Round 3 (Optional): If some groups finish earlier than others, they may start a new round to build on the first two rounds.

Step 4: If directed by your instructor, discuss the following questions about the uses of dialogue:

1. What did you learn about people who have a positive influence on the development of others?
2. How did it feel to have a talking stick mechanism that allowed only one person to speak at a time?
3. What was it like as the speaker, when you knew you could tell your story without interruptions?
4. How was it listening, when you were really forced not to interact?
5. How is dialogue different from typical conversations or discussions?
6. What are the best times to use dialogue?
7. When should you *not* use dialogue?

FIELD TEAM EXERCISE

How Are Public Conflicts Resolved?

Step 1: Divide into groups of three to five.

Step 2: Each group develops a plan to individually search relevant media (Internet, TV news programs, business magazines, newspapers, etc.) that cover politics, sports, and business to find stories about conflict. Each team member is responsible to find at least one unique story that involves a conflict between individuals or groups.

Step 3: Meet as a group, with each member bringing at least one conflict story.

Step 4: By using a format similar to that on the following page, discuss and answer as a group the following questions about the conflict stories.

	Story 1	Story 2	Story 3
Briefly describe the story			
Who is involved in the conflict?			
What is the underlying cause of the problem or conflict?			
What conflict and communication styles are used to resolve the issue?			
What conflict styles might be more effective in this situation?			

Step 5: What patterns (similarities, differences) does your group notice in causes, communications, conflict management styles, or their effectiveness across all the conflict situations?

Step 6 (Optional): Your instructor may ask you to write a report of what you found.

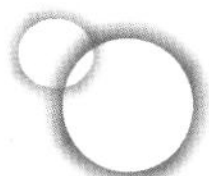

TEST YOUR METTLE

ROLE PLAY SIMULATIONS

Appraisal Inflation

Background: Re-read the written Video Incident at the beginning of the chapter.

Instructions: Divide into groups of three. One person will play the role of Jane Sutton, general manager, one will play the role of Carlos Hernandez, CFO, and one will be an observer.

Round 1: Use the first lines from the incident for each person, as follows:

Jane: "We have some problems here. You are rating your people too generously."

Carlos: "Are you saying I'm not telling the truth?"

Continue the role play using your own words. Spend five minutes role playing the situation.

Now, try the role play with a different opening line from Jane. Come up with a new opening line for Jane that you think would be more effective.

Debrief: Spend five minutes hearing from the observer and talking as a small group about how well Jane and Carlos managed to have a reasoned discussion. How often did one or both of them get defensive?

Rounds 2 and 3: Switch roles so that everyone has a chance to play each role. Spend five minutes role playing and five minutes debriefing.

Round 4: Class role play (optional). Your instructor may choose to have some people come to the front and role play Jane and Carlos.

After the role play rounds, discuss these questions:

1. What makes it easy for someone to get defensive?
2. How can you notice when you, yourself, get defensive? What can you do to stop being defensive in that moment?
3. How can you communicate to reduce the likelihood that the other person might get defensive?

Negotiating a Business Opportunity

This Role Play Simulation is available online at www.cengagebrain.com.

VIDEO APPLICATION

Conflict During *In Good Company*

A corporate takeover brings Mark Steckel (Clark Gregg) as the boss of Dan Foreman (Dennis Quaid) and Carter Duryea (Topher Grace). Although young, Duryea is marketing chief over the older Foreman at the sports magazine. Steckel is upset with Foreman's comments to the CEO and Duryea joins the conflict.

SHUTTERSTOCK #53973379

Discussion Questions

1. What conflict handling style is used by Steckel? Explain.
2. Do you think it's appropriate for Steckel to raise issues with Foreman when he is upset and angry? Would it be better to have this conversation when he is calm and rational? Why? How would you start the conversation to achieve a better result?
3. At what point did the confrontation become a negotiation? What negotiation leverage did Duryea use to forestall the firing of Foreman?

CASE INCIDENTS

"What I Like to Hear"

Tracy rushed past executive assistant Sharon Craig on his way into the boardroom. "Is the boss here, yet?" he asked.

"No. He tweeted to say he's stuck in traffic and will be a few minutes late," Sharon replied.

"Whew!" Tracy entered the room and saw Myers, James, and Deon gathered around the coffee and donuts. "Morning, guys. Sharon said the boss is running late."

"Yeah," James answered. "We got the tweet, didn't you?"

"Oops! I had the phone turned off while I met with Katie's day-care director," Tracy answered, switching on the device.

"He'll come bounding in here all fired up for this switch," Deon said. "But I still have serious reservations about this deal . . . "

"The idea of switching suppliers for some key components is a bit unsettling," Myers cut in.

"Especially when the new supplier is further away," Deon continued. "I can't figure out why he wants to do this. I hate messing with the logistics of on-time delivery on important parts. And our guys are being asked to make a number of adjustments in order to get this to work. I just don't get it . . . .

"Ah, maybe it'll work out," Tracy said. "But I don't see a good reason to make the change either."

"It's our heads, if it gets screwed up," Deon moaned.

"Top management has looked at it and they seem satisfied, but they don't have to meet the specs every day," James said. "Oh. I hear him coming."

The group took their seats as David Parker noisily entered the room, removed his jacket, and sat at the head of the conference table. "Good morning, gentlemen. Traffic was hell—a big wreck on the south loop." He clapped his huge hands together and rubbed them enthusiastically. "Now, let's get down to business. As you know, we've gone to considerable effort to make some major logistical changes for delivery of key components—adjustments that, I believe, will greatly improve the manufacturing process. And now, I want your feedback. What do you think? Be honest, now. Tracy?"

"Well, I know you've all worked hard . . . "

"Sure have!" David said enthusiastically.

" . . . and I don't see any glaring problems. I'm sure there will be a few kinks to work out initially," continued Tracy.

"Of course! Of course! That's true of anything that's new," replied David. "Hell, Moses busted up the Ten Commandments and had to go back up the mountain and

get them again!" It was the boss's favorite saying regarding change and they had all heard it a thousand times before, but they laughed, *again*. "Myers, what do you think? I've always said that you have a good head on your shoulders. Do you see a major problem here? Some reason we should just *not* do this?"

"Thanks, David. I'm like Tracy. I say, let's give it a try," conceded Myers. "Our new partners have a great company, great reputation. Although we didn't have any problems with the previous company—they were dependable and on time and offered good quality parts, this may be a major improvement."

David was pleased. "That's what I like to hear. I like to think of us as a company that sees *possibilities* and is willing to move ahead—glass half full and all of that. James?"

James hesitated, and then responded, "As you say—glass half full. There may be some problems, but . . . "

"But, I know you men and I know your teams. You'll have everything up and running smoothly in no time. Deon, you're my realist. What do you say?" David asked.

Deon responded, "Realistically?"

Everyone laughed nervously and Deon continued. "Well, I have a few concerns about the increased distance between our production plant and the delivery timing given the worsening traffic, but . . . "

"But you think your team can make it work," David continued.

"Well, yeah, of course. Our employees are the best anywhere. We can make this work," agreed Deon.

"Great!" David shouted, enthusiastically rapping his knuckles on the table.

Deon interrupted, "I am concerned that their components will require some machine adjustments on our end. I mean, have we *tried* this yet with our machines?"

"Oh, we've looked into it and have been assured that these are minor tweaks," David said. "You can read it all right there in the report. We feel that our teams can handle this until we install the upgraded machinery over the next year to eighteen months. I think to calm whatever worries you have, this issue has been explored and addressed adequately. Your teams can handle all of this during the transition, don't you think?"

"Oh, sure . . . "

"Well, then, any questions?" David asked, briefly. "Gentlemen, I've looked forward to your feedback and I look forward to seeing improved company performance and product quality as we put the new suppliers in place. You all impress me with the way you've embraced this change. Thank you."

Discussion Questions

1. Was this conversation effective? Why? What do you think is happening?
2. Who would you say is more responsible for the communication failure among the participants? Why?
3. What communication process would you recommend to get more of the information and true opinions of the participants out in the open? How would you guide that process?

Decision Time

Ben Dooley and Casey Stringer had agreed to stop for coffee in the atrium Starbucks before heading up to the 35th floor for a board meeting.

"You seem deep in thought," Ben said, placing the two cups of hot coffee on the table.

"Watching Johnna and Robert in previous board meetings helps me to understand why the folks in Congress can't get anything done," Casey mused. "Both sides have stated their positions and nothing, *nothing* will budge them. I dread this meeting. I'd rather have a root canal."

"Well, while the two giants battle it out, the rest of us will have to work out some sort of compromise. We outsourced manufacturing operations to China several years ago to cut costs and now things are changing rapidly and we have a major decision. Does Bishop's Engineered Plastics make the best of the situation in China?"

" . . . Or do we re-shore?" Casey added.

"Someone will have to be the voice of reason today," Ben said. "Robert Ma has overseen the outsourcing to China and, initially, it was a great move."

"I agree the cost savings were pretty amazing. The retooling and creation of a state-of-the-art factory in Wenzhou by the Chinese really propelled us to a new level within the industry," said Casey.

"Well, 2012 is the Year of the Dragon, and the dragon is having a problem," Ben replied.

"Yes, Robert is going to have to face the fact that if we stay in China, we have to move from Wenzhou," Casey pointed out. "The worker shortage is bad and getting worse. The last estimate for that region was one million workers short. As wages go up and other opportunities present themselves, manufacturing jobs are losing their appeal in the cities. In our plant, the managers have to come down and work on the lines. That's not good. Now, to try to stave off a mass industrial exodus, the Chinese are offering a stimulus to industries to relocate into the interior of the country. The interior offers more workers and lower wages."

"And a factory move will delay manufacturing and make shipping even more difficult," Ben replied. "Add to that the Chinese insistence on full payment before shipping, and we're looking at some potentially serious delays."

"Johnna, on the other hand, is going to argue that the situation in China is an indication that now is the perfect time to re-shore—bring the jobs back to the good old U.S.," Casey added. "She's going to dig in her heels on this one and you and I know that at least two members of our illustrious board are going to back off and let her have her way with no careful analysis of the pros and cons. I sometimes think Frank is a people pleaser, always agreeable, especially toward Johnna because she is the chair. And Martha usually doesn't say anything, much less offer an opinion. She stares down at her hands when the going gets heavy."

"The pros for Johnna are obvious—bring jobs home where jobs are needed; shorten the supply line, reduce shipping costs, offer faster response to customers, and, I believe, offer a better quality product. It is worth a little higher labor cost," admitted Ben.

"And what are the cons?" Casey asked.

"The problems are the higher wages here and the cost of retooling factories in this country that have been down for a few years," replied Ben.

"But," Casey asked, "Would we have to build a new factory deep in China's interior? No. And will their interior workforce be adequately trained? I would guess not. The Chinese government will help with building and relocation costs, but still. . . ."

"So both Johnna and Robert have a strong argument and some glaring weaknesses. Is there room here for a compromise? That's what I would like to see. They would both get something," stated Ben.

"I don't know," Casey responded. "I'm eager to see what each one of them presents. It should be an interesting conversation."

"Or an afternoon in hell," Ben said as the two headed for the elevator. "I wonder what you and I might do to help Johnna and Robert resolve this conflict. What do you think we should do, Casey?"

Discussion Questions

1. What styles for handling conflict appear among the board members? Explain.
2. What options do Ben and Casey have for helping resolve the conflict between Johnna and Robert? What conflict management styles might they adopt for this meeting?
3. What suggestions would you make to help board members arrive at a good decision?

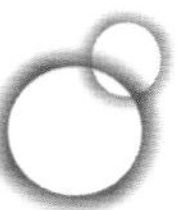

PERSONAL SKILLS LOG

Directions: Fill in the rows below based on what you learned from each part of the chapter that you completed.

	What is my key takeaway or insight from this activity?	What do I personally do well (strength) regarding this activity?	What could I improve (weakness) about myself regarding this activity?	How might I use what I've learned from this activity in the future?
Manager Challenge Incident:				
Discover Yourself Questionnaires:				
Deliberate Practice Exercises:				
In-Class and/or Field Team Exercises:				
Role-Play Exercises:				
Case Incidents:				

REFERENCES

Discover Yourself

1 Based on Roy J. Lewicki and Robert J. Robinson, "Ethical and Unethical Bargaining Tactics: An Empirical Study," *Journal of Business Ethics* 17 (1998): 665–662.

Discover Knowledge

2 Robert A. Guth, "Gates-Ballmer Clash Shaped Microsoft's Coming Handover," *The Wall Street Journal*, June 5, 2008.

3 Linda Ellinor and Glenna Gerard, *Dialogue: Rediscover the Transforming Power of Conversation* (New York: John Wiley & Sons, Inc., 1998), p. 13.

4 Scott Kirsner, "Want to Grow? Hire a Shrink!" *Fast Company* (December–January 1998): 68, 70.

5 Jerry B. Harvey, *The Abilene Paradox and Other Meditations on Management* (Lexington, MA: Lexington Books, 1988).

6 Based on Ellinor and Gerard, *Dialogue: Rediscover the Transforming Power of Conversation*, p. 24.

7 Richard L. Daft, *The Executive and the Elephant* (New York: John Wiley & Sons, Inc., 2010), p. 99.

8 Ellinor and Gerard, *Dialogue*, pp. 26–27.

9 Deborah L. Flick, *From Debate to Dialogue: Using the Understanding Process to Transform Our Conversations* (Boulder, CO: Orchid Publications, 1998), p. 22.

10 Ellinor and Gerard, *Dialogue: Rediscover the Transforming Power of Conversation*; David Bohm, *On Dialogue* (Ojai, CA: David Bohm Seminars, 1989); and William Isaacs, *Dialogue and the Art of Thinking Together* (New York: Currency Doubleday, 1999).

11 Glenna Gerard and Linda Teurfs, "Dialogue and Organizational Transformation," in *Community Building: Renewing Spirit and Learning in Business*, Kazimierz Gozdz, ed. (Pleasanton, CA: New Leaders Press, 1995); and Edgar Schein, "On Dialogue, Culture, and Organizational Learning," *Organizational Dynamics* 22, no. 2 (Fall 1993): 40–51.

12 Kerry Patterson, Joseph Grenny, Ron McMillan, and Al Switzler, *Crucial Conversations: Tools for Talking When Stakes Are High* (New York: McGraw-Hill, 2002).

13 These examples are from Patterson et al., *Crucial Conversations*.

14 *Ibid.*, p. 20.

15 Based on Jean-Francois Manzoni, "A Better Way to Deliver Bad News," *Harvard Business Review* (September 2002): 114–119.

16 Daft, *The Executive and the Elephant*, pp. 132–133.

17 Stephen R. Covey, *The 7 Habits of Highly Effective People* (New York: Free Press, 2004).

18 This discussion is based partly on Patterson et al., *Crucial Conversations*. The ILETS model was developed from several sources.

19 Peter J. Frost, "Handling the Hurt: A Critical Skill for Leaders," *Ivey Management Journal* (January–February 2004): 1–6.

20 This conversation is adapted from Edwin A. Locke, *Handbook of Principles of Organizational Behavior*, 2nd ed. (New York: John Wiley & Sons, 2009), pp. 97–99.

21 These are based on Holly Weeks, "Taking the Stress Out of Stressful Conversation," *Harvard Business Review* (July–August 2001): 113–119; Patterson et al., *Crucial Conversations*, pp. 27–32; and Douglas Stone, Bruce Patton, and Sheila Heen, *Difficult Conversations: How to Discuss What Matters Most* (New York: Viking Penguin, 1999).

22 Susan Hackley, "How to Say What Matters Most," *Negotiation* (August 2005): 3–5.

23 Stephen P. Robbins, *Managing Organizational Conflict: A Nontraditional Approach* (Inglewood Cliffs, NJ: Prentice Hall, 1974).

24 Based on K. A. Jehn, "A Multi-method Examination of the Benefits and Determinants of Intragroup Conflict," *Administrative Science Quarterly* 40 (1995): 256–282; and K. A. Jehn, "A Qualitative Analysis of Conflict Types and Dimensions in Organizational Groups," *Administrative Science Quarterly* 42 (1997): 530–557.

25 Linda A. Hill, "A *Note for Analyzing Work Groups*," Harvard Business School, Industry and Background Note, Product #496-026, August 28, 1995, http://hbr.org/product/note-for-analyzing-work-groups/an/496026-PDF-ENG (accessed April 14, 2011).

26 A. Amason, "Distinguishing the Effects of Functional and Dysfunctional Conflict on Strategic Decision Making: Resolving a Paradox for Top Management Teams," *Academy of Management Journal* 39, no. 1 (1996): 123–148.

27 This discussion is based on Kenneth W. Thomas, "Towards Multi-Dimensional Values in Teaching: The Example of Conflict Behaviors," *Academy of Management Review* 2, no. 3 (July 1977): 484–490, and Nan Peck, "*Conflict 101: Styles of Fighting*," North Virginia Community College Web site, September 20, 2005, http://www.nvcc.edu/home/npeck/conflicthome/conflict/Conflict101/conflictstyles.htm (accessed April 13, 2011)

28 This discussion is based on Richard L. Daft, *The Leadership Experience*, 5th edition (Mason, OH: South-Western Cengage Learning, 2011), pp. 317–318; and Don Hellriegel and John W. Slocum, Jr., *Organizational Behavior*, 13th ed. (Mason, OH: South-Western, 2011), pp. 390–394.

29 Example based on Deepak Malhotra and Max H. Bazerman, "Investigative Negotiation," *Harvard Business Review* (September 2007): 72–78.

30 This discussion is based on Rob Walker, "Take It or Leave It: The Only Guide to Negotiating You Will Ever Need," *Inc.* (August, 2003): 74–82; and Robert Adler, Benson Rosen, and Elliot Silverstein, "Thrust and Parry: The Art of Tough Negotiating," *Training & Development* (March 1996): 43–47.

31 Robb Mandelbaum, "How to Negotiate Effectively," *Inc.*, November 1, 2010, http://www.inc.com/magazine/20101101/how-to-negotiate-effectively.html (accessed April 12, 2011).

32 This discussion is based on Mandelbaum, "How to Negotiate Effectively"; Walker, "Take It or Leave It"; and Michael Wheeler, "*Negotiation Analysis: An Introduction*," Harvard Business School, Industry and Background Note, Product #801156, August 29, 2000, http://hbr.org/product/negotiation-analysis-an-introduction/an/801156-PDF-ENG (accessed April 14, 2011).

33 Roger Fisher and William Ury, *Getting to Yes; Negotiating Agreement without Giving In* (New York: Penguin, 1999), p. 106.

34 As discussed in Walker, "Take It or Leave It."

35 This discussion is based on Walker, "Take It or Leave It"; "Negotiation Types," The Negotiation Experts, http://www.negotiations.com/articles/negotiation-types/ (accessed February 6, 2012); "The Negotiation Process: The Difference Between Integrative and Distributive Negotiation," La Piana Associates Inc., http://www.lapiana.org/resources/tips/negotiations (accessed April 11, 2011); and Hellriegel and Slocum, *Organizational Behavior*, p. 399.

36 This familiar story has been reported in many sources, including in "The Negotiation Process: The Difference Between Integrative and Distributive Negotiation," La Piana Associates Inc.

37 This discussion is based on Walker, "Take It or Leave It"; Mandelbaum, "How to Negotiate Effectively"; and Adler et al., "Thrust and Parry: The Art of Tough Negotiating."

38 This discussion is based on Richard L. Daft, *Management*, 9th ed. (Mason, OH: South-Western Cengage Learning, 2010), p. 521; Michelle Maiese, "*Interests, Positions, Needs, and Values*," Beyond Intractability Web site, http://www.beyondintractability.org/essay/interests/?nid=1026 (accessed April 13, 2011); Howard Schwartz, May Ping Szeto, and Carol Stewart, "*Conflict Resolution*," Nonprofit Coordinating Committee of New York Web site, http://www.npccny.org/info/pmei7.htm (accessed April 14, 2011); and Malhotra and Bazerman, "Investigative Negotiation."

39 This example is from Malhotra and Bazerman, "Investigative Negotiation."

40 This discussion is based on Walker, "Take It or Leave It"; Mandelbaum, "How to Negotiate Effectively"; and Malhotra and Bazerman, "Investigative Negotiation."

CHAPTER 11
Managing Your Boss

Chapter Outline

RYAN LASH

MANAGER CHALLENGE

VIDEO INCIDENT: PUSHBACK?

Jane Sutton, general manager of Caffeine and Crullers in Madison, Wisconsin, was called to a meeting with her boss, Edmund Daniels, COO in the Milwaukee corporate headquarters. Jane arrived a few minutes early for the 3:00 P.M. appointment and waited in the reception area thinking about her strategy for the meeting. Jane knows Edmund is an "idea person," always dreaming up new ways to do things. The purpose of this meeting is to discuss the draft of his newest idea, this one for restructuring the Madison locations, which would involve reassignment of responsibilities based more on a matrix structure than the current functional design. With only twelve locations in Madison, Jane believes the burden of a matrix structure will compromise productivity. Edmund feels passionately for his new ideas, but he never works out the details. It falls on Jane and her employees to work out execution details, usually wasting lots of time and resources. Edmund never seems to notice that most of his ideas fail, because he's off on a new one by that time. Jane has decided to be more forceful with Edmund this time. She agrees that a review of C&C's structure might be a good thing, but she wants to stop the possible implementation of a matrix structure. Jane is thinking about how she can confront Edmund in a way that prevents him from getting defensive and losing respect for her.

Initial Thoughts

1. If you were Jane, what would you do?

2. What is a direct report's responsibility when responding to new ideas from the boss that often seem unrealistic?

Your instructor may ask you to be part of a role play based on the "Pushback?" incident.

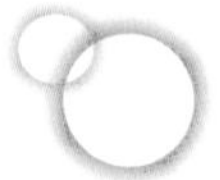

DISCOVER YOURSELF

For those students using CourseMate or CengageNOW, you can access the Daft/Marcic Assessment Library to take the questionnaires online and view dynamically updated comparative data.

Questionnaire 1

Instructions: Think of a typical job situation in which you are working under a manager. Considering that typical situation, rate how accurately each statement describes you based on whether the statement is clearly true or accurate, clearly false or inaccurate, or in the middle as somewhat true and somewhat false.

Part A

	True	Somewhat	False
1. I usually feel like I don't want help from my boss or other people.	○	○	○
2. I trust myself more than other people to get something done.	○	○	○
3. I find it difficult to feel really close to other people.	○	○	○
4. I don't think I could make a long-term commitment to any boss.	○	○	○
5. I prefer to struggle with something myself rather than ask for help.	○	○	○
6. I am not very touchy or huggy.	○	○	○

Total Score Part A ________. (Sum your answers to questions 1–6 by giving 3 points for each True, 2 points for each Somewhat, and 1 point for each False.)

Part B

	True	Somewhat	False
7. I have a hard time asserting myself toward my boss.	○	○	○
8. I hate it if my boss does not approve of me.	○	○	○
9. I am reluctant to "tell it like it is" to my boss.	○	○	○
10. I feel responsible to keep my boss happy.	○	○	○
11. I tend to give in to my boss to avoid conflict.	○	○	○
12. I find myself saying "Yes" to my boss when I want to say "No."	○	○	○

Total Score Part B ________. (Sum your responses to 7–12 by giving 3 points for each True, 2 points for each Somewhat, and 1 point for each False.) Go to page 409 to interpret your scores.

Questionnaire 2[1]

Instructions: Think of a specific boss for whom you have worked, and then answer the questions below with respect to your relationship with that particular boss. Indicate whether each item is Yes, Maybe, or No for you.

	Yes	Maybe	No
1. Did you go out of your way to avoid your boss?	○	○	○
2. Did your boss play favorites?	○	○	○
3. Did your boss rarely, if ever, express appreciation?	○	○	○
4. Did your boss criticize people in public?	○	○	○
5. Did you hesitate to offer an opinion because it wasn't welcomed or listened to?	○	○	○
6. Was the only feedback you received when things went wrong, if then?	○	○	○
7. Did your boss often say something such as "Handle it," without any explanation?	○	○	○
8. Did your boss allow numerous interruptions when you tried to talk to him or her?	○	○	○
9. Did your boss take credit for the work of you or the team?	○	○	○
10. Did your boss frequently cancel meetings at the last minute because of something "important"?	○	○	○

Total Score ________. (Give yourself 3 points for each Yes, 2 points for each Maybe, and 1 point for each No.) Go to page 412 to interpret your score.

Questionnaire 3[2]

Instructions: For each of the following statements, think of a specific situation in which you worked for a boss in an organization. Then indicate whether each item is True, Somewhat, or False.

Part A	True	Somewhat	False
1. I commented to my manager on the broader importance of data or events.	○	○	○
2. I thought carefully and expressed my opinion about critical issues.	○	○	○
3. I frequently suggested ways to improve my and others' ways of doing things.	○	○	○
4. I challenged my manager to think about an old problem in a new way.	○	○	○
5. Rather than wait to be told, I would figure out the critical activities for achieving my unit's goals.	○	○	○
6. I independently thought up and championed new ideas.	○	○	○
7. I tried to solve the tough problems rather than expect my manager to do it.	○	○	○
8. I played devil's advocate if necessary to demonstrate the downside as well as the upside of initiatives.	○	○	○

Total Score Part A ________. (Sum questions 1–8 by giving yourself 3 points for each True, 2 points for each Somewhat, and 1 point for each False.)

DISCOVER YOURSELF

Part B

	True	Somewhat	False
9. My work fulfilled a higher personal goal for me.	○	○	○
10. I was enthusiastic about my job.	○	○	○
11. I understood my manager's goals and worked hard to meet them.	○	○	○
12. The work I did was significant to me.	○	○	○
13. I felt emotionally engaged throughout the day.	○	○	○
14. I had the opportunity to do what I do best each day.	○	○	○
15. I understood how my role contributed to company success.	○	○	○
16. I was willing to put in a great deal of effort beyond what was normally expected.	○	○	○

Total Score Part B ________. (Sum questions 9–16 by giving yourself 3 points for each True, 2 points for each Somewhat, and 1 point for each False.) Go to page 418 to interpret your scores.

Questionnaire 4[3]

Instructions: Think of a job you have held, and indicate how frequently you have used each social tactic below to influence a boss or colleague to undertake a new action that you wanted. Answer each question twice—once for Boss and once for Colleague.

	Frequently	Occasionally	Seldom
1. I mentioned the names of key people who endorsed the proposed activity.			
a. To influence a boss	○	○	○
b. To influence a colleague	○	○	○
2. I said my requested activity was consistent with official rules and practices.			
a. To influence a boss	○	○	○
b. To influence a colleague	○	○	○
3. I used facts and logic to make a persuasive case for a new activity.			
a. To influence a boss	○	○	○
b. To influence a colleague	○	○	○
4. I described benefits the person would gain from a proposed activity.			
a. To influence a boss	○	○	○
b. To influence a colleague	○	○	○
5. I asked the person to express any ideas or concerns about a proposed activity.			
a. To influence a boss	○	○	○
b. To influence a colleague	○	○	○

	Frequently	Occasionally	Seldom
6. I talked about my vision and values when proposing a new activity.			
a. To influence a boss	○	○	○
b. To influence a colleague	○	○	○
7. I offered to do something in return for the person carrying out my request.			
a. To influence a boss	○	○	○
b. To influence a colleague	○	○	○
8. I repeatedly reminded the person about what I wanted.			
a. To influence a boss	○	○	○
b. To influence a colleague	○	○	○

Total Score for Boss ________. Total Score for Colleague ________. (Sum your Boss score ("a" answers) and Colleague score ("b" answers) separately. Give 3 points for each Frequently, 2 points for each Occasionally, and 1 point for each Seldom.) Go to page 419 to interpret your scores.

GO ONLINE to find additional questionnaires at www.cengagebrain.com, search for Daft/Marcic Building Management Skills 1e, click on Free Online Resources, click on Additional Self-Assessments.

- Destructive Boss

DISCOVER YOURSELF

SHUTTERSTOCK #53973379

Chapter 11: Managing Your Boss

DISCOVER KNOWLEDGE

After steadily rising through the ranks at Westwood Industries, Kumar Chopra has just been fired. The president of Westwood was reluctant to fire him, but during Chopra's 14 months in his new position, a series of problems led to the company reporting a net loss for the first time in almost a decade. In sorting out the events, the president discovered a chain of misunderstandings, miscommunications, and hurt feelings between Chopra, in charge of new products, and his boss, Frank Bennington, head of manufacturing. The company was bringing out a major new product that required exceptionally close coordination among sales, engineering, and manufacturing. But misunderstandings between Chopra and Bennington had caused planning to go haywire. Consequently, the company built a new plant that couldn't produce the new product as it was designed by engineering, in the quantity needed by sales, and at the cost approved by the board. Bennington blamed Chopra for the mistake, whereas Chopra blamed Bennington. Westwood's president had promoted Chopra because of his excellent track record and his reputation for working well with everyone. What had gone so wrong? Pondering the failure, he noted that over his 13 years with the company Chopra had always worked with bosses who were excellent managers. Bennington, on the other hand, was a manufacturing genius but not a very good manager of people. Perhaps, he thought, Chopra simply didn't have the experience or the skills to work with a different kind of boss. Chopra later said he had never considered managing his boss to be a part of the job.[4]

When most people consider what it means to be a manager, they automatically think of *managing down*—building good relationships with subordinates, effectively directing activities, and influencing employees to accomplish goals. They fail to realize that *managing up* is an equally important skill. As Kumar Chopra discovered at Westwood Industries, your ability to understand and manage your boss can make the difference between success and failure. An immediate supervisor can have a significant impact on one's happiness, motivation, and effectiveness. If you can't develop a productive and satisfying work relationship with your boss, your work performance, commitment, and well-being will be limited.

Managing up means consciously and deliberately developing a meaningful, task-related, mutually respectful relationship with your direct superiors; offering insight, information, guidance, and initiative; and challenging your superiors when necessary in order to enable everyone to do their best work for the organization.[5] You might already understand that managing your boss can be vital to advancing your career, but it is also important to your productivity and effectiveness, as well as to the productivity and effectiveness of your boss and your subordinates.

THE ART OF MANAGING UP

Managing up presents unique challenges and requires a different set of skills than does managing down. Some people are quite good at managing relationships with their subordinates but fail miserably when it comes to effectively interacting with their superiors. You need to know how to do both.

You'll be more successful if you learn to manage effectively both up and down the hierarchy. Why is managing up so important? For one thing, people at higher organizational levels depend on their subordinates for information, support, and assistance in accomplishing the organization's goals, so your boss needs you to manage up. In addition, your subordinates depend on you to help them get the information, resources, support, and recognition they need and deserve from higher levels. People like working for managers who have influence with their superiors because it enhances their own status in the organization and helps them get what they need to do their jobs well.[6] You can't be a really good manager unless you manage the boss as skillfully as you manage employees.

Many people are uncomfortable with the idea of managing the boss. Their overriding concern is pleasing the boss and keeping him or her happy. Therefore, they hesitate to pass along any information that might not be welcome, and they avoid questioning any of their superior's assumptions, ideas, or decisions.[7] In

LEADING WORDS

"Followers who tell the truth and leaders who listen to it are an unbeatable combination."
—**Warren G. Bennis**
leadership expert, professor, and consultant

"Everyday courage has few witnesses. But yours is no less noble because no drum beats for you and no crowds shout your name."
—**Robert Louis Stevenson**
Scottish novelist and poet, author of *Treasure Island*

"Smart people instinctively understand the dangers of entrusting our future to self-serving leaders who use our institutions . . . whether in the corporate or social sectors . . . to advance their own interests."
—**Jim Collins**
business consultant and speaker, author of bestsellers including *Good to Great*

"The key to being a good manager is keeping the people who hate you away from those who are still undecided."
—**Casey Stengal**
Major League baseball player and manager, member of the Baseball Hall of Fame

© CENGAGE LEARNING 2014

the long run, these self-protective strategies hurt the employee, the boss, and the organization.

One reason we may have difficulty managing upward is that we're not "in control" in this relationship as we are in our relationships with subordinates. It is natural that we try to protect ourselves in a relationship in which we feel we have little control and little power.[8] Yet in reality we have more power than we know. Bosses need our support—our talent, information, ideas, and honesty—in order to do their jobs well, just as we need their support to do our best work. Everyone benefits when we learn to effectively manage relationships with our superiors as well as our subordinates.

WHY DO YOU TENSE UP AROUND THE BOSS?

Harrison Bradford is a bright, energetic middle manager at a consumer products company. Bradford thought everything was fine in his world except for one aspect: His new boss disliked him and didn't appreciate his hard work and commitment. He finally hired an outside coach from a consulting firm to help him learn how to cope with working for a boss who considered him inconsequential. "She ignores me," Bradford told his coach. "I see her talking to other managers, but she never talks to me." After a couple of months of coaching, Bradford finally took steps to find out what he could do to make the relationship with his boss better. He was shocked when his boss told him that he was one of her most trusted managers. "Harrison, you're one of the few people here I don't feel that I have to watch over all the time," she said. "I've had so much to deal with since I started this job that it has been such a relief to know there's at least one person I can trust to do what needs to be done without my constant attention."[9]

Harrison Bradford learned a valuable lesson. Our interpretations of our boss's behavior are sometimes way off the mark. Fortunately, Bradford found the courage to ask his boss why she seemed to ignore him. Many times, however, people sabotage their relationships with superiors by acting based on misunderstandings.

Different people can interpret the same behavior from a boss in different ways; that is, any action can typically be interpreted either positively or negatively based on one's attitude and viewpoint. Consider the following examples[10]:

	Interpretation by Subordinate	
Boss Action	**Positive**	**Negative**
Gives critical feedback	Interested in my development	Harsh and unkind
Asks lots of questions	Curious and informed	A micromanager
Gives unsolicited advice	Helpful	Meddlesome
Instructs that work be redone	Demanding	Impossible to please
Goes back on a previous decision	Pragmatic	Erratic
Loses temper	Passionate	Temperamental
Limits interaction time	Structured, disciplined	Unapproachable

There are many reasons why people might interpret a behavior as either positive or negative. Most relationships between bosses and employees are characterized by emotions and behaviors based on our attitudes toward authority and submission. As authority figures, bosses sometimes play a disproportionately large role in our minds.

The relationships between bosses and employees are not unlike those between parents and children, and people often engage old family patterns at work.[11] When we're managing down, we're the one in control (the parent), but managing up puts us in the role of the child. In this situation, many people feel somewhat apprehensive and become much more hesitant to openly express themselves, to speak up about difficult issues, or even to be their true selves. Personal "baggage," learned anxieties, and fears are much more likely to affect our relationships with bosses than our interactions with subordinates or peers. A major stumbling block for some people is that they have gut reactions toward authority that are not conducive to developing an effective boss-subordinate relationship. Others approach authority with a more productive mindset. Four ways of thinking about and interacting with authority are illustrated in Exhibit 11.1.[12]

Unhelpful Attitudes toward the Boss

In "The Authority Song" from the early 1980s, John Mellencamp sang "I fight authority; authority always wins. . . . Been doin' it since I was a young kid and I come out grinnin'; I fight authority; authority always wins." We've all known people who constantly fight authority. They seem to instinctively resent, rebel against, or even despise any authority figure. These people display a pattern called *counterdependence*.

Counterdependence

Counterdependence is an exaggerated and distorted attempt at self-reliance. The psychological use of the term **counterdependence** refers to a deep-seated aversion to being assisted or supported by anyone. Counterdependent people subconsciously overcompensate for feelings of weakness. They go out of their way to maintain their independence, rejecting help and emotional support and maintaining an emotional distance from others.[13] Psychologists suggest that counterdependence develops in early childhood when an individual's needs are routinely not met. These individuals learn that they can't depend on authority figures (parents or primary caretakers) to meet their needs. Thus, they learn to view authority figures as irrelevant at best, or even as obstacles or problems to be overcome.

In organizations, counterdependent people are the ones who habitually criticize bosses as incompetent or worthless and can't develop respectful and trusting relationships with their superiors. They see the boss as an enemy and often pick fights just for the sake of fighting. They are what former General Electric CEO Jack Welch has referred to as boss haters, approaching every boss with "barely repressed cynicism" and conveying a steady tone of negativity toward any authority figure.[14]

Overdependence

In contrast to counterdependent people, individuals who display a pattern of **overdependence** can't seem to get enough help and support. These people are needy, insecure, and submissive. They have little trust in their own abilities and ideas, and they never criticize or disagree with authority figures because they fear losing their attention and emotional support. One psychological explanation for overdependence is that children who grow up with inconsistent caregivers—those who are accessible and caring sometimes but distant, cold,

Exhibit 11.1 Four Attitudes toward Authority

Pattern	Trust in Self	Trust in Others	Approach to Boss
Counterdependence	High	Low	Rebels; sees as a problem
Overdependence	Low	High	"Whatever you say"
Independence	High	Moderate	Takes positive action
Interdependence	High	High	Mutually dependent; help one another

and unhelpful at others—develop abandonment anxiety, which then carries over into all aspects of their lives.

DISCOVER YOURSELF

Interpret Your Score:
Counterdependence, Dependence
(Questionnaire 1)

Your score for Part A represents your degree of unconscious "counterdependence." A higher score means that you do not want to be dependent on authority, and thus may resist or fight authority as described in the text. Comparative data for **Counterdependence** (Part A): Thirty-person Mean score = 10.3; Top Quartile = 12–15; Bottom Quartile = 6–8. Your Part B score represents your unconscious desire for "dependence" and approval from others, especially authority figures. A high score on Part B may signal overdependence, which would make it hard to confront or deal with a boss as an equal. Comparative data for **Dependence** (Part B): 30-person mean score = 0.0; Top Quartile = 00–00; Bottom Quartile = 00–00. A high score on either dimension may complicate your feelings toward your boss. Compare your scores to other students. What do your scores mean to you? CNOW and CourseMate users can access dynamically updated comparative data through www.cengagebrain.com.

© CENGAGE LEARNING 2014

In organizations, these are the people who always want to please the boss, the "Yes Men" who are "so full of follow that they can't lead."[15] If their boss makes a decision they believe is unwise or even unethical, they swallow their anger or uneasiness and act very compliant, treating the boss almost as a parent who always knows best.[16] Unfortunately, in many organizations, even people who aren't typically overdependent develop a mindset of dependency, expecting someone else to take care of everything and make all the decisions.

Helpful Attitudes toward the Boss

Both counterdependence and overdependence reflect a view that the boss is somehow inherently superior. Therefore, the counterdependent person rebels and the overdependent one grovels. People who develop effective boss-subordinate relationships, on the other hand, typically perceive themselves as the equals of their bosses, not inherently subordinate to them.

Independence

A person with a pattern of **independence** has developed a sense of self-worth and a healthy attitude of self-reliance. Independent people accept personal responsibility and get what they want through their own actions. Psychologists believe that when children grow up with caregivers who are consistent and responsive to their needs, they feel secure and develop an accompanying sense of trust in authority figures. Secure children grow into independent adults. These individuals don't need to continually strive for attention or approval, like the overly dependent, nor do they exhibit an ongoing resistance to authority like the counterdependent.

Interdependence

Being truly effective and successful in organizations also requires a further step beyond independence to **interdependence,** the realization that the best things happen by working cooperatively with others, that life and work are better when one experiences the richness of close interpersonal relationships. Individuals who are independent can move easily to interdependence because they are secure in their own worth and have the attitude that authority figures are trustworthy and dependable unless proven otherwise. Their sense of self-worth enables them to more easily develop mutually trusting and respectful relationships and an attitude of "we're all in this together."

Although changing your attitudes toward authority isn't easy, just being aware of these differences and how they affect behavior can help you better understand and manage your own relationships.

WHAT YOUR BOSS WANTS FROM YOU

When Ken Montgomery worked for the CEO of a Silicon Valley outsourcing company in the dot-com heyday, the company was getting press coverage in many major publications. But Montgomery knew what his boss *really* wanted was a splash in one of the new-economy magazines that focused on the CEO's personal contribution to the emerging world of e-business. Montgomery could have rolled his eyes and grumbled about his boss's ego, but instead

he made sure his boss got the coverage he wanted. It was good for the company, and it was good for Montgomery. "Doing that small thing for him . . . bought me credibility as an achiever," he says. It also led to a relationship of stronger trust and respect and helped Montgomery get the boss's support for projects he considered important.[17]

Ken Montgomery realized what his boss wanted and helped him achieve it. Rather than seeing it as feeding his boss's ego, Montgomery saw it as a way to show his boss that he could make things happen. Any boss appreciates that, because our bosses depend on us much more than many of us realize. If we don't do our jobs well, our bosses suffer. Any manager's performance depends on the performance of his or her subordinates.[18]

The first aspect of managing your boss is simply to understand what your boss wants and needs from you. It's in your own best interest to help your boss do a good job. When you work for a winner, your own effectiveness and career success is enhanced. Every boss and every organizational situation is different, but the following paragraphs give a few clues to what every boss wants.[19]

Keep a make-it-happen attitude. Bosses don't want excuses. They want results. The boss's job becomes smoother when he or she has followers who are positive and self-motivated, who can get things done, who accept responsibility, and who excel at required tasks. Supervisors value those people who take action when they see something that needs to be done or a problem that needs to be solved. In addition, people who are innovative and creative, who propose ideas and alternatives for the boss to consider, are highly important to the boss's success. Have you ever sat in a meeting where everyone, including the boss, seems confused and uncertain—and then one person introduces a significant new idea or insight? Right then, the tempo changes and things move forward. Remember that your boss is a fallible human being just like you. He or she can't know everything or do everything. Bosses depend on the ideas and actions of their subordinates.

Be willing to collaborate. Your boss is responsible for much more in the organization than your concerns, your feelings, and your performance. You're a part of the boss's larger system and your actions affect the whole. Larry Bossidy, former chairman and CEO of AlliedSignal and of Honeywell, tells about a conflict between the heads of manufacturing and marketing at one organization. Because the two managers didn't communicate with one another, inventories were always out of whack. The CEO finally had to fire them both because their refusal to cooperate was hurting the organization. They got their jobs back when they jointly called and said they got the point and would change their behavior. They did, and the performance of both units and the overall organization improved considerably.[20]

Lead initiatives for change. New initiatives are important for organizations, but many people fear the uncertainty associated with leading change initiatives: What if things go wrong? Will I be blamed? Is my career in jeopardy if the initiative doesn't succeed? Bosses want people who are willing to step up to the plate, to take a chance on a new idea or program, and to assume a leadership role in making change happen.

Stay up-to-date. Bosses expect you to know what's happening in your industry or field of endeavor. In addition, they want you to know your customers, your competition, and how changes in technology or world events might affect the organization. Most of us try to learn all we can in order to get a job we really want, but we sometimes grow complacent and fail to stay current with what's going on outside the narrow confines of our day-to-day work. It's frustrating for bosses to work with people who don't stay current and keep their knowledge and skills up to date.

Drive your own growth. Similarly, bosses like people who continually seek to enhance their own education and development rather than depending on the boss to do it. This might mean taking classes or seminars, but there are many other ways to drive your own professional growth. Anything that exposes you to new people and ideas can enhance your development.

For example, taking on difficult assignments demonstrates your willingness to face challenges, stretch your limits, and learn.

BOSS MANAGEMENT RULE #1: UNDERSTAND YOUR BOSS

If you're "single and looking," what do you do when you want to start a relationship with an attractive person you've recently met? If you're smart, you strive to understand what that person's interests are; what he or she needs, wants, and cares about; and how you can modify your behavior to create a good impression and

7 STEPS TO . . .
Infuriating the Boss

Many people annoy or even enrage their boss without realizing it. Here we describe some of the most common ways to do it, as well as the contrasting approaches of effective subordinates.

1. **Hide your mistakes.** You've made a mistake in an important piece of work and you're wondering what to do. If you want to infuriate the boss, hide it and try to smooth it over before anyone finds out. Effective managers always fess up, knowing it is better to share your concerns as far in advance as possible so the boss has time to help you out.
2. **Surprise the boss with bad news.** Yep, if you hadn't figured it out from Number 1, bosses don't like surprises, especially bad ones. It's your job to protect the boss against surprises by keeping him or her informed and up to date.
3. **Take everything personally.** Your boss was abrupt with you, and now you're whimpering in your office wondering why he doesn't like you or if you're about to be fired. Grow up and get on with your job. Bosses have a lot more to think about than your feelings.
4. **Interrupt the boss's personal time.** You've been trying to get some face time with the boss and finally run into her in the employee restroom. If you want to keep a good relationship, don't even think about it! Never grab a chance to schmooze with the boss by interrupting his or her personal time.
5. **Bad-mouth your "dopey boss."** Humorous grousing about the boss can ease stress, but don't let it get out of hand. You can be sure anything negative you say will eventually get back to the boss. It's the fastest way to destroy trust.
6. **Hover at the door when she's on the phone.** Sure, what you've got to say is important, but this is a sure-fire abuse of the "open door" policy. If the boss is busy, leave a note or come back later.
7. **Whine.** If you really want to annoy the boss, whine about how tough it is to get your work done, your problems with your landlord, and the fight you had with your girlfriend. Whining isn't appealing even in a five-year-old child, so what makes you think your boss will find it appealing in you?

Sources: Based on Peter F. Drucker, "Drucker on Management: How to Manage the Boss," *The Wall Street Journal*, August 1, 1986; Judith Sills, "When You're Smarter Than Your Boss," *Psychology Today* (May–June 2006): 58–59; Liz Ryan, "10 Things Your Manager Wants You to Know," *USA Today*, December 10, 2003; and William Speed Weed, Alex Lash, and Constance Loizos, "30 Ways to Annoy Your Boss," *MBA Jungle* (March–April 2003): 51–55.

develop a good connection. Let's say you're successful and the two of you end up married. If it's going to be a good and lasting marriage, the process of seeking to understand one another will continue throughout the rest of your lives.

Most of us probably don't like the image of our boss as a romantic partner, but the process of building a good relationship with him or her is similar. "Managing the boss is a constant, like being in a good marriage," says Deborah Singer Dobson, coauthor of *Managing Up*.[21] We all spend time and energy trying to understand people who are important to us, so it only makes sense that you do the same with your boss if you want to have a productive working relationship. It is up to you to take the initiative to learn about your boss: What are her primary goals? What pressures might he be under from his own boss or from customers? What does she need from you in order to do the best job she can do? In the following sections, we talk about some ways to gain a better understanding of your boss.

Observe and Analyze the Boss's Work Style

Understanding and being sensitive to your boss's work style can be crucial to an effective relationship.[22] No two individuals work alike or behave alike under the same circumstances. Every boss you have will be different, but it's up to you to observe and analyze your boss objectively so that you can work with him or her

more effectively. Pay close attention to your boss's behavior. Here are some of the key things[23] to look for:

- Does your boss like to know all the details of your plans, projects, and problems or does she just want the big picture?
- Does your boss typically have a positive or a cynical attitude?
- Is he more people focused or task focused? Some bosses enjoy dealing with the human and emotional needs of employees, whereas others prefer to focus on directing employees' activities toward accomplishing tasks.
- Is she open or defensive? Is she receptive to different ideas and opinions or does she become suspicious of people's motives and easily take offense?
- Is your boss controlling or empowering? Does he need to feel that he's always on top of what's going on, or does he use a more delegating style, preferring that subordinates keep him informed of important issues but handle the details on their own?
- Does your boss like to carefully analyze information and alternatives before making a decision or is she more inclined to make quick decisions and take action?
- What's your boss's orientation to time? Does he typically take quick action or take a more open-ended approach to time and tend to put things off?
- Is your boss a morning person, or is late afternoon a better time for her? This helps you know the best time to approach the boss with important or difficult issues.
- Is your boss a reader or a listener? Does he like to have materials presented in written form so he has time to study and analyze them by himself first, or does he prefer an oral presentation where he can ask questions on the spot?
- Is she a numbers person or a word person? Does she want statistics and figures to back up your report or request?
- Is your boss an extravert or an introvert? Is he outgoing and talkative or somewhat shy and quiet? Do interactions with large groups of people energize or tire him? Does he like to be involved with people all day or need time alone to think and recharge?

Effective managers seek out all the information they can about their boss, from talking with the boss, talking with others, and paying attention to clues in the boss's behavior, so that they are sensitive to the boss's work style and needs. Learning to adapt to the boss's style can help you improve as a manager and maintain more control over your own career. "Once you have that skill," says Anita Belani, senior human resources manager at a large high-tech firm, "you need never feel apprehensive about working for anyone."[24] Belani once worked for a difficult boss but found a way to adapt her approach. Together, she and her boss accomplished amazing business results, which eventually led to Belani being offered a higher-level job at a different company.

Understand the Types of Bosses

Individuals' personalities, work styles, and other personal characteristics define what type of boss they will be. Here we define several common behavioral types, the problems they can potentially create for subordinates, and how you can most effectively work with each type.[25]

The Natural

Some people seem custom made to be managers. They display all the positive qualities we expect from someone we want to follow, and their behavior inspires us to give our best. These managers are thoughtful, self-reflective, and competent. They are honest, they can be trusted to follow through on their commitments,

DISCOVER YOURSELF

Interpret Your Score: The Good Boss (Questionnaire 2)

For these questions, a low score means a good boss. Comparative data for **Good Bosses:** Thirty-person Mean score = 17.5; Top Quartile = 23–30; Bottom Quartile = 10–13. Here's hoping that you had no "Yes" answers. If you had more than three, you were likely very unhappy working for your boss. Typically people don't quit companies, they quit bosses. A good boss adds a lot to your job satisfaction and growth compared to a bad boss. Did your boss fit one of the "types" described in the chapter? CNOW and CourseMate users can access dynamically updated comparative data through www.cengagebrain.com.

© CENGAGE LEARNING 2014

and they genuinely care about employees. Instead of always talking, they know how to listen. Managing a Natural is relatively easy, because this type of boss will always meet you halfway. If only we could be so lucky to always have bosses who exhibit characteristics associated with this type. But the fact is that most bosses have at least a few behavioral characteristics that can create stress and difficulties for their subordinates.

The Politician

The Politician is also a good listener and is quite skilled at discerning people's wants, needs, and emotions. Politician managers can be highly effective, and all good managers use political skills. However, managers who illustrate the extreme of this type get so busy playing politics that they forget they even have subordinates. These managers spend all their time and energy managing their own bosses, negotiating favorable upward and horizontal relationships, and expanding their networks outside the office. To work effectively with a Politician, find ways to make the best use of what limited time you have with the boss. Set a time when you can meet periodically, even if it's only for ten minutes at a time. Keep a running list of questions or requests so you'll be prepared whenever you get a few unexpected minutes of the boss's time. Do some politicking of your own, so that you keep the boss aware of your responsibilities and accomplishments.

The Wimp

These are the bosses who can't take charge, who do whatever they can to avoid conflict, and who often have difficulty making decisions. Lorrie Bartlett worked for this type of manager in the accounts receivable department of a packaging company. Bartlett says her boss was so afraid to ask employees to do their jobs that he worked day and night to handle everything himself.[26] Wimps are also typically "Yes Men," as described earlier. They are unlikely to go to bat for their employees because they can't risk standing up to their superiors. Working for a Wimp can be particularly challenging. One tip is to provide support in any way you can and try to boost the boss's confidence. For example, if your boss needs to make a request to a higher-up for something you or your department needs, supply the boss with plenty of hard data and facts that can lend assurance and make it easier for him to present the request. Compliment the boss on his effectiveness any time he manages to step through his fears. Joe Herring, now CEO of drug development services company Covance, once worked for a boss who rarely came out of his office. One day, after the boss had initiated a rare interaction with staff, Herring told him it had really improved morale, and everyone hoped he would do it more often. The compliment worked and the boss started interacting more frequently.[27]

The Workaholic

Managers typically work long hours, but some bosses go far beyond what would already be considered a grueling schedule—and they expect their subordinates to do the same. When working for this type of boss, people begin to feel like slaves rather than employees. If you have a workaholic boss, it's important to set boundaries. The best approach is to frame it in a way that benefits the boss, such as explaining that you can't do your best work for him or her unless you have a more balanced schedule. In many cases, workaholics back down easily when people set limits. For example, one woman who had been pulling long hours for two straight weeks finally had enough when she got a text message from her boss late in the day asking for something that would require her to once again work until midnight. After telling the boss this grueling pace was destroying her positive attitude toward work, the boss sent her home for a well-needed rest, and the two never again had a problem.[28] Some workaholics, however, are prone to outbursts and bullying behavior. The best thing you can do in that case is to remain civil; you can't beat your boss by being nasty and argumentative in return.

The Micromanager

Perhaps the most common type of difficult boss is the micromanager. The "micromanagement pandemic" is so widespread that 79 percent of people say they've had to deal with this type of boss.[29] These bosses want to closely monitor and control every minute of their subordinates' workday. One manager tells of a boss who insisted employees sign everything only in black ink and deleted any e-mails she felt they shouldn't answer. The micromanager's need to be in constant control often reflects a degree of insecurity about results. This is a case where it can be highly important to adapt to your boss's style. If he wants a lot of communication so that he stays informed about every detail, give it to him. In addition, the more you can do to give the boss a sense of trust in your work, the better off you'll be with a micromanager.

BOSS MANAGEMENT RULE #2: EMPLOY SPECIFIC TACTICS

Marcia Reynolds worked for a micromanaging boss. He was always criticizing and correcting the work of Reynolds and her colleagues. Everyone resented him. But one day, Reynolds decided she would stop resenting her boss's micromanaging and instead "act as though he were the world's best boss with the world's best employee." She started trying to understand why her boss needed to keep such close tabs on the work, and she decided she was going to be as helpful as she could to him. Rather than complaining and pushing back when her boss micromanaged, she was cheerful and accommodating. Soon, an interesting thing happened. "When I stopped resisting," Reynolds says, "he started trusting me." By doing what she could to help rather than resisting, Reynolds allowed her boss to relax and appreciate her contributions. "Doing that really empowered me," Reynolds says. As her boss increasingly trusted Reynolds, his micromanaging continued to abate.[30]

Even when working for a difficult boss, Marcia Reynolds used her understanding of the boss to develop strategies that helped overcome the authority-based relationship and build an effective, respectful association. There are a number of strategies, shown in Exhibit 11.2 and discussed in detail below, that you can use to improve your relationship with your boss.[31]

Help Your Boss Be a Good Boss

The primary strategy for managing the boss is to help him or her be a good boss. This means you have to do the job the boss wants and needs you to do, not the job you think you should be doing. Effective managers find out what their boss's needs and goals are. Rather than assuming you know what the boss wants, solicit information about your boss's problems and priorities. Initiate a discussion that helps the boss clarify and communicate exactly what he or she expects from you and the goals you can help accomplish.

With information about problems and goals and a clear set of expectations, you will know how to direct work activities to give the boss what she wants and needs. You won't agree with every decision your boss makes, but your job is to perform the tasks your boss needs you to do. When you do your job well, you establish yourself as a dependable and dedicated employee. This makes you look good, which in turn makes the boss look good. You can also seek the boss's advice and look for ways she can help you improve your skills, abilities, and value to the organization. Managers like to feel needed, and when they believe subordinates value

Exhibit 11.2 Tactics for Managing the Boss

Help Your Boss Be a Good Boss
- Initiate discussion of the boss's needs and goals
- Do a good job
- Ask for advice and assistance
- Tell the boss what you think
- Confront the boss when necessary

Be a Resource
- Tell the boss your strengths & weaknesses
- Understand your boss's pressures
- Zig where the boss zags
- Come up with solutions, not just problems

See Your Boss Realistically
- Give up idealized expectations
- Don't hide anything
- Don't criticize the boss to others
- Disagree occasionally

Build a Relationship
- Learn to listen
- Ask for feedback
- Find things to compliment
- Tell your boss of your accomplishments

© CENGAGE LEARNING 2014

their counsel, they are more likely to give constructive guidance rather than unconstructive criticism.

Another important aspect of helping the boss be a good boss is to tell him what you think and what you need to be a good follower. Informing the boss of your ideas, beliefs, needs, and constraints enhances the relationship and makes you both stronger. Occasionally, telling the boss what you think involves confronting him if you believe he is doing something that hurts the team or organization. This can be a little scary, but bosses need followers who let them know if they're really messing up. If you feel that you should confront the boss, don't get personal. Remain objective, back up your analysis of the situation with facts, and give specific examples that illustrate the behavior you're critiquing.

Be a Resource for the Boss

Every boss appreciates it when someone is a source of genuine strength and support. To be a resource for your boss, develop an understanding of her strengths and weaknesses, as well as your own. It is likely that there are some things your boss does extremely well and other things she's not so good at. When you know where your boss needs reinforcement, you can find ways to compensate for the boss's weaknesses with your own strengths (zig where the boss zags). It's not likely that your boss is going to openly admit that she's terrible at some aspect of her job and needs your help. Good managers identify where their bosses are weak and find ways to provide support in those areas, without making a big deal about it.

To enhance your value, you can understand the pressures on your boss and see the job through his or her eyes. Bosses have limited time and resources and a variety of pressures from both inside and outside the organization. Therefore, they'll appreciate anyone who makes their job easier. There will be times you'll have problems you need to discuss, but you'll be a more valuable resource for your boss if, when you let him know about the problems, you offer some proposed solutions as well. You should never hide problems from the boss. Bosses need to know about the failures as well as the successes, the bad news as well as the good. However, remember to present them appropriately and try to offer ideas for how to make things better.

Build a Relationship with Your Boss

The most important key to building a good relationship with your boss is to learn to listen. Asking questions that encourage a give-and-take conversation helps you understand how the boss views things. Everyone looks

What's Your Problem?

Q: I'm happy with the type of work I am doing, I make a good salary, and the location suits my family. But my boss is driving me nuts. Rose is a decent, ethical person, but she has trouble focusing and setting priorities. Our meetings go on and on, jumping from one topic to the other. There is no follow-up on her part, and she has a hot new priority practically every day. This has been going on for two years, despite my requests to her for more clarity. It's such a waste of time when her goals change constantly and my work ends up being useless. It's never clear where we are going. I don't know how much more of this I can stand, but I can't quit my job.

A: You have discovered that indecisiveness and authority are a dangerous combination. Given your history of making appeals and the length of time this has gone on, there is little hope Rose will change. And it seems like her bosses are not working to change her, so you need to supply your own focus. During each meeting with Rose, confirm her stated priority. After each meeting, send her an e-mail outlining what you saw as the main points, the steps you are taking for implementation, and your timeline. You will have to provide the detailed planning to keep her on track as that is not her strength. Be humble and not bossy with your plans. She must know she is disorganized, so try to fill in her gaps. Help Rose look good and enable your group to become more organized. In a few months, she will depend on you, and rewards will come your way.

Source: This example is adapted from Jeremy Bullmore, "What's Your Problem?" *Management Today* (July 2008): 71.

at the world differently, and it's important that you understand the boss's mindset. Subtle differences in how people perceive and think about events can hinder communication and often create damaging misunderstandings.[32] Active listening is an essential skill for all managers, as discussed in Chapter 5.

Listening is important for learning more about yourself as well. Seeking feedback and constructive criticism from the boss shows that you value his or her advice and want to learn and grow in your position. Many people fear feedback because they expect the worst. One human resources consultant says at least half of the managers his firm works with *never* ask for feedback.[33] This cuts off a valuable source of learning, and it leaves people trying to guess what the boss is thinking or what he wants from them. Building a relationship with the boss means genuinely striving to learn how you are doing in your position and what you can do better. At the same time, you should make sure you keep the boss informed about your projects, activities, and accomplishments.

A final way to build rapport with your boss is to find ways to compliment him or her when it is appropriate. Everyone appreciates a compliment, bosses included, and you can learn to praise your boss's accomplishments without becoming a sycophant. Sincerity is the key, and calling attention to your boss's strengths in the presence of people who are important to the boss creates an environment that benefits both of you.

See the Boss Realistically

One of the biggest barriers to an effective boss-subordinate relationship is that we often have unrealistic expectations of our bosses. When we're managing subordinates, we typically accept that people have weaknesses as well as strengths, but curiously we expect our bosses to be totally competent and utterly infallible. We also usually recognize that our subordinates have some expertise or knowledge that we don't have, and we appreciate it when they take responsibility and help us out in certain areas. Yet we often resent it when our boss appears to know less than we do about a subject or when we're asked to help out in areas we think the boss should handle.[34]

Viewing your boss realistically means giving up idealized images of him or her. Your boss, just like you, has flaws and limitations and will make many mistakes. And, just like you, he needs the knowledge and assistance of his subordinates in certain areas. Accepting this fact lays the groundwork for an equitable relationship. Brian DesRoches, author of *Your Boss Is Not Your Mother*, reminds us that we sometimes revert to parent-child patterns in our interactions with superiors. We tend to turn into irritable teenagers when the boss doesn't meet our idealized expectations, and we fail to consider that the boss is under pressures of his or her own.[35] It is important that you also present a realistic image of yourself to the boss too. Don't try to hide your weaknesses or cover your mistakes.

Finally, never criticize your boss to others. Bosses highly value loyalty; hearing that you've been criticizing him behind his back can destroy the trust your boss has in you.[36] Instead of criticizing, it's far more constructive to directly and appropriately disagree with your boss on matters relevant to the department's or organization's work. In fact, occasionally disagreeing can be good for the relationship because it shows that you can think for yourself.

BOSS MANAGEMENT RULE #3: UNDERSTAND YOURSELF

Irvin D. Yalom is a professor of psychiatry and author of the novels *Lying on the Couch* and *When Nietzsche Wept*. He has also counseled numerous patients in individual and group therapy. One patient of Yalom's ranted at length in a group therapy session about her boss, who never listened and refused to pay her any respect. Interestingly, though, as the patient continued her work with Yalom, her complaints about her terrible boss persisted through three different jobs with three different supervisors. Sometimes, we need to look in the mirror before blaming our boss for an unsatisfying or unproductive relationship.[37]

Developing insight into your boss is only half the equation. That insight is useless unless you also have an understanding of yourself. In Chapter 2, we discussed self-awareness and some of the key areas you should know about, including your personality characteristics, thinking style, and personal values. You can understand your work style and how it can mesh with the boss's style. You can use your strengths to compensate for your boss's weaknesses and turn to the boss for greater assistance in areas in which you are weak and the boss is strong. And, as we learned earlier in this chapter, you can determine your basic orientation toward authority figures and how it might be a hindrance to effective working relationships.

In addition, when we're assessing the boss's management style, it is crucial to spend some time reflecting on our subordinate style.[38] One model that can help you understand how you behave as a subordinate is illustrated in Exhibit 11.3. Robert E. Kelley conducted extensive interviews with managers and their subordinates and came up with five *follower styles*, which are categorized according to two dimensions.[39]

The first dimension is the quality of independent, **critical thinking** versus dependent, **uncritical thinking.** Independent critical thinkers are mindful of the effects of their own and others' behavior on achieving organizational goals. They can weigh the impact of their boss's and their own decisions and offer constructive criticism, creativity, and innovation. Conversely, a dependent, uncritical thinker does not consider possibilities beyond what he or she is told, does not contribute to the cultivation of the organization, and accepts the boss's ideas without thinking.

The second dimension of subordinate style is **active versus passive behavior.** An active individual participates fully in the organization, engages in behavior that is beyond the limits of the job, demonstrates a sense of ownership, and initiates problem solving and decision making. A passive individual, by contrast, is characterized by a need for constant supervision and prodding by superiors. Passivity is often regarded as laziness; a passive person does nothing that is not required and avoids added responsibility.

Exhibit 11.3 Five Types of Followers

Source: Based on Robert E. Kelley, *The Power of Followership* (New York: Doubleday Business, 1992), p. 97

The extent to which you are active or passive and are a critical, independent thinker or a dependent, uncritical thinker determines whether you will be an alienated follower, a passive follower, a conformist, a pragmatic survivor, or an effective follower in your relationship with your boss, as shown in Exhibit 11.3.

The **alienated follower** is a passive, yet independent, critical thinker. Alienated employees are often effective followers who have experienced setbacks and obstacles, perhaps promises broken by their superiors. Thus, they are capable, but they focus exclusively on the shortcomings of their boss. Often cynical, alienated followers are able to think independently, but they do not participate in developing solutions to the problems or deficiencies they see. These people waste valuable time complaining about their boss without offering constructive feedback.

The **conformist** participates actively in a relationship with the boss but doesn't use critical thinking skills. In other words, a conformist typically carries out any and all orders regardless of the nature of the request. The conformist participates willingly, but without considering the consequences of what he or she is being asked to do—even at the risk of contributing to a harmful endeavor. A conformist is concerned only with avoiding conflict. This subordinate style might reflect an individual's overdependent attitude toward authority, yet it can also result from rigid rules and authoritarian environments that create a culture of conformity.

The **pragmatic survivor** has qualities of all four extremes—depending on which style fits with the prevalent situation. This type of person uses whatever style best benefits his or her own position and minimizes risk. Pragmatic survivors often emerge when an organization is going through desperate times, and managers find themselves doing whatever is needed to get themselves through the difficulty. Within any given company, some 25 to 35 percent of people tend to be pragmatic survivors, avoiding risks and fostering the status quo.[40]

The **passive follower** exhibits neither critical, independent thinking nor active participation. Being passive and uncritical, these people show neither initiative nor a sense of responsibility. Their activity is limited to what they are told to do, and they accomplish things only with a great deal of supervision.

Passive followers leave the thinking to the boss. Often, this style is the result of a micromanaging boss who encourages passive behavior. People learn that to show initiative, accept responsibility, or think creatively is not rewarded, and may even be punished by the boss, so they grow increasingly passive.

The **effective follower** is both a critical, independent thinker and active in the organization. Effective followers behave the same toward everyone, regardless of their position in the organization. They develop an equitable relationship with the boss and do not try to avoid risk or conflict. These people are capable of self-management, they discern strengths and weaknesses in themselves and their bosses, they are committed to something bigger than themselves, and they work toward competency, solutions, and a positive impact. Effective followers recognize that they have power in their relationships with superiors; thus, they have the courage to manage upward, to initiate change, and to put themselves at risk or in conflict with the boss if they believe it serves the best interest of the team or organization.

DISCOVER KNOWLEDGE

DISCOVER YOURSELF

Interpret Your Score: Followership (Questionnaire 3)

Your score for Part A represents your critical-thinking qualities as a follower, as described in the chapter. Comparative data for **Critical Thinking** (Part A): Thirty-person Mean score = 20.3; Top Quartile = 23–24; Bottom Quartile = 11–20. Your score for Part B represents your active-engagement approach as a follower. Comparative data for **Active Engagement** (Part B): Thirty-person Mean score = 19.8; Top Quartile = 23–24; Bottom Quartile = 9–16. You can assess your followership style below based on whether your score is high, in the middle, or low compared to average scores. CNOW and CourseMate users can access dynamically updated comparative data through www.cengagebrain.com.

Followership Style	Critical-Thinking Score	Active-Engagement Score
Effective	High	High
Alienated	High	Low
Conformist	Low	High
Pragmatist	Middle	Middle
Passive	Low	Low

How do you feel about your followership style? What might you do to be more effective as a follower?

© CENGAGE LEARNING 2014

FINDING POWER AND COURAGE FOR MANAGING UP

James Copeland, who retired as CEO from Deloitte & Touche in 2003, said that over the course of his career he gave so much "constructive criticism" to his superiors that one boss jokingly told Copeland that supervising him was the most painful part of his job.[41] You might not feel comfortable giving constructive criticism to your boss, but as we've discussed throughout this chapter, bosses need subordinates who are willing and able to manage up. Managing your boss takes courage.

Finding the courage to effectively manage up comes easier when you realize that the relationship with your boss is one of *mutual* dependence (interdependence).[42] Your boss depends on you. For example, Douglas Emond was chief operating officer at BankBoston when Fleet Financial acquired the company. Many senior managers quickly headed for new jobs, not wanting to be involved in the difficult changes that would be required in integrating the two companies. Emond, though, agreed to stay and help his boss with the challenges. When Emond disagreed with one of the boss's decisions, he faced a dilemma: He didn't want to be disloyal to his boss, but if he simply followed the orders from above, he risked alienating his own subordinates. Emond decided to explain to people that he was given orders and that this was the way it was going to go, without badmouthing his superiors or complaining about the decision. His frank, straightforward approach helped prepare subordinates for what was coming and won him the trust and support of managers both below and above him in the hierarchy.[43]

It is a fact that our bosses typically have more power than we do. After all, in most organizations, they have the power to fire us, but we can't fire them. Yet, as a subordinate, you have more power than you

Exhibit 11.4 Sources of Power for Managing Up

Personal Sources	Position Sources
• Knowledge, skills • Expertise • Effort • Persuasion	• Visible position • Flow of information • Central location • Network of relationships

© CENGAGE LEARNING 2014

probably realize. The boss is dependent on you just as much as you are dependent on him or her, and perhaps even more so. In fact, without the hard work and cooperation of subordinates, your boss is up the creek without a paddle. Think about what happens when union employees go on strike. If subordinates refuse to do their jobs, the whole organization shuts down. In almost all cases, subordinates have information that the boss needs to do his or her job well. Furthermore, bosses depend on subordinates doing a good job to make them look good to their own bosses.

Exhibit 11.4 outlines several sources of power that you can use when managing up.

Personal Sources

One personal source of upward influence is your knowledge, talents, and skills that are valuable to the organization. A subordinate with useful *knowledge* is of real benefit to the boss, and his or her departure would be a loss. In addition, someone who has a demonstrated record of performance often develops *expertise* and in this way can influence the boss's decisions. A record of successes and a history of contributions can gain you expert status, from which you can derive the power to influence activities and establish yourself as an indispensable resource to the boss. The power to influence is also associated with the *effort* you put forth. By demonstrating a willingness to learn, to accept difficult or undesirable projects, and to initiate activities beyond the scope of expected effort, you can increase your power.[44]

Another way to influence up is with *persuasion*, which refers to the direct appeal to your boss for desired outcomes.[45] Rational persuasion—using facts and reason—is typically the most effective approach when trying to influence upward. However, managers use a variety of influence tactics, depending on their own personalities and styles. In addition, smart managers tailor their choice of tactics to the work styles of their bosses.[46] We discussed a range of influence tactics in Chapter 8.

Speaking truthfully to your boss can sometimes be a source of power.[47] Rob Hummel, head of international post-production at Dreamworks SKG, once promoted a manager who was known for being "difficult" because he always challenged his superiors. The fact that this manager was willing to speak truthfully to higher-ups based on his own knowledge and creative brilliance gave him increased power.[48]

Position Sources

Your formal position also provides sources of power. For example, your job and physical location can render you visible to numerous individuals. A position that is key to the *flow of information* can establish that position and the person in it as critical—thus,

DISCOVER KNOWLEDGE

DISCOVER YOURSELF

Interpret Your Score: InfluenceTactics to Manage the Boss (Questionnaire 4)

Influence tactics described in statements 1 and 2 of this questionnaire are called coalition and legitimation, which are typically used more often toward the boss than toward a colleague. Statements 3, 4, and 5 refer to tactics called rational, apprising, and consultation. These tend to be used about equally toward a boss or a colleague. Influence tactics in statements 6, 7, and 8 are called inspirational appeal, exchange, and assertive, and are used more often toward a colleague than toward the boss. Frequently using a wide range of influence tactics is called a shot-gun style. Frequently using selective rational tactics is called a tactician style. Using few if any tactics is called a bystander style. Comparative data for **Boss Influence:** Thirty-person Mean score = 19.0; Top Quartile = 22–24; Bottom Quartile = 8–16. For **Colleague Influence:** Thirty-person Mean score = 18.6; Top Quartile = 21–24; Bottom Quartile = 8–17. Did you have the courage to influence your boss as much as your colleague? If you did, which tactics did you use? How would you describe your style? CNOW and CourseMate users can access dynamically updated comparative data through www.cengagebrain.com.

© CENGAGE LEARNING 2014

influential—to those who need the information. A *central location* provides influence because you become known to many people and contribute to the work of many. Access to people and information in an organization provides you a means to establish relationships with a broad range of people both inside and outside the organization. With a *network of relationships*, you'll have more clout with your boss and more opportunity to persuade and make significant contributions.

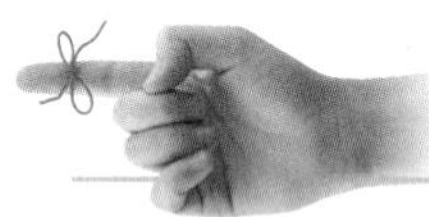

NEED TO KNOW

- Being an effective and successful manager requires that you manage up as well as down the hierarchy. If you cannot develop a meaningful, task-related, mutually respectful relationship with your direct superiors, your effectiveness and well-being as a manager will suffer. We often misinterpret our boss's behavior, and we allow personal "baggage," learned anxieties, and fears to affect our relationships with bosses more so than with our subordinates or peers.
- Four ways of thinking about and interacting with authority are counterdependence, overdependence, independence, and interdependence. Counterdependent people rebel against bosses and overdependent people rely on bosses too much. Effective subordinates are independent, and they move to interdependence to work cooperatively with authority figures and build trusting, respectful relationships.
- Five things a boss wants from you are a make-it-happen attitude, a willingness to cooperate, the courage to lead change, the effort to stay up to date in your job, and the commitment to drive your own growth and development.
- To manage up, learn about your boss's work style so you know how to work with him or her most effectively. Develop an understanding of five types of bosses—the Natural, the Politician, the Wimp, the Workaholic, and the Micromanager—and steps you can take to make working with each type smoother and more productive. Strategies for managing up include helping the boss be a good boss, acting as a resource for the boss, building a personal relationship with the boss, and seeing the boss realistically.
- You also have to understand yourself—your work style, personality characteristics, and so forth. One consideration is what type of follower you are. Five follower styles are effective, alienated, passive, conformist, and pragmatic survivor. Strive to be an effective follower, which means being an independent, critical thinker and making an active contribution to the organization.
- Managing up requires courage because bosses typically have more power than we do. However, our bosses depend on us more than we realize, which gives us power as well. Recognizing personal and positional sources of power can give you the courage to successfully manage up and be an effective follower.

ACTION LEARNING

DELIBERATE PRACTICE EXERCISES

Help the Boss

Step 1: Choose three of these activities that you will perform during the following week with someone who is some kind of "boss" for you:

1. Start a discussion about your relationship and how you can help your boss achieve his or her goals.
2. Help your boss be a good boss. Consider that part of your job is to serve the boss. Offer to help in extra ways—above and beyond.
3. Be a resource. Find out information the boss needs. Anticipate what the boss will want before the boss asks.
4. Help create change. If the boss is starting a new project, get in there and be supportive and work hard.
5. Work on your relationship with your boss. Ask questions, request feedback, find out the boss's concerns, and listen to the boss's problems.
6. See the positive in the boss. Write down the boss's strengths.
7. Understand the boss's weaknesses and try compensating for them, so that when the boss "zigs," you "zag."

Step 2: Practice the behaviors and fill in the table below as you go through the week.

Which behavior are you trying?	How did the first attempt go?	Second and other attempts?	What was difficult?	What went well?
1.				
2.				
3.				

Step 3: What did you learn about managing the boss? How did it feel?

Step 4 (Optional): Share your insights with a partner, and ask your partner what insights he or she gained.

What Kind of Boss Am I?

This Deliberate Practice Exercise is available online at www.cengagebrain.com.

Looking Up

Step 1: Think of the relationships you've had with up to three bosses or authority figures (not your parents; you will consider those in Step 2). These authority figures can include professors, dorm supervisors, coaches, club officers, team leaders, managers at work, and so on. Think of a word or two that would describe the type of interactions you had with each of the three—for example, cordial, combative, supportive, punitive, tense, or uplifting. Fill in the table below.

Name of boss	Describe your relationship in a word or two	Was it in general positive or negative?	Did you tilt toward being over-dependent or counter-dependent?	What positive things did you get out of the relationship?
1.				
2.				
3.				
Your parents				

Step 2: Now think about the kind of relationship you've had with your parents and fill in the bottom row of the table.

Step 3: Are there similarities in the way you behave toward the various authority figures? What are they?

Step 4 (Optional): Share your insights with a partner, and ask your partner what insights he or she gained.

ACTION LEARNING

SHUTTERSTOCK #53973379

IN-CLASS TEAM EXERCISE

Boss Dilemmas

Step 1: Divide into groups of four to five people. Each individual reads the following two situations and writes down a few sentences after each one, indicating how he or she would handle the situation.

Step 2: In a group, each member shares his or her response; then the group discusses and agrees on one best course of action for each situation.

Situation 1: The Procrastinating Boss

You are a technical writer for a software company and you regularly get good evaluations from your supervisor. But she gets on your nerves. When you know an assignment is coming, you ask her for the details, but she tends to put things off until the last minute. Then, a day before your work is due, she gives you the details. You have to race to finish your work and can't really polish it the way you would like. You've asked your boss on two occasions to give you more lead time, but she keeps saying the situation is out of her hands. How would you try to influence the boss?

Your response	
Group response	

Situation 2: The Boss Who Plays Favorites

You are on a financial analysis team with four other people, each of whom has unique and strong skills. For some reason, your boss seems to favor Michael over the other team members. She is always praising Michael in front of everyone and giving him the plum assignments, which of course makes his work look even better. You wonder if she even knows she is playing favorites. You've been working really hard for two years, trying to show the boss what a great job you are doing, but you can't seem to get the kind of attention Michael does. How would you try to influence the boss?

Your response	
Group response	

Step 3: As a team, analyze each individual's responses and categorize the responses according to the types of followers in Exhibit 11.3 (alienated, conformist, pragmatic, passive, effective). What are the most frequent follower types in the pattern of individual responses to the two situations? Then analyze the pattern of the group's responses to

the situations to determine the type of "follower" the group would be. Complete the table below.

The most frequent follower type among individual responses:	
The second most frequent follower type among individual responses:	
The follower type identified in the group's responses:	

Step 4 (Optional): Your instructor may choose to have a class discussion about the boss situations.

FIELD TEAM EXERCISE

Getting Along with the Boss

Step 1: Divide into groups of three to five, and schedule a time for a group meeting.

Step 2: Before your group meeting, each individual should briefly interview someone who has had a positive relationship with a boss and someone who has had a negative relationship with a boss. (Note: The same interviewee may have had both the positive and negative boss relationships.) Ask questions and take notes so you can fill in the table below with details about the two relationships.

	Good Boss Relationship	Bad Boss Relationship
Describe the person you interviewed (who it is, where the person works, etc.).		
Describe the boss as that person sees him or her.		
Refer to the "Understand the Types of Bosses" section in the text. What type of boss was this individual?		
Refer to Exhibit 11.4 (Sources of Power for Managing Up). How did the interviewee manage the relationship with the boss? What sources of power did he or she try to use?		

Step 3: At your group meeting, have each person report on the two relationships. As a group, look for patterns in the relationships and fill in the table below.

	Good Boss Relationships	Bad Boss Relationships
Common characteristics of the bosses		
What were similarities in the relationships between the bosses and subordinates?		
What "managing upward" behaviors by subordinates were most helpful?		
What "managing upward" behaviors by subordinates were least helpful?		

Step 4: Based on the evidence your group gathered, what advice would you give to people to manage their bosses more effectively?

Step 5 (Optional): Your instructor may ask you to write a report or present your findings in class.

TEST YOUR METTLE

ROLE PLAY SIMULATIONS

Pushback?

Background: Re-read the written Video Incident at the beginning of the chapter. Caffeine and Crullers general manager Jane Sutton is in the office of her boss, Edmund Daniels, who is the COO at the corporate office. He has called her to a meeting to discuss his new idea for restructuring the Madison locations.

Instructions: Divide into groups of two or three. One person will be Edmund and one will be Jane. If there are three, the third person is an observer. Each person reads only his or her confidential role, but the observer reads both. Spend ten minutes on the role play.

Confidential information for Jane: Your boss, Edmund Daniels, asked to meet with you about his proposal (which is 30 pages, single-spaced, with ten diagrams) to restructure your twelve Madison, Wisconsin, locations. You know Edmund just attended another workshop, this one on corporate design. No doubt the "matrix" speaker was enthusiastic and convincing, because this is now Edmund's latest idea that he is trying to get you and your people to implement. You can't even count the hundreds of hours you've wasted in the past on his crazy ideas—things such as poker-playing incentives and virtual Sudoko as motivators. Because the corporate office is in Milwaukee, you asked to meet at the end of the day so you won't lose the commute both ways during working hours. You arrived a little early and are sitting and thinking about how you can suggest to Edmund that his idea might not be a good solution without upsetting him. Frankly, you don't see a problem with the current structure, but Edmund has gotten upset in the past if you don't agree with his ideas. You do think the idea of looking at the structure may be okay, but it would be better for you to go back to your team and for everyone to discuss the best way to reorganize. But Edmund loves to tell everyone how to do everything when he is hot on a new idea. You've thought and thought how to communicate your concerns without him getting upset or even throwing you out of his office.

Confidential information for Edmund: You work in the corporate office of Caffeine and Crullers in Milwaukee. The Madison locations have had a drop in sales and you've called the Madison general manager, Jane Sutton, in to see you. After some recent reading you've done, plus attending a workshop on corporate design, you've come to see the problem and it is so clear. The Madison locations are structured in a way that reduces coordination and hinders them from increasing their sales. The answer: a matrix structure. That gives more flexibility and freedom to employees and provides better coordination across locations for advertising, sharing personnel, and so on. Right now, with the functional structure, people are limited to a specific job in one location. You've talked to your management guru, Steven Watkins, and he agrees with you. Why haven't you seen this before? Well, better late than never. And writing the proposal really helped you solidify your thoughts. Jane will be here any minute, and you want to get her excited about this wonderful idea. Sometimes she can be such a Debby Downer, so you've got to work to bring out her positive side. After all, isn't that what a boss is supposed to do?

After the role play, discuss what happened and answer these questions:

1. How difficult was it for Jane to confront the boss with something he doesn't want to hear? How might she have said things differently?
2. What happens when one person is so completely convinced of the rightness of his or her ideas that he or she has trouble listening to other opinions?
3. How often do people go along with ideas just to avoid confrontation?

The Hovering Boss

A second Role Play Simulation is available online at www.cengagebrain.com.

VIDEO APPLICATION

Barcelona Restaurant Group

Andy Pforzheimer, co-owner, and Scott Lawton, COO, of Barcelona Restaurant Group, strive for success by *not* trying to make their employees happy.

Discussion Questions

1. How would you characterize Pforzheimer and Lawton as bosses? What do you see as their strengths and weaknesses?
2. What does Pforzheimer mean when he says to wait staff, "When customers walk in the door, I don't want them looking for me, I want them looking for you." Is this a form of empowerment? Explain.
3. If you were a Barcelona employee, what techniques would you use to manage upward to Pforzheimer? Lawton? Which one would you rather work for? Why?

CASE INCIDENTS

Waiting for Lift-off

He wanted the help. But CEO Tony Bussard apparently wanted to relinquish none of the power when he agreed with board members of Alvon Biometrics to maintain control over the financial and administrative side of the company, while naming a COO to oversee day-to-day operations.

Everyone agreed that the job was too big for one guy. After months of assessments, interviews, and discussion, Juan Carlos De la Vega was hired as COO for the company.

De la Vega came over to Alvon from a smaller rival company and was initially excited about his new position and the future of Alvon. De la Vega trained in military security investigations and became interested in the measuring and statistical analysis of biological data that included fingerprints, eye retinas and irises, voice patterns, and facial patterns that could be used in security systems. He had worked his way up through rival bio-tech companies to a position in middle management and jumped at the opportunity to guide a major company in the field about which he was so passionate.

"That is *so cool*," was a De la Vega trademark comment as he delighted in the giant leaps of each system's gadgetry.

But De la Vega's exciting new position came with its own set of frustrations as he tried to plunge into the rapidly changing technology while simultaneously fitting into the organization and tip-toeing around Tony Bussard's ego.

Bussard welcomed De la Vega with the gusto of an under-fire field officer who looks up to see reinforcements riding into the fray. He enthusiastically introduced the new COO to everyone and raved, almost to the point of embarrassment, about De la Vega's experience and level of expertise in the field of biometrics.

"You've made my job a whole lot easier," Bussard gushed. "We're all thrilled to have you."

Now, one year into the job, De la Vega was still wondering what was expected of him and where Bussard's duties ended and his duties began. Those things were never actually spelled out in an agreement, and the boundaries remained vague and confusing. Even during the initial job interviews, Bussard and board members showed great interest in De la Vega's background and talked endlessly about Bussard's vision for the future. But now, in retrospect, the COO realized there was little or no discussion of *his* vision or any mention about how he would fit into the future being laid out for him.

With no clear agreement, De la Vega's earnest efforts to get guidance about his responsibilities seemed to be brushed aside by the CEO, who remained elusive and vague.

"If he tells me one more time, 'Yeah, yeah, we'll talk,' I think I will scream," De la Vega complained. "I want to feel like a COO, not a sidekick to the CEO. At the same time, I don't want to push so hard that Bussard and the board members become concerned that they made a mistake in selecting me."

The confusion about De la Vega's role also filtered down the ranks. Employees, expecting initiative from De la Vega, remained uncertain about his range of responsibilities. People looked almost exclusively to Bussard for direction, by-passing the new COO. Workers liked De la Vega and admired his industry experience. But old habits die hard, and the habit of yielding to Bussard's leadership remained intact. Even one year later, employees were reluctant to take a chance on angering Bussard by shifting even a portion of their attention and allegiance to De la Vega.

For his part, De la Vega knew the time for clarity was now, but he hesitated, not knowing exactly how or when to approach the CEO from a position of strength.

Discussion Questions

1. If you were De la Vega, what would you do at this point? Why?
2. What are Bussard's characteristics as a boss? Explain.
3. What sources of influence might De la Vega draw upon to improve his relationship with Bussard? Do you think De la Vega has waited too long to make a substantial change in this situation? Why?

Finding What's Still Salvageable

WesTex Financial Group survived the mortgage crisis. There was a period when the company endured bad publicity about its mortgage department because of local television reporting and government investigations. There were claims that WesTex made loans to unqualified applicants to earn fees from selling the loans to large banks and other investors. Some loans went bad and houses went into foreclosure. Nothing illegal

happened, but the publicity had been difficult as employees tried to explain to family, friends, panicking customers, and even total strangers that the company had done nothing wrong and that, in the end, WesTex's corporate reputation would be salvaged.

"Looking my kids in the face and telling them that we are not crooks was unbearably emotional," Rebecca Lynch said later. "Yes, we got off with a fine and a slap on the wrist, but the fact is that some in the public still think we were running a crooked mortgage relief service. It hurts."

Although WesTex was now enjoying a mild resurgence in business and public trust, the company culture had suffered a serious blow. What had been an environment of close-knit, easy-going staff was now a workplace manned by jittery, uptight employees who second-guessed every decision and faced still uncertain futures. "The other day, a car with government tags parked out front and you could just see the panic on the faces," one employee said. "It turns out, the guy was just dropping off his sister's mortgage payment."

The most obvious impact was on long-time mortgage manager Darren Conrad. Certain that an 'insider' had either been the source behind the government investigations or had been too cooperative with the government and media, Darren had changed dramatically from a trusting, back-slapping, my-door-is-always-open leader into an increasingly suspicious boss. At one point during the crisis, he had to be dissuaded from his plan to require all employees to sign pledges of loyalty to the company.

As the dust settled and business picked up, the "loyalty level" should have been obvious as the entire staff remained intact. However, Darren's attitude failed to improve. Not knowing the source of the allegations against his company, Darren was determined to watch his back. As he replayed events over and over in his mind, he developed a belief that *his* reputation had been attacked; *his* credibility had been damaged. He became increasingly defensive and private.

In his effort to regain control over the organization, Darren demonstrated a sudden reluctance to trust the decisions of employees and insisted on reviewing every major transaction over and over again. "Managerial directives" replaced weekly staff meetings. He began micro-managing the activities of all employees, including those with 15 or more years of service with the company. Darren monitored employee e-mails and online activity. On occasion, he would appear suddenly to interrupt casual conversations between employees, demanding, "Let's break this up and get back to work," as if they were fomenting workplace revolution.

As the months passed, dissatisfaction within the organization reached a critical point. Three of the company's longest-serving employees (Rebecca Lynch, Bailey Worsham, and Sam Garrett) met privately to discuss how to deal with the situation.

"I thought the three of us should get together and explore how we can reset the culture here and maybe bring back the camaraderie and level of trust we had before all of this happened," Sam Garrett said. "I think we should have some sort of intervention with Darren to wake him up to the damage he's doing to morale. Let's hit him with the facts and wake him up."

"Look, I know that Darren has been through a lot," Bailey remarked. "We all have. But it's time to put the past behind us and move on. I think that maybe, if we're patient with him a little longer, things will improve. I think a confrontation is too strong, too risky. He's the boss. We should do things his way."

"We've been patient," Rebecca said. "I'm tired of it. I'm an adult and dedicated to my work and to my customers who are dealing with their own difficult situations. I've put in 15 years with this company, and I will not be treated like a child who has to be monitored in order to do my job."

Sam responded, "You're saying?"

"I'm saying that I am quitting unless something changes soon. I think I can find some other way to support myself if Darren doesn't change his style."

Sam and Bailey looked shocked. "But, Rebecca, you've been the heart and spirit of this organization. If you walk out, everyone will question whether they should stay. You might be able to go with another company, but most here would have a difficult time in this economy finding another job," Bailey said.

"It's your decision, of course," Sam added. "And I can't say that I blame you. But I think that if we talk to Darren together, and other staff members see even small changes, we can turn this around. This *is* still salvageable, Rebecca."

"Okay, we don't wait, like Bailey suggested," Rebecca said.

"And we don't quit, like you suggested," Bailey chimed in.

Sam picked up the conversation. "Let's put together a series of logical, well-thought-out steps, starting with how we will confront Darren and get him back in the loop and back to the level of leadership he's demonstrated over the years."

Discussion Questions

1. What type of boss has Darren become? If you reported to him at WesTex, how would you handle the relationship? Why?
2. What follower styles do you think are illustrated by the suggestions to wait, quit, or confront in response to Darren's behavior? Which approach do you think would work out the best? Why?
3. What sources of influence and courage are available to Sam, Rebecca, and Bailey? To what extent should they take it upon themselves to try to create a better organization?

PERSONAL SKILLS LOG

Directions: Fill in the rows below based on what you learned from each part of the chapter that you completed.

	What is my key takeaway or insight from this activity?	What do I personally do well (strength) regarding this activity?	What could I improve (weakness) about myself regarding this activity?	How might I use what I've learned from this activity in the future?
Manager Challenge Incident:				
Discover Yourself Questionnaires:				
Deliberate Practice Exercises:				
In-Class and/or Field Team Exercises:				
Role-Play Exercises:				
Case Incidents:				

REFERENCES

Discover Yourself

1 Based in part on presentations by Professor Lico Reis, "Managing Your Boss," http://licoreis.com/wp-content/uploads/2010/10/task-4157-presentation-managing-your-boss.pdf (accessed April 26, 2012); and "What Is Your Boss Like?" http://licoreis.com/wp-content/uploads/2009/07/task-1608-presentation-boss.pdf (accessed April 26, 2012).

2 Based on Douglas R. May, Richard L. Gilson, and Lynn M. Harter, "The Psychological Conditions of Meaningfulness, Safety and Availability and the Engagement of the Human Spirit at Work," *Journal of Occupational and Organizational Psychology* 77 (March 2004): 11–38; Robert E. Kelley, *The Power of Followership: How to Create Leaders People Want to Follow and Followers Who Lead Themselves* (New York: Doubleday, 1992); and Towers Perrin HR Services, "Working Today: Understanding What Drives Employee Engagement: The 2003 Towers Perrin Talent Report," http://www.towersperrin.com/tp/getwebcachedoc?webc=hrs/usa/2003/200309/talent_2003.pdf (accessed February 20, 2012).

3 Based on Gary Yukl and J. Bruce Tracey, "Consequences of Influence Tactics Used With Subordinates, Peers, and the Boss," *Journal of Applied Psychology* 77, no. 4 (1992): 525–535; and David Kipnis, Stuart M. Schmidt, and Ian Wilkinson, "Intraorganizational Influence Tactics: Explorations in Getting One's Way," *Journal of Applied Psychology* 65, no. 4 (1980): 440–452.

Discover Knowledge

4 Adapted from a true story in John G. Gabarro and John P. Kotter, "Managing Your Boss," Best of HBR 1980, *Harvard Business Review*, January 2005, http://hbr.org/2005/01/managing-your-boss/ar/1 (accessed April 18, 2011).

5 Based on Gabarro and Kotter, "Managing Your Boss."

6 Rosabeth Moss Kanter, "Power Failure in Management Circuits," *Harvard Business Review* (July–August, 1979): 65–75.

7 Ronald J. DeLuga, "Kissing Up to the Boss: What It Is and What to Do About It," *Business Forum* 26 (2003): 14–18; and Bennett Tepper, "Upward Maintenance Tactics in Supervisory Mentoring and Nonmentoring Relationships," *Academy of Management Journal* 38, no. 4 (1995): 1191–1205.

8 Liz Simpson, "Why Managing Up Matters," *Harvard Management Update* (August 2002): 3–5; and Stanley Bing, *Throwing the Elephant* (New York: HarperCollins, 2002).

9 Based on a story in Christopher Hegarty, *How to Manage Your Boss* (Mill Valley, CA: Whatever Publishing, Inc., 1982), pp. 58–59.

10 These examples are from Table 1, Same Behaviors, Different Takes, in Jean-François Manzoni and Jean-Louis Barsoux, "The Interpersonal Side of Taking Charge," *Organizational Dynamics* 38, no. 2 (2009): 106–116.

11 This discussion is based on William Kahn and Kathy Kram, "Authority at Work: Internal Models and Their Organizational Consequences," *Academy of Management Review* 19, no. 1 (1994): 17–50; Judith Sills, "When You're Smarter than Your Boss," *Psychology Today* (May–June 2006): 58–59; Frank Pittman, "How to Manage Mom and Dad," *Psychology Today* (November–December 1994): 44–74; Sarah Kershaw, "My Other Family Is the Office," *The New York Times*, December 4, 2008; and Kerry J. Sulkowicz, "The Corporate Shrink," *Fast Company* (September 2003): 50.

12 The discussion of these four styles is based on Gabarro and Kotter, "Managing Your Boss"; and Diane Zimberoff and David Hartman, "Four Primary Existential Themes in Heart-Centered Therapy," *Journal of Heart-Centered Therapies* 4, no. 2 (2001): 3–64.

13 Zimberoff and Hartman, "Four Primary Existential Themes in Heart-Centered Therapy."

14 Gabarro and Kotter, "Managing Your Boss"; and Jack Welch with Suzy Welch, *Winning* (New York: HarperBusiness, 2005), p. 303.

15 Jared Sandberg, "How Do You Say 'No' to a Yes Man? Often Unsuccessfully" (Cubicle Culture column), *The Wall Street Journal*, July 25, 2006.

16 Gabarro and Kotter, "Managing Your Boss."

17 Story told in Simpson, "Why Managing Up Matters."

18 Peter F. Drucker, "Drucker on Management: How to Manage the Boss," *The Wall Street Journal*, August 1, 1986.

19 These are based on Larry Bossidy, "What Your Leader Expects of You," *Harvard Business Review* (April 2007): 58ff; and Drucker, "Drucker on Management: How to Manage the Boss."

20 Bossidy, "What Your Leader Expects of You."

21 Quoted in Simpson, "Why Managing Up Matters"; Michael and Deborah Singer Dobson, *Managing Up: 59 Ways to Build a Career-Advancing Relationship with Your Boss* (New York: AMACOM, 1999).

22 Gabarro and Kotter, "Managing the Boss"; and Hegarty, *How to Manage Your Boss.*

23 Based on Jo Owen, "Manage Your Boss," *Industrial and Commercial Training* 39, no. 2 (2007): 79–84.

24 Story told in Simpson, "Why Managing Up Matters."

25 This discussion of types of bosses is based on Stefan Stern, "How to Manage Your Boss," *Management Today* (October 2004): 50–52; Julie Amparano Lopez and Catherine Romano, "The Boss from Hell—and How to Tame Him," *Working Woman* (December 1999): 68–71; and Paul Kaihla, "Getting Inside the Boss's Head," *Business 2.0* (November 2003): 49.

26 Lopez and Romano, "The Boss from Hell."

27 Reported in Del Jones, "Should Workers Suck Up to the Boss or Not?" *USA Today*, November 18, 2009, http://www.usatoday.com/money/workplace/2009-11-18-brownnosing18_CV_N.htm (accessed November 18, 2009).

28 Story told in Paul O'Donnell, "Stop Being a Wimp," *MBA Jungle* (September 2003): 53–56.

29 The discussion of the micromanager is based on Robert McGarvey, "And You Thought Your Boss Was Bad," *American Way* (May 1, 2006): 69–74. The survey statistic is reported in Harry Chambers, *My Way or the Highway: The Micromanagement Survival Guide* (San Francisco: Berrett-Koehler, 2004).

30 Reported in McGarvey, "And You Thought Your Boss Was Bad."

31 These are based on Ira Chaleff, *The Courageous Follower: Standing Up to and for Our Leaders* (San Francisco: Berrett-Koehler, 1995); Robert E. Kelley, "In Praise of Followers," *Harvard Business Review* (November–December 1988): 142–148; Gabarro and Kotter, "Managing Your Boss"; Hegarty, *How to Manage Your Boss*; and Pittman, "How to Manage Mom and Dad."

32 James Billington, "The Fundamentals of Managing Up," *Harvard Management Update* (September 1997): 3–4.

33 Jay M. Jackman and Myra H. Strober, "Fear of Feedback," *Harvard Business Review* (April 2003): 101ff.

34 Kevin P. Kearns, "Managing Upward: Working Effectively with Supervisors and Others in the Hierarchy," *Information Outlook* (October 1997): 23–28.

35 Shari Caudron, "The Boss from Hell: Coping with a Bad Boss," *Industry Week* (September 4, 1995): 12–16.

36 Wayne Turk, "The Art of Managing Up," *Defense AT&L* (March–April 2007): 21–23; Chris Pearce, "Ten Steps to Managing Your Boss," *Nursing Management* 14, no. 3 (June 2007): 21; and Jo Owen, "Manage Your Boss," *Industrial and Commercial Training* 39, no. 2 (2007): 79–84.

37 Irvin D. Yalom, with Ben Yalom, "Mad About Me," *Inc.* (December 1998): 37–38.

38 Gene Boccialetti, *It Takes Two: Managing Yourself When Working with Bosses and Other Authority Figures* (San Francisco: Jossey-Bass, 1995).

39 Robert E. Kelley, *The Power of Followership* (New York: Doubleday, 1992).

40 *Ibid.*, pp. 117–118.

41 Reported in Jones, "Should Workers Suck Up to the Boss or Not?"

42 Gabarro and Kotter, "Managing Your Boss."

43 Carol Hymowitz, "When You Disagree with the Boss's Order, Do You Tell Your Staff?" (In the Lead column), *The Wall Street Journal*, April 16, 2002.

44 Peter Moroz and Brian H. Kleiner, "Playing Hardball in Business Organizations," *Industrial Management* (January/February 1994): 9–11.

45 Warren Keith Schilit and Edwin A. Locke, "A Study of Upward Influence in Organizations," *Administrative Science Quarterly* 27 (1982): 304–316.

46 Deepti Bhatnagar, "Evaluation of Managerial Influence Tactics," *Journal of Managerial Psychology* 8, no. 1 (1993): 3–9; and Daniel M. Cable and Timothy A. Judge, "Managers' Upward Influence Tactic Strategies: The Role of Manager Personality and Supervisor Leadership Style," *Journal of Organizational Behavior* 24 (2003): 197–214.

47 Chaleff, *The Courageous Follower: Standing Up to and for Our Leaders.*

48 "Open Mouth, Open Career," sidebar in Michael Warshaw, "Open Mouth, Close Career?" *Fast Company* (December 1998): 240.

PART 3

Managing Your Team

FANCY ALAMY

CHAPTER 12
Managing Teams

Chapter Outline

RYAN LASH

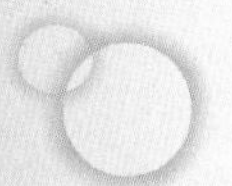

MANAGER CHALLENGE

VIDEO INCIDENT: REWARDING WHAT?

Madison-area Caffeine and Crullers general manager Jane Sutton has just gotten word from corporate that bonuses are no longer going to be based totally on individual achievement, but also on how the entire team of managers in her region performs. Now half of each manager's year-end bonus will be calculated based on the average of how each team member's department delivers on its goals. Most of Jane's managers do not like this because they all see themselves as above-average performers. They started making references to the "unfair practice of group grades, just like in school," and they've been saying unkind things to one another, stressing their own department's superior performance and the desire not to be "dragged down by other departments." Jane knows these are signs of deep fears about the new reward system.

Initial Thoughts

1. **If you were Jane, how would you handle the team's resistance to team rewards?**

2. **Do you think team or individual rewards are better for a management team? Why?**

Your instructor may ask you to be part of a role play based on the "Rewarding What?" incident.

DISCOVER YOURSELF

For those students using CourseMate or CengageNOW, you can access the Daft/Marcic Assessment Library to take the questionnaires online and view dynamically updated comparative data.

Questionnaire 1[1]

Instructions: Respond to the statements below based on your preferences for working on your job or school assignments. Rate how accurately each statement describes you based on whether the statement is clearly true or accurate, clearly false or inaccurate, or in the middle as somewhat true and somewhat false.

	True	Somewhat	False
1. I prefer to work on a team rather than do tasks individually.	○	○	○
2. Given a choice, I try to work by myself rather than face the hassles of group work.	○	○	○
3. I enjoy the personal interaction when working with others.	○	○	○
4. I prefer to do my own work and let others do theirs.	○	○	○
5. I get more satisfaction from a group victory than an individual victory.	○	○	○
6. Teamwork is not worthwhile when people do not do their share.	○	○	○
7. I feel good when I work with others, even when we disagree.	○	○	○
8. I prefer to rely on myself rather than others to do a job or assignment.	○	○	○
9. I find that working as a member of a team increases my ability to perform well.	○	○	○
10. It annoys me to do work as a member of a team.	○	○	○

Total Score ________. (Sum your answers to odd-numbered items, giving 3 points for each True, 2 points for each Somewhat, and 1 point for each False. Reverse the scoring for even-numbered items: 3 points for each False, 2 points for each Somewhat, and 1 point for each True, and add the two numbers for your total score.) Go to page 442 to interpret your score.

Questionnaire 2[2]

Instructions: Think back to a specific team you were part of that completed a major project or task. Respond to each statement below about how the team functioned, marking each as True, Somewhat, or False.

Part A

	True	Somewhat	False
1. We spent time defining the parameters of the task to be accomplished.	○	○	○

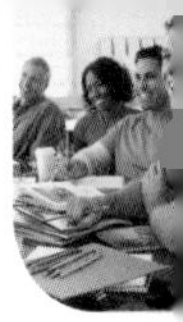

	True	Somewhat	False
2. We had abstract discussions of issues, concepts, and organizing.	○	○	○
3. I felt some excitement to be on the team.	○	○	○

Total Score Part A ________. (Sum questions 1 through 3, giving 3 points for each True, 2 points for each Somewhat, and 1 point for each False.)

Part B

4. There was disorder and friction about how to proceed.	○	○	○
5. We generated lots of ideas without much agreement.	○	○	○
6. Team members were pushing their own ideas about how the team should work.	○	○	○

Total Score Part B ________. (Sum questions 4 through 6, giving 3 points for each True, 2 points for each Somewhat, and 1 point for each False.)

Part C

7. We became a functioning unit.	○	○	○
8. Members accepted team goals and plans.	○	○	○
9. We experienced mostly harmony and little conflict.	○	○	○

Total Score Part C ________. (Sum questions 7 through 9, giving 3 points for each True, 2 points for each Somewhat, and 1 point for each False.)

Part D

10. Team members felt shared responsibility for achieving success.	○	○	○
11. We enjoyed working together and were highly productive.	○	○	○
12. We understood and took advantage of each other's strengths and weaknesses.	○	○	○

Total Score Part D ________. (Sum questions 10 through 12, giving 3 points for each True, 2 points for each Somewhat, and 1 point for each False.) Go to page 447 to interpret your scores.

Questionnaire 3[3]

Instructions: Think about your behavior as a member of various student or work teams and indicate whether each statement below is True, Somewhat, or False for you.

Part A

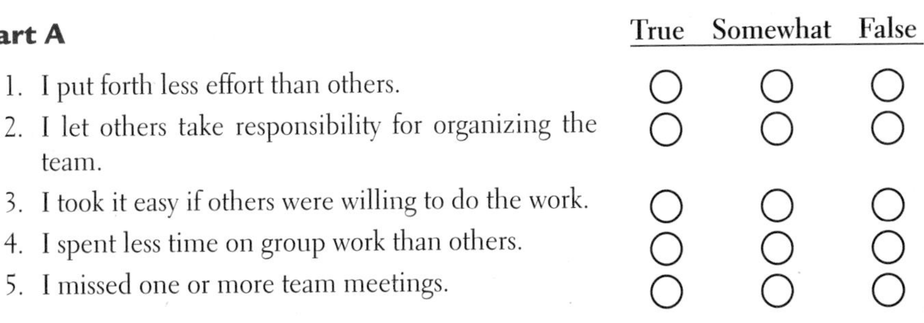

	True	Somewhat	False
1. I put forth less effort than others.	○	○	○
2. I let others take responsibility for organizing the team.	○	○	○
3. I took it easy if others were willing to do the work.	○	○	○
4. I spent less time on group work than others.	○	○	○
5. I missed one or more team meetings.	○	○	○

Total Score Part A ________. (Sum questions 1 through 5, giving 3 points for each True, 2 points for each Somewhat, and 1 point for each False.)

Part B

	True	Somewhat	False
6. I kept silent about my misgivings on a topic.	○	○	○
7. I was mentally critical of someone who challenged the majority opinion.	○	○	○
8. I, along with other members, strongly believed our solution was right.	○	○	○
9. I felt that there was no time or interest in hearing every possible idea or opinion.	○	○	○
10. I did not want to spend time seeking outside information or opinions about our team's solution.	○	○	○

Total Score Part B ________. (Sum questions 6 through 10, giving 3 points for each True, 2 points for each Somewhat, and 1 point for each False.) Go to page 449 to interpret your scores.

Questionnaire 4

Instructions: Think about how you have typically behaved as a member of student or work teams. Respond to the statements below based on that behavior.

Part A

	Usually	Sometimes	Rarely
1. I proposed a clear vision of team purpose.	○	○	○
2. I initiated up-front discussions of team goals and objectives.	○	○	○
3. I suggested a clear statement of where the team should be going.	○	○	○

Total Score Part A ________. (Sum answers 1 through 3, giving 3 points for each Usually, 2 points for each Sometimes, and 1 point for each Rarely.)

Part B

4. I engaged the team in clarifying plans and deadlines.	○	○	○
5. I suggested corrective actions to improve performance.	○	○	○
6. I kept the discussion focused on relevant items.	○	○	○
7. I suggested roles for team members.	○	○	○
8. I helped coordinate team members.	○	○	○

Total Score Part B ________. (Sum questions 4 through 8, giving 3 points for each Usually, 2 points for each Sometimes, and 1 point for each Rarely.)

Part C

9. I came to meetings well prepared.	○	○	○
10. I knew other members would complete their work on time.	○	○	○

	Usually	Sometimes	Rarely
11. I followed through on promises and commitments.	○	○	○
12. Team objectives were more important than my personal objectives.	○	○	○
13. I shared all relevant information and resources.	○	○	○

Total Score Part C ________. (Sum questions 9 through 13, giving 3 points for each Usually, 2 points for each Sometimes, and 1 point for each Rarely.)

Part D

14. I was a focused, active listener.	○	○	○
15. I verbalized insights and recommendations.	○	○	○
16. I provided constructive feedback to others.	○	○	○
17. I handled feedback and disagreements non-defensively.	○	○	○
18. I actively engaged others in problem solving.	○	○	○

Total Score Part D ________. (Sum questions 14 through 18, giving 3 points for each Usually, 2 points for each Sometimes, and 1 point for each Rarely.)

Part E

19. I did not shy away from disputes.	○	○	○
20. I knew when to stop pushing for my own position.	○	○	○
21. I promoted constructive intervention or mediation when conflicts arose.	○	○	○

Total Score Part E ________. (Sum questions 19 through 21, giving 3 points for each Usually, 2 points for each Sometimes, and 1 point for each Rarely.)

Part F

22. I gave team members appreciation and support.	○	○	○
23. I celebrated the accomplishments of others.	○	○	○
24. I praised people for a job well done.	○	○	○

Total Score Part F ________. (Sum questions 22 through 24, giving 3 points for each Usually, 2 points for each Sometimes, and 1 point for each Rarely.) Go to page 451 to interpret your scores.

GO ONLINE to find additional questionnaires at www.cengagebrain.com, search for Daft/Marcic Building Management Skills 1e, click on Free Online Resources, click on Additional Self-Assessments.

- Team Cohesion
- Leading Team Meetings

DISCOVER YOURSELF

SHUTTERSTOCK #53973379

Chapter 12: Managing Teams

DISCOVER KNOWLEDGE

In the spring of 2010, LeBron James, Dwyane Wade, and Chris Bosh were the top scorers on their respective basketball teams. The next year, they were all playing for the Miami Heat. With that kind of talent, the team should have been tough for anyone to beat, right? Well, not really. The Heat's dream team opened with a humiliating loss and stumbled through the early weeks of the season. Then they hit a three-month winning streak, but faltered again, losing six out of the next seven games. Star players who were used to being in charge at crunch time found themselves working at cross-purposes. Discussing the Heat's loss to the New York Knicks, former Chicago Bulls player Steve Kerr said, "It was a total meltdown. It was 'I'm so talented, I'll take over.' They looked awful." It just goes to show that individual stars don't necessarily make a great team. The Miami Heat is struggling with issues that all teams face: how to get star performers to sublimate their egos and sacrifice their individual goals, how to bring together the right set of specialties and skills, how to define roles, how to promote collaboration and cohesiveness, and how to create a team that is united in a common mission and willing to fight hard to cover one another's backs.[4]

The sports world provides numerous examples of teams with superstar players who flounder or put in only average performances, whereas other teams that have only average players perform like superstars. The Miami Heat has excellent players, but they are still learning to work together as a team. The same phenomenon can be seen in business and other types of organizations. Good teams can be highly productive, but teams aren't always successful. In a survey of manufacturing organizations, about 80 percent of respondents said they used teams of some type, but only 14 percent of those companies rated their teaming efforts as highly effective. Just over half of the respondents said their efforts were only "somewhat effective," and 15 percent considered their efforts not effective at all.[5] Teams are a central aspect of organizational life, and your ability to manage them so that they are productive will be a vital component of your success.

DISCOVER YOURSELF

Interpret Your Score: Individual versus Team Preference (Questionnaire 1)

Your score indicates your preference for working as part of a team versus working as an individual. A high score suggests a clear preference for working with others on a team. Comparative data for **Individual versus Team Preference:** Thirty-person Mean score = 20.0; Top Quartile = 22–28; Bottom Quartile = 12–16. Teamwork can be both frustrating and motivating depending on your preference. On a team you will lose some autonomy and have to rely on others who may be less committed than you. On a team you have to work through other people and you lose some control over work procedures and outcomes. On the other hand, teams can accomplish tasks far beyond what an individual can do, and working with others can be a major source of satisfaction. How do you think your preference will affect your career choices and your potential role as a manager? CNOW and CourseMate users can access dynamically updated comparative data through www.cengagebrain.com.

© CENGAGE LEARNING 2014

THE VALUE OF TEAMS

Many people get their first experience managing other people in a team setting. But what's the purpose of using teams? You might think of an organization as just a collection of individuals doing their own jobs. But no, organizations are made up of various individuals and groups that have to work together and coordinate their activities to accomplish objectives. There are challenges as well as benefits related to teamwork.

A **team** is a unit of two or more people who interact and coordinate their work to accomplish a common goal for which they are committed and hold themselves mutually accountable. Several key features distinguish a team.[6] For example, a team of engineers at

Cisco Systems had a clear purpose (*common goal*) of creating a multimedia device to compete with Apple's iPad. Team members in North Carolina, Texas, and California had to coordinate their efforts and *work interdependently* to design, test, and develop the Cius business tablet.[7] The Cius development team was a *distinct unit* with membership distinct from other teams. Members of the Cius development team worked together for a period of 18 months to complete the early design, concept development, and testing of the Cius. The team disbanded after completing its work.

A team is a group of people, but not all groups are teams. For example, a group of students attending a campus lecture would not be considered a team, nor would a group of people waiting in line at a local fast-food restaurant. Even a group of employees whose work is related is not a team unless the members share a common purpose that requires them to work interdependently. In addition, the concept of teamwork implies that people sublimate their individual needs, desires, and egos and synthesize their knowledge, skills, and efforts toward accomplishing a common goal. Recall the opening example of the Miami Heat, in which individual star players are still learning how to work together as a real team. The sports world is full of stories of underdog teams that have won championships against a group of players who were better individually but did not make up a better team.[8]

Teams are found at every level of today's organizations. At Cirque du Soleil, the CEO, chief operating officer, chief financial officer, and vice president of creation function as a top management team to develop, coordinate, and oversee acrobatic troupes that travel to approximately 100 cities on four continents a year. Google assembles teams of three or four employees to assess new ideas and recommend whether they should be implemented. IBM uses teams of people specializing in hardware, software, research, and sales to solve specific problems for clients such as Walmart, Charles Schwab, and the Mayo Clinic. And at the Ralston Foods plant in Sparks, Nevada, teams of production workers handle all team hiring, scheduling, quality, budgeting, and disciplinary issues.[9]

Organizations use teams to meet certain internal needs or external challenges. Exhibit 12.1 lists some functions of teams in which you might participate rather than doing work as an individual employee.

Special purpose teams, sometimes called *project teams*, focus on a specific purpose and disband once the project is completed. They are created outside the formal organization structure to undertake a project of special importance or complexity. An example is the team at Georgetown Preparatory School that developed a preparedness plan to address the threat of potentially devastating influenza epidemics such as the avian flu and swine flu.[10] The school needed to include the viewpoints and ideas of teachers, coaches, administrators, support staff, parents, and outside consultants to come up with an effective plan for prevention, communication, and quick response.

Exhibit 12.1 Three Functions of Teams

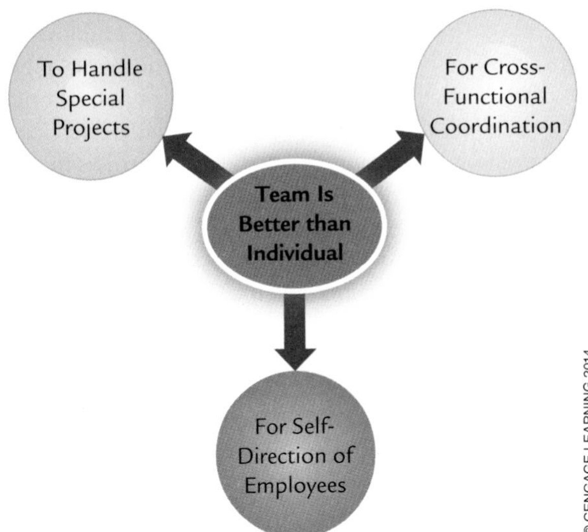

© CENGAGE LEARNING 2014

Cross-functional teams are made up of members from different functional departments within the organization. They facilitate information sharing across organizational boundaries and generate ideas for coordinating the departments represented. Jet Blue put together a cross-functional team made up of crew schedulers, systems operators, dispatchers, reservations agents, and other employees to revise how the airline handles and recovers from "irregular operations," such as severe weather. How effectively airlines manage and recover from these events dramatically affects performance and customer satisfaction, but effectiveness requires close coordination. At the first team meeting, leaders presented a simulated emergency and asked the team to map out how it would respond. As team members went through the process, they began to spot problems. The team spent months in intense meetings working out solutions that helped

JetBlue improve its regular on-time performance and its recovery time from major events.[11]

Self-directed teams are made up of employees who work with minimum supervision and rotate jobs to produce an entire product or service, or at least one complete aspect or portion of a product or service. Imagination Ltd., Britain's largest design firm, is made up entirely of self-directed teams. Teams composed of creative, information technology (IT), and marketing experts complete projects such as staging a launch event for the *Harry Potter and the Prisoner of Azkaban* DVD release. Eight hundred guests toured an historic London building housing re-creations of four movie sets, including the Great Hall at the Hogwarts School of Witchcraft and Wizardry.[12]

WHAT DOES A HIGH-PERFORMING TEAM LOOK LIKE?

Mark Gray knew he was facing an uphill battle when he was put in charge of leading a failing development project. He had no credibility with the development team, and team members fully expected the project to fail no matter what. Gray began by bringing the team together to clarify objectives and develop more effective communications. It quickly became clear that a couple of members with "alpha male" personalities were creating a lot of conflict and tension. At an off-site meeting Gray had scheduled in hopes of building some trust, these two members were arguing heatedly by the pool. Looking for a way to defuse the situation, Gray pushed them both into the pool. When they recovered from the shock, the two pulled Gray in as well. Soon, all the other team members were jumping in, laughing and jostling one another. Later, Gray ordered food and beer, and the soggy team sat around talking about the project. Pushing the fighting team members into the pool was a spur-of-the-moment, almost desperate reaction, but it worked. It turned out to be the move that helped people get beyond their conflicts and start creating bonds of trust and commitment to the project.[13]

Pushing your team members into a swimming pool might not always be a great idea, but one important job of a team leader is to get people to trust one another and communicate effectively. A great deal of research and team experience over the past few decades has produced significant insights into what causes teams to succeed or fail. The evidence shows that how teams are managed plays the most critical role in determining how well they function.[14] Exhibit 12.2 lists five dysfunctions that are common in teams and describes the contrasting desirable characteristics that effective team leaders develop.

Exhibit 12.2 Five Common Dysfunctions of Teams

Dysfunction	Effective Team Characteristics
Lack of Trust—People don't feel safe to reveal mistakes, share concerns, or express ideas.	**Trust**—Members trust one another on a deep emotional level; feel comfortable being vulnerable with one another.
Fear of Conflict—People go along with others for the sake of harmony; don't express conflicting opinions.	**Healthy Conflict**—Members feel comfortable disagreeing and challenging one another in the interest of finding the best solution.
Lack of Commitment—If people are afraid to express their true opinions, it's difficult to gain clarity and true commitment to decisions.	**Commitment**—Because all ideas are put on the table, people can eventually achieve genuine buy-in around important goals and decisions.
Avoidance of Accountability—People don't accept responsibility for outcomes; engage in finger-pointing when things go wrong.	**Accountability**—Members hold one another accountable rather than relying on managers as the source of accountability.
Inattention to Results—Members put personal ambition or the needs of their individual departments ahead of collective results.	**Results Orientation**—Individual members set aside personal agendas and focus on what's best for the team. Collective results define success.

Source: Based on Patrick Lencioni, *The Five Dysfunctions of a Team* (New York: John Wiley & Sons, 2002); and Patrick Lencioni, "Dissolve Dysfunctions: Begin Building Your Dream Team," *Leadership Excellence* (October 2009): 20.

As a manager or a team leader, you can focus on six elements that contribute to effective and successful teamwork.[15]

1. *A compelling purpose and clear objectives*. To succeed, team members have to know what is expected of them and commit to accomplishing it. High-performing teams have a specific, clearly defined purpose and a well-defined set of goals, enabling people to come together in a shared undertaking.

2. *Metrics that enable the team to assess progress*. Team members need to know how well they are progressing toward meeting goals. At Xerox, a customer service team devised metrics that enabled people to assess their work on a day-to-day basis. "Instead of waiting for [top managers] to send us information on how we'd done, we could check any time . . . and see where we were," said one member.[16]

3. *Clear roles and diversity of skills*. Effective teams contain the diverse mix of skills, knowledge, and experience needed to perform all the components of the team's project.[17] In addition, diversity in terms of race, gender, ethnic or cultural background, and other dimensions can contribute to greater innovation and better decision making because the team can draw from wider perspectives.[18] Within this diverse mix, however, individual roles and responsibilities are clearly defined. Clarity of roles leads to enhanced cooperation because people aren't butting up against one another in confusion over their duties and responsibilities.[19]

4. *Streamlined team size*. Although most researchers agree there is no optimal team size, teams function best when they contain just enough members to perform the job, and most experts recommend that teams should err on the side of having too few members rather than too many.[20] Much research has shown that small teams (six or fewer members) perform better than large ones.[21] Small teams typically ask more questions, exchange more opinions, and exhibit more cooperative behavior. In addition, people in small teams report higher motivation, more job satisfaction, and a greater sense of belonging and cohesiveness. A Gallup poll in the United States found that 82 percent of employees agree that small teams are more productive.[22]

5. *Decision authority over how to achieve goals*. Although teams need clearly defined goals that are spelled out unambiguously by leaders, the team itself should have the authority to decide how it will reach those goals. People can act as a team only if they have genuine responsibility, which includes the power to determine how they will work cooperatively to accomplish objectives and achieve the team's purpose.

6. *Open culture and ongoing training*. An open, trust-based culture is essential for the cooperative behavior of effective teamwork. When people trust one another, they want the team to succeed, even if individual members have to make sacrifices. Team members are willing to hamper their own individual progress to help out a teammate if it's in the best interest of the team. They don't feel a need to jockey with one another for attention, resources, or credit.[23] Everyone is focused on doing what needs to be done for the team to accomplish its task. To keep these open relationships, people need ongoing training in how to work togerther as a team. Periodic training that teaches skills such as communication, building relationships, team leadership, developing productive team norms, and resolving conflicts can have a significant impact on team collaboration and performance.[24]

IT TAKES TIME TO DEVELOP A HIGH-PERFORMING TEAM

Many construction projects are characterized by conflicts, frantic scheduling, and poor communications. Not at McDevitt Street Bovis, though, where the company's contractors, designers, suppliers, and other partners function as a true team—putting the success of the project ahead of their own individual interests. Managers bring all the players together for a couple of days of team building at the beginning of any new project. The process gives everyone an opportunity to get to know one another; explore the ground rules; and clarify roles, responsibilities, and expectations. The team is first divided into separate groups that may have competing objectives—such as the clients in one group, suppliers in another, engineers and architects in a third, and so forth—and asked to come up with a list of their goals for the project. By talking about conflicting goals and interests, as well as what all the groups share, facilitators help the team gradually come together around a common purpose and begin to develop shared values that will guide the project. After jointly writing a mission statement for the team, each party says what it expects from the others, so that roles and responsibilities can be clarified.[25]

Why do managers at McDevitt Street Bovis put so much emphasis on team building? They realize that teams go through stages of development, and by helping people move more quickly to the "performing" stage, they get better results. "We prevent conflicts from happening," says team facilitator Monica Bennett. If you have participated in teams to do class assignments, you probably noticed that the team changed over time. All teams follow a predictable life cycle, with distinct stages of development. By recognizing these stages, you can help teams move through them successfully.[26]

A model of the stages of team development is shown in Exhibit 12.3.[27] These five stages typically occur in sequence, although there can be overlap. Each stage presents team members and leaders with unique problems and challenges.

Forming

The **forming** stage of development is a period of orientation and getting acquainted. Team members find out what behavior is acceptable to others, explore friendship possibilities, and determine task orientation. Uncertainty is high because no one knows what the ground rules are or what is expected of them. Members will usually accept whatever power or authority is offered by either formal or informal leaders. As a team leader, your challenge at this stage of development would be to facilitate communication and interaction to help people get acquainted and establish guidelines for how the team will work together. It is important at this stage that you try to make everyone feel comfortable and like a part of the team. Leaders can draw out shy or quiet team members to help them establish relationships with others.

Storming

During the **storming** stage, individual personalities emerge more clearly. People become more assertive in clarifying their roles. This stage is marked by conflict and disagreement. Team members may differ in their perceptions of the team's mission or goals. They may jockey for position or form subgroups based on common interests. The team is characterized by a general lack of unity and cohesiveness. If teams can't successfully move beyond this stage, they will never achieve high performance. As team leader, your role would be to encourage participation by each team member and help members find their common vision and values. People need to debate ideas, bring conflicts to the surface, disagree with one another, and work through the uncertainties and conflicting perceptions about team tasks and goals.

Exhibit 12.3 The Life Cycle of a Team

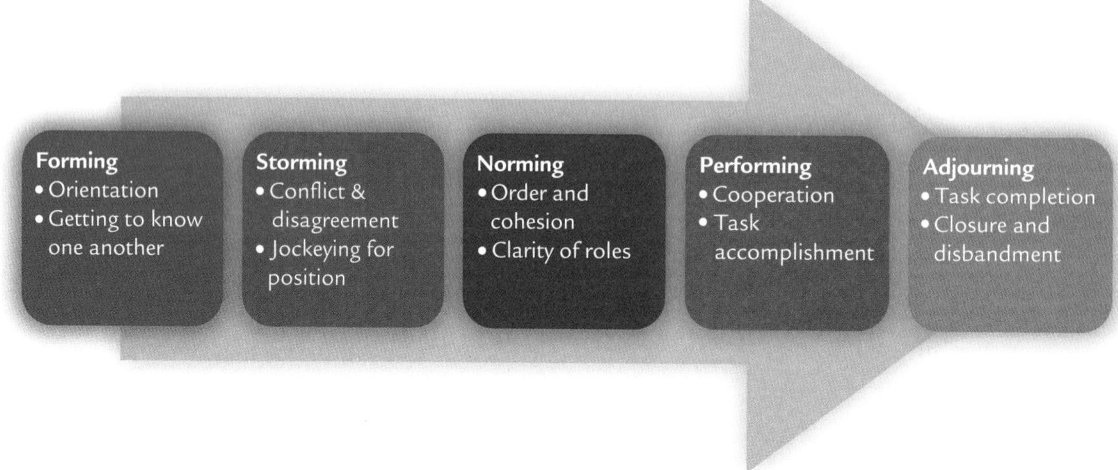

Sources: Based on the stages of small-group development in Bruce W. Tuckman, "Developmental Sequence in Small Groups," *Psychological Bulletin* 63 (1965): 384–399; and B. W. Tuckman and M. A. Jensen, "Stages of Small-Group Development Revisited," *Group and Organizational Studies* 2 (1977): 419–427.

Norming

At the **norming** stage, conflict has been resolved and team unity and harmony emerge. Consensus develops as to who the natural leaders are, and members' roles are clear. Team members come to understand and accept one another. Differences are settled and members develop a sense of cohesiveness. This stage typically is of short duration and moves quickly into the next stage. As team leader, you should emphasize openness within the team and continue to facilitate communication and clarify team roles, values, and expectations.

DISCOVER YOURSELF

Interpret Your Score: Stages of Team Development (Questionnaire 2)

Your scores on this questionnaire help you assess the stage of development in which your team functioned, as described in the chapter. Comparative data for **Forming** (Part A): Thirty-person Mean score = 8.2; Top Quartile = 9–9; Bottom Quartile = 5–8. **Storming** (Part B): Thirty-person Mean score = 4.7; Top Quartile = 6–9; Bottom Quartile = 3–3. **Norming** (Part C): Thirty-person Mean score = 8.3; Top Quartile = 9–9; Bottom Quartile = 3–8. **Performing** (Part D): Thirty-person Mean score = 8.2; Top Quartile = 9–9; Bottom Quartile = 4–8. If your four scores are about equal, then your team probably passed through each stage of development. If one score is higher, it indicates the stage your team normally operated in. If one score is lower than others, it may indicate a stage your team skipped over. How well do the four stages describe what happened in your team? Can you think of any team experiences that represent each of the four stages? CNOW and CourseMate users can access dynamically updated comparative data through www.cengagebrain.com.

© CENGAGE LEARNING 2014

Performing

During the **performing** stage, the major emphasis is on accomplishing goals. Members are committed to the team's mission. They interact frequently, coordinate their actions, and handle disagreements in a mature, productive manner. Team members confront and resolve problems in the interest of task accomplishment. At this stage, the team leader should concentrate on facilitating high task performance and helping the team self-manage to reach its goals.

Adjourning

The **adjourning** stage occurs in teams that have a limited task or project and disband after it is completed. During this stage, the emphasis is on wrapping things up and gearing down. Task performance is no longer a top priority. Members may feel heightened emotionality, strong cohesiveness, and regret or sadness over the team's disbandment. At this point, as a team leader you should help members reflect on what they've learned and how to apply it in the future. You might also identify and honor the team's accomplishment, perhaps holding a celebration or giving out awards to signify closure and completeness.

Not all teams pass through the stages of develoment in the same way. Yet understanding the team life cycle is important because it helps us look at teamwork as a process that changes over time, thus enabling leaders to anticipate possible problems that could interfere with effective performance. Navigating the team's development is a clear responsibility of team leaders.

THE PERSONAL DILEMMA OF TEAMWORK

If you've been in a class where the teacher announced that part of your grade would be based on a team project, you probably heard a few groans—maybe even emitted one yourself. The same thing happens in organizations. At one medical products company, the CFO was so chagrined when the company implemented teams that he quit.[28] Some people love the idea of teamwork, others hate it, and most have both positive and negative emotions about it.

Many of us have had negative experiences with teams. An anthropologist studying people's feelings about teamwork found that some individuals have deep-seated fears or apprehensions about teamwork related to childhood experiences, such as always being picked last for the softball team at recess or being hurt, teased, or rejected by teammates in a gym class.[29] Other people have had negative experiences with teams in a high school or college class. They may have felt that they could have done a better job and received a higher grade working on their own, or they may have believed they did most of the work while other team members got equal credit for the results. Negative experiences with work teams can also color a person's attitudes toward teamwork. Work teams don't always function well. A civilian worker at a large U.S. Air Force base tells of an experience in which a team "streamlined" the process of handling mail by changing it from 8 steps to a ridiculous 19, meaning official mail was handled by more people and getting to its intended recipient even later than before.[30]

The idea of teamwork may conflict with our values. Another reason teams present a dilemma is that the idea of teamwork conflicts with the dominant values of some cultures. Managers have had trouble implementing empowered, self-directed teams in Mexico, for example, because traditional values in that country support the idea that there should be status and power differences in organizations.[31] Cultural values in the United States highly prize individualism, and many of the cultural heroes are strong individuals who succeed by their own wits and hard work. Yet, when people are part of a team, their success depends on the team's success; therefore, they are dependent on how well other people perform, and not just on their own individual initiative and actions. People often have a hard time giving up their individual freedom and choice to truly function as part of a team. In contrast, Japanese companies have had tremendous success with teams because traditional Japanese culture highly values the group over the individual.

There may be a conflict between what employees want and what managers want. Particularly in countries that value individualism, a related problem is a conflict between what the individual wants and expects from participating on a team and what managers want and expect.[32] Most people are comfortable with the idea of making sacrifices in order to achieve their own individual success, yet teamwork demands that they make sacrifices for *group* success. When people are assigned to work on a team, they typically want to see benefits for themselves. That is, they want a personal reward for their efforts and often want the team to be a mechanism for increasing their own status, success, or reputation in the organization. Managers, on the other hand, want people to sublimate their individual desires for the good of the team. The idea is that each person should put the team first, even if at times it hurts the individual. Many employees in the United States have a hard time appreciating and accepting that concept.

As a manager, it is essential that you understand the dilemma teamwork creates. As with other aspects of management, you should remember that people's

DISCOVER KNOWLEDGE

What's Your Problem?

Q: I'm part of a team at work and one of the members is driving me crazy. We are supposedly a "self-directed team" so we have no formal leader. But Renaldo acts like he's in charge. He talks the most, sits at the head of the table during meetings, always asks our opinions (as we were taught to do in training), but then he "decides" what the solution is. He says he is just summarizing, but why is he always the one with the last word? A couple of people, including me, have joked with him about being the CEO of our group, but he just sloughs it off and says someone had to take initiative. What can I do?

A: You should first look at yourself to see if the problem is that you wish you were more of the leader and maybe have a power struggle going on with Renaldo. If others, though, are also bothered by his behaviors, you need to call a meeting to talk about your group's dynamics. Make clear to everyone the meeting's focus and that you will be in charge of this session. Ask every team member to describe what is working for them (first round of sharing) and what is not working for them (second round). When it is your turn, make sure you bring up—in a very calm and reasonable tone—that you think there is an imbalance of leadership in the group. See what other people say. Expect Renaldo to get defensive, but don't let that rile you. If no one else brings up the problem of unbalanced leadership, then either it is your issue with Renaldo, or they like having someone in charge. The worst that can happen is that you know where you stand. Good luck!

© CENGAGE LEARNING 2014

emotions are involved and will influence how they behave. Some people will be energized and excited by the idea of working as part of a team, while others will be apprehensive, cynical, or annoyed. How you deal with these emotions will play a role in how effective a team will be. Smoothly functioning teams don't just happen. They are built by managers who take specific actions to help people come together and perform well as a team.

FRUSTRATIONS WITHIN TEAMS

Now let's explore some of the potential threats to effective teamwork. Two of the primary frustrations within teams relate to the equity of members' contributions and social pressures that sometimes prevent good decision making.

Reduced Effort

Teams are usually made up of people who have different work ethics and styles, which can sometimes lead to conflict if some members do more work than others. The term *free rider* refers to a team member who attains benefits from team membership but does not actively participate in and contribute to the team's work. You might have experienced this frustration in a student project team, where one member put little effort into the group project but benefited from the hard work of others when grades were handed out.

Free riding is also called **social loafing** because members do not exert equal effort.[33] A classic experiment by German psychologist Max Ringelmann first identified the free rider tendency. Ringelmann asked people to pull on a rope as hard as they could, first individually and then as a group. Ringelmann found that, on average, individuals exerted less effort when they were members of a group than they did individually, and effort continued to decrease as more people joined the group.[34] Similarly, experiments have found that when people are asked to clap and make noise, they make more noise on a per person basis when working alone or in small groups than they do in a large group.[35]

Most people want to feel that work is shared equitably, so social loafing is a real threat to team harmony and effectiveness. It is important that leaders shape norms that discourage social loafing, as well as make sure work activities are distributed equitably. The team might also establish guidelines for peer evaluations and agreed-upon ways to deal with free riders.

Loss of Diverse Thinking

Team harmony is good, but sometimes teams go too far in their efforts to maintain harmony. **Groupthink** refers to the tendency of members in highly cohesive teams to suppress contrary opinions.[36] When a team slips into groupthink, the desire for harmony outweighs concerns over decision quality. Team members emphasize maintaining unity rather than realistically evaluating problems and alternatives. People censor their personal opinions and are reluctant to criticize or challenge the opinions of others. Recall our discussions of the Abilene Paradox in Chapters 6 and 10. Pressures for conformity exist in almost any group. It is important for team leaders and members to keep in mind that some disagreement and conflict is much healthier than blind agreement.

DISCOVER YOURSELF

Interpret Your Score: Social Loafing, Groupthink (Questionnaire 3)

These questions assess whether you may have contributed to group frustrations via social loafing (free riding) and groupthink as described in the chapter. Your Part A score pertains to social loafing, which means you may have carried less than a full share of the group's workload and responsibilities. Comparative data for **Social Loafing** (Part A): Thirty-person Mean score = 5.9; Top Quartile = 6–10; Bottom Quartile = 3–5. Your Part B score pertains to groupthink, which welcomes conformity, efficiency, and apparent cohesion over lengthy and open discussions of issues. Comparative data for **Groupthink** (Part B): Thirty-person Mean score = 8.3; Top Quartile = 9–10; Bottom Quartile = 6–7. How do you feel about your scores? Were you aware that your behavior may have been considered free riding or may have contributed to groupthink? What changes would you like to make for your participation in future groups? CNOW and CourseMate users can access dynamically updated comparative data through www.cengagebrain.com.

DISCOVER KNOWLEDGE

© CENGAGE LEARNING 2014

Wrong Rewards

Individual versus group rewards can have different effects on the level of motivation and cooperation among team members. *Individual-based rewards*, in which people are paid based on individual performance, tend to encourage competition among members. For example, salespeople at Ann Taylor Stores earn individual commissions, which encourages people to work hard for themselves but not to spend time cooperating with fellow employees. In contrast, software development team members at Great Plains Software and production workers on the waste-reduction teams at RR Donnelley & Sons all share equally in any rewards the group earns, which encourages people to cooperate with one another. This *group-based reward* means that people are paid based on the team's performance. Although this encourages cooperation, a group reward can also encourage free riding because it does not provide a clear link between individual effort and individual outcome. With a group reward, individuals are rewarded whether or not they work hard.[37]

DISCOVER KNOWLEDGE

Thus, individual rewards discourage cooperation, and group rewards may lead to social loafing. When should a team leader use each type of reward? The general rule is that when people are required to work independently to complete the team's task, individual-based rewards are more effective. Each member is rewarded based on his or her own work contribution so there is little social loafing. However, when team members depend heavily upon one another to complete the team's task, then group-based rewards tend to be appropriate because cooperation is important. A simple example is a group of waiters in a restaurant. If each waiter is independently responsible for all services provided to his or her own set of tables, then the waiter is motivated to serve customers well and the best reward is to keep all the tips from those tables. Sharing the tips with wait staff working on another set of tables, and who may not work as hard, is demotivating. However, in another more exclusive restaurant, a team of three or four people may together serve a set of tables, with each person depending on the others for certain tasks. Because interdependence among this group of waiters is high, group-based rewards—dividing the tips among the team members—will likely reward members more accurately for their contributions and encourage cooperation with other members who also serve the tables.

Interdependence refers to the extent to which team members depend on each other for information, resources, or ideas to accomplish their tasks. The responsibility of the manager in charge is to assess the level of work interdependence among team members and design rewards accordingly. In some cases, managers may use a mix of individual-based and group-based rewards to spur better performance, providing incentives for both cooperation and individual performance.

WHAT MAKES A VALUABLE TEAM MEMBER?

In early August of 2010, a copper mine in San José, Chile, collapsed, trapping 33 miners. The men endured 69 days of little food, scant water, dusty conditions, and frayed nerves. The situation could have led to chaos, but these men quickly perceived that teamwork offered them the best chance to survive. The miners organized into several teams in charge of critical activities such as communication with rescue workers, the transport of supplies from above ground, rationing and distribution of food, managing health concerns, and securing the mine to prevent further rockfalls. Some people were good at coordinating activities, others focused on solving problems, and still others made their best contribution by helping the group maintain a sense of solidarity and hope as days stretched into weeks and weeks into months. Experts agree that good teamwork was a key to the miners' survival.[38]

Most of us will never face the kind of crisis situation these 33 miners endured and the urgent need to work together for our very survival. However, the Chilean miners illustrate how important it is for members of a team to possess a variety of capabilities and meet a variety of needs. It is rare to find a single individual who naturally possesses all the technical and interpersonal skills a team needs for high performance and long-term success. Yet almost everyone has the potential to develop effective teamwork skills, and teams can be structured so that all the necessary technical and interpersonal requirements are met by someone on the team.

What Team Members Must Contribute

Research has identified a number of key competencies needed to make up an effective team.[39] To function well as a team, members of the team should together display each of the following five competencies.

1. **Goal Setting and Performance Management.** First and foremost, team members must have the ability to establish and execute specific, challenging team objectives, as well as ways to monitor and evaluate performance toward meeting objectives.
2. **Planning and Coordination.** The ability to plan and coordinate is an important determinant of team effectiveness.[40] Members must tightly cooordinate and synchronize activities, information, and resources in order to accomplish goals.
3. **Collaborative Problem Solving.** Team members need to be able to recognize when a problem requires group participation and then appropriately involve team members in searching for alternatives and devising solutions.
4. **Communication.** Employees working on individual jobs can sometimes get by with poor communication skills, but the wheels of teamwork keep rolling only with good communication. Members speak their minds, ask questions, seek and provide feedback, and make skillful presentations.
5. **Conflict Resolution.** Last, but by no means least, teams need to know how to effectively manage and resolve disagreements. Even in the most cohesive of teams, conflicts will inevitably arise.

DISCOVER YOURSELF

Interpret Your Score: Contributing Team Member (Questionnaire 4)

An effective team must have contributing members. A team must have someone performing each part, but no member is expected to perform all parts. Indeed, if you scored well on most questions you would be playing a leader role on the team. Comparative data for team membership ability: **Goal and Direction Setting** (Part A): Thirty-person Mean score = 8.2; Top Quartile = 9–9; Bottom Quartile = 5–8. **Performance Management** (Part B): Thirty-person Mean score = 12.5; Top Quartile = 15–15; Bottom Quartile = 5–11. **Interdependence with Other Members** (Part C): Thirty-person Mean score = 13.5; Top Quartile = 14–15; Bottom Quartile = 10–13. **Communication and Problem Solving-Skills** (Part D): Thirty-person Mean score = 13.8; Top Quartile = 15–15; Bottom Quartile = 9–13. **Approach to Task Conflict** (Part E): Thirty-person Mean score = 7.4; Top Quartile = 9–9; Bottom Quartile = 4–6. **Meeting Others' Relationship Needs** (Part F): Thirty-person Mean score = 8.8; Top Quartile = 9–9; Bottom Quartile = 6–9. Parts A, B, and F are skills often associated with a team leader role. How do you feel about your contribution to teams? In what ways do you take the initiative to be an effective member? What might you do to be more effective? How would you describe your approach to team membership? CNOW and CourseMate users can access dynamically updated comparative data through www.cengagebrain.com.

DISCOVER KNOWLEDGE

© CENGAGE LEARNING 2014

Team Member Roles

Another aspect of effective teams is that they have members who meet the important needs of the team for both accomplishing its tasks and fostering member unity, satisfaction, and well-being. People tend to take on different roles in teams based on their personalities and interests, but every team needs members who fill both social and task roles. A **role** can be thought of as shared expectations of how an individual behaves in fulfilling the requirements of his or her job. Some people naturally lean more toward behaviors that aid in accomplishing tasks, whereas others tend toward behaviors that maintain group harmony and satisfaction.

Members often fill nine important types of roles that blend each member's natural strengths to accomplish the work of an effective team:[41]

- *Organizer* Clarifies tasks and objectives, identifies ways to proceed toward task accomplishment, and assigns necessary actions. Frequently initiates goals and ideas for solving problems.
- *Encourager* Encourages contributions from other team members, drawing out others' ideas by showing warmth and acceptance. Promotes compromise and cooperation, mediates differences among members, and strives to create harmonious relationships so that everyone participates.
- *Enforcer* Concerned with establishing and enforcing rules for member behavior and how things should be done. Helps reinforce the team's standards and maintains agreed-upon procedures for getting things done.

- *Resource Developer* Outgoing, enthusiastic, explores opportunities inside and outside the group, exudes enthusiasm, builds a network of resources, motivates others toward greater effort.
- *Creator* Imaginative, unorthodox, sees things from a different angle, suggests novel solutions to difficult problems.
- *Coordinator* A good chairperson, delegates well, coordinates people and tasks, confident, mature, guides team toward ultimate result. Helps team make decisions and achieve progress toward deadlines.
- *Implementer* Disciplined, conscientious, finds and corrects errors, translates ideas into practical actions. Concerned with progress, corrective actions, details, accountability. Reliable, on time, can be counted on.
- *Teamworker* Cooperative, helpful, completes assigned tasks, avoids friction, listens, does own part, seldom asserts leadership, dislikes extreme positions and conflict. Mild-mannered and focused on completing own task despite differences that might exist.
- *Specialist* Prefers to work apart from group. Self-starting, does own thing well, dislikes coordination and compromise, contributes from independent skill set, often introverted, has particular skills, likes to do things own way.

Reflect on these roles and think about the ones you are most likely to play when working as part of a group. Which roles do you feel least qualified to play?

WHAT MAKES A GOOD TEAM LEADER?

Whitworth Manufacturing was facing a problem many companies have. The marketing and sales department was making promises to customers that the production and distribution departments couldn't meet. Adam Richards was energized and excited to be assigned to lead a cross-functional team that would better integrate the three departments so everyone was on the same page. At the first team meeting, he urged everyone to focus on the good of the company rather than their own departments. Representatives from all three departments expressed their support for the goal of identifing reasons for the lack of coordination and finding ways to solve the problem. The team met once a week and everyone seemed to be getting along fine. Richards didn't attend every meeting because he wanted the group to feel free to discuss and debate ideas. After three months, though, nothing had changed. Coordination was still woefully inadequate and the team hadn't come up with any concrete ideas for fixing it. Team members had agreed on some general targets but no one would commit to any specific actions or hold one another accountable. Members seemed more interested in protecting their own turf than increasing cross-functional coordination. Richards grew more and more frustrated, and the CEO eventually assigned a new team leader.[42]

A team member might fill any of the roles discussed in the previous section, and people typically fill more than one role. So what is the role of the team leader? Some managers make the mistake of acting like traditional bosses when they become team leaders. Others, like Adam Richards, err in the other direction, taking a hands-off approach. Harvard professor J. Richard Hackman, who has studied teams extensively, advises that effective team leaders "maintain an appropriate balance of authority" between themselves and their teams.[43] In the following sections, we discuss some specific areas in which leaders make a critical contribution to team success.

Recognize the Importance of a Compelling Purpose

As mentioned earlier, a clear, compelling purpose and direction is one of the key elements of effective teams. Who decides the purpose and direction varies depending on the situation—in some cases it is top management, in others it is the team leader, and in rare instances the direction might be decided within the team. However it's decided, it is the responsibility of the team leader to articulate a clear and compelling vision so that everyone is moving in the same direction rather than floundering around wondering why the team was created and where it's supposed to be going. Even in self-directed teams, effective self-management can't happen unless the leader marks out a clear direction for the team's work.[44]

Learn to Truly Share Power

Good team leaders embrace the concept of teamwork in deeds as well as words.[45] This means sharing power, information, and responsibility. It means letting team members who do the work have a say in how to do it. Sharing power requires the leader to have faith that team members will make good decisions, even if those decisions might not be the ones the leader would make. This isn't always easy for most managers. One leader of a sales team received a limited number of much-coveted tickets to a golf outing and turned them over to the team, suggesting that they give one of the tickets to a manager from another department. When the team instead gave all the tickets to exceptionally hard-working team members, the leader exploded. Only after he openly admitted that he was wrong was the team able to pull together again and effectively resume its work.[46] Effective team leaders know that it is *example*, not command and control, that holds a team together.[47]

The trend in effective teams, especially when tasks are complicated and interdependence is high, is toward decentralized communication, so that everyone is involved in important communications and decisions, as illustrated in Exhibit 12.4.[48] In a **centralized network,** team members communicate through one individual, such as a team leader, to solve a problem or make a decision. Centralized communication can be effective for large teams because it limits the number of people involved in decision making. The result is a faster decision that involves fewer people. In a **decentralized network,** however, individuals communicate directly with other team members and process information equally among themselves until a decision is reached.

In laboratory experiments, centralized communication networks achieved faster solutions to simple problems when people worked independently. A

LEADING WORDS

"Coming together is a beginning.
Keeping together is progress.
Working together is success."
—Henry Ford
American industrialist and founder of Ford Motor Company

"Most dysfunctional teams don't even realize they are dysfunctional. It's always the leader's responsibility to model the right behavior, or the team won't follow suit."
—Keith Carlson
former president and CEO of Innotas

"Individual commitment to a group effort—that is what makes a team work, a company work, a society work, a civilization work."
—Vince Lombardi
legendary NFL football coach

"The ratio of We's to I's is the best indicator of the development of a team."
—Lewis B. Ergen

Exhibit 12.4 Team Communication Networks

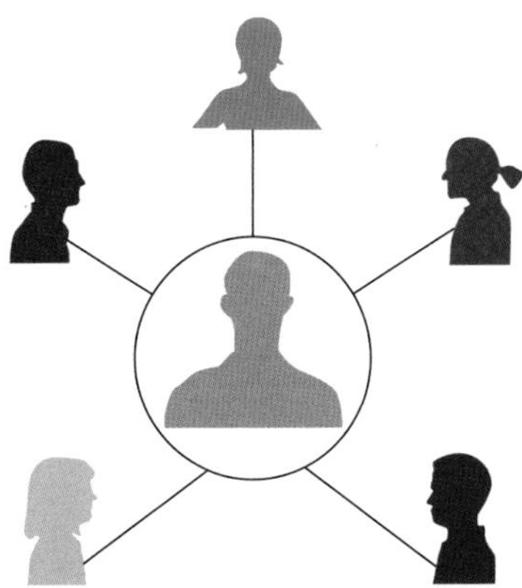
Centralized Network

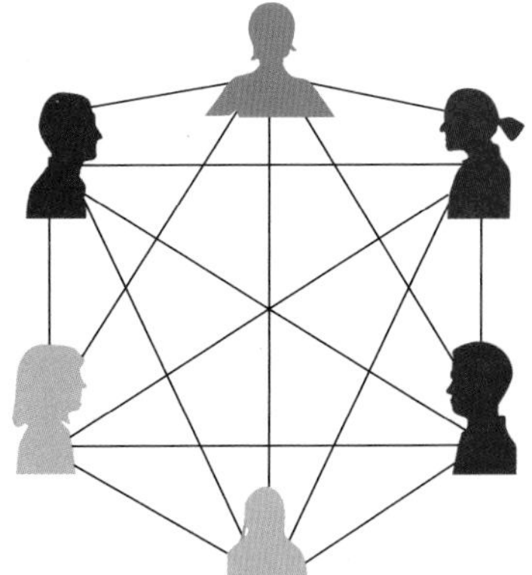
Decentralized Network

Source: Joel Spolsky, "A Little Less Conversation," *Inc.* (February 2010): 28–29. Used with permission of Inc. magazine. Copyright © 2012. All rights reserved.

DISCOVER KNOWLEDGE

decentralized communication structure took longer to include everyone and share everyone's perspective. The decentralized network provided greater input and brainpower for more complicated problems.[49] As a practical matter, most problems that organization teams deal with are complicated. That's why a team was created—so the decentalized sharing of information works better most of the time.[50] Decentralized communication also contributes to higher team satisfaction because people feel like an important part of the team and feel that their opinions count.

Shape Norms of Conduct and Performance

From a team's first days, the leader should begin building a healthy culture that clarifies expectations and establishes informal norms of collaboration and shared responsibility for collective outcomes.[51] A **team norm** is a standard of conduct that is shared by members and guides their behavior.[52] Norms are important because they define the boundaries of acceptable behavior and provide a frame of reference for team members.

For example, the team orientation of a commercial aircraft crew is brought to life by the actions of the captain. The captain's actions during the crucial first moments when the crew comes together carry forward throughout the life of the crew. Crews with captains who reviewed crew members' roles, emphasized safety and timeliness goals, and reviewed support systems available to the crew fared better than crews that received no briefing or crews for which the captain behaved in ways that undermined the team mindset. Best of all were those with captains who went beyond team affirmation to engage their crews in discussions of the unique circumstances of the trip that was about to begin. These captains used the first moments when members came together to establish norms that transformed individual pilots into an actual flying team.[53]

RUNNING A TEAM MEETING

Every morning at 9:30 sharp, the top management team at Bishop-Wisecarver Corporation, a manufacturer of machine components, gathers in the boardroom. As they stand around the table, each person fires off a brief review of the most critical items on his or her agenda. Ten minutes later, everyone is back in the office armed with the information needed to efficiently blast through the work day. President Pamela Kan credits the information sharing of the morning huddle for averting numerous snafus. For example, if the manufacturing director reports trouble with a machine, the sales director can adjust his delivery schedule. If the controller says there's a problem with a particular supplier, Kan can intercede before things reach a crisis. For Bishop-Wisecarver, a huddle a day helps keep chaos away.[54]

Bishop-Wisecarver managers start each day with a short, highly productive meeting. But when most of us think of meetings, that's not what comes to mind. A major source of frustration for teams relates to pointless, unorganized, or unproductive meetings. Some teams feel like they spend so much time in meetings that they never get any work done. One survey of 1,000 managers found that they spent an average of 17 hours a week in meetings and considered at least one third of that time wasted.[55] In another study, 70 percent of managers reported that many of the meetings they attend are a waste of time.[56] These results reflect the widespread exasperation we feel about this unavoidable aspect of organizational life.

Bad meetings are not inevitable. Meetings can be excellent avenues to solving problems, sharing information, and achieving shared goals. As a manager, you can learn to make meetings worthwhile and productive. Effective managers follow the five keys to effective meetings outlined in Exhibit 12.5.[57] As illustrated in the exhibit, much of what goes into a good meeting occurs before the event rather than during the meeting itself.

Have a Clear Purpose

The first key is to identify the reason for holding a meeting. *If a meeting isn't essential, don't have it.* Can the information or action needed be handled through means other than a meeting, such as an exchange of telephone calls and e-mail messages? If a meeting is essential, clearly define and communicate its purpose.

Invite the Right People

Meetings fail when too many, too few, or the wrong people are involved. If the meeting gets too big, it

Exhibit 12.5 Five Keys to Effective Meetings

Clear Purpose
- Operational review?
- Information sharing?
- Problem solving?
- Action?

Right People
- Who needs to be there?
- Who should *not* be there?
- Invite well ahead of time

Good Preparation
- Distribute agenda: state purpose, note begin and end times
- Distribute any materials needed
- Let people know what's expected of them at meeting
- Clarify expected outcome
- Pick the right time and place

Right Processes
- Start & end on time
- Set ground rules
- Create involvement
- Manage conflicts
- Keep it moving
- Summarize decisions and assignments

Follow-up
- Distribute simple minutes
- Describe decisions made
- Recap assignments and agreed activities

© CENGAGE LEARNING 2014

won't be productive. However, you need to be sure everyone with a stake in the topic or who has a contribution to make is represented. Does the full team or department need to attend, or is the matter one that concerns only a few people? It's also wise to consider if there are people who might feel offended if they are left out, as well as to think about people who might not be directly involved but have useful experience or insight that could contribute to the meeting.

Be Prepared

Good meetings are focused and efficient, and many problems can be averted with adequate preparation. After clearly defining the purpose of the meeting and deciding who should attend, advance preparation should include preparing a concise agenda that provides a clear description of the meeting's purpose. This agenda should be distributed ahead of time and it should set a definite beginning and ending time for the meeting. People need to know in advance what to expect and how to prepare. Participants should also be given any materials they need to study in advance, as well as be advised of what will be expected of them at the meeting.

Use the Right Processes

During the actual meeting, certain techniques can bring out the best in people and ensure a productive session rather than a waste of time and energy.

- *Start and End on Time.* It is amazing what a difference simply starting and ending on time and keeping the meeting moving at a rapid pace can make in people's attitudes, morale, and willingness to participate in meetings.[58] Starting promptly and moving the meeting along has symbolic value because it tells people that the meeting is important and that you value their time.
- *Set Ground Rules.* Effective meetings begin with a statement of the purpose, review of the agenda, and the setting of ground rules. At ICU Medical, a maker of medical devices, every team follows a core set of ground rules for interaction, shown in Exhibit 12.6. Teams establish further rules for meetings if participants believe they're needed.
- *Create Involvement.* Some people like to go around the room and get each person's perspective on an issue. Others prefer a more subtle approach in which the leader brings shy or reticent

Exhibit 12.6 ICU Medical's Rules of Engagement for Teams

- Challenge the issue, not the person.
- Consider all options.
- Stand up for your position, but don't argue against the facts.
- Allow yourself the opportunity to seriously consider all views.
- Lose the words "I" and "They" once a decision is reached.

Source: Erin White, "How a Company Made Everyone a Team Player," *The Wall Street Journal,* August 13, 2007.

people into the discussion in an encouraging and non-threatening way. For example, a leader might say, "Yuan, I know this is in your area of expertise, so I'm interested to hear your views." When leading a meeting, encourage a cross-current of discussion and debate, but control disruptive conflicts and make sure people stick to the topic rather than getting sidetracked.

- *Summarize.* End the meeting with a summary of the discussion and decisions made and a review of any follow-up assignments. Everyone needs to understand their post-meeting roles and responsibilities to prevent misunderstandings.

Follow-Up

Swift follow-up is critical to the value of the entire meeting process. You should send simple minutes that include the topic discussed, any decisions made, the agreed-upon activities, a recap of assignments, and suggested schedules for implementation.

A Special Note on Virtual Meetings

In today's world of advanced technology, it is possible to bring people together for a meeting even if they are spread all over the world. The procedures for effective meetings generally apply to virtual meetings as well, but there are also some special challenges to meeting in virtual as opposed to physical space. Here are some additional guidelines for making virtual meetings effective.[59]

- *Pay attention to the niceties.* In many cases, people attending a face-to-face meeting already know one another and they mingle and talk among themselves as they enter the meeting room. In a virtual environment, however, where some participants might never have met face-to-face, it is highly important to make sure everyone is properly introduced at the start of the meeting.

7 STEPS TO... Running a Great Meeting

1. Make clear that everyone is expected to participate.
2. Establish ground rules for how people interact and treat one another.
3. Provoke discussion with open-ended questions and by inquiring into differing opinions so everyone feels heard.
4. Listen to each person carefully and seriously.
5. Encourage the clash of ideas but not of personalities. If needed, anticipate trouble and intervene with potentially difficult people in advance.
6. Defuse an unpleasant or hostile atmosphere with humor.
7. Stay cool, calm, and collected. Remember that you are in charge of the meeting and have the authority to move it along as needed to meet time constraints.

Sources: Based on Suzanne Bates, "Learning to Lead: Five Steps to Pain Free, Productive Meetings," *Supervision* (August 2006): 18–19; John Wareham, "My Gangbuster Meeting," *The Conference Board Review* (March–April 2007): 20–24; "Expert's View: Ros Jay on Conducting Effective Meetings," sidebar in Martin Couzins and Scott Beagrie, "How To . . . Conduct Effective Meetings," *Personnel Today* (June 3, 2003): 31; and T. L. Stanley, "Make Your Meetings Effective," *Supervision* (April 2006): 6–8.

DISCOVER KNOWLEDGE

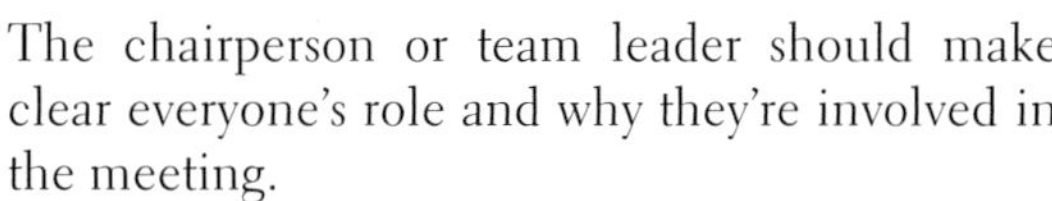

The chairperson or team leader should make clear everyone's role and why they're involved in the meeting.

- *Don't skimp on the rules of engagement.* The tone of a virtual meeting often is a bit more formal because there have to be more rules of interaction. Things can easily be misunderstood online, for example, leading to anger or hard feelings, so people need guidelines about how to effectively communicate. Is joking and teasing okay, for instance, or should people stick to business? What's the protocol for making sure everyone has the same understanding of a comment or suggestion? In conference calls, the chairperson or team leader has to be particularly vigilant that people don't talk over one another, because participants can't see when someone else is starting to talk.
- *Make everything explicit.* When communicating online or via conference call, people need ways to let colleagues know when they're shifting mental gears, pausing to think, or needing more feedback. Without visual cues, a few seconds of silence following a team member's presentation can seem interminable. The member might be wondering "Are they upset? Did they misunderstand my comment? Do they think I haven't done a good job?" and so forth.
- *Consider new-generation videoconferencing for critical issues.* The latest videoconferencing systems use advanced video, audio, and transmission technologies to create a lifelike meeting experience. The price tag is still steep, but for highly important, complex, or difficult issues, these "telepresence" systems are the next best thing to a flesh-and-blood, face-to-face meeting.

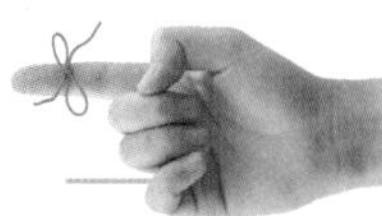

NEED TO KNOW

- Teams are a central aspect of today's organizations, and you will likely get your first experience managing people in a team setting. A team is a unit of two or more people who interact and coordinate their work to accomplish a common goal for which they are committed and hold themselves mutually accountable. Teams have a clear purpose, well-defined boundaries, and stability of membership. Teams are frequently used to handle special projects, to enhance cross-functional coordination and get buy-in, and to decentralize decision making and empower employees.
- Teams present a dilemma for most people because many of us have had negative experiences with teams, teams may conflict with our values, and we may be uncomfortable with the idea that our individual success depends on how well others perform. Social loafing (free riding) and groupthink also create frustrations among team members and may reduce effectiveness.
- Individual rewards for team members are effective when people are required to work independently to complete the group's task. Group rewards are more appropriate when team members depend heavily upon one another to complete the group's task and cooperation is important. Managers assess the level of work interdependence among team members and design rewards accordingly, often using a mix of individual and group rewards.
- Six team leader behaviors that contribute to effective teamwork are: a compelling purpose and clear objectives, metrics that enable the team to assess progress, clear roles and diversity of skills, streamlined team size, decision authority over how to achieve goals, and an open culture and ongoing training. On every team, someone must possess the following competencies: goal setting and performance management, planning and coordination, collaborative problem solving, communication, and conflict resolution.
- Team members may take on one or more of nine different roles that help the team meet its needs for task accomplishment and positive relationships.
- Other important areas in which leaders make a critical contribution to team success are in articulating a compelling purpose, learning to truly share power, and shaping productive norms for conduct and performance.
- Running an effective team meeting requires identifying a clear reason for having the meeting, inviting the right people, preparing well ahead of time, setting ground rules and creating involvement during the meeting, and following up after the meeting.

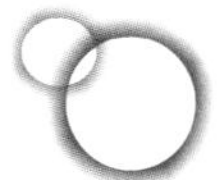

ACTION LEARNING

DELIBERATE PRACTICE EXERCISES

Birth Order and Team Roles

Step 1: Answer the following questions:

1. What is your birth order in your family? First-born, middle child, youngest, etc.?
2. How does your birth order influence your attitude and behavior when working in groups? (Respecting group authority, sharing power, tendency toward groupthink, social loafing/over-responsibility, etc.)

Step 2: Think about your strengths and weaknesses that you might attribute to your birth order and answer the following questions:

1. What are your strengths that you can attribute to your birth order?
2. How can you leverage these strengths as a group member?
3. What are your weaknesses that you can attribute to your birth order?

Step 3: How does your birth order make you the person you are today?

Step 4 (Optional): Share your insights with a partner, and ask your partner what insights he or she gained.

Group Skills

Step 1: Review the text discussion of group member roles related to meeting a group's task and relationship needs on pages 451–452.

Step 2: Think of at least two activities that you will be involved in with one or more persons during the next week. Choose one of the following behaviors to practice in these settings (choose the behavior that stretches you, one that does not come naturally to you):

1. "Make sure the group stays on task." This might include ensuring there is an agenda, that the agenda is followed, that ideas are summarized, that distractions are minimized, that decisions are made promptly, and that follow-up actions are defined.
2. "Make sure the group has an effective interpersonal process." This might include asking questions of others, making sure everyone participates, mediating during a conflict, encouraging others through positive feedback, displaying humor, showing members how they are actually in agreement, creating unity, and so on.

Step 3: Complete the following table:

What are the activities during which you will practice the behavior?	1.
	2.
List the behavior (task, interpersonal process) you chose to practice.	
Outcome of your behavior in situation #1	
Outcome of your behavior in situation #2	
What struggles did you have practicing the behavior?	
What feedback did you get, either verbal or nonverbal?	
What insights have you gained on being a more effective group participant?	

IN-CLASS TEAM EXERCISES

Wilderness Survival

Step 1: Read the Background and Situation regarding the exercise:

Wilderness Survival Background

Sometimes team/group decision making is more effective than individual decision making. Research shows that if the decision is simple, it is better to have one person responsible; however, if the problem is more complex, group decision making is more effective. In this exercise, you'll get a chance to compare the results of individual and group decision making.

Wilderness Survival Situation

You have gone on a Boundary Waters canoe trip with five friends to upper Minnesota and southern Ontario in the Quetico Provincial Park. Your group has been traveling the Saganaga Lake to Kawnipi Lake following through Canyon Falls and Kennebas Falls and Kenny Lake. See the map on page 462.

The closest road is 15 to 18 miles away, accessible by paddling through lakes and rivers and usually portaging (taking the land path) around numerous falls. Saganaga Lake is impossible to cross in bad weather, generally because of heavy rain. The nearest town is Grand Marais, Minnesota, 60 miles away. That town has plenty of camping outfitters, but limited medical help, so citizens rely on hospitals farther to the south.

ACTION LEARNING

The terrain is about 70 percent land and 30 percent water, with small patches of land here and there between the lakes and rivers. Bears are not uncommon in this region. It is now mid-May, when the temperature (daytime) ranges from about 25 to 70 degrees, often in the same day. Nighttime temperatures can be in the 20s.

Rain is frequent during the day (nights too) and is life threatening if the temperature is cold. It is unusual for the weather to stay the same for more than a day or two. Generally, it will rain one day and be warm and clear the next, with a third day windy—and it is not easy to predict what type of weather will come next. In fact, it may be clear and warm, rainy and windy, all in the same day.

Your group of six was in two canoes going down the river and came to a rapids. Rather than taking the portage route on land, the group foolishly decided to shoot the rapids by canoe. Unfortunately, everyone fell out of the canoes and some were banged against the rocks. Luckily no one was killed, but one person suffered a broken leg and several members had cuts and bruises.

Both canoes were severely damaged. Both were bent clear in half, one with an open tear of 18 inches, while the other had two tears of 12 and 15 inches long. Both had broken gunwales (upper edges on both sides). You lost the packs that held the tent, most clothing, nearly all the food, cooking equipment, fuel, first aid kit, and flashlight. Your combined possessions include one jackknife, four canoe paddles, a pocketful of hard candies, five dollar bills, and 65 cents in coins.

You had permits to take this trip, but no one knows for sure where you are. There is no cell phone signal and the closest land line is in Grand Marais. You are scheduled back four days from now. It is likely a search party will be sent out in about five days (as you may have been delayed a day or so in getting back). Just now it has started to drizzle and it looks like rain will follow.

Your task is to figure out how to survive in these unpredictable and possibly harsh conditions until you can get help.

SHUTTERSTOCK #53973379

Step 2: Rank order, completely by yourself, the 14 items listed in the table below in terms of their "survival value." The most important item would get a "1" and the least important a "14." Put your rank ordering in Column A.

	A	B	C	D	E	F
			(A–B)		(A–D)	(B–D)
Items	**Your Ranking from 1–14 (1 is most important)**	**Group Ranking**	**Your Persuasion Score**	**Expert Ranking**	**Individual Difference Score**	**Group Difference Score**
Fanny pack of food: cheese, salami, GORP						
Plastic-covered map of boundary waters						
6 PDFs (personal flotation devices)						
2 fishing poles, broken						
Set of clothes for 3 (wet)						
One yellow Frisbee®						
Water purification tablets						
Duct tape, one 30' roll						
Whiskey, one pint, 180 proof						
Insect repellant						
Matches, 30, dry						
Parachute chord, 35 feet						
Compass						
6 sleeping bags, synthetic, medium weight						

Step 3: Divide into groups of five to six members and decide the rank order of each item's "survival value" as a group. Record the group's ranking in Column B. Do not change your individual ranking after discussion begins. You have approximately 30 minutes for this activity.

Step 4: Your instructor will give you the expert's ranking. Enter the expert's ranking in Column D and then compute the following scores using *absolute* differences to compute all scores—*ignore pluses and minuses.*

1. Your individual score as the total of Column E _________
2. The average individual score of your group's members _____________
3. The best individual score (lowest score) in your group __________
4. Your group's score as the total of Column F _______________
5. The influence of your ranking on the group's ranking as the total score of Column C ____________

Step 5: Discuss the following questions:

1. To what extent was the group's score, which was based on the group's discussion, more accurate than the average of individual scores? Why do you think that happened?
2. Which behaviors of members helped or hindered the group's decision-making process?
3. What happened if a person had a very accurate individual score, but was not very persuasive in the group? And conversely, what if a person had a poor individual score and was very persuasive in the group?
4. What roles did you observe during your group's discussion? Which group members played which roles described on pages 451–452?

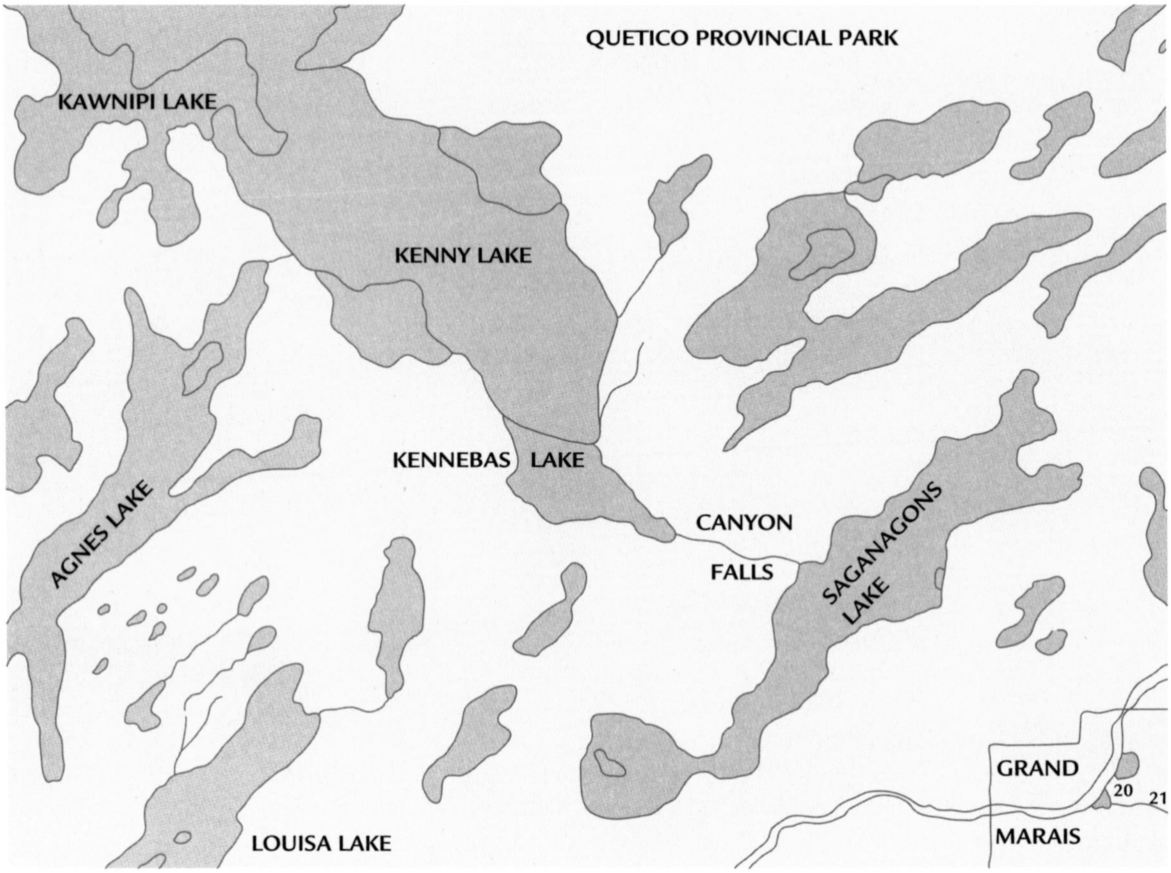

QUETICO PROVINCIAL PARK
KAWNIPI LAKE
KENNY LAKE
KENNEBAS LAKE
CANYON
FALLS
AGNES LAKE
SAGANAGONS LAKE
LOUISA LAKE
GRAND
MARAIS
20
21

© CENGAGE LEARNING 2014

Running a Meeting

This In-Class Team Exercise is available online at www.cengagebrain.com.

FIELD TEAM EXERCISE

Cooking Your Team

Step 1: Form into groups of six or seven. It works best if you are in a group with diverse people and people you don't know well. Your team will need to set aside time for two meetings: one for decision making and one for cooking, cleanup, and discussion.

Step 2: Each individual will bring to the first group meeting his or her favorite recipe, something that has at least 12 ingredients, including spices. Each person should also bring a second-favorite recipe, in case the group needs backups.

My favorite recipe:	My second favorite recipe:
List ingredients:	List ingredients:

Step 3: Schedule your meetings. During the process, you will take detailed notes on the team development process and the roles each person plays. Fill out the tables below as you go along.

Stages of Development: (Review the text on pages 446–447 and the statements in Questionnaire 2 at the beginning of this chapter for more information.)

Stage	Describe what happened during each stage. How did people behave? What issues emerged?
Forming	
Storming	
Norming	
Performing	
Adjourning	

Team Roles: Identify who played which roles and list some behaviors that showed that role. (Refer to the text discussion of team roles on pages 451–452 for more information.)

SHUTTERSTOCK #53973379

Team Roles	Member 1	Member 2	Member 3	Member 4	Member 5	Member 6	Member 7
Organizer							
Encourager							
Enforcer							
Resource Developer							
Creator							
Coordinator							
Implementer							
Teamworker							
Specialist							

Step 4: First meeting, part I: Your first job as a team is to choose one recipe you will make together. It must be something that everyone can eat—and wants to eat. Consider food restrictions (religious, health, choice, or other), food allergies, and so on. Everyone should not only be able to eat the final product, but look forward to eating it. Choose a second-choice or back-up recipe, just in case something goes wrong in trying to prepare the first one.

Recipe the group chose:
Second choice of group:

ACTION LEARNING

Step 5: First meeting, part II: Planning. As a team, decide how the work will be divided. Everyone should have to buy at least one item and everyone needs to be involved somehow in the food preparation and the cleanup.

Step 6: Second meeting, part I: Cooking and cleanup. Cook the food with everyone present and working.

Second meeting, part II: Eat and enjoy.

Second meeting, part III: Clean up.

Step 7: Second meeting, part IV: Group process. Talk about what happened in your group. What worked? What did not? What roles did people take on? Talk about the stages of development. What did you learn from the process?

Step 8: As an individual, what did you learn about teams from this cooking exercise?

TEST YOUR METTLE

ROLE PLAY SIMULATIONS

Rewarding What?

Background: Reread the written Video Incident at the beginning of this chapter.

Instructions: Divide into groups of six to seven members. Assign people to play the roles of general manager Jane Sutton, CFO Carlos Hernandez, director of operations Carrie Fishman, HR director Heather Carreau, and sales manager Jason Wong. All other members of the group are observers who should look for the types of behavior and strategies each person employs. Each person reads only his or her confidential role, but observers read all. Spend 10 to 15 minutes on the role play.

Confidential information for Jane: You know this is sudden, going from an individual-based merit system to team-based rewards, but corporate won't back down on this, no matter how much everyone complains. Anyway, you think this is a good thing, because your managers could learn a thing or two about functioning as a high-performing team.

Confidential information for Carlos: You've always done a good job and gotten great reviews on the technical parts of your job. Why should the other department managers pull you down? Everyone knows you have way more years with the company than any of the other managers. Of course that means your contributions are more valuable. You count on those bonuses every year and this year it's even more important because you'll have two kids in college. No time to be punished for other people's lack of a work ethic.

Confidential information for Carrie: You've discovered that the people you work with don't always learn very fast, and you know they are going to pull you down when it comes time to hand out bonuses. They keep asking dumb questions and can never seem to get their work done on time. And they demand to be treated the same, even though it takes them twice as long to get anything done. Why should their naïveté make you suffer? And why doesn't Jane fight more with corporate about this insane new system? Besides, your mother has stage four cancer and her insurance doesn't cover everything. So you need every penny of that bonus.

Confidential information for Jason: You've only been on this job for a few months, but you've never experienced so much chaos. Talk about making mountains out of molehills! Why spend so much time arguing over who gets which office? Everyone should be talking about how to increase sales, not how many more cubic feet someone has, or how many windows. You want to get sales up and a new campaign is needed, now. Carrie and Carlos are especially resistant. Why should their dragging their feet be the cause of you getting a lower bonus? Your wife just broke her leg and she is completely incapacitated. You've got help during the week, but it costs money. Moving here really set you back, even though the company did pay some of the expenses. And you and your wife are both still paying off student loans.

Confidential information for Heather: You think this new reward system is a great idea. All the studies show that a united team produces more. You've seen a lot of data on high-performing teams and the positive effects of group rewards. What a great

incentive. You plan to call corporate soon and thank them for helping create a more positive work environment.

After the role play, observers report to the group and then everyone discusses the following questions:

1. What can general manager Jane Sutton do to create team spirit in this situation?
2. What's a fair approach to rewards on a group project? Do you think the new reward system seems appropriate for Caffeine and Crullers?

Creating a High-Performance Team

This Role Play Simulation is available online at www.cengagebrain.com.

VIDEO APPLICATION

Striving for More Teamwork at Holden Outerwear

Owner Mikey LeBlanc encourages the employees at his fashionable outerwear company to take steps toward more teamwork.

Discussion Questions

1. Why do you think the owner Mikey LeBlanc is encouraging the idea of "team" among his employees? LeBlanc said it is hard to bring new people onto the team. Why do you think that would be the case?
2. Nikki Brush switched from freelancer to design manager. What conflicts might she feel about being part of a team? What advantages do you think a designer would experience by working alone?
3. Working as a team is fairly new at Holden. At what stage of team development do you think they are? Why?

TEST YOUR METTLE

CASE INCIDENTS

"*We* Are the Dream Team"

Germaine Kemp, team leader and director of branding, answered the call from Leroy Winstead, CEO of Winstead & Griffiths, and switched to speaker phone so that everyone could hear.

"Well, my dream team has done it again," Leroy raved. "You guys just keep nabbing top accounts and I'm just amazed—again! You folks are the best example of what a team can accomplish on a consistent basis. I look forward to seeing all of you when you return from Paris." A few more words were exchanged before the call ended. For a moment, no one spoke.

"Yes, we've *done it again*," said Whitney Caulfield, "If he tells us one more time how we exemplify teamwork, I think I'll scream."

"Well I, for one, appreciate his call," said Jessie Barnhardt, one of two creative directors on the global ad team.

SHUTTERSTOCK #53973379

Germaine and Jessie, along with team members Whitney (accounting) and Lew Casey (production), had gathered at a fabulous Paris restaurant along the famous Champs Elysées to celebrate another success in securing major clients for the global advertising firm. Only creative director Marlena Brando was absent. A high-energy, non-stop, and apparently non-sleeping dynamo, Brando came to Winstead & Griffiths two years before and had become a force on the team. Fluent in five languages, Brando moved easily through the global marketplace, charming potential clients and communicating W&G's vision. Her unusual, easy-to-remember name evoked images of Marlon Brando, and team members had become accustomed to hearing clients humming the *Godfather* theme when she was introduced. "It was funny for maybe the first five thousand times we had to hear it," Whitney said. "But it's really gotten old. The worst part is that they think they are being so original. So we always have to laugh at the potential client's lame attempt at humor."

"I propose a toast," Lew stood and said, adding sarcastically, "To advertising's greatest team." The group drained their glasses and again fell silent. "We're missing the presence of our *star*, folks."

"We really should be grateful," Germaine said. "Brando has come through for us and saved our butts several times and we all know it. She works hard. She can make a last minute change that really carries the proposal over the top and clinches the deal."

"*She* does it," Lew complained. "This is supposed to be a team effort. Yes, I'm glad we're getting these deals and that the CEO thinks we're the greatest thing since sliced bread, but I, for one, feel like a fraud. I work hard on these proposals, too. But when the client says yes, they're saying yes to her work, not to mine. Mine got lost somewhere."

"Ok, let's chill. This is supposed to be a celebration for getting the account, even if she did it her way," Germaine said. "We all worked on these deals and we all share the credit. She does not claim the credit and she never complains about her workload. I believe she probably likes all of us and thinks of us as a team."

"Think so?" Lew asked.

"We *were* a team before Brando came," Whitney pointed out. "We each contributed . . ."

"But now, when I look at the finished product, I barely recognize my contribution. I see her stamp all over it, redoing our stuff to fit her needs," Lew insisted.

"I don't think it's that simple, Lew," Jessie said. "Germaine sets our objectives and is always open to our ideas and the adjustments we make to move the project. You and Whitney do an excellent job of coordinating production and costs, and Brando and I design the visual presentations. We all contribute to a successful presentation."

"Ah, you forgot all of the little last minute tweaks and changes she makes to *improve* all of that great work. She hardly works in partnership with us. I think we are her support staff."

"You're the official team leader, Germaine." Whitney said. "I think you should talk to her or talk to Leroy."

"Yeah, how do we go into Leroy's office and say 'Oh, your dream team does not really see itself as a *team*,'" Germaine responded. "We'll sound like a bunch of whiners. He's going to *love* that."

"Well, do we continue as we are—riding along on her coattails to glory-land? Or do we find a way to look at our various roles and realign into a *real* dream team?" Jessie asked.

"And how do we do that without giving the appearance of ganging up on someone who contributes so much to our effort?" Germaine asked. "If we confront her about

this, will it shake her confidence, or piss her off, and make her pull back on her effort? Wouldn't we be the losers?"

"Not if we do it right," Jessie said.

Discussion Questions

1. Should team members take their concerns to Leroy or discuss them directly with Brando? Exactly how should they bring up and discuss the issue with either person?
2. Review and analyze the list of contributions for team members in the chapter and analyze which are or are not being performed on this team. Which members are doing what?
3. Are these people really a team? If you were one of the members, what would you do to increase cohesiveness? Why?

Class Project

John Taylor was angry. In less than ten hours' time he was scheduled to make the in-class presentation of a marketing project on behalf of his five-member team (including Brittany Jones, Marty Greenlow, Kim Ma, and Khalid Khalil). The project was the majority of the final course grade. After sitting through over half of the class presentations, he knew that the project he would be presenting was superior to anything developed by other teams. Yet, his confidence in the final product was countered by his mounting anger. At last, he picked up the phone and called team member Khalid Khalil. A sleepy voice answered.

"Khalid, I'm sorry to wake you up, man, but I wanted to ask you something about our project presentation tomorrow."

"It's okay. I don't mind making the presentation for you if you're nervous about it. You saw the others; ours is much better and I think everyone will agree we did some great work on this."

"That's just my point. *We* worked hard—you and me. It's *our* work," John said. "The rest of our so-called team didn't come close to pulling their weight on this. I don't think we should include their names."

"But it's a group grade," Khalid replied, suddenly wide awake after hearing John's unexpected remark.

"You and I know these people are just coasting and letting the two of us carry the project and get the grade for them. It's not fair and we should not let them get away with it."

Khalid held the phone as his friend continued his rant, pointing out all of the ways the others had failed to "man up" for this important project. Khalid was sympathetic and in total agreement—in principle.

He barely knew John when they were placed on the five-member team. During the initial brief meeting team members introduced themselves and agreed to return days later to exchange ideas for the project. However, John and Khalid met for coffee after class and, over the next few days, created their vision for the project. At the second team meeting, other members tossed around ideas, but gave in to the well-developed concepts presented by John and Khalid. Drawing upon Khalid's native Arabic and knowledge of marketing throughout the Middle East, the project expanded the marketing plan beyond America (the focus of projects by other teams) and into the global marketplace. It was, the two men agreed, a master stroke.

Taking charge, John made assignments based on what he perceived as the strengths of the various team members, drawn from the team's introductory meeting.

"Did Dr. Armistead designate *you* as the team leader?" Kim had challenged.

"No," John answered. "But since our idea for the project is going forward, either Khalid or I should lead."

"I agree with John," Brittany said. "This is their concept and since much of Khalid's time will be needed to translate materials into Arabic, John seems to be the logical team director. The important thing here is for everyone to work together." Aside from that one brief dispute, the group appeared united.

But over the weeks, the motivation of the other team members waned as Marty and Kim questioned the Middle Eastern focus and urged Brittany's support for their mounting concerns. "How can we provide insight or feedback when we know nothing about the region; when we're writing text for the presentation that we're not even sure will translate well?" Kim complained. Brittany's frustrations as head of visual design emerged in trying to meet overly optimistic deadlines while also encouraging excitement for the project and mediating the mounting tensions among group members. Increasingly, John and Khalid worked toward their goals, assigned work to others, and then hustled to make changes in the work submitted by others for the final presentation.

Khalid's attention now snapped back as he heard John say, "Hell, half the time we couldn't even pull everyone together for a meeting. And now, after we carried the load, they all want to share our grade. It's not going to happen."

"So you're planning to just drop them without letting them know."

"Yes. I'm thinking about removing their names and explaining to the class their lack of contribution to the final product."

"Whew! I don't know if that's wise, man. The project and the presentation are the major portions of the grade, but Dr. Armistead is also looking at how we worked together as a team. You know that at the conclusion of each presentation, he asks team members to tell about their individual contributions and how they would evaluate the team experience. If we drop member names and announce that they didn't contribute, I'm afraid we will lose some valuable points."

"And if he asks what they contributed, what will they say?" John asked frantically. "Do we just make up a lie for each one? If these guys get away with this; if we cover for them . . ."

"So what do we do?" Khalid asked. "They did what we told them, even if we had to redo things the way we wanted. We have only a few options at this late stage. We cover for them and act like nothing happened. Or we call them right now and tell them they had better come up with some way to talk about their contribution, or we announce to the class that, yes, we have this fantastic marketing project, but we failed as a team."

"I just don't know which way we should go," John moaned.

"There's one more option," Khalid said. "We meet privately with Dr. Armistead before class to explain what happened."

"No!" John said. "I don't think that's a good idea. Maybe we should have done that a few weeks ago."

"Well, we have to decide now, man."

Discussion Questions

1. Which of the five dysfunctions of a team in Exhibit 12.2 are apparent in this team. Why?
2. What team roles are recognizable, and what roles are needed but missing in this scenario?
3. What factors do you think caused the breakdown of the team? What should John and Khalid do now?

PERSONAL SKILLS LOG

PERSONAL SKILLS LOG

Directions: Fill in the rows below based on what you learned from each part of the chapter that you completed.

	What is my key takeaway or insight from this activity?	**What do I personally do well (strength) regarding this activity?**	**What could I improve (weakness) about myself regarding this activity?**	**How might I use what I've learned from this activity in the future?**
Manager Challenge Incident:				
Discover Yourself Questionnaires:				
Deliberate Practice Exercises:				
In-Class and/or Field Team Exercises:				
Role-Play Exercises:				
Case Incidents:				

REFERENCES

Discover Yourself

1 Based on Eric M. Stark, Jason D. Shaw, and Michelle K. Duffy, "Preference for Group Work, Winning Orientation, and Social Loafing Behavior in Groups," *Group & Organization Management* 32, no. 6 (December 2007): 699–723; and Alvin Hwang and Anne Marie Francesco, "The Influence of Individualism-Collectivism and Power Distance on Use of Feedback Channels and Consequences for Learning," *Academy of Management Learning and Education* 10, no. 2 (2010): 243–257.

2 Adapted from "Teamwork Survey," Big Dog & Little Dog's Performance Juxtaposition Web site, http://www.nwlink.com/~donclark/leader/teamsuv.html (accessed February 8, 2012); and Diane L. Miller, "The Stages of Group Development: A Retrospective Study of Dynamic Team Processes," *Canadian Journal of Administrative Sciences* 20, no. 2 (June 2003): 121–134.

3 Based on Jennifer M. George, "Extrinsic and Intrinsic Origins of Perceived Social Loafing in Organizations," *Academy of Management Journal* 35, no. 1 (1992): 191–202; Charles H. Allen, "Developing an Assessment Process for Determining If Groupthink Characteristics Are Present in a Military Unit," research paper submitted in partial fulfillment for a Master of Science degree, University of Wisconsin – Stout (November 2001); and Jin Nam Choi and Myung Un Kim, "The Organizational Application of Groupthink and Its Limitations in Organizations," *Journal of Applied Psychology*, 54, no. 2 (1999): 297–306.

Discover Knowledge

4 Chuck Salter, "What LeBron James and the Miami Heat Teach Us About Teamwork," *Fast Company*, April 2011, http://www.fastcompany.com/magazine/155/the-worlds-greatest-chemistry-experiment.html (accessed April 25, 2011).

5 Industry Week/Manufacturing Performance Institute's Census of Manufacturers for 2004, reported in Traci Purdum, "Teaming, Take 2," *Industry Week* (May 2005): 41–43.

6 This definition is based on J. Richard Hackman, *Leading Teams: Setting the Stage for Great Performances* (Boston: Harvard Business School Press, 2002); and Dawn R. Utley and Stephanie E. Brown, "Establishing Characteristic Differences between Team and Working Group Behaviors," *Institute of Industrial Engineers Annual Conference Proceedings* (2010): 1–6.

7 John Murawski, "Cisco Unveils 'Business Tablet,'" *The News and Observer*, June 30, 2010, http://www.newsobserver.com/2010/06/30/558049/cisco-unveils-business-tablet.html (accessed April 21, 2011).

8 Lee G. Bolman and Terrence E. Deal, "What Makes a Team Work?" *Organizational Dynamics* (August 1992): 34–44.

9 Telis Demos, "Cirque du Balancing Act," *Fortune* (June 12, 2006): 114; Erin White, "How a Company Made Everyone a Team Player," *The Wall Street Journal*, August 13, 2007; David Kirkpatrick, "Inside Sam's $100 Billion Growth Machine," *Fortune* (June 14, 2004): 80–98; Daniel R. Kibbe and Jill Casner-Lotto, "Ralston Foods: From Greenfield to Maturity in a Team-Based Plant, *Journal of Organizational Excellence* (Summer 2002): 57–67.

10 Margaret Frazier, "Flu Prep," *The Wall Street Journal*, March 25, 2006.

11 Dan Heath and Chip Heath, "Blowing the Baton Pass," *Fast Company* (July–August 2010): 46–48.

12 Charles Fishman, "Total Teamwork: Imagination Ltd.," *Fast Company* (April 2000): 156–168; and Kelly Wardle, "Confetti: Imagination Creates One Enchanted Evening," *Special Events*, February 1, 2006, http://specialevents.com/corporate/events_one_enchanted_evening_20060203/ (accessed February 14, 2012).

13 Based on a story in Sara Fister Gale, "The Turn Around Artist," *PM Network* (October 2007): 28–35.

14 "Why Some Teams Succeed (and So Many Don't)," *Harvard Management Update* (October 2006): 3–4.

15 These factors are based partly on "Why Some Teams Succeed (and So Many Don't)" and Ruth Wageman, "Critical Success Factors for Creating Superb Self-Managing Teams," *Organizational Dynamics* (Summer 1997): 49–61.

16 "Why Some Teams Succeed."

17 J. Polzer, W. Swann Jr., and L. Milton, "The Benefits of Verifying Diverse Identities for Group Performance," in M. Neale, E. Mannix, and J. Polzer, eds., *Research on Managing Groups and Teams: Identity Issues in Groups*, Vol. 5 (Stamford, CT: JAI Press, 2003), pp. 91–112.

18 Warren E. Watson, Kamalesh Kumar, and Larry K. Michaelsen, "Cultural Diversity's Impact on Interaction Process and Performance: Comparing Homogeneous and Diverse Task Groups," *Academy*

of Management Journal 36 (1993): 590–602; and Gail Robinson and Kathleen Dechant, "Building a Business Case for Diversity," *Academy of Management Executive* 11, no. 3 (1997): 21–31.

19 Lynda Gratton and Tamara J. Erickson, "Eight Ways to Build Collaborative Teams," *Harvard Business Review* (November 2007): 2–10.

20 Jeffrey T. Polzer, "Leading Teams," *Harvard Business Publishing for Educators*, Background Note, Product #403094-PDF-ENG (ordered at http://cb.hbsp.harvard.edu/cb/product/403094-PDF-ENG).

21 This summary of team size research is based on Martin Hoegl, "Smaller Teams—Better Teamwork: How to Keep Project Teams Small," *Business Horizons* 48 (2005): 209–214; Lillian Chaney and Julie Lyden, "Making U.S. Teams Work," *Supervision* (January 2000): 6; Jia Lynn Yang, "The Power of Number 4.6," part of a special series, "Secrets of Greatness: Teamwork," *Fortune* (June 12, 2006): 122; M. E. Shaw, *Group Dynamics*, 3rd ed. (New York: McGraw Hill, 1981); and G. Manners, "Another Look at Group Size, Group Problem Solving, and Group Consensus," *Academy of Management Journal* 18 (1975): 715–724.

22 Gallup poll results reported in "Viva La Difference," box in Julie Connelly, "All Together Now," *Gallup Management Journal* (Spring 2002): 13–18.

23 Polzer, "Leading Teams."

24 Gratton and Erickson, "Eight Ways to Build Collaborative Teams."

25 Thomas Petzinger Jr., "Bovis Team Helps Builders Construct a Solid Foundation," *The Wall Street Journal*, March 21, 1997.

26 Kenneth G. Koehler, "Effective Team Management," *Small Business Report* (July 19, 1989): 14–16; Connie J. G. Gersick, "Time and Transition in Work Teams: Toward a New Model of Group Development," *Academy of Management Journal* 31 (1988): 9–41; and John Beck and Neil Yeager, "Moving Beyond Myths," *Training & Development* (March 1996): 51–55.

27 Bruce W. Tuckman and Mary Ann C. Jensen, "Stages of Small-Group Development Revisited," *Group and Organizational Studies* 2 (1977): 419–427; and Bruce W. Tuckman, "Developmental Sequences in Small Groups," *Psychological Bulletin* 63 (1965): 384–399. See also Linda N. Jewell and H. Joseph Reitz, *Group Effectiveness in Organizations* (Glenview, IL: Scott, Foresman,1981).

28 White, "How a Company Made Everyone a Team Player."

29 Study by G. Clotaire Rapaille, reported in Karen Bernowski, "What Makes American Teams Tick?" *Quality Progress* 28, no. 1 (January 1995): 39–42.

30 Jared Sandberg, "Some Ideas Are So Bad That Only Team Efforts Can Account for Them," Cubicle Culture column, *The Wall Street Journal*, September 29, 2004.

31 Chantell E. Nicholls, Henry W. Lane, and Mauricio Brehm Brechu, "Taking Self-Managed Teams to Mexico," *Academy of Management Executive* 13, no. 2 (1999): 15–27.

32 Rapaille study reported in Bernowski, "What Makes American Teams Tick?"

33 Robert Albanese and David D. Van Fleet, "Rational Behavior in Groups: The Free-Riding Tendency," *Academy of Management Review* 10 (1985): 244–255.

34 D. A. Kravitz and B. Martin, "Ringelmann Rediscovered: The Original Article," *Journal of Personality and Social Psychology* 50, no. 5 (1986): 936–941.

35 Studies reported in R. A. Baron, *Behavior in Organizations*, 2nd ed. (Boston: Allyn & Bacon, 1986).

36 Irving L. Janis, *Groupthink: Psychological Studies of Policy Decisions and Fiascoes*, 2nd ed. (Boston: Houghton Mifflin, 1982).

37 Christopher M. Barnes et al., "Mixing Individual Incentives and Group Incentives: Best of Both Worlds or Social Dilemma?" *Journal of Management* 37, no. 6 (November 2011): 1611–1635; and Bianca Beersma et al., "Cooperation, Competition, and Team Performance: Toward a Contingency Approach," *Academy of Management Journal* 46, no. 5 (2003): 572–590.

38 Matt Moffett, "Trapped Miners Kept Focus, Shared Tuna—Foiled Escape, Bid to Organize Marked First Two Weeks Underground in Chile," *The Wall Street Journal*, August 25, 2010; and "Lessons on Leadership and Teamwork—From 700 Meters Below the Earth's Surface," Universia Knowledge @ Wharton, September 22, 2010, http://www.wharton.universia.net/index.cfm?fa=viewArticle&id=1943&language=english (accessed September 29, 2010).

39 These are based on Michael J. Stevens and Michael A. Campion, "The Knowledge, Skill, and Ability Requirements for Teamwork: Implications for Human Resource Management," *Journal of Management* 20, no. 2 (1994): 503–530.

40 R. Oser, G. A. McCallum, E. Salas, and B. B. Morgan, *Toward a Definition of Teamwork: An Analysis of Critical Team Behaviors*, Technical Report NTSC 89-004 (Arlington, VA: Office of Naval Research, 1989); A. S. Glickman, S. Zimmer, R. C. Montero et al., *The Evolution of Team Skills: An Empirical*

Assessment with Implications for Training, Technical Report NTSC 87-016 (Arlington, VA: Office of Naval Research, 1987).

41 These roles are drawn from ideas in Meredith R. Belbin, *Team Roles at Work* (London: Taylor & Francis, 2010); G. Margerison and D. McCann, *Team Management: Practical New Approaches* (London: Mercury Books, 1990); R. N. Lussier, *Human Relations in Organizations*, 6th ed. (Boston: McGraw-Hill Irwin, 2005): 408; Baron, *Behavior in Organizations*; G. A. Yukl, *Leadership in Organizations* 4th ed. (Upper Saddle River, NJ: Prentice Hall, 1998): 384–387; and E. H. Schein, "What to Observe in a Group," in C. R. Mill and L. C. Porter, eds., *Reading Book for Human Relations Training* (Bethel, ME: NTL Institute, 1976).

42 Based on a story in Mansour Javidan, Mary Teagarden, and David Bowen, "Making It Overseas," *Harvard Business Review* (April 2010): 109–113.

43 Quoted in "Why Some Teams Succeed (and So Many Don't)."

44 J. Richard Hackman, *Leading Teams* (Boston, MA: Harvard Business School Press, 2002): 62.

45 Based on Susan Caminiti, "What Team Leaders Need to Know," *Fortune* (February 20, 1995): 93–100; and J. Thomas Buck, "The Rocky Road to Team-Based Management," *Training & Development* (April 1995): 35–38.

46 Jeanne M. Wilson, Jill George, and Richard S. Wellings, with William C. Byham, *Leadership Trapeze: Strategies for Leadership in Team-Based Organizations* (San Francisco: Jossey-Bass, 1994).

47 Bolman and Deal, "What Makes a Team Work?"

48 E. M. Rogers and R. A. Rogers, *Communication in Organizations* (New York: Free Press, 1976); and A. Bavelas and D. Barrett, "An Experimental Approach to Organization Communication," *Personnel* 27 (1951): 366–371.

49 Bavelas and Barrett, "An Experimental Approach"; and M. E. Shaw, *Group Dynamics: The Psychology of Small Group Behavior* (New York: McGraw-Hill, 1976).

50 Richard L. Daft and Norman B. Macintosh, "A Tentative Exploration into the Amount and Equivocality of Information Processing in Organizational Work Units," *Administrative Science Quarterly* 26 (1981): 207–224.

51 Polzer, "Leading Teams."

52 J. Richard Hackman, "Group Influences on Individuals," in M. Dunnette, ed., *Handbook of Industrial and Organizational Psychology* (Chicago: Rand McNally, 1976).

53 R. C. Ginnett, "Crews As Groups: Their Formation and Their Leadership." In E. L. Wiener, B. G. Kanki, and R. L. Helmreich, eds., *Cockpit Resource Management* (Orlando, FL: Academic Press, 1993), pp. 71–98; and J. Richard Hackman and Ruth Wageman, "Foster Team Effectiveness by Fulfilling Key Leadership Functions." In Edwin A. Locke, ed., *Handbook of Principles of Organizational Behavior* (New York: Wiley-Blackwell, 2009), pp. 275–294.

54 Leigh Buchanan, "The Art of the Huddle: How to Run a Prompt, Productive, and Painless Morning Meeting," *Inc. Magazine* (November 2007): 40–43.

55 American Media Incorporated Video "Meetings Bloody Meetings," reported in Beth Bratkovic, "Running an Effective Meeting," *Government Finance Review* (April 2007): 58–60.

56 Frank Basil, "Advance Planning Is Key to Successful Meetings," *Indianapolis Business Journal* (March 13, 2000): 21.

57 The discussion of these keys to effective meetings is based on Martin Couzins and Scott Beagrie, "How To . . . Conduct Effective Meetings," Career Wise column, *Personnel Today*, June 3, 2003, http://www.personneltoday.com/articles/2003/06/03/19133/how-to.-conduct-effective-meetings.html (accessed April 27, 2011); Sally N. Katz, "Power Skills for Effective Meetings," *Training & Development* (July 1991): 53–55; Suzanne Bates, "Learning to Lead: Five Steps to Pain Free, Productive Meetings," *Supervision* 67, no. 8 (August 2006): 18–19; Beth Bratkovic, "Running an Effective Meeting," *Government Finance Review* (April 2007): 58–60 ; John Wareham, "My Gangbuster Meeting," *The Conference Board Review* (March–April 2007): 20–24; "How to Make Meetings More Effective," *Credit Union Executive Newsletter* (May 8, 2006): 4; Richard Axelrod, Emily M. Axelrod, Julie Beedon, and Robert "Jake" Jacobs, "Creating Dynamic, Energy-Producing Meetings," *Leader to Leader* (Spring 2005): 53–60; and T. L. Stanley, "Make Your Meetings Effective," *Supervision* (April 2006): 6–8.

58 Bates, "Learning to Lead: Five Steps to Pain Free, Productive Meetings."

59 These guidelines are based on information in "Expert's View: Ros Jay on Conducting Effective Meetings," sidebar in Couzins and Beagrie, "How To . . . Conduct Effective Meetings"; Terri L. Griffith and Margaret A. Neale, "Information Processing in Traditional, Hybrid, and Virtual Teams: From Nascent Knowledge to Transactive Memory," *Research in Organizational Behavior* 23, (2001): 379–421; and Roger O. Crockett, "The 21st Century Meeting," *BusinessWeek* (February 26, 2007): 72–79.

Chapter Outline

CHAPTER 13

Achieving Desired Outcomes: Getting the Right People and Managing Performance

RYAN LASH

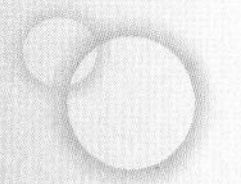

MANAGER CHALLENGE

VIDEO INCIDENT: THE SCORECARD

Madison's Caffeine and Crullers bakery chain has been in trouble since the new competitor, Scone Prone, opened. General manager Jane Sutton has been trying to meet the competition and to increase C&C's productivity, so when director of operations Carrie Fishman came to her office and suggested they implement a performance management "scorecard," she thought it sounded like a good idea. If store managers could learn to measure not only financial performance, but customer service, internal business processes, and C&C's capacity for learning and growth, this could propel them forward. Jane started talking about this informally with her team. She thought everyone would welcome this new system. However, CFO Carlos Hernandez is very upset. He says it cost the company $50,000 to implement a new telecom system and C&C can't possibly take on another expensive project until it is paid off. Sales manager Jason Wong thinks it will take more focus away from making sales, which he emphasizes is the only way to improve the bottom line. Jane thinks improved accountability would boost performance and wonders why her team doesn't get it.

Initial Thoughts

1. If you were Jane, how would you proceed to get your team on board for implementing a new performance scorecard?

2. What value do you think there is in a performance management system that measures outcomes other than financial indicators?

Your instructor may ask you to be part of a role play based on "The Scorecard" incident.

DISCOVER YOURSELF

For those students using CourseMate or CengageNOW, you can access the Daft/Marcic Assessment Library to take the questionnaires online and view dynamically updated comparative data.

Questionnaire 1

Instructions: This questionnaire can help you diagnose your approach to dealing with others when you adopt a formal or informal leadership role in a group. Think about how you usually behave in a group to get an assignment completed. If you have been a leader with direct reports, think back to that experience. Please answer honestly about how frequently you display each behavior.

Part A	Usually	Sometimes	Rarely
1. I make people's work on the job more pleasant.	○	○	○
2. I go out of my way to be helpful.	○	○	○
3. I show respect for others' feelings and opinions.	○	○	○
4. I work hard to maintain a friendly atmosphere on the team.	○	○	○
5. I think a lot about people's personal welfare.	○	○	○
6. I treat a person's failure as a chance for me to coach and help that individual.	○	○	○
7. I make it a point to be approachable and friendly toward others.	○	○	○
8. I am concerned more with relationships than with results.	○	○	○
9. I focus more on being pleasant with people than on execution of tasks.	○	○	○
10. People consider me cooperative and easy to work with.	○	○	○

Total Score Part A ________. (Sum questions 1–10 by giving 3 points for each Usually, 2 points for each Sometimes, and 1 point for each Rarely.)

Part B	Usually	Sometimes	Rarely
11. I focus more on execution of tasks than on being pleasant with people.	○	○	○
12. I hold people accountable for their performance.	○	○	○
13. I clearly tell people what I expect of them.	○	○	○
14. I check up on people to know how they are doing.	○	○	○
15. I assign people to specific roles and tasks.	○	○	○

	Usually	Sometimes	Rarely
16. I insist that people observe established agreements and deadlines.	○	○	○
17. I treat a person's failure as a time to think about replacing him or her.	○	○	○
18. I am firm with others about achieving outcomes.	○	○	○
19. I am concerned more with results than with relationships.	○	○	○
20. I like to get to the "bottom line" of things.	○	○	○

Total Score Part B ________. (Sum questions 11–20 by giving 3 points for each Usually, 2 points for each Sometimes, and 1 point for each Rarely.) Go to page 482 to interpret your scores.

Questionnaire 2

Instructions: Respond to each statement below based on the type of organization in which you would like to manage people. Rate how accurately each statement describes you based on whether the statement is clearly true or accurate, clearly false or inaccurate, or in the middle as somewhat true and somewhat false.

	True	Somewhat	False
1. Superiors have the right to tell people what to do based on their formal position rather than depending on personal relationships.	○	○	○
2. Managers are able to make things difficult for people if they don't comply.	○	○	○
3. Managers are able to give rewards or special benefits to people for doing what they are told.	○	○	○
4. Departments use a formal hierarchy rather than act like a family.	○	○	○
5. Team and organization members are loyal to their managers.	○	○	○
6. Employees conform to rather than debate company policies.	○	○	○
7. Bosses have the formal authority to make decisions rather than having to discuss issues with everyone.	○	○	○
8. People do what they are told rather than object and resist.	○	○	○
9. People are clear about whether they are superior or subordinate to others.	○	○	○
10. Employees obey their bosses regardless of their personal feelings.	○	○	○

Total Score ________. (Sum questions 1–10 by giving 3 points for each True, 2 points for each Somewhat, and 1 point for each False.) Go to page 484 to interpret your score.

DISCOVER YOURSELF

DISCOVER YOURSELF

Questionnaire 3

Instructions: Think about your strengths and preferences based on how you handle challenges and issues at school or work. Mark (a) or (b) for each of the following items, depending on which is more descriptive of you. There are no right or wrong answers.

1. For weekend activities, I prefer to
   _____ a. Plan in advance
   _____ b. Be free to do what I want
2. The work elements I prefer are
   _____ a. Creative
   _____ b. Organizing
3. It is more natural for me
   _____ a. To hold people accountable
   _____ b. To let people get away with things
4. I think it is more important
   _____ a. How something looks (form)
   _____ b. How well something works (function)
5. When keeping records, I tend to
   _____ a. Be careful about documentation
   _____ b. Be haphazard about documentation
6. I can best contribute to a strategy by encouraging
   _____ a. Openness to a wide range of assumptions and ideas
   _____ b. Thoroughness when implementing ideas and plans
7. If I run a group or a project, I
   _____ a. Try to figure out specific goals, timelines, and expected outcomes
   _____ b. Have the general idea and let others figure out how to do the tasks
8. When running a group or project, I
   _____ a. Encourage people to do their own thing
   _____ b. Make people accountable for their part
9. One of my strengths is
   _____ a. Commitment to making things work
   _____ b. Commitment to a dream for the future
10. To understand how something works, I prefer
    _____ a. A general impression
    _____ b. Measurements and metrics
11. I am good at
    _____ a. Setting specific goals in various areas of my life
    _____ b. Moving ahead without specific goals
12. When running a group or a project, I usually
    _____ a. Trust that things will work out in the end
    _____ b. Seek specific feedback after each incremental step

Total Score _______. Score one point for each "a" answer to odd-numbered questions and one point for each "b" answer to even-numbered questions. Go to page 488 to interpret your score.

Questionnaire 4[1]

Instructions: As a manager, how much emphasis will you give to each of the behaviors described in the statements below? Find out by indicating whether each statement is True, Somewhat, or False for you, based on your realistic expectations and beliefs for handling your management job.

	True	Somewhat	False
1. I will readily confront and fire someone who isn't working out for the interests of my team or organization.	○	○	○
2. Selecting the right people for a winning business team is as important to me as getting the best athletes for a winning sports team.	○	○	○
3. I expect to spend 40 to 50 percent of my management time on issues such as recruiting, developing, and placing people.	○	○	○
4. I will paint a realistic picture of negative job aspects that will help scare off the wrong people for the job.	○	○	○
5. My priority as a manager is first to hire the right people, second to put people in the right positions, and third to decide strategy and vision.	○	○	○
6. With the right people on my team, problems of motivation and supervision will largely go away.	○	○	○
7. I expect that hiring the right people will be a lengthy and arduous process.	○	○	○
8. I view firing someone as helping them find a new position where they will find fulfillment.	○	○	○
9. I will evaluate my people based as much on building a positive culture as on meeting metrics for results.	○	○	○
10. I will prefer people who are humble and demonstrate more concern for the team than for themselves.	○	○	○

Total Score ________. (Sum questions 1–10 by giving 3 points for each True, 2 points for each Somewhat, and 1 point for each False.) Go to page 491 to interpret your score.

GO ONLINE to find additional questionnaires at www.cengagebrain.com, search for Daft/Marcic Building Management Skills 1e, click on Free Online Resources, click on Additional Self-Assessments.

- Authority Role Models
- Locus of Control

DISCOVER YOURSELF

SHUTTERSTOCK #53973379

Chapter 13: Achieving Desired Outcomes: Getting the Right People and Managing Performance

DISCOVER KNOWLEDGE

Clay Harris, a math teacher at Beers Elementary School, recently had one of the most harrowing experiences in his 20-year career in the Washington, D.C., public school system. It wasn't a fight in the classroom, a challenge from a student, or even a conflict with the principal. The event that put this veteran teacher on edge was his evaluation by a master educator from IMPACT, a new system that uses rigorous standards to appraise teacher performance—an evaluation that could have cost him his job. Harris is passionate about teaching, and he even spends weekends mentoring and tutoring his students, many of whom come from low-income families and are several grade levels behind. Yet, Harris scored low on several of the nine specific standards used by the IMPACT system. Washington D.C.'s evaluation system is part of a growing educational reform movement to try to hold teachers in America's public schools accountable for student progress.[2]

Many people think America's public schools are failing, so they welcome the new evaluation systems. Others argue that the systems are biased toward teachers in wealthier schools and will ultimately hurt rather than help school and student performance. School administrators will continue searching for the right way to assess and improve teacher performance. For any organization to succeed, managers have to have systems that hold people accountable for achieving specific desired results. This chapter describes how managers design systems to select the right people, make sure everyone's actions are aligned toward achieving the organization's goals, and hold people accountable for producing specific measurable outcomes.

TWO PATHS TO HIGH PERFORMANCE

Performance management is "a continuous process of identifying, measuring, and developing the performance of individuals and teams and aligning performance with strategic goals of the organization."[3] Managing performance means keeping everyone moving in the same direction and accountable for attaining specific results that help the company meet its overall goals. There is a clear correlation between effective performance management systems and an organization's strategic performance. All managers have to be skilled in performance management.

Effective managers pay attention to two paths to high performance: meet the needs of the work and meet the needs of the people who do the work. That is, managers have to be sure people can both accomplish their tasks and find some personal enjoyment and satisfaction in their work. To succeed as a manager, you need to be aware of the inherent tensions between the needs of work and the needs of people, be able to recognize which need is stronger in a specific situation, and understand your own personal preference for focusing either on work or on people. Exhibit 13.1 illustrates various needs a manager has to meet to achieve a team's or department's purpose.

Meet Task Needs

A major part of your job as a manager will be to develop a disciplined approach that accomplishes work on time and within budget, while also aligning the work of your team or department with the needs and goals of the larger organization. In many organizations, government regulations, industry standards, and special guidelines have to be followed that also shape work procedures.[4] As illustrated in Exhibit 13.1, meeting task needs first involves setting goals and defining desired outcomes for the team's work. In addition, you need to ensure that the structure of work is clear, the roles for team members are well-defined, and mechanisms exist for lateral communication and coordination. A plan of action gives people specific details about where they are headed and how to get there. To keep work progressing as desired, you will periodically monitor the team's work, which requires developing metrics to measure operations and evaluate the performance of individuals as well as the team

Exhibit 13.1 Two Paths to High Performance

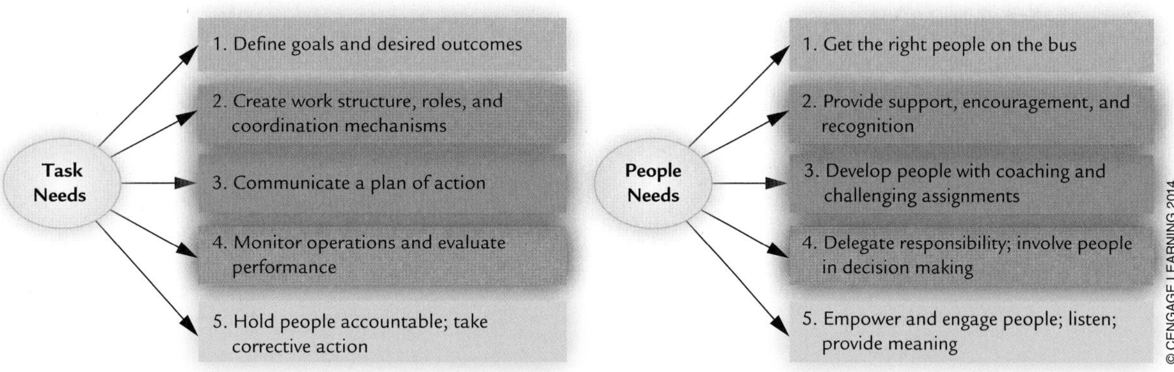

as a whole. You can establish benchmarks to measure performance and see if progress conforms to expected standards. The final task need shown in Exhibit 13.1 is to hold people accountable for outcomes and take any needed corrective actions.

Meet People Needs

The second set of needs you must meet as a manager—the needs of people—is also illustrated in Exhibit 13.1.[5] The importance of personal relationships has been emphasized throughout this book. Particularly in Chapters 7 through 10, we have presented some of the challenges managers face and techniques for resolving issues when dealing with the needs of people. People and relationship issues take up a large portion of a manager's time and attention. The first people need is the need to get the right people on the bus, which means hiring people who fit the team's culture and the requirements of the job. Once you get them on board, you have to support, encourage, motivate, recognize, and develop team members as they carry out their tasks. As we discussed in Chapter 9, one way to meet people needs is by coaching and developing people, including offering challenging assignments and delegating work so that people grow to be capable of larger responsibilities. Another approach is to consult with people on decisions to engage them in management responsibility as well as task accomplishment. Engagement and empowerment, as described in Chapter 7, are key ways to meet the needs of people so they are motivated to work, grow, and learn.

Do You Have a Task or a People Orientation?

Researchers have identified two meta-categories, or broadly defined behavior categories, that all managers apply to some extent to drive performance.[6] These two basic behavior patterns are called *task-oriented behavior* and *relationship-oriented behavior*. Exhibit 13.2 describes typical task and relationship behaviors depending on whether a manager focuses primarily on work tasks, primarily on people, relatively equally on both, or on neither. As a manager, you might naturally lean toward one behavioral style and be able to adapt your style to fit other categories shown in Exhibit 13.2.

A high-task and low-relationship style (Quadrant 1 of the exhibit) means that a manager focuses primarily on work structure such as planning short-term activities and monitoring operations and performance, while giving little attention to the people needs of team members. A low-task and high-relationship style (Quadrant 3), on the other hand, means a manager focuses on providing personal support, involvement, and recognition to people while paying little attention to the structure and operational needs of the work. A Quadrant 2 manager would be focused on both work and people fairly equally, and a Quadrant 4 manager would not be focused on either.

Studies have also looked at the situations in which a specific management style tends to be effective. The effectiveness of a manager's focus and behavior is *contingent* upon organizational situations. Thus, a manager's style that is effective in one situation might be ineffective in another. The nature of the work and

Exhibit 13.2 Two Broad Categories of Leader Focus and Style

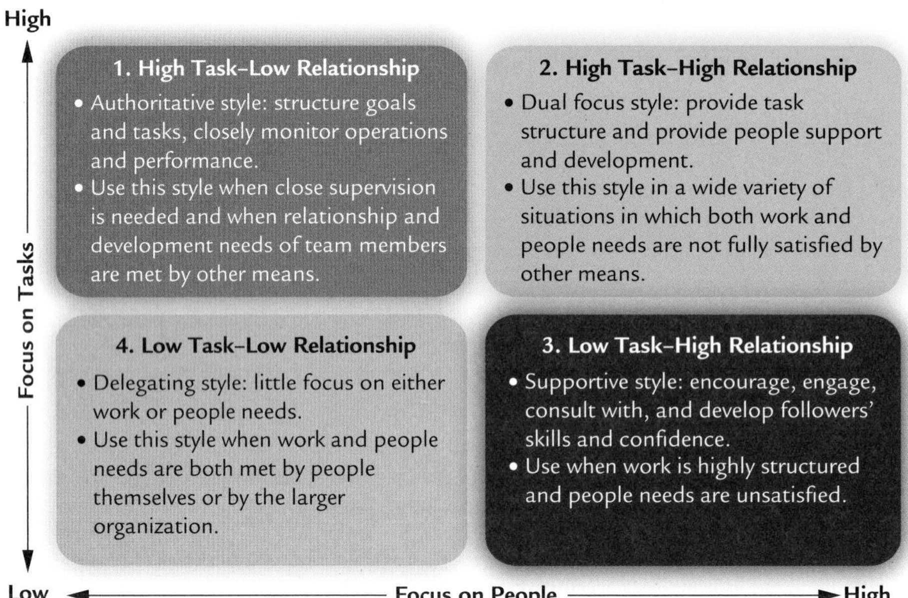

Source: Based on Gary Yukl, Angela Gordon, and Tom Taber, "A Hierarchical Taxonomy of Leadership Behavior: Integrating a Half Century of Behavior Research," *Journal of Leadership and Organization Studies* 9, no. 1 (2002): 15–32.

the maturity and cohesiveness of team members are two variables that make a significant difference to the most effective style of management.[7] The high-task style in Quadrant 1 works best when people are not mature enough to work on their own, for example. A high focus on relationships in Quadrant 3 is effective on an assembly line where work is highly structured but the interpersonal needs of people are not met. A dual focus in Quadrant 2 works well when both work and people needs have to be met by the manager. And a style of complete delegation in Quadrant 4 fits a situation where neither work structure nor people needs have to be met by the manager to facilitate high performance, such as with employees who have high levels of

DISCOVER KNOWLEDGE

DISCOVER YOURSELF

Interpret Your Score: Task vs. People Orientation (Questionnaire 1)

Comparative data for **Orientation toward People and Relationships** (Part A): Thirty-person Mean score = 25.8; Top Quartile = 28–30; Bottom Quartile = 19 to 24. An above-average score suggests that you are "high" on relationship behavior. A below-average score suggests that you are "low" on relationship orientation. Comparative data for **Orientation toward Tasks and Outcomes** (Part B): Thirty-person Mean score = 23.4; Top Quartile = 26–29; Bottom Quartile = 10–21. An above-average score here suggests that you are "high" on task-oriented behavior. A below-average score suggests that you are "low" on task orientation.

Check which of the following best represents your leadership style. Look at Exhibit 13.2 to see the quadrant in which you fit.

______Low Task, Low Relationship

______Low Task, High Relationship

______High Task, Low Relationship

______High Task, High Relationship

Does your quadrant seem correct to you? How would you like to change your orientation? What steps can you take to do so? CNOW and CourseMate users can access dynamically updated comparative data through www.cengagebrain.com.

© CENGAGE LEARNING 2014

education, experience, and commitment. If a manager can properly diagnose a situation and find the flexibility to apply the appropriate style, a successful performance outcome is likely. If the manager has an inflexible style, high performance is likely only when the manager is in a situation that fits his or her particular style.

THE ROLE OF HARD POWER AND FORMAL AUTHORITY

When George Schaefer took over as CEO of Caterpillar in the mid-1980s, the maker of large construction equipment, engines, and power systems was losing $1 million a day seven days a week. Schaefer knew something had to be done, and fast. One problem he saw was that people weren't being held accountable for meeting specific targets. Schaefer changed the authority structure to give division managers the freedom to design their own products, develop their own manufacturing processes, and set their own prices rather than getting permission or directives from headquarters. However, the new freedom came with responsibility to meet stringent profitability goals. The division managers would be held strictly accountable. Schaefer told them their bonuses would be based on meeting the targets, and any division that couldn't demonstrate 15 percent ROA (return on assets) was subject to elimination.[8]

George Schaefer used the power and authority granted by his position as CEO to establish new guidelines for performance at Caterpillar. Even as a lower-level manager, you will sometimes have to rely on the power and authority of your formal position to manage employee performance and accountability. For managers to hold people accountable means that they require them to meet specific standards of performance and produce specific results, which often depends on the use of power.

Power is the potential ability of one person in an organization to influence other people to bring about desired outcomes.[9] Recall from Chapter 8 that there are five types of manager power, categorized as either *hard power* or *soft power*. Soft power was discussed in detail in Chapter 8. The source of soft power is a manager's ability to earn respect, trust, and commitment based on the manager's personal style and expertise. People are willing to work harder, be more cooperative, and collaborate with team members when they genuinely admire their manager's competence and style.[10] In this chapter, we turn our attention to the use of hard power, which is power that stems largely from a person's position of authority in the organization. Hard power, or positional power, includes legitimate, reward, and coercive power, as described in Exhibit 13.3.

Managers can use the power of their position to get compliance from those in a lower position on the hierarchical ladder. When managers absolutely have to achieve the results mandated by their position, they may use their hard power to do so, as George Schaefer

DISCOVER KNOWLEDGE

Exhibit 13.3 Sources of Hard Power for Managers

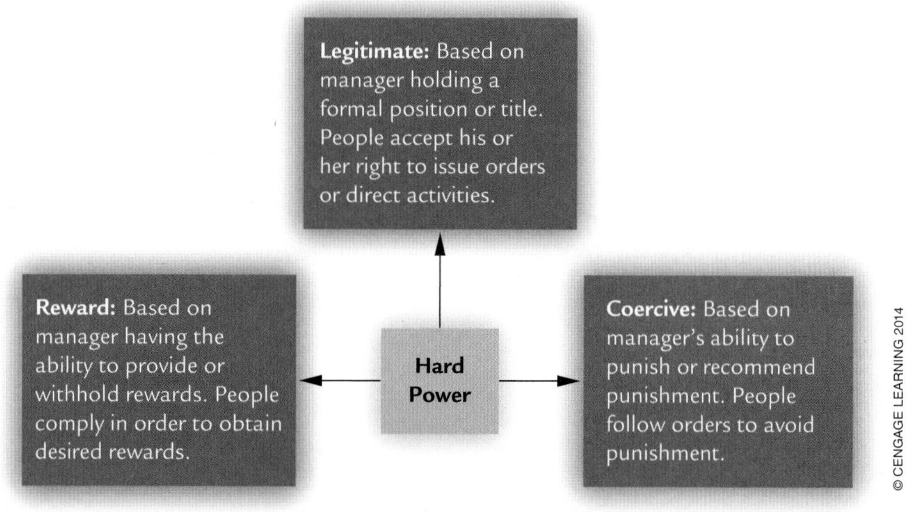

did at Caterpillar. A manager has the right to expect directives to be followed, for example (legitimate power), and can use rewards and punishment to motivate direct reports (reward power, coercive power). At Caterpillar, George Schaefer used all three types of hard power to get results: issuing directives to meet specific targets (legitimate); offering bonuses tied to meeting goals (reward); and threatening to close divisions that didn't meet the standards (coercive).

Legitimate Power of Position

Legitimate power stems from the authority granted via a formal position in an organization. Once a person has been made a supervisor, most employees accept that they are obligated to follow that person's direction with respect to work activities. A manager's formal authority is a force for achieving desired outcomes, but only as prescribed by the organizational hierarchy and reporting relationships. Three properties[11] identify authority:

1. *Authority is vested in organizational positions.* People have authority because of the positions they hold, not because of personal characteristics or resources.
2. *Subordinates accept authority.* Subordinates comply because they believe position holders have a legitimate right to exercise authority.
3. *Authority flows down the vertical hierarchy.* Authority exists along the formal chain of command, and positions at the top of the hierarchy are vested with more formal authority than are positions at the bottom.

Resources: Rewards and Punishments

Organizations allocate huge amounts of resources. Buildings are constructed, salaries are paid, and equipment and supplies are distributed. These resources are allocated downward from top management.[12] Managers have control over resources that can be used as rewards and punishments and are thus sources of power.

Reward Power

Power that stems from the authority of a manager to bestow rewards on people is called **reward power.** As a manager, you might have access to formal rewards such as pay increases or promotions. You can use rewards to influence behavior because lower-level employees are motivated to receive rewards and depend on managers for the financial and physical resources to perform their jobs.

Coercive Power

The negative side of reward power is **coercive power.** This refers to the power to punish or recommend punishment. Managers have coercive power when they have the right to fire or demote subordinates, criticize, or withhold pay increases and promotions. For example, if you are the sales manager and a salesperson does not perform as well as expected, you would have the coercive power to criticize, reprimand, put a negative letter in the salesperson's employment file, and affect the person's chances for a raise or promotion. The use of coercive power is sometimes necessary, but good managers limit their use of this negative type of power.

DISCOVER YOURSELF

Interpret Your Score: Formal Authority (Questionnaire 2)

Your score for this questionnaire reveals your attitude and preference for having formal authority and a formal hierarchy as a manager. Comparative data for **Formal Authority Attitudes:** Thirty-person Mean score = 22.6; Top Quartile = 25–28; Bottom Quartile = 15–20. In an organization that emphasizes a formal hierarchy, power and status are clear, and people are more likely to do what they are told. In an organization that is more informal, manager power is based more on discussion, consensus building, and personal relationships, which are messier and less clear-cut. If your score is high, you would likely be more comfortable managing with formal authority rather than managing in an egalitarian setting. If your score is low, you would probably prefer to be a manager in a more informal, collegial organizational culture.

Compare your score here to your score for using soft-power tactics in Questionnaire 4 in Chapter 8. What type of industry would have organization power relationships in which you would be most comfortable? Do you think most organizations today rely more on formal authority or soft-power? Why? CNOW and CourseMate users can access dynamically updated comparative data through www.cengagebrain.com.

© CENGAGE LEARNING 2014

ACCOUNTABILITY-BASED MANAGEMENT

Effective managers use both hard and soft power in organizations. Soft power is excellent for building coalitions and personal support for a manager's decisions and actions, as discussed in Chapter 8. Hard power, such as formal authority and reward power, plays an important role in setting up and applying systems for holding people accountable for their performance. **Accountability** means that people with various responsibilities in organizations are subject to reporting and justifying task outcomes to those above them in the chain of command.[13]

The Need for Accountability

Alan Robbins, founder of Plastic Lumber Company, believed if he treated people right, they would do a good job. When he started the company, which converts plastic milk and soda bottles into fake lumber, Robbins tried to be both a boss and a friend to his employees. Things soon went haywire. Some workers were frequently absent or late without calling, showed up drunk or under the influence of drugs, and even started fights on the factory floor. Production quotas were rarely met, and employees who genuinely wanted to do a good job were frustrated by the lack of order and the fact that some employees seemed to get away with anything. Robbins learned quickly that he had to take a different approach to management.[14]

Here is a fact you will have to face as a manager: Human beings have bad habits and weaknesses, and these can come out on the job when people are not held accountable for their behavior and work outcomes. When there is a lack of accountability for subordinates' actions and behavior, it creates problems for managers, employees, and the organization. Who picks up the slack if you don't hold your subordinates accountable? More than likely it will be the responsible workers who end up cleaning up the messes that the less-stellar performers leave behind. After a while the best workers will burn out, resent carrying the extra workload, reduce their efforts, and maybe even leave the organization. Team and individual performance suffers and an atmosphere of blame develops. When no one is accountable, then anyone can be blamed for errors, missed deadlines, and not reaching goals.

The *blame game* is easy to play when a culture of not holding people accountable is present in an organization. Here are a few ways people play the blame game:

- *It's Not My Job* – People narrowly define their job as doing a specific task instead of getting the result: "That's not what I am paid to do."
- *Finger Pointing* – People blame others or events for their own failures: "Marketing gave us the wrong forecasts."
- *Tell Me What To Do* – People insist that the decision was above their pay grade and they have patiently been awaiting instructions from on high: "Of course I wanted to take action but I've been held up by the dummies upstairs."[15]

An Accountability Cycle

Mark Pincus, founder and chief executive of Zynga, uses a valuable accountability tool he learned from venture capitalist John Doerr. The technique, called O.K.R. (Objectives and Key Results), was originally developed at Intel and is also used at Google. The whole company, as well as each individual, team, or department, has one objective and three measurable key results. If two out of the three results are achieved, the overall objective has been reached. If all three have been achieved, then the individual or team has hit a homerun. "We put the whole company on that, so everyone knows their O.K.R.s," Pincus said. "And that is a good, simple organizing principle that keeps people focused on three things that matter—not the top ten." At the beginning of each week Pincus asks each employee to write down his or her three priorities for the week. Then on Friday everyone checks to see how much was accomplished on the three priorities. Three priorities is just the right number to help people stay focused, not burn out, and have a sense of accomplishment at the end of the week.[16]

A manager's direct action is required to counter the tendency people sometimes have to let things slide or play the blame game. Managers like Mark Pincus use specific tools and techniques to keep people focused on performance. For organizations to function well, everyone needs to know what they are accountable for and accept the responsibility for performing it. One system you can use to manage people and projects is called the **accountability cycle,** illustrated in Exhibit 13.4. There are five essential steps that are explained in detail in the following sections.[17]

Exhibit 13.4 The Accountability Cycle

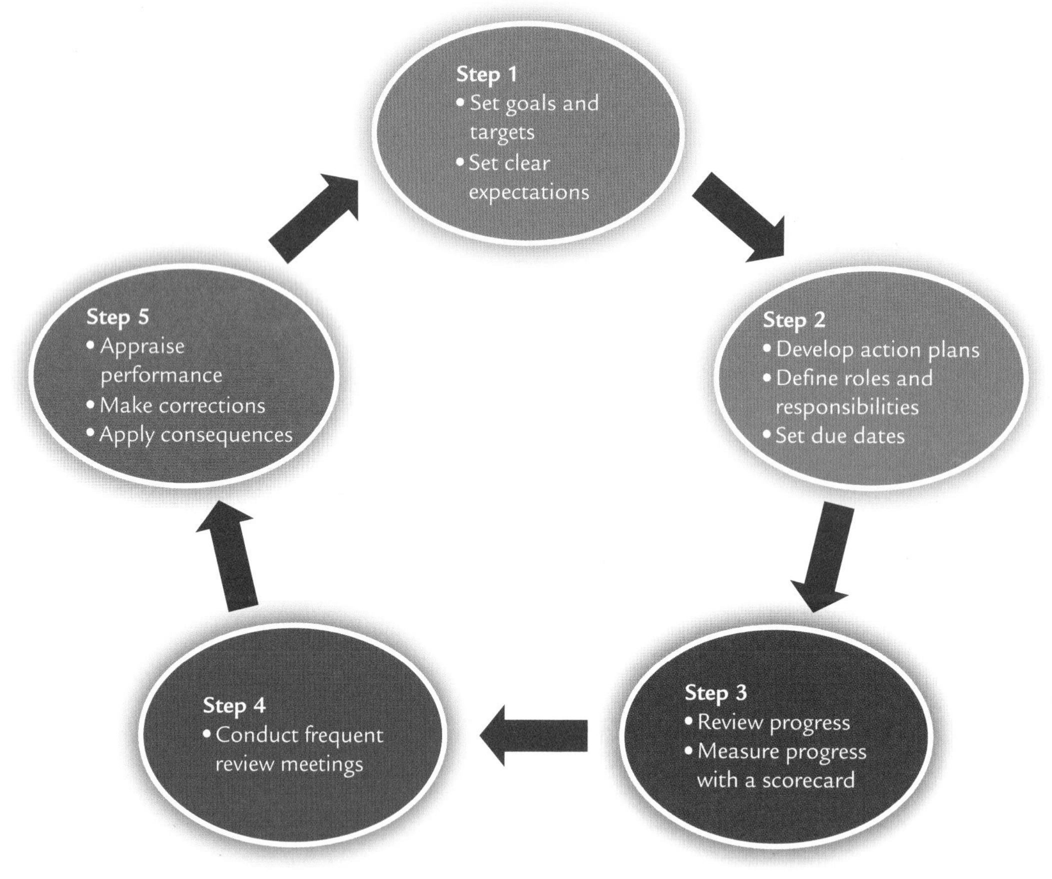

© CENGAGE LEARNING 2014

Set Goals and Expectations

Goals promote success. When we don't have them, we are rudderless and prone to wander off course. They define a context and a focus for the work to be done. As discussed in Chapter 7, goals can increase incentive, motivation, drive, and energy.

At the beginning of any project, it is important to set clear goals, expectations, and targets. This engages employees to look beyond day-to-day activities to answer the question "What are we trying to accomplish?"

However, managers and team leaders sometimes fall short when it comes to setting goals that effectively engage employees and spur them to high performance. They may set goals that are too broad, for example, or set goals without clear measures and deadlines. Research has found that effective goal setting entails SMART goals, an acronym used to encompass five criteria that are essential to defining and applying goals that people can embrace and accomplish.[18] The SMART criteria for effective goals, as illustrated in Exhibit 13.5, are:

Specific:	What exactly will you accomplish with this goal?
Measurable:	How will you know when you have accomplished the goal?
Achievable:	Is the action required to achieve the goal realistic, with effort and commitment? Do you have the needed resources?
Relevant:	Why is this goal significant to your job or organization?
Time-Bound:	When will you complete the achievement of the goal?

Making goals SMART goals enhances their power. For example, the manager of a university administrative department coordinating the annual Education in the Arts conference set a goal of increasing attendance for the 2010 event. The staff knew how many people

Exhibit 13.5 SMART Criteria for Effective Goals

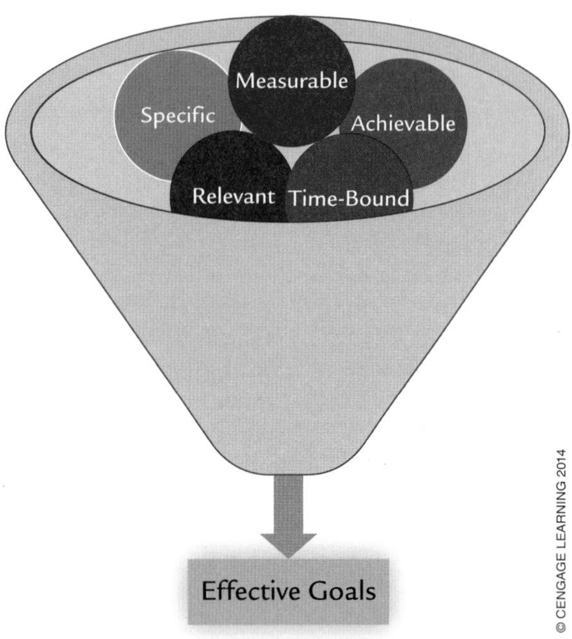

© CENGAGE LEARNING 2014

had attended the previous conference held in 2008, but the goal was too vague to be motivating or provide a standard for high performance. Employees became actively engaged in striving for the goal when the manager revised it into a SMART goal: "To achieve attendance of at least 150 guests at the Education in the Arts conference on May 15, 2010 by directly contacting previous attendees and sending a promotional email to all relevant education professionals by September 30, 2009, with a follow-up on January 15, 2010."

In addition to the SMART goal criteria, goals should be jointly derived to the extent possible. Goals that are mutually agreed upon between employee and supervisor create stronger commitment and a higher level of motivation and performance, as discussed in Chapter 7. Brainstorming as a team helps employees to feel part of the future of an organization and increases their accountability. As a manager, you will find that your direct reports have valuable insights and information that can balance out goals and make them more realistic and achievable.

Develop Action Plans

This step involves defining specific plans, roles, responsibilities, and due dates. An action plan describes the detailed course of action people will follow to achieve the stated goals. Managers at various levels of the hierarchy create action plans for individuals, departments, and the whole organization. Each individual, for example, plays a role in helping the organization accomplish its goals and purpose. When roles and responsibilities are clearly defined, people can be accountable for the benchmarks they need to accomplish. Due dates establish a firm commitment between parties.

Measure Progress with a Scorecard (Metrics)

People need to know how well they are progressing toward meeting goals. To encourage accountability, managers measure results by gathering data and comparing activities against previous statistics or standards. Are people making adequate progress toward goals? Are there performance gaps that need attention? One way you can keep people focused on goals is to give them a way to monitor their own progress on a regular basis. There are different options for creating a scorecard that measures progress and indicates what still needs to be accomplished.

Many organizations use performance dashboards that keep people informed of progress toward goals. You can see numerous examples of dashboards by typing "performance dashboard images" into your Internet search engine. The scorecard can be a graph, a bar chart, a pie chart, or even a simple thermometer image that shows

DISCOVER YOURSELF

Interpret Your Score: Accountability Preference (Questionnaire 3)

Your score for this questionnaire indicates your accountability preference, which is your inclination toward setting goals, developing action plans, measuring progress, and holding people accountable in alignment with the accountability cycle described in the chapter. Comparative data for **Accountability Preference:** Thirty-person Mean score = 8.7; Top Quartile = 11–12; Bottom Quartile = 3–7. A high score means that developing and using an accountability system would be rather natural for you. A low score suggests that your orientation is less toward strict standards of accountability and more toward other qualities such as creativity and spontaneity. If your score is low, you may want to think more about accountability if you aspire to become a manager. What would be the ideal role of accountability thinking in your life? Can you think of disadvantages to accountability? CNOW and CourseMate users can access dynamically updated comparative data through www.cengagebrain.com.

© CENGAGE LEARNING 2014

DISCOVER KNOWLEDGE

progress toward the goal. Nonprofit organizations seeking community donations for a specific cause, such as restoring a historic church, for example, often put up a big thermometer image indicating the level of funds raised. As people see the thermometer going up, energy and enthusiasm builds for reaching the goal. The same thing can happen in an organization. The important point is to make the scorecard something people see on a regular basis. The team leader can also discuss progress daily to help build buzz. As results of the scorecard improve, people become more engaged and compelled to work toward the goals.[19]

Review Progress

To keep people progressing, managers carefully review progress frequently, at least once a month, rather than waiting for an annual performance review. This intense and frequent focus keeps goals in constant sight and attainable. Progress reviews enable managers and employees to see whether they are on target or whether corrective action is needed. If review shows that adequate progress toward goals isn't being made, action plans can be changed.

Appraise Performance

The final step in the accountability cycle is to appraise performance and apply corrections and consequences. Managers carefully evaluate whether goals have been achieved for both individuals and departments. Success or failure to achieve goals can become part of the performance appraisal system and be linked to salary increases and other rewards. The appraisal of departmental and overall corporate performance shapes goals for the next cycle. After an appraisal, a review of success and failure is important so that everyone can learn and improve. If an individual fails to deliver, for instance, the manager holds the employee accountable to come up with a solution to the problem. But the manager also wants to encourage learning. Here are some questions[20] that you as a manager can get people to ask themselves as they review their failure to meet objectives:

- Present: What can I do to get back on track?
- Future: What can I do to prevent this problem from happening again?
- Past: What could I have done to prevent this problem?

LEADINGWORDS

"To be a manager means sharing in the responsibility for the performance of the enterprise."
—Peter Drucker
management expert, consultant, and author

"The growth and development of people is the highest calling of leadership."
—Harvey S. Firestone
American businessman, founder of The Firestone Tire & Rubber Company

"I've learned that hinting or trying to dance around issues is probably the worst thing you can do for somebody whose performance you're responsible for. . . . Assuming I have all the right people in the right positions, I think the most important thing I can do for them is provide direct, honest, clear feedback."
—Tiffany Cooper Gueye
CEO of BELL (Building Educated Leaders for Life)

"Great companies have high cultures of accountability."
—Steve Ballmer
CEO of Microsoft

© CENGAGE LEARNING 2014

The accountability cycle can repeat itself on a weekly, monthly, quarterly, or annual basis. Using a performance measurement system such as the five-step accountability cycle outlined in Exhibit 13.4 helps people see how their jobs and performance contribute to the business, giving them a sense of ownership and commitment. Performance is improved when employees are committed to attaining the goal, are motivated because they help decide what is expected, and are free to be resourceful. Goals at lower levels are aligned with and enable the attainment of goals at top management levels.

GET THE RIGHT PEOPLE ON THE BUS

When revenues went from $2.6 million to $4 million in one recent year, Michael Mahoney, CEO of Brittenford Systems of Reston, Virginia, was so busy that he no longer had time for the things he was really good at—strategy, client relationships, and achieving results. He decided to hire a strong second-in-command who was good at operations and project management. However, in his rush to find help, Mahoney hired the wrong person three times in succession. The entire company was traumatized and demoralized from the ups and downs of these bad hires. Mahoney decided to step back and revamp the software company's approach to hiring. The next time, he took the following steps to find the right person for his second-in-command:

1. *Define the position.* Mahoney worked with other managers and employees to create a detailed list of the top six to eight things for which the new hire would be accountable during the first year on the job.
2. *Determine skills, education, and behavioral profile.* Next, they identified how much education and experience the person needed to perform well in the No. 2 position, and listed the key skills and behaviors needed to effectively perform in the job.
3. *Post the job in the right places.* Mahoney learned to find the best outlets for posting the job based on the nature of the job. Mahoney's open position was for a software company executive, so he posted the job on Monster.com and in a local industry newsletter.
4. *Go through a process of elimination.* After receiving candidates' applications, Mahoney eliminated 80 percent of applicants based on insufficient résumés or their online behavioral profile score.
5. *Conduct preliminary phone interviews.* Next, Mahoney's staff designed a set of ten questions for phone interviews that were conducted by an administrative person. This information eliminated another 15 percent of applicants.
6. *Conduct second phone interviews and then in-person interviews.* Mahoney personally interviewed the remaining applicants by phone, and later held face-to-face interviews with those who passed his phone interview.
7. *Have team do the final interview.* Mahoney had his team members conduct the final interview of each candidate. After the interviews, the team members e-mailed Mahoney with a "yea" or "nay" vote on the candidates.
8. *Assign homework—the last step.* Before making the final decision, Mahoney asked the two remaining candidates to write a one-page strategy for the company.

The result of Michael Mahoney's four-month hiring odyssey was a terrific hire. Within 90 days, the new No. 2 increased Brittenford's sales pipeline, ramped up recruiting, and brought a new sense of optimism to the team.[21]

Michael Mahoney's approach may seem like a long and arduous process to hire the right person, but the four-month time period was insignificant compared to the many months he had spent hiring, working with, and then having to terminate the *wrong* people. Recent bestsellers such *Winning*, by Jack Welch, *Good to Great*, by Jim Collins, and *Execution: The Discipline of Getting Things Done*, by Larry Bossidy and Ram Charan, all make the same point: For an organization to succeed, managers have to get the right people on the bus. All organizations need a systematic process, such as that used at Brittenford Systems, to find and hire the right people for their specific needs and culture. There is no 100-percent guarantee that you will end up with a great hire every time by following the right steps. However, without a systematic and disciplined hiring model, there's a pretty good bet that you will end up with some bad hires that damage your team's culture and performance.[22] The following sections describe the key aspects of an effective hiring model.

Clearly Define the Position

To find the right person for any job, managers have to clearly define the position, just as Mahoney did at Brittenford Systems. Matching a person to the job starts with creating a clear understanding of the skills, attitudes, and aptitudes needed by the organization.[23] Assessing a job often falls in the jurisdiction of the human resources (HR) department, but other managers are involved too, especially for higher-level positions. HR may help with a formal *job analysis*, which is a procedure for gathering and interpreting information about the key duties, tasks, and responsibilities of a job. A *job description* summarizes duties, tasks, and responsibilities so the hiring manager can focus recruitment and selection efforts. A *job specification* offers details about knowledge, skills, education, and other requirements an applicant would need to perform the job.

Get the Word Out

Managers use both external and internal recruiting.[24] *External recruiting* is when the organization looks outside its ranks to fill a job position. Managers may use online job sites, social media, newspapers, industry newsletters, professional journals, job fairs, college recruiting, employee referrals, employment agencies, and other sources to get the word out. Sometimes, organizations offer incentives to current employees to recommend someone from outside the organization to apply for an opening. Current employees can use their networks, social media sites, and contacts to help the company fill vacant positions. Employee referrals are often one of the best sources for finding people who fit with the company culture.

Internal recruiting is when managers search within the organization for potential candidates. This promote-from-within approach is often used to fill managerial or higher-level positions. Internal candidates already have organizational experience and know-how. They are a proven commodity with a desire and commitment to grow with an organization. Internal hiring is also a morale booster because employees receive opportunities for career advancement and professional growth.

Select the Best Person

Some combination of interviews and testing is typically used to select the best person for the job.[25] Almost all managers use some type of interview as part of the hiring process. Exhibit 13.6 provides specific

Exhibit 13.6 Interviewing: What to Ask and What Not to Ask

Subject	Okay to Ask	Not Okay to Ask
Race	• Nothing	• Race or color of skin
National Origin	• Name of applicant • Did applicant ever work under a different name	• The origin of applicant's name • Ancestry or ethnicity
Age	• If applicant is over 18 years of age	• Age of applicant • When applicant graduated from high school
Disabilities	• If applicant has any disabilities that will prevent him or her from doing the job	• If applicant has any physical or mental defects • If applicant has ever filed a worker's compensation claim
Criminal Record	• If applicant has ever been convicted of a crime	• If applicant has ever been arrested
Religion	• Nothing	• Religious affiliation • Religious holidays applicant observes
Marital Status	• Nothing	• Marital status
Family Status	• Nothing	• Number of children or planned children • Childcare needs or arrangements in place
Education	• Where applicant went to school • Prior work experience	• When applicant graduated • Hobbies
Citizenship	• If applicant has a legal right to work in the United States	• If applicant is a citizen of another country

Sources: Based on George Bohlander, Scott Snell, and Arthur Sherman, *Managing Human Resources*, 12th ed. (Cincinnati, OH: South-Western, 2001), p. 207; and "Guidelines to Lawful and Unlawful Preemployment Inquiries, Appendix E," in Robert L. Mathis and John H. Jackson, *Human Resource Management*, 2nd ed. (Cincinnati, OH: South-Western, 2002), pp. 189–190.

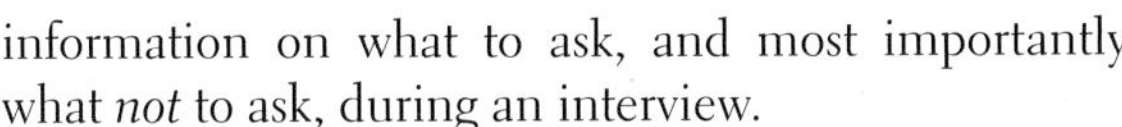

information on what to ask, and most importantly what *not* to ask, during an interview.

Managers use a variety of interviewing approaches to identify the right match for the position. Many organizations use multiple people to conduct interviews. Usually an HR representative will conduct an interview, along with the hiring manager, perhaps senior managers, and key staff members who will work with the new hire. Different eyes and ears will see and hear different aspects of the candidate to predict the person's fit with the job and the culture. Likewise, personality assessments provide a different perspective on a candidate. Some organizations provide candidates with a *realistic job preview (RJP)*. The RJP gives candidates a comprehensive view of the job and the organization. After reviewing the positive and negative aspects of the position, candidates can determine if they feel suited for the work, which helps determine a correct match.

Take Your Time

Hiring the wrong people is costly, time consuming, and discouraging. Following the steps of a disciplined hiring system slows things down and reduces the urgency to fill a position quickly. Rushing the hiring process usually leads to a poor decision. In addition to the techniques described above, most managers check references and many also do some snooping online, such as checking out a candidate's online profile on social media sites. Some organizations require drug screening, credit checks, and criminal background investigations.

Getting the right people on the bus takes time and effort. Sam Walton, the iconic founder of Walmart, said the primary criterion he looked for when hiring was common sense. He knew it when he saw it, so Walton selected people based on whether they had what he considered common sense and then developed them into leaders. He knew who to put on the bus.[26] Managers of consistently successful businesses—whether it's Walmart or a local convenience store—focus intensely and relentlessly on finding the right people.[27]

A Manager's Toughest Job: Getting Rid of Poor Performers

When Bob Keegan took over as CEO of Goodyear, he replaced 23 of the company's 24 top managers.[28] Keegan realized that getting the right people on the bus sometimes means you have to get rid of the wrong ones.

DISCOVER YOURSELF

Interpret Your Score: Getting the Right People on the Bus (Questionnaire 4)

Most new managers are shocked by the large amount of time, effort, and skill required to recruit, place, and retain the right people. The right people can make an organization great; the wrong people can be catastrophic. For example, when you have the right people, they can decide strategy and vision (item 5) and they will be naturally motivated and need little supervision (item 6). A high score on this questionnaire means you understand the importance and difficulty of finding the right people to work for you. A low score means you may assume that most people hired will work out or that it is pretty easy to find good people to work for you. Comparative data for **Hiring Attitudes:** Thirty-person Mean score = 22.3; Top Quartile = 24–28; Bottom Quartile = 16–20. Don't underestimate how hard it is to hire the right people. Your success as a manager will largely depend on the quality of the people around you. Do you think the emphasis placed on getting the right people on the bus is overrated? Why? CNOW and CourseMate users can access dynamically updated comparative data through www.cengagebrain.com.

DISCOVER KNOWLEDGE

© CENGAGE LEARNING 2014

As a manager, you may occasionally have to fire people. Managers who want to run great companies have to get rid of the poor performers, the people who simply cannot do the job, even after exhaustive training, coaching, and counseling.[29] Firing people is never easy or pleasant, but managers have a responsibility to get rid of people who aren't suited for the job and are not pulling their weight. Keeping poor performers isn't fair to other employees or to the organization's customers and other stakeholders. Tolerating poor performance, such as consistently missing goals, being sloppy, refusing to accept responsibility, or being dishonest creates a culture that forces the best people to pick up the slack. This leads to resentment, a demoralized staff, and a weaker organization. Even the most skillful and experienced manager may sometimes make hiring mistakes. How do you know if you need to get someone off the bus? If you would be relieved if the person quit, you know: It is time to be accountable as a manager and do what needs to be done.

DISCOVER KNOWLEDGE

HOW TO EVALUATE PEOPLE

John Donohoe, president and chief executive of eBay, says one thing he has learned as a manager is that you can't change people. All you can do, Donohoe says, is try to help them help themselves. Donohoe doesn't bother trying to make people do something they either can't do or don't want to do. Instead, he spends his time clarifying what needs to be done. Those who won't or can't do it have to be shifted to other positions where they can make a contribution or be fired. When Donohoe was CEO of Bain & Company, his performance was appraised by a committee that interviewed 40 partners and would then present Donohoe with a 20-page document highlighting everything he could do better. Donohoe says he felt a great sense of freedom when he got that feedback. About a third of the suggestions were "right on the money" and Donohoe started immediately working on making the changes.[30]

As this example shows, even CEOs get evaluated. Most organizations have some sort of system by which they evaluate the performance of individual employees. Most managers prepare a written evaluation, and some also have employees write a self-appraisal to rate their own performance. A self-evaluation by an employee gives the individual the opportunity to look at his or her strengths, weaknesses, successes, and failures. This is a more productive approach than just the manager presenting a one-sided story. Once the written evaluations are finished, the manager and employee meet and discuss the results.

Conducting a Performance Appraisal

No matter what appraisal system is used, most managers and employees dread the performance appraisal discussion. Giving and receiving critical feedback isn't always easy, but having a better understanding of what a performance appraisal is and how best to conduct one can help alleviate some of the apprehension. **Performance appraisal** is the process by which a manager evaluates an employee's work effectiveness by using objective criteria, provides feedback to the employee, and shows where improvements are needed. The objective is not to get an employee's agreement during the appraisal discussion, but rather to help the employee understand why his or her performance was rated as it was and how the individual can improve weak points. Performance appraisal is a tool that can leverage the strengths people have, help them correct their weaknesses, and deepen what they do really well. It can be a time to build trust and mutual respect between employee and manager.[31] The following sections offer suggestions for making the performance appraisal experience beneficial to both the individual and the organization.

Be Prepared

Preparation is the key to a smooth appraisal interview. Both the manager and the employee should take the appraisal process seriously and put forth a sincere effort in completing their written evaluations. As a manager, you should keep track of how each employee is performing throughout the year. Don't wait until evaluation time to start observing people's performance. It is easy to forget both positive and negative behaviors, so smart managers keep notes so they have easy recall at evaluation time. To be most effective, feedback needs to be linked to specific examples instead of vague impressions.

Set the Tone

During the appraisal interview, you should set a tone for the meeting that is amicable and conducive to having a positive outcome. This can be a time to show commitment and partnership toward working together over the next year. It is important to set aside adequate time for the appraisal interview so you won't be rushed or distracted. Remember that your behavior during this interview can either improve or damage your relationship with the individual employee.

Conduct the Interview

You might want to review the ILETs model for conducting difficult conversations that we described in Chapter 10. Usually, it is best to let the employee speak first about his or her self-appraisal and work performance. Listen closely, express thanks for the time the individual took to complete the evaluation, and acknowledge the subordinate's perspective. After you have listened, it is time to give your opinion of the individual's performance. Here are some guidelines:

- *Show appreciation.* Through the appraisal process, it is important to let people know they are valued

7 STEPS TO...

Turning a Performance Review into a Fight

1. **Don't show your human side.** Making the interview "all business" makes an already-stressful situation even more intimidating. Good managers genuinely care about the well-being and development of their employees, and the performance review is a time to sincerely let people know that.
2. **Save up all the bad stuff.** A performance review isn't the place to hit a person with tons of negative feedback on issues that have never been raised before. Good managers give a continuous flow of feedback throughout the year.
3. **Play dirty politics.** Giving a review that will hurt a team member's chance for promotion because you don't want to lose her, or playing team members against one another are *not* behaviors that benefit employees or the organization.
4. **Quickly shut down disagreement.** True, the purpose is not to get the employee to agree with you—or to change your evaluation—but you should let the other person tell his or her side of the story. Some experts say that as soon as a disagreement pops up, the manager should shift into active listening mode.
5. **Make it all about the paperwork.** The interview isn't a time for filling out forms and preparing documents. Save that for later so you can focus completely on the employee—his or her goals, contributions, weaknesses, needs, concerns, capabilities, and potential.
6. **Compare team members with one another.** If you want to damage both your relationship with the employee and your team's cohesiveness, open with a statement such as, "You and Sarah have the same level of experience, but she's delivering twice the results!" Good managers approach each employee as an individual, not by comparing people.
7. **Sweat the small details.** Pointing out every minor problem you've noticed, including that the employee leaves his dirty coffee cup in the break room sink, wastes time and loses sight of the issues that truly matter for individual, team, and organizational performance.

Sources: Based on ideas in Aastha Dogra, "Performance Review Tips," *Buzzle.com*, http://www.buzzle.com/articles/performance-review-tips.html (accessed December 24, 2010); Margaret Steen, "Performance Review: Meeting with the Boss," *Monster.com*, http://career-advice.monster.com/in-the-office/workplace-issues/performance-review-meeting-with-the-boss-hot-jobs/article.aspx (accessed December 24, 2010); and "Performance Review Meetings: Common Ground for Constructive Feedback System," *Leadership Champions*, June 29, 2009, http://leadershipchamps.wordpress.com/2009/06/29/performance-review-meetings-common-ground-for-constructive-feedback-system/ (accessed December 26, 2010).

DISCOVER KNOWLEDGE

and respected. Appraisal shouldn't be a time for focusing only on what someone has done poorly. Find the individual's strengths and successes and build them up at the same time as you acknowledge any weaknesses and shortcomings.

- *Be candid.* Performance appraisals that lack frankness and honesty or that fail to focus clearly on developmental needs are a waste of time for everyone. Good managers don't avoid difficult issues in hopes that poor performance will improve on its own.[32]
- *Compare performance to goals.* This is safe ground. Do not discuss character, personality, or rumors. If your appraisal has found a "gap" between the employee's goal and actual performance, make this the focus of your discussion and feedback. As a starting point, identify a larger organizational goal to explain how the employee's goal supports it. People can change when they understand the consequences of their behavior and performance for the larger team and organization.[33] Work together to address any problems and together find the reasons for the performance gaps.
- *Come up with a workable plan.* Once gaps have been identified, let the employee propose a solution instead of immediately jumping in with your ideas. Success is more likely if the employee is the architect developing the plan. However, if the employee is struggling to come up with a solution, offer some suggestions and make the plan together. Create a plan that has specific goals, timelines, and benchmarks to measure success.

- *Document everything.* Document what was discussed during the interview and make certain the action plan is put in writing and signed by both you and the employee. Both the manager and employee should have a copy of the documents, and a copy should also be kept in the employee's work record.

Follow Up

You should periodically follow up with the employee throughout the year to see how the plan is moving forward. This will make the next appraisal interview easier because there will be accomplished goals and employee satisfaction. The best managers meet formally with their direct reports at least three or even four times a year; once to set goals, once or twice to get an update on progress toward the goals, and finally to review performance at year-end. Meeting more often provides a better chance to tweak goals if necessary and minimizes surprises at the end of the year.[34]

A Controversial Appraisal System

Some companies have gone to a forced ranking system as a way to evaluate and reward people, particularly those at supervisory and management levels. The **forced ranking system** ranks employees according to their relative performance: 20 percent would be placed in the top group of performers; 70 percent have to be ranked in the middle; and 10 percent are ranked at the bottom. The bottom tier are given a set period of time to improve their performance, and if they don't improve, they are fired. The idea behind the forced ranking of employees is that everyone will be motivated to improve their performance.

However, forced ranking of employees is controversial because it compares people to people rather than comparing each person to a standard of performance. The advantages of a forced ranking system are that it: (1) forces reluctant managers to make difficult decisions and identify the best and worst performers; and (2) creates and sustains a high-performance culture in which people continuously improve. The disadvantages are that the forced ranking system: (1) may increase cut-throat competition among employees; (2) discourages collaboration and teamwork; and (3) potentially harms morale.[35] Many companies have dropped the forced ranking system or modified it so that it doesn't insist on quotas for underperformers. A study by the Institute for Corporate Productivity found

DISCOVER KNOWLEDGE

What's Your Problem?

Q: I've been a manager in a retail men's clothing store for two years. Our turnover, as in most retail, is high, and I don't want to do anything to make it higher, because it costs money to replace someone. One of my employees, Seth, is a pretty decent salesman. He meets or exceeds weekly goals half the time and the other half, he falls short. In other words, he is quite uneven. I've observed him carefully and I know exactly why he falls below the mark so often. He slacks off, becomes introverted and unfocused at those times, and just does not seem to care. His annual review is coming up, and I am thinking I need to point out to him these weaknesses so he will do better. I think he should be more like Melinda, who never fails to meet her goals. What do you think?

A: Unless you want Seth to become part of your turnover statistics, I suggest you hold off on the review dumpfest and the comparisons with other employees. Such tactics will only push Seth further away and will not lead to the result you expect. Instead, analyze what Seth does right when he meets his goals. Talk to him about his specific behavior (energy, focus, extroversion) during those weeks when he exceeds goals. Build on those behaviors and strategies. Ask him to write down the desired behaviors on a chart, which the two of you can sketch while talking. The chart can have a checklist to remind him to follow those behaviors. You need to set up regular meetings with Seth to go over (and adjust, if necessary) his checklist and to review his progress, always pointing him toward the positive. You can provide feedback on what you see as his weaknesses, but remember to focus on what he does well and help him do that more consistently.

© CENGAGE LEARNING 2014

that only 14 percent of companies surveyed reported using a strict forced ranking system in 2010, down from 42 percent a year earlier.[36]

As a manager, you will have to meet business goals and financial targets. However, don't allow yourself to get trapped into a sole focus on numbers, task results, and rankings that ignore the development and care of people who work with and for you.[37] Being a good manager requires paying attention to both task needs and people needs, which means helping people understand what is expected from them, monitoring and measuring performance, developing people, and holding yourself and your team members accountable for results.

NEED TO KNOW

- A system for performance management identifies, measures, and develops the performance of individuals and teams and aligns performance with organizational goals. Effective managers pay attention to two paths to high performance: meet the needs of the work and meet the needs of the people who do the work. Two broad categories of manager behavior are task oriented and relationship oriented. Managers can be high or low on either task or relationship behavior, but both are needed to some extent. The effectiveness of a manager's focus and behavior is contingent upon the organizational situation.
- Accountability means that people with various responsibilities in organizations are subject to reporting and justifying task outcomes to those above them in the chain of command. Managers hold people accountable by requiring them to meet specific standards of performance and produce specific results, depending often on the use of "hard power," which is the power granted by a manager's formal position in the organization. Three types of hard power are legitimate, reward, and coercive.
- A lack of accountability creates problems for managers, employees, and the organization. A good system for managing people and projects is the accountability cycle, which includes five steps: setting goals and expectations, developing action plans, measuring progress, reviewing progress, and appraising performance.
- For an organization to succeed, managers have to "get the right people on the bus." Key aspects of an effective approach for hiring the right people are to clearly define the position, advertise the open position, use appropriate selection criteria, and be sure to take time to follow systematic procedures that can increase the chance of getting the right person for the job and the culture. Getting the right people in the organization also means that managers have to reposition or sometimes get rid of the ones who won't or can't perform as needed.
- Organizations need systems to evaluate the performance of all individuals in the organization, from the top to the bottom. Performance appraisal is a tool that can leverage the strengths people have and help them correct their weaknesses. Some companies use a forced ranking system to evaluate and reward people, but the practice is controversial.

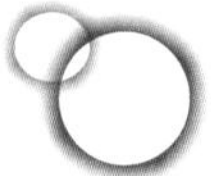

ACTION LEARNING

DELIBERATE PRACTICE EXERCISES

Holding Yourself Accountable

Step 1: Choose some behavior you want to change about yourself, something you can begin to do within the next week. Write down where you are now and where you want to be in one week.

Behavior you want to change:	The new behavior you want to exhibit in one week:

Step 2: Fill in the table below, which asks you to develop a system of accountability about your change process. It will be helpful to refer to Exhibit 13.4 (The Accountability Cycle).

Write down your goal, stated clearly and precisely:	
What reward will you apply to yourself if you meet your goal? What will you do if you do not meet your goal?	
What is your action plan? List a minimum of five little steps you can take to reach your goal:	1. 2. 3. 4. 5.
Devise a metric or "count" about your behavior that will show your progress. Record your count each day:	
Specify the due date for completion of the change:	
Midway to your due date, assess your progress:	
On your due date, assess your progress:	

Step 3: What did you learn from this exercise that you can apply later when holding direct reports accountable for a change?

Step 4 (Optional): If you have the chance, sit down with a friend or classmate and go over what you did, and what your struggles and achievements were.

Your instructor may ask you to write a report about this exercise.

Tasks versus Relationships

Step 1: Think about how you spend a typical week, including time at work, studying, doing chores, running errands, and leisure activities alone or with other people. Fill in the table below by identifying how many hours you spend on each type of activity. Account for as many hours as possible.

	List the specific activities you engaged in:	How many hours do you spend on this in a typical week?	Would you rather spend more or less on this particular activity?
Activities in which the major focus is task/work related (job activity, study, hobby, etc.)			
Activities in which the major focus is relationship/people related (going to a movie together, having a meal with someone, etc.)			

Step 2: Using a rough estimate, indicate below what percentage of your time is spent in task activities and what percentage in relationship activities. In the second column, indicate what would be your preferred allocation.

	What percentage of your time is currently used on this kind of activity?	What percentage would you prefer to spend on this kind of activity?
Task		
People/Relationships		

Step 3: What can you do to gradually change your time allocation between task and people to where you want it to be?

Steps you will take to change percentage
1.
2.
3.
4.

ACTION LEARNING

Step 4 (Optional): Compare your time allocation to other students. What do you conclude about your task-versus-people orientation compared to other people?

IN-CLASS TEAM EXERCISES

Performance Evaluation Plan

This exercise will help you understand how to prepare, as a manager, for a performance evaluation.

Step 1: Form into groups of four to five. Each group will plan for a performance evaluation of Jane Sutton, the general manager of Caffeine and Crullers from the opening videos. You should consider your group is acting as Edmund Daniels, Jane's boss.

Step 2: Going back over the material in the chapter, develop a list of the skills and tasks on which you will evaluate Jane Sutton and write them in the first column of the table below.

Step 3: After you have the list, decide as a group how you would rate Jane on each item. Use a scale of 1 to 5, with 5 being the highest. Complete the rest of the table.

Jane Sutton's Performance Evaluation Form			
Task or skill	**Rate 1–5**	**Your comments on the task or skill**	**Advice for Jane on this task or skill**

Step 4: Answer the following questions:

1. **What are Jane's greatest strengths?**

2. **What are her greatest weaknesses?**

Step 5: What advice would you give Jane so that she can grow and improve? How would you coach her to become a better manager?

The De-Luxe Boat Shipyard: Group Construction and Accountability

This In-Class Team Exercise is available online at www.cengagebrain.com.

FIELD TEAM EXERCISE

Getting the Right People on the Bus

Your job will be to interview a manager to assess how that individual personally "gets the right people on the bus" in his or her department or business.

Step 1: Divide into groups of three to five. Choose the owner or manager of a small business or the head of a single department of a larger organization.

SHUTTERSTOCK #53973379

Step 2: Your primary data collection method will be to conduct a group interview with the head of the department or small business. Meet as a group to determine your strategy, the person to interview, and how to allocate your work among members.

Step 3: Prepare your questions in advance. All group members should be present for the interview. You can start the interview with a general question, such as "How do you go about hiring a new person for your organization?" For follow-up questions, review the table below to be sure you cover the essential topics.

Step 4: After your research is done, meet again as a group to evaluate your department or organization. Fill in the table.

Topical Area	
What was the position to be filled?	
Were skills, education, and behavior requirements defined?	
In what ways did the organization get the word out?	
Of the applications received, how did the company choose promising candidates to interview?	
How many applicants were interviewed by phone and by whom were they interviewed?	
How many were invited for in-person interviews?	
Who did the interviews? What types of questions were asked?	
Were candidates given any tests or assignments? What were they?	
How was the final decision made?	
What provisions does the organization make for getting rid of someone who does not work out?	

Step 5: Assess as a group what you learned from this exercise and answer the following questions:

1. **What did you learn about their hiring practices for getting the right people on the bus?**
2. **What recommendations would you make to improve their hiring system?**

Step 6 (Optional): Your instructor may ask you to share your findings with the whole class to discover themes across groups.

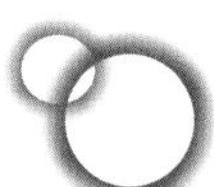

TEST YOUR METTLE

ROLE PLAY SIMULATIONS

The Scorecard

Background: Caffeine and Crullers has been experiencing poor financial performance since a new competitor came to Madison. General manager Jane Sutton wants to follow director of operations Carrie Fishman's idea to use a performance scorecard as a means of improving productivity and results, but she is faced with some opposition by two members of her management team. Because Carrie is more familiar with the scorecard, Jane has decided to have Carrie present the proposal in a meeting with the team.

Instructions: Form into groups of five to six. Review the written Video Incident at the beginning of the chapter. Assign members of the group to play general manager Jane Sutton, director of operations Carrie Fishman, HR director Heather Carreau, sales manager Jason Wong, and CFO Carlos Hernandez. If there are six people in your group, the sixth person will be an observer. Each person reads only his or her confidential role, but the observer reads all. Spend 15 to 20 minutes on the role play.

Confidential information for Carrie: C&C is still in trouble. You think the management team has been overly focused on financial goals and is missing the bigger picture. How can you have overall financial well-being if you don't put energy and resources into customer service, business processes, and learning? It seems so narrow to consider only the bottom line. You've got data from several other companies that started doing better after they implemented a performance scorecard that measures results in all areas. You know that if C&C's management team develops its own metrics and then regularly monitors them, there is no way they cannot improve. You just have to prove it to them, so they see the point. The biggest problem is that Jason and Carlos care only about sales and the bottom line. Your job is to help them get a broader perspective.

Confidential information for Jane: You've about exhausted yourself trying to turn around C&C. What you've tried has helped, but C&C is still operating in the red. Carrie's idea of using a performance scorecard makes sense. You've seen other companies that have implemented such a system, and it has helped them get to financial solvency. You and Carrie know it, but Jason and Carlos are totally against the idea. You've got to anticipate their objections and give them answers that make sense and will persuade them to take on this new approach. You could, of course, just tell them to do it, but you know from past experience that is not the way to get buy-in on a comprehensive plan such as this. They need to be on board and enthusiastic, or it won't work.

Confidential information for Jason: Scone Prone has decimated your sales. This management group can't let a new competitor keep outselling C&C. So what everyone needs to focus on is sales, sales, sales. That's the only way to get the company out of the hole it's in. Jane keeps coming up with all these wacky ideas, but all you want to say to her is, "Show me the money!" After sales go up, then everyone can focus on those nice things such as customer satisfaction. And you have to let them know that all these meetings are taking you away from concentrating on increasing sales. You just want them to leave you alone.

Confidential information for Carlos: You feel that C&C is just starting to recover from the last hare-brained idea of a new communications model, which cost $50,000 to implement. Now Jane wants another wasteful program. Some scorecard or something that makes no sense. There's one and only one way to measure a company's success: Does it make a profit? If not, you go out of business. It is that simple, so why can't Jane see this? You've got to educate her, again, about the purpose of business. This isn't some social program to make everyone feel better, after all.

Confidential information for Heather: You like that Jane is always looking for ways to improve C&C, but sometimes she goes too far. This whole scorecard idea makes little sense. Measuring capacity for learning and growth, that's good, but haven't they already looked at their business processes? And surely the whole financial piece has been overworked again and again. Why do they need another whole system? Just look at the learning. That will help all of you see how well the company can adapt to the changes in the business environment and the new competition.

After the role play, discuss what happened and answer these questions:

1. What were the obstacles to implementing a performance scorecard that measures results in the areas of financial performance, customer service, internal processes, and capacity for learning and growth?
2. Did the group overcome the obstacles? If not, how might Jane and Carrie convince others to go along with the scorecard idea?

The CEO's Decision

This Role Play Simulation is available online at www.cengagebrain.com.

VIDEO APPLICATION

The Right People at Barcelona Restaurant Group

Barcelona Restaurant Group's COO, Scott Lawton, explains how the organization keeps performance high by getting the right people on the bus.

Discussion Questions

1. What do you think of a company that is "always firing," encourages 60–70 percent turnover among managers, and is continuously "culling out the bottom 20 percent of wait staff"? Would you want to work there? Why?
2. COO Lawton says he has no faith in his interviews with prospective employees and uses the interview to talk more than listen, so he can explain Barcelona's philosophy and mission. Explain the possible advantages and disadvantages of this approach.
3. Barcelona managers set high expectations for employees and believe the company gets better by hiring better people. Does this sound like an accountability system? Explain.

TEST YOUR METTLE

SHUTTERSTOCK #53973379

CASE INCIDENTS

"What's Wrong with the Team?"

What's wrong with the team? What's wrong with the team? Nichole Dyer's words repeated over and over in Henry Rankin's mind as he boarded the plane from Los Angeles to Chicago.

Rankin was responsible for the technical implementation of the new customer relationship management (CRM) software being installed for western and eastern sales offices in both cities. The software was badly needed to improve follow-up sales for his company, Reflex Systems. Reflex sold exercise equipment to high schools and colleges, as well as to small and midsize businesses for recreation centers, through a national force of 310 salespeople. The company's low prices won a lot of sales; however, follow-up service was uneven and the new CRM system promised to resolve those problems with historical data, inquiries, reminders, and updates going to sales reps daily. The CEO of Reflex ordered the CRM system installed with all possible haste.

Rankin pulled a yellow pad and pen from the side pocket of his carry-on bag and tossed it in the seat beside the window, stashed the bag in the overhead compartment, and sat down as other passengers filed past. In an effort to shut out his thoughts, he closed his eyes and concentrated on the muffled voices and low whooshing sound of the air vents. His thoughts were suddenly interrupted as a kid around 10 or 11 years old plopped into the seat beside him, shot him one of those pre-teen, "Do I have to ride with you?" looks, opened a Harry Potter book, and started reading. Rankin was grateful to have the kid as his seatmate rather than the non-stop talkers he was sometimes paired with on flights. He needed time to think, and doodling on a pad was his way of sorting his thoughts.

He wrote *what's wrong with the team* three times and began drawing arrows to circles bearing the names of his team members: Barry Livingston and Max Wojohowski in LA, and Bob Finley, Lynne Johnston, and Sally Phillips in Chicago. He marked through Sally's name. She had jumped ship recently, taking her less-than-stellar but much-needed talents with her to another company. It was on a previous LA-to-Chicago flight that Sally had pumped him for feedback on her future with Reflex. She had informed him that she had another job offer. She admitted it was less money, but she was feeling under pressure as a member of the team and she wanted more "quality of life." Rankin told Sally bluntly that her technical expertise, on which he placed top importance, was slightly below that of her peers, so future promotion was less likely despite her impressive people and team skills.

He wrote *quality of life*, circled it, and then crossed it out and wrote *what the hell?* "Why should she get quality of life?" he mused. "I've barely seen my wife and kids since this project started." Rankin's team was under a great deal of pressure and he had needed Sally to stick it out. He told her so, but the plane had barely touched down when she went directly to the office and quit, leaving the team short-handed and too close to deadline to add another body.

What's wrong with the team? Rankin furiously scribbled as his thoughts raced: (1) *The deadline is ridiculously short.* Dyer had scheduled a ten-week completion deadline for the new CRM software, including installation and training for both cities. He suddenly stopped writing and drew a rider and horse, then returned to his list. (2) *I feel like some frazzled pony-express rider running back and forth across the country, trying to develop, build, set up, and work the kinks out of a new system that everyone at Reflex is eager to see* NOW.

He was interrupted by the flight attendant. "Would you care for a drink, sir?"

"Yes. Make it a scotch and water. And be light on the water." The boy beside him shot a grimacing look and for a brief moment, Rankin felt—then squelched—the impulse to stick out his tongue at the kid.

Rankin took his drink and continued to write. (3) *Thank God for LA.* From the outset, Barry and Max had worked feverishly while avoiding the whining and complaining that seemed to overwhelm members of the Chicago team. The atmosphere was different. Although the project moved forward, meeting deadlines, there appeared to be less stress. The LA guys focused tirelessly on work, with no families to consider, alternating intense work with joking around. "Those are my kind of people," Rankin thought. (4) *But there is Chicago*, he wrote. Earlier in the day, Sam Matheny from sales had e-mailed, then called, Rankin to tell him the two remaining members of the Chicago team appeared to be alternating between bickering and avoiding one another. Apparently this had been going on for some time. "What's with that?" Rankin wondered. "And why did Sam know and I didn't?" So that morning, before his flight, Rankin had to make time to call and text both Finley and Johnston. Finley admitted he had overreacted to Johnston.

"Look, man. I'm tired and stressed out," Finley said. "We've been working non-stop. My wife is not happy."

"Just get along until this project is completed," Rankin ordered.

"When will *that* be?" Finley asked before hanging up.

Rankin thought about Dyer's persistent complaints to him that the team appeared to have a lack of passion, and she admonished him to "get your people to understand the urgency of this project." Her complaints only added to his own stress level. He had long considered himself the frontrunner for Dyer's job when she retired in two years. But had his team ruined that opportunity? The sense of urgency could be measured now in the level of stress and the long hours they had all endured. He admitted his team members were unenthusiastic, but they seemed committed.

Rankin scribbled a final note on the pad: *Is it too late to turn around and restore the level of teamwork?* He tore off the sheet, crumpled it in his hand, and stared out the window.

Discussion Questions

1. How would you characterize Rankin's leadership approach (task/results versus people/values)? What approach do you think is correct for this situation? Why?
2. What would you do now if you were Rankin? How might you awaken more enthusiasm in your team for completing this project on time? Specify the steps you would take.
3. How would you suggest that Rankin modify his leadership style if he wants to succeed Dyer in two years? Be specific.

Five Stars—Really??

Cousins Jeri Lynn DeBose, Tish Hoover, and Josephine (Joey) Parks looked forward to meeting up during the Christmas holidays to compare notes on the results of midyear statewide teacher evaluations.

All were public school teachers in districts scattered over the state. In the pressured search for new levels of teacher accountability demanded by legislators, the state department of education joined 16 other states in implementing a new teacher evaluation

system. The goal is to hold teachers accountable for student learning progress in the classroom. Under the guidance of the National Council for Teacher Quality, criteria varied by state, but in most cases 50 percent of each teacher's accountability score would be based on the principal's evaluation/ranking, with the other half divided between student test score gains (roughly 40 percent) and other data such as ACT or SAT scores (another 10 percent). In preparation, the state, like others, conducted intensive training sessions for principals or other district officials who would conduct the evaluations based on four class observations per teacher. Officials use standardized achievement tests to derive value-added scores that measure student learning over the year.

Teacher ratings were 1–5, with 1 being the lowest and 5 representing near perfection. The publication of the first evaluations stirred interest and controversy, particularly among teachers who worried about the possible long-term effects on job retention and tenure.

Now, with the half-year evaluations in hand, the three cousins pored over their experiences. The three represented different types of school systems within the state. Jeri Lynn worked for a metropolitan system in the state capital. The system included many low-income and English language learning students, and several schools within the system were teetering on the brink of state takeover if improvement in student scores didn't materialize this school year. Tish worked in a county system dominated by upper-income residents. Joey taught in the rural community in which all three grew up. The rural community had high unemployment and a low percentage of graduates went on to college. As a result, the cousins came to the table with differing teaching experiences.

"The numbers are all over the place," Jeri Lynn remarked as she went through the pages.

"The whole system is flawed and they need to make changes before the end of the year," Joey said. "It's too subjective. With the principals conducting the observations and writing up the evaluations, there are personal factors that affect a true outcome."

"Yeah, look at the numbers from your upper income district," Jeri Lynn said to Tish. "How can 60 percent of the teachers score 5s?"

Tish chuckled. "Yeah, lucky us. Our schools are overflowing with children from wealthy families. These are the kids who will apply to Ivy League schools. I can tell you that the principals are going to avoid confrontation on all fronts. No principal is going to give any indication that their students are receiving an education under anyone less than perfect and that means cramming the rankings with 5s. They claim a higher level of motivation for students and thus the selection of an elite team of educators. So with those pressures, I don't think we get personal feedback that is accurate."

"At the other end of the spectrum, we have my rural district," Joey said. "We have principals on a power surge. And the big problem is that they know everyone and have long-standing relationships with everyone in the county, so I think they give scores based on personal history. We could almost predict who would get high or low scores *before* the observations. For the principals, it can go back as far as 'his daddy and my daddy hated each other in high school and now I get to evaluate his daughter.'"

"I think that in many cases principals feel pressure to align scores with state expectations. The state *expected* my district to have high scores and *expected* rural schools such as yours to be lower," Tish said.

"The key to the accountability system is the principal in each school," Jeri Lynn suggested. "With several of the schools in Metro teetering on the edge of state takeover by the end of the year, we have lots of strict principals who want to hold our feet to the fire, especially during this first round of scoring. I expect the scores to go up in the second round, whether or not they are accurate, in order to show improvement."

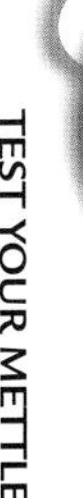

"I thought the whole idea was to provide the teachers with feedback so that we would know the areas in which we need improvement," Tish said.

Jeri Lynn laughed. "That was the idea. But it's sort of like all of those post-session evaluation forms we have to fill out at education workshops. You know and I know most attendees just go down the form and mark 4s and 5s."

"I've done that many times," Tish admitted.

"Why?" Joey asked.

"Well, for one thing, I don't want to hurt the feelings of the speakers and for another, I don't want to take the time to write something. I just want to get out and move to the next session."

"The principals were supposed to conduct two observations in the fall and two more in the spring," Jeri Lynn said. "I think that's asking too much of them when they already have so much on their plates. I think a lot of them are skimping on their visits. I know I only had one observation last semester and I'm sure Mr. Talley just faked the second set of numbers."

"I'm wondering, too, how principals measure performance in a course area outside their area of expertise, such as math" Joey said. "If the guy has a phobia about math, anything the teacher says or does is going to look brilliant—thus a 5."

Tish and Jeri Lynn looked at each other and laughed. "Maybe we picked the wrong subjects," Tish said.

"My question is one of perception," Jeri Lynn said. "A large percentage of my students are ELL. That affects their scores. How do you measure a 3 in my situation against a 5 for Tish? At the end of the school year, little Carlos is thrilled that his reading in English has improved, but there's no Big Bang here. It's a slow, steady improvement that may not actually show up in big strides for a couple of years."

"So the question is *how do they create a system that is fair?*" Tish asked.

"*And accurate*," added Jeri Lynn.

Discussion Questions

1. What do you see as the major flaws in the accountability system for the schools? What changes do you recommend to improve the system?
2. Is a 1–5 grading system by principals a valuable part of performance feedback to teachers? Why?
3. How might the state manage the accuracy of principals who are conducting teacher evaluations?

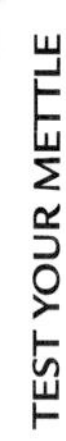
TEST YOUR METTLE

PERSONAL SKILLS LOG

Directions: Fill in the rows below based on what you learned from each part of the chapter that you completed.

	What is my key takeaway or insight from this activity?	What do I personally do well (strength) regarding this activity?	What could I improve (weakness) about myself regarding this activity?	How might I use what I've learned from this activity in the future?
Manager Challenge Incident:				
Discover Yourself Questionnaires:				
Deliberate Practice Exercises:				
In-Class and/or Field Team Exercises:				
Role-Play Exercises:				
Case Incidents:				

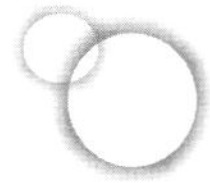

REFERENCES

Discover Yourself

1 This questionnaire is based on ideas in Jim Collins, *Good to Great: Why Some Companies Make the Leap . . . and Others Don't* (Harper Business, 2001), and other publications.

Discover Knowledge

2 Stephanie McCrummen, "Evaluation of D.C. Teachers Is a Delicate Conversation," *The Washington Post*, March 17, 2011, http://www.washingtonpost.com/local/education/evaluating-teachers-is-a-delicate-conversation/2011/03/09/ABpPILn_story.html (accessed March 18, 2011).

3 H. Aguinis, *Performance Management* (Upper Saddle River, NJ: Pearson Prentice Hall, 2007). See also Troy V. Mumford, "Developing Performance Management Competence: An Exercise Leveraging Video Technology and Multisource Feedback," *Journal of Management Education* 33, no. 5 (2009): 617–644.

4 This discussion is based on Gary Yukl, Angela Gordon, and Tom Taber, "A Hierarchical Taxonomy of Leadership Behavior: Integrating a Half Century of Behavior Research," *Journal of Leadership and Organization Studies* 9, no. 1 (2002): 15–32.

5 This discussion is based on "Consultancy Skills Toolkit: Adair Leadership Model," *Lindsay Sherwin Ltd. Web site*, http://www.lindsay-sherwin.co.uk/guide_consultancy_skills/html_consultancy_skills/15_adair.htm (accessed April 27, 2011); and Yukl et al., "A Hierarchical Taxonomy of Leadership Behavior."

6 Yukl et al., "A Hierarchical Taxonomy of Leadership Behavior."

7 See Fred E. Fiedler, *A Theory of Leadership Effectiveness* (New York: McGraw-Hill, 1967); Fred E. Fiedler, "Assumed Similarity Measures As Predictors of Team Effectiveness," *Journal of Abnormal and Social Psychology* 49 (1954): 381–388; Paul Hersey and Kenneth H. Blanchard, *Management of Organizational Behavior: Utilizing Human Resources*, 4th ed. (Englewood Cliffs, NJ: Prentice-Hall, 1982); Ken Blanchard, "Situational Leadership," *Leadership Excellence* (May 2008): 19; K. H. Blanchard, *Leading at a Higher Level* (Upper Saddle River, NJ: Prentice Hall, 2007).

8 Gary L. Neilson and Bruce A. Pasternack, "The Cat That Came Back," *Strategy + Business*, no. 40 (August 17, 2005): 32–45.

9 This definition and discussion is based on Earle Hitchner, "The Power to Get Things Done," *National Productivity Review* 12 (Winter 1992–1993): 117–122; Robert A. Dahl, "The Concept of Power," *Behavioral Science* 2 (1957): 201–215; W. Graham Astley and Paramijit S. Pachdeva, "Structural Sources of Intraorganizational Power: A Theoretical Synthesis," *Academy of Management Review* 9 (1984): 104–113; and Gerald R. Salancik and Jeffrey Pfeffer, "The Bases and Use of Power in Organizational Decision Making: The Case of the University," *Administrative Science Quarterly* 19 (1974): 453–473.

10 Tony Alessandra, "High Performance: Your Leadership Can Help Create It," *Leadership Excellence* (November 2010): 17.

11 Based on A. J. Grimes, "Authority, Power, Influence, and Social Control: A Theoretical Synthesis," *Academy of Management Review* 3 (1978): 724–735; and Astley and Sachdeva, "Structural Sources of Intraorganizational Power."

12 Sydney Finkelstein, "Power in Top Management Teams: Dimensions, Measurement, and Validation," *Academy of Management Journal* 35 (1992): 505–538.

13 Michael G. O'Loughlin, "What Is Bureaucratic Accountability and How Can We Measure It?" *Administration & Society* 22, no. 3 (November 1990): 275–302; and Brian Dive, "When Is an Organization Too Flat?" *Across the Board* (July–August 2003): 20–23.

14 Timothy Aeppel, "Personnel Disorders Sap a Factory Owner of His Early Idealism," *The Wall Street Journal*, January 14, 1998.

15 Roger Conners and Tom Smith, *Journey to the Emerald City: Achieve a Competitive Edge by Creating a Culture of Accountability* (Upper Saddle River, NJ: Prentice Hall, 2002), pp. 28–30.

16 Adam Bryant, "Are You a C.E.O. of Something?" (Corner Office column, an interview with Mark Pincus), *The New York Times*, January 31, 2010.

17 This discussion is based on Richard L. Daft, *Management*, 9th ed. (Mason, OH: South-Western Cengage Learning, 2010), pp. 168–171; Stephen R. Covey, "Hold Everyone Accountable—All the Time," *Chief Learning Officer* (October 2004): 20; Lois Zachary, "Hold People Accountable: Monitor Progress and Measure Results," *Leadership Excellence* (January 2005): 18; Richard Lepsinger, "No Accountability?" *Leadership Excellence* (December 2010): 14–15; and Gina Pellegrini, "Leading Your Team to the Top," *National Underwriter: Life & Health* (June 18, 2007): 20–21.

18 "Effective Goal Setting; Applying SMART Goals," *Healthcare Registration* (September 2010): 5–6; and Joan Lloyd, "Linking Employee Goals to Organization Goals," *The Receivables Report* (April 2011): 9–11.

19 Stephen R. Covey, "Create a Compelling Scoreboard," *Chief Learning Officer Web site*, May 17, 2004, http://clomedia.com/index.php?url=articles/view/create_a_compelling_scoreboard/ (accessed April 27, 2011).

20 Richard Lepsinger, "Building Accountability and Commitment," *Industrial Management* (November–December 2010): 21–25.

21 Michael Mahoney, "Perfect Match," *Fortune Small Business* (March 20, 2006): 100.

22 Jeff Williford, "Get the Right People on Your Bus," *Journal of Property Management* 70, no. 3 (May–June, 2005): 72.

23 This discussion is based on Williford, "Get the Right People on Your Bus," and Luis Gomez-Mejia, David Balkin, and Robert Cardy, *Managing Human Resources*, 7th ed. (Upper Saddle River, NJ: Prentice Hall, 2011), Chapter 6.

24 Gomez-Mejia et al., *Managing Human Resources.*

25 This discussion is based on Gomez-Mejia et al., *Managing Human Resources*; and Timothy T. Baldwin, William H. Bommer, and Robert S. Rubin, *Developing Management Skills* (New York: McGraw-Hill Irwin, 2008), p. 172.

26 Ram Charan, "Business Acumen: Get the Right People in the Right Jobs," *Leadership Excellence* (September 2010): 3.

27 Larry Bossidy and Ram Charan, *Execution: The Discipline of Getting Things Done* (New York: Crown Business, 2002), p. 110.

28 Joann S. Lublin, "Ram Charan: Message to CEOs: Do More to Keep Your Key Employees" (Managing & Careers Boss Talk column), *The Wall Street Journal*, December 27, 2010.

29 This discussion is based on Jay Goltz, "The Dirty Little Secret of Successful Companies," *The New York Times*, February 3, 2011, http://boss.blogs.nytimes.com/2011/02/08/the-dirty-little-secret-of-successful-companies/ (accessed May 2, 2011).

30 Adam Bryant, "There's No Need to Bat .900," (Corner Office column, an interview with John Donohoe), *The New York Times*, April 5, 2009.

31 Dick Grote, "Passing: Why We Still Can't Get Performance Appraisal Right," *The Conference Board Review* (September–October 2008): 38.

32 "Talent Tutor: Ram Charan's List of Biggest Corporate Talent-Management Issues," in Joann S. Lublin, "Ram Charan: Message to CEOs: Do More to Keep Your Key Employees," *The Wall Street Journal*, December 27, 2010.

33 Harvard Business Essentials, "Coaching and Mentoring: How to Develop Top Talent and Achieve Stronger Performance" (Boston: Harvard Business School Press, 2004), p. 133.

34 Jena McGregor, "The Struggle to Measure Performance," *BusinessWeek* (January 9, 2006): 26–28.

35 "Forced Ranking (Forced Distribution)," *HR Management Web site*, http://www.humanresources.hrvinet.com/forced-ranking-forced-distribution/ (accessed January 21, 2012).

36 Leslie Kwoh, "'Rank and Yank' Retains Vocal Fans," *The Wall Street Journal*, January 31, 2012.

37 Bethany Detrich, "Accountable Leadership: To Survive, Develop Real Leaders," *Leadership Excellence* (June 2009): 5.

Chapter Outline

CHAPTER 14
Managing Cross-Culturally

RYAN LASH

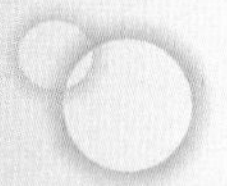

MANAGER CHALLENGE

VIDEO INCIDENT: GETTING RESPECT

Caffeine and Crullers general manager Jane Sutton has suspected for a long time that one member of her management team, Carlos Hernandez, doesn't respect her. He often disagrees with her in front of others, rolls his eyes in meetings when she says something, or just plain ignores her by addressing other people with his comments in meetings. When Jane talks to Carlos, he often doesn't even look at her. She wonders if it is gender related, because she's seen situations before where male managers don't respect her as a boss because she is female—no matter how competent she is. Jane is agonizing over how to deal with Carlos on this issue. She is thinking about confronting him about his behavior the next time it happens in a meeting. She could also try humor by making a joke now and then about how Carlos won't look her in the eye.

Initial Thoughts

1. If you were Jane, what would you do about Carlos's behavior?

2. What reasons can you come up with for Carlos behaving in this way?

Your instructor may ask you to be part of a role play based on the "Getting Respect" incident.

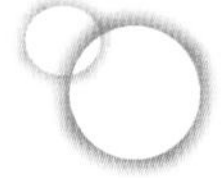

DISCOVER YOURSELF

For those students using CourseMate or CengageNOW, you can access the Daft/Marcic Assessment Library to take the questionnaires online and view dynamically updated comparative data.

Questionnaire 1[1]

Instructions: Rate how accurately each statement describes you based on whether the statement is clearly true or accurate, clearly false or inaccurate, or in the middle as somewhat true and somewhat false. Describe yourself as you are now, not as you wish to be. There are no right or wrong answers.

Part A

	True	Somewhat	False
1. Achieving one's personal goals is more important than achieving team or organization goals.	○	○	○
2. Children should take great pride in the individual accomplishments of their parents and vice versa.	○	○	○
3. Pay and bonus systems should be designed to maximize individual interests over mutual interests.	○	○	○

Total Score Part A ________. (Sum questions 1–3 by giving 3 points for each True, 2 points for each Somewhat, and 1 point for each False.)

Part B

	True	Somewhat	False
4. I believe that orderliness and consistency should be stressed in society, even at the expense of experimentation and innovation.	○	○	○
5. Organizations work better when people do not break rules.	○	○	○
6. Organizations should spell out job requirements in detail so that employees know what they are supposed to do.	○	○	○

Total Score Part B ________. (Sum questions 4–6 by giving 3 points for each True, 2 points for each Somewhat, and 1 point for each False.)

Part C

	True	Somewhat	False
7. I want to compete for high level jobs and high earnings.	○	○	○
8. People should be encouraged to be assertive rather than nonassertive.	○	○	○
9. In an organization, people should be encouraged to be tough rather than tender.	○	○	○

Total Score Part C ________. (Sum questions 7–9 by giving 3 points for each True, 2 points for each Somewhat, and 1 point for each False.)

Part D	True	Somewhat	False
10. As a manager, I would want an egalitarian working relationship with my direct reports rather than maintaining distance from them.	○	○	○
11. Organizations should encourage followers to question their leaders.	○	○	○
12. Authority should be based on one's ability and contribution rather than on one's position in the hierarchy.	○	○	○

Total Score Part D ________. (Sum questions 10–12 by giving 3 points for each True, 2 points for each Somewhat, and 1 point for each False.)

Part E			
13. People in society will be happier if they accept the status quo rather than try to change things for the days ahead.	○	○	○
14. I prefer a norm of taking life events as they occur rather than constantly planning ahead.	○	○	○
15. I believe in focusing on current problems rather than trying to make things happen for the future.	○	○	○

Total Score Part E ________. (Sum items 13–15 by giving 3 points for each True, 2 points for each Somewhat, and 1 point for each False.) Go to page 520 to interpret your scores.

Questionnaire 2[2]

Instructions: To what extent does each of the following statements characterize your behavior? Please honestly answer each item below as True, Somewhat, or False.

Part A	True	Somewhat	False
1. I think about how I'm going to relate to people from a different culture before I meet them.	○	○	○
2. I understand the major religions and how they influence other cultures.	○	○	○
3. I know about the geography, history, and cultural leaders of several countries.	○	○	○
4. I regularly discuss world events with family and friends.	○	○	○

Total Score Part A ________. (Sum questions 1–4 by giving 3 points for each True, 2 points for each Somewhat, and 1 point for each False.)

Part B

	True	Somewhat	False
5. I seek out opportunities to interact with people from different cultures.	○	○	○
6. I can adapt to living in a different culture with relative ease.	○	○	○
7. I am confident that I can befriend locals in a culture that is unfamiliar to me.	○	○	○
8. I find work on a multicultural team very satisfying.	○	○	○

Total Score Part B ________. (Sum questions 5–8 by giving 3 points for each True, 2 points for each Somewhat, and 1 point for each False.)

Part C

	True	Somewhat	False
9. I regularly associate with people from cultural backgrounds different from my own.	○	○	○
10. I alter my facial expressions and gestures as needed to facilitate a cross-cultural interaction.	○	○	○
11. I am quick to change the way I behave when a cross-cultural encounter seems to require it.	○	○	○
12. I take pleasure in talking with someone whose English is limited.	○	○	○

Total Score Part C ________. (Sum questions 9–12 by giving 3 points for each True, 2 points for each Somewhat, and 1 point for each False.) Go to page 522 to interpret your scores.

Questionnaire 3[3]

Instructions: How do you typically manage projects or conduct business at school or work? To what extent do you display the behaviors below? Please indicate whether each item is True, Somewhat, or False for you.

Are You Typically:

	True	Somewhat	False
1. Impatient? Do you have a short attention span? Do you want to keep moving to the next topic?	○	○	○
2. A poor listener? Does your mind think about what you want to say next?	○	○	○
3. Uncomfortable with long silences?	○	○	○
4. Argumentative? Do you enjoy arguing for its own sake?	○	○	○
5. Uncomfortable negotiating a deal with someone who cannot make a final decision?	○	○	○
6. Placing more emphasis on the short-term than on the long-term in your thinking and planning?	○	○	○
7. Thinking that it is a waste of time getting to know someone personally before discussing business?	○	○	○

	True	Somewhat	False
8. Legalistic to win your point?	○	○	○
9. Holding others to an agreement regardless of changing circumstances?	○	○	○
10. Thinking "win/lose" when negotiating? Of trying to win a negotiation at the other's expense?	○	○	○

Total Score Questionnaire 3 ________. (Sum questions 1–10 by giving 3 points for each True, 2 points for each Somewhat, and 1 point for each False.) Go to page 523 to interpret your score.

Questionnaire 4[4]

Instructions: Circle all the words below that you associate with your personal response to the idea of workplace diversity.

Abnormal	Dispute	Oppose
Accommodate	Dissatisfaction	Optimistic
Aggravation	Dread	Partake
Appreciative	Eager	Perplexed
Assist	Gratified	Pleased
Baseless	Hostile	Reasonable
Belittle	Impractical	Retreat
Beneficial	Irritation	Right
Biased	Join	Suitable
Committed	Just	Sympathetic
Comprehend	Listen	Uneasy
Corrupt	Necessary	Unfounded
Criticize	Noble	Valueless
Dislike	Obstinate	Welcoming

Total Score 4A ________. Add 1 point for each of the following words circled: Beneficial, Just, Necessary, Noble, Reasonable, Right, Suitable. Subtract 1 point for each of the following words circled: Abnormal, Baseless, Biased, Corrupt, Impractical, Unfounded, Valueless.

Total Score 4B ________. Add 1 point for each of the following words circled: Appreciative, Committed, Eager, Gratified, Optimistic, Pleased, Sympathetic. Subtract 1 point for each of the following words circled: Aggravation, Dislike, Dissatisfaction, Dread, Irritation, Perplexed, Uneasy.

Total Score 4C ________. Add 1 point for each of the following words circled: Accommodate, Assist, Comprehend, Join, Listen, Partake, Welcoming. Subtract 1 point for each of the following words circled: Belittle, Criticize, Dispute, Hostile, Obstinate, Oppose, Retreat. Go to page 527 to interpret your scores.

DISCOVER YOURSELF

Questionnaire 5[5]

Instructions: Indicate below whether each of the following statements is True, Somewhat, or False for you.

	True	Somewhat	False
1. I would feel more comfortable if the pilot of an airplane I was traveling on were male.	○	○	○
2. In general, I would rather work for a man than for a woman.	○	○	○
3. If I were being sentenced in court, I would prefer that the judge be a woman.	○	○	○
4. The people I look up to most are women.	○	○	○
5. I probably prefer that the U.S. president is a man versus a woman.	○	○	○
6. When it comes to politics, I would rather vote for women than for men.	○	○	○
7. For most college courses, I prefer a male professor to a female professor.	○	○	○
8. In general, I think women make better leaders than men do.	○	○	○
9. In most areas, I would rather take advice from a man than from a woman.	○	○	○
10. In general, I feel more comfortable when a man (versus a woman) is in charge.	○	○	○

Total Score Questionnaire 5 ________. (Sum items 1, 2, 5, 7, 9, and 10 by giving 3 points for each True, 2 points for each Somewhat, and 1 point for each False. Reverse score items 3, 4, 6, and 8 by summing 3 points for each False, 2 points for each Somewhat, and 1 point for each True and add the numbers for your total.) Go to page 530 to interpret your score.

GO ONLINE to find additional questionnaires at www.cengagebrain.com, search for Daft/Marcic Building Management Skills 1e, click on Free Online Resources, click on Additional Self-Assessments.

- Passive Bias
- Values Balancing

See It Online

SHUTTERSTOCK #53973379

Chapter 14: Managing Cross-Culturally
DISCOVER KNOWLEDGE

Ann Bennett loves Japan. Bennett had taken a course in Japanese in college, so she had an edge when her company was looking for someone to lead a project developing an interface for a U.S. and Japanese customer-data system. She was thrilled with her first overseas assignment and determined to make it a success. While working late one night, Bennett discovered some flaws in the system that could significantly disrupt company operations. She immediately sent an e-mail to her boss back in the United States and followed up with e-mails to all team members. The next day she got a message from the boss thanking her for her quick warning and asking that she keep him updated. When she tried to discuss the problem with her Japanese team members, though, Bennett got little cooperation. Things didn't improve as the weeks passed. As the project neared a critical phase, Bennett found her access to the people and information she needed to adequately monitor progress on the project severely restricted. By the end of the project, Japanese managers had moved Bennett's desk into a storage room, literally as well as figuratively isolating her from important communication networks. The new system was launched on time and problem-free, but Bennett wonders how things went so wrong in her relationships with her Japanese colleagues.[6]

Like many American managers, Ann Bennett failed to appreciate that the values and behaviors that typically govern how business is done in the United States don't translate to the rest of the world. Bennett's Japanese colleagues were humiliated by her direct approach. By going straight to the boss with the problem, she had violated a cultural norm of indirectly presenting information to the group and collaboratively uncovering and discussing problems.

Working with and managing diverse people has been a matter of concern for organizations in the United States for years, but today's managers are confronting diversity issues on a broader scale than ever before. A global mindset and international experience are quickly becoming prerequisites for managerial success.

At the same time, cultural diversity within the United States is dramatically increasing. Exhibit 14.1

Exhibit 14.1 Changes in the U.S. Population

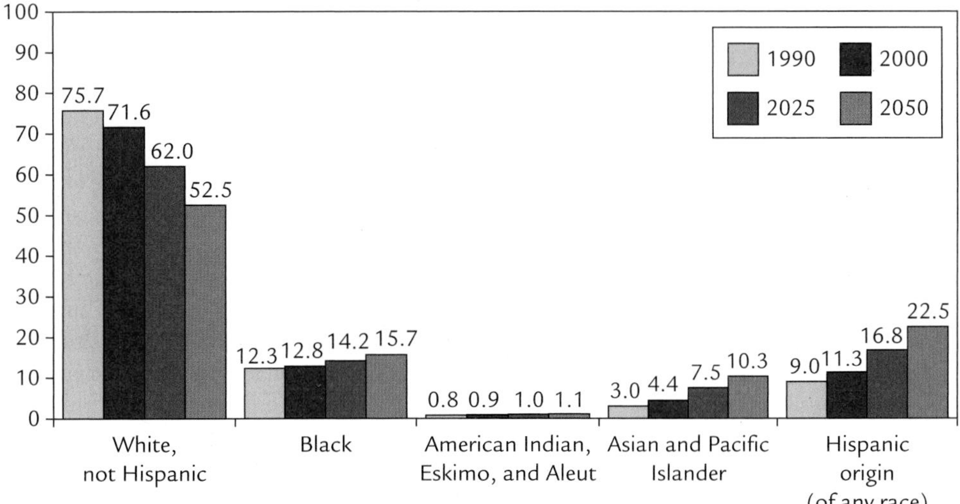

Source: Jennifer Cheeseman Day, "National Population Projections," Population Profile of the United States, U.S. Census Bureau, http://www.census.gov/population/www/pop-profile/natproj.html (accessed May 6, 2011).

illustrates the U.S. population by race from 1990 projected to 2050, showing a steady decline in the non-Hispanic white population and a steady increase in the Hispanic and Asian populations. About a third of current population growth in the United States is due to immigration, and immigration is expected to continue being a positive element over the time period shown in Exhibit 14.1.[7] As the population changes, so does the labor force. The number of Hispanics in the U.S. workforce is expected to increase by 7.3 million between 2008 and 2018, and Hispanics will make up 17.6 percent of the workforce by 2018.[8] In addition to greater racial and cultural diversity in the workplace, women became the majority of the workforce for the first time in U.S. history in 2010.[9]

Thus, managers in the United States, and indeed in every country, deal with cross-cultural and diversity issues both at home and abroad. In this chapter, we first examine some of the challenges managers face working internationally and describe some skills and techniques for handling them. Later in the chapter, we'll talk about some important diversity issues in the United States, including the problems minority and female managers often face in organizations.

LEADING WORDS

"Diversity may be the hardest thing for a society to live with, and perhaps the most dangerous thing for a society to be without."

—**William Sloane Coffin, Jr.**

American clergyman, civil rights activist, and antiwar campaigner

"If you judge people, you have no time to love them."

—**Mother Teresa**

Roman Catholic nun who ministered to the poor and sick for more than 45 years

"Diversity without unity makes about as much sense as dishing up flour, sugar, water, eggs, shortening, and baking powder on a plate and calling it a cake."

—**C. William Pollard**

chairman emeritus and former CEO of ServiceMaster; author of *The Soul of the Firm*

"Diversity is not about how we differ. Diversity is about embracing one another's uniqueness."

—**Ola Joseph**

motivational speaker and author

© CENGAGE LEARNING 2014

MANAGING GLOBALLY: THE CULTURE DIFFERENCE TRAP

It was one of the costliest blunders in commercial aviation history: In designing the Airbus A380 double-decker jet, factories in Germany and those in France used incompatible design software. That meant the wiring produced in Hamburg didn't fit into the plane on the assembly line in France. This was only one of several cross-cultural problems that delayed the plane's development for more than two years and threw Airbus into a financial and management tailspin. Cross-border rivalries and lack of information sharing among the company's French, German, British, and Spanish employees plagued Airbus, turning the dream of a seamless, pan-European company into a nightmare. Managers in each country had their own ideas about how things should be done. In addition, efforts to integrate operations ran afoul of politicians and legislators concerned over the loss of jobs or status in their respective countries. Airbus survived this complicated "stew of cultures" but it wasn't easy. When Louis Gallois took over as chief executive of Airbus in October of 2006, one of the first things he did was ban the use of national symbols in PowerPoint presentations. "It is because of national pride that we have the problem of the A380," Gallois said.[10]

If you have any management experience—even managing a class project—you know how tough it can be to successfully coordinate people, resources, and information to get something done. Think about doing it on a global scale, managing and coordinating the work of people who are thousands of miles apart, working in different time zones, speaking different languages, and interpreting instructions or behaviors in different ways. Managers face a tremendous challenge in finding how to capitalize on the incredible opportunities and avoid the pitfalls of global business.

Perhaps the most difficult aspect of managing globally relates to cultural

Exhibit 14.2 How Do You Shake Hands?

Culture	Preferred Style of Handshake
Asian	Gentle (shaking hands is unfamiliar and uncomfortable for some Asians; the exception is the Korean, who usually prefers a firm handshake)
British	Soft
French	Light and quick; repeated on arrival and departure; not offered to superiors
German	Brusque and firm; repeated on arrival and departure
Latin American	Moderate grasp; repeated frequently
Middle Eastern	Gentle; repeated frequently
North American	Firm

Source: Lillian H. Chaney and Jeannette S. Martin, *Intercultural Business Communication* (Englewood Cliffs, NJ: Prentice-Hall, 1995), p. 115.

differences. The opportunities for new resources and markets are appealing, but then culture differences assert themselves. Numerous definitions of the term "culture" exist, but for our purposes, **culture** consists of values, assumptions, norms, and patterns of thought that are shared by all or most members of a social group, that are passed on from existing to new members of the group, and that shape group members' behaviors and perceptions of the world.[11]

Even something that seems simple, such as a handshake, can be very dissimilar from culture to culture, as described in Exhibit 14.2. If the proper way to shake hands can vary so widely, it is no wonder managers have trouble knowing how to act when doing business in other countries. Some managers who have faced difficulties in overseas assignments or with cross-cultural mergers refer to it simply as "the C word." Culture is intangible, pervasive, and difficult for outsiders to learn. As perplexing as political or economic factors can be in another country, cultural differences can cause more problems than almost anything else.

One way you can get a handle on varied cultures and work within them more effectively is to understand how cultures differ in terms of values. The classic study of how national value systems influence organizational life and employee working relationships was done by Geert Hofstede, who studied 116,000 IBM employees working in 40 countries. More recent research from Project GLOBE (Global Leadership and Organizational Behavior Effectiveness) has significantly extended Hofstede's assessment and offers a broader understanding for today's managers. Project GLOBE used data collected from 18,000 managers working in 62 countries. Based on these two major research projects and the books and articles that have explored and expanded on these ideas, here are some critical areas of value differences[12] that you will need to pay attention to as a manager:

1. *Individualism and collectivism.* **Individualism** is a strong American value. People define themselves in terms of personal characteristics and value individual success and welfare over that of the group. Other countries with strong individualist values include Canada, Great Britain, and Australia. In Japan, by contrast, **collectivism** is highly valued. People define themselves in terms of the group and place common goals, group harmony, and collective welfare above individual success. China, Thailand, and Costa Rica are other countries that place a strong emphasis on collectivism.

2. *Power distance.* In countries with a high value for **power distance,** people accept inequality in power among people, organizations, and institutions. Traditional values in countries such as Malaysia, Mexico, and India, for example, support inequality in power relationships. In countries with a low value for power distance, such as Denmark, Austria, and Israel, on the other hand, people expect equality in power.

3. *Uncertainty avoidance.* High **uncertainty avoidance** means that people feel uncomfortable with ambiguity and thus support beliefs that ensure certainty and conformity. Countries with high uncertainty avoidance include Greece, France, and Uruguay. In countries with low uncertainty avoidance, people have a high tolerance for the unstructured, the unclear, and the unpredictable. Low uncertainty avoidance countries include Sweden, Jamaica, and Singapore.

4. *Assertiveness.* A high value on **assertiveness** means people in that society encourage toughness, assertiveness, and competitiveness. High assertiveness countries include Spain, Germany (former East), and Austria. In countries with low assertiveness, such as Switzerland, Denmark, and Norway, people value relationships, tenderness, and concern over being tough and competitive.

5. *Time Orientation.* **Time orientation** refers to whether a country is most strongly oriented toward the past, present, or future. Many European countries are past oriented. They believe ideas, plans, and goals should be evaluated in terms of how they fit with the society's customs and traditions. People tend to emphasize preserving history and honoring traditions. Other countries are strongly present oriented, which means people want quick gratification, don't like to follow strict schedules, and don't depend on tradition to dictate behaviors. Future-oriented societies encourage and reward planning for the long term over quick gratification and short-term results. The United States is oriented toward the present and near future. Even when managers formulate 10-year plans, they typically do whatever it takes to achieve this quarter's results. Future-oriented societies include Japan and Bahrain. In 1932, Konosuke Matsushita formulated an ambitious 250-year plan for Japan's Matsushita Electric, perhaps an all-time record for long-range planning![13]

6. *Doing and Being.* For some countries, including Sweden, Canada, and the United States, the goal of existence is **doing.** People take action, emphasize achieving measurable outcomes, and believe in the idea of working as much as possible to make more money or accomplish more results. In contrast, some countries emphasize **being** as the goal. People in Malaysia and Mexico, for example, are typically more interested in extra time with family and friends than in earning overtime pay or accomplishing more business goals. "Being" countries stress living and working for the moment, letting ideas and events flow spontaneously. The difference between doing and being is captured beautifully in a promotional spot featuring Spanish dancers on the History International television channel: "Americans live to work," the announcer says and

DISCOVER KNOWLEDGE

DISCOVER YOURSELF

Interpret Your Score: Cultural Values (Questionnaire 1)

These scores represent a measure of five cultural values as described by Geert Hofstede and Project GLOBE. Comparative data for **Individualism-Collectivism** (Part A): Thirty person Mean score = 6.5; Top Quartile = 7–13; Bottom Quartile = 3–6. A high Part A score represents a belief toward individualism; a low score indicates a belief more toward collectivism. Comparative data for **Uncertainty Avoidance** (Part B): Thirty person Mean score = 6.7; Top Quartile = 8–9; Bottom Quartile = 4–6. A higher Part B score means a value for low uncertainty in life; a lower score means a value for higher uncertainty. Comparative data for **Assertiveness** (Part C): Thirty person Mean score = 6.5; Top Quartile = 8–9; Bottom Quartile = 0–5. A higher Part C score means a value for people being assertive; a lower score means a value for people being nonassertive. Comparative data for **Power Distance** (Part D): Thirty person Mean score = 7.3; Top Quartile = 9–11; Bottom Quartile = 0–6. A higher Part D score means a value for low power distance; a lower score means a value for high power distance. Comparative data for **Time Orientation** (Part E): Thirty person Mean score = 5.1; Top Quartile = 6–9; Bottom Quartile = 3–4. A high Part E score means an orientation toward the present; a lower score represents a future orientation.

Your scores have both individual and societal meaning. Compare your scores to other students to understand your perception of the different values in your colleague group. On which of the five values would you personally like to score higher? Lower? The five culture values also differ widely across national cultures. Go to the Web site http://www.geert-hofstede.com/hofstede_dimensions.php and compare your native country's scores on the five values to the scores of other countries. (Note that on this Web site, the term masculinity is used instead of assertiveness.) What surprises you about the differences across countries? CNOW and CourseMate users can access dynamically updated comparative data through www.cengagebrain.com.

© CENGAGE LEARNING 2014

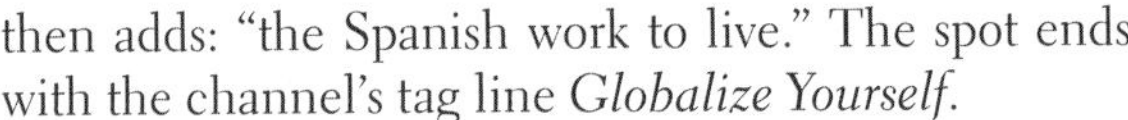

then adds: "the Spanish work to live." The spot ends with the channel's tag line *Globalize Yourself*.

7. *Performance orientation*. A society with a high **performance orientation** places great emphasis on performance and rewards people for excellence and performance improvements. High performance countries include the United States and Taiwan. In countries with a low performance orientation, such as Russia and Venezuela, people pay less attention to performance and more attention to loyalty, belonging, and background.

These seven dimensions are broad generalizations, but they provide some insight into how widely cultures vary. Not every person in a society, of course, will subscribe to the dominant values. There is extreme variety in the United States, for example, with regard to each of the dimensions above, as there is in many countries. Understanding these dimensions is important, though, because the dominant values do tend to influence organizational functioning, management styles, and employee behavior in a given country. Recall from Chapter 12 how U.S. managers in Mexico have had trouble implementing self-managed teams because of that country's emphasis on high power distance and a low tolerance for uncertainty, characteristics that conflict with the American concept of teamwork.

PERSONAL QUALITIES FOR BEING A SUCCESSFUL GLOBAL MANAGER

Even managers in companies that have many years of global experience make mistakes. Consider the following blunders:

- When U.S. chicken entrepreneur Frank Perdue translated a successful advertising slogan into Spanish, "It takes a tough man to make a tender chicken" came out as "It takes a virile man to make a chicken affectionate."[14]
- It took McDonald's managers more than a year to figure out that Hindus in India do not eat beef. The company's sales took off only after McDonald's started making burgers sold in India out of lamb or chicken.[15]
- In Africa, the labels on bottles show pictures of what is inside so illiterate shoppers can know what they are buying. When a baby-food company showed a picture of an infant on its label, the product didn't sell very well.[16]
- Managers at United Airlines discovered that even colors can doom a product. The airline handed out white carnations when it started flying from Hong Kong, only to discover that, to many Asians, these flowers represent death and bad luck.[17]

Some of these examples might seem humorous, but there's nothing funny about them to managers trying to operate in a highly competitive global environment. There is no way you can ever understand all the value differences of every person in every culture in every country, in addition to knowing all the varied languages, laws, and customs. So what's a manager to do? Avoiding cross-cultural interactions isn't an option if you want to succeed in today's world. The new global environment demands globally competent managers. How prepared are you to work in a different country or to manage people from a variety of countries working on your own native soil?

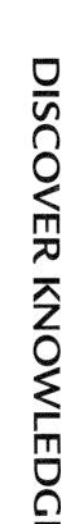

DISCOVER KNOWLEDGE

The Curse of Ethnocentrism

Ethnocentrism refers to a natural tendency among people to regard their own culture as inherently superior and to downgrade or dismiss other cultural values. Ethnocentrism is found in all countries among all types of people, yet American managers in particular are frequently accused of having strong ethnocentric attitudes that presume that the American way is the best way.

Ethnocentrism makes it impossible to value and benefit from the broad diversity of the world. With an ethnocentric attitude, managers recognize cultural differences only as a source of problems.[18] The goal for successful cross-cultural managers is ethnorelativism rather than ethnocentrism. **Ethnorelativism** is the attitude that cultures and subcultures are inherently equal. It recognizes that "our way and their way differ, but neither is inherently better." A manager with an attitude of ethnorelativism finds creative ways to combine "our way and their way" to achieve the best approach to working together effectively. Managers can learn to recognize cultural differences, see potential advantages and disadvantages of different ways of doing things, and leverage cultural variety to best serve the organization.

Developing Cultural Intelligence

Pat McGovern is the founder and CEO of IDG, a technology publishing and research firm in Massachusetts that owns magazines such as *CIO* and *Computerworld*. IDG operates in 85 countries and gets 80 percent of profits from outside the United States. When McGovern goes to a country for the first time, he spends the weekend just wandering around observing people. By watching how people in a foreign country behave, McGovern says he gets a sense of the culture—how fast people walk, how much they gesture, what they wear, how they treat one another, and so forth.[19] McGovern believes you can be in sync anywhere if you pay attention.

Managers like Pat McGovern who are successful working cross-culturally are flexible and able to adapt easily to new situations and ways of doing things. In other words, they have high cultural intelligence. **Cultural intelligence** refers to a person's ability to use reasoning and observation skills to interpret unfamiliar gestures and situations and devise appropriate behavioral responses.[20] Developing a high cultural-intelligence quotient (CQ) will enable you to interpret unfamiliar situations and adapt quickly. Rather than a list of global "dos and don'ts," this is a practical learning approach that enables a person to ferret out clues to a culture's shared understandings and respond to new situations in culturally appropriate ways.

DISCOVER KNOWLEDGE

Cultural intelligence includes three components that work together: cognitive, emotional, and physical.[21] The *cognitive* component involves your observational and learning skills and the ability to pick up on clues to understanding. The *emotional* aspect concerns your self-confidence and self-motivation. That is, you have to believe in your ability to understand and assimilate into a different culture. Difficulties and setbacks are triggers to work harder, not a cause to give up. The third component, the *physical*, refers to an ability to shift your speech patterns, expressions, and body language to be in tune with people from a different culture. Most people aren't equally strong in all three areas, but maximizing cultural intelligence requires that you draw upon all three facets. In a sense, a high CQ requires that the head, heart, and body work in concert.

A high CQ requires that you be open and receptive to new ideas and approaches. One study found that people who adapt to global management most easily are those who have grown up learning how to understand, empathize, and work with others who are different from themselves. For example, Singaporeans consistently hear English and Chinese spoken side by side. The Dutch have to learn English, German, and French, as well as Dutch, to interact and trade with their economically dominant neighbors. English Canadians must not only be well-versed in American culture and politics, but they also have to consider the views and ideas of French Canadians, who, in turn, must learn to think like North Americans, members of a global French community, Canadians, and Quebecois.[22] People in the United States who have grown up without this kind of language and cultural diversity typically have more difficulties with foreign assignments, but willing managers from any country can learn to open their minds and appreciate other viewpoints.

DISCOVER YOURSELF

Interpret Your Score: Cultural Intelligence (Questionnaire 2)

Comparative data for aspects of cultural intelligence: **Head or Cognitive CQ** (Part A): Thirty person Mean score = 8.8; Top Quartile = 10–12; Bottom Quartile = 4–7. **Heart or Emotional CQ** (Part B): Thirty person Mean score = 8.8; Top Quartile = 10–12; Bottom Quartile = 5–7. **Body or Behavioral CQ** (Part C): Thirty person Mean score = 8.1; Top Quartile = 10–12; Bottom Quartile = 4–7. If you have sufficient international experience and understanding to have scored above average on all three parts, then consider yourself to have a high CQ. If you scored below average on all three parts, it is time to learn more about other national cultures. Hone your observational skills, take courses, look for international travel opportunities, and learn to pick up on clues about how people from a different country respond to various situations. Compare your scores to those of others students. If you are not fascinated by diverse people and cultures, how might you develop greater interest and understanding of people who are different from you? CNOW and CourseMate users can access dynamically updated comparative data through www.cengagebrain.com.

© CENGAGE LEARNING 2014

You can develop a higher cultural intelligence quotient. Ways to increase your CQ include studying other languages and cultures and forming relationships with people from different countries. You can learn to be sensitive to differences in social value systems, and find creative ways to address delicate diversity issues.

DISCOVER YOURSELF

Interpret Your Score: Managing a Global Team (Questionnaire 3)

Are you ready to manage a global team with members from other countries? American managers often display cross-cultural ignorance during team interactions, compared to counterparts in other countries. American habits can be disturbing, such as impatience, rushing to results, emphasizing areas of disagreement over agreement, spending little time understanding the views and interests of others, and adopting an adversarial attitude. Americans often like to leave a discussion thinking they won, which can be embarrassing to the other side. Comparative data for **Global Team Style:** Thirty person Mean score = 16.2; Top Quartile = 18–23; Bottom Quartile = 10–14. For this quiz, a low score shows better international presence—a style that will serve you well on an international team. If you have a high score, it is time to learn more about other national cultures before participating in or managing a global team. Try to develop greater focus on other people's needs and an appreciation for different viewpoints. Be open to compromise and develop empathy for people who are different from you. CNOW and CourseMate users can access dynamically updated comparative data through www.cengagebrain.com.

© CENGAGE LEARNING 2014

WHAT PEOPLE ACROSS CULTURES EXPECT FROM MANAGERS

The cross-cultural team manager's biggest job often is to integrate differences in unspoken assumptions about norms and language. For example, Johanna Rothman led a global software team that stumbled over the word "fixed." The team's job was to fix defects in software that were critical for users. European members would tell customers a problem was "fixed" when they took action on the defect, even if the repair was not complete. The U.S. team members used the notation "fix" to mean a defect had been investigated, the cause understood, and final repair was in progress. To complicate things further, it never occurred to the Europeans that when U.S. counterparts said "fixed" it might not mean something was truly fixed. Rothman spent much of her time sorting out these small but importance differences in respective assumptions and meanings.[23]

There is tremendous variation across countries in what people expect managers to do and be. For example, should managers be experts who provide precise answers to their employees' questions and concerns or should they instead be problem solvers who help employees discover solutions rather than providing them with direct answers? The answer varies from country to country, and problems can occur when unaware managers from one culture interact with employees from another. For example, most managers in the United States think merely providing answers limits subordinates' initiative and creativity. In France, though, managers believe they should give exact answers in order to maintain their credibility as experts. If a manager from the United States working in France tells an employee she doesn't know the answer and suggests the employee consult with someone else about the problem, the employee might conclude that the U.S. manager is incompetent. Similarly, employees in the United States working for a French boss might consider the boss egotistical when he continually provides specific answers rather than offering suggestions on how to find solutions to a problem.[24] Exhibit 14.3 gives some examples of how the manager's role varies across countries based on whether managers are expected to provide answers to employee questions.

Four other areas in which you should be aware of cultural differences that influence effective management are communication, decision making, motivation, and negotiation.

Communication

After China's Lenovo Group acquired IBM's PC business, managers experienced some challenging communication breakdowns. In meetings and conference calls, Western executives were frustrated by their

Exhibit 14.3 Are Managers Expected to Be Experts?

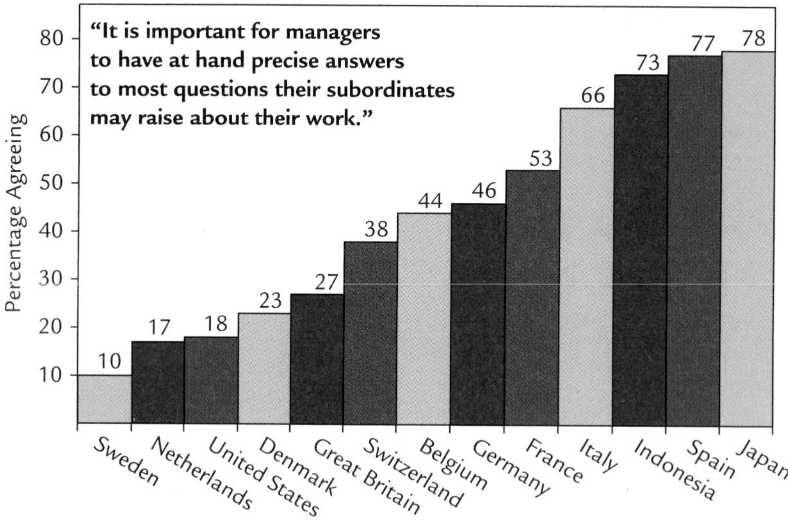

Source: From André Laurent, "The Cultural Diversity of Western Conceptions of Management," in *International Studies of Management and Organization* 13, no. 1–2 (Spring–Summer, 1983): 75–96. Adapted from ADLER, International Dimensions of Organizational Behavior, 5E. © 2008 Cengage Learning.

Chinese counterparts' reluctance to speak up, while the Chinese managers were irritated by the Americans' propensity to "just talk and talk," as one vice president of human resources put it.[25] As this example shows, there can be many barriers to effective communication in addition to language differences. One communication difference is that people from some cultures pay more attention to the social context (social setting, nonverbal behavior, social status) of their verbal communications than do other cultures. In some countries, social context is considerably more important than it is in the United States, and American managers have to suppress their impatience and devote time to establishing personal relationships.

Exhibit 14.4 indicates how the emphasis on social context varies among several countries. In a **high-context culture**, people are sensitive to circumstances surrounding communications. People in high-context cultures tend not to express feelings and thoughts explicitly, and they expect others to have the ability to detect and discern subtle cues. People focus on building personal social relationships, and meaning is derived from context—setting, status, nonverbal behavior—more than from explicit words. Relationships and trust are more important than business; and the welfare and harmony of the group are valued. In a **low-context culture,** such as in the United States, on the other hand, people use communication primarily to exchange facts

Exhibit 14.4 A Scale of High- and Low-Context Cultures

Sources: Based on Edward T. Hall and M.R. Hall, *Understanding Cultural Differences* (Yarmouth, ME: Intercultural Press, 1990); and Martin Rosch, "Communications: Focal Point of Culture," *Management International Review* 27, no. 4 (1987).

and information; everything is made more explicit so meaning is derived primarily from words. Business transactions are more important than building relationships and trust; and individual welfare and achievement are more important than the group.[26]

When people from low-context cultures communicate with people from high-context cultures, there is tremendous potential for misunderstandings. The low-context people might think those from high-context cultures are not being open with them. The high-context people, in turn, don't understand why the low-context people aren't picking up on what is *not* being said.

Decision Making

Although many international organizations use similar decision-making norms, cultures can vary tremendously in terms of how quickly decisions should be made, who should be involved, and how much analysis is required beforehand. American managers typically like to make decisions quickly, with relatively little analysis. Managers in Korea, on the other hand, want to take a long time to consider and reconsider all the issues and alternatives.[27] In France, top executives typically make all major decisions and issue specific instructions.[28] In some Arab and African countries, though, managers are expected to use consultative decision making in the extreme.

Motivation

Many of the ideas about motivation in the United States are based on Abraham Maslow's hierarchy of needs theory, as described in Chapter 7. Maslow suggested that individuals are motivated by multiple needs and that people will seek to satisfy these needs in a particular hierarchical order. Yet research has shown that people in different cultures are not motivated by the same things.[29] One study found, for example, that factors such as challenge, recognition, and the work itself (considered higher-level needs) are not as effective in countries that value high power distance. It may be that employees in these cultures perceive manager recognition and support as manipulative and therefore demotivating.[30] In places such as the United States and the United Kingdom, by contrast, these factors can be highly motivating. Similarly, in countries with higher uncertainty avoidance, such as Greece and Japan, the desire for security motivates people more strongly than does a need for developing one's potential or solving challenging problems.

As a manager, you should recognize that your own culture's ways of motivating don't always apply cross-culturally, and motivation should fit the incentives of the particular culture. There may be a universal aspect of human needs, but the importance of needs and their impact on motivation can vary tremendously.

Negotiation

Global managers, by one estimate, spend more than half their time involved in formal or informal negotiations.[31] As described in Chapter 10, negotiation is a process whereby two parties with different goals and viewpoints try to reach agreement on matters of mutual interest. When the parties involved come from different cultures, the differing ways of thinking and feeling can lead to problems if managers don't understand how effective negotiating styles vary from country to country.[32]

For example, Americans typically negotiate in a strictly businesslike way. This is related to their low-context communication style. Emotional sensitivity to nuances of the situation and the other parties isn't highly valued, and decisions are based on cost-benefit analysis and objective factors. In contrast, emotional sensitivity is considered highly important in many Asian and Latin American countries, and the concept of saving face plays a crucial role in negotiation decisions. For example, an American manager nearly blew a deal with a Korean company because he complained directly to higher-level managers when he had difficulty getting the information he needed from his Korean counterparts. In the United States, such an approach would be acceptable, but in Korea, it was seen as a sign of disrespect. The lower-level Korean managers were horrified and embarrassed; the upper-level managers were offended; and the crisis was resolved only when top-level managers from the United States made a trip to Korea to apologize and show respect.[33] In Latin America, as well, face saving is considered crucial to preserving one's honor and dignity.[34]

As with our discussion of value differences, the information in these sections on communication, decision making, motivation, and negotiation are generalizations. The point is that, as a manager, you need to be aware that cultural differences exist and can influence how to interact most effectively with people from different countries and cultures.

WHAT ABOUT DIVERSE CULTURES IN A SINGLE COUNTRY?

City Fresh Foods in Boston ships out 4,000 meals a day to institutional customers ranging from nursing homes to charter schools. Many of the employees who prepare and deliver those meals don't speak English, but CEO Glynn Lloyd has found ways to make sure they work together smoothly. Nearly 70 percent of City Fresh Foods' employees are immigrants from places such as Brazil, Nigeria, the Dominican Republic, or Cape Verde, off the West Coast of Africa. Lloyd found that trying to get everyone to learn English was too massive a challenge, so City Fresh focuses on teaching people the limited language they need to work together—terms like "delivery ticket," "checkout sheet," or "ice pack." Job training is done by demonstration rather than verbally, and managers use numerical checklists that anyone, whatever their native language, can understand. Anyone who wants to move into management, though, has to learn English. And City Fresh helps by providing employees up to $1,000 a year for education.[35]

Many people reading this text will certainly work in a country other than their native land at some point in their careers. Others, though, might never leave their home country. Do these ideas about cross-cultural management apply to them? Most definitely. All of us know it's not necessary to go abroad to meet someone who has a cultural background different from our own.

In almost any country today, people of different nationalities, ethnicities, and cultural beliefs work side by side. The workforce of Canadian organizations is so diverse that it has jokingly been referred to as the "United Nations."[36] The United States is equally heterogeneous, with people from around the world working together on a daily basis. In addition to different national origins, people in organizations reflect various races, religions, and social and economic backgrounds, among other differences. Diversity and multiculturalism is a fact of life no manager can afford to ignore.

Valuing Diversity

Workforce diversity means a workforce made up of people who have different human qualities or who belong to different cultural groups. This includes not only different nationalities and races, but things such as gender, physical ability, and age, as well as people's varying social backgrounds, educational levels, or marital status.

The definition of diversity has been expanded. Decades ago, most companies defined diversity in terms of a very limited set of dimensions, but today's organizations are embracing a much more inclusive definition that recognizes a spectrum of differences that influence how people approach work, interact with each other, derive satisfaction from their work, and define who they are as people in the workplace.[37] Exhibit 14.5 illustrates the difference between the traditional model and a more inclusive model of diversity. The dimensions of diversity shown in the traditional model reflect primarily inborn differences that are immediately observable, such as race, gender, age, and physical ability. However, the inclusive model of diversity embraces *all* of the ways in which people differ, including dimensions of diversity that can be acquired or changed throughout one's lifetime. These dimensions may have less impact than those in the traditional model but nevertheless affect a person's self-definition and world view and influence the way the person is viewed by others. Secondary dimensions such as work style, communication style, and educational or skill level are particularly relevant in the organizational setting.[38]

Managers value diversity for many reasons. In the United States, managers say their companies value diversity because it gives the organization access to a broader range of opinions and viewpoints, it spurs greater creativity and innovation, it reflects an increasingly diverse customer base, and it enables the company to obtain the best talent and compete more effectively in a global marketplace.[39] A study of diversity management in the United Kingdom, Scandinavia, and continental Europe found managers reporting similar motives, as well as a desire to enhance the company's image and to improve employee satisfaction.[40] Indeed, a survey commissioned by *The New York Times* found that 91 percent of job seekers think diversity programs make a company a better place to work, and nearly all minority job seekers said they would prefer to work in a diverse workplace.[41]

Many managers are ill-prepared to handle diversity issues. Many Americans grew up in ethnically or racially unmixed neighborhoods and had little exposure to people substantially different from

DISCOVER KNOWLEDGE

Exhibit 14.5 Traditional versus Inclusive Models of Diversity

Source: Based on Anthony Oshiotse and Richard O'Leary, "Corning Creates an Inclusive Culture to Drive Technology Innovation and Performance," *Global Business and Organizational Excellence* 26, no. 3 (March–April 2007): 7–21, From DAFT/MARCIC, Understanding Management, 8E. © 2013 Cengage Learning.

themselves. The challenge is particularly great when working with people from other countries and cultures. One recent challenge at IBM involved a new immigrant, a Muslim woman who was required to have a photo taken for a company identification badge. She protested that her religious beliefs required that, as a married woman, she wear a veil and not expose her face to men in public. A typical American manager, schooled in traditional management training, might insist that she have the photo taken or hit the door. Fortunately, IBM has a well-developed diversity program and managers worked out a satisfactory compromise.[42]

Similar complicated issues occur for managers in other organizations and in other countries. Deutsche Bank's CEO Josef Ackerman came under attack in Germany, for example, for joking that including women on the bank's all-male executive board would make it "more colorful and prettier."[43] For female and minority managers, organizational life can sometimes be quite challenging. It is important that all managers understand the difficulties minorities face in organizations.

Management Challenges

What is it like for an African American managing a primarily white workforce, a woman supervising a group of men, or a 30-year-old immigrant promoted to manage a group of mostly 50- to 60-year-old middle managers? Many minority managers struggle daily with the problem of delegating authority and responsibility to employees who show them little respect. For many career women and minority managers, their experience suggests that no matter how many college degrees they earn, how many hours they work, how they dress, or how much effort and enthusiasm they invest, they are never perceived as "having the right stuff."

> **DISCOVER YOURSELF**
>
> **Interpret Your Score: Valuing Workplace Diversity** (Questionnaire 4)
>
> Comparative data for attitudes toward workplace diversity, which are reflected in your personal diversity values: **Intellectual Judgments** (Part A) Thirty person Mean score = 0.0; Top Quartile = 00–00; Bottom Quartile = 00–00. **Affective (Emotional) Reaction** (Part B) Mean = 0.0; Top Quartile = 00–00; Bottom Quartile = 00–00. **Behavioral Response** (Part C) Mean = 0.0; Top Quartile = 00–00; Bottom Quartile = 00–00. If your scores are near zero, then your attitudes and values are neutral. Higher positive scores mean that you hold positive values toward diversity and will likely deal sympathetically with bias in the workplace. Higher negative scores mean you hold negative values toward diversity and may be ill-prepared to deal with diversity issues that arise in your role as manager. What experiences have led to your diversity values? How do you think your values will contribute to a career in management? CNOW and CourseMate users can access dynamically updated comparative data through www.cengagebrain.com.

DISCOVER KNOWLEDGE

© CENGAGE LEARNING 2014

7 STEPS TO... Not Being Taken Seriously

All managers are judged by their body language as well as by what they say. Here are some nonverbal signals that can cause female and minority managers to be perceived as less powerful and credible in U.S. organizations.

1. **Tilt your head a lot.** Body language experts say keeping one's head straight and the chin high when talking with someone connotes power, while head tilting indicates submissiveness.
2. **Avoid direct eye contact.** Some cultures consider direct eye contact rude or disrespectful. But in most U.S. organizations, not looking people in the eye is taken as either a sign of submissiveness or evidence that you have something to hide.
3. **Physically condense yourself.** Women and some ethnic minorities tend to literally pull in their bodies to minimize their size and dominance. Look at high-status white men, and you'll notice they *expand*. Claiming space is a sign of power.
4. **Wait your turn.** The powerful talk more and interrupt more frequently. When asked what advice she would give professional women, former U.S. Secretary of State Madeleine Albright replied, "Learn to interrupt."
5. **Use a dead-fish handshake.** People with a delicate or too-gentle handshake are often judged to be passive, less confident, and less effective. In the United States, use a firm, full-palm handshake, while fully facing the other person.
6. **Speak "up."** Speaking with a low-pitched, slow-paced, downward-inflected voice commands people to listen. Many women's voices tend to rise at the end as if asking a question or seeking approval. Keep it down.
7. **Keep a rigid stance.** In general, people with a calm, relaxed posture are perceived as more powerful. If you have a rigid demeanor, people may perceive you as nervous and uncertain of yourself as a manager.

Sources: Based on Carol Kinsey Goman, "Body Language," *Leadership Excellence* (August 2010): 9; "Body Language Signs Exhibiting Confidence/Authority and Power," Body Language Magic Web site, http://www.improvementtower.com/bodylanguage/Body_Language_Signs_Exhibiting_Confidence_Authority_Power.html (accessed May 10, 2011); Gerry McMahon, "Good Body Language Can 'Do the Business'—A Large Percentage of the Messages We Send Out to Others Is Through Our Body Language," *Irish Times* (May 7, 2001); Patricia D. Palleschi, "The Hidden Messages Managers Send," *Manage* (July 1981): 8; and "Body Language Speaks Volumes without Saying a Word, Class Told," *The Salt Lake Tribune*, February 13, 1991.

DISCOVER KNOWLEDGE

Bias in Today's Workplace

Although blatant discrimination is not as widespread as it was in the past, bias in the workplace often shows up in subtle ways—a lack of choice assignments, the disregard by a subordinate of a minority manager's directions, or the ignoring of comments made by women and minorities at meetings. A survey by Korn Ferry International found that 59 percent of minority managers surveyed had observed a racially motivated double standard in the delegation of assignments.[44] Minority managers may spend more time waiting for a chance, and then have to prove themselves over and over again with each new assignment. Minority managers typically feel that they have to put in longer hours and extra effort to achieve the same status as their white colleagues.

Another study found that white managers gave more negative performance ratings to black managers and white subordinates, and more positive ratings to white managers and black subordinates, affirming the widespread acceptance of these employees in their stereotypical roles.[45] Bruce Gordon, who was president of Bell Atlantic's enterprise group before Bell was purchased by Verizon, once said, "It's not enough to be as good as the next person. We have to be better."[46]

Biculturalism

Another problem is that many minority managers feel they have to become bicultural in order to succeed. **Biculturalism** can be defined as the sociocultural skills and attitudes used by racial minorities as they move back and forth between the dominant culture and their own ethnic or racial culture.[47] Research on differences between whites and blacks has focused on issues of biculturalism and how it affects employees' access to information, level of respect and appreciation, and relation to superiors and subordinates. In general, African Americans feel less accepted in their organizations, perceive themselves to have less discretion on their jobs, receive lower ratings on job performance, experience lower levels of job satisfaction, and reach career plateaus earlier than whites. They find themselves striving to adopt behaviors and attitudes that will help them be successful in the white-dominated corporate world while at the same time maintaining their ties to the black community and culture.

Other minority groups struggle with biculturalism as well. For example, Asian Americans who aspire to management positions are often frustrated by the stereotype that they are hardworking but not executive material because they are too quiet and deferential. Assertiveness and pressing your views in a group is seen as a characteristic of leadership in American culture, but Asians typically view this behavior as inappropriate and immature.[48] Some Asian Americans feel they have a chance for career advancement only by becoming bicultural or abandoning their native cultures altogether.

Challenges to Women Managers

Female managers face significant challenges too. In recent years, many women have been choosing to step off the career ladder. This so-called *opt-out trend* has provoked quite a debate. Some say that many women have decided corporate success isn't worth the high price in terms of reduced family and personal time, greater stress, and negative health effects.[49] These observers and researchers argue that most women just don't want to work as hard, aggressively, and competitively as most men want to work.[50] Critics, however, charge that this is just another way to blame women themselves for the dearth of female managers at higher organizational levels.[51]

Although some women are voluntarily leaving the fast track, there are many more who genuinely want to move up the corporate ladder but find their paths blocked. Consider that 55 percent of executive women surveyed by Catalyst said they aspire to senior management levels.[52] In addition, a survey of 103 women voluntarily leaving executive jobs in *Fortune* 1000 companies found that corporate culture was cited as the No. 1 reason for leaving.[53] Top-level corporate culture

DISCOVER KNOWLEDGE

What's Your Problem?

Q: I work in senior management at a pharmaceutical company and have been doing very well these past years, steadily working up the corporate ladder. Several months ago, a man seven years younger than me was hired in a position equal to mine. From the beginning, I could see the ease with which he interacted with the long-time male executives, whether it was playing golf, going to Friday night poker, or just gabbing on about sports teams. What is most striking to me is his natural sense of entitlement, how he casually delegates tasks to me and others who are more senior than he is. Then he'll redo some of the work I've turned in. Though I know I could learn a lot from this guy about how to get my own sense of entitlement, I feel I am being swallowed in this mostly male environment. What should I do?

A: Some people might advise talking to your colleague about your concerns, but that is risky, because some people will take the vulnerability you show and the information you give and use it against you later, so be careful. On the other hand, remember that leadership is about doing the right thing and taking risks. You can try to see if anyone else is experiencing what you are or if it is only you. Quietly find out what your firm's record is in promoting women to higher levels, pay ranges, types of access to the boss, and so on. Without creating a fuss, check with other women to see if they are frustrated. If you find you are not alone and have evidence to back this up, find a sympathetic executive—someone you really trust—and share a little bit of your concern, just to test the waters. If this executive is open, schedule a meeting with him, you, and another of the women. See if you can make any headway in making the organization more open to women. In the process, if you have conducted yourself professionally and competently, you may just gain some admiration from a male colleague or two.

Source: This problem is adapted from "Confronting Gender Bias Head-on, Part II," *Washington Post,* July 15, 2009, http://views.washingtonpost.com/leadership/leadership_house_call/2009/07/confronting-gender-bias-head-on-part-ii.html?referrer=emaillink (accessed July 15, 2009).

© CENGAGE LEARNING 2014

in the United States still revolves around white, heterosexual, American males, who tend to hire and promote people who look, act, and think like them. Few companies have role models and mentors for women who want to move into high-level positions.[54]

Among women who have managed to reach top levels of organizations, fully 96 percent said adapting to a predominantly white male culture was necessary for their success.[55]

Thus, many women find themselves in a double bind. They have learned that they need to act and think like men to succeed, but they are criticized when they do so. The band of acceptable behavior is much more narrow for women managers than for men. When women managers are assertive and competitive like their male colleagues, they are often judged in performance reviews as being too tough, abrasive, or not supportive of their employees. Conversely, if they behave in stereotypical feminine ways of showing care and concern for others, they're typically judged as less competent. One study found that women managers are rarely perceived by their peers and supervisors as both competent and likable.[56]

WAYS WOMEN LEAD

Cindy Szadokierski quit her job teaching high school French 25 years ago and went to work as a reservations agent for United Airlines. Today, she is vice president in charge of operations for United's largest hub at O'Hare International Airport. As she oversees 4,000 employees and 600 flights a day, Szadokierski's favorite times are the weekly afternoon walkabouts on the O'Hare ramp and the weekly morning strolls through the terminal. Why? Because they give her a chance to connect with employees and customers. Pete McDonald, chief operating officer of United's parent, UAL Corporation, says there were serious operations problems at O'Hare, so they put "the most communicative person" in the job. In addition to learning from employees and customers during her weekly ramp and terminal outings, Szadokierski meets regularly with her management team to talk about what's going right, what's going wrong, and how the team can collaboratively fix any problems.[57]

Cindy Szadokierski is a highly effective and successful manager, with her own unique style of leading, but she shares some characteristics with other successful female managers, such as an emphasis on good communication and personal relationships. Despite the challenges women face, some people think they might actually make better managers, partly because of a more collaborative, relationship-oriented approach that is in tune with today's global and multicultural environment.[58]

As attitudes and values change with changing generations, the qualities women seem to naturally possess may lead to a gradual role reversal in organizations. For example, there's a dramatic gender reversal in U.S. education, with girls taking over almost every leadership role from kindergarten to graduate school. In addition, women of all races and ethnic groups are outpacing men in earning bachelor's and master's degrees. Women are rapidly closing the M.D. and Ph.D. gap, and they make up about half of all U.S. law students, half of all undergraduate business majors, and about 30 percent of MBA candidates. Overall, women's participation in both the labor force and civic affairs has steadily increased since the mid-1950s, while men's participation has slowly but steadily declined.[59] As mentioned earlier, women are now the majority in the U.S. workforce. However, there are still significantly fewer women than men in

> **DISCOVER YOURSELF**
>
> **Interpret Your Score: Gender and Authority** (Questionnaire 5)
>
> Research indicates that women often are considered to have better leadership skills than men, yet implicit attitudes may link men to high-authority roles and women to low-authority roles. Comparative data for **Gender Attitudes:** Thirty person Mean score = 17.6; Top Quartile = 19–27; Bottom Quartile = 10–17. A score above 20 would mean that you tend to favor men in authority roles. A score below 20 would mean you tend to favor women. A score of exactly 20 means you have a balanced attitude toward men and women in authority roles. How do you account for your score? What experiences have led to your attitude toward men and women in authority roles? How will your attitude fit your chosen career? CNOW and CourseMate users can access dynamically updated comparative data through www.cengagebrain.com.

© CENGAGE LEARNING 2014

management positions, particularly at higher organizational levels.[60]

Women As Managers

According to James Gabarino, an author and professor of human development at Cornell University, women are "better able to deliver in terms of what modern society requires of people—paying attention, abiding by rules, being verbally competent, and dealing with interpersonal relationships in offices."[61] His observation is supported by the fact that female managers are typically rated higher by subordinates on interpersonal skills as well as on factors such as task behavior, communication, ability to motivate others, and goal accomplishment.[62] Research has also found a correlation between balanced gender composition in companies (that is, roughly equal male and female representation) and higher organizational performance. Moreover, a study by Catalyst indicates that organizations with the highest percentage of women in top management financially outperform, by about 35 percent, those with the lowest percentage of women in higher-level jobs.[63]

Is Management Style Gender Driven?

Several researchers have looked at the differences between male and female managers. Traits traditionally associated with white, American-born males include aggressiveness or assertiveness, rational analysis, and a "take charge" attitude. Male leaders tend to be competitive and individualistic and prefer working in vertical hierarchies. They rely on formal authority and position in their dealings with subordinates. Of course, women may also demonstrate these traits, but research has found that, in general, women prefer less competitive environments than men, tend to be more collaborative, and are more concerned with relationship building, inclusiveness, participation, and caring.[64] Women managers are often more willing to share power and information, to encourage employee development, and to strive to enhance others' feelings of self-worth.

Professor and author Judy B. Rosener has called women's approach **interactive leadership.**[65] The manager favors a consensual and collaborative process, and influence derives from relationships rather than position power and authority. Although the values associated with interactive leadership, such as inclusion, relationship building, and caring, are generally considered "feminine" values, interactive leadership is not gender-specific. These values are becoming increasingly valuable for both male and female managers. Today's team-based and global organizations are no longer looking for top-down authority figures but for more collaborative and inclusive approaches.[66] Any manager can learn to adopt a more inclusive style by paying attention to nonverbal behavior and developing skills such as listening, empathy, cooperation, and collaboration.[67]

YOUR CHALLENGE AS A MANAGER

For a manager today, the goal is to ensure that *all* people—women, ethnic minorities, younger people, gays and lesbians, the disabled, older people, racial minorities, as well as white males—are given equal opportunities and treated with fairness and respect. Strong, culturally sensitive managers can move organizations toward a more inclusive culture, where all individuals are valued and respected for the unique abilities they bring to the workplace. Here are four tips[68] to keep in mind:

1. *Develop a personal, long-range vision that supports diversity.* As a manager, work to include individuals of various ethnic and cultural groups, races, ages, and so on at all levels of the organization. Whenever you have a decision to make, take differing perspectives into account.
2. *Commit to cross-cultural understanding and gain a general knowledge of the dimensions of diversity.* Inclusive managers consciously avoid the curse of ethnocentrism and appreciate the benefits of different ways of thinking and behaving. You should develop a broad understanding of the various dimensions of diversity and how differences affect working relationships.
3. *Be open to changing yourself.* To be effective working in a diverse environment, encourage feedback from employees, learn to accept criticism in the spirit of learning, and be willing to change your behavior as needed.
4. *Make a serious effort to mentor diverse employees.* Take an active role in creating opportunities for all employees to use their unique abilities. Offer honest feedback and coaching as needed to help diverse employees advance in the organization.

NEED TO KNOW

- As a manager, you will likely work with people from other countries and cultures. Even if you never leave the United States, diversity within the nation is rapidly increasing. Both the Hispanic and Asian populations are growing while the white, non-Hispanic population is declining.
- Cultural differences can create major problems for managers working in foreign countries. Culture consists of values, assumptions, norms, and patterns of thought that are shared by members of a social group and shape people's behaviors and perception of the world. Seven critical areas of cultural value differences are individualism versus collectivism, power distance, uncertainty avoidance, assertiveness, time orientation, doing versus being, and performance orientation.
- Personal qualities for being an effective multicultural manager include an attitude of ethnorelativism and a high CQ (cultural intelligence quotient).
- What people expect from managers varies culturally. One key area of difference relates to high-context versus low-context communications. A high-context culture is one in which people use communication to build personal relationships. In a low-context culture, people use communication primarily to exchange facts and information. As a manager, you should also be aware of cultural differences in the areas of decision making, motivation, and negotiation. What works in one culture might not work in another.
- Within any country, such as the United States, people of different ethnicities, ages, races, genders, and so forth work side by side. Workforce diversity means a workforce made up of people with different human qualities or who belong to different cultural groups. Three specific diversity challenges in the United States are subtle bias in the workplace, biculturalism, and problems women managers face.
- Because many women use an interactive leadership style, they may make better managers in today's world. An interactive style means using a consensual and collaborative process and influencing people based on relationships rather than position power and authority. The values associated with interactive leadership are considered feminine values, but interactive leadership is *not* gender-specific. Many men also use this style of leadership, and anyone can learn to be an interactive leader.
- The goal for today's managers is to ensure that all people are given equal opportunities and treated with fairness and respect. Four characteristics for being an inclusive leader are a personal vision that supports diversity; a commitment to cross-cultural understanding and knowledge of the dimensions of diversity; openness to changing oneself; and a serious effort to mentor and develop diverse employees.

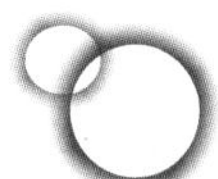

ACTION LEARNING

DELIBERATE PRACTICE EXERCISES

Understanding Cultural Differences

Step 1: Identify three people you will talk to over the course of the next week who are members of a different racial, ethnic, religious, or national group from you. Try to choose people from school or work, so you know you can safely sit and talk with them. Each person should be from a different group.

Step 2: Ask each person the following questions and write their answers in the table below. Explain that you are doing some research on diversity for coursework.

Question	Person #1	Person #2	Person #3
Where are you from?			
Does your name have cultural or religious significance?			
How would you describe your group versus my group?			
What are some customs you have that might be different from what I do?			
What are some foods you eat that people in my group don't eat often?			
What do people in my group sometimes do that is unknowingly disrespectful?			
How can I learn to be more appreciative of your group?			

Step 3: Your instructor may ask you to write a report or share your results in class.

The Ups and the Downs[69]

When people are in a minority, whether it is because of racial, ethnic, or gender differences, there is often an up-down relationship, with the minority being in the down position in terms of power and status.

Step 1: In order to help you understand more about this dynamic, read the following parable from Dr. Robert Terry.

The Parable of the Ups and the Downs

What makes an "Up" an Up and a "Down" a Down is that an Up can do more to a Down than a Down can do to an Up. That's what keeps an Up up and a Down down. The Ups tend to talk to each other and study the Downs, asking the Downs "what's up?" or "what's coming down?" for that matter. The Downs spend a lot of time taking the Ups out to lunch or dinner, to explain their downness. The Ups listen attentively (sometimes), often in amazement about the experiences of being a Down. They contrast one's down experience with another's down experience, and at times don't worry too much about what the Downs are up to, because the Downs never seem to get together. If they did, the Ups would have to shape up.

After a while, the Downs grow weary of talking to the Ups. They tire of explaining and justifying their downness. They think, "If I have to explain my downness one more time, I'll throw up." And so they form a process they call "networking and support groups." This act makes the Ups nervous. Three Ups together is a board meeting, but three Downs together is a revolution. Some Ups hire Downs, dress them up, and send them down to see what the other Downs are up to. They sometimes call this "inclusion training." This creates a serious problem for the Down who is dressed up with nowhere to go. The Down doesn't know whether he/she is up or down. That's why Downs in the middle often burn out.

Sometimes what the Ups do to smarten up is to ask the Downs to come into a program one at a time to explain their downness. The Ups call this "diversity coaching." Of course, the Ups never have to explain their upness. That's why they're Ups rather than Downs.

The good news is that we are both Ups and Downs, depending on the situation. The bad news is that when we are Ups, it often makes us stupid. We call that "dumbupness." It's not because Ups are not smart. It's that Ups don't have to pay attention to Downs the way Downs have to pay attention to Ups. Downs always have to spend time figuring out what the Ups are up to. The only time Ups worry about Downs is when Downs get uppity, at which time they're put down by the Ups. The Ups' perception is that Downs are overly sensitive; they have an attitude problem. It is never understood that Ups are "underly" sensitive and have an attitude problem.

Step 2: Complete the following table:

List a few situations where you felt like an "Up."	
What about situations when you felt like a "Down"?	
Give two examples of times when you've seen the up-down dynamic.	1. 2.
When you are an Up, how do you behave toward Downs?	
When you are a Down, how do you behave toward Ups?	
What are the prices organizations (and society) pay for having Ups and Downs?	
How could we learn to work more side by side?	

IN-CLASS TEAM EXERCISE

Gender Differences in Communication

Numerous studies (most notably Deborah Tannen's work) have shown that males and females have different styles of communication. This exercise will help you explore that theory.

Step 1: The instructor asks people in the class if they think there are any differences in communication between males and females, and, if so, what they are.

Step 2: Divide into groups of eight to ten. Two people will be observers and the rest will be part of the simulation. Each group (not counting observers) should be as evenly balanced between male and female as possible. If you have more males or more females in the class, assign more of that gender to be observers. *Observers ONLY read their confidential instructions below* while the rest of the group moves to Step 3.

Step 3: Each group chooses a controversial topic to discuss. Make sure you have people in the group who already disagree on the topic. If it is controversial, but you all agree, that issue won't work. Try to pick a topic for which there is almost complete disagreement in your group. Some possible topics are the death penalty, smoking bans, the wearing of fur, legalization of marijuana, abortion laws, current political candidates, the use of animals in research, the value of cosmetic surgery, legalization of gay marriage, importance of getting top grades versus actual learning, the adage that blonds have more fun, the importance of being thin, the value of growing up in a big city versus a small town. *Do not pick an issue that is repulsive to any group member.*

Possible issues for our group to discuss:	The issue we decided on:

Step 4: The instructor makes sure each group has chosen an issue, and that the observers are ready. Groups discuss their issue for 20 minutes, while observers take notes. The instructor calls time after 20 minutes.

Step 5: Observers go to the side to discuss their findings and prepare to give their results to the group. While observers are talking, the rest of the group debriefs what happened with the group dynamics, making notes in the table below of any differences in male and female communication that were noticed.

How did females communicate?	How did males communicate?

Step 6: Each observer group writes down results and gives a copy to the instructor, and then observers go back to their groups and report.

Step 7: Each group talks about male–female behaviors in class.

Step 8: The instructor leads a class discussion on gender and communication.

Confidential Instructions for Observers

1. You must have at least two observers. Make sure each of you has access to a stopwatch (on your phone, perhaps) or something with a second hand.

2. Assign one of you to watch the males and the other to watch the females.
3. On a sheet of paper, write down every person's name that is in the group you are to watch (either males or females, depending on your assignment). Leave enough space after each name to make notes. Be sure you know everyone's name.
4. When the group starts to discuss, put a check mark beside each person's name whenever that person talks. Use your second-hand measure to count how long that person "has the floor." If two are talking at the same time and are equally listened to, try to get both, but if one is dominant, only count that person. Your numbers will be approximate, so don't worry if you can't be exact under these conditions.
5. Talk with the other observer to make sure you both understand the instructions. You will be doing all of this while the group is selecting their topic.
6. Take notes as your group discusses its issue.
7. After the group is done and you've talked with your observer partner, fill out the report below and make a copy on a separate paper for the instructor.

Person's name (list each group member)	Number of times this person spoke	Length of each speaking time (list them)	Approximate average of time talked; divide cumulative time by number of times spoken

FIELD TEAM EXERCISE

Becoming a Minority[70]

In today's globalized, flat business world, skills for dealing with people from different cultures, ethnic groups, or countries are vital to your success as a manager. One way to learn how to interact effectively with people from different backgrounds is to have empathy, to know how it feels to be different. This field exercise will help you develop this kind of empathy.

Step 1: Divide into groups of two people each. Choose a place to go that is "foreign" or "different" to both of you. Ideas include a different church or synagogue, a place where people mostly from another racial group go, young people going to a nursing home,

attending an organization's meeting for disabled people, going to a wedding of someone from another country, and so on. DO NOT go to any dangerous place. Be careful.

Step 2: Go to your chosen place. Do not talk to each other while you are there. You will be permitted to talk before or after, but not during, unless there is some emergency.

Step 3: Afterwards, both of you discuss what you experienced.

Step 4: Fill in the table below. Your instructor may also ask you to write a report of your experience.

What were the similarities between this place and your normal life?	
What were the differences?	
How did you feel as a minority?	
How did people treat you?	
What did you learn about what it is like to be a minority?	

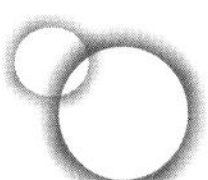

TEST YOUR METTLE

ROLE PLAY SIMULATIONS

Getting Respect

Background: Re-read the written Video Incident at the beginning of the chapter. Women and minorities sometimes feel discounted in group situations or with certain coworkers. If women and minorities move into management, there are often certain employees who have a hard time respecting them. This role play explores these dynamics at work in the opening Video Incident.

Instructions: Divide into groups of three. One person will be general manager Jane Sutton, one CFO Carlos Hernandez, and one an observer. Each person reads only his or her confidential role, but the observer reads both. Spend 15 minutes on the role play.

Confidential information for Jane: You've put up with Carlos's put-downs for too long. He's dismissive when you make comments or express ideas and he seems to enjoy disagreeing with you on almost anything. Because of his cultural background and its emphasis on the need for "saving face," you've decided to talk to him alone rather than call him out in a team meeting. You need to let him know that respecting you is part of his job. But you have to be careful not to come on too strong, because it might create more negative feelings. He also won't want to lose face to you, personally. Therefore, you need to gently but firmly let Carlos know which behaviors are not acceptable, as well as let him know how much you value him as a team member.

Confidential information for Carlos: Jane's on another one of her rampages and wants to talk to you. Either she has another wacked-out idea, or she's upset with you for something she thinks you did. She never seems to check anything out before she calls you in. She'll hear a rumor that you were complaining about her decisions, but she doesn't bother to find out that you actually did not say those things. You have no idea how she got promoted to this position, because she clearly is not up to the task. They need someone older, with more authority, more decisiveness. Jane tries hard, but she just isn't cut out to be a leader. And let's face it, you think, few women are. You'd never say that to Jane, of course, because she'd jump all over you and maybe even file a lawsuit. She's got a temper, that one. Uses the law, rather than her own abilities, to maintain control. You've learned to humor her, just agree with everything, and then go about your business as usual.

After the role play, the observer gives feedback and then the group discusses these questions:

1. What parts of the role play felt familiar to you?
2. What role did gender expectations play?
3. Is it ever necessary to harshly call someone on their patronizing or condescending behavior?

SHUTTERSTOCK #53973379

The Management Consultant from Appazit

This Role Play Simulation is available online at www.cengagebrain.com.

VIDEO APPLICATION

See It Online

Mitchell Gold + Bob Williams

Mitchell Gold + Bob Williams (MG+BW) leads the furniture manufacturing industry with its generous benefits and trendsetting diversity policies. With over $100 million in sales, the company's policies seem to be working.

Discussion Questions

1. Maria Thompson, store manager, said that her gender has no bearing on her performance evaluations or relationships with coworkers, and there is no glass ceiling at MG+BW. How typical do you think that is in furniture manufacturing and sales?
2. At MG+BW all employees receive the same generous benefits. There are nondiscrimination policies, diversity training, a wellness program, a gym, a daycare, a café, and scholarships for employees' children. The idea is to make employees happy. Do you think the company may go too far, in the sense of paying out more to employees than they can get back in profit?
3. Would you want to work at MG+BW? Why?

CASE INCIDENTS

True to Myself

Ethney Gentry was thrilled to have infiltrated the ultimate good old boy network, landing a job with a mid-sized Tulsa-based oil company. Armed with solid credentials and what she considered the strengths of female leadership—listening, collaboration, consensus building, and organization—Ethney looked forward to her first meeting with the company's retiring first female manager, Alexis Bale.

Alexis offered a firm, almost painful, handshake and a cup of coffee.

"I've been looking forward to meeting you, Alexis," Ethney said.

"It's Alex."

"Oh, I didn't know." Ethney took a sip of piping hot coffee with a sudden vague feeling of discomfort. The first moments of this much-anticipated meeting seemed awkward and somewhat strained.

"I'll be honest with you," Alex said as she walked around and sat in the oversized chair behind her desk. "You're here for the same reason I was here. When our founder Champ Luman died 12 years ago, his three middle-aged daughters, referred to throughout the company as *the girls*, became major shareholders. They pushed hard for the inclusion of a woman in management. That *was* me. Now it's you."

Ethney tried to show no reaction as she set her cup on the desk. "Are you implying that I was selected over more qualified male candidates?"

"No. I was not on the selection team. I've seen your résumé, and you are an excellent addition to the organization. But qualifications aside, you and I fulfill, shall we say, the 'diversity' requirements for an otherwise all-male club."

Ethney could not believe the undisguised cynicism of the woman across the desk. She was torn between a desire to get up and march out of the office and a desire to stay and hear the entire lecture. She decided to take the high road. "My understanding was that you have been very successful here," she said.

SHUTTERSTOCK #53973379

"I suppose so." Alex gazed up at the numerous photographs showing oil rigs scattered across the Oklahoma plains. "I learned to play the game," she said somewhat wistfully and then suddenly turned and looked at Ethney. "I'm not trying to intimidate you. But I think that coming in, you should understand some things."

"Such as?"

"Such as . . . don't be too eager with your ideas or opinions. When I started, I intended to jump right in and contribute. The men resented it. I was considered a 'pushy broad' as one *gentleman* told me to my face. The reaction to me was harsh. They may have been stuck with me, but these guys could marginalize me—make sure I didn't count, and make sure I knew it."

"What did you do?" asked Ethney.

"I stewed awhile and finally tried the opposite tactic. I jumped up to get coffee for everyone. I sought the *wise counsel* of their opinions before daring to make a suggestion in meetings. I played the female image that was in their minds. I felt like an idiot. I kowtowed till I thought I would throw up," Alex said.

"How did they react?"

"I was no longer marginalized. But I wasn't respected either. I had quietly stepped back and accepted *my place*."

"Why didn't you just quit?"

"Because I knew that's exactly what they wanted me to do. And I'm just mean enough and stubborn enough not to give them what they wanted."

Ethney took a deep breath and shook her head. "This sounds like the 1950s. I can't believe men in management act like this."

"Uh-huh. It may be a little better now, but they are still throwbacks to *Mad Men*."

"So how did you develop this reputation for success if you went from being ignored to being a doormat?" Ethney asked.

"Have you met Bill Ledson?"

Ethney nodded, took a sip of coffee, and leaned forward, waiting to hear the secret of success.

"At an industry meeting in Houston, his wife, Margaret, got drunk, cornered me, and drawled, '*Listen, Honey. I've been around oil men all my life. My daddy and his daddy were oil men. You're going to have to wise up and take the plunge—become one of the boys. It's the only way you'll ever be accepted.*' She reminded me that I was on *their* turf. Margaret told me, '*Honey, as a wife and hostess for this crowd, I've talked more football than you can imagine. I hate football. I hang on for the commercials. But they don't know that. Bill doesn't know that. Me and God—we're the only ones who know that. Trust me,*' she said. '*These guys do get down to some serious business, but not until they grouse about how Oklahoma State was robbed of its chance to play LSU for the national championship.*'"

"Isn't that trivializing the men in this company?" Ethney asked.

Alex shrugged. "It worked. I became Alex and I became one of the guys. And, over time, I came to be treated with grudging respect, and promotions followed. I held the room spellbound for 15 minutes at the last board meeting with my theory that Texas A&M joined the Southeastern Conference in order to up their chances for better bowls because the BCS favors the SEC. Later, when I submitted my ideas for improving coordination of teams in the oil fields, they thought it was *brilliant*! I'm one of them!"

Ethney nodded, somewhat impressed.

"Take my advice. Change your name. Ethney is too girlie. What's your middle name?"

"Madison."

"Be Madison." Alex walked Ethney to the door and shook her hand. The meeting was over.

As the door closed behind her, Ethney's feelings about what she had just heard ranged from bewilderment to anger to depression.

She sold out. All of these women sold out. They can't even be who they are. I am an experienced, educated, qualified, capable woman. I don't want to be Madison, Ethney thought confidently and pushed the elevator button.

The elevator opened and she stepped inside. *What have I gotten myself into?*

Discussion Questions

1. If you were Ethney, how would you try to conduct yourself at the oil company? Why do you think your approach would be successful?
2. Do you think women have to plot a strategy to be accepted in male-dominated corporate cultures? Would you adopt a strategy in which you acted differently from your normal personality? Why?
3. What does it mean to be "true to yourself"? Is being true to yourself more important than achieving personal career success in a male-dominated company? Is it okay to enable the continuation of an "unhealthy" work environment for women? Why?

Diversity Nightmare

Stephen Gulliford jumped at the chance to take over management of the southeastern regional manufacturing plant for Jordan (pronounced *jər-dən*) Carpets. With corporate headquarters and the main manufacturing facility located outside Tucson, Arizona, the company expanded four years earlier, with a new facility located in the Antioch section of metropolitan Nashville, Tennessee.

Since its founding in 1990, the company prided itself on utilizing the knowledge and carpeting/weaving skills of a diverse workforce. The Tucson facility was largely composed of Mexican Americans and Native Americans whose cultures boasted outstanding weaving and carpeting traditions.

In an effort to improve production and quality, Stephen had successfully developed and implemented manufacturing teams in the Tucson plant, providing cross-functional coordination and opening greater opportunity for task variety and responsibility for workers. An environment of friendly competition developed between teams, and the plant had experienced improved output through a more inclusive work environment. Native American and Mexican American employees had worked well together and communication within and across departments had improved dramatically.

Stephen hoped to bring that same success to the Antioch plant, which suffered from slow production and numerous complaints from both management and workers about the effect of the work environment on morale and performance.

Antioch had been selected as a site for manufacturing because, like Tucson, it offered a community rich in diversity. The southeast corner of Nashville/Davidson County running from Antioch Pike, spreading west toward Nolensville Road and east to Murfreesboro Pike, was teeming with diverse immigrant populations dominated by Hispanics, but including Somali and Sudanese refugees, an estimated 30,000 Egyptians, and the largest Kurdish population outside the Middle East, as well as scatterings of other ethnic groups. An astonishing 93 languages were spoken in metro schools. Small businesses had popped up across the city, but particularly along this southeast corridor. Local government, universities, and organizations around the city encouraged dialogue and celebrated diversity, highlighted by Centennial Park's annual Celebration of Cultures. A potential employment pool of hardworking immigrants from cultures rich in carpet-making traditions and in need of jobs made the city a perfect expansion location for Jordan.

Stephen was certain that, as in Tucson, the implementation of manufacturing teams throughout the Antioch plant would result in a turnaround in production and overall quality. However, within months of his arrival, one highly respected Antioch department manager resigned in anger, accusing Stephen and other company representatives of undercutting his authority. Another manager who transferred to Antioch from Tucson likewise resigned, claiming the diversity within this plant's workforce made it impossible to build teams or to develop communication. "This is an impossible situation," he reported to Tucson. "The people want to work and need to work. They show up and work hard. But they stick together with others from their own culture, often speaking a native language. I cannot train people or create and manage cross-department teams when I cannot be understood and I cannot understand them. It's chaos down here."

"We're trying," Stephen assured Tucson. "But communication problems are unbelievable. Just getting information to workers is challenging. We abandoned the overwhelming task of providing basic instructions in a variety of languages and tried the IKEA method of using picture instructions that could be understood by everyone. That works for signage, but not for training materials for team development."

Stephen and his managers' use of onsite interpreters from among the workers was time consuming and costly, and on occasion, the translations were flawed, leading to mistakes and more delays, particularly in regard to machine maintenance issues.

"We thought we had lucked out," Stephen explained. "Because within each immigrant population in the plant, we have a number of highly educated, English-speaking people who can't get certified here in America in their fields of expertise and so they take whatever jobs are available. So, for example, I have a guy with a master's degree in architecture and another with an automotive engineering degree. But without going back to school to get the certifications required here in America, they can't get jobs in those fields. So we took these educated people and assigned them as leaders of the various teams. Did that solve our problems? No. Because within the various cultures groups recognize their *own* leaders and they may be members of a certain family. We have entire neighborhoods from 'back home' that can completely monopolize that ethnic group. So some teams will listen to and follow my hand-picked educated English-speaking guy and some teams will brush him off."

"If you need a visual representation of the problem," one Antioch manager explained to Carson Anderson, the head of HR in Tucson, "you only have to look at the lunchroom. The Egyptians are all sitting together in one section; the Sudanese are together in another; the Hispanics are somewhere else—and everyone is chattering away in their language . . ."

"And I'm supposed to take all of this and create working teams?" Stephen complained. "Now I understand why international treaty negotiations break down."

"Okay, let's all take a breath here," COO Travis Collins suggested. "Diversity is working in Tucson. You have lots of examples. So why can't we model what's already working and create a workable structure for this plant?"

Discussion Questions

1. What do you think is the problem in the Antioch plant? What is the cause of that problem?
2. How do you think Stephen and his team of managers might cut through the cultural and language differences to create a more collaborative and productive workforce?
3. How might Stephen and his management team work through their own discomfort and frustration with other languages and cultures?

PERSONAL SKILLS LOG

Directions: Fill in the rows below based on what you learned from each part of the chapter that you completed.

	What is my key takeaway or insight from this activity?	What do I personally do well (strength) regarding this activity?	What could I improve (weakness) about myself regarding this activity?	How might I use what I've learned from this activity in the future?
Manager Challenge Incident:				
Discover Yourself Questionnaires:				
Deliberate Practice Exercises:				
In-Class and/or Field Team Exercises:				
Role-Play Exercises:				
Case Incidents:				

PERSONAL SKILLS LOG

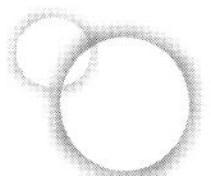

REFERENCES

Discover Yourself

1 Based on Robert J. House, Paul J. Hanges, Mansour Javidan, et al., eds., *Culture, Leadership, and Organizations: The GLOBE Study of 62 Societies* (Thousand Oaks, CA: Sage Publications, 2004); Geert Hofstede, *Culture's Consequences* (London: Sage Publications, 1984); and D. Matsumoto, M. D. Weissman, K. Preston, B.R. Brown, and C. Kupperbausch, "Context-Specific Measurement of Individualism-Collectivism on the Individual Level: The Individualism-Collectivism Interpersonal Assessment Inventory," *Journal of Cross-Cultural Psychology* 28, no. 6 (1997): 743–767.

2 Based on P. Christopher Earley and Elaine Mosakowski, "Cultural Intelligence," *Harvard Business Review* (October 2004): 139–146; Soon Ang, Lynn Van Dyne, Christine Koh, et al., "Cultural Intelligence: Its Measurement and Effects on Cultural Judgment and Decision Making, Cultural Adaptation, and Task Performance," *Management and Organization Review* 3 (2007): 335–371; and David C. Thomas and Kerr Inkson, *Cultural Intelligence: People Skills for Global Business* (San Francisco: Berrett-Koehler, 2004).

3 Adapted from Cynthia Barnum and Natasha Wolniansky, "Why Americans Fail at Overseas Negotiations," *Management Review* (October 1989): 54–57.

4 Based on Kenneth P. De Meuse and Todd J. Hostager, "Developing an Instrument for Measuring Attitudes Toward and Perceptions of Workplace Diversity: An Initial Report," *Human Resource Development Quarterly* (Spring 2001): 33–51; and Alfred B. Heilbrun, "Measurement of Masculine and Feminine Sex Role Identities as Independent Dimensions," *Journal of Consulting and Clinical Psychology* 44 (1976): 183–190.

5 Laurie A. Rudman and Stephan E. Killanski, "Implicit and Explicit Attitudes Toward Female Authority," *Personality and Social Psychology Bulletin* 26(11), pp. 1315–1328, copyright © 2000. Reprinted by Permission of SAGE Publications.

Discover Knowledge

6 Based on an example in Jeanne Brett, Kristin Behfar, and Mary C. Kern, "Managing Multicultural Teams," *Harvard Business Review* (November 2006): 84–91.

7 Jennifer Cheeseman Day, "National Population Projections," Population Profile of the United States, U.S. Census Bureau, http://www.census.gov/population/www/pop-profile/natproj.html (accessed May 6, 2011); and Laura B. Shrestha and Elayne J. Heisler, "The Changing Demographic Profile of the United States," Congressional Research Service, March 31, 2011, http://www.fas.org/sgp/crs/misc/RL32701.pdf (accessed May 6, 2011).

8 "Employment Projections: 2008–2018 Summary," U.S. Department of Labor, Bureau of Labor Statistics, December 10, 2009, http://www.bls.gov/news.release/ecopro.nr0.htm (accessed September 21, 2010).

9 Hanna Rosin, "The End of Men," *The Atlantic Monthly*, July–August 2010, http://www.theatlantic.com/magazine/archive/2010/07/the-end-of-men/8135/ (accessed December 25, 2010).

10 Nicola Clark, "Turnaround Effort Is Challenging at Airbus; A Stew of European Cultures," *The New York Times*, May 18, 2007; Carol Matlack, "Snafus: Wayward Airbus," *BusinessWeek* (October 23, 2006): 46–48; Nicola Clark, "A Humbled Airbus Learns Hard Lessons," *The New York Times*, December 14, 2006.

11 Based on Nancy J. Adler, *International Dimensions of Organizational Behavior*, 4th ed. (Cincinnati, OH: South-Western, 2002), p.16.

12 The description of these values is based on Geert Hofstede, "The Interaction Between National and Organizational Value Systems," *Journal of Management Studies* 22 (1985): 347–357; "Retrospective: Culture's Consequences," a collection of articles focusing on Hofstede's work, *The Academy of Management Executive* 18, no. 1 (February 2004): 72–93; Robert J. House, Paul J. Hanges, Mansour Javidan, et al., *Culture, Leadership and Organizations: The GLOBE Study of 62 Societies* (Thousand Oaks, CA: Sage, 2004); M. Javidan and R. J. House, "Cultural Acumen for the Global Manager: Lessons from Project GLOBE," *Organizational Dynamics* 29, no. 4 (2001): 289–305; and Adler, *International Dimensions of Organizational Behavior*, pp. 20–34.

13 Anne B. Fisher, "Is Long-Range Planning Worth It?" *Fortune* (April 23, 1990): 281–284.

14 Cited in Gary Ferraro, *Cultural Anthropology: An Applied Perspective*, 3rd ed. (Belmont, CA: West/Wadsworth, 1998), p. 68.

15 Jim Holt, "Gone Global?" *Management Review* (March 2000): 13.

16 *Ibid.*

17 "Slogans Often Lose Something in Translation," *The New Mexican*, July 3, 1994.

18 This discussion is based partly on Adler, *International Dimensions of Organizational Behavior*, pp. 113–118.

19 Pat McGovern, "How to Be a Local, Anywhere," *Inc.* (April 2007): 113–114.

20 The discussion of cultural intelligence is based on P. Christopher Earley and Elaine Mosakowski, "Cultural Intelligence," *Harvard Business Review* (October 2004): 139–146; Ilan Alon and James M. Higgins, "Global Leadership Success through Emotional and Cultural Intelligence," *Business Horizons* 48 (2005): 501–512; P.C. Earley and Soon Ang, *Cultural Intelligence: Individual Interactions Across Cultures* (Stanford, CA: Stanford Business Books, 2003); and David C. Thomas and Kerr Inkson, *Cultural Intelligence: People Skills for Global Business* (San Francisco: Berrett-Koehler, 2004).

21 These components are from Earley and Mosakowski, "Cultural Intelligence."

22 Karl Moore, "Great Global Managers," *Across the Board* (May–June 2003): 40–43.

23 Johanna Rothman, "Managing Global Teams," Dr. Dobbs: The World of Software Development Website, August 1, 1998, http://drdobbs.com/184415624 (accessed February 22, 2012).

24 Based on Adler, *International Dimensions of Organizational Behavior*, pp. 51–52.

25 Jane Spencer, "Lenovo Goes Global, But Not without Strife," *The Wall Street Journal*, November 4, 2008.

26 J. Kennedy and A. Everest, "Put Diversity in Context," *Personnel Journal* (September 1991): 50–54; Edward T. Hall and M.R. Hall, *Understanding Cultural Differences* (Yarmouth, ME: Intercultural Press, 1990).

27 Brett et al., "Managing Multicultural Teams."

28 Richard M. Hodgetts and Fred Luthans, *International Management: Culture, Strategy, and Behavior*, 5th ed. (Boston: McGraw-Hill Irwin, 2003), p. 340.

29 Fons Trompenaars, *Riding the Waves of Culture* (London: The Economist Books, 1993); and Geert Hofstede, "Motivation, Leadership, and Organization: Do American Theories Apply Abroad?" *Organizational Dynamics* 9, no. 1 (1980): 42–63.

30 Xu Huang and Evert Van De Vliert, "Where Intrinsic Job Satisfaction Fails to Work: National Moderators of Intrinsic Motivation," *Journal of Organizational Behavior* 24 (2003): 159–179.

31 Howard Perlmutter, "More than 50 Percent of International Managers' Time Is Spent in Negotiating—in Interpersonal Transaction Time Influencing Other Managers," statement made at Academy of Management Meetings, Dallas, TX, August 1983, and at The Wharton School, University of Pennsylvania, 1984, reported in Adler, *International Dimensions of Organizational Behavior*.

32 Pierre Casse, *Training for the Cross-Cultural Mind*, 2nd ed. (Washington, D.C.: Society for Intercultural Education, Training, and Research, 1981), p. 152.

33 Reported in Brett et al., "Managing Multicultural Teams."

34 Pierre Casse, *Training for the Multicultural Manager* (Yarmouth, ME: Intercultural Press, 1982).

35 Joshua Hyatt, "Found in Translation: How to Make the Multicultural Work Force Work," *Inc.* (October 2006): 41–42.

36 Lionel Laroche, "Teaming Up," *CMA Management* (April 2001): 22–25.

37 Anthony Oshiotse and Richard O'Leary, "Corning Creates an Inclusive Culture to Drive Technology Innovation and Performance, *Global Business and Organizational Excellence* 26, no. 3 (March–April 2007): 7–21.

38 Frances J. Milliken and Luis I. Martins, "Searching for Common Threads: Understanding the Multiple Effects of Diversity in Organizational Groups," *Academy of Management Review* 21, no. 2 (1996): 402–433.

39 Roy Harris, "The Illusion of Inclusion," *CFO* (May 2001): 42–50; C. J. Prince, "Doing Diversity: The Question Isn't Why to Do It—But How," *Chief Executive* (April, 2005): 46; and results of a study conducted by the Society for Human Resource Management and *Fortune* magazine, reported in "Diversity Hiring in 2005: Are You in the Minority?" *Fortune* (January 24, 2005): 57–58.

40 Val Singh and Sébastien Point, "Strategic Responses by European Companies to the Diversity Challenge: An Online Comparison," *Long Range Planning* 37 (2004): 295–318.

41 Survey results reported in "Diversity Initiatives Shown to Be Critical to Job Seekers," (part of a special advertisement, "Diversity Works") *The New York Times Magazine* (September 14, 2003), p. 100.

42 Edward Iwata, "Companies Find Gold Inside Melting Pot; Diverse Staff Helps Business Run Smoothly Across Borders," *USA Today*, July 9, 2007.

43 Laura Stevens, "German CEO's Call for a 'Prettier' Board Flops," *The Wall Street Journal*, February 8, 2011.

44 Reported in Harris, "The Illusion of Inclusion."

45 Jennifer L. Knight, Michelle R. Hebl, Jessica B. Foster, and Laura M. Mannix, "Out of Role? Out of Luck: The Influence of Race and Leadership Status on Performance Appraisals," *The Journal of Leadership and Organizational Studies* 9, no. 3 (2003): 85–93.

46 Stephanie N. Mehta, "What Minority Employees Really Want," *Fortune* (June 10, 2000): 181–186.

47 Robert Hooijberg and Nancy DiTomaso, "Leadership in and of Demographically Diverse Organizations," *Leadership Quarterly* 7, no. 1 (1996): 1–19.

48 Harris, "The Illusion of Inclusion"; and Lee Smith, "Closing the Gap," *Fortune* (November 14, 2005): 211–218.

49 Lisa Belkin, "The Opt-Out Revolution," *The New York Times Magazine* (October 26, 2003): 43–47, 58.

50 See John Byrne, "The Price of Balance," *Fast Company*, February 2004, http://www.fastcompany.com/magazine/79/edlet.html (accessed May 11, 2011); LindaTischler, "Where Are the Women?" *Fast Company* (February 2004): 52–60; Patricia Sellers, "Power: Do Women Really Want It?" *Fortune* (October 13, 2003): 80–100.

51 C. J. Prince, "Media Myths: The Truth About the Opt-Out Hype," *NAFE Magazine* (Second Quarter, 2004): 14–18; Sellers, "Power: Do Women Really Want It?"

52 Sheila Wellington, Marcia Brumit Kropf, and Paulette R. Gerkovich, "What's Holding Women Back?" *Harvard Business Review* (June 2003): 18–19.

53 The Leader's Edge/Executive Women Research 2002 survey, reported in "Why Women Leave," *Executive Female* (Summer 2003): 4.

54 Barbara Reinhold, "Smashing Glass Ceilings: Why Women *Still* Find It Tough to Advance to the Executive Suite," *Journal of Organizational Excellence* (Summer 2005): 43–55; Alice H. Eagly and Linda L. Carli, "The Female Leadership Advantage: An Evaluation of the Evidence," *The Leadership Quarterly* 14 (2003): 807–834; Douglas A. Ready and Jay A. Conger, "How to Fill the Talent Gap," *The Wall Street Journal*, September 15, 2007.

55 C. Soloman, "Careers under Glass," *Personnel Journal* 69, no. 4 (1990): 96–105; Belle Rose Ragins, Bickley Townsend, and Mary Mattis, "Gender Gap in the Executive Suite: CEOs and Female Executives Report on Breaking the Glass Ceiling," *Academy of Management Executive* 12, no. 1 (1998): 28–42.

56 Catalyst study, "Damned If You Do, Doomed If You Don't," results reported in Lisa Belkin, "The Feminine Critique," *The New York Times*, November 1, 2007; and in Carol Hymowitz, "Looking at Clinton, Seeing Themselves—Executive Women Identify with the Scrutiny She's Facing" (In the Lead column), *The Wall Street Journal*, November 12, 2007.

57 Susan Carey, "More Women Take Flight in Airline Operations," *The Wall Street Journal*, August 14, 2007; and Ann Therese Palmer, "Teacher Learns All About Airline; United VP Began as Reservations Clerk, Rose Through Ranks," *Chicago Tribune*, December 24, 2006.

58 Eagly and Carli, "The Female Leadership Advantage"; Reinhold, "Smashing Glass Ceilings"; Sally Helgesen, *The Female Advantage: Women's Ways of Leadership* (New York: Doubleday Currency, 1990); Rochelle Sharpe, "As Leaders, Women Rule: New Studies Find that Female Managers Outshine Their Male Counterparts in Almost Every Measure," *BusinessWeek* (November 20, 2000): 75–84; and Del Jones, "2003: Year of the Woman Among the Fortune 500?" *USAToday*, December 30, 2003.

59 Michelle Conlin, "The New Gender Gap," *BusinessWeek* (May 26, 2003): 74–82; Tamar Lewin, "The New Gender Divide: At Colleges, Women Are Leaving Men in the Dust," *The New York Times*, July 9, 2006; and Mary Beth Marklein, "College Gender Gap Widens: 57% Are Women," *USA Today*, October 20, 2005.

60 Catherine Rampell, "Still Few Women in Management, Report Says," *The New York Times*, September 27, 2010.

61 Quoted in Conlin, "The New Gender Gap."

62 Kathryn M. Bartol, David C. Martin, and Julie A. Kromkowski, "Leadership and the Glass Ceiling: Gender and Ethnic Group Influences on Leader Behaviors at Middle and Executive Managerial Levels," *The Journal of Leadership and Organizational Studies* 9, no. 3 (2003): 8–19; Bernard M. Bass and Bruce J. Avolio, "Shatter the Glass Ceiling: Women May Make Better Managers," *Human Resource Management* 33, no. 4 (Winter 1994): 549–560; and Sharpe, "As Leaders, Women Rule."

63 D.D. Frink, R.K. Robinson, B. Reithel, et al., "Gender Demography and Organization Performance: A Two-Study Investigation with Convergence," *Group & Organization Management* 28, no. 1 (March 2003): 127–147; Catalyst research project cited in Reinhold, "Smashing Glass Ceilings."

64 The study on competitiveness was reported in Hal R. Varian, "The Difference Between Men and Women, Revisited: It's About Competition," *The New York Times*, March 9, 2006. For reviews and analyses of the research on gender differences in leadership, see Nicole Z. Stelter, "Gender Differences in Leadership: Current Social Issues and Future Organizational Implications," *The Journal of Leadership Studies* 8, no. 4 (2002): 88–99; and Alice H. Eagly, Mary C. Johannesen-Schmidt, and Marloes L. van Engen, "Transformational, Transactional, and Laissez-Faire Leadership Styles: A Meta-Analysis Comparing Women and Men," *Psychological Bulletin* 129, no. 4 (July 2003): 569ff.

65 Based on Judy B. Rosener, *America's Competitive Secret: Women Managers* (New York: Oxford University Press, 1997), pp. 129–135.

66 Susan J. Wells, "A Female Executive Is Hard to Find," *HR Magazine* (June 2001): 40–49; and Helgesen, *The Female Advantage*.

67 M. Fine, F. Johnson, and M. S. Ryan, "Cultural Diversity in the Workforce," *Public Personnel Management* 19 (1990): 305–319; and Dawn Hill, "Women Leaders Doing It Their Way," *New Woman* (January 1994): 78.

68 Based on Martin M. Chemers and Roya Ayman, *Leadership Theory and Research: Perspectives and Directions* (San Diego, CA: Academic Press, 1993), p. 209; and Robert T. Moran and John R. Riesenberger, *The Global Challenge* (London: McGraw-Hill, 1994), pp. 251–262.

Action Learning Exercises

69 Adapted from the work of Dr. Robert Terry, the Action Wheel Leadership Group, St. Paul, MN. Used with permission of The Action Wheel Leadership Group.

70 Adapted from an exercise by Renate Mai-Dalton, University of Kansas School of Business.

CHAPTER 15
Positive Leadership

Chapter Outline

RYAN LASH

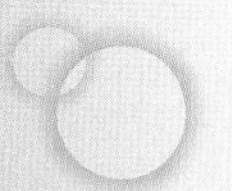

MANAGER CHALLENGE

VIDEO INCIDENT: JUST SAY NO!

Caffeine and Crullers general manager Jane Sutton is frustrated. Sales manager Jason Wong has just gone into one of his negative tirades. No one else is doing a good job except for him, according to Jason. Carlos is too prickly, Carrie has too much of an edge, and Heather doesn't even know what the term "on time" means. Jane has noticed that Jason gets like this periodically, maybe every month or so, but she can't figure out if something in particular is causing his behavior. What she does know is that it puts a damper on the other members of the management team and makes it hard for people to connect positively with Jason. Jane knows if she does nothing, the negativity will stop after a few days—until next month.

Initial Thoughts

1. **If you were Jane, what would you do?**

2. **Why do you think a manager's disposition might change periodically? Should anything be done about it?**

Your instructor may ask you to be part of a role play based on the "Just Say No!" incident.

DISCOVER YOURSELF

For those students using CourseMate or CengageNOW, you can access the Daft/Marcic Assessment Library to take the questionnaires online and view dynamically updated comparative data.

Questionnaire 1[1]

Instructions: Respond to each of the following statements based on how you behave when dealing with other people. Rate how accurately each statement describes you based on whether the statement is clearly true or accurate, clearly false or inaccurate, or in the middle as somewhat true and somewhat false. Describe yourself as you are now, not as you wish to be. There are no right or wrong answers.

	True	Somewhat	False
1. I usually ask how a person's day is going.	○	○	○
2. I act cheerful and positive toward others.	○	○	○
3. I attempt to make interactions enjoyable.	○	○	○
4. I am cooperative in handling disagreements.	○	○	○
5. I look past annoying behaviors to see the good qualities in people.	○	○	○
6. I am seldom critical of others.	○	○	○
7. I frequently express appreciation and give compliments.	○	○	○
8. I always look for the silver lining in people and situations.	○	○	○
9. Things typically work out the way I want them to.	○	○	○
10. I'm always optimistic about my future.	○	○	○

Total Score Questionnaire 1 ________. (Sum questions 1–10 by giving 3 points for each True, 2 points for each Somewhat, and 1 point for each False.) Go to page 555 to interpret your score.

Questionnaire 2

Instructions: Think back to how you typically behave toward others at work or in student groups. Please respond to the following items based on whether you frequently displayed each behavior.

Part A[2]	True	Somewhat	False
1. I challenged people to think about old problems in new ways.	○	○	○
2. I challenged people's basic assumptions about the work.	○	○	○
3. I was willing to start new initiatives even if they might fail.	○	○	○

	True	Somewhat	False
4. I liked experimenting with new concepts.	○	○	○
5. I came to my own conclusion despite what others thought.	○	○	○
6. I encouraged others to express opposing ideas and arguments.	○	○	○
7. I asked questions to prompt others to think more deeply about an issue.	○	○	○

Total Score Part A ________. (Sum questions 1–7 by giving 3 points for each True, 2 points for each Somewhat, and 1 point for each False.)

Part B

	True	Somewhat	False
8. I was more devoted to my group's success than to my own.	○	○	○
9. I acted with quiet modesty rather than personal assertiveness.	○	○	○
10. I came across as a simple, unassuming person.	○	○	○
11. I acted with quiet but great determination.	○	○	○
12. I was relentless to help the group succeed.	○	○	○
13. I pursued persistent high standards for my group's performance.	○	○	○

Total Score Part B ________. (Sum questions 8–13 by giving 3 points for each True, 2 points for each Somewhat, and 1 point for each False.) Go to page 560 to interpret your scores.

Questionnaire 3

Instructions: Think about a situation in which you played a leadership role in a group. To what extent do the following statements describe what you did as an informal or formal leader?

	True	Somewhat	False
1. I thought of my role as creating a vision and mission for the group.	○	○	○
2. I initiated a discussion to establish a clear understanding of our purpose and goals.	○	○	○
3. I explained to others the importance of working toward a common vision.	○	○	○
4. I verbalized for others my ideas for the future.	○	○	○
5. I recognized others when their work was consistent with the vision.	○	○	○
6. I created a big picture for others.	○	○	○
7. I explained the "why" of what we were doing.	○	○	○
8. I worked to get others to commit to our purpose.	○	○	○

DISCOVER YOURSELF

Total Score Questionnaire 3 ________. (Sum items 1–8 by giving 3 points for each True, 2 points for each Somewhat, and 1 point for each False.) Go to page 561 to interpret your score.

Questionnaire 4[3]

Instructions: The following items describe the experience of what you may think or feel while you perform a specific task. *Respond to each item twice*—the first time for doing a particular task, hobby, or sports activity you enjoy, and the second time for doing specific work (or homework) that is not your favorite. Consider each item thoughtfully and respond according to your inner motivation and experience.

	True	Somewhat	False
1. I knew clearly what I wanted to accomplish.			
Task I liked:	○	○	○
Task I didn't like:	○	○	○
2. I knew how well I was doing while performing the task.			
Task I liked:	○	○	○
Task I didn't like:	○	○	○
3. I felt capable to meet the challenge of the situation.			
Task I liked:	○	○	○
Task I didn't like:	○	○	○
4. I was not distracted by anything going on around me.			
Task I liked:	○	○	○
Task I didn't like:	○	○	○
5. I lost track of time.			
Task I liked:	○	○	○
Task I didn't like:	○	○	○
6. I was not concerned with what others would think of my results.			
Task I liked:	○	○	○
Task I didn't like:	○	○	○
7. I was so "in the zone" that I was not conscious of myself.			
Task I liked:	○	○	○
Task I didn't like:	○	○	○
8. The experience left me feeling great.			
Task I liked:	○	○	○
Task I didn't like:	○	○	○

Total Scores Questionnaire 4: Task I liked ________. (Sum answers 1–8 for the task you liked by giving 3 points for each True, 2 points for each Somewhat, and 1 point for each False.)

Task I didn't like ________. (Sum answers 1–8 for the task you didn't like by giving 3 points for each True, 2 points for each Somewhat, and 1 point for each False.) Go to page 568 to interpret your scores.

GO ONLINE to find additional questionnaires at www.cengagebrain.com, search for Daft/Marcic Building Management Skills 1e, click on Free Online Resources, click on Additional Self-Assessments.

- Servant Leadership
- Spirituality

DISCOVER YOURSELF

SHUTTERSTOCK #53973379

Chapter 15: Positive Leadership

DISCOVER KNOWLEDGE

After Patrick Charmel resigned from Griffin Hospital, the organization went through a tumultuous period that manifested itself in backbiting, criticism, and negative feelings among the staff. A number of employees appealed to the board of directors to get rid of the new CEO and bring back Charmel. Charmel's persona projected hope and positive energy for the future, and he was considered an innovative and effective administrator. The board listened and persuaded Charmel to return as CEO and president. Unfortunately, the financial condition of the hospital had deteriorated in Charmel's absence, which required that managers lay off 10 percent of the workforce. Layoffs usually lead to a decline in employee loyalty, low morale, anger, blaming, less productivity, and anxiety about the future. But at Griffin, Charmel fostered a positive climate. He showed genuine concern for everyone's well-being by openly sharing information, behaving with integrity, and focusing on the positive, thereby enabling people to embrace their work in a meaningful way. For instance, nurses helped design and install double beds for maternity patients so fathers could sleep with mothers instead of sleeping in a chair. Employees put Jacuzzis in the maternity ward and welcomed pets to visit and cheer up patients. They also carpeted hallways and hung original works of art on the walls to create a warmer environment. All these improvements pushed Griffin onto the list of *Fortune* magazine's "The 25 Best Places to Work," and the hospital was ranked 12th nationwide on the "Top 100 Quality Award" list.[4]

Thanks to Patrick Charmel's positive leadership, Griffin Hospital overcame pervasive negativity, resolved problems, brought out the best in people, increased competitiveness, and achieved profitability, which seemed like a miracle to employees. Organizations cannot survive without good management. But they also need positive leadership. Leadership provides vision and inspiration, and management offers expert planning, organizing, motivation, communication, and negotiation. People in organizations want to be inspired, but they also need a coherent structure, milieu, and focus for their efforts. Leadership's power comes from building on the solid foundation of a well-managed organization.[5]

Like other skills, leadership can be learned and developed. This chapter will focus on developing your leadership ability. We describe positive leadership qualities and examine the importance of leadership vision, as well as discuss how managers can shape culture and values for a positive and productive work environment.

LEADERSHIP WITH A POSITIVE PREFERENCE

Patrick Charmel's turnaround of Griffin Hospital was largely due to his own optimism. He exuded positive energy that drove away the negativity normally associated with downsizing. Negativity is widespread in many organizations. You may have heard people moaning and complaining about the company, the boss, or the benefits, and you may have done so yourself. The truth is that you can't build a great organization on pessimism and complaints. Would you want to follow a leader who would only find fault with you, other people, the organization, and the work? A leader's job is to find and promote the positive. The leader sets the tone for the culture, attitudes, and desired future of the organization. As a manager, you can address the prevalent issue of negativity in organizations and learn to embrace positive leadership.

Face Your Negativity Problem

Negativity bias is the term used in psychology to describe how the human mind reacts more quickly and strongly to perceived bad things than it does to good things. Consequently, if there are even minimal bad feelings associated with a task or person, your mind will notice and focus on those rather than on the existing good feelings or qualities.

People pay more attention to negative happenings than to positive ones. Psychologists have confirmed that "bad is stronger than good" because the human mind is biased toward negativity.[6] Negative events such as losing $100, being betrayed by a friend, or getting criticized are felt more intensely than positive events such as finding $100, gaining a friend, or receiving praise. In early stages of human evolution, negative events could be life threatening, which is probably why humans still react more strongly to them. From an early age, we learn that negative words, physical actions, or feedback can hurt. Moreover, news programs are dominated by negative events because people are more interested in negative events that might influence their lives. More attention is given to bankruptcies, scandals, thefts, and the financial ruin of businesses than to how well a company is doing or how an organization has contributed to society. A study of the business press over a 17-year time period found that positive terms seldom appeared over the 17 years, while negative words increased fourfold over that period.[7]

Leaders in organizations are bombarded with problems, threats, and obstacles. Leaders are charged with beating the competition and finding, analyzing, and fixing glitches and difficulties. Hence, it is easy for a leader's mind to focus more on the negative than on the positive. Leaders can easily pay more attention to solving problems than to supporting and developing people. For example, a survey of two million people found that only 20 percent got to use some aspect of their strengths every day at work.[8] Can you be an effective leader when your mind is constantly finding fault with people and projects? A positive leader has to counteract the negative trend to be encouraging and optimistic in the face of continuous problems and difficulties. Otherwise, leaders may fail in their effectiveness and career goals. In Chapter 1, we presented research findings from the Center for Creative Leadership revealing that 75 percent of managers with promising careers who derailed did so because they displayed qualities such as an abrasive or insensitive style, arrogance, being difficult to work with, constant disagreements with senior management, and being poor at team building or involving staff.[9] A leader's challenge is to learn how to lead from a positive mindset and perspective.

Develop Positive Leadership Qualities

Southwest Airlines has remained profitable for 39 consecutive years and is the most successful airline in the industry. Southwest's astonishing record of top performance is attributed to founder and former CEO Herb Kelleher, who built a positive corporate culture and who was able to connect with employees and earn their loyalty. His style was to fly on planes to meet and form close bonds with employees. Kelleher motivated people to come up with timely and creative ways to better serve customers. Their "above and beyond the call of duty" performance stemmed from the high regard in which they held the CEO. Kelleher's style was eccentric, and his first boss tried to change him to fit more into the mold of the traditional airline management type. Fortunately, this well-meaning attempt to improve Kelleher's performance failed and his positive leadership style prevailed. His characteristics of eccentricity and charisma enabled Kelleher to lead Southwest to outstanding performance year after year.[10]

Positive leadership is an outgrowth of a new academic field called positive psychology. **Positive leadership** uses theoretically grounded principles to promote outcomes such as thriving at work, interpersonal flourishing, positive emotions, and energized teams. The field of organizational behavior that studies people in organizations has often taken a negative perspective—trying to fix what is wrong with managers and employees and concentrating on deficiencies and weaknesses. "Positive Organizational Behavior" is an emerging field that concentrates on people's strengths rather than their weaknesses, especially on the positive characteristics of people and organizations such as confidence, optimism, positive choices, positive thought patterns,

DISCOVER YOURSELF

Interpret Your Score: Positivity (Questionnaire 1)

Your score for these questions represents your positivity and optimism in relationships with others. Comparative data for **Positivity:** Thirty person Mean score = 25.0; Top Quartile = 27–30; Bottom Quartile = 18–23. A high score would mean lower susceptibility to the negativity bias described in the chapter and more frequent affirmative bias and facilitating intrinsic goodness in your relationships. A higher score would mean greater potential for positive leadership compared to a lower score. Do you want to be a positive leader? How do you feel about your score? In what way would you change the way you relate to others? CNOW and CourseMate users can access dynamically updated comparative data through www.cengagebrain.com.

© CENGAGE LEARNING 2014

hope, and well-being.[11] Three aspects of positive leadership are: an affirmative bias, facilitating intrinsic goodness, and exceeding performance expectations.[12]

Affirmative Bias

When a leader's internal thought process sees the strengths and capabilities of individuals, and affirms human potential, this is considered an *affirmative bias*. Affirmative bias occurs within the leader. Positive leadership makes it possible for people and organizations to thrive and flourish by not emphasizing the difficulties they must overcome. Positive leaders place the emphasis on positive communication, optimism, appreciation, and strengths. They don't ignore problems and weaknesses, but they view them through a positive lens as valuable opportunities rather than hindrances. As a leader with an affirmative bias, for instance, you would pay attention to negative elements of an employee's performance, but with the emphasis on how to turn them into positives. Positive leaders combine personal attributes such as being nice, trustworthy, and affirmative with behaviors that provide strengths-based positive energy. You can learn and develop greater optimism and an affirmative bias. People who are neutral or naturally pessimistic can become more optimistic. Optimism is a desirable trait for leaders. It leads to happiness, perseverance, achievement, and good health.[13]

Facilitating Intrinsic Goodness

To facilitate intrinsic goodness means the leader reaches out to cultivate the goodness in other people, promotes happiness, and has a goal and focus to create an environment that promotes people's well-being. The positive leader creates strategies that encourage and support traits such as honesty and virtuousness in others. Aristotle called this collection of higher traits "that which is good in itself and is to be chosen for its own sake."[14] There is no master list of what is good, but each culture accepts some traits more than others as being virtuous. But what happens when there is a downturn in the economy and the leader has to lay off people, or a company is being sold and half of the department is being let go? Deficit thinking can trap people into fear, disorientation, negative thinking, and competition for scarce resources. Positive leaders try to create mental abundance in workplaces by giving people meaning, purpose, hope, and pleasure. These leaders look at the heart of the organization and engage workers by showing them the higher purpose of their work. When you act as a positive leader, focusing on opportunity and synergy, you can bring order out of chaos and create intrinsic value for workers, who in turn serve customers and the broader society.[15]

Exceeding Expectations

Exceeding performance expectations means that the results of positive leadership often are spectacular—way above the norm. The reason for this is illustrated in Exhibit 15.1. In an emotionally toxic work environment, most of an individual's or team's effort is used for emotional survival. In a positive environment, on the other hand, most of the team's effort is available for work. When a leader is able to unlock positive emotions of joyfulness, appreciation, or love, people's

Exhibit 15.1 Positive Leadership and Performance

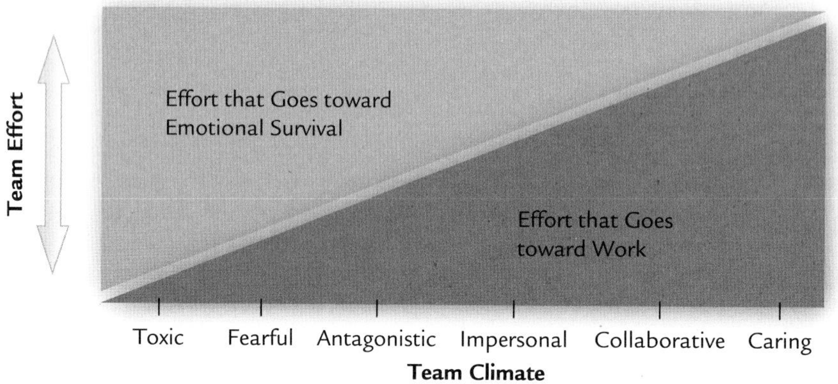

Source: Adapted from "Success & the Team Climate," Team Leadership Toolkit, *Lindsay-Sherwin Company Web site*, http://www.lindsay-sherwin.co.uk/guide_team_leadership/html_team_development/1_success_and_team_climate.htm (accessed May 13, 2011).

energy, creativity, and intellectual commitment expand. Employees are able to grasp more data, be more creative and resourceful in their solutions, and produce superior results. Positive emotions mean the decline of negative emotions such as sadness, anger, anxiety, and fear. Positive emotions "broaden people's . . . repertoires and build their enduring personal resources."[16] Positive instead of negative emotional responses enable individuals to perform to the best of their abilities. A positive workplace increases employee engagement, productivity, and collaboration, thereby supporting a thriving enterprise.

Leaders apply the three aspects of positive leadership to build positive organization relationships and cultures. But what behaviors and activities do positive leaders use that enable them to build the right kind of organization? In the remainder of the chapter, we discuss specific ways in which you can act as a leader to build positive, high-performance teams and organizations. First we examine personal qualities and relationships of leaders. Succeeding sections will look at how to create positive vision, foster positive communication, create the right corporate culture, and help people find positive energy and meaning in their work.

POSITIVE PERSONAL QUALITIES AND RELATIONSHIPS

Positive leadership can be learned, but it is more than a specific set of skills. Leadership relies on a number of subtle personal qualities that are hard to see but are very powerful.

7 STEPS TO...

A Toxic Workplace

With deadlines to meet, resources that have to be shared, and competition for promotions, people in organizations sometimes have a hard time being nice. Here are some common ways to create a toxic workplace and the contrasting positive leader behaviors:

1. **Belittle others' efforts.** Positive leaders build people up rather than tear them down. When compliments and credits come their way, good leaders spread them around to everyone in the group.
2. **Never apologize.** When you make a mistake, hurt someone's feelings, or take a stand and later realize you were wrong, be big enough to say you're sorry. An apology helps the hurt go away and increases people's trust in you.
3. **Leave a mess for others to clean up.** It's a simple thing, but merely cleaning up your own mess in the break room or shared office space sends a message that you care about others and respect their time.
4. **Stick with your own crowd.** "Elite" cliques that shut people out are a sure route to demoralization. A positive approach is to step out of your usual zone and have a casual chat with someone you rarely interact with. Eat lunch with different people instead of the same group every day.
5. **Judge others.** Positive leaders resist the urge to jump to conclusions about people and their motives. Instead, they go to the source and get the facts before making an evaluation.
6. **Don't keep promises.** It hurts everyone when leaders make grand promises and then don't follow through. Promise only what you can deliver; if results fall short, explain why.
7. **Never express gratitude.** Positive leaders say "thank you" a lot. Showing sincere appreciation is powerful—as consultant and motivational speaker Tom Terez points out, it's "feedback, recognition, and respect all wrapped in one."

Sources: Tom Terez, "Civility at Work: 20 Ways to Build a Kinder Workplace," Tom Terez Workplace Solutions, Inc., 2002, http://www.betterworkplacenow.com/civilityart.html (accessed May 15, 2011); Christine Pearson and Christine Porath, *The Cost of Bad Behavior: How Incivility Is Damaging Your Business and What to Do About It* (New York: Portfolio Penguin, 2009); and Susan G. Hauser, "The Degeneration of Decorum," *Workforce Management* (January 11, 2011): 16–18, 20–21.

Practice Mindfulness

As a leader, how can you remain positive when you're faced with problems and obstacles every day? How can you keep from being sucked into a tide of negativity, blame, and fault finding that can easily take hold in an organization? One answer is to think for yourself and keep your mind open to different ways of doing things. **Independent thinking** means questioning assumptions and interpreting data and events according to one's own beliefs, ideas, and thinking, not according to pre-established rules, routines, or categories defined by others. When you think independently, you're willing to stand apart, to have opinions, to say what you think, and to determine a course of action based on your own understanding.

Independent thinking is one part of what is called leader mindfulness.[17] **Mindfulness** can be defined as continuously reevaluating previously learned ways of doing things in the context of evolving information and shifting circumstances. Mindfulness is the opposite of *mindlessness*, which means blindly accepting rules and labels created by others. Mindless people let others do the thinking for them, but mindful leaders are always looking for new ideas and approaches. Mindful leaders also apply critical thinking to explore a situation, problem, or question from multiple perspectives and integrate all the available information into a possible solution. When leaders think mindfully, they question current assumptions, vigorously seek divergent opinions, and are willing to try new thinking to move an organization in a positive direction.[18]

DISCOVER KNOWLEDGE

Thinking Independently Takes Intentional Effort

Independent thinking is hard work, and most of us can easily relax into temporary mindlessness, accepting black-and-white answers and relying on the standard way of doing things. One approach to independent thinking is to try to break out of the mental boxes, the categorized thinking patterns we have been conditioned to accept as correct in an organization. The power of the conditioning that guides our thinking and behavior is illustrated by the *Pike Syndrome*. In an experiment, a northern pike is placed in one half of a large glass-divided aquarium, with numerous minnows placed in the other half. The hungry pike makes repeated attempts to get the minnows, but succeeds only in battering itself against the glass, finally learning that trying to reach the minnows is futile. The glass divider is then removed, but the pike makes no attempt to attack the minnows because it has been conditioned to believe that reaching them is impossible. When you assume that you have knowledge of a situation and don't keep your mind open to unusual choices, you exhibit the Pike Syndrome. The trained incapacity comes from inflexible commitment to what was true in the past and a refusal to consider novel alternatives and different perspectives.[19]

Positive Leaders Break Free of Preconceived Barriers

Positive leaders work to overcome their conditioned ideas, strive to keep open minds, and cultivate an organizational environment that encourages curiosity and learning. They understand the limitations of past experience and reach out for better ways to engage employees. These leaders encourage everyone throughout the organization to openly debate assumptions, confront paradoxes, question perceptions, and express feelings.[20]

Demonstrate Humility and Will

When he was promoted to CEO of Kimberly-Clark, Darwin Smith questioned whether the board really wanted to appoint him because he didn't believe he had the qualifications a CEO needed. When Smith took over, Kimberly-Clark was a stodgy paper company with a rapidly falling stock price. Under his tenure, it became the leading consumer paper products company in the world, beating rivals Scott Paper and Procter & Gamble. The company generated cumulative stock returns that were 4.1 times greater than those of the general market. When asked after his retirement about his exceptional performance, Smith said simply, "I never stopped trying to become qualified for the job."[21]

Darwin Smith, who led Kimberly-Clark from 1971 to 1991, is a classic example of what researcher Jim Collins calls a *Level 5 leader*. Few people have ever heard of Darwin Smith—and that's probably just the way he wanted it. A key characteristic of Level 5 leaders is their humility and lack of ego, coupled with a fierce resolve to do what is best for their organizations.

As described by Collins in his book *Good to Great*, Level 5 leadership refers to the highest level in a hierarchy of manager capabilities, as illustrated

Exhibit 15.2 Level 5 Hierarchy

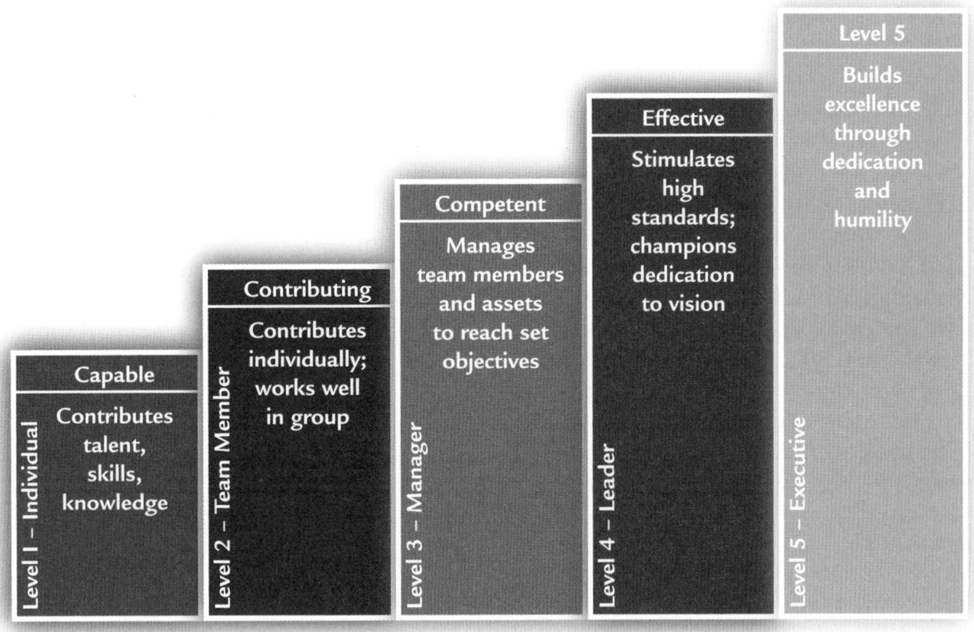

Source: Based on Jim Collins, *Good to Great: Why Some Companies Make the Leap . . . and Others Don't* (New York: HarperCollins, 2001), p. 20.

in Exhibit 15.2.[22] Two primary qualities of Level 5 leaders are humility and will. Humility means being unpretentious and modest rather than arrogant and prideful. Humble leaders don't have to be in the center of things. They quietly build strong, enduring companies by developing and supporting others rather than touting their own abilities and accomplishments. In contrast to the view of great leaders as larger-than-life personalities with strong egos and big ambitions, Level 5 leaders often seem shy and unpretentious. Although they accept full responsibility for mistakes, poor results, or failures, Level 5 leaders give credit for successes to other people.

Yet despite their personal humility, Level 5 leaders have a strong will to do whatever it takes to produce great and lasting results for their organizations. That is, they are extremely ambitious for their companies rather than for themselves. This becomes particularly evident in the areas of employee development and succession planning. Level 5 leaders cultivate a solid corps of leaders throughout the organization, so that when they leave the company it can continue to thrive and grow even stronger. Egocentric leaders, by contrast, often set their successors up for failure because it will be a testament to their own greatness if the company doesn't perform well without them. Level 5 leaders want everyone in the organization to develop to their fullest potential.

Lead with Love, not Fear

Jeff Immelt, now CEO of General Electric, still remembers what Jack Welch, the former CEO and Immelt's boss, told him once when he'd had a bad year and hadn't made his numbers: "I love you and I know you can do better." Welch was known as something of a hard-nosed manager, but he understood the power of leading with love rather than with fear. Welch genuinely cared about his managers and their career development and success, and they responded, contributing to growth and success for the organization.[23]

Many executives are wary of feelings in the workplace, but real leaders know that emotion is what drives people, for either good or ill. An environment that reflects care and respect for employees is much

DISCOVER YOURSELF

Interpret Your Score: Positive Personal Qualities (Questionnaire 2)

Comparative data for the personal qualities of positive leaders: **Mindfulness** (Part A): Thirty person Mean score = 17.3; Top Quartile = 19–20; Bottom Quartile = 11–15. **Humility and Will** (Part B): Thirty person Mean score = 13.4; Top Quartile = 15–18; Bottom Quartile = 6–12. A higher Part A score would mean the ability to think independently and go against the crowd to behave in a positive way. A lower score typically is associated with going along with current norms of behavior. A higher Part B score would be closer to a Level 5 leader, whereas a low score might imply more self-interest. Your first three answers in Part B pertain to humility and the second three to will. You might compute separate scores for questions 1–3 and 4–6 to see on which aspect you score higher. How do you feel about your scores on these two dimensions? Are you attracted to these qualities of positive leadership or would you prefer a different approach to leadership? CNOW and CourseMate users can access dynamically updated comparative data through www.cengagebrain.com.

© CENGAGE LEARNING 2014

DISCOVER KNOWLEDGE

more effective than one in which people are anxious and fearful. Bringing love into the workplace, as Jack Welch did at GE, means genuinely caring for others and sharing your knowledge, understanding, and compassion to enable people to grow and succeed.

Leadership in many organizations has been based on fear. An unspoken notion among many senior-level executives is that fear is a good thing and benefits the organization.[24] Indeed, fear can be a powerful motivator. However, fear-based motivation doesn't engage people emotionally in solving problems and striving to make the organization successful. From an employee's perspective, love versus fear has different motivational potential:

- **Fear-based motivation:** "I need a job to pay for my basic needs (fulfilling lower needs of the body). You give me a job, and I will give you just enough to keep my job."
- **Love-based motivation:** "If the job and the leader make me feel valued as a person and provide a sense of meaning and contribution to the community at large (fulfilling higher needs of the heart and mind), then I will give you all I have to offer."[25]

Certainly, as a manager, you can rely on negative emotions such as fear to fuel productive work, but by doing so you may slowly destroy people's spirits, which ultimately is bad for you, your employees, and the organization.[26] Fear prevents people from doing their best, from taking risks, and from challenging and changing the status quo. It creates an atmosphere in which people feel powerless, so that their confidence, commitment, enthusiasm, imagination, and motivation are diminished. As we illustrated in Exhibit 15.1 earlier in this chapter, when people are fearful and in a threatening environment, most of their energy gets used for emotional survival rather than being channeled toward doing a good job. Consider, for example, that two-thirds of employees surveyed said their performance declined after being the victim of rudeness or hostility at work. Four out of five said they lost work time fretting about the unpleasant incident, three-quarters said their commitment to their employer declined, and 12 percent even quit their jobs.[27]

In addition, when fear is high, managers destroy the opportunity for feedback, blinding them to reality and denying them the chance to correct damaging decisions and behaviors. The relationship between an employee and direct supervisor is the primary factor determining the level of fear experienced at work, and you can learn to bind people together for accomplishing a shared purpose through more positive forces such as caring and compassion, listening, and connecting to others on a personal level.

CREATE POSITIVE VISION AND MEANING

Now let's turn our attention to some of the specific activities positive leaders undertake within organizations. One of the most important functions of leadership is to articulate and communicate a compelling vision that will motivate and energize employees. A

vision is an ambitious view of the future that everyone involved can believe in, one that can realistically be achieved, yet one that offers a future that is dramatically better than what now exists. Inspiring visions offer an ideal, attractive image of the future that is credible and meaningful but not readily attainable, thus giving people something to reach for. For example, when President John F. Kennedy announced a vision of putting a man on the moon by the end of the 1960s, NASA had only a small amount of the knowledge it would need to accomplish the feat. Yet in July 1969 that inspiring vision became a reality.

Good visions are associated with higher organizational performance.[28] Employees who have a sense of clarity and confidence in where the organization is headed are more likely to be motivated and committed to staying with the organization.[29] And when people are inspired by a picture of what the organization can be in the future, they can help take it there. To be motivating and effective, a vision is linked with action and defines a noble purpose that gives meaning to people's work.

Link Vision with Action

Hopes and dreams for the future are what keep people moving forward. Yet leadership means linking those hopes and dreams to specific goals, objectives, and plans so that people can take action toward achieving the future. An old English churchyard saying applies to organizations as it does to life:

> *Life without vision is drudgery.*
>
> *Vision without action is but an empty dream.*
>
> *Action guided by vision is joy and the hope of the earth.*[30]

Exhibit 15.3 illustrates four possibilities of leadership in providing direction. Four types of leader are described based on their attention to vision as a basis for action.[31] A person who is low both on providing vision and stimulating action is *uninvolved*, not really a leader at all. The leader who is all action and little vision is a *doer*. This leader may be a hard worker and dedicated to the job and the organization, but the doer is working blind. Without a sense of purpose and direction, activities have no real meaning and do not truly serve the organization, the employees, or the community. The *dreamer*, on the other hand, is good at providing a big idea with meaning. This leader effectively inspires others with a vision, yet he or she is weak on implementing strategic action. The vision in this case is only a dream, a fantasy, because it has little chance of ever becoming reality. To be an *effective leader*, you need to both dream big *and* transform those dreams into significant strategic action, either through your own activities or by hiring other people who can effectively implement the vision and strategy.

Exhibit 15.3 Linking Vision with Action

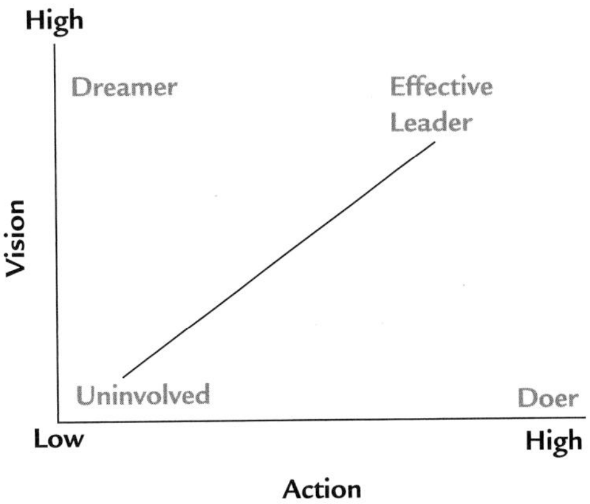

Source: Based on William D. Hitt, *The Leader-Manager: Guidelines for Action* (Columbus, OH: Batelle Press, 1988), p. 7.

DISCOVER KNOWLEDGE

DISCOVER YOURSELF

Interpret Your Score: Vision (Questionnaire 3)

Comparative data for **Visionary Leadership:** Thirty person Mean score = 21.1; Top Quartile = 24–24; Bottom Quartile = 16–19. Vision has to do with thinking about the team's purpose and future and engaging others in pursuing that future. Many managers have a hard time with vision because they are focused primarily on solving immediate problems. A higher score probably means that thinking about vision is natural for you, while a lower score means that you will have to make a special effort to express and engage people in the team's purpose and vision. Do you like it when a leader articulates a clear and inspiring vision for your work? Can you provide that same inspiration to others? CNOW and CourseMate users can access dynamically updated comparative data through www.cengagebrain.com.

© CENGAGE LEARNING 2014

Provide a Noble Purpose

A good vision captures people's idealistic motivations for what the organization is striving to achieve. People like to have a sense of meaningful work that makes a positive difference in the world.[32] Visions such as discovering a drug to cure cancer or creating a breakout product that revives the U.S. auto industry clearly strive for an honorable purpose. Leaders in any type of organization can tap into people's desire to contribute and make a difference. Even employees performing routine tasks can find pride and meaning in their work when leaders create a good vision.[33] Leaders at ServiceMaster, a company that cleans and maintains hospitals, schools, and other buildings, use vision to help people feel a sense of meaningfulness, dignity, and responsibility in menial labor. One housekeeper at a hospital explained that her job wasn't just scrubbing floors. She considered herself a member of a team dedicated to helping sick people get well. Without exceptional cleaning, she emphasized, the hospital could not serve its patients effectively and would soon be out of business.[34]

Exhibit 15.4 describes four basic approaches you can take in framing a noble purpose that helps people feel that their work is worthwhile.

Discovery

Discovery for its own sake can serve as a noble purpose, as it did for NASA in the 1960s. As another example, people at Google are energized by the psychic rewards they get from working on intellectually stimulating and challenging technical problems. Leaders at Google stress a vision of unifying data and information around the world, one day totally obliterating language barriers via the Internet.[35] With this approach, a vision inspires people to see the adventure in their work and experience the joy of a pioneering or entrepreneurial spirit.

Excellence

This approach focuses people on being the best, both on an individual and organizational level, even if that means turning some customers away. For example, Apple has always built high-quality, cleverly designed computers, but the company still holds less than 5 percent of the personal computer market. Managers would like to increase their share of the market, but they aren't willing to sacrifice their commitment to high quality and what they consider superior technology.[36] In companies that use excellence as a noble purpose, people are treated as valuable resources and provided with support to perform at their peak. Employees are motivated by the opportunity to achieve personal fulfilment in what they do.

Altruism

Many nonprofit organizations have visions that reflect an altruistic purpose, but businesses use this approach as well. IKEA wants to provide stylish, high-quality furniture for people with limited budgets. Panera Bread aims to be a comfortable gathering place for the 70 percent of office workers who don't really have an office but spend their days in cramped cubicles.[37] Most people feel good when they are doing something to help others or make their communities a better place.

Heroism

The final category, heroism, means the vision is based on being strong, aggressive, and effective. Bill Gates, for example, started Microsoft with a vision of putting the Windows operating system into every personal computer in the world. Southwest Airlines was founded with a vision of winning against much larger competitors such as American and Delta. With this approach, the basis of action is *efficacy*, which means people like to feel capable of being effective and producing results.

Exhibit 15.4 A Framework for Defining Noble Purpose

Purpose	Description	Basis for Action	Examples
Discovery	Finding the new	Pioneer, entrepreneur	Google, 3M, Virgin
Excellence	Being the best	Fulfillment	Berkshire Hathaway, Apple, BMW
Altruism	Providing service	Happiness	ServiceMaster, Dollar General
Heroism	Being effective	Achievement	Microsoft, Dell, ExxonMobil

Source: Based on Nikos Mourkogiannis, *Purpose: The Starting Point of Great Companies* (New York: Palgrave Macmillan, 2006); and Nikos Mourkogiannis, "The Realist's Guide to Moral Purpose," *Strategy + Business* 41 (Winter 2005): 42–53.

FOSTER A HIGH POSITIVITY RATIO IN COMMUNICATIONS

A powerful way to influence a team is for the leader to use positive communications that counter the natural human tendency toward negativity. Research in diverse social settings has revealed that without special effort, negative statements typically outweigh positive statements. For example, one study observed the ratio of negative to positive statements in family dynamics as 13:1; that is, there were 13 negative statements for each positive statement![38] A similar study of people in business revealed a negative to positive ratio of 8:1. The mental preference for the negative was also found in a study of college student gossip, which showed a relative frequency of 9:1.[39]

These are alarming findings, because our language influences our thinking and behavior. There is strength in positive communication. A direct connection exists between team performance and the use of positive or negative statements. The **positivity ratio** is the ratio of positive to negative statements. High-performing teams typically show a strong positivity ratio. Indeed, research found that the ratio of positive statements to negative statements was an important factor in forecasting the performance of an organization. Exhibit 15.5 shows the results of research that looked at the varying communication styles among 60 top management teams and how well teams and their organizations performed.[40] The study looked at four different communication categories: the ratio of positive to negative comments; the ratio of inquiry (asking questions) to advocacy (telling one's own opinion); the ratio of whether statements focus on others compared to a focus on self; and a measure of connectivity, which concerns the interaction, engagement, and information exchanged in a team.

The results in Exhibit 15.5 show that the higher-performing organizations had a ratio of 5.6 positive statements for each negative statement, which is pretty remarkable. Positive statements express approval, compliments, appreciation, support, or helpfulness, whereas negative statements express cynicism, disparagement, criticism, disapproval, or dissatisfaction. On the other hand, low-performing organizations had a ratio of 0.36 positive statements for each negative statement, which is about 3 to 1 in a negative direction. Managers in the higher-performing organizations clearly were more complimentary and supportive of each other. Managers in high-performing organizations also asked many more questions (inquiry/advocacy ratio) and showed much greater focus on others compared to self (others/self ratio) than in low-performing organizations. The last column in Exhibit 15.5 is the connectivity average, which expresses

Exhibit 15.5 Team Performance Is Influenced by Positive Communication and Connectivity

Performance Level	Positivity Ratio	Asking/Telling Ratio	Other/Self Ratio	Connectivity Average
High	5.6 to 1	1.1 to 1	0.94 to 1	32
Medium	1.9 to 1	0.67 to 1	0.62 to 1	22
Low	0.36 to 1	0.05 to 1	0.03 to 1	18

Source: Based on Marcial Losada and Emily Heaphy, "The Role of Positivity and Connectivity in the Performance of Business Teams: A Nonlinear Dynamics Model," *American Behavioral Scientist* 47, no. 6 (February 2004): 740–765, Table 1: Ratios for the Three Bipolar Dimensions.

What's Your Problem?

Q: I've worked really hard to make sure my employees are happy. And I think I can confidently say they are. But now my bottom-line-obsessed boss says I need to focus more on cutting costs or increasing revenues. He says I spend too much time on "tree-hugging, airy-fairy activities" with my direct reports. How can I convince him that satisfied employees are more productive and that this actually helps the company to invest in this?

A: You and your boss are both right. It is true that numerous studies have shown that employees who experience well-being can be up to 100 percent more productive than their unhappy counterparts. But how much does it cost? Creating shared purpose and positive relationships among coworkers doesn't have to cost anything, and the positive emotional energy can go directly into cost cutting or revenue generating. It's not necessary to install expensive cappuccino machines, enroll everyone in hot-coal walks, or take the team on international expeditions to create unity. Try to have a talk with your boss, acknowledging that costs can be cut and that you will, at the same time, find ways to keep the employees happy. Then everyone wins.

Source: This problem is based on Miranda Kennett, "First-Class Coach," *Management Today* (May 1, 2011): 62.

© CENGAGE LEARNING 2014

DISCOVER KNOWLEDGE

the flow of mutual influence, information, and coordinated action. In the higher-performing organizations, social connectivity was greater, which means that social capital and synchronicity were encouraged. In summary, frequent positive and connective statements made by leaders are associated with better performance. Leaders in the higher-performing organizations did, of course, make some negative comments, but not sufficient to overwhelm the positive.

BUILD A POSITIVE TEAM CULTURE AND VALUES

Once leaders have framed a compelling vision and established a positive communication style, they are on their way to shaping the culture and values needed to achieve the visiion. **Organizational culture** is the set of key values, assumptions, understandings, and norms that is shared by members of the organization and taught to new members as correct.[41] **Norms** are shared standards that define what behaviors are acceptable and desirable within a group of people. Some people think of organizational culture as the character or personality of an organization. How an organization looks and "feels" when you enter it is a manifestation of the organizational culture. At its most basic, culture is a pattern of shared assumptions about how things are done. Culture gives employees a sense of organizational identity and generates a commitment to particular values and ways of doing things.

Culture Strength

Culture strength refers to the level of agreement among employees about the importance of specific values and norms. If widespread consensus exists, the culture is strong and cohesive; if little agreement exists, the culture is weak.[42] A strong culture is typically desirable, but the effect of a strong culture is not always a positive one. Sometimes a strong culture can encourage the wrong values and cause harm to the organization and its members. Think of Bear Stearns, for example, which failed partly because senior leaders built a strong culture that supported pushing everything to the limits and bending rules, standards, and laws for the sake of achieving personal gain and status.[43]

Thus, a strong culture increases employee cohesion and commitment to the values, goals, and strategies of the organization, but companies can sometimes have unethical values or values that are unhealthy for the organization because they don't fit the needs of the environment. Research at Harvard into some 200 corporate cultures found that a strong culture does not ensure success unless it also encourages a healthy adaptation to the external environment.[44]

The High-Performance Culture

A strong culture that encourages adaptation and change enhances organizational performance by energizing and motivating employees, unifying people around shared goals, and shaping and guiding employee behavior so that everyone's actions are aligned with strategic priorities. Thus, culture plays a tremendous role in enabling learning and innovative response to challenges, competitive threats, or new opportunities.

The right culture can drive high performance.[45] A number of studies have found a positive relationship between culture and performance.[46] You can help build a strong adaptive culture that facilitates high performance by incorporating the following values:

- *The whole is more important than the parts, and boundaries between parts are minimized.* People are aware of the whole system, how everything fits together, and the relationships among various organizational parts. All members consider how their actions affect other parts and the total organization. This emphasis on the whole reduces boundaries both within the organization and with other companies, allowing for a free flow of people, ideas, and information that facilitates coordinated action and continuous learning.
- *Equality and trust are primary values.* The culture creates a sense of community and caring for one another. The organization is a place for creating a web of relationships that helps people take risks and develop to their full potential. The emphasis on treating everyone with care and respect creates a climate of open communication, safety, and trust that allows experimentation, frequent mistakes, and learning. At the small company Ternary Software Inc., for example, the culture is based on egalitarianism. Everyone has full access to all company information and has an equal voice in decisions.[47] The culture helps support an entrepreneurial and innovative environment that is critical to Ternary's success.
- *The culture encourages risk taking, change, and improvement.* A basic value is to question the status quo. Constant questioning of assumptions opens the gates to creativity and improvement. The culture rewards and celebrates the creators of new ideas, products, and work processes.

In addition to these three characteristics, high-performance cultures emphasize both values and solid business performance as the drivers of organizational success. Leaders align values with the company's day-to-day operations—hiring practices, performance management, budgeting, criteria for promotions and rewards, and so forth. A study of corporate values by Booz Allen Hamilton and the Aspen Institute found that managers in companies that report superior financial results typically put a high emphasis on values and link them directly to the way they run the organization.[48]

How to Shape Culture

Canada's WestJet Airlines ranked in a survey as having Canada's most admired corporate culture. WestJet employees regularly see top leaders putting the values of equality, teamwork, participation, and customer service into action. At the end of a flight, everyone on hand pitches in to pick up garbage—even the CEO. Top executives spend much of their time chatting informally with employees and customers, and they regularly send notes of thanks to people who have gone above and beyond the call of duty. Top executives have been known to visit the call center on Christmas Day to pitch in and to thank people for working the holiday. Leaders don't receive perks over and above anyone else. There are no assigned parking spaces and no club memberships. Every person at WestJet is treated as first class, exactly the way leaders want employees to treat every passenger on a WestJet flight.[49]

As a manager, how can you influence norms and values to build a high-performance team and organization? A primary way is to use cultural leadership, as leaders at WestJet Airlines do. A *cultural leader* defines and uses signals and symbols to influence corporate culture. Cultural leaders influence culture in two key areas:

1. *The cultural leader articulates a vision for the organizational culture that employees can believe in.* This means the leader defines and communicates central values that employees believe in and will rally around.
2. *The cultural leader heeds the day-to-day activities that reinforce the cultural vision.* The leader makes sure that work procedures and reward systems match and reinforce the values. Actions speak louder than words, so cultural leaders "walk their talk."[50]

For values to guide the organization, leaders model them every day, as they do at WestJet. Creating and maintaining a high-performance culture is not easy, but through their words—and particularly their actions—cultural leaders let everyone in the organization know what really counts. Here are some mechanisms you can use to enact cultural values:

LEADING WORDS

"Always recognize that human individuals are ends, and do not use them as means to your end."

—Immanuel Kant
18th-century German philosopher

"Leaders really think about others first. They think about the people who are on the team, trying to help them get the job done. . . . Your thoughts are always there first . . . and you think last about 'what does this mean for me?'"

—Clarence Otis, Jr.
chairman and CEO of Darden Restaurants (Olive Garden, Red Lobster)

"What I've really learned over time is that optimism is a very, very important part of leadership. . . . People don't like to follow pessimists."

—Robert Iger
chairman and CEO of The Walt Disney Company

"It's very important in a leadership role not to place your ego at the foreground and not to judge everything in relation to how your ego is fed."

—Ruth J. Simmons
18th president of Brown University; professor of comparative literature and Africana studies

"I believe the real difference between success and failure in a corporation can be very often traced to the question of how well the organization brings out the great energies and talents of its people."

—Thomas J. Watson, Jr.
American businessman; second president of IBM

© CENGAGE LEARNING 2014

- *Ceremonies.* A **ceremony** is a planned activity that makes up a special event and is generally conducted for the benefit of an audience. You can use ceremonies to provide dramatic examples of what the company values.[51]
- *Stories.* A **story** is a narrative based on true events that is repeated frequently and shared among employees. As a leader, you can use stories to connect with people on an emotional level and transmit and reinforce important values.
- *Symbols.* A **symbol** is an object, act, or event that conveys meaning to others. In a sense, stories and ceremonies are symbols, but as a leader you can also use physical artifacts to symbolize particular values.
- *Specialized Language.* Leaders sometimes use **slogans** or sayings to express key corporate values. For example, at Averitt Express, the slogan "Our driving force is people," applies to customers and employees alike. Leaders also express and reinforce cultural values through written public statements, such as corporate mission statements or other formal statements that express the core values of the organization.
- *Selection and Socialization.* You can strive to hire people who will fit the cultural values, and then socialize them into the culture. **Socialization** is the process by which a person learns the values, norms, perspectives, and expected behaviors that enable him or her to successfully participate in the group or organization.[52] When people are effectively socialized, they "fit in," because they understand and adopt the norms and values of the group.
- *Daily Actions.* One of the most important ways to build and maintain the cultural values you want is by signaling and supporting these values through your daily actions. Employees learn what is valued most in a company by watching what attitudes and behaviors managers pay attention to and reward, how managers react to organizational crises, and whether the manager's own behavior matches the espoused values.[53]

DESIGN POSITIVE WORK

Another way leaders create a positive work environment that keeps people energized and focused is by designing jobs and assigning tasks in such a way that people are using their natural abilities, doing tasks they enjoy, and finding intrinsic satisfaction and personal growth in the work they do. Positive leaders want people to be able to use their strengths and find a state of flow where work seems effortless and enjoyable.

Focus on Strengths

Tachi Yamada, a physician and president of the Bill & Melinda Gates Foundation's Global Health Program, has learned a thing or two about building a positive team culture. Yamada has gone into many different organizations with people from all walks of life, and he has adopted the philosophy that some people are very good at what they do, others are average, and some are not so good. Yamada knows if he spends all his time dwelling on the bad, he won't get anything accomplished. He tries to discover and then focus on the best qualities of the people he already has in place. His prescription for building a great organization is to ask, "What makes them great, and how can I really improve them one or two notches? [I]f I spend my time on that, then I'll have a great organization. If you bring out the worst in everybody, you're going to have a bad organization."[54]

Tachi Yamada understands the positive leadership aspect of finding and building on people's strengths, which was discussed in Chapter 1. He knows that managers can't just fire everyone who comes up short in an organization. Managers have to work to develop and improve the strengths of the people on board. You can be more productive by focusing and building on an individual's strengths rather than by dwelling on his or her shortcomings. There is value in identifying a person's gaps in performance and offering developmental challenges along with training, coaching, and support as described in Chapter 9. When you recognize and refine employees' strengths and help people use their strengths at work, they can perform at a high level doing what they do naturally. Their feelings of credibility and competence increase, and their commitment and contributions to the organization expand.[55]

Help People Find Flow

Have you ever been so totally immersed in something that time stands still and you experience an overall feeling of enjoyment and satisfaction? This is a state of flow. Many people experience flow when involved in a sport or leisure activity such as skiing, tennis, gardening, or birdhouse building. People can also experience a state of flow when performing their jobs, which contributes to engagement and satisfaction at work.

Psychologist Mihaly Csikszentmihalyi and his colleagues have performed many studies of the flow experience.[56] They have interviewed over 10,000 people from all over the world to better understand a person's consciousness when he or she is in a state of flow. As a manager, you can create conditions that are conducive to enabling the flow experience.

Creating Conditions for Flow

Creating an environment that enables flow requires that managers be committed to the emotional well-being of employees as well as to getting the job done. Many managers are already implementing conditions that are conducive to flow because these are some of the fundamentals of good management:

- *Make sure goals are clear.* To become deeply involved in an activity, people must have a clear goal to reach for and know the tasks they perform moment to moment are taking them toward the goal. People have to understand and commit to deliberately taking each step toward the goal. Yes, reaching the top of the mountain is important, but deep concentration on each step taken to get there is the key to flow. Unfortunately, when people spend their energy focusing on the outcome rather than appreciating each step on the path, they feel less satisfaction. Involving people in setting goals and giving them leeway in how they perform the activities to reach them can help employees feel more committed to and energized by their work.
- *Give frequent feedback.* As we discussed in Chapter 13 on performance management, people need to know how well they are progressing toward meeting goals. Poor managers often allow people to flounder because they don't give them information about how well they're doing. The best condition for flow to occur is when people get immediate feedback from the activity itself. Take, for

example, a surgeon, who gets immediate feedback from each action. He or she knows when something is going well and when it isn't. Musicians, too, can sense if their performance is exceptional or if it isn't up to par. Not every job can provide this type of immediate feedback from the work itself. To be a positive leader, make sure you provide specific, frequent feedback so people know how they are performing and how close they are to the goal.

- *Make sure challenges and skills match.* For flow to happen, the individual needs a challenge, but it should be one that he or she has the skills to meet. When a person feels that a task is beyond his or her capacity, anxiety impedes a flow experience. To enable flow, you can put people in jobs in which they can use their strengths, stretch themselves, and refine and grow their skills. As skills improve, a person can take on greater challenges. As people focus on learning and become proficient and confident with an activity, they are more likely to experience flow.

DISCOVER YOURSELF

Interpret Your Score: Flow
(Questionnaire 4)

This questionnaire pertains to the concept of flow. The first three questions pertain to the conditions for flow—clear goals (question 1), immediate feedback (2), and fit between challenge and skills (3). The remaining five questions pertain to the internal state during flow—deep concentration (question 4), present moment (5), loss of ego or self (6 and 7), and self-fulfillment (8). What is the difference between your two scores? Comparative data for **Flow** ("Like" questions): Thirty person Mean score = 20.5; Top Quartile = 23–24; Bottom Quartile = 12–18. **Forced** ("Don't Like" questions): Thirty person Mean score = 15.6; Top Quartile = 17–23; Bottom Quartile = 8–13. Typically, a task you have to force yourself into involves little flow. Things that we like engage us in flow more readily. How often do you experience flow? Does it occur more often in mental or physical activities? Will you select a career based on your ability to achieve flow or on other criteria? CNOW and CourseMate users can access dynamically updated comparative data through www.cengagebrain.com.

© CENGAGE LEARNING 2014

What Happens with Flow?

The flow experience provides benefits to both the individual and the organization. Based on Csikszentmihalyi's research, here are some outcomes[57] of the flow experience:

- *Concentration deepens.* Deep concentration is like a seamless wave of energy with no distinction between the individual and the activity. This rarely happens day to day because there are so many distractions that compete for our attention. One rock climber describes the feeling of flow as "a one-pointedness of mind . . . when things become automatic [and] . . . somehow the right thing is done without your ever thinking about it or doing anything at all . . . it just happens."[58] When you focus your attention on a specific task so completely that you don't notice anything else, you are in flow.
- *The present is what matters.* In flow, the routine pressures and problems of life disappear. They don't even register in our minds. A mountaineer who is a physicist describes his experience: "When I start to climb it is as if my memory input has been cut off. All I can remember is the last thirty seconds, and all I can think ahead is the next five minutes."[59] When a person's mind isn't focused on the present moment, it thinks randomly about threats, unfinished business, failures, and unfilled desires. In flow, there is no room for such mental wandering.
- *Ego disappears.* Focusing attention pushes anything that is not directly related to the task out of the way. During flow, people forget their job titles, their degrees, their status—they don't think about themselves at all. This frees people from their self-consciousness, fears, and failures as well as from their ambitions, desires, and conceits. Yet, even though an individual forgets the "self" during flow, self-esteem grows from the experience. Austrian psychiatrist Viktor Frankl wrote that happiness isn't attained by wanting to be happy, but comes instead as an unintended consequence of working for a goal greater than oneself.[60]

Flow offers an opportunity to develop employees' leadership skills, improve the quality of their lives, and boost their performance. It isn't easy to create flow within organizations, but as a manager you can strive to provide the conditions that enable people to find it. "You have to give [employees] as much freedom and trust as possible and generate a culture of learning and development," says Utho Creusen, chief human resources officer for European electronics superstores Media Markt and Saturn, who spoke at a workplace symposium on positive psychology and leadership. His company's strategy to find and develop talented people is based on four pillars: participation, vision, strengths orientation, and the state of full engagement, or flow. To encourage flow, individual store managers are given a high degree of autonomy, a financial stake in the performance of the stores, and the responsibility of keeping staff members fully engaged by continually developing their potential.[61]

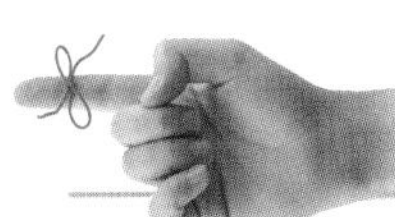

NEED TO KNOW

- A leader's job is to find and promote the positive. Like other skills, positive leadership can be learned. People have a natural tendency, called a negativity bias, to pay more attention to bad things than to good ones. Leaders counteract this tendency by being encouraging and optimistic in the face of organizational problems and difficulties. Three aspects of positive leadership are an affirmative bias, facilitating intrinsic goodness, and exceeding performance expectations.
- Leaders apply the two aspects of positive leadership to build positive organizations: acting on personal qualities such as being mindful, and displaying personal humility combined with a will to do what is best for the organization.
- Leaders create a positive vision for people to follow. A vision is an ambitious view of the future that everyone can believe in, that can realistically be achieved, and that offers a future that is dramatically better than what now exists. Good visions are linked with action and define a noble purpose that gives meaning to people's work. Four frameworks for defining noble purpose are discovery, excellence, altruism, and heroism.
- Positive leaders strive to use more positive than negative statements, which leads to happier, more committed employees and higher organizational performance. Positive communication contributes to a positive culture. Leaders work to build strong cultures that encourage high performance and a healthy adaptation to the environment. Cultural leaders use ceremonies, stories, symbols, language, selection and socialization, and daily actions to build and maintain the right cultural values. In addition, positive leaders help people understand and apply their strengths and find a state of flow in their work.

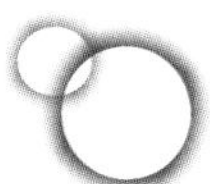

ACTION LEARNING

DELIBERATE PRACTICE EXERCISES

Check Your Ego[62]

Through humility people find nobility, something bigger than themselves. To be humble, you must surrender your outer pretensions and your ego's desire to be right, to get the credit, or to grab things for yourself.

Step 1: For this exercise, you will practice humility for one full day to develop your leadership potential. Start by choosing at least three of the activities below to complete during your egoless day.

1. *Seek no approval from others.* Try to live up to your own standards for your work without the compulsion to please others.
2. *Make no comparisons of yourself or your work to others.* If you find yourself feeling superior or inferior to someone else, say to yourself, "Make no comparisons" and get on with what you are doing.
3. *Seek no recognition or reward.* Do your work well because it pleases you to do it well. If you find yourself motivated primarily by recognition or reward, say to yourself, "Seek no recognition or reward" and get on with your work.
4. *Work hard and do your best, for its own sake.* To be humble is not to lower your standards and become a sloth. To be humble is to honor your internal standards more than what the rest of the world thinks. Take pleasure in the *process* of doing your work to the best of your ability.
5. *Ask someone, "How can I do better?"* Ask your spouse, "How can I do better as a husband/wife?" Ask a fellow club officer, "How can I do better as an officer?" Ask a team member, "How can I be a better team member (or leader)?"
6. *Perform a random act of kindness.* When you feel the urge to serve yourself first, such as when driving or waiting in line, put another person ahead of yourself. Provide one deliberate act of kindness when the recipient will know you and another act in which you are anonymous.

Step 2: Practice your activities and keep a log of what you do and what happens as a result.

Your Ego-Free Day Log

Describe incidents during which you practiced humility.	1.
	2.
	3.
How did you feel?	
What was the reaction of the other person(s)?	
What did you learn from practicing this?	
How can you remember to keep doing this?	

Step 3 (Optional): Share your insights with a partner, and ask your partner what insights he or she gained.

Caring Relationships[63]

Supportive relationships and love form a foundation of positive leadership. This exercise asks you to consider how well you do with relationships and how you can do better.

Step 1: Fill out the table below, considering two people at your school or workplace and one personal relationship.

Name of person with whom I want a better relationship	Describe current relationship	What would I rather have in the relationship?	What steps can I take to make the relationship more positive?
1.			
2.			
3. (Personal)			

Step 2: Answer the following questions.

1. **What has been keeping me from making these relationships more positive?**
2. **Do I see any patterns in the dynamics of the different relationships?**
3. **How easy or difficult will it be for me to implement the steps I've laid out?**
4. **How can I get support from others to make sure I do these things?**

Step 3 (Optional): Share your insights with a partner, and ask your partner what insights he or she gained.

IN-CLASS TEAM EXERCISE

Car Wash

This is an exercise to help you see the power of positive communication and recognition.

Step 1: Divide into groups of four to five. You should preferably be with people you know fairly well, or at least somewhat.

Step 2: Each individual fills out the following table about the other people in his or her group.

	Person #1	Person #2	Person #3	Person #4
List two things you like/admire about this person.				
What positive adjectives would you use to describe this person to someone else?				
Describe a situation when this person did something really nice.				
What positive feelings do you have when this person is around?				

Step 3: Each person in the group gives his or her positive feedback in the following manner, so that each person gets his or her compliments as if in a "car wash":

1. Choose one person to start receiving feedback.
2. Person #2 shares the positive comments he or she wrote about Person #1.
3. Person #3 shares positive feedback about Person #1, etc., until everyone has given what they wrote about Person #1.
4. Then go around and everyone give their positive feedback to Person #2.
5. Then do Person #3, Person #4, and Person #5 in the same manner.

Step 4: As a group, discuss how it felt to get positive feedback.

Step 5: Write down two names of people you will give positive feedback to within the next three days.

Name	What will you tell them?

FIELD TEAM EXERCISE

Anthropological Hunt[64]

The purpose of this exercise is to familiarize you with the symbols, ceremonies, stories, language, and so on of your university so you will have a greater awareness of how these cultural artifacts help the university achieve its goals.

Step 1: Form into groups of three to four. Preferably, you should do the entire work as a group. But you may also divide up the work outlined in Step 2 as you see fit and then meet together to go over what you have and how each item helps tell the story of your university's culture.

Step 2: Spend time, as if you were an anthropological team, looking for artifacts of your university's culture and values:

1. Look for any images, items, or statements that help you identify areas such as:
    a. The goals and mission of the university
    b. Types of student or academic programs
    c. Sports and athletics
    d. Donors and funders
    e. Cognitive dissonance (any areas that look hypocritical or where there have been scandals)
2. List any words, slogans, or language unique to your university.
3. You can use any printed materials, cartoons on faculty members' offices (use your phone and take photos), t-shirts (photos are fine), flyers, pictures of ceremonies or mascots, and so on.
4. Interview students and faculty to find stories that tell something about the university, especially stories (which may or may not be true) that are repeated over and over, year after year.

Step 3: After you've gathered everything, meet as a group and discuss the meanings of what you found.

Step 4: Choose four things you think are most representative of the culture:

Four most representative things you found:
1.
2.
3.
4.

Step 5: As a group, design a ceremony and write a story that shows the university as it wants to be.

Your ceremony	
Your story	

Step 6: How can leaders use stories, ceremonies, and symbols to create a more productive organization?

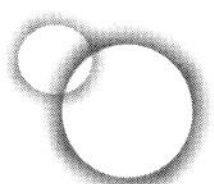

TEST YOUR METTLE

ROLE PLAY SIMULATIONS

Just say NO!

Background: Re-read the written Video Incident at the beginning of the chapter. Caffeine and Crullers sales manager Jason Wong has a habit of putting a negative spin on his colleagues, which does not help elevate the work environment. General manager Jane Sutton has to figure out what, if anything, to do about it.

Instructions: Form into groups of three. One person will be Jason, one Jane, and the third an observer. Each person reads only his or her confidential role, but the observer reads both. Spend 15 minutes on the role play.

Confidential information for Jason: You've only been at this C&C job for what—maybe seven months now?—but it sure seems like seven years. People are so lazy, so stupid, and no one seems to care. They turn in sloppy work, show up late (especially Heather), resist new ideas (especially yours), mouth off (there goes Carrie again), and are afraid to stand up to anyone (Carlos, do you recognize yourself?). And it's like they don't even know they are behaving this way or that it hurts the company. The illustrious boss, Jane, doesn't get on their case enough. If you were in charge, you'd really tell them where they are going wrong. But everyone is *soooo* sensitive. You can hardly say "boo" without an angry look or a pouty mouth. You think it's time you had a talk with Jane and let her know how she needs to straighten everyone out. Thank goodness she's asked to see you. She probably wants to hear your wisdom on this matter.

Confidential information for Jane: Your sales manager, Jason Wong, is in one of his negative moods again. You've always let it slide before, because you saw early on that it only lasts a few days. But this time and last, it's been worse. He just can't say a nice thing about anybody, or any project. He acts like he's the only one who cares about C&C, or the only one who knows how to solve problems. You think it's time you had a long talk with Jason. But how can you do it without also being negative? You've been talking to the staff lately about being more positive, so you can't exactly try to resolve this situation by being negative. The bottom line, though, is that you have to talk to Jason and help him see the harmful effect he's having on the others. He's coming to see you in five minutes and you've got to find a way.

After the role play, observer gives feedback and then the group discusses these questions:

1. How well did Jane handle this situation?
2. What is the most effective way to deal with negativity in other people?
3. Discuss some positive approaches Jane could take.

The Ho-Hum Job

This Role Play Simulation is available online at www.cengagebrain.com.

SHUTTERSTOCK #53973379

VIDEO APPLICATION

See It Online

Positive Leadership at Camp Bow Wow

Heidi Ganahl uses her leadership style to create a distinct corporate culture at Camp Bow Wow.

Discussion Questions

1. Do you think Heidi Ganahl can be considered a positive leader? Why? To what extent does Ganahl illustrate humility, service, and love as part of her leadership style? Explain.
2. To what extent do you think Ganahl's vision for Camp Bow Wow reflects her personality? What role does her leadership style and vision play in shaping the culture of Camp Bow Wow?
3. Which of the four noble purposes does Camp Bow Wow seem to exhibit? Explain.

CASE INCIDENTS

One Size Fits All?

In their three years at Vreeland Pharmaceuticals, Vitorio Nuños and Gary Shaw had rarely crossed paths and they had exchanged no more than a dozen sentences. But here they were, seatmates on a plane headed to company headquarters in Kansas City, Missouri. And suddenly, they had a lot to say to each other.

"What I'd like to know is why we're wasting a trip to Kansas City to thrash out some new model of leader competencies," Vitorio said.

"Because Connie Wyland *is* HR at Vreeland and you and I both know that forms and models and all of that touchy-feely people stuff is the life blood of HR," Gary replied. "I also think a lot of this is the result of panic on the heels of the scandals in sales last year."

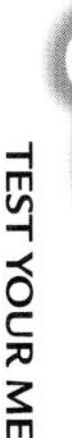

"I don't think there's cause for panic. The company fired the guys, apologized, and then you just move on," said Vitorio.

Gary laughed sarcastically. "No, you fire them, you apologize, and then you analyze the whole thing *ad nauseam*, and *then* you hamstring your management team with endless rules and standards of conduct just to make sure it doesn't happen again."

"So we all pay for their mistakes," replied Vitorio.

"We pay because HR feels guilty that those guys moved up so high in the system," Gary said. "So now Connie and her staff have devised the ultimate solution to the problem. I don't know why we all have to go in to discuss it; she's already decided what she's going to do and she's positive this is the cure-all to prevent any further embarrassment to the company."

"Let's look at the document," Vitorio said. He reached under the seat, retrieved and unpacked his tablet, placed it on the tray table, and turned it on.

"Too much glare," Gary said, peeking over. Vitorio pulled down the window shade.

"Is that better?"

Gary nodded. The two men read through the document.

"I resent the term 'rogue leaders,'" Gary remarked, pointing to the phrase.

Vitorio shrugged. "It's a rough draft. They'll clean up the language . . . I think."

"It's really just a re-hash of the mission statement and all of the things we learned in training. This is stuff we all learned in business school. I feel like I'm being lectured."

"Yeah," Vitorio scrolled up and down the document. "Any business student could have written this."

"I hear the HR crew put in lots of overtime," said Gary.

Vitorio smirked. "For this? I'll tell you . . . and this is just between you and me, but I really resent this and we're some of the newer members of management. I would love to hear what the older managers are saying."

"I know Connie," Gary said. "She and her staff are going to come in tomorrow all gung-ho on this." He turned the tablet in order to see it easier. "We already *know* what's expected of us." He scrolled down, stopping at key phrases. "Look at this . . . 'critical values' . . . 'core competencies' . . . 'fostering conflict resolution' . . . and here's one—'implementing employee involvement strategies.' How does she think we got these jobs in the first place?" Gary paused. "What really makes me angry is that I heard Connie is going to start manager training sessions where she will teach us the behaviors associated with each value! Can you believe that? She will have us role-playing and stuff. I will fight this if it goes beyond general value statements that we can follow in our own way.

"I can't wait to hear what Vreeland says," Vitorio remarked.

"Are you kidding? He'll go along with it. He'll spend ten to fifteen minutes telling us how great we all are and insinuating that we don't really need this, and then he'll back Connie all the way. Face it, this is the way it's going to be and he really doesn't *need* our input or approval. It just looks good," commented Gary.

Vitorio turned off and closed the tablet. "I just feel that imposing something like this on management is a slap at every one of us. We know what's expected. We don't need training. We also know our people, and we have to have some flexibility within a broad set of boundaries. This sort of thing just hamstrings us. Connie wants the Stepford Wives."

"I just hope a couple of senior managers speak up at this meeting and voice some concerns. Maybe it will be toned down a little," Gary said. "You and I are middle management, and we haven't been with the company long enough. All we can do at this meeting is sit and nod."

Discussion Questions

1. Are Connie and her staff on the right track to a positive culture by defining a new list of core competencies and core values? Explain your answer.
2. Do you think positive leadership practices and a positive culture can be imposed on managers with value statements and training sessions? Why or why not?
3. Why do you think Vitorio Nuños and Gary Shaw are on the defensive? Might the extra emphasis on core leadership competencies be handled in a different way? What do you suggest?

Culture Clash

When you think of a culture clash, you usually associate it with global expansion or cultural diversity within the organization. But in the case of our company, the clash between the old culture and the new comes to a head tomorrow. CEO Jane Lionel has some hard decisions to make with regard to some of the company's older hands, and even on the eve of that decision; I believe she is wavering about what she should do. I will be in that meeting, assisting with that decision, and I'm not certain which way to go either. And so here I am, sorting through and writing down my thoughts.

When Jim Lionel started manufacturing heavy-duty construction equipment here in Alaska 40 years ago, his personal management style reflected the ruggedness of Alaska and the construction business. He understood that he was producing tough equipment for tough men working in an unforgiving environment. At 6'5" and over 300 pounds, Lionel personified the bigger-than-life image of Alaskan workers. He had a no-nonsense management style. He coddled no one. Jim Lionel expected and got results. He chewed—not smoked—a cigar. I swear that in the 30 years I worked for him, I never saw that thing lit up as he barked—yes, *barked*—orders.

I'd have to say that Jim Lionel gained respect because he always delivered and his word was his bond. But he never achieved admiration. There was no finesse. A new HR director once mentioned to me that Jim should create bonds with his workers through techniques such as management by walking around. I said, "Believe me, you do *not* want him walking around—that simply means he's stressed and he's mad." You could actually *feel* him and hear him before you saw him and as one employee said, "When he barked your name, your heart stopped, because until that moment you were certain that he did not *know* your name." We all figured that his temper would explode one day and he would die on the shop floor from a heart attack. Then suddenly, he did.

Following his death, we were certain that the company would have to be sold in order to continue operations. But Jim's one true friend and confidante was his wife Jane, and with unanimous board approval, she moved in to take his place as the head of the company. The initial concerns and fears of employees were soon calmed. Jane knew the company to a degree that surprised employees. But her management style, developed over 20 years as head of marketing for a regional health-care organization, was in stark contrast to that of her husband.

While Jane shared her husband's goals and high standards for quality and on-time delivery, she also believed in the importance of demonstrating to employees their value to the company. She not only communicated her vision, but she took the time to listen to the employees, to give them opportunities to voice opinions, express concerns, and submit ideas. She met regularly with individual departments and assisted line workers in the movement toward self-managed teams. The reaction from workers was positive. And a year later, we can see a huge change. Production is up slightly, but the real change can be seen in the employees' attitudes and pride in their jobs. Communication and the overall level of civility among workers have improved dramatically. But while these cultural changes have been embraced by the majority of workers and supervisors, there are two glaring exceptions.

Supervisors Curtis Willett and Morgan Elder were among the first employees hired by Jim Lionel. Their long service to the organization and their consistency in meeting all production goals and deadlines is impressive. They take pride in their ability to push themselves and their crews relentlessly. But their management styles are a throw-back to the old culture. They succeed by intimidation. The civility and cooperation that characterizes other parts of the plant is shoved aside or drowned out in a barrage of yelling. "Shock and Awe," the joint nickname briefly given to the two men by employees following the 2003 U.S. aerial assault on Iraq, has been revived. If these men are aware of the label, they are probably proud.

So here's our dilemma: They are too old to change. Curtis and Morgan not only do not fit the new culture, but through tactics of control and intimidation, they also encourage workers to ignore the new cultural initiatives. Everyone is on board except the

workers in these two adjoining areas of the plant. So we cannot reach the full potential of the new culture while the old culture pulls us back. Fire them? Demote them? I don't think so. They've done nothing wrong. Their crews are meeting their production and quality targets. Furthermore, these two guys have been with the company for 40 years. A move on our part that appears unjustified opens us to an age-discrimination suit. But I also don't see how we can change the culture unless they leave.

So, we meet tomorrow to determine what we can do. Writing about a problem usually helps me to sort things out. When I finish, I generally have an answer or at least an idea about how to proceed. I've finished writing. And I haven't got a clue.

Discussion Questions

1. What options do you think Jane and her management team should consider with regard to these two long-time supervisors? Make a list and discuss the positives and negatives of each.
2. Do you agree that it is appropriate to remove two managers in order to create a positive culture for everyone else? Which do you think is more important—the culture or two people? Why?
3. What do you recommend that Jane do? Why?

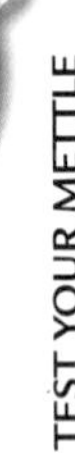

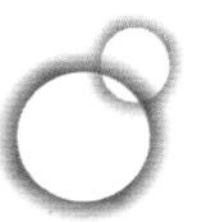

PERSONAL SKILLS LOG

Directions: Fill in the rows below based on what you learned from each part of the chapter that you completed.

	What is my key takeaway or insight from this activity?	What do I personally do well (strength) regarding this activity?	What could I improve (weakness) about myself regarding this activity?	How might I use what I've learned from this activity in the future?
Manager Challenge Incident:				
Discover Yourself Questionnaires:				
Deliberate Practice Exercises:				
In-Class and/or Field Team Exercises:				
Role-Play Exercises:				
Case Incidents:				

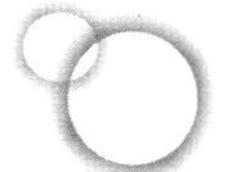

REFERENCES

Discover Yourself

1 Adapted from Laura Stafford and Daniel J. Canary, "Maintenance Strategies and Romantic Relationship Type, Gender and Relational Characteristics," *Journal of Social and Personal Relationships* 8, no. 2 (May 1991): 217–242; and Michael F. Scheier and Charles S. Carver, "Optimism, Coping, and Health: Assessment and Implications of Generalized Outcome Expectancies," *Health Psychology* 4, no. 3 (1985): 219–247.

2 These questions are based on ideas from R.L. Daft and R.M. Lengel, *Fusion Leadership* (Berrett Koehler, 2000), Chapter 4; B. Bass and B. Avolio, *Multifactor Leadership Questionnaire*, 2nd ed. (Mind Garden, Inc.); and Alannah E. Rafferty and Mark A. Griffin, "Dimensions of Transformational Leadership: Conceptual and Empirical Extensions," *The Leadership Quarterly* 15 (2004): 329–354.

3 Adapted from Susan A. Jackson and Herbert Marsh, "Development and Validation of a Scale to Measure Optimal Experience: The Flow State Scale" *Journal of Sport & Exercise Psychology* 18, no. 1 (March 1996): 17–35; and Kevin Money, Carola Hillenbrand, and Nuno da Camara, "Putting Positive Psychology to Work in Organizations," *Journal of General Management* 34, no. 2 (Winter 2008): 21–36.

Discover Knowledge

4 This example is from Kim Cameron, *Positive Leadership: Strategies for Extraordinary Performance*, (San Francisco: Berrett-Koehler Publishers, Inc., 2008), pp. 10–13.

5 Gary Yukl and Richard Lepsinger, "Why Integrating the Leading and Managing Roles Is Essential for Organizational Effectiveness," *Organizational Dynamics* 34, no. 4 (2005): 361–375; and Martha H. Peak, "Anti-Manager Named Manager of the Year," *Management Review* (October, 1991): 7.

6 This discussion is based on R.F. Baumeister, E. Bratlavsky, C. Finenauer, and K.D. Vohs, "Bad Is Stronger Than Good," *Review of General Psychology* 5 (2001): 323–370; P. Rozin and E.B. Royzman, "Negativity Bias, Negativity Dominance, and Contagion," *Personality and Social Psychology Review* 5 (2001): 296–320; Kim S. Cameron, "Paradox in Positive Organizational Change," *The Journal of Applied Behavioral Science* 44, no. 1 (March 2008): 7–24; and Kim Cameron, *Positive Leadership*, pp. 10–13.

7 J.P. Walsh, "Business Must Talk about Its Social Role," in T. Dixon, ed., *Mastering Strategy* (London: Prentice Hall, 1999), pp. 289–294.

8 Marcus Buckingham and Donald O. Clifton., "The Strengths Revolution: Two Assumptions at the Foundation of Great Organizations," *Gallup Management Journal*, January 22, 2001, http://gmj.gallup.com/content/547/the-strengths-revolution.aspx (accessed February 24, 2012).

9 Morgan W. McCall, Jr. and Michael M. Lombardo, "Off the Track: Why and How Successful Executives Get Derailed," *Technical Report No. 21* (Greensboro, NC: Center for Creative Leadership, January 1983).

10 Gretchen M. Spreitzer, "Leadership Development Lessons from Positive Organizational Studies," *Organizational Dynamics* 35, no. 4 (2006): 305–315; and Debra Benton, "Southwest Airlines Culture Drives Profitability and Community Caring," *BusinessWeek Online*, September 22, 2010, http://bx.businessweek.com/corporate-social-responsibility/view?url=http%3A%2F%2Fbclc.chamberpost.com%2F2010%2F09%2Fsouthwest-airlines-culture-drives-profitability-and-community-caring.html (accessed May 12, 2011).

11 Fred Luthans, "Positive Organizational Behavior: Developing and Managing Psychological Strengths," *Academy of Management Executive*, 16, no. 1 (2002): 57–75.

12 This discussion in these three sections is based heavily on Kim Cameron, *Positive Leadership*.

13 M.E.P. Seligman, *Learned Optimism* (New York: Pocket Books, 1998); Fred Luthans, "Positive Organizational Behavior."

14 Cited in Cameron, *Positive Leadership*, p. 3.

15 Dave Ulrich and Wendy Ulrich, "Creating Abundance," *Leadership Excellence* (June 2010): 8–9.

16 Barbara L. Fredrickson, "What Good Are Positive Emotions?" *Review of General Psychology* 2, no. 3 (1998): 300–319.

17 Ellen Langer and John Sviokla, "An Evaluation of Charisma from the Mindfulness Perspective," unpublished manuscript, Harvard University. Part of this discussion is also drawn from Richard L. Daft and Robert H. Lengel, *Fusion Leadership: Unlocking the Subtle Forces that Change People and Organizations* (San Francisco: Berrett-Koehler, 1998).

18 T.K. Das, "Educating Tomorrow's Managers: The Role of Critical Thinking," *The International Journal of Organizational Analysis* 2, no. 4 (October 1994): 333–360.

19 The Pike Syndrome has been discussed in multiple sources.

20 Chris Argyris, *Flawed Advice and the Management Trap* (New York: Oxford University Press, 2000); Eileen C. Shapiro, "Managing in the Cappuccino Economy," (review of *Flawed Advice*), *Harvard Business Review* (March–April 2000): 177–183.

21 This example is from Jim Collins, "Level 5 Leadership: The Triumph of Humility and Fierce Resolve," *Harvard Business Review* (January 2001): 67–76.

22 The discussion of Level 5 leadership is based on Collins, "Level 5 Leadership"; James C. Collins, *From Good to Great: Why Some Companies Make the Leap . . . and Others Don't* (New York: HarperCollins, 2001); Jim Collins, "Good to Great," *Fast Company* (October 2001): 90–104; and A.J. Vogl, "Onward and Upward" (an interview with Jim Collins), *Across the Board* (September–October 2001): 29–34.

23 Geoffrey Colvin, "What's Love Got to Do with It?" *Fortune* (November 12, 2001): 60.

24 Kathleen D. Ryan and Daniel K. Oestreich, *Driving Fear Out of the Workplace: How to Overcome the Invisible Barriers to Quality, Productivity, and Innovation* (San Francisco: Jossey-Bass, 1991).

25 Madan Birla with Cecilia Miller Marshall, *Balanced Life and Leadership Excellence* (Memphis, TN: The Balance Group, 1997), pp. 76–77.

26 This discussion is based on Ryan and Oestreich, *Driving Fear Out of the Workplace*; Therese R. Welter, "Reducing Employee Fear: Get Workers and Managers to Speak Their Minds," *Small Business Reports* (April 1991): 15–18; and David E. Dorsey, "Escape from the Red Zone," *Fast Company*, (April-May 1997): 116–127.

27 Susan G. Hauser, "The Degeneration of Decorum," *Workforce Management* (January 11, 2011): 16–18, 20–21.

28 R.J. Baum, E.A. Locke, and S. Kirkpatrick, "A Longitudinal Study of the Relations of Vision and Vision Communication to Venture Growth in Entrepreneurial Firms," *Journal of Applied Psychology* 83 (1998): 43–54.

29 Hay Group study, reported in Edward Prewitt, "Watch What You Say," *CIO* (November 1, 2005): 26.

30 Quoted in Pat McHenry Sullivan, "Finding Visions for Work and Life," *Spirit at Work* (April 1997), p. 3.

31 William D. Hitt, *The Leader-Manager: Guidelines for Action* (Columbus, OH: Batelle Press, 1988).

32 The discussion of noble purpose is based on Nikos Mourkogiannis, "The Realist's Guide to Moral Purpose," *Strategy + Business* 41 (Winter 2005): 42–53.

33 Roger E. Herman and Joyce L. Gioia, "Making Work Meaningful: Secrets of the Future-Focused Corporation," *The Futurist* (December 1998): 24–26.

34 Stephen J. Garone, "Motivation: What Makes People Work?" *Across the Board* (May–June 2001): 79–80.

35 Alan Deutschman, "Can Google Stay Google?" *Fast Company* (August 2005): 62–68.

36 Steve Lohr, "Apple, a Success at Stores, Bets Big on Fifth Avenue," *The New York Times* (May 19, 2006); and Michael V. Copeland, "The Apple Ecosystem," *Fortune* (November 23, 2009): 102–109.

37 Kerry Capell, "IKEA: How the Swedish Retailer Became a Global Cult Brand," *BusinessWeek* (November 14, 2005): 97–106; [The CEO Interview] Jérôme Barthélemy, "The Experimental Roots of Revolutionary Vision," *MIT Sloan Management Review* 48, no. 1 (Fall 2006): 81–84; and Corey Hajim, "Not by Bread Alone," *Fortune* (July 10, 2006): 126.

38 Eric Klein and John Izzo, *Awakening Corporate Soul: Four Paths to Unleash the Power of People at Work* (Beverly, MA: Fair Winds Press, 1999); John Izzo, Leadership Speaker, *YouTube*, September 25, 2008, http://www.youtube.com/watch?v=R9C3wJbjsN4 (accessed May 13, 2011).

39 Holly Hom and Jonathan Haidt, "The Bonding and Norming Functions of Gossip," (in preparation, University of Virginia), cited in Jonathan Haidt, *The Happiness Hypothesis: Finding Modern Truth in Ancient Wisdom* (New York: Basic Books, 2006), p. 54.

40 Marcial Losada and Emily Heaphy, "The Role of Positivity and Connectivity in the Performance of Business Teams: A Nonlinear Dynamics Model," *American Behavioral Scientist* 47, no. 6 (February 2004): 740–765.

41 Edgar H. Schein, "Organizational Culture," *American Psychologist* 45, no. 2 (1990): 109–119; W. Jack Duncan, "Organizational Culture: Getting a 'Fix' on an Elusive Concept," *Academy of Management Executive* 3 (1989): 229–236; Linda Smircich, "Concepts of Culture and Organizational Analysis," *Administrative Science Quarterly* 28 (1983): 339–358; and Andrew D. Brown and Ken Starkey, "The Effect of Organizational Culture on Communication and Information," *Journal of Management Studies* 31, no. 6 (November 1994): 807–828.

42 Bernard Arogyaswamy and Charles M. Byles, "Organizational Culture: Internal and External Fits," *Journal of Management* 13 (1987): 647–659.

43 Michiko Kakutani, "The Tsunami That Buried a Wall Street Giant," *The New York Times*, March 10, 2009.

44 John P. Kotter and John Heskett, *Corporate Culture and Performance* (New York: The Free Press, 1992).

45 Jennifer A. Chatman and Sandra Eunyoung Cha, "Leading by Leveraging Culture," *California Management Review* 45, no. 4 (Summer 2003): 20–34; and Jeff Rosenthal and Mary Ann Masarech, "High-Performance Cultures: How Values Can Drive Business Results," *Journal of Organizational Excellence* (Spring 2003): 3–18.

46 Kotter and Heskett, *Corporate Culture and Performance*; Abby Ghobadian and Nicholas O'Regan, "The Link Between Culture, Strategy and Performance in Manufacturing SMEs," *Journal of General Management* 28, no. 1 (Autumn, 2002): 16–34; G.G. Gordon and N. DiTomaso, "Predicting Corporate Performance from Organisational Culture," *Journal of Management Studies* 29, no. 6 (1992): 783–798; and G.A. Marcoulides and R.H. Heck, "Organizational Culture and Performance: Proposing and Testing a Model," *Organization Science* 4 (1993): 209–225.

47 Jaclyne Badal, "Can a Company Be Run as a Democracy?" *The Wall Street Journal*, April 23, 2007.

48 Reggie Van Lee, Lisa Fabish, and Nancy McGaw, "The Value of Corporate Values: A Booz Allen Hamilton/Aspen Institute Survey," *Strategy + Business*, Issue 39 (Summer 2005): 52–65.

49 Andrew Wahl, "Culture Shock," *Canadian Business* (October 10–23, 2005): 115–116; and Calvin Leung, Michelle Magnan, and Andrew Wahl, "People Power," *Canadian Business* (October 10–23, 2005): 125–126.

50 Rosenthal and Masarech, "High-Performance Cultures"; Patrick M. Lencioni, "Make Your Values Mean Something," *Harvard Business Review* (July 2002): 113–117; and Thomas J. Peters and Robert H. Waterman, Jr., *In Search of Excellence* (New York: Warner, 1988).

51 Harrison M. Trice and Janice M. Beyer, "Studying Organizational Culture Through Rites and Ceremonials," *Academy of Management Review* 9 (1984): 653–669.

52 D.C. Feldman, "The Multiple Socialization of Organization Members," *Academy of Management Review* 6 (1981): 309–318; J. Van Maanen, "Breaking In: Socialization to Work," in *Handbook of Work, Organization, and Society*, R. Dubin, ed. (Chicago: Rand-McNally, 1976), p. 67; and Blake E. Ashford and Alan M. Saks, "Socialization Tactics: Longitudinal Effects on Newcomer Adjustment," *Academy of Management Journal* 39, no. 1 (February 1996): 149–178.

53 Deanne N. Den Hartog, Jaap J. Van Muijen, and Paul L. Koopman, "Linking Transformational Leadership and Organizational Culture," *The Journal of Leadership Studies* 3, no. 4 (1996): 68–83; and Schein, "Organizational Culture."

54 Adam Bryant, "Talk to Me. I'll Turn Off My Phone," *The New York Times*, February 28, 2010.

55 Charles A. Millick, "Leadership and the Science of Happiness," *Industrial Management* (September-October 2008): 18–20.

56 This section is based on Mihaly Csikszentmihalyi, *Good Business* (New York: Viking, 2003), pp. 105–139.

57 *Ibid.*, pp. 46–56.

58 *Ibid.*, p. 47.

59 *Ibid.*, p. 49.

60 *Ibid.*, p. 56.

61 Steve Crabtree, "How Good Feelings Boost Bottom Lines" *Gallup Management Journal Online*, December 14, 2006, http://gmj.gallup.com/content/25852/how-good-feelings-boost-bottom-lines.aspx (accessed May 13, 2011).

Action Learning Exercises

62 A special thanks to Michael Ray for providing his "Live-With" exercise from which this exercise is adapted.

63 From Dorothy Marcic, *Love Lift Me Higher* (United Kingdom: George Ronald Press, 2010).

64 Inspired by an exercise originally created by Lizabeth A. Barclay and Kenneth M. York.

CHAPTER 16

Managing Personal and Organizational Change

Chapter Outline

RYAN LASH

MANAGER CHALLENGE

VIDEO INCIDENT: LIGHT THE FIRE

Jane Sutton, general manager of Caffeine and Crullers, has seen the enthusiasm of her staff dwindle each week as Scone Prone takes more and more market share. At the last meeting, Jane soft-pedaled the threat so her team didn't get upset, and people were arguing, doodling, and texting—anything but solving the big problem of how to win back customers. No one seemed to care. Then it hit her: Her management team was acting as if they didn't understand the seriousness of the situation. They didn't seem to get that C&C could go out of business and they would all lose their jobs. Moreover, the team didn't seem to share the vision of what this company could become if they innovated and worked harder to take back market share. Jane is thinking to herself that at the next meeting, she has to change her approach. The company is sinking fast.

Initial Thoughts

1. **If you were Jane, what would you do at the next meeting?**

2. **How do you think a manager could get a team "on fire" to make changes to improve a company? Why would this be important?**

Your instructor may ask you to be part of a role play based on the "Light the Fire" incident.

DISCOVER YOURSELF

For those students using CourseMate or CengageNOW, you can access the Daft/Marcic Assessment Library to take the questionnaires online and view dynamically updated comparative data.

Questionnaire 1[1]

Instructions: Think carefully about each of the following statements and indicate your answers based on how you respond to day-to-day issues. Be as honest as possible. Please indicate whether each item is clearly true or accurate for you, clearly false or inaccurate, or in the middle as somewhat true and somewhat false.

	True	Somewhat	False
1. I generally consider changes in my life to be a negative thing.	○	○	○
2. When I am told of a change of plans, I may tense up a bit.	○	○	○
3. Once I have made plans, I am not likely to change them.	○	○	○
4. I often change my mind.	○	○	○
5. Whenever my life fits a stable routine, I look for ways to change it.	○	○	○
6. I feel less stress when things go according to plan.	○	○	○
7. I sometimes avoid making personal changes even when the change would be good for me.	○	○	○
8. My views are very consistent over time.	○	○	○
9. I prefer a routine day to a day full of unexpected surprises.	○	○	○
10. If I were informed of a significant change in my work, I would tighten up.	○	○	○
11. When someone pressures me to change something, I tend to resist it.	○	○	○
12. Once I have come to a conclusion, I stick to it.	○	○	○

Total Score Questionnaire 1 ______. (Sum items 1–3 and 6–12 by giving 3 points for each True, 2 points for each Somewhat, and 1 point for each False. Reverse score items 4 and 5 by giving 3 points for each False, 2 points for each Somewhat, and 1 point for each True, and add to the total.) Go to page 592 to interpret your score.

Questionnaire 2[2]

Instructions: Think about a specific behavior change—for example, stop smoking, schedule regular exercise, adopt a healthier diet, drop a bad habit—that you have considered making in your life. With that specific behavior or habit in mind, carefully mark each item below as True, Somewhat, or False for you.

Part A

	True	Somewhat	False
1. To be honest, my problem is not so bad that it needs changing.	○	○	○
2. The behavior may be a fault, but it is nothing that I really need to change.	○	○	○
3. I am aware of the issue, but I am fine with it.	○	○	○

Total Score Part A ________. (Sum questions 1–3 by giving 3 points for each True, 2 points for each Somewhat, and 1 point for each False.)

Part B

	True	Somewhat	False
4. I have been thinking that I would like to change that behavior.	○	○	○
5. I wish I knew more about how to solve that problem.	○	○	○
6. I would like to understand better that behavior to start changing it.	○	○	○

Total Score Part B ________. (Sum questions 4–6 by giving 3 points for each True, 2 points for each Somewhat, and 1 point for each False.)

Part C

	True	Somewhat	False
7. I am actually doing something about it right now.	○	○	○
8. I am really starting to change, but I am not there yet.	○	○	○
9. I am in the process of changing, but I want to be more consistent.	○	○	○

Total Score Part C ________. (Sum questions 7–9 by giving 3 points for each True, 2 points for each Somewhat, and 1 point for each False.)

Part D

	True	Somewhat	False
10. I have already completed the change, and I do not plan to backslide.	○	○	○
11. The change has become part of my day, and I feel wrong if I do not stay with it.	○	○	○
12. The new behavior is now a part of my life, and I do not think about it anymore.	○	○	○

Total Score Part D ________. (Sum questions 10–12 by giving 3 points for each True, 2 points for each Somewhat, and 1 point for each False.) Go to page 594 to interpret your scores.

Questionnaire 3[3]

Instructions: Think of a job you held for a period of time. Respond to the statements below according to your behaviors *over a typical six-month period.*

DISCOVER YOURSELF

Part A

	Often	Sometimes	Rarely
1. I tried to adopt improved procedures for doing my job.	○	○	○
2. I felt a personal sense of responsibility to bring about changes.	○	○	○
3. I attempted to remove a barrier to making things more effective for the company.	○	○	○
4. I noticed problems and would solve them to execute work more efficiently.	○	○	○
5. I went to my boss to try to change organizational rules or policies that were counterproductive.	○	○	○
6. I felt it was up to me to bring about improvement in my workplace.	○	○	○
7. I made constructive suggestions for improving how things operated.	○	○	○
8. I tried to implement new ideas for pressing organizational problems.	○	○	○
9. I felt a personal obligation to challenge or change the status quo.	○	○	○
10. I tried to introduce new structures, technologies, or approaches that would improve efficiency.	○	○	○

Total Score Questionnaire 3 ________. (Sum items 1–10 by giving 3 points for each Often, 2 points for each Sometimes, and 1 point for each Rarely.) Go to page 600 to interpret your score.

Questionnaire 4[4]

Instructions: Think about day-to-day projects or hobbies that you initiate at school, work, or home. Indicate whether each of the following statements is True, Somewhat, or False for you. Respond as honestly as possible.

	True	Somewhat	False
1. I often set a goal but later choose to pursue a different one.	○	○	○
2. I have been obsessed with a certain idea or project for a short time but later lost interest.	○	○	○
3. I have difficulty maintaining my focus on projects that take more than a few months to complete.	○	○	○
4. New ideas and projects sometimes distract me from previous ones.	○	○	○
5. I finish whatever I begin.	○	○	○
6. Setbacks don't discourage me.	○	○	○
7. I am diligent.	○	○	○
8. I am a hard worker.	○	○	○

Total Score Questionnaire 4 ________. (Sum items 5–8 by giving 3 points for each True, 2 points for each Somewhat, and 1 point for each False. Reverse score items 1–4 by giving 3 points for each False, 2 points for each Somewhat, and 1 point for each True, and add to the total.) Go to page 601 to interpret your score.

GO ONLINE to find additional questionnaires at www.cengagebrain.com, search for Daft/Marcic Building Management Skills 1e, click on Free Online Resources, click on Additional Self-Assessments.

- Personal Innovativeness
- Work Innovativeness

SHUTTERSTOCK #53973379

Chapter 16: Managing Personal and Organizational Change

DISCOVER KNOWLEDGE

Robert Viega knows that uncontrolled diabetes is a sure route to blindness, heart disease, circulation problems, kidney failure, and other devastating health problems. After all, he watched his mother die from complications of the disease. Yet the 32-year-old Viega maintains his own fight against Type II diabetes only sporadically: He checks his blood sugar only two or three times a week, has continued his diet of hot dogs, doughnuts, and beer, and stopped taking his diabetes pills because he doesn't like taking medicine. Viega says it's just so hard to adapt to new patterns of living—especially when the new ways seem so much less appealing than the old ones.[5]

Many people assume that knowing the cold, hard facts is enough to convince someone to change. But anyone who has ever tried to lose a significant amount of weight, kick the smoking habit, or break an addiction to computer games knows what Viega is talking about. You realize you'd feel much better, have more fun, and improve your health by losing weight, but you keep eating fried foods and drop out of your exercise program after a couple of weeks. You know smoking is going to kill you, but you think there's nothing better than a cigarette after a meal. You have been told over and over that your obsession with online gaming is destroying your family relationships, but you can't wait to get online after dinner every night. The brutal reality is that, for most people, change is remarkably difficult. Some health-care studies suggest that nine out of ten people can't change their habits even when their lives depend on it.[6]

FACE THE FACTS: PEOPLE HAVE A HARD TIME CHANGING

Most of us think if we were given a clear choice—change or die—we'd change in a hurry. But in fact, scientific studies demonstrate that most people, just like Robert Viega, have a hard time changing even when told that *not* changing will lead them to an early grave. People who have had coronary-artery bypass surgery, for example, know they can avoid the return of pain and arrest the course of heart disease before it kills them by making some simple lifestyle changes. Yet study after study shows that 90 percent of patients don't change their habits. Even seemingly simple changes can be hard to stick with. Two-thirds of patients prescribed anti-statin drugs for reducing cholesterol stop taking them within a year. A group of top executives looking at ways to solve the health-care crisis in America were stunned when experts said the root cause of the crisis is not lack of scientific knowledge or limited access to care, but rather the behavioral habits that people just can't seem to change.[7]

Although it usually isn't a matter of life and death, most managers and employees in organizations find change just as challenging. Manufacturing plants shut down because management and production workers can't forge trusting relationships or adapt to new ways of working that will keep the plant competitive. Service companies falter because people have a hard time shifting to a new approach to customer service. People lose their jobs because they refuse to learn new technologies or go along with new requirements. Most organizations have many people who simply seem unable or unwilling to change. Changing the behavior of people is just as big a challenge in businesses, nonprofit organizations, and government agencies as it is in the health-care system.

The big question is, why is changing our ways so difficult?[8]

Change Typically Involves a Personal Ending and Loss

For something new to begin, something old has to end. For example, an individual who commits to losing weight might have to give up a cherished ritual such as eating chocolate cake at midnight or having a large buttered popcorn and soda every Saturday at the cinema. To stop drinking and live an alcohol-free life means no more rowdy Friday nights bar-hopping with friends. For a couple to start a family means their carefree days of coming and going as they please are over.

You Can't Get to a New Beginning without Dealing with an Ending

Most of us have a hard time letting go of something we value, even if we want something new. We want to lose weight, but giving up the chocolate cake seems too much to ask. Rather than focusing on a new beginning and what we might gain from a change, our emotions are stuck on the ending of our current situation and what we might lose. Changing behavior always depends on changing people's emotions about the situation. People have to psychologically and emotionally let go of the old before they can embrace the new.[9] Exhibit 16.1 illustrates the transition individuals have to go through to make a successful change. To help someone change, or to change yourself, means first dealing with the emotions associated with endings and losses, rather than denying those emotions or trying to talk people out of feeling them. Then, people move into a neutral zone, where they've let go of the old but the new hasn't yet gelled into an accepted pattern. Finally, they transition into a new beginning. No one gets to a new beginning without first dealing with an ending.

Managers who want to implement change always have to ask "who's going to lose what?"[10] Many people view change as loss. In organizations, changes in job design, technology, or structure may mean that some people will no longer have the same type of power or prestige they once had, for example. At Best Buy, many managers resisted the shift to a "results-oriented work environment" (ROWE) that allows employees to work when and where they like as long as they get the job done. The ROWE system meant that managers would lose some of their control, which many perceived as also losing some of their power and prestige.[11] In addition, when changes are imposed from outside the individual, many people feel a loss of control over their own lives and circumstances, which provokes a strong emotional reaction. Sometimes a change conflicts with the goals of some individuals or departments. At pharmaceuticals company Pfizer, top managers wanted to implement a computerized system for collecting and processing trial data, which could cut 40 percent off the cost of new drug development. Research and development managers balked, citing their concern that the automation and standardization of case report forms would hamper their flexibility and creativity.[12]

Exhibit 16.1 Endings Precede Beginnings for Successful Change

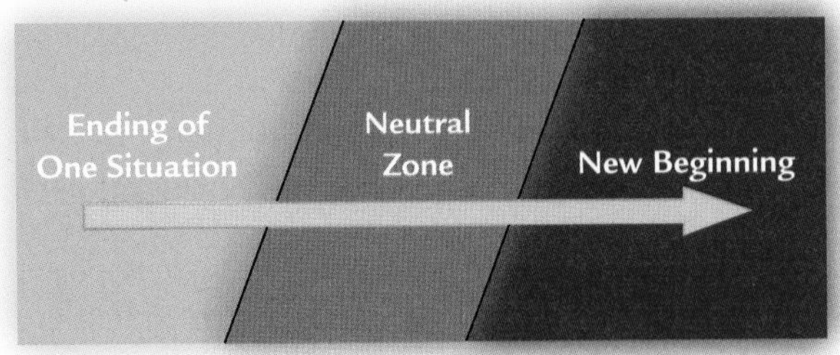

Source: Based on ideas in William Bridges, *Managing Transitions: Making the Most of Change* (Cambridge, MA: Da Capo Lifelong Books, 2009).

Change means giving up our stable routines. Hospitals that have spent millions of dollars adopting electronic medical records are having a hard time getting doctors and caregivers to use them. One reason is that electronic records require doctors to change how they go about their daily work, and many are having trouble giving up their standard routine.[13] Most people have at least some fear of the unknown and are more comfortable dealing with the tried-and-true. Particularly

DISCOVER KNOWLEDGE

LEADING WORDS

"All changes, even the most longed for, have their melancholy; for what we leave behind us is a part of ourselves; we must die to one life before we can enter another."
—**Anatole France**
French novelist

"A ship is safe in harbor, but that's not what ships are for."
—**William Shedd**
nineteenth-century theologian

"It is not the strongest of the species nor the most intelligent, but the most responsive to change that survives."
—**Charles Darwin**
naturalist, author of *On the Origin of Species*

"There is nothing more difficult to take in hand, or perilous to conduct, or more uncertain in its success than to take the lead in the introduction of a new order of things."
—**Niccolò Machiavelli**
fifteenth-century historian, philosopher, and politician

© CENGAGE LEARNING 2014

when people don't understand how a change will affect them, they find it more reassuring to stick with what they know, even if it is unpleasant, than to jump into the unknown. At work, for instance, employees might worry that a needed change in work procedures will mean an end to the camaraderie among their work group or fear that a new technology might cause them to lose autonomy or status. At SuperShuttle, a national transportation provider, drivers were opposed to using GPS-enabled phones. The drivers felt that the new technology meant an end to their freedom, since managers could track their movements. SuperShuttle learned that, "if you don't tell employees what to expect, they'll invent something, and inevitably, it will be bad."[14]

Even good changes begin with losses. Many times, people will resist a change or have a hard time making a change even when they deeply want the change and know it will benefit them in the long run. A middle-aged bachelor was thrilled to finally find someone to share his life with. He had been lonely for so long and genuinely wanted to be married. Yet, he found himself bemoaning the fact he could no longer stay after work for drinks without calling home, or go in after a long day and take a nap without someone being in the house. In a work situation, a promotion or a new job can bring an increase in pay, but it also brings greater stress, which means the individual loses the comfortable, easy job he or she was accustomed to.

You Have to Let People Grieve the Endings

Especially for major changes, people go through a process of grieving similar to Elisabeth Kübler-Ross's five stages of grief. Although the model was originally applied to the process of coming to terms with the death of a loved one, the five stages have often been applied in change management, specifically the emotions felt by those affected by change.[15] A person facing a change that requires giving up something of value might go through the stages as such: Denial (This isn't happening. I don't have to give this up.); Anger (Why is this happening to me? Why should I have to give this up?); Bargaining (I'll change if I don't have to give up *all* of this.); Depression and reflection (I'm sad over what I have to give up. How can I give this up?); and Acceptance (I'm ready to face the reality that I have to give this up and more forward.). Managers who try to bypass the first four stages and get people to accept changes without grieving the endings often fail in their change efforts.

DISCOVER YOURSELF

Interpret Your Score: Resistance to Change Scale (Questionnaire 1)

Everyone feels some resistance to change because of painful "endings," but people do differ in their tolerance for frequent change. Comparative data for **Resistance to Change:** Thirty person Mean score = 25.8; Top Quartile = 29–34; Bottom Quartile = 18–23. A higher score on this scale means you probably prefer a predictable and routine life. Frequent or dramatic changes at work may be difficult for you, probably creating feelings of stress and tension. If you received a lower score, your resistance to change may be low, so you probably find surprises and changes to be somewhat stimulating.

For additional insight, there are four subscales in the Resistance to Change scale. (Don't forget to reverse score items 4 and 5 in calculating these.) A high score for items 1, 5, and 9 reflects a preference for the routine over the non-routine in daily life. For items 2, 6, and 10, it shows a negative emotional reaction to unexpected changes. Scoring high on items 3, 7, and 11 suggests a preference for short-term consequences rather than long-term benefits of a change. A high score forz items 4, 8, and 12 indicates cognitive persistence, which means a reluctance to change your mind based on new information. How do your scores on these subscales differ from one another? Compare your scores to others in your class. What are your conclusions about your personal response to change? What could managers do to make change easier for people to accept? CNOW and CourseMate users can access dynamically updated comparative data through www.cengagebrain.com.

© CENGAGE LEARNING 2014

A New Beginning

At the Delancey Street Foundation in the heart of San Francisco, 500 ex-convicts, almost all of whom came to Delancey after committing serious crimes and having serious problems with alcohol or drug addiction, live and work peacefully together. They run the top-rated moving company in the San Francisco Bay area and manage a thriving upscale restaurant, a bookstore-café, and a print shop. And they run it all by themselves, without guards or supervisors except for one 63-year-old psychologist, Dr. Mimi Silbert, who stands 4 feet 11 inches and weighs 95 pounds. Nearly 60 percent of the residents who enter Delancey successfully complete the four-year program and sustain productive lives once they "graduate."[16]

Psychologists and criminologists alike typically agree that trying to rehabilitate criminal offenders is a losing battle. Most hard criminals, they say, aren't capable of significantly changing their lives and becoming productive members of society. More than six out of ten convicts eventually return to their old criminal ways.[17]

Yet, as the Delancey Street Foundation example shows, people *can* leave their old ways behind and move into a new beginning. A new beginning doesn't necessarily mean the change is accomplished and there won't be "backsliding," but it does mean people have dealt with the losses and endings of the old situation and are ready for something fresh, new, and hopeful.

LEARN THE KEYS TO HELPING INDIVIDUALS CHANGE

Dr. Dean Ornish, a professor of medicine at the University of California at San Francisco and founder of the Preventative Medicine Research Institute, has worked with plenty of critically ill patients who wouldn't change their bad habits even though it meant they would die. So, instead of motivating with the "fear of dying," Dr. Ornish began inspiring people with a clear vision of the "joy of living." His studies show that when people feel convinced that they can enjoy life more—such as taking long walks without pain, playing with their grandchildren, enjoying intimacy with their spouse again—they are much more likely to make significant changes in their lifestyle and stick with the changes over the long term. Dr. Ornish worked with 194 patients to help them quit smoking and follow an extreme vegetarian diet that derived fewer than 10 percent of its calories from fat. For a year, the patients participated in group conversations twice a week and took classes in relaxation, meditation, yoga, and aerobic exercise as part of their daily routine. Three years after the program ended, 77 percent had stuck with the lifestyle changes, halting—and in some cases reversing—the progress of their heart disease.[18]

Dr. Ornish gave these patients the keys to effective personal change. You might wonder how change ever happens, as many people seem to want so deeply *not* to change. Changing our thinking and behavior is possible, and the keys to doing so incorporate three elements: a positive emotional attractor, supportive relationships, and repetition of new behaviors.[19]

The first key to change is having a *positive emotional attractor (PEA)*, such as Dean Ornish provided for heart patients. A PEA awakens an individual's hopes and dreams about the future, about possibilities of what could be, rather than focusing on trying to "fix" weaknesses or shortcomings. People learn and change because they *want to*, not because they *ought to*, which means they need an inspiring picture of what the future can be.[20]

The second key, a *support system*, involves establishing new, emotional relationships with people who give you hope, make you believe that you can change, and inspire you with the expectation that change will happen. Effective leaders of social movements, for example, are highly skilled at giving people hope and faith that change is possible. This emotional relationship with a leader, a mentor, or a community helps people learn and practice the new skills and habits needed to change. This is what Alcoholics Anonymous or Weight Watchers meetings are all about, for example.

The third key, *repetition*, means people experiment and practice the new skills and habits until new patterns of behavior become automatic. If the change was to stop smoking, you eventually reach a point at which you never even think about the morning cigarette you wish you could have. A person shifting to a healthier diet eats healthy low-fat foods as a matter of routine rather than having to count calories.

RECOGNIZE THE STAGES OF PERSONAL CHANGE

When an individual is attempting significant behavioral change, it is helpful to understand that the mind and body go through stages. Change doesn't happen all in one big leap. Most people try to quit smoking numerous times before they finally quit for good, for example. James Prochaska and Carlo DiClemente at the University of Rhode Island studied how smokers successfully kicked the habit and came up with the Stages of Change model shown in Exhibit 16.2.[21] Since that time, the model has been used in efforts to

Exhibit 16.2 Typical Stages of Individual Change

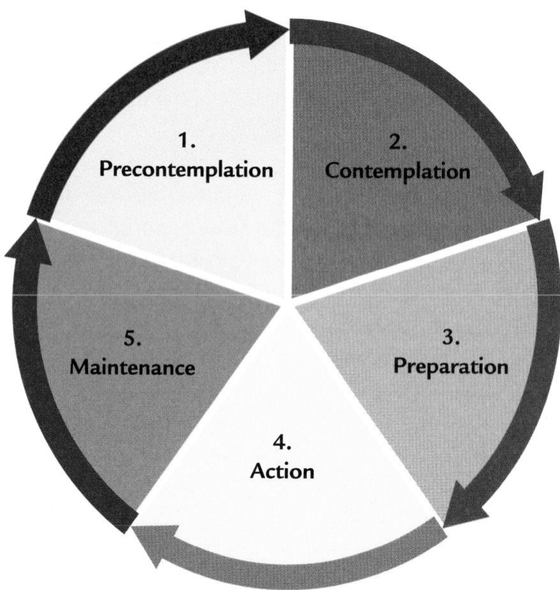

Sources: Based on James O. Prochaska, John Norcross, and Carlo DiClemente, *Changing for Good: The Revolutionary Program That Explains the Six Stages of Change and Teaches You How to Free Yourself from Bad Habits* (New York: William Morrow, 1994); Mark F. Kern, "Stages of Change Model," AddictionInfo.org, April 19, 2008, http://www.addictioninfo.org/articles/11/1/Stages-of-Change-Model/Page1.html (accessed May 20, 2011); and "Stages of Change Model," BupPractice.com, Clinical Tools, Inc., http://www.buppractice.com/node/1367 (accessed May 20, 2011).

change a broad range of behaviors, including overeating, alcohol addiction, and drug problems.

- *Precontemplation.* A person in the precontemplation stage isn't interested in changing and tends to defend his or her current behavior or habits. The person may be "in denial" or may just not yet believe there is problem with his or her behavior.
- *Contemplation.* In this stage, the individual admits there's a problem, but he or she isn't ready to do anything about it. A smoker might admit that she needs to quit for her health but is still weighing the pros and cons of giving up cigarettes. In this stage, people are more open to hearing information from others and might seek out information as they weigh their decision about changing. Many people wanting to change can spend a significant amount of time, even many years, in contemplation.
- *Preparation.* This is the stage at which a person makes a commitment to change. A smoker might set a quit date, stock up on nicotine replacement products, or see a doctor for stop-smoking aids. An overweight individual might plan to join a health club or set a date for going on a diet. Some people can get stuck at this stage, continually planning for change but never taking the next step to action.
- *Action.* This is when people actively try to change and believe they have the ability to change. This is typically the shortest of the change stages, during which people consciously attempt to change their habits. This stage can be a real emotional rollercoaster, as people try to keep up their motivation and sustain their willpower. At this stage, many people wanting to change actively seek the help of others.
- *Maintenance.* Maintenance means avoiding the temptations to return to old habits. At this stage, people tend to remind themselves of how far they've come and consciously strive to avoid situations that could cause a relapse. They feel that the change is beneficial and meaningful, but they recognize that letting go of old habits is a long process. They continually practice new behavior

DISCOVER YOURSELF

Interpret Your Score: Readiness for Personal Change (Questionnaire 2)

Comparative data for Readiness for Change: **Pre-contemplation Stage** (Part A): Thirty person Mean score = 4.5; Top Quartile = 5–7; Bottom Quartile = 3–3. **Contemplation Stage** (Part B): Thirty person Mean score = 7.4; Top Quartile = 9–9; Bottom Quartile = 3–6.5. **Action Stage** (Part C): Thirty person Mean score = 6.9; Top Quartile = 9–9; Bottom Quartile = 3–6. **Maintenance Stage** (Part D): Thirty person Mean score = 4.8; Top Quartile = 6–9; Bottom Quartile = 3–3. Which of your four scores is highest? The highest score indicates the stage you are in for that specific change. If you are in the contemplation or action stages, you have a good chance of making the change. If you are in the maintenance stage, congratulations for already making the personal change. Answer the questions again for any other specific behavior you would like to change. How difficult do you find it to make personal changes? Do you think making personal changes is easier or harder than making an organizational change? Discuss your results with others in the class. CNOW and CourseMate users can access dynamically updated comparative data through www.cengagebrain.com.

© CENGAGE LEARNING 2014

patterns so that they become second nature. The danger of relapsing to old ways of behavior is still present, and people will often go back to a previous stage and try again.

It is important to remember that individuals progress through these stages at their own rate. Trying to convince an alcoholic who isn't willing to admit he has a drinking problem (in the precontemplation stage) is like trying to stop the tide. In addition, the impetus for change and for moving from one stage to the next has to come from within the individual rather than being imposed from outside. However, inspirational leaders or mentors can help people move through the stages more quickly by remembering the keys to personal change and the reasons people typically have a hard time changing, which were discussed previously in this chapter.

CHANGING THE TEAM OR ORGANIZATION

Now that we understand a little about how individuals change, let's discuss how managers can apply this understanding as they attempt to implement the many changes organizations need to remain vital and successful. Two effective approaches that incorporate these ideas for making organizational changes are appreciative inquiry and Kotter's eight-stage model of change.

Appreciative Inquiry

When Jerry Sternin arrived in Vietnam with the Save the Children organization to fight malnutrition, the foreign minister told him bluntly that he had six months to make a difference. Rather than looking at the problems and how to fix them, Sternin decided to look at what was going *right*. Rather than looking at what caused malnourished babies, he looked for healthy babies and found out what their mothers were doing that made them healthy. He went to a local village and enlisted mothers to weigh and measure every child in the village. "Did you find any very, very poor kids who are bigger and healthier than the average child?" he asked. When the answer was *yes*, Sternin said, "Then let's go see what they're doing." Based on this understanding, Sternin's team implemented a program to get other families to provide better nutrition. Rather than telling mothers about nutrition, the program focused on changing behavior. Malnourished families, in groups of ten, would meet each day and prepare food together. They were required to bring shrimp, crabs, and sweet potato greens (foods the healthy children were normally fed but the malnourished ones were not). The mothers had to first wash their hands with soap and they cooked the meal together. Six months after Sternin's visit to the village, 65 percent of the kids were better nourished—and they stayed that way.[22]

Numerous experts had previously analyzed the problem of poor nutrition among children in Vietnam but had failed to make any significant changes. The problems—for example, widespread poverty, poor sanitation, lack of clean drinking water—just seemed too big. Sternin's Save the Children team effected change by looking at the positive—what mothers were doing that made some kids healthy—rather than focusing on the negative.

Sternin adopted a line of attack known as appreciative inquiry, one of the most exciting approaches to leading change in groups and organizations. **Appreciative inquiry** (AI) engages individuals, teams, or the entire organization in creating change by reinforcing positive messages and focusing on learning from success.[23] Rather than looking at a situation from the viewpoint of what is wrong and who is to blame for it, AI takes a positive, affirming approach by asking, "What is possible? What do we want to achieve?" For example, rather than looking at a problem such as decreasing sales, AI would investigate what makes sales increase. Appropriately framing a topic—to investigate what is right rather than what is wrong—is critical to the success of appreciative inquiry because it gets people away from blame, defensiveness, and denial and sets a positive framework for change.

Appreciative inquiry can accelerate large-scale organizational change by positively engaging a large group of people in the change process, including managers and employees, as well as people from outside the organization, such as customers or clients, partners, and other stakeholders. Once a topic has been identified for exploration, the group follows a four-stage appreciative inquiry process, as illustrated in Exhibit 16.3.[24]

1. Discovery. In the discovery stage, people identify "the best of what exists"—the team's or organization's key strengths and best practices. This stage is about discovering the unique qualities of the group

Exhibit 16.3 The Appreciative Inquiry Process

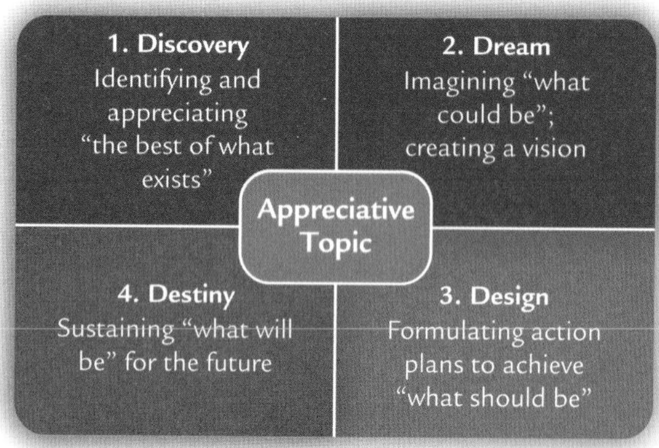

Source: Based on Gabriella Giglio, Silvia Michalcova, and Chris Yates, "Instilling a Culture of Winning at American Express," *Organization Development Journal* 25, no. 4 (Winter 2007): 33–37.

DISCOVER KNOWLEDGE

that have contributed to success. Managers interview people, asking them to tell stories that identify the best of their experiences with the organization. During an AI session focused on building a winning culture at American Express, for example, managers asked people to describe a situation in which they felt the most proud working for the company. Based on these stories, people together identify common themes.

2. **Dream.** Next, people reflect on what they learned during the discovery stage and imagine what it would be like if these extraordinary experiences were the norm. What if people at American Express, for instance, experienced the kind of environment every day that made them feel proud of working for American Express? The dream stage is about imagining "what could be" and creating a shared vision of the best possible future, grounded in the reality of what already exists. By allowing people to express their dreams for the future, AI inspires hope and energy for change.

3. **Design.** The design stage formulates action plans for transforming dreams into reality. This involves people making decisions about what the team or organization needs to do in order to be what it wants to be. At American Express, people identified the values that would support the kind of culture they wanted, the leadership behaviors that would instill and support the values, and the structures, systems, and processes that would keep the new cultural values alive.

4. **Destiny.** The final stage of AI is creating a destiny by translating the ideas identified in the previous stages into concrete action steps. This involves both celebrating the best of what exists and pushing forward to realize the dream by creating specific programs, activities, and other tangible forces that will implement the design and ensure the continuation of change begun during the AI process. For example, specific changes in training programs, performance evaluation, and reward systems were part of the destiny stage at American Express.

A wide variety of organizations, including businesses, school systems, churches and religious organizations, communities, government agencies, and social service organizations, have used AI for large-scale change.[25]

Leading Everyday Change with Appreciative Inquiry

As a manager, you can also apply appreciative inquiry every day on a smaller scale. To be a good manager means influencing people in many small ways on an ongoing basis—working daily to gradually shift attitudes, assumptions, and behavior toward a desired future.[26]

You can use the tools of appreciative inquiry for a variety of everyday change initiatives, such as developing followers, strengthening teamwork, solving a particular work issue, or resolving conflicts.[27] Again, the key is to frame the issue in a positive way and keep people focused on improvement rather than looking at what went wrong. For example, Jim (Gus) Gustafson, currently Leadership Scholar-in-Residence and Director of Executive Education in the Center for Values-Driven Leadership at Benedictine University, uses appreciative inquiry to develop followers. One example comes from the time Gustafson took over as director of sales and marketing for a major electrical manufacturer. While sitting in on several employees' performance reviews with the outgoing executive, Gustafson noticed that two employees in particular were treated by the outgoing manager with disrespect and disinterest as they were given poor evaluations of their performance. Gustafson used appreciative inquiry by asking the two employees questions such as, "What have you done in the last six months that you are most proud of?" "What is your greatest source of job satisfaction?" and "What motivates you to excel?" He worked with the two to identify how they could

be satisfied and productive, carrying forward the best from their past but moving toward a better future. Thanks to Gustafson's coaching and the use of AI, both employees were eventually promoted to management positions in the organization.[28]

A Checklist for Planned Organizational Change

Dealing with the complexities of change can feel like being lost in a dense fog. Managers need a systematic checklist to follow that keeps team and organizational efforts moving in the right direction. One model that keeps the focus on change so that people are less likely to get "lost in the fog" is an eight-stage model developed by John Kotter, illustrated in Exhibit 16.4.[29]

Exhibit 16.4 The Eight Stages of Planned Organizational Change

Source: Based on John P. Kotter, *Leading Change* (Boston: Harvard Business School Press, 1996), p. 21.

1. Light a fire for change. People have to believe that change is really needed. To be effective managing change, communicate the urgency for change in a way that touches people's emotions—in other words, help them *feel* the need for change rather than just giving them facts and figures. To get people to see the need for radical change at Nokia, new CEO Stephen Elop compared the company's plight to a man standing on a burning platform. Nokia has fallen way behind Apple and Google's Android in the market for sophisticated mobile phones, and even its share of the lower-end phone market is declining. The company's future rests on the ability of managers to lead successful change.[30]

2. Get the right people on board. Considering the complexities of change, no single person can implement a change, especially a major one, alone. For successful change, reach out to others in the organization and build a strong coalition with a shared commitment to the need for and possibility of change. Include people with enough power to make sure the change happens, as well as people who can make the change more acceptable to end users.

3. Paint a compelling picture. Develop a clear picture and strategy to inspire people that a better future is possible and they can achieve it through their actions. The energy for true change comes from seeing how the change can be positive for individuals and the organization. Create a vision that helps people understand why the organization is undertaking the effort and how the change will help achieve long-term goals. It's also important to develop a strategy for achieving the vision and let people know how they fit into the big picture.

4. Communicate, communicate, communicate. Tell the message not just once, but over and over again. You need to communicate about the change at least ten more times than you think necessary. Change throws everyone into doubt and uncertainty, and people don't listen well when they feel anxious. Another point to remember is that actions speak louder than words. Model the new behaviors needed from employees.

5. Get rid of obstacles and empower people to act. Give people the time, knowledge, resources, and discretion to take steps and make the change happen.

This might mean revising structures, systems, or procedures that hinder or undermine the change effort.

6. **Achieve and celebrate quick wins.** Unless people see positive results of their efforts, energy and motivation can wane during a major change project. To keep the momentum going, identify some short-term accomplishments that people can recognize and celebrate. A highly visible and successful short-term accomplishment boosts the credibility of the change process and renews everyone's enthusiasm and commitment.

7. **Keep it moving.** Don't get stuck on short-term wins. One study suggests that nearly 50 percent of all change initiatives crumble simply from lack of attention.[31] It's important to build on the credibility of early accomplishments and keep the change process moving forward. At this stage, confront and change any remaining issues, structures, or systems that are getting in the way of achieving the vision. Look for and deploy the people who can implement the vision for change.

8. **Find ways to make the changes stick.** At this stage, look for ways to institutionalize the new approach. Strive to integrate the new values and patterns into everyone's work habits. At Del-Air, a Florida heating, ventilation, and air conditioning contractor, managers linked a new GPS-enabled time-tracking system with the company's bonus system. Employees who are more efficient with their time get rewarded for it. Managers hit on the idea of an incentive after a previous tracking system had failed. After a short period, managers had stopped promoting the benefits of that system, leading to a rapid decline in employee use. By integrating the change with the incentive system, managers made the new time-tracking system an accepted, integral part of everyone's daily work.[32]

EFFECTIVE TECHNIQUES USED BY CHANGE MANAGERS

By now, you should have an understanding of why people find it so hard to change, some basic knowledge of how individuals can change, and insight into applying appreciative inquiry and an eight-stage model to guide major team and organizational change. What could be simpler, right? Okay, it's admittedly not an easy job. Change isn't easy for many experienced managers either, but there are some tips and techniques that can make managing change in organizations easier.

Always Have a Sponsor

Exhibit 16.5 illustrates three key roles involved in organizational change: the target of change, the change agent, and the sponsor.[33] The target of change is the individual or group who must actually make the behavioral change. When you need to implement a

What's Your Problem?

Q: I have this great idea for my department, which involves how we divide the work among ourselves. Because I took several courses in college in industrial engineering, I have a good background to make these kinds of assessments. Although I am the manager in the department, I need to get the managers in other departments we work with to sign off on this type of change. But none of my co-managers seems interested in making things better. They just tell me they are too busy to waste their time. The thing is: I know this would lead to higher productivity. What should I do?

A: Your attempt to build a coalition to support your change is moving slowly, so the next thing to do is find a senior-level sponsor for your change project. Talk to your immediate supervisor or someone else you know in the company who has the clout to provide resources and voice support for your ideas. Try to figure out who the change will help most and find a sponsor there. After you round up a high-level sponsor who can help you sell others on the benefits of your ideas, you will find your peer managers more agreeable, giving you a much better chance of being successful.

© CENGAGE LEARNING 2014

Exhibit 16.5 Key Change Roles

Source: Based on Daryl R. Conner, *Managing at the Speed of Change* (New York: Villard Books, 1992), pp. 108–109.

change in your team, you are the change agent. But you usually can't implement change alone. It's important that you have a sponsor. A **sponsor** is a person or group with the power to authorize, provide resources, and legitimize the change. This might be the department head, the division vice president, the CEO, or the board of directors, depending on the nature of the change. This is the person or group who has the authority to decide which changes will happen in the organization, can communicate the change to employees as a priority, and has the ability to provide resources and reinforcement to make sure the change is successful.

Leverage Both the Hard and Soft Sides of Change

When Sam Palmisano took over as CEO of IBM, the computer industry was shifting dramatically and IBM faced a tremendous challenge to remain relevant and thriving. Palmisano wanted to implement a new "e-business on demand" strategy, which required developing deep relationships with large corporate clients and helping them improve their planning, operations, marketing, and customer service. To support this massive shift from a supermarket of technology to a provider of on-demand services, Palmisano addressed both "hard" issues such as the structure and systems and "soft" issues such as culture and manager attitudes. He asked all IBM employees to get involved in determining and shaping new cultural values, thereby enabling them to be owners of the new culture. He dismantled the executive committee and set up three cross-functional, cross-hierarchical teams for strategy, operations, and technology. The structure was shifted so that teams of employees work across functional boundaries and directly with customers. Palmisano set aside $800 million for employee training programs and professional growth and development. Part of that amount went toward helping managers learn how to inspire and lead people rather than manage and control them. Teams also revised performance evaluation systems, career paths, training programs, and reward systems to be in line with the new strategy, structure, and culture.[34]

Effective change managers like Sam Palmisano leverage two parts of any change issue: the hard side and the soft side, as illustrated in Exhibit 16.6.[35] Most managers feel comfortable dealing with the hard side, including changes in formal structures and systems, policies and procedures, measurements, and the basic tools, processes, and resources that the organization uses to accomplish goals. Yet, as anyone who has tried to implement a major change knows, until employee

Exhibit 16.6 Address the Hard and Soft Sides of Change

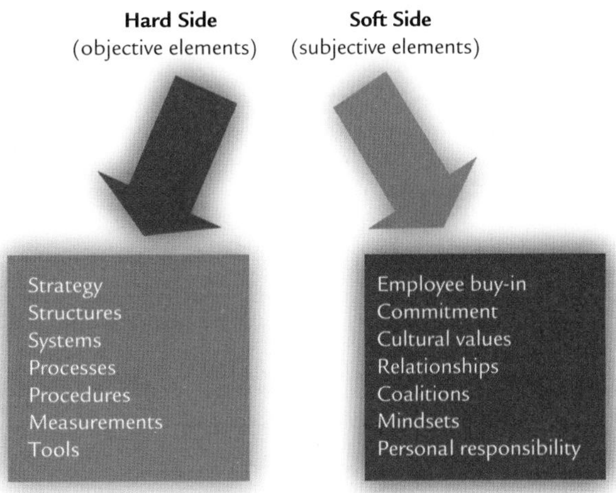

Source: Based on Ed Oakley and Doug Krug, *Enlightened Leadership: Getting to the Heart of Change* (New York: Simon & Schuster, 1993), pp. 44–48.

attitudes, values, and beliefs are shifted, the changes won't stick.

As shown in Exhibit 16.6, major change requires addressing both hard and soft, objective and subjective, issues. Hard issues focus on the exterior, objective world. Managers analyze the organization and the environment to determine what strategy or course of action can help reach desired goals. They consider questions such as: Is the structure appropriate for the desired change? Do planning, budgeting, and control systems support or undermine the desired change? How can performance and reward systems support the new direction?

The soft side of change focuses on interior, subjective issues, including employee commitment and buy-in, cultural values, manager attitudes and leadership abilities, and the nature of organizational relationships. Managers consider what personal development training is needed to shape employee attitudes and values toward those needed for the change. How can people expand their mindsets and grow into acceptance of new roles and responsibilities? Are the values that bind people together adaptive or unadaptive? Does the culture embrace or resist change? What shared values are needed?

Changes in the objective, exterior elements often fail because managers fail to address these deeper, subtle issues. For example, a shift to a team-based structure will be unsuccessful if the organization's cultural values encourage individual accomplishment, internal competition, and hoarding of knowledge. On the other hand, changing only the soft aspects doesn't work, either. Attempts to build a corporate culture that values teamwork, knowledge-sharing, and collaboration will fail if structures and systems still support and reward individual accomplishment. For successful change, managers expand their focus to address both exterior, objective issues *and* interior, subjective forces at the same time.

DISCOVER KNOWLEDGE

DISCOVER YOURSELF

Interpret Your Score: Taking Charge of Change (Questionnaire 3)

Comparative data for **Willingness to Initiate and Take Charge of Change:** Thirty person Mean score = 22.3; Top Quartile = 25–30; Bottom Quartile = 12–19.5. A higher score probably means that you have a natural ability to see the need for changes and to take charge of making improvements. A low score probably means you are willing to let other people worry about change. Note that items 2, 6, and 9 pertain to a felt responsibility to initiate changes, and the other items pertain to change actions. A felt responsibility may be the trigger to take charge of making changes. Compare your score for items 2, 6, and 9 to your score for the other items. Do you consider yourself a change leader? You may want to become more active or aggressive at taking charge of change. In what kind of situations would you be more likely to initiate changes? CNOW and CourseMate users can access dynamically updated comparative data through www.cengagebrain.com.

© CENGAGE LEARNING 2014

Don't Be Deceived by Despair

Many front-line supervisors, mid-level managers, and top executives find the process of change as frightening, confusing, and overwhelming as do the people they're trying to guide through the process. To be an effective change agent, you can understand and appreciate the *curve of change*. The change curve, illustrated in Exhibit 16.7, is the psychological process people go through during a significant change.[36] Remember, every change looks dark in the middle.

For example, a supervisor sees a need for a change in work procedures in her department and initiates the change with high expectations for a smooth implementation and a positive outcome. As time progresses, the complexities of altering people's attitudes and behaviors begin to overwhelm the supervisor, who may even reach a point of despair that change is really possible. Performance may decline dramatically as people wrestle with the new procedures and resist the shift to a new way of working. Effective managers don't allow this period of despair to overwhelm them and sabotage the change effort. With effective change management, the changes can take hold and lead toward better performance. For example, managers at Procter & Gamble prepare themselves for a "60-day immune response" from users of a new technology. They expect that it takes 60 days to overcome resistance, work out the bugs in the new work process, and reach the light at the end of the tunnel, when everyone begins to see positive results of the change.[37]

One quality that enables managers to persist through the dark days of a change project is called grit. **Grit** is an individual's passion and persistence

Exhibit 16.7 The Change Curve: Watch Out for Despair

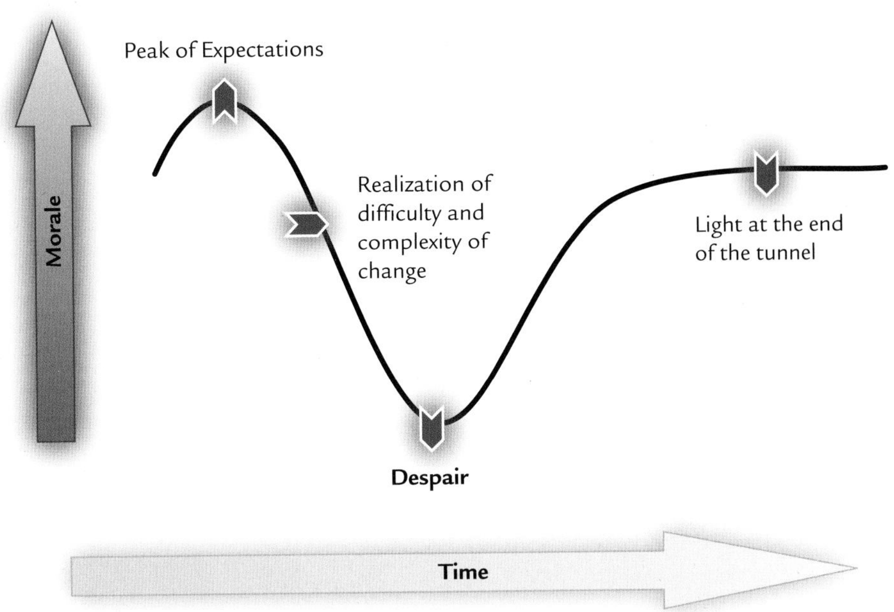

Sources: Based on "Gartner Hype Cycle: Interpreting Technology Hype," Gartner Research, http://www.gartner.com/technology/research/methodologies/hype-cycle.jsp (accessed May 20, 2011); "The Change Equation and Curve," 21st Century Leader Website, http://www.21stcenturyleader.co.uk/resources/turbulent-times/the-change-equation-and-curve/ (accessed May 22, 2012); and David M. Schneider and Charles Goldwasser, "Be a Model Leader of Change," *Management Review* (March 1998): 41–45.

DISCOVER KNOWLEDGE

DISCOVER YOURSELF

Interpret Your Score: Grit
(Questionnaire 4)

The score on this questionnaire measures your grit, which is defined as your perseverance and passion for long-term goals. The grit score predicted achievement in challenging situations among cadets at West Point and among final round contestants of a national spelling bee. Comparative data for **Grit:** Thirty person Mean score = 19.6; Top Quartile = 20–24; Bottom Quartile = 12–17. Individuals high in grit do not swerve from their change-implementation goals. The grit scale is composed of two parts. Questions 1–4 measure "consistency of interest" and questions 5–8 measure "perseverance of effort," so you can compare your scores on those two subscales. The average score for a group of students 25–34 was approximately 15.2 for grit, 6.9 for consistency of interest, and 8.4 for perseverance of effort. CNOW and CourseMate users can access dynamically updated comparative data through www.cengagebrain.com.

© CENGAGE LEARNING 2014

for achieving a long-term goal.[38] Grit is a key trait for change agents who must persevere through resistance and setbacks to succeed with implementing a significant change in an organization. The ability to stick with and pursue a goal over a long period is also associated with career success.[39]

STRIVE TO CREATE A LEARNING ORGANIZATION

Medtronic is the world's largest medical technology company, with $15.9 billion in revenues for the year ended April 30, 2011. But managers don't focus employees' attention and actions on increasing sales or shareholder value. Instead, they align everyone's behaviors toward "alleviating pain, restoring health, and extending life" for people with serious medical problems. The structure at Medtronic is based on teamwork rather than a rigid hierarchy, and teams work directly with customers and are empowered to come

7 STEPS TO...
Stacking the Odds against Change

1. **Pick the wrong thing to change.** You should decide and define with care what, specifically, needs to change. Change is tough, so putting people through the trauma associated with major change needs to be worth it.
2. **Focus on immediate circumstances rather than purpose and meaning.** Effective change agents focus people on a clear sense of purpose, value, and meaning to rise above immediate challenging circumstances.
3. **Doubt your people.** People *can* change, and good managers trust that most employees genuinely want to do what is best for the organization. To be effective, inspire people with what they can do rather than doubting their abilities and commitment.
4. **Crush resistance.** Effective change agents relish resistance because it gives them a chance to understand opponents, address their concerns, and bring them on board—or sometimes shift the change for the better based on their input.
5. **Try to hide your true motives.** In times of change, people need to trust in the integrity and authenticity of their leaders, not be trying to guess what they're thinking or questioning what the proposed change is all about.
6. **Skip the rewards.** Rewards answer everyone's big question about a change, "What's in it for me?" People need to see some results from their efforts. It is surprising how often managers forget to reward people for changing their behavior.
7. **Delude yourself about what it will take.** Change often fails because change agents underestimate the time and effort it requires and fall prey to frustration and despair.

Sources: Based on Kevin Cashman, "Change Smart," *Leadership Excellence* (July 2009): 14; Marshall Goldsmith, "Rules of Change," *Leadership Excellence* (July 2009): 10–11; and "Your Route to the Top: Managing Change," *Management Today* (March 3, 2009): 19.

up with new ideas and bring them to fruition. The culture treats every idea—no matter where it comes from—as equally worthy. Experimentation is encouraged, and failure is seen as a route to learning and adaptability. Physicians, health-care providers, organizational partners, and others are an important part of Medtronic's communication networks. Managers and employees are urged to network across boundaries and communicate with anyone inside or outside the organization who can help the company meet goals and fulfill its mission. Rather than being fearful of change, Medtronic employees have learned to thrive on it because continual change is the best way to serve critically ill people with a broad range of health-care needs.[40]

One of your most important challenges as a manager will be to keep people focused on adaptive change to meet the demands of a turbulent and rapidly changing world. Few problems come with ready-made solutions, and people throughout the organization need to be able to think in new ways and learn new values and attitudes.[41] To keep people poised for change and adaptation, as they are at Medtronic, managers strive to create the conditions of a learning organization.

Managers began thinking about the concept of the learning organization after the publication of Peter Senge's book, *The Fifth Discipline: The Art and Practice of Learning Organizations*.[42] Senge described the kind of changes managers needed to undergo to help their organizations adapt to an increasingly chaotic world. These ideas gradually evolved to describe characteristics of the organization itself.

The **learning organization** can be defined as one in which everyone is engaged in identifying and solving problems, enabling the organization to continuously experiment, change, and transform itself. To develop a learning organization, managers make changes in all the subsystems of the organization. Four important elements to promote continuous learning and change are a team-based structure, empowered employees, personal networks, and an adaptive culture, as illustrated in Exhibit 16.8.

Exhibit 16.8 Four Elements of a Learning Organization

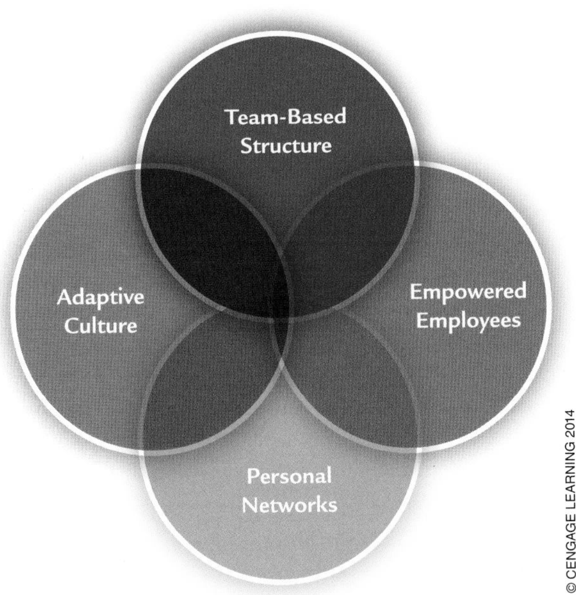

© CENGAGE LEARNING 2014

Team-Based Structure

An important value in a learning organization is collaboration and communication across departmental and hierarchical boundaries. As we discussed in Chapter 12, managers use teams to enhance coordination, to connect the best people for a project, and to give employees greater autonomy and decision-making authority. Self-directed teams are the basic building blocks of a learning organization structure. Traditional management tasks are pushed down to lower levels of the organization, with teams often taking responsibility for training, safety, scheduling, and decisions about work methods, pay and reward systems, and coordination with other teams. People on the team are given the skills, information, tools, motivation, and authority to make decisions central to the team's performance and to respond creatively and flexibly to new challenges or opportunities that arise.

Empowered Employees

As defined in Chapter 7, empowerment means unleashing the power and creativity of employees by giving them the freedom, resources, information, and skills to make decisions and perform effectively. In a learning organization, empowerment may be reflected in self-directed work teams, quality circles, job enrichment, and employee participation groups as well as through decision-making authority, training, and information so that people can perform jobs without close supervision. People are valued as a manager's primary source of strength, and not a cost to be minimized. Companies that adopt this perspective believe in treating employees well by providing competitive wages and good working conditions, as well as by investing time and money in training programs and opportunities for personal and professional development. In addition, they often provide a sense of employee ownership by sharing gains in productivity and profits.[43]

Personal Networks

In a learning organization, informal personal networks, as described in Chapter 8, are the basis for information sharing and getting things done. Rather than having most information controlled by managers, information is dispersed throughout the organization. Everyone is responsible for networking, sharing information across boundaries, and reaching out to those who can further the goals of the team and organization. Managers not only spend time networking with people inside and outside the organization, but they also invest significant energy in nourishing the personal networks of others. They know networks are essential to keep information flowing freely across departmental and hierarchical boundaries. People are valued and rewarded not just for what they know, but for how much knowledge they share with others.

Adaptive Culture

In Chapter 15, we talked about how managers build a positive organizational culture that encourages high performance and adaptation to the external environment. A strong, adaptive culture is one of the most important qualities for a learning organization because it builds learning and change into the fabric of the organization. People value risk-taking, experimentation, questioning, and changing rather than maintaining the status quo. Many organizations have become "stuck" in outmoded cultures that no longer work for a shifting environment. Changing cultural values to support adaptation and change is one of the most important "soft" elements managers pay attention to as they strive to create a learning organization in which people are perpetually poised for change.

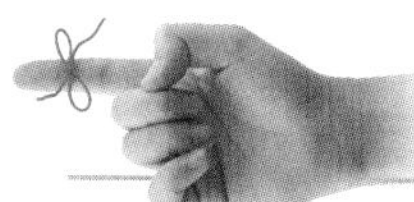

NEED TO KNOW

- Most people have a really tough time changing. The primary reason is that change requires that something come to an end and people experience an emotional loss. To successfully change, people have to grieve the ending of one thing and be ready to move to a new beginning. When managers want to make changes in the organization, they have to ask "who's going to lose what?"
- Three keys to helping individuals change successfully are a positive emotional attractor, supportive relationships, and repetition of new behaviors. Change doesn't happen all in one big leap. People go through the stages of precontemplation, contemplation, preparation, action, and maintenance.
- Two organizational approaches that incorporate the ideas about how people change are appreciative inquiry and Kotter's eight-stage model of change. Appreciative inquiry engages people in creating change by reinforcing positive messages and focusing on learning from success. It looks at what is right rather than looking at a situation from the viewpoint of what is wrong and who is to blame for it. Managers can use appreciative inquiry for both large-scale change and everyday change. Kotter's model for leading change gives managers a systematic way to make sure change efforts keep moving in the right direction.
- Effective change managers always have a sponsor, a person or group with the ability to authorize and legitimize the change. Successful organizational change requires addressing both hard aspects, such as structures and systems, and soft aspects, such as values and attitudes. To be successful, managers understand the change curve and don't allow themselves to be overwhelmed by frustration and despair.
- One of your most important jobs as a manager will be to keep people focused on adaptive change. Managers want to create the conditions of a learning organization, in which everyone is engaged in solving problems and is poised for change. Four elements critical to a learning organization are a team-based structure, empowered employees, personal networks, and an adaptive culture.

ACTION LEARNING

DELIBERATE PRACTICE EXERCISES

Do What You Love[44]

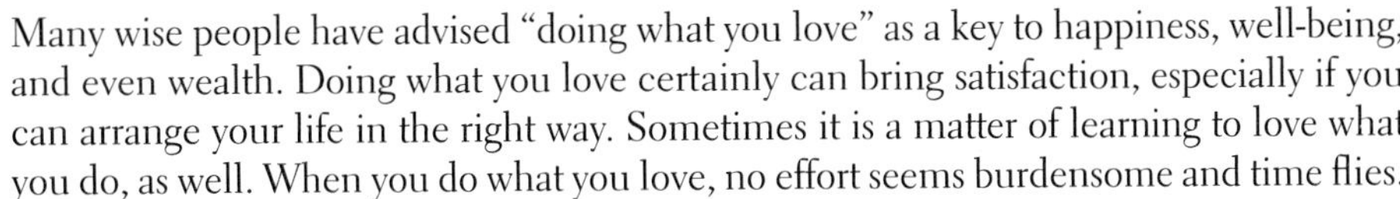

Many wise people have advised "doing what you love" as a key to happiness, well-being, and even wealth. Doing what you love certainly can bring satisfaction, especially if you can arrange your life in the right way. Sometimes it is a matter of learning to love what you do, as well. When you do what you love, no effort seems burdensome and time flies.

Step 1: For this exercise, imagine having a life that is filled with a sense of purpose, where you are contributing to the betterment of the world and doing what you love. Think of some small changes you could make in your life that move you toward doing what you love.

Step 2: During the next week, spend some time EACH DAY on one activity that gets you close to doing what you love. You may choose a different activity each day or the same thing over and over. It is up to you, as long as each day you perform an activity that fulfills at least one of the eight criteria listed below:

1. It is intensely meaningful to you.
2. It is easy, effortless, and enjoyable.
3. It makes time go by quickly.
4. It feels natural to do.
5. It makes you feel good about yourself.
6. It is what you would rather be doing over anything else.
7. It is enjoyed for itself, rather than as a means to an end.
8. It helps you feel a sense of contributing to something greater than yourself.

Step 3: Complete the table below. It will be easiest if you complete this each day.

Day	What was the activity?	Which criterion did it fulfill? (There can be more than one.)	Describe the experience and how you felt during and after.
Day 1			
Day 2			
Day 3			
Day 4			
Day 5			
Day 6			
Day 7			

Step 4: What did you learn about doing what you love from this exercise?

Step 5 (Optional): Share your insights with a partner, and ask your partner what insights he or she gained.

You Can Change!

Personal change is often difficult. This is an exercise to help you go through a process that research has shown increases the chances of actually changing. Refer to the chapter discussion of the keys to personal change and the stages of personal change, including Exhibit 16.2.

Step 1: Identify one thing about yourself you want to change. Write that here:

Step 2: Identify what you have or what you need for each of the three "keys to personal change," and fill in the table:

ACTION LEARNING

Key to Change	What do you have for this key?	How can you do better with this key?
Positive Emotional Attractor: Awaken your hopes and dreams		
Support System: Who provides the loving, supportive relationships you need to make this change?		
Repetition: How can you practice and experiment with new skills, perhaps in tiny steps?		

Step 3: Identify the forces for and against your change. In a change process, an effective tool for analysis is called *force-field analysis*. For the personal change you listed in Step 1, think about the forces that are working in your favor (driving forces) and those that are working against the change (barriers or restraining forces). For example, if your change is to lose weight, a factor helping you (driving force) might be that you get motivated by enjoying how you look in smaller clothes as you gradually lose weight, whereas a factor against the change (restraining force) might be that people are always bringing cookies, muffins, and brownies to work. Complete the following table by listing your driving and restraining forces and what you can do to increase the driving forces and decrease restraining forces.

What are the driving forces for your desired change?	How can you enhance driving forces?	What are the restraining forces?	How can you minimize restraining forces?

Step 4: What will you do to ensure success in your change endeavor?

Step 5 (Optional): Share your insights with a partner, and ask your partner what insights he or she gained.

IN-CLASS TEAM EXERCISE

An Ancient Tale[45]

To be more effective in bringing change in organizations, it is a good idea to understand the dynamics of what is currently happening. This can also have the effect of helping to "light a fire for change" (see Exhibit 16.4). In this exercise, you'll also be examining whether you have the right people on board.

Step 1: Form into groups of four to six members. Each person reads the "Situation" below.

Situation

Long ago in an ancient kingdom, there lived a princess who was very young and very beautiful. The princess, recently married, lived in a large and luxurious castle with her husband, a powerful and wealthy lord. The young princess was not content, however, to sit and eat strawberries by herself while her husband took frequent and long journeys to neighboring kingdoms. She felt neglected and soon became quite unhappy. One day, while she was alone in the castle gardens, a handsome vagabond rode out of the forest bordering the castle. He spied the beautiful princess, quickly won her heart, and carried her away with him.

Following a day of dalliance, the young princess found herself ruthlessly abandoned by the vagabond. She then discovered that the only way back to the castle led through the bewitched forest of the wicked sorcerer. Fearing to venture into the forest alone, she sought out her kind and wise godfather. She explained her plight, begged forgiveness of

the godfather, and asked his assistance in returning home before her husband returned. The godfather, however, surprised and shocked at her behavior, refused forgiveness and denied her any assistance. Discouraged but still determined, the princess disguised her identity and sought the help of the most noble of all the kingdom's knights. After hearing the sad story, the knight pledged his unfailing aid—for a modest fee. But alas, the princess had no money and the knight rode away to save other damsels.

The beautiful princess had no one else from whom she might seek help, and decided to brave the great peril alone. She followed the safest path she knew, but when she was almost through the forest, the wicked sorcerer spied her and caused her to be devoured by the fire-breathing dragon.

Step 2: In the following table, please make a check mark in each column to show which person you think is most responsible, which is second most responsible, and which is least responsible for the death of the princess.

Character	Most responsible	Next most responsible	Least responsible
Princess			
Husband			
Vagabond			
Godfather			
Knight			
Sorcerer			

Step 3: Answer the following questions in your group.

1. Was there a "lit fire" for change, considering the betrayals and loss?
2. What were your criteria for the above decisions about who was most and least responsible for the princess's demise?
3. What interventions would you suggest to prevent a recurrence of this kind of tragedy?
4. How important is it to "get the right people on the bus" for running a safe kingdom? (See Exhibit 16.4 and associated text.)
5. Whose job is it to paint a compelling picture of a better kingdom?
6. How might the kingdom get rid of obstacles and empower people to act?
7. How can they find ways to make the changes stick?

FIELD TEAM EXERCISE

Appreciative Inquiry

Appreciative inquiry questions provide a powerful way to connect with others and to discover new information. Sometimes AI helps people identify what they actually want and feel, which might have been hidden below the conscious surface. You will get a chance in this exercise to practice asking appreciative inquiry questions. See Exhibit 16.3 and the supporting text for more information.

Step 1: Divide into groups of two. Outside of class, find someone to interview, such as a student, coworker, or family member.

Step 2: Read through the questions below with your partner, deciding which five you want to ask.

Questions you might want to ask in your interview:

1. Tell me about a time when you were absolutely performing at your best. What were you doing and how did it make you feel?
2. What is your purpose today? What higher purpose are you serving?
3. What is the most valuable asset you bring to a collaboration? Describe the best collaboration you've had.
4. What would you most like to do if you didn't feel afraid?
5. What was your most meaningful experience over the past year as a student or employee—a time when you felt most alive and fulfilled? How might you repeat that level of meaningfulness? How do you feel right now recalling that experience?
6. What is working in your life right now? What would you like more of?
7. Is there some way I can help? How can I support you?

Step 3: Conduct the interview. You can have one person ask all the questions, or take turns with your partner.

Step 4: Now, ask the person you interviewed to ask five questions of each of you from the list.

Step 5: With your partner, discuss what you each discovered about yourself from the exercise. What did you learn from asking and answering the appreciative inquiry questions?

Learned from asking the questions:
Learned from answering the questions:

TEST YOUR METTLE

ROLE PLAY SIMULATIONS

Light the Fire

Background: Reread the written Video Incident at the beginning of the chapter. In this role play, Caffeine and Crullers general manager Jane Sutton tries to get her staff to feel the urgency of C&C's competitive decline and get excited about the company's vision for the future. She knows she has to do something, or C&C will go under. She's called a meeting of her leadership team.

Instructions: Form into groups of five to six. One person will be general manager Jane Sutton, one CFO Carlos Hernandez, one sales manager Jason Wong, one director of operations Carrie Fishman, and one HR director Heather Carreau. If there are six people in the group, the sixth will be an observer. Each person reads only his or her confidential role, but the observer reads all. Spend 20–25 minutes on the role play.

Confidential information for Jane: You are at the end of your rope. Scone Prone has been taking away your customers for months. If you don't do something now, you don't see how you can stay in business. Your managers seem so disengaged, but that's not the way to solve problems. You've read about this appreciative inquiry method (see Exhibit 16.3) and think you should try it with the staff at the meeting coming up in a few minutes.

Confidential information for Jason: C&C is dying and there's nothing you or anyone else can do about it. You've tried, you have, to give them ideas on how to get out of this mess. But no one would listen, so you've had it. If Jane comes up with something at this late hour, she's crazy and stupid to think anyone will go along with her. It's too little, too late.

Confidential information for Carlos: C&C's been bleeding for months now. No one seemed to listen when you kept talking about getting the bottom line in shape. You suppose Jane will come crawling to you now to ask for advice on how to get out of this mess. Maybe you'll help. The first thing is to cut costs. You've got to close a couple of the locations. No question. Otherwise, they all close. You've got to make Jane and the others see the truth, the real world.

Confidential information for Carrie: You know C&C is in trouble. Everyone knows that. The only solution now is to cut staff and work out some systems in which you can survive with fewer employees. It will take some work putting the models and reports together, but you know you can do it. Otherwise, we all lose our jobs. Jane better not have another hare-brained scheme of hers. Because this is really, really serious.

Confidential information for Heather: You've seen a steady decline in employee motivation in recent weeks, as sales have slacked and no one seems to be directly addressing the problem. You've got to make sure they don't use this as an excuse to slice jobs. That's always the first idea. But there are so many other ways to cut costs. Trim hours, especially in a couple of the locations that cater mostly to business people during the day. And reduce the variety of drinks and bakery items offered, so there is less waste. So many things like that. You've got to stand firm for your people.

After the role play, the observer gives feedback and then the group discusses these questions:

1. What happened in the role play?
2. How can appreciative inquiry help the group get unstuck in this or a similar situation?
3. What is the difference between asking questions and giving opinions? How does it affect the group process and decision outcomes?

"An Ancient Tale" Role Play

This Role Play Simulation is available online at www.cengagebrain.com

VIDEO APPLICATION

Theo Chocolate

Top managers at Theo Chocolate decided to implement a change in strategy.

Discussion Questions

1. How did Theo managers learn that a change in strategy was needed? What level of urgency (low, medium, high) do you think Theo managers felt in order to undertake the change? Explain.
2. What aspects of the organization would have to change in order to implement the new strategy?
3. Which elements within Theo Chocolate will remain stable and not change? Do you think Theo Chocolate could be considered a learning organization? Why?

CASE INCIDENTS

TEST YOUR METTLE

Agents of Change

I am the CEO of Pac-Rim Consulting. We *are* agents of change. Our consulting teams work with a variety of U.S. organizations seeking expansion throughout the Pacific Rim, particularly into Asian markets. Over the past decade, I've gathered around me a talented, dynamic, and multilingual workforce for our two offices—one in San Francisco and the other in Los Angeles. Our employees understand the various markets and have established impressive networks to match their skills, creating a formidable team. The result of all of this expertise and vitality is a large and diverse clientele and a reputation for molding successful ventures.

Into this group of go-getters, I brought an Asian-American named Fen Xiao for our San Francisco office. With an MBA degree as well as a degree in international law, this slender, quiet man with a constant smile grasps and understands details and nuances that escape most managers.

From the outset, Xiao's cheerful willingness to pitch in and do what had to be done was greatly appreciated and he quickly became a staff favorite. It did not escape my

SHUTTERSTOCK #53973379

notice on frequent trips to San Francisco that many evenings Xiao would be the last to leave as he meticulously worked through research or details for a team presentation. Although he was not a high profile member of the team, he seemed to have found and settled into his niche.

Our team members have a tendency for falling all over themselves for choice assignments that highlight their areas of expertise, as well as for opportunities to make important presentations. But along with the high-profile side of consulting, there is a great deal of research and administrative paperwork—necessary chores that are less glamorous but have to be done. Over time, more and more of this detail work seems to have fallen to Xiao. I admit that I occasionally felt a twinge of sympathy for the guy as I observed the inequality of his workload. I mentioned this once to Xiao and several times to other members of the team, but the consensus seemed to be that he appeared to be okay with the situation. I decided that some people get a great deal of satisfaction working in the background.

One evening on my way out of a late meeting, I passed Xiao's office and noticed Chelsea Brooks huddled with him over the computers. I thought nothing of it until Chelsea approached me during my next visit two weeks later.

"I think you should have a talk with Xiao," she suggested.

"What's the problem? I saw the two of you working together a couple of weeks ago."

"I felt sorry for the guy and thought I would help him out with some of the research for the Beijing project. I think he should have a higher profile for that job than just conducting research. He has all of that education and, quite frankly, he's treated like an intern."

I was shocked by her remark, and my expression must have reflected my shock.

Chelsea shrugged. "Just saying . . . maybe it's not my place to speak up."

"I thought he liked the details," I responded.

"I'm sure it's okay . . . to a point."

"Has he said anything?"

"He's not one to complain, but I got the impression that evening that he's starting to feel trapped in the less-than-fulfilling role that the rest of us have been all too happy to hand over to him because *we* don't want to have to do it." She raised her brow, gave me the *what are you going to do about it* look, and as she walked away called back to me, "It's just a heads-up."

So now I'm standing here in the hallway, wondering what I should do next.

Why didn't he speak up if he was so miserable? Is he afraid to change his situation? Or is he ready to expand his role in the company and show a more assertive side that reflects his talents and expertise? Do I talk to him now or should I wait until he decides to change and comes to me with his concerns?

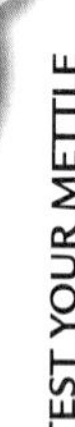

Discussion Questions

1. In what stage of readiness for change is Xiao in regard to making a change toward becoming more assertive? Why?
2. What steps might the CEO take to help Xiao start to change himself? Should the CEO take steps now or wait until Xiao asks for help?
3. To what extent do you think Xiao has to change his role on the team by himself rather than have someone like the CEO help him? Why?

"From This Point On . . ."

Bernini Foods is one of several companies offering healthy, frozen-packaged meals in the once-laughable and nutritionally challenged frozen dinner industry. Meeting the

changing needs of modern, on-the-go, budget-conscious consumers, the new generation of meals offered by Bernini faces unprecedented competition from long-time industry leaders including Bertolli, Marie Callender's, Healthy Choice, Lean Cuisine, and others.

Cutthroat competition within the industry means every corporation must hustle for high-quality ingredients, improved packaging, efficiency in delivery systems, and decreased cooking times. Like its competitors, Bernini strives for increased market share through a combination of price cuts and the introduction of new products.

To meet these challenges, CEO Roberto Bernini created a new management position to monitor pricing and purchasing. Vice president for finance Ted McCann hired Lucian Wilkes, a retired army colonel, for the new position, giving him wide latitude for setting up new rules and procedures. With an announcement from CEO Bernini, Wilkes was introduced to the company. Following an intense period of in-house research and information gathering, Wilkes zeroed in on what he saw as the major problems—the fragmentation of pricing and purchasing decisions, with managers in various regions devising their own standards and making their own contracts.

The process sent up red flags for Wilkes. He made an across-the-board e-mail announcement for new standardized procedures, basically informing each regional office that "from this point on . . . " regional managers must inform his office of any price change above 3 percent. In addition, all local purchase contracts above $10,000 must also be approved by Wilkes's office prior to implementation.

Directives for these new procedures were issued to regional managers for their policy manuals. These managers, according to their immediate feedback, were all in agreement with the changes. But as one month followed another, Wilkes's concern and level of frustration grew, and everyone seemed to carry on with a culture of "business as usual." Managers did not resist. Frequent correspondence across the various regions, including e-mails, faxes, and conference calls, brought repeated assurances that change was coming.

"We just need time to make the changes," one manager said.

But time dragged on and the situation remained unaltered. Complicating the situation, Wilkes appeared to have no vocal support from company executives, who were busy with their own concerns. While both Bernini and McCann offered lukewarm comments about the need for new initiatives to spur efficiency, neither demonstrated wholehearted support for the changes. The new plan was going nowhere, and Wilkes was aware that the failure of the company to increase profits could result in the loss of his own position.

"If nothing changes," Wilkes complained to his wife, "the regional managers will remain on the job. My job will be cut."

Wilkes wondered what his next move should be. In how many ways could he inform the managers to implement the new procedures? What pressures could he apply? How could he impress upon Bernini and McCann the importance of their support for the changes? He felt at a loss for what he should do. Did Bernini Foods want these new standards implemented or not?

Discussion Questions

1. Why do you think the regions are not responding to Wilkes's initiative for change? What did Wilkes do wrong with respect to implementing the change?
2. Should Wilkes solicit more active support from Bernini and McCann for the change he is attempting to implement? How might he do that?
3. Develop a plan that Wilkes can use to successfully restart the implementation of this change.

PERSONAL SKILLS LOG

PERSONAL SKILLS LOG

Directions: Fill in the rows below based on what you learned from each part of the chapter that you completed.

	What is my key takeaway or insight from this activity?	What do I personally do well (strength) regarding this activity?	What could I improve (weakness) about myself regarding this activity?	How might I use what I've learned from this activity in the future?
Manager Challenge Incident:				
Discover Yourself Questionnaires:				
Deliberate Practice Exercises:				
In-Class and/or Field Team Exercises:				
Role-Play Exercises:				
Case Incidents:				

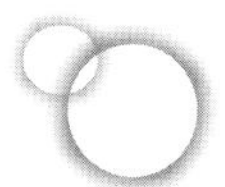

REFERENCES

Discover Yourself

1. Shaul Oreg, "Resistance to Change: Developing an Individual Differences Measure," *Journal of Applied Psychology* 88, no. 4 (2003): 680–693. Copyright © 2003 by the American Psychological Association. Adapted with permission. No further reproduction or distribution is permitted without written permission from the American Psychological Association.
2. Based on Eileen A. McConnaughy, James O. Prochaska, and Wayne F. Velicer, "Stages of Change in Psychotherapy: Measurement and Sample Profiles," *Psychotherapy: Theory, Research and Practice* 20, no. 3 (1983): 368–375; and Stephen Rollnick, Nick Heather, Ruth Gold, and Wayne Hall, "Development of a Short 'Readiness to Change' Questionnaire for Use in Brief, Opportunistic Interventions among Excessive Drinkers," *British Journal of Addiction* 87 (1992): 743–754.
3. Based on Elizabeth W. Morrison and Corey C. Phelps, "Taking Charge at Work: Extra-Role Efforts to Initiate Workplace Change," *Academy of Management Journal* 42 (1999): 403–419; and Michael Frese, Wolfgang Kring, Andrea Soose, and Jeannette Zempel, "Personal Initiative at Work: Differences between East and West Germany," *Academy of Management Journal* 39 (February 1996): 37–63.
4. Angela Lee Duckworth and Patrick D. Quinn, "Development and Validation of the Short Grit Scale (Grit-S)," *Journal of Personality Assessment* 91, no. 2 (2009): 166–174. Reprinted by permission of the publisher (Taylor & Francis Ltd, http://www.tandf.co.uk/journals).

Discover Knowledge

5. This example is based on information in N. R. Kleinfield, "Living at an Epicenter of Diabetes, Defiance, and Despair," *The New York Times*, January 10, 2006, http://www.nytimes.com/2006/01/10/nyregion/nyregionspecial5/10diabetes.html (accessed May 19, 2011).
6. Studies reported in Alan Deutschman, "The Three Keys to Change," *Fast Company*, January 2, 2007, http://www.fastcompany.com/articles/2007/01/change-or-die.html (accessed July 23, 2008); and Alan Deutschman, "Change or Die," *Fast Company*, May 1, 2005, http://www.fastcompany.com/magazine/94/open_change-or-die.html (accessed July 23, 2008).
7. This discussion is based on Deutschman, "The Three Keys to Change" and "Change or Die."
8. The following discussion is based on William Bridges, *Transitions; Making Sense of Life's Changes* (Reading, MA: Addison-Wesley, 1980); and Shaul Oreg, "Resistance to Change: Developing an Individual Differences Measure," *Journal of Applied Psychology* 88, no. 4 (2003): 680–693.
9. Bridges, *Transitions; Making Sense of Life's Changes*; and William Bridges, "Three Questions," *Leadership Excellence* (February 2010): 11.
10. Bridges, "Three Questions."
11. Jyoti Thottam, "Reworking Work," *Time* (July 25, 2005): 50–55.
12. Todd Datz, "No Small Change," *CIO* (February 15, 2004): 66–72.
13. Katherine Hobson, "Getting Docs to Use PCs," *The New York Times*, March 15, 2011.
14. Christopher Lindquist, "Watch Carefully," *CIO*, June 8, 2005, http://www.cio.com.au/article/181417/watch_carefully/ (accessed May 19, 2011) .
15. Elisabeth Kübler-Ross, *On Death and Dying* (New York: Touchstone, 1969); Maria Vakola and Ioannis Nikolaou, "Attitudes towards Organizational Change: What Is the Role of Employees' Stress and Commitment?" *Employee Relations* 27, no. 2 (2005): 160–174; Jeff Hiatt, "Change Management: An Introduction; Managing the People Side of Change," *knol.google*, August 5, 2008, http://knol.google.com/k/change-management-an-introduction# (accessed May 17, 2011); Meg Schoolfield and Aubray Orduña, "Understanding Staff Nurse Responses to Change: Utilization of a Grief-Change Framework to Facilitate Innovation," *Clinical Nurse Specialist* (September 2001): 224–229; and John Brady, "The Two Key Rules of Change," *Executive Excellence*, July 2009, http://www.johnbradyconsultants.com/Exec%20Excellence%20-%20Change%20Ldershp%20v4.5.pdf (accessed May 17, 2011).
16. This story is told in detail in Deutschman, "The Three Keys to Change."
17. Reported in Deutschman, "The Three Keys to Change."
18. Story told in Deutschman, "Change or Die."

19 Based on Richard E. Boyatzis, "How People Change; Create Positive Attractors," *Leadership Excellence* (October 2010): 17; and Deutschman, "The Three Keys to Change."

20 Boyatzis, "How People Change."

21 Based on James O. Prochaska, John Norcross, and Carlo DiClemente, *Changing for Good: The Revolutionary Program That Explains the Six Stages of Change and Teaches You How to Free Yourself from Bad Habits* (New York: William Morrow, 1994); and Marc F. Kern, "Stages of Change Model," April 19, 2008, http://www.addictioninfo.org/articles/11/1/Stages-of-Change-Model/Page1.html (accessed May 21, 2007).

22 This story is from Chip Heath and Dan Heath, *Switch: How to Change Things When Change Is Hard* (New York: Broadway, 2010).

23 David L. Cooperrider and Shuresh Srivastva, "Appreciative Inquiry in Organizational Life," in R. Woodman and W. Pasmore, eds., *Research in Organizational Change and Development*, Vol. 1 (Greenwich, CT: JAI Press, 1987); and D. Cooperrider and D. Whitney, *Appreciative Inquiry: A Positive Revolution in Change* (San Francisco, CA: Berrett-Koehler, 2005).

24 This discussion draws from Sarah Lewis, Jonathan Passmore, and Stefan Cantore, "Using Appreciative Inquiry in Sales Team Development," *Industrial and Commercial Training* 40, no. 4 (2008): 175–180; Steven J. Skinner and Scott W. Kelley, "Transforming Sales Organizations Through Appreciative Inquiry," *Psychology & Marketing* 23, no 2 (February 2006): 77–93; and Gabriella Giglio, Silvia Michalcova, and Chris Yates, "Instilling a Culture of Winning at American Express," *Organization Development Journal* 25, no. 4 (Winter 2007): 33–37.

25 See "Outstanding Cases," Appreciative Inquiry Commons Web site, http://appreciativeinquiry.case.edu/intro/bestcases.cfm for numerous examples of the uses of appreciative inquiry (accessed March 12, 2012).

26 Debra Meyerson, *Tempered Radicals: How People Use Difference to Inspire Change at Work* (Boston: Harvard Business School Press, 2001).

27 William B. Locander and David L. Luechauer, "Leader as Inquirer: Change Your Approach to Inquiry," *Marketing Management* (September–October 2007): 46–49; and Skinner and Kelley, "Transforming Sales Organizations Through Appreciative Inquiry."

28 Thomas J. Griffin, "In the Eye of the Beholder: Interview with Jim 'Gus' Gustafson," *Appreciative Leadership Interviews*, The Taos Institute, http://www.taosinstitute.com/resources/gustafson.html (accessed July 16, 2009); and "Getting to Know . . . Gus Gustafson, CCL Donor and Alumnus," in *Making a Difference: A Report on Activities and Impact from the Center for Creative Leadership*, Center for Creative Leadership, January 2009, http://www.ccl.org/leadership/pdf/news/newsletters/mad0109.pdf (accessed July 16, 2009).

29 Based on John P. Kotter, *Leading Change* (Boston: Harvard Business School Press, 1996), pp. 20–25; John P. Kotter, "Leading Change: Why Transformation Efforts Fail," *Harvard Business Review* (March–April, 1995): 59–67; and John P. Kotter and Dan S. Cohen, *The Heart of Change: Real-Life Stories of How People Change Their Organizations* (Boston: Harvard Business School Press, 2002).

30 Eric Pfanner, "Nokia Chief Sees Company on 'Burning Platform,' According to Leaked Memo," *The New York Times*, February 9, 2011.

31 Larry Hirschhorn, "Campaigning for Change," *Harvard Business Review* (July 2002): 98–104.

32 Lindquist, "Watch Carefully."

33 Daryl R. Conner, *Managing at the Speed of Change* (New York: Villard Books, 1992), chapter 7.

34 Steve Lohr, "Big Blue's Big Bet: Less Tech, More Touch," *The New York Times*, January 25, 2004; Spencer E. Ante, "The New Blue: Lou Gerstner Saved Big Blue. Now It's Up to New CEO Sam Palmisano to Restore It to Greatness," *BusinessWeek* (March 17, 2003): 80ff; and Kevin Maney, "Homebred CEO Summons IBM's Past, Present, Future," *USA Today*, November 19, 2003, http://www.usatoday.com/tech/techinvestor/2003-11-19-palmisano-cover_x.htm (accessed May 19, 2011).

35 This discussion of the hard and soft sides of change is based on "The McKinsey 7S Framework; Ensuring That All Parts of Your Organization Work in Harmony," *Mind Tools*, http://www.mindtools.com/pages/article/newSTR_91.htm (accessed May 19, 2011); and Ed Oakley and Doug Krug, *Enlightened Leadership: Getting to the Heart of Change* (New York: Simon & Shuster, 1993), pp. 44–48.

36 Oakley and Krug, *Enlightened Leadership: Getting to the Heart of Change.*

37 Datz, "No Small Change."

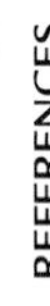

38 Duckworth and Quinn, "Development and Validation of the Short Grit Scale (Grit-S)."

39 Angela L. Duckworth, Christopher Peterson, Michael D. Matthews, and Dennis R. Kelly, "Grit: Perseverance and Passion for Long-Term Goals," *Personality Processes and Individual Differences* 92, no. 6 (2007): 1087–1101.

40 Tim Stevens, "Heart & Soul," *Industry Week* (May 4, 1998): 44–49; Bill George, *Authentic Leadership: Rediscovering the Secrets to Creating Lasting Value* (San Francisco: Jossey-Bass, 2003); and Medtronic Web site pages, "Medtronic at a Glance," http://wwwp.medtronic.com/Newsroom/MedtronicAtAGlance.do?lang=en_US, and "Our Mission," http://www.medtronic.com/about-medtronic/our-mission/index.htm (accessed May19, 2011).

41 Ronald A. Heifetz and Donald L. Laurie, "The Leader as Teacher: Creating the Learning Organization," *Ivey Business Journal*, January–February 2003, http://www.iveybusinessjournal.com/topics/leadership/the-leader-as-teacher-creating-the-learning-organization (accessed March 12, 2012).

42 Peter Senge, *The Fifth Discipline: The Art and Practice of Learning Organizations* (New York: Doubleday/Currency, 1990).

43 Khoo Hsien Hui and Tan Kay Chuan, "Nine Approaches to Organizational Excellence," *Journal of Organizational Excellence* (Winter 2002): 53–65; Leon Martel, "The Principles of High Performance—And How to Apply Them," *Journal of Organizational Excellence* (Autumn 2002): 49–59; and Jeffrey Pfeffer, "Producing Sustainable Competitive Advantage through the Effective Management of People," *Academy of Management Executive* 9, no. 1 (1995): 55–69.

Action Learning

44 Thanks to Michael Ray for providing his thinking for this exercise.

45 Adapted from J. B. Ritchie and Paul Thompson, *Organization and People: Readings, Cases and Exercises in Organizational Behavior* (St. Paul, MN: West Publishing, 1980), pp. 68–70. All rights reserved. In Dorothy Marcic, *Organizational Behavior: Experiences and Cases*, 4th ed. (St. Paul, MN: West Publishing, 1992), pp. 378–79. Reprinted with permission.

GLOSSARY

A

accountability state of being subject to reporting and justifying task outcomes to those above in the chain of command

accountability cycle a five-step system used to manage people and projects by setting goals, developing action plans, measuring outcomes, reviewing progress, and appraising performance

active versus passive behavior the second dimension of follower style: an active individual participates fully in the organization and engages in behavior that is beyond the limits of the job; a passive individual, by contrast, is characterized by a need for constant supervision and prodding by superiors and is often regarded as lazy

adaptive learning cycle experienced by all living organisms, starting with action to feedback to synthesis and then to a new action

adjourning stage of development period during which the emphasis is on wrapping things up and gearing down; occurs in teams that have a limited task or project and disband after it is completed

after-action reviews quick sessions during which managers review the outcome of activities to see what worked, what didn't, and what can be learned from the experience

agility ability to revise and adjust your plans and change course when faced with obstacles, setbacks, new data, or mistakes

agreeableness degree to which a person is able to get along with others by being good-natured, likable, cooperative, forgiving, understanding, and trusting

alienated follower a passive, yet independent, critical thinker

appreciative inquiry (AI) engages individuals, teams, or the entire organization in creating change by reinforcing positive messages and focusing on learning from success

assertiveness toughness and competitiveness

B

being a cultural value that places greater emphasis on leisure and spending time with family and friends than on earning overtime pay or accomplishing more business goals; "being" cultures stress living and working for the moment

best alternative to a negotiated agreement (BATNA) the course of action that will be taken by a party if the current negotiations fail and an agreement cannot be reached; successful negotiators understand their options so they have leverage in the negotiation

biculturalism the sociocultural skills and attitudes used by racial minorities as they move back and forth between the dominant culture and their own ethnic or racial culture

Big Five personality dimensions an individual's extraversion, agreeableness, conscientiousness, emotional stability, and openness to experience

brainstorming a face-to-face interactive group that spontaneously suggests a wide range of creative ideas

C

centralized network team members communicate through one individual, such as a team leader, to solve a problem or make a decision

ceremony a planned activity that makes up a special event and is generally conducted for the benefit of an audience

channel richness the amount of information that can be transmitted during a communication episode

coaching feedback information about work or personal performance that enables a person to change his or her behavior

coercive power negative side of reward power; managers have coercive power when they have the right to fire or demote subordinates, criticize, or withhold pay increases and promotions

collectivism a cultural preference for a tightly knit social group in which individuals put common goals, group harmony, and collective welfare above individual success

communication champion one who is philosophically grounded in the belief that good communication is essential to building trust, gaining commitment, and inspiring and uniting people to work together to accomplish a common purpose

communication channel the medium by which a message is carried from one person to another

conflict antagonistic interaction in which one party, in order to achieve its goals, will prevent or block the intentions or goals of another

conformist a type of follower who participates actively in a relationship with the boss but doesn't use critical thinking skills; a conformist typically carries out any and all orders regardless of the nature of the request

conscientiousness degree to which a person is careful, organized, self-disciplined, responsible, dependable, persistent, and achievement-oriented

counterdependence a deep-seated aversion to being assisted or supported by anyone

courage ability to act in spite of doubt or fear

creativity the generation of new and potentially useful ideas

critical thinking being mindful of the effects of your own and others' behavior on achieving organizational goals; weighing the impact of your boss's and your own decisions and offering constructive criticism, creativity, and innovation

cross-functional team a group made up of members from different functional departments within the organization

cultural intelligence ability to use reasoning and observation skills to interpret unfamiliar gestures and situations and devise appropriate behavioral responses

culture values, assumptions, norms, and patterns of thought that are shared by all or most members of a social group, that are passed on from existing to new members of the group, and that shape group members' behaviors and perception of the world

culture strength the level of agreement among members of a group about the importance of specific values and norms

D

decentralized network individuals communicate directly with other team members and process information equally among themselves until a decision is reached

devil's advocate one who challenges the assumptions and assertions made by another individual or group to stimulate creative thinking and prevent premature consensus

dialogue communication process in which participants suspend their attachment to a particular point of view so that a deeper level of listening, synthesis, and meaning can emerge from the group

difficult conversation a discussion between two or more people in which (a) outcomes are important, (b) viewpoints differ, and (c) emotions run high

distributive approach a competitive and adversarial negotiation approach in which each party strives to get as much as it can, usually at the expense of the other party

doing a cultural value that places emphasis on taking action and achieving measurable outcomes; "doing" cultures emphasize working as much as possible to make more money or accomplish more results

E

effective follower one who is both a critical, independent thinker and active in the organization

emotional intelligence ability to perceive, identify, understand, and successfully manage emotions in self and others

emotional stability degree to which a person is calm, enthusiastic, positive, and self-confident rather than moody, fearful, negative, or insecure

empathy ability to put yourself in other people's shoes, sense their emotions, and understand their perspective

empowerment power sharing; the delegation of power or authority to subordinates in an organization

end values beliefs about the kind of goals or outcomes that are worth pursuing; sometimes called *terminal values*

engagement state in which employees enjoy their jobs, are satisfied with their work conditions, contribute enthusiastically to meeting team and organizational goals, and feel a sense of belonging and commitment to the organization

equity theory proposes that people are motivated to seek social equity in the rewards they receive for performance; that is, they want to feel that they are receiving fair compensation for their contributions as compared to others

escalating commitment a tendency to continue investing time, money, and energy in something despite strong evidence that it is not working

ethical dilemma a situation concerning right or wrong when values are in conflict

ethnocentrism a natural tendency among people to regard their own culture as inherently superior and to downgrade or dismiss other cultural values

ethnorelativism the attitude that cultures and subcultures are inherently equal

expectancy theory suggests that high motivation depends on an individual's belief, or expectation, that he or she has the ability to perform tasks and receive desired awards

extraversion degree to which a person is outgoing, sociable, assertive, and comfortable meeting and talking to new people

F

five whys a question-asking approach used to understand cause-effect relationships underlying a problem that has an unknown cause

forced ranking system grades employees according to their relative performance: 20 percent would be placed in the top group of performers; 70 percent have to be ranked in the middle; and 10 percent are ranked at the bottom

forming stage of development period of orientation and getting acquainted; team members find out what behavior is acceptable to others, explore friendship possibilities, and determine task orientation

G

goal setting establishing specific, challenging goals that are accepted as valid by employees, and then helping people track their progress toward goals by providing timely feedback

grit an individual's passion and persistence for achieving a long-term goal

groupthink the tendency of members in highly cohesive teams to suppress contrary opinions

H

hierarchy of needs Maslow's concept of human motivation characterized by five general types of needs: physiological, safety, belongingness, esteem, and self-actualization

high-context culture a culture in which people are sensitive to circumstances surrounding communications and communication is used to enhance personal relationships

hygiene factors characteristics that influence job dissatisfaction, such as working conditions, pay, company policies, and interpersonal relationships

I

ILETS model a step-by-step technique used when leading a difficult conversation: Introduce the topic, Listen to the other person, Empathize, Talk, and Solve the problem

independence a sense of self-worth and a healthy attitude of self-reliance

independent thinking questioning assumptions and interpreting data and events according to one's own beliefs, ideas, and thinking, not according to pre-established rules, routines, or categories defined by others

individualism a value in which people define themselves in terms of personal characteristics and value individual success and welfare over that of the group

instrumental values beliefs about the types of behavior that are appropriate for reaching end goals; for example, being helpful to others, being honest, or exhibiting courage

integrative approach a collaborative approach to negotiation that combines the needs of both sides; based on a win-win assumption that tries for a creative solution to benefit both parties

interactive leadership management that favors a consensual and collaborative process, in which influence is derived from relationships rather than position power and authority

interdependence a step beyond independence to the realization that the best things happen by working cooperatively with others

intrinsic rewards rewards experienced by an employee as a result of the work itself; for example, a feeling of accomplishment, self-esteem, and personal or professional growth

intuitive problem identification the use of experience and judgment to recognize problems

J

job characteristics model proposes that certain core job dimensions create positive psychological reactions within employees, leading to higher motivation and better performance

job design structuring jobs in a way to meet higher-level needs and increase motivation toward the accomplishment of goals

Johari Window tool managers can use to move toward greater transparency and alignment with others; the four quadrants of the Johari Window each represent a self-awareness "window"

K

knowledge facts, information, and experiences that are linked together to become meaningful

L

learning organization a group in which everyone is engaged in identifying and solving problems, enabling the organization to continuously experiment, learn, and adapt

legitimate power power that stems from the authority granted via a formal position in an organization

listening consciously striving to grasp and interpret a message's genuine meaning by paying attention not only to facts but also to feelings, observing facial expressions and body language as well as hearing the words that are being spoken

low-context culture a culture in which people use communication primarily to exchange facts and information

M

manager communication process by which information is exchanged and understood by two or more people, usually with the intent to influence or motivate behavior

managing up consciously and deliberately developing a meaningful, task-related, mutually respectful, and mutually beneficial relationship with your direct superiors

mentoring a relationship between a senior or experienced manager and a new or less-experienced manager that focuses on guiding the protégé's career development

metacognition ability to observe and think about your own thinking and assert some control over your cognitive processes

mindfulness continuously reevaluating previously learned ways of doing things in the context of evolving information and shifting circumstances

moral leadership leading by distinguishing right from wrong and doing right; seeking the just, the honest, the good, and the right conduct in achieving goals and fulfilling purpose

motivators factors that influence job satisfaction based on meeting higher-level needs such as achievement, challenging work, recognition, responsibility, and opportunity for growth

Myers–Briggs Type Indicator (MBTI) assessment instrument that measures differences among individuals based on their preferences for introversion vs. extraversion, sensing vs. intuition, thinking vs. feeling, and judging vs. perceiving

N

negativity bias term used in psychology to describe how the human mind reacts more quickly and strongly to perceived bad things than to good things

negotiation a formal process of discussion used to reach an agreement between parties in conflict

networking proactive attempts by individuals to develop and maintain personal and professional relationships with others for the purpose of mutual benefit in their work or career

nonverbal communication process of transmitting messages through action and behavior; accounts for at least half of the entire message received in a personal encounter

norming stage of development period during which conflict has been resolved, team roles are clear, and team unity and harmony emerge

norms shared standards that define what behaviors are acceptable and desirable within a group of people

O

open communication sharing all types of information throughout the organization, across functional and hierarchical boundaries

openness to experience degree to which a person has a broad range of interests and is curious, imaginative, and willing to consider new ideas

organizational culture the set of key values, assumptions, understandings, and norms that is shared by members of an organization and taught to new members as correct

overdependence the psychological inability to get enough help and support

P

passive follower one who exhibits neither critical, independent thinking nor active participation in the organization

performance appraisal process by which a manager evaluates an employee's work effectiveness by using objective criteria, provides feedback to the employee, and shows where improvements are needed

performance management a process of monitoring and developing the performance of individuals and teams so that everyone is aligned toward strategic goals and accountable for attaining specific results

performance orientation placing emphasis on high performance and rewarding people for excellence and performance improvements

performing stage of development period during which the major emphasis is on accomplishing goals; team members are committed to the team's mission and coordinate their actions to achieve it

person-job fit matching job characteristics to an employee's interests, personality, and abilities

point-counterpoint a decision-making technique that divides a group into two subgroups that are assigned to express competing points of view

positive leadership uses theoretically grounded psychological principles to focus on the positive and promote outcomes such as thriving at work, interpersonal flourishing, positive emotions, and energized teams

positivity ratio the ratio of positive to negative statements; high performing teams typically show a strong positivity ratio

power the potential ability of one person in an organization to influence other people to bring about desired outcomes

power distance a cultural value that expects and accepts inequality in power among people, organizations, and institutions

pragmatic survivor a type of follower who adjusts his or her approach depending on which style fits with the prevalent situation and minimizes personal risk

problem a gap between actual performance and desired performance—when things are not operating as they should

problem consensus agreement about the nature of a problem and about which goals to pursue

problem solving process of taking corrective action to meet objectives and achieve desired results

procrastination delay in starting or completing an intended task or course of action even when the delay may have negative consequences

professional network a set of relationships critical to one's ability to get things done, get ahead, and develop personally and professionally

R

reinforcement anything that causes a certain behavior to be repeated or inhibited

relationship conflict interpersonal incompatibility that creates tension and personal animosity among people

reward power power that stems from the authority of a manager to bestow rewards on people

role shared expectations of how an individual should behave in fulfilling the requirements of his or her job

root cause analysis (RCA) a systematic approach to finding out what the "true" or root cause of a problem is instead of continuing to address symptoms of the problem

S

satisficing accepting a satisfactory outcome rather than trying to maximize or achieve an optimal outcome or level of performance

search seeking out alternatives to solve a problem within the organization's repertoire of solutions

self-awareness being conscious of the internal aspects of one's nature, such as personality traits, beliefs, emotions, values, strengths, and limitations, and appreciating how those patterns affect other people

self-confidence assurance in one's own ideas, judgments, and capabilities

self-directed team a group made up of employees who work with minimum supervision and rotate jobs to produce an entire product or service

self-disclosure act of sharing your fears, thoughts, emotions, and concepts of yourself with others

self-management ability to engage in self-regulating thoughts and behavior to handle difficult or challenging situations

self-restraint ability to think before you speak or act

skills accumulated knowledge that has been formalized into behavior steps needed to adequately perform an activity

social loafing situation in which team members do not exert equal effort; also called *free riding*

soft power power that stems from one's personal credibility and a network of positive relationships rather than being based on formal authority granted by the organization

special purpose team a group that focuses on a specific purpose and disbands once the project is completed; sometimes called a *project team*

sponsor a person or group with the power to authorize, provide resources, and legitimize a decision or change in the organization

storming stage of development period in which individual personalities emerge within a group, along with resulting conflicts and disagreements

story a narrative based on true events that is repeated frequently and shared among employees

strength individual attribute that arises from a natural talent that is supported and reinforced with both learned knowledge and skills

stress an individual's physiological, mental, and emotional response to external stimuli that place physical or psychological demands on the individual and create uncertainty and lack of personal control when important outcomes are at stake

stretch goals highly ambitious goals that are so clear, compelling, and imaginative that they get people fired up about meeting the challenge

symbol an object, act, or event that conveys meaning to others

system a set of interacting elements that continually affect one another over time and work toward a common purpose

systemic thinking seeing the synergy of the whole rather than just the separate elements of a system

T

talents naturally recurring patterns of thought, feeling, or behavior; instinctive abilities

targeted self-talk a repeated intentional mental statement that is directed toward yourself

task conflict disagreements among people about the goals to be achieved or the tasks to be performed

task interdependence the extent to which team members depend on each other for information, resources, or ideas to accomplish their tasks

team a unit of two or more people who interact and coordinate their work to accomplish a common goal for which they are committed and hold themselves mutually accountable

team norm a standard of conduct that is shared by members and guides their behavior

theory of constraints the idea that every system or process has one or a few weaknesses that prevent it from achieving maximum performance

time management use of techniques that enable you to get more done in less time and with better results, be more relaxed, and have more time to enjoy your work and your life

time orientation area of value differences concerning whether a culture is most strongly oriented toward the past, present, or future

two-factor theory Herzberg's concept of human motivation characterized by the differences between dissatisfaction/low motivation and satisfaction/high motivation

U

uncertainty avoidance a cultural value characterized by people being uncomfortable with ambiguity and thus supporting beliefs that ensure certainty and conformity

uncritical thinking thought process that does not consider possibilities beyond what one is told; accepting others' ideas without thinking

V

values fundamental beliefs that an individual considers to be important, that are relatively stable over time, and that influence attitudes, perception, and behavior

values-based management supervision that provides a shared foundation of ethical values and beliefs that guide individual behavior and organizational actions

vision an ambitious view of the future that everyone involved can believe in, one that can realistically be achieved, yet one that offers a future that is dramatically better than what now exists

visualization creation of a vivid picture in your mind of the action you desire

W

whistleblowing employee disclosure of illegal, immoral, or unethical practices in the organization

Whole Brain Model system that considers a person's preference for right-brained versus left-brained thinking and for conceptual versus experiential thinking to identify four basic thinking styles

work redesign altering jobs to increase both the quality of employees' work experience and their productivity

workforce diversity an organizational workforce made up of people who have different human qualities or who belong to different cultural groups

NAME INDEX

Exhibits are indicated by *exh* following the page number.

X

Y

Z

SUBJECT INDEX

Exhibits are indicated by *exh* following the page number.

A

B

C

G

H

I

J

K

Y